NAVIGATING WORLDS

NAVIGATING WORLDS

COLLECTED ESSAYS

(2006-2020)

BEZALEL NAOR

OROT/KODESH

2021/5781

NAVIGATING WORLDS
Collected Essays
(2006-2020)

© Bezalel Naor 2021
978-1-947857-57-5

Paperback edition

All rights reserved.
Except for brief quotations in printed reviews,
no part of this publication may be reproduced,
stored in a retrieval system, or transmitted in any form or by any means
(printed, written, photocopied, visual electronic, audio, or otherwise)
without the prior permission of the publisher.

For permission requests, write to the Publisher:
Kodesh Press LLC
New York, NY
www.kodeshpress.com
kodeshpress@gmail.com
sales@kodeshpress.com

Layout, design, and typesetting by
Dynagrafik Design Studio, Monsey, NY
Printed in the United States of America

לאמי מורתי

חנה גיטל שתחי'

מוגש באהבה

To my mother

H ELEN

With love

TABLE OF CONTENTS

INTRODUCTION

I. TORAH

    Vayyera: 'Akedat Yitzhak: The Binding of Isaac   19
    Vayyera: The Ashes of Isaac   25
    Vayyigash: Bittul Yitsra de-Sin'at Hinam (An End to Infighting)   31
    Shemot: Exile of the Word   35
    Yitro: Jethro: A Double Epiphany   39
    Yitro: Through a Field-Glass: Jacob's Ladder and the Altar's Ramp   47
    Ki Tissa: Moses and Bezalel: The "Servant of the Lord" and the Architect of the Soul   55
    Vayyakhel-Pekudei: Nahmanides on the Tabernacle   63

II. TALMUD

    The Head Movements of *Shema'* (*b. Berakhot* 13b)   71
    The Carnal Kippur (*b. Yoma* 19b-20a)   77
    A Meditation on *Masekhet Megillah* (*b. Megillah* 5b-6b)   87
    First Fruits and the Talmudic View of Capital: An *Essai* in the Philosophy of *Halakhah* (*b. Gittin* 47b)   97
    Mindfulness and the Cities of Refuge (*b. Makkot* 10a)   107
    Moses Enters the Divine Superconscious (*b. Menahot* 29b)   123

III. CHRISTIANITY AND ISLAM: JUDAISM'S STRUGGLE WITH SUPERSESSIONISM

The Theological Boldness of Nahmanides:
Israel's Reaffirmation of Vows 137

From Deicide to Calf-Worship: Islam and Judaism 147

The Cain-Korah-Christianity Connection 157

IV. MAIMONIDES

The Religious Phenomenology of Maimonides 163

When Rambam Met the Izhbitser Rebbe: Response to a
Straussian Reading of *Hilkhot Teshuvah* 181

V. KABBALAH

The Orality of *Shir ha-Shirim* and of *Tikkunei Zohar* 197

The Anonymous Author of *Tikkunei Zohar*
and *Ra'ya Mehemna*: An Antinomian
or a Radical Maimonidean? 203

Kabbalah—Escape from Reality or Affirmation of Life?—
A Response to Lippman Bodoff, "Jewish Mysticism:
Medieval Roots, Contemporary Dangers
and Prospective Challenges" 221

VI. HASIDISM

Rabbi Nahman's *Shir Na'im* as a Reply to Maimonides 237

A Discourse of Rabbi Aharon Halevi Hurwitz
of Staroshelye for the Day of Atonement 247

The Rebbe of Radzyn and Rav Kook on Doubt 261

Bati le-Gani ("I Came to My Garden"): Two Discourses
of Rabbis Schneersohn and Hutner Compared 279

VII. The Thought of Rav Kook

Reflections on *Yom ha-'Atsma'ut*   299

Searching for the Lost Dimensions of Judaism   307

The Scribal Art of Rabbi Meir:
    A Study in Metanomianism   311

The Hasidism of Rav Kook   327

The Universalism of Rav Kook   341

Rav Kook's Space Odyssey   351

Rav Kook on Teaching Torah to Girls   365

Rav Kook and Rav Harlap—
    Truth and the Pursuit of Truth   377

Zion and Jerusalem: The Secular and the Sacred   393

Rav Kook's Shattered Vessels and Their Repair   411

VIII. Rav Kook: Historical Studies

Rav Kook's Missing Student   431

When Rav Kook Was the Zealot (*Kana'i*)
    and His Opponent the Advocate (*Melits Yosher*)   445

IX. Messiah

The Two Faces of Messianism   463

"My Beloved is Like a Gazelle" (*Domeh Dodi li-Tsevi*):
    The Esthetic Messiah   485

The Philosopher King and the Poet Messiah:
    Hellenic and Hebrew Republics Compared   503

Messiah's Donkey of a Thousand Colors   513

X: Book Reviews

The Maggid of Kozhnits,
   Rabbi Israel ben Shabtai Hopstein. *'Avodat Yisrael*   521

The Jackals and the Lion:
   Animal Fables of Kafka and Rav Kook   531

Bridging the Kabbalistic Gap:
   Nefesh HaTzimtzum by Avinoam Fraenkel   537

*Maimonides Between Philosophy and Halakhah
Rabbi Joseph B. Soloveitchik's Lectures
on the* Guide of the Perplexed
   Edited with an Introduction by Lawrence J. Kaplan   551

Hallel from Heaven and *Hallel* from Hell:
   The Post-Holocaust Responses of Paul Celan,
   Aharon Appelfeld and Meshulam Rath   561

When Elijah's Mantle Fell:
   The Judaism of Leonard Cohen   567

The Religious-Zionist Manifesto
   of Rabbi Yehudah Leib Don Yahya   573

Of Priests and Prophets: The Way of Knowing
   and the Way of Not Knowing
   Shnayor Z. Burton. *Mishnat Ya'akov*   591

The Two Luminaries: Rabbi Nahman of Breslov
   and Rav Kook
   Moshe Nahmani. *Shnei ha-Me'orot*   599

Etatism and Halakhah: Family Feud and Political Theory
   Rabbi Yitzhak Goldstoff. *Mikdash ha-Kodesh*   609

Rav Yosef Dov Soloveitchik on the *Seder ha-'Avodah*
   of *Yom ha-Kippurim:* A Synopsis of the Rav's
   Yiddish *Teshuvah Derashah* 5736 (1975)   615

A King's Palace
   Aharon Hayyim Zimmerman. *Agra la-Yesharim*   625

Bibliography   631

In Loving Memory of

Albert Allen a"h

Mr. Albert Allen was born in Cairo, Egypt,
and was involved for many years
in supporting and furthering Sephardic causes.
He was a founding member and gabbai
of the Sephardic Minyan of Englewood, NJ,
as well as being involved in many other Jewish organizations
including Yeshiva University, Yeshiva of North Jersey,
Congregation Ahavath Torah
and the Jewish Outreach Network.
His endeavors were conducted
with warmth, wisdom and generosity,
and he is greatly missed by his family
and all who came in contact with him.

DEDICATED BY
THE ALLEN FAMILY

Introduction

The present work is the sequel to the earlier volume of collected essays, *From A Kabbalist's Diary* (2005). In addition to essays which appeared over the years in various journals, both scholarly and popular, our collection contains hitherto unpublished essays. Essays already published very likely appear here in updated versions. *"Panim hadashot ba'u le-khan."*

It is my pleasant duty to thank my publisher Rabbi Alec Goldstein, *shelit"a*, a young man of unusual vision and unflagging commitment to disseminating the wisdom of Torah, for undertaking this project and seeing it through to completion. To Alec and Caroline at Kodesh Press, *berakhah ve-hatslahah!*

I would be remiss in my duty if I did not express my gratitude to the tireless staff of Dynagrafik Design Studio who have succeeded in creating a beautiful "vessel" for the "lights."

My one-time student and present colleague Rabbi Eliyahu Allen, *shelit"a*, has dedicated this volume in loving memory of his father Avraham (Albert) Allen. As his namesake, Avraham was a man of extraordinary kindness. *"Hesed le-Avraham."* Yehi zikhro barukh.

Israel's narrative of an ongoing romance between God, a nation, a Torah and a land, is as unpopular today as it was in the past. Yet empires—Babylonian, Persian, Greek, Roman—come and go. Lonely Israel endures.

> *And the earth was desolate*—This is the exile of Babylonia.
> *and empty*—This is the exile of Persia.
> *and darkness*—This is the exile of Greece.
> *[was] upon the face of the deep*—This is the exile of Rome.
> *and the spirit of God hovers*—This is the spirit of King Messiah.
> (*Genesis Rabbah* 2:4)

Bezalel Naor

SPINOZA
Las traslúcidas manos del judio
Labran en la penumbra los cristales
Y la tarde que muere es miedo y frío.
(Las tardes a las tardes son iguales.)
Las manos y el espacio de jacinto
Que palidece en el confín del Ghetto
Casi no existen para el hombre quieto
Que está soñando un claro laberinto.
No lo turba la fama, ese reflejo
De sueños en el sueño de otro espejo,
Ni el temeroso amor de las doncellas.
Libre de la metáfora y del mito
Labra un arduo cristal: el infinito
Mapa de Aquél que es todas Sus estrellas.
—Jorge Luis Borges

SPINOZA
The Jew's hands, translucent in the dusk,
Polish the lenses time and again.
The dying afternoon is fear, is
Cold, and all the afternoons are the same.
The hands and the hyacinth-blue air
That whitens at the Ghetto edges
Do not quite exist for this silent
Man who conjures up a clear labyrinth—
Undisturbed by fame, that reflection
Of dreams in the dream of another
Mirror, nor by maidens' timid love.
Free of metaphor and myth, he grinds
A stubborn crystal: the infinite
Map of the One who is all His stars.
(Transl. Richard Howard and Cesar Rennert)

... we can take our places in the Sanhedrin and determine what is to be done with those great cubes of diamond that our teacher Moses shouldered down the mountain. You want to place them in such a way that the sun by day, and the moon and stars by night, will shine through them. I suggest another perspective which would include the light of the celestial bodies within the supernal radiance of the cubes. We lean toward each other over the table. The dust mingles with the mist, our nostrils widen. We are definitely interested; now we can get down to a Jew's business.
—Leonard Cohen, *Book of Mercy*, Psalm 13

I

TORAH

Vayyera

'Akedat Yitzhak: The Binding of Isaac

For the Ascent of the Souls of the Eleven 'Akedot of Pittsburgh

In the Torah portion of *Vayyera* there are contained two epics that are diametrically opposed: the Destruction of Sodom and the Binding of Isaac.

When the LORD reveals to Abraham His plan to destroy the city of Sodom, Abraham proves adversarial, as he attempts to intercede on behalf of the people of Sodom. As it were, Abraham summons the Almighty to appear in a court of law: "Shall the Judge of the entire earth, not do justice?!"[1]

At the conclusion of the Torah portion, we read of the Binding of Isaac. On that occasion, Abraham is asked by the Almighty to take his only son, whom he loves, Isaac, and offer him up on one of the mountains. And on that occasion, Abraham remains silent. He does not utter a peep in protest. No remonstrance. How is that possible?

The contradiction between the two narratives is glaring, and several solutions have been offered by interpreters.

The truth is that whoever has grown up in the study-house of Rabbi Moses Hayyim Luzzatto, the great Paduan mystic, will immediately recognize that these two stories adhere to two different divine governances: the Governance of Justice (*Hanhagat ha-*

Mishpat) and the Governance of Unity (*Hanhagat ha-Yihud*).² In the course of history, there are two tracks. There are times that the LORD conducts His world through a lens of justice. Then "reward and punishment" are the order of the day. The righteous prosper and the wicked suffer. In such a chapter in history, the LORD actually invites His creations to summon Him to court, as it were. Then the appropriate response is to throw up in God's face the rhetorical question, "Shall the Judge of the entire earth, not do justice?!"

Then there are other times when the LORD arises from the Throne of Justice and sets Himself down upon the Throne of Unity. In regard to this mysterious behavior, Job said: "And it goes roundabout by His schemes."³ In that scenario, it is more than likely that the righteous will suffer and the wicked prosper. (At least in the short term.) In this paradoxical arrangement, God does not play by the rules of "reward and punishment." The LORD has an overarching interest: the Secret of Unity (*Sod ha-Yihud*). At the conclusion of human history, at the end of the proverbial "six millennia of the world," there will be revealed retroactively that "All that the Merciful One does—is done for good."⁴

At that time, man will sincerely bless "the Good and the Benefactor" (*Ha-Tov ve-ha-Metiv*). This will not be merely "lip service"; it will be wholehearted conviction. But in the meantime, within the span of the "six millennia," upon hearing evil tidings we are obligated to recite the blessing "the Truthful Judge" (*Barukh Dayyan ha-Emet*).⁵ And Abraham, our forefather, must maintain a self-imposed silence; he must accept the divine decree and not second-guess the Holy One, blessed be He. It is called *"Tsidduk ha-Din."* "Justification of the Law."

The Return of Evil to Good (*Hahzarat ha-Ra' la-Tov*), in the parlance of Luzzatto, is part of the agenda of the Secret of Unity (*Sod ha-Yihud*). This was already laid out in the Talmud:

> "The LORD shall be a king upon the entire earth; on that day the LORD shall be one and His name one."[6]
>
> Does that mean that today He is not one?
>
> Said Rabbi Aha bar Hanina: This world is not like the World to Come. In this world, upon hearing good tidings, one says, "Blessed is the Good and the Benefactor," and upon hearing bad tidings, one says, "Blessed is the Truthful Judge." But in the World to Come, it is all "the Good and the Benefactor."[7]

So far, we have briefly surveyed the Secret of Unity as it is expressed on the ethical horizon. From here on, we shall attempt to penetrate the Secret of Unity as it is expressed on the existential horizon.

To do so, we must journey from the city of Padua, Italy, to the hamlet of Staroshelye in Belarus; we must temporarily take leave of the study-house of Rabbi Moses Hayyim Luzzatto and transport ourselves to the study-house of the favorite pupil of the *"Alter Rebbe"* (founder of HaBaD Hasidism)—that beloved disciple for whom the *Alter Rebbe* would pray, "Seekers of unity (*Doreshei*

Yihudekha), watch over them as the apple of Your eye"[8]—Rabbi Aharon Halevi Hurwitz, author of *'Avodat Halevi*.

Innumerable times in his works, Rabbi Aharon will revisit the theme of the ultimate unity, the final frontier: "the equation of being and nothingness" (*hashva'at yesh va-'ayin*). This great "Seeker of Unity" will point out that the division between existence and non-existence is a mental construct of the human brain. Rabbi Aharon will explain—as only he can—that in the World of Unity (*'Alma de-Yihuda*), "the darkness is even as the light"[9]; non-existence is even as existence.

We return to our point of departure, the Binding of Isaac. This epic is enveloped in mystery. Did Isaac survive or succumb? The Written Torah is most clear that Isaac survived the ordeal. But in the Oral Torah there are deposited the "ashes of Isaac" (*efro shel Yitzhak*).[10] Which is to say that in truth, Isaac was offered up on the altar as a burnt offering, a "holocaust." It is precisely for this reason that there was instituted the second of the Eighteen Benedictions (*Shemoneh 'Esreh*): "Who revives the dead" (*mehayeh ha-metim*). (The first blessing, "the Shield of Abraham," corresponds to the first patriarch, Abraham; the third blessing, "the holy God," corresponds to the third patriarch, Jacob; while the intervening blessing, "Who revives the dead," refers to the immolation of the second patriarch, Isaac.)

This paradoxical situation—this interpenetration of life and death; this blurring of the boundaries of being and non-being—is precisely the objective of the Secret of Unity.

VAYYERA

And all of us, Children of Abraham and Isaac, are referred to collectively as "Seekers of Unity."

"Seekers of Unity, watch over them as the apple of Your eye."

"Doreshei yihudekha, ke-vavat shomrem."

---

[1] Genesis 18:25.
[2] The concepts were clarified by Rabbi Yosef Avivi in his work, *Zohar Ramhal* (Jerusalem, 1997).
[3] Job 37:12.
[4] *b. Berakhot* 60b.
[5] *b. Pesahim* 50a.
[6] Zechariah 14:9.
[7] *b. Pesahim* 50a.
[8] From the prayer *"Ana be-Kho'ah"* attributed to Rabbi Nehunyah ben ha-Kaneh. For more information concerning the "Seeker of Unity," see below page 247.
[9] Psalms 139:12.
[10] See *b. Berakhot* 62b; *y. Ta'anit* 2:1; *b. Ta'anit* 16a; *Zevahim* 62a. See the solution offered by Rabbi David Luria, *Be'ur ha-RaDaL* to *Pirkei de-Rabbi Eliezer* (Warsaw, 1852), chap. 31, note 59 (71c-d).

Vayyera
The Ashes of Isaac

The Torah is very explicit concerning the items that Abraham took with him as he embarked on the journey to sacrifice his beloved son Isaac:

> And Abraham took the wood of the burnt-offering, and laid it upon Isaac his son; and he took in his hand the fire and the knife; and they went both of them together.[1]

There arises a halakhic question. Just as Abraham took a knife to slaughter the sacrifice,[2] by the same token he should have taken a vessel (*keli sharet*) in which to receive the blood of the sacrifice subsequent to its slaughter.[3] Why is there no mention of this equally important instrument?[4]

One of the great Talmudists of Poland between the two World Wars, Rabbi Isaac Judah Trunk of Kutno, rose to the challenge of this conundrum.[5] While proffering several solutions, one sticks out as the boldest—and the one that hews closest to the truth.

According to Rabbi Trunk, even if the angel from heaven had not stayed Abraham's hand, and Abraham had actually executed the slaughter of his son, there would have followed no "receiving of the blood" (*kabbalat ha-dam*). Why not? Unlike sacrifices in general, whose focal point is the blood which serves as atonement (*kaparah*),⁶ this sacrifice, the sacrifice of Isaac, was not about blood, but about ashes!

In Rabbi Trunk's understanding of the divine mandate, there would not have been four services (*'avodot*) as is the norm, but one: ritual slaughter (*shehitah*). This alone would have given full expression to Abraham's *"mesirut nefesh,"* his willingness to give his all for the Almighty. In this reading, not only the blood would be deemed "the portion of the Above" (*helek gavo'ah*), but the flesh as well.

The motif that recurs throughout Rabbinic literature is the "ashes of Isaac" (*efro shel Yitzhak*).⁷

There are varying opinions as to which merit of Israel convinced God to curtail the plague that raged as punishment for King David having conducted a census of the people. The *amora* Samuel offered that the LORD beheld the ashes of Isaac (*efro shel Yitzhak*).⁸

On a public fast day it was customary to place ashes on the head. According to one *amora*, this was done to commemorate the ashes of Isaac (*efro shel Yitzhak*).⁹

When the exiles returned from Babylonian captivity and built the Second Temple in Jerusalem, they had to locate the exact spot where once the altar had been situated. There are three opinions of the *amora'im* how they were able to locate the former site of the altar. Rabbi Yitzhak Nappaha opined that they saw the ashes of Isaac (*efro shel Yitzhak*) resting in that place.¹⁰

What is there about this motif of the ashes of Isaac?

Ashes symbolize the ultimate destruction. Paradoxically, having reached this ultimate destruction, one becomes, as it were, indestructible. Having reached the bottommost depth, one can only rise up.

Isaac becomes synonymous with resurrection of the dead. The first three blessings of the *Shemoneh 'Esreh* (or *'Amidah*) correspond to the three patriarchs, Abraham, Isaac and Jacob. The first benediction is the "Shield of Abraham." The third blessing, "the holy God," corresponds to Jacob.[11] The second blessing, "Who resurrects the dead," corresponds to Isaac.[12]

The symbol of the "ashes of Isaac" is most appropriate for our post-Holocaust generation. A nation that was reduced to ashes in the crematoria, can only rise up. Having suffered the ultimate destruction, Israel has become, as it were, indestructible.

Isaac is the patriarch of the future.

We are told that there will come a time when Abraham and Jacob will wash their hands of their progeny. When the Holy One, blessed be He, will tell Abraham, "Your children have sinned against me," Abraham's response will be: "Let them be erased for the sanctity of Your name." Jacob's response will be the same: "Let them be erased for the sanctity of Your name." Only Isaac will rise to our defense. At that point, the nation of Israel will embrace

Isaac, saying: "For you are our father, for Abraham did not know us and Israel did not recognize us."[13]

Isaac truly represents the indestructibility of the Children of Israel.

---

[1] Genesis 22:6.

[2] Abraham's knife for ritual slaughter becomes paradigmatic in Halakhah. The Talmud (*Zevahim* 97b) derives from our verse in Genesis that a burnt-offering (*'olah*) requires a knife (*keli sharet*). See also *Tosafot* ibid., s.v. *ve-hatam 'olah hu*, citing *Hullin* 16a.

[3] The stipulation that the blood be received in a vessel (*keli sharet*) is derived from the verse in Exodus 24:6: "And Moses took half of the blood and placed [it] in basins." See *Zevahim* 97b, and earlier 13a and Rashi there, and 47a and Rashi there, s.v. *bi-kheli sharet*; also Maimonides, *MT, Hil. Ma'aseh ha-Korbanot* 5:1. See also *Hil. Ma'aseh ha-Korbanot* 4:7 and the discussion in *Tosefot ha-ROSh 'al Masekhet Sotah*, ed. Rabbi Ya'akov ha-Levi Lifshitz (Jerusalem: Makhon Harry Fischel, 1968), *Sotah* 14b, s.v. *'af 'al gav de-kadishteh sakin be-tsavar behemah* (quoting Rabbeinu Ephraim).

[4] This question was raised by Rabbi Pinhas Menahem Justman of Piltz (Pilica), *Siftei Tsaddik, Vayyera*, paragraph 66, and earlier par. 63. The author reasons that since the slaughter was to take place upon the altar itself, no vessel was required to convey the blood to the altar; Isaac would have bled directly onto the altar. (Normally, ritual slaughter would take place on the side of the altar and the vessel would be required for the conveyance of the blood to be thrown upon the altar.)

Rabbi Pinhas Menahem Justman (1848-1920) was the grandson of Rabbi Isaac Meir Alter (*Hiddushei ha-RIM*), progenitor of the Gur Hasidic dynasty, and the brother-in-law of Rabbi Judah Aryeh Leib Alter (*Sefat Emet*). After the demise of the *Sefat Emet*, some of the Gerrer Hasidim accepted the *Siftei Tsaddik* as their rebbe.

[5] Rabbi Isaac Judah Trunk (1879-1939), succeeded his famed grandfather Rabbi Israel Joshua Trunk (known popularly as "Reb Yehoshua'leh Kutner") as rabbi of Kutno. He was responsible for the publication of his grandfather's responsa, *Yeshu'ot Malko*.

The young Rabbi Trunk was married to the daughter of Rabbi Samuel Bornstein, the Rebbe of Sochatchov (Sochaczew). Unlike most of Poland's rabbis, who were affiliated with *Agudat Yisrael*, the young Rabbi of Kutno was a prominent member of the *Mizrahi* movement. For this reason, he suffered marginalization by his rabbinic peers.

Rabbi Trunk's remarks are included in his response to Rabbi Moshe Rotenberg's work, *Bikkurei Aviv*. See *Bikkurei Aviv* (St. Louis, MO, 1942), chap. 10, par. 10 (65d-66a).

[6] The four services (*'avodot*) that comprise the process of offering a sacrifice are: slaughter (*shehitah*); receiving the blood (*kabbalat ha-dam*); walking the blood

(*holakhat ha-dam*) and throwing the blood (*zerikat ha-dam*). (See *m. Zevahim* 1:4; Maimonides, *MT, Hil. Ma'aseh ha-Korbanot* 4:10.) It should be pointed out that even the initial step of slaughtering the animal is purposed solely for extracting the blood, the "portion of Above" (*"helek gavo'ah"*). See Rashi, *Zevahim* 13b, s.v. *bi-shelama komets*.

[7] The passage in *Mekhilta, Bo*, would seem to be an exception to the rule. There we read: "'And I shall see the blood' [Exodus 12:13]—I see the *blood* of the binding of Isaac."

[8] 1 Chronicles 21:15; *b. Berakhot* 62b.

[9] *y. Ta'anit* 2:1; *b. Ta'anit* 16a.

[10] *b. Zevahim* 62a.

[11] *Pirke deRabbi Eliezer*, translated and annotated Gerald Friedlander (New York: Sepher-Hermon, 1981), end chap. 35 (p. 267, n. 4).

[12] According to *Pirkei de-Rabbi Eliezer* (chap. 31), Isaac was the first to recite the blessing, "Who resurrects the dead." See Rabbi David Luria's commentary there, *Be'ur ha-RaDaL*, note 59; and Friedlander ed., p. 228, n. 7.

[13] Isaiah 63:16; *b. Shabbat* 89b.

Vayyigash
Bittul Yitsra de-Sin'at Hinam
(An End to Infighting)

We read in this week's Torah portion of the rapprochement between feuding brothers, specifically Joseph and Judah. This theme is reflected in the *Haftarah*, the reading from the Prophets, which is designed to act as a mirror image of the Pentateuchal reading.[1]

By the time of the Prophet Ezekiel, the nation of Israel had been divided into two kingdoms: the Kingdom of Israel (or Joseph) in the North, and the Kingdom of Judah in the South. Ezekiel is commanded by God to perform a symbolic act (referred to in Nahmanidean terminology as a *"po'al dimyoni"*).[2] He is to take two sticks. Upon one he is to write: "For Judah." Upon the other he must write: "For Joseph." He is then to bind the two sticks together as one. This is to symbolize that the LORD will reunite Joseph and Judah.

> When the children of your people will say to you, Will you not tell us what these are to you? Speak to them, Thus said the LORD, Behold I am taking the Tree of Joseph...and the tribes of Israel, his companions, and placing them together with the Tree of Judah, and I shall make them into one tree, and they shall be one in my hand.[3]

The brothers' sin of selling Joseph into slavery was so grievous that one of the great teachers of Torah who perished in the Holocaust, Rabbi Elhanan Wasserman (*Rosh Yeshivah* of Baranovich), opined that the blood libels brought against the Jews throughout the centuries were divine retribution for the nation's collective guilt in having sold the righteous Joseph![4]

Unfortunately, the Satan of *sin'at hinam* (literally, "free hatred"), senseless hatred and infighting between members of our own people, still dances among us. How does one eradicate this bane?

The Talmud tells us that the First Temple was destroyed on account of the three cardinal sins rampant during the First Temple era: idolatry, sexual immorality and murder. The Second Temple, on the other hand, was destroyed due to the sin of *sin'at hinam*, internal strife, hatred of Jew for Jew.[5]

Rav Kook is famous for having said that the corrective to *sin'at hinam* ("free hatred") is *ahavat hinam* ("free love"). Just as the Temple was destroyed on account of senseless hatred, so it will be rebuilt by the power of senseless love that one Jew has for another.

Rav Kook had a dear friend, a fellow kabbalist, by the name of Pinhas Hakohen Lintop (1852-1924), Rabbi of Birzh (Biržai), Lithuania.[6] Rabbi Lintop had a different idea how we might solve the ongoing problem of *sin'at hinam*.

According to the Talmud, at the very onset of the Second Temple, a Great Assembly was convened to abolish the *yitsra da-'avodah zarah*, the drive for idolatry. The *Anshei Knesset ha-Gedolah* (Men of the Great Assembly) knew that it would be pointless to erect a Second Temple as long as the compulsion for idolatry was yet intact. As long as Jews were yet drawn to idolatry, it was a foregone conclusion that this new temple would suffer the same fate as its predecessor. So the *Anshei Knesset ha-Gedolah* came together and through their power of prayer, abolished the entire phenomenon of idolatry.[7]

Rabbi Lintop reasoned that what is required in our own day—so that we may rebuild the Temple—is to once again convene a *Knesset ha-Gedolah*, a Great Assembly, this time to abolish the *yitsra de-sin'at hinam*, the driving compulsion for senseless, irrational hatred so rampant among us.[8]

In fact, Rabbi Lintop hoped that the *Knessiyah ha-Gedolah* of the World Agudath Israel movement, convened in Vienna in the month of Ellul, 5683 (1923), would be the golden opportunity for doing away with infighting, once and for all. To this end, he wrote an address to that great congress, in which he outlined his plan. He requested of Rabbi Hayyim Ozer Grodzenski of Vilna, the acknowledged leader of the generation, that he read the address from the podium![9]

Needless to say, Rabbi Lintop was sorely disappointed when the *Knessiyah ha-Gedolah*, despite its truly remarkable achievement in unifying disparate elements of the Jewish People—*Hasidim* and *Mitnagdim*, Hirschians from Frankfurt and Mussarites from Slabodka, et al—failed to live up to the potential that the visionary expected of it.

Perhaps the saddest commentary on the failure of the *Knessiyah Gedolah* was the fact that at the convention itself, abuse was heaped upon Rav Kook of Jerusalem, Rabbi Lintop's dearest friend and soul "brother." For that reason, the elder statesman, the saintly Rabbi Israel Meir Hakohen (author of *Hafets Hayyim*), felt forced to walk out of the convention in demonstrative protest, locking himself away in his hotel room, awaiting his return to Radin.

Sadly enough, the lion of senseless hatred continues to roar with all its might.

---

[1] See Maimonides, *MT*, *Hil. Tefillah* 13:3.

[2] See Nahmanides' commentary to Genesis 12:6 (Chavel ed. p. 77). One might wish to draw parallels between Nahmanides' theory of prophecy and the practice of sympathetic (or imitative) magic.

[3] Ezekiel 37:18-19.

[4] Rabbi Elhanan Bunim Wasserman, *"Divrei Aggadah,"* appended to *Kovets He'arot le-Masekhet Yevamot* (Piotrków, 1932), chap. 6, par. 7.

[5] *b. Yoma* 9b.

[6] See Bezalel Naor, *Kana'uteh de-Pinhas* (Spring Valley, NY: Orot, 2013).

[7] *b. Yoma* 69b; *Sanhedrin* 64a.

[8] See Rabbi Pinhas Hakohen Lintop, *Yalkut Avnei Emunat Yisrael* (Warsaw, 1895), 18b-19b; idem, *Binyan ha-'Ummah* (Piotrków, 1907), 13a-14a.

[9] Facsimile in *Kana'uteh de-Pinhas*, p. 101.
Remarkably, the Rebbe of Gur, Rabbi Abraham Mordechai Alter (*"Imrei Emet"*), one of the pillars of Agudat Yisrael, wrote in a somewhat similar vein that the Agudah must steer clear of controversy and the *yetser ha-ra'* of *sin'at hinam*. See his *Mikhtevei Torah*, ed. Abramovitz and Alter, 2nd enlarged edition (Tel-Aviv, 1987), Letter 139 (pp. 204-205). See also Rabbi Judah Aryeh Leib Alter, *Sefat Emet*, *Vayyakhel* 5646, s.v. *'od*, and the correction in *Mikhtevei Torah*, p. 228, n. 24.

Shemot
Exile of the Word

According to the *Zohar*, speech was in exile in Egypt.[1] The French Jewish thinker Andre Neher adopted this theme from the *Zohar* as the title of one of his studies, *L'Exil de la parole*, translated into English as *Exile of the Word*.

Developing this idea, Rabbi Isaac Luria punned that the deliverance from Egypt, *Pesah* (Passover), is actually two words: *Peh sah* ("talking mouth").[2] The redemption consists in the liberation of the word.

Whereas the Torah itself discusses only the speech impediment of Moses, who by his own admission was a stutterer and stammerer (*kevad peh u-khevad lashon*),[3] our great thinkers portray the existential condition of the Children of Israel in Egypt as one of collective muteness. Rabbi Joseph Baer Soloveitchik of Boston once remarked that the expressions the Torah employs to describe the Children of Israel's reaction to the oppression of slavery (*ze'akah, shav'ah, na'akah*)[4] evoke the anguished outcry, the moaning and groaning of a wounded animal; nothing even approaching the eloquence of prayer. One might go so far as to say that their response is "preverbal." (Rabbi Soloveitchik was preceded in this observation by Rabbi Abraham Tsevi Margaliyot, eminent disciple of the Hasidic Rabbi Tsadok Hakohen of Lublin.)[5]

One muses aloud that this is perhaps the symbolism of the custom of eating eggs during the meal at the *Seder* table on the night of the fifteenth of Nissan.[6] Eggs have no "mouth." They symbolize muteness. For this reason, traditionally they are eaten by mourners.[7] As a result of the loss of a loved one, the mourner is plunged into a state of muteness. The eggs would come to remind us of the exile of the word in Egypt.

The one Hebrew who stands out as an exception to the muted, "silent picture" of Egypt is: Shelomit bat Divri. Rashi interprets her name in the following manner:

Shelomit—For she would chatter, "Shalom to you! Shalom to you!" She would chatter on, extending greeting to all.

Bat Divri—She was (overly) talkative, speaking with everyone....[8]

Rashi goes on to explain that Shelomit's behavior led to her undoing, whereby she bore a son to an Egyptian. (This Egyptian man was none other than the Egyptian overseer slain by Moses.)[9] But short of committing adultery, her talkativeness alone was inappropriate behavior in that state of "exile of the word." Just as it is improper in a house of mourning (*beit ha-'evel*) to extend the greeting of "Shalom,"[10] so in Egypt the greeting of "Shalom" was certainly out of character.

---

[1] *Zohar* II, 25b.
[2] Rabbi Hayyim Vital, *Sha'ar ha-Kavvanot, 'Inyan ha-Pesah, Derush* 3.
[3] Exodus 4:10. Interesting is Onkelos' Aramaic version of *"kevad lashon"*: *"'amik lishan"* (literally, "deep of tongue"). Might this be an allusion to the Rabbinic tradition that Moses had a very deep voice? See Rashi to Exodus 2:6, s.v.

ve-hinneh na'ar bokheh: "His voice like that of a lad." While yet an infant, Moses possessed the voice of a pubescent boy. However, this is a matter of controversy between Rabbi Judah and Rabbi Nehemiah in *b. Sotah* 12b. See Nahmanides' commentary, Exodus 2:6, s.v. *ve-hinneh na'ar bokheh* (Chavel ed., p. 283), and Rabbi Menahem Kasher, *Torah Sheleimah*, Exodus 2:6 (p. 65, n. 46).

Upon closer inspection, Onkelos' *'amik lishan* reflects the phrase "*'imkei safah ve-khivdei lashon*" in Ezekiel 3:5,6. See Rabbi Abraham son of the Vilna Gaon, *Tirgem Avraham* (Jerusalem, 1896), Exodus 4:10 (8b).

[4] Exodus 2:23-24.
[5] See Rabbi Abraham Tsevi Margaliyot, *Keren 'Orah* (Jerusalem, 1986), *Va'era*, p. 81. The author compares the outcry in Egypt to the sound of the *shofar*, and to the roar of the lion (see *Zohar* III, 191a). Rabbi Margaliyot further explains that Moses, who represented the collective Israel, was afflicted with their collective muteness, whereas his brother Aaron, who was not identified with the collective but had a private identity, was spared this fate.
[6] Gloss of Rabbi Moses Isserles to *Shulhan 'Arukh, Orah Hayyim* 476:2. This custom was preserved in the Lithuanian community.
[7] Ibid.
[8] Rashi, Leviticus 24:11.
[9] See Rashi, Exodus 2:11 and Leviticus 24:10.
[10] *b. Mo'ed Katan* 21b; Maimonides, *MT, Hil. Evel* 5:1, 20; *Shulhan 'Arukh, Yoreh De'ah* 385:1.

YITRO:

JETHRO: A DOUBLE EPIPHANY

"Jethro heard...." (Exodus 18:1)
What did he hear that prompted him to come?
The Splitting of the Reed Sea and the War of Amalek.
(Rashi)

Jethro, the Priest of Midian, father-in-law of Moses, is described in the Midrashic literature as a lifelong spiritual seeker, a man who researched every religion until he arrived at the faith of Israel.[1] The question, what motivated him to relinquish his past and adopt the new faith, is especially poignant. And the solution of the sage, that he gravitated to the camp of Israel because of two specific events—the Splitting of the Sea and the War with Amalek—must be of great significance.

One might simply say that it was the cumulative effect of the two events that vindicated Israel's cause, as the verse continues: "....all that God (*Elohim*) did for Moses and for His people Israel, that the LORD (*YHVH*) brought Israel out of Egypt."[2]

However, it is possible that each event represented a different dimension, and that it was the combination of these two disparate dimensions, the synthesis of two opposed values, that convinced Jethro that he had finally discovered the true faith.

If we examine closely, we find that the two events—the Splitting of the Sea and the War of Amalek—are diametrically opposed. The Splitting of the Sea was an openly miraculous event. Man did not partner with God in this event. The people were instructed by Moses to remain passive, to forgo armed resistance against the approaching hordes of Pharaoh: "The LORD shall fight for you, and you shall remain silent."[3] The battle with Amalek, on the other hand, was an event cloaked in natural raiment[4]: "Moses said to Joshua: 'Choose for us men and go do battle with Amalek….'"[5]

In the Splitting of the Sea, Jethro heard the miraculous, the suspension of the laws of nature. In Israel's victory over Amalek in battle, a natural occurrence, Jethro heard the manifestation of God in nature.

Rashi has been accused of conflating two different opinions of the sages, that of Rabbi Eliezer who attributed Jethro's conversion to the Splitting of the Sea, and that of Rabbi Joshua, who attributed it to the victory over Amalek.[6]

I humbly submit that Rashi is responding to the challenge of the verse itself: "Jethro heard all that God (*Elohim*) did for Moses and for His people Israel, that the LORD (*YHVH*) brought Israel out of Egypt." In the first half of the verse, *Elohim* authors the event; in the second half, the Tetragrammaton, *YHVH*, is responsible for the deliverance of Israel from Egypt. Logically, the first event described is the natural victory over Amalek.[7] "*Elohim be-gematria ha-Teva'*," goes the saying. "*Elohim* has the same numerical value as Nature."[8] The Exodus from Egypt, a miraculous event, is the incursion of the supernatural aspect of the divinity, signified by the name YHVH.[9]

And it was this combination—the manifestation of the God of Israel in both the miraculous and natural realms—that prevailed upon Jethro to come to take shelter under the "wings of the *Shekhinah*."

Jethro overheard a snippet of what would be recurring themes within the ongoing conversation between God and His people Israel. He witnessed a single cycle of a repetitive process. Moments of miracle and of nature would alternate in the divine history of this people right up to the modern era.

Roughly around the time of the Balfour Declaration in 1917, there came to Rav Kook (then living in London) as if in a reverie, the Talmudic proverb, *"Tav le-meitav tan du, mi-le-meitav armelu"* ("Better to dwell as two, than dwell as a widow").[10] This mundane statement about relations between man and woman, Rav Kook interpreted symbolically as bespeaking the relation between Israel and the Holy One, blessed be He. Rather than reside in a state of "widowhood" in the exile, Israel would emerge from that *galut* through a process involving both the natural and the miraculous, thus *TaN*, the initials of *Teva'-Nes* (nature-miracle).[11]

---

[1] This background was derived from the words of Jethro: "Now I know that the LORD is greater than all the gods" (Exodus 18:11). See *Mekhilta, Yitro,* quoted in Rashi ad loc.
  According to Rabbi Isaac Meir Rothenburg-Alter of Gur, this was Jethro's intention when, according to the Midrash, he made Moses swear that his first son would worship idolatry. Jethro wished his grandson to follow his path of

spiritual experimentation in order to finally appreciate the veracity of the Israelite faith, and to be able to utter these words: "Now I know that the LORD is greater than all the gods." See *Mekhilta de-Rabbi Ishmael, Yitro, Masekhta da-'Amalek*, chap. 1; Rabbi Samuel of Shinawa (Sieniawa), *Ramatayim Tsofim* (on *Tanna de-Vei Eliyahu*), ed. Shmuel Tsevi Zinger (Jerusalem, 2016), chap. 2, par. 27 (pp. 30-31); *Hiddushei ha-RIM 'al ha-Torah*, ed. Judah Leib Levin (Jerusalem, 2010), *Shemot*, s.v. *Vayyoel Moshe* (Exodus 2:21), p. 83 (quoting *Si'ah Sarfei Kodesh*, part 4). (It is highly ironic that Rabbi Menahem Mendel Kasher, himself a *hasid* of Gur, did not mention this solution of the *Hiddushei ha-RIM* to the puzzling Midrash, in addition to all the other attempted solutions. See *Torah Sheleimah* to Exodus 2:21, par. 166 [pp. 97-98].)

See now Rabbi Abraham Isaac Hakohen Kook, *Metsi'ot Katan* (Jerusalem: Maggid, 2018), para. 127 (p. 208), who also interpreted the Middrash thus.

[2] The Kamenitzer Maggid, Rabbi Hayyim Zundel Maccoby, interpreted Rashi in the following manner. Rashi's question is what caused Jethro to act with such alacrity. His answer is that Jethro reasoned that just as the Egyptians and Amalek had gone very far out of their way to pursue Israel to destroy them, so he must pick himself up and act with alacrity to join Israel. Sometimes one must learn a lesson from the behavior of the wicked; one must apply their method to the execution of good deeds. The Maggid quotes in this regard the verse in Psalms 119:98: "From my enemies teach me Your commandments." (This interpretation of the verse was misattributed to Bahya's *Hovot ha-Levavot*.) See Rabbi Hayyim Zundel Maccoby, *Imrei Hayyim*, ed. Max Mansky (Tel-Aviv, 1929), p. 193, par. 31.

[3] Exodus 14:14.

[4] Nahmanides developed the concept that "nature" (*"teva'"*) is in fact "hidden miracles" (*"nissim nistarim"*). See Nahmanides' commentary to the Pentateuch, Exodus 13:16 (Chavel ed., pp. 346-347), and his sermon, *"Torat Hashem Temimah,"* in *Kitvei Rabbeinu Moshe ben Nahman*, ed. C.B. Chavel, vol. 1 (Jerusalem: Mossad Harav Kook, 1968), pp. 152-155.

[5] Exodus 17:9.

[6] *Mekhilta*; and *Zevahim* 116a. See the numerous supercommentaries to Rashi. Another issue raised by the supercommentaries is that Rashi disregarded the third opinion, that of Rabbi El'azar ha-Moda'i; who attributed Jethro's conversion to the event of the giving of the Torah on Mount Sinai. The consensus is that Rashi follows the sequence of the Torah whereby Jethro appeared before the giving of the Torah, whereas Rabbi El'azar ha-Moda'i evidently subscribed to the opinion that the events narrated in the Torah do not appear in chronological order (*"Ein mukdam u-me'uhar ba-Torah"*) and that Jethro appeared after the giving of the Torah. (However, see Rashi, Exodus 18:9, s.v. *'al kol ha-tovah*, who seems to imply that Jethro arrived after the giving of the Torah.)

Most curious is a letter of the Rogatchover Gaon, Rabbi Joseph Rosen, in which he supposedly finds elements of the ongoing struggle with Amalek—within the event of the Splitting of the Sea! In this respect, he adduces the comment of the *Mekhilta, Beshallah*, 1: "'It was told to the King of Egypt that the people fled' [Exodus 14:5]—Some say, Amalek told him." See *She'elot u-Teshuvot Tsafnat Pa'ne'ah ha-Hadashot*, vol. 2 (Modi'in 'Ilit, 2012), Letter 15 (pp. 456-457). The letter is datelined "Dvinsk, *Motsa'ei Hag ha-Matsot*,

5693 [i.e., 1933].

The Rogatchover was probably responding to the latest anti-Semitic laws of the newly installed Nazi regime, which was clearly hell-bent on the destruction of the Jewish People, and thus worthy of the appellation "Amalek," Israel's mortal enemy.

[7] The reference in the verse to Moses may be an allusion to the part played by the "hands of Moses" in the victory over Amalek. See Rashi to Exodus 17:11, quoting *m. Rosh Hashanah* 3:8.

[8] Both have the numerical value of 86. See Rabbi Shneur Zalman of Liadi, *Tanya, Sha'ar ha-Yihud ve-ha-Emunah*, chap. 6. See earlier Rabbi Moses Cordovero, *Pardes Rimonim* 12:2; Rabbi Elijah de Vidas, *Reshit Hokhmah, Sha'ar ha-Teshuvah* (Munkatch, n.d.), chap. 6 (121b); and the response of Rabbi Tsevi Ashkenazi to Rabbi David Nieto, *Hakham* of the Spanish and Portuguese community of London, in *She'elot u-Teshuvot Hakham Tsevi*, no. 18.

See also Rabbeinu Bahaye's commentary to Genesis 2:4, s.v. *be-yom 'asot YHVH Elohim* (Chavel ed., p. 59), and compare earlier Rabbi Joseph Chiquitilla, *Ginat Egoz*, ed. Rabbi Mordechai Attiyah (Jerusalem: Yeshivat Ha-Hayyim ve-ha-Shalom, 1989), Part One, *Sha'ar ha-Havayah* (p. 32).

[9] *Elohim* is a homonym which, besides signifying the divinity, may refer to either an officer, a judge, or the court, depending on context. See Rashi to Exodus 4:16, 7:1, and 21:6. YHVH, on the other hand, refers exclusively to the divinity.

For Rashi's attitude toward miracles, see Avraham Grossman, *Rashi: Religious Beliefs and Social Views* (Hebrew) (Alon Shevut, 2016), pp. 124-134.

On the opposition of the names *Elohim* versus *YHVH*, see Rabbi Judah Halevi, *Kuzari* IV, 1-3; Rabbi Abraham ibn Ezra, *Yesod Mora ve-Sod Torah*, ed. Joseph Cohen and Uriel Simon (Ramat-Gan: Bar-Ilan University Press, 2002), *Sha'ar* 12, par. 2 (pp. 197-199); Maimonides, *Guide of the Perplexed* I, 2, 61; II, 6; idem, *MT, Hil. Yesodei ha-Torah* 1:1-6 (as explained in my work, *Shod Melakhim* [Jerusalem: Makhon RaMHaL, 2018], pp. 15-17); Rabbi Shneur Zalman of Liadi, *Tanya, Sha'ar ha-Yihud ve-ha-Emunah*, chaps. 4, 6; Rabbi Hayyim of Volozhin, *Nefesh ha-Hayyim*, ed. Yissachar Dov Rubin (B'nei Berak, 1989), III, 10-12.

Though there is a famous disagreement between the authors of *Tanya* and *Nefesh ha-Hayyim* how to employ the terms *memalei kol 'almin* and *sovev kol 'almin*—so that for *Tanya*, *Elohim* is equated with *memalei kol 'almin* and YHVH with *sovev kol 'almin*; and for *Nefesh ha-Hayyim* it is the exact opposite, whereby *Elohim* becomes *sovev kol 'almin* and YHVH becomes *memalei kol 'almin* (see *Nefesh ha-Hayyim* III, 4, 11 [Rubin ed., pp. 156, 177-178]) —they would come together to regard *Elohim* as nature and YHVH as miracle. (On the controversy between the *Sefer ha-Tanya* and *Nefesh ha-Hayyim*, see Rabbi Shelomo Fisher, *Beit Yishai: Derashot* [Jerusalem, 2003], 355a.)

The appropriateness of attaching the name YHVH to the event of the Splitting of the Sea is borne out by the novel suggestion of the Rogatchover Gaon that the reliving of the event on the seventh day of Passover satisfies the halakhic requirement of "before the LORD" (Deuteronomy 26:13) in regard to the recitation of *viddui ma'aser* on that day. Maimonides had written that one recites *viddui ma'aser* even when there is no Temple in Jerusalem. RABaD of Posquières objected that there is a stipulation that it be recited "before the

LORD," which is possible only in the presence of the Temple. (See Maimonides, *Hil. Ma'aser Sheni* 11:4 and RABaD's animadversion there.) The Rogatchover rose to the defense of Maimonides by saying that since the day to recite *viddui ma'aser* is the seventh day of Passover (see *m. Ma'aser Sheni* 5:10), which just so happens to be the commemoration of the Splitting of the Sea, that epiphany, reenacted every year, serves the purpose of reciting "before the LORD." It is hard to know whether the Rogatchover intended this in a strictly halakhic vein or was writing in an aggadic, or homiletic, vein. The Rogatchover's letter is cited above note 6.

Inter alia, Rabbi Elijah David Rabinowitz-Te'omim (ADeReT) and his son-in-law, Rav Kook, promoted the recitation of *viddui ma'aser* on the seventh day of Passover, in conformity with the opinion of Maimonides and *Shulhan 'Arukh* (over and against the opinion of RABaD). See ADeReT's work, *Aharit ha-Shanim*, and Rabbi Abraham Isaac Hakohen Kook, *Mishpat Kohen*, no. 56.

However, for the sake of objectivity, it is possible that attributing this construal of the names *Elohim* and *YHVH* (whereby *Elohim* is to be equated with the natural order and *YHVH* with the supernatural or miraculous) to Rashi is unlawful. The sources I cited—*Kuzari*, *Yesod Mora*, *Moreh ha-Nevukhim*—belong to what has come to be known as the Andalusian or Sefardic tradition, whereas Rashi is the bearer of Ashkenazic tradition.

Furthermore, Rabbi Moshe Maimon has brought to my attention that even within the so-called Andalusian tradition, there was great reluctance to account for the Torah's usage of the two names *Elohim* and *YHVH*. Thus, Abraham Maimonides wrote: "We cannot know why in one place a certain name was employed and in a different place another name; and if we can understand this in a few verses, we cannot understand it in all the verses" (Rabbeinu Avraham ben ha-RaMBaM, *Peirush ha-Torah*, ed. Rabbi Moshe Maimon, *Bereishit* [Monsey, NY, 2020], Genesis 2:4 [pp. 122-123]). Earlier, Sa'adyah Gaon seems to have downplayed the difference between the two names; see the sources quoted by Rabbi Maimon, ibid., note 165.

[10] This statement of Reish Lakish occurs in several instances in the Talmud with practical halakhic ramifications. (See *b. Yevamot* 118b; *Ketubot* 75a; *Kiddushin* 7a, 41a; *Bava Kamma* 111a.) The import of the adage is that a woman prefers the companionship of any husband rather than dwelling alone. Today, there is lively discussion whether this halakhic psychology of woman still applies. Rabbi J.B. Soloveitchik of Boston was adamant that this is an existential principle not subject to the vagaries of society.

Unlike the rest of the adage which is Aramaic, the phrase *"tan du"* is Farsi, meaning "two bodies" or "two persons." (*"Tan"* is the word for body or person; *"du"* is two.) See Alexander Kohut, *Aruch Completum*, s.v. *tandur*. Clearly, this adage is a rhyme (*tan du/armelu*).

[11] This reverie is recorded in *Kevatsim mi-Ketav Yad Kodsho*, ed. Boaz Ofen, vol. 1 (Jerusalem, 2006), *Pinkas "Reshimot London,"* par. 23 (p. 200):

> *"Tav le-meitav TaN du,"* says Ecclesia Israel. Better that nature (*teva'*) and miracle (*nes*) should be combined together, initials *TaN*, in order that there sprout a horn of salvation, rather than dwell as a widow, "She has become as a widow" [Lamentations 1:1]. Rather build the House of Israel in the Land of Israel through all the opportune ways. And the LORD will return to His people. And "you shall call [Me] 'my man'" [Hosea 2:18].

Yitro

The Balfour Declaration was issued on November 2, 1917 (or 17 Heshvan, 5678 in the Hebrew reckoning). Two entries down from the reverie (par. 25), Rav Kook recorded his (telepathic) thought of Rabbi Ya'akov Moshe Harlap in Jerusalem, which occurred on 5 Kislev. That would have been November 20, 1917, assuming that the Hebrew year (unstated) was 5678. (The problem with that is that Rav Kook wrote that the thought occurred on a Monday, while 5 Kislev, 5678 was a Tuesday!)

Cf. Rav Kook's earlier letter to Rabbi Pinhas Hakohen Lintop, quoting the Ba'al Shem Tov to the effect that one must expect salvation to come through all different ways. See *Iggerot ha-RAYaH*, vol. 1 (Jerusalem: Mossad Harav Kook, 1962), Letter 112 (pp. 141-142).

Yitro

Through a Field-Glass:
Jacob's Ladder and the Altar's Ramp

> Do not ascend by steps to My altar, [so] that your nakedness be not exposed upon it.　　(Exodus 20:23)

In order to observe the injunction that there be no steps leading up to the *mizbe'ah*, or altar, in the Temple, rabbinic tradition demanded construction of an access ramp known as the *kevesh*.[1]

Now there arises a thorny problem. When it comes to the *menorah*, or candelabrum, received tradition dictated the exact opposite: "Make for it steps!"[2] And indeed, there were three steps leading up to the *menorah*.[3] (Why exactly three is not spelled out in the tradition.)[4]

What is one to make of this diametric opposition? When it comes to the altar, we are enjoined: "Make a ramp for the altar!"[5] And when it comes to the candelabrum, we are told the exact opposite: "Make for it steps!"

One approach is to simply chalk the difference up to *"gezeirat ha-katuv"* (scriptural decree). This was the approach of the Tripolitan exegete to Maimonides' code, Rabbi Mas'ud Hai Raccah (1690-1768).[6] It is a time-honored approach. There are some matters of Halakhah that simply defy rational explanation.

Yet it is possible that an anonymous Tosafist living in the Middle Ages did pursue the matter. He writes: "It is a bit difficult why Scripture was more insistent upon the honor of the altar than all the other vessels of the Temple. This requires study."[7]

The thought occurs to this writer (BN) that there is a very good reason why the Torah should have insisted that there be no steps approaching the altar, when there was no such insistence in regard to the other vessels of the Temple.

Very much alive in the historical consciousness of the People of Israel was Jacob's dream of a ladder perched upon the earth, with its head reaching to the heavens, and the angels of God ascending and descending upon it.[8]

Factor in the romanticization of the *kohen*, the priest—which peaked in the prophet Malachi's hyperbole, "For the lips of a priest safeguard knowledge, and they shall seek Torah from his mouth, for he is the angel of the LORD of hosts"[9]—and you begin to get the picture why the Torah forbade steps to the altar.

The image of priests ascending and descending the steps to the altar (halakhically, the prohibition extends to descending the steps as well),[10] would easily have evoked the memory of the angels of God ascending and descending Jacob's ladder to heaven.[11] And this would have led to the divinization of the priests.[12] You will counter that Malachi himself equated priest with angel. Yes, but the prophet was merely employing a figure of speech. The fine line between the figurative and the literal is likely to be crossed by the gullible masses, so the danger of ascribing superhuman qualities to the priestly class is real.[13]

Yitro II

By substituting a ramp for stairs, the Torah broke the connection between the scene in the Temple and the imagery of Jacob's dream.

So far, things appear clear-cut. There is still a major obstacle in our way, and that is the ancient Midrash that established a direct link between the two vistas, the imaginal and the actual:

> Rabbi El'azar ha-Kappar says: How do you know that the Holy One, blessed be He, showed Jacob our father the Temple built, sacrifices being offered, priests serving, and the *Shekhinah* resting?
>
> For it says, "And behold, a ladder standing on the earth, and its head reaching to the heavens, and behold, angels of God ascending and descending upon it" [Genesis 28:12].
>
> There is no dream devoid of interpretation:
>
> *A ladder standing on the earth*—This is the Temple.
>
> *And its head reaching to the heavens*—These are the sacrifices whose aroma ascends to heaven.
>
> *And behold, angels of God*—These are the ministering priests who ascend and descend the ramp (*kevesh*).
>
> *And behold, the LORD stands over it* [Genesis 28:13]— "I saw the LORD standing over the altar" [Amos 9:1].
>
> (*Sifré, Korah,* 119)[14]

What we have are the two ends of a field-glass or binoculars. Through the "right" end, the image is maximized; through the "wrong" end, the image is minimized. When Father Jacob looks from his end, the image is miniscule; the discrepancy between his own steps and the ramp of the future altar is hardly noticeable. He makes the connection, and then, the priests are indeed as angels. However, we, his descendants, look from the end of the glass whereby images are blown up in all their detail. The glaring difference between our own ramp and Jacob's ladder with its steps is emphasized; the connection is broken beyond repair. And deliberately so, for this is the Torah's stratagem for heading off any idolatrous leanings that would make a man into a god, or at least, an angel.

The Torah's ingenuity is highly reminiscent of Jacob's own when discrediting his son Joseph's dream. On the one hand, Jacob knew Joseph's dream to be true. "And his father watched the thing."[15] On the other hand, Jacob wished to poke a hole in the dream so as not to arouse the jealousy of his other children, Joseph's brothers. Joseph dreamt the sun and the moon and eleven stars bowing down to him.[16] The message was transparent enough. One day in the future, the sun (Jacob), the moon (Joseph's mother) and eleven stars (Joseph's eleven brothers) would prostrate themselves before him. Cleverly seizing upon the one detail askew—the moon or mother (for Joseph's mother, Rachel, was already deceased)—

Yitro II

Jacob was able to dismantle the entire dream.[17] "And his father rebuked him, and said unto him: 'What is this dream that you have dreamed? Shall I and your mother and your brothers come to bow down to you to the earth?'"[18]

So the Torah, by altering a single element of the scenario[19]—simply substituting ramp for stairs—was able to disrupt the association with Jacob's ladder, and thus, prevent the popular imagination from transforming the priestly class into some sort of demigods.[20]

---

[1] Maimonides, *MT*, *Hil. Beit ha-Behirah* 1:17.
[2] *Sifré*, *Beha'alotekha*, 59 (Numbers 8:1).
[3] *m. Tamid* 3:9; *b. Menahot* 29a; Maimonides, *MT*, *Hil. Beit a-Behirah* 3:11.
[4] Rabbeinu Obadiah Bertinuro in his commentary to the *Mishnah* posits that the three steps correspond to the three expressions of "raising up" (*ha'ala'ah*) found in the Torah in regard to lighting the *menorah*, but he provides no source for his assertion.
[5] *Mekhilta*, *Yitro* (Exodus 20:23).
[6] *Ma'aseh Rokah*, *Hil. Beit ha-Behirah* 3:11.

An elementary explanation for the difference would be that no service is to be performed upon the ramp itself. It is merely the prelude to the altar where the service is to take place. Thus, there is no reason for the priest to stand still in one place on the ramp. However, the reason for the steps to the candelabrum is to enable the priest to clean and light the candelabrum. (See Maimonides, Commentary to the Mishnah, *Tamid* 3:9; idem, *MT*, *Hil. Beit ha-Behirah* 3:11.) To do so, the priest must stand still, which is physically challenging on a ramp with its incline.

[7] *Moshav Zekenim*, ed. Rabbi Solomon David Sassoon (London, 1959), Exodus 20:23.

Rabbi Mordechai Ilan understood that the Tosafist was comparing the altar to the candelabrum with its steps. See Rabbi Mordechai Ilan, *Torat ha-Kodesh*, vol. 1 (B'nei Berak, 2006), chap. 34 (p. 164, right column). However, it seems more likely that the question was not posed in regard to the construction of the ramp, but rather to the prohibition, derived from the second half of the verse, not to take large steps or run on the altar. See *Mekhilta* to Exodus 20:23:

> *That your nakedness be not exposed upon it*—Upon it, you may not take a large step, but you may take a large step in in the *Heikhal* and in the *Kodesh ha-Kodashim* (Holy of Holies). Logic would have dic-

tated that if on the altar, which is minor, it is forbidden to take a large step, all the more so the *Heikhal* and the *Kodesh ha-Kodashim*, which are major. Therefore it is written, "that your nakedness be not exposed upon it." Upon it, you may not take a large step, but you may take a large step in the *Heikhal* and in the *Kodesh ha-Kodashim*.

The *Mekhilta* goes on to explain that taking a large step is considered a sign of disrespect to the altar:

> And we may deduce by *kal va-homer* (a fortiori): If in regard to stones [of the altar] that have no knowledge, neither good nor bad, the Holy One, blessed be He, said not to behave disrespectfully toward them, then your companion, who is in the likeness of the One who said and the world came into being, one must not behave disrespectfully toward him!

[8] Genesis 28:12.
[9] Malachi 2:7.

Later, Ben Sira wrote a panegyric to the high priest Simeon; see *Ben Sira*, chap. 50. Historians debate whether Ben Sira's "Simon" is the much celebrated Simeon the Just (*Shim'on ha-Tsaddik*) or a descendant by the same name.

Ben Sira's romantic portrayal of the high priest echoes later in the immensely popular medieval liturgical poem, *"Mar'eh Kohen,"* recited in Ashkenazic congregations at the conclusion of the *Seder ha-'Avodah*, commemorating the Temple ritual, recited during the *Musaf* (Additional Service) of Yom Kippur.

[10] *Mekhilta* ad loc.
[11] Rabbeinu Meyuhas paraphrased the verse in Exodus 20:23: "Do not be accustomed to ascend it by *ladder* (*sulam*), step by step, rather make a sloped ramp, and ascend it."
[12] It should be of interest in this connection that according to the Targumim (Pseudo-Jonathan and Yerushalmi), the prohibition of ascending steps to the altar was directed strictly at the priests. This line of thinking is borne out in one of the solutions provided by *Tosafot Yeshanim*, Yoma 22a, s.v. *bi-zeman she-hen merubin ratsin ba-kevesh*. See Rabbi Mordechai Ilan, *Torat ha-Kodesh*, vol. 1, 34:6 (p. 165, right column).
[13] Rabbi Hayyim of Volozhin, reacting to excesses of the Hasidic movement in Eastern Europe, wrote that even submission to the divine spirit of a prophet constitutes *'avodah zarah* (idolatry). See *Nefesh ha-Hayyim* III, 9.
[14] See also *Genesis Rabbah* 68:12:

> *And behold, a ladder*—This is the ramp (*kevesh*).
> *Standing on the earth*—This is the altar, "An altar of earth you shall make for Me" [Exodus 20:21].
> *And its head reaching to the heavens*—These are the sacrifices whose aroma ascends to heaven.
> *And behold, angels of God*—These are the priests,
> *Ascending and descending upon it*—who ascend and descend the ramp.
> *And behold, the LORD stands over it* [Genesis 28:13]—"I saw the LORD standing over the altar" [Amos 9:1].

Also *Tanhuma Vetus, Vayyetse* 7; and the sources cited in Rabbi M.M. Kasher, *Torah Sheleimah*, vol. 5 (Jerusalem, 1936), p. 1130 (Genesis 28:12), par. 69.

[15] Genesis 37:11.
[16] Genesis 37:9.
[17] Rashi, Genesis 37:10.
[18] Genesis 37:10.
[19] The *Halakhah* may be instructive in this regard. It is forbidden to make an exact replica of one of the vessels in the Temple, such as the table of showbread (*shulhan*), or the candelabrum (*menorah*). However, this prohibition can be avoided by altering one of the details, such as fashioning a *menorah* of five, six, or eight branches, as opposed to the original seven-branched *menorah*; or retaining the seven branches but making the *menorah* of a non-metallic substance (such as wood). See *b. 'Avodah Zarah* 43a; Maimonides, *Hil. Beit ha-Behirah* 7:10; *Shulhan 'Arukh, Yoreh De'ah* 141:8.

(Rav Kook suggested—to answer the famous question of the *Beit Yosef*—that we light Hanukkah candles for eight nights—though in reality, the miracle was only for seven nights, because the cruse of oil would have sufficed normally for one night—to prevent us from fashioning a seven-branched *menorah*, which is forbidden by Torah law. See *Mitsvat RAYaH, Orah Hayyim* 670:1 [p. 84].)

[20] We might add that in Maimonides' construal, the altar upon which the sacrifices were offered, is the focal point of the Temple in Jerusalem. See *MT, Hil. Beit ha-Behirah* 1:3; 2:1-2; and the letter of Rabbi Yitzhak Ze'ev Soloveitchik datelined "12 Adar, 5693," regarding the chosenness of the site of the altar (based on the verse in 1Chronicles 22:1); appended to *Hiddushei Maran RIZ ha-Levi ('al ha-RaMBaM)*.

Ki Tissa
Moses and Bezalel:
The "Servant of the Lord"
and the Architect of the Soul

See, I have called by a name, Bezalel son of Uri, son of Hur, of the tribe of Judah. And I have filled him with a spirit of God, with wisdom, understanding and knowledge ....

(Exodus 31:2, 3)

Said Rav Yehudah in the name of Rav: "Bezalel knew [how] to combine the letters with which heaven and earth were created."

(b. Berakhot 55a)

The letters with which heaven and earth were created.—Through their combination (*tseirufan*), and in *Sefer Yetsirah* (the *Book of Creation*) they were taught.

(Rashi)

Bezalel the master artisan was tasked with crafting the various vessels of the Tabernacle in the wilderness.

In the Book of Chronicles we find a most puzzling account. For some unexplained reason, Moses is credited with the making of the Tent of Meeting (*ohel mo'ed*), while Bezalel is credited with making the altar of bronze (*mizbah ha-nehoshet*):

> So Solomon, and all the congregation with him, went to the high place that was at Gibeon, for there was the Tent of Meeting of God, which Moses the servant of the LORD had made in the wilderness.[1]
> And the altar of bronze, that Bezalel the son of Uri, the son of Hur, had made, was there before the tabernacle of the LORD....[2]

This assignation appears to us totally arbitrary. Moses, in his capacity of overseer or supervisor of the entire project might very well have been credited with the altar of bronze as well.[3] On the other hand, Bezalel's purview was certainly not restricted to the altar; it extended to the sundry vessels within the Tent of Meeting, as detailed in Exodus 31:7-11: the ark; the table; the candelabrum (*menorah*); the incense altar; the laver; the priestly vestments, etc.—besides the outer bronze altar upon which the sacrifices were offered.

It seems that the Book of Chronicles has a special relation with the altar. It trains its attention on the altar like no other book of the Bible.[4] This focus, one is almost tempted to say fascination, is later picked up by the great Maimonides. In his Laws of the Temple (*Hilkhot Beit ha-Behirah*), he quotes another defining verse from the Book of Chronicles:

Ki Tissa

This altar—its place is very precise, and [we] must never change it, for it says: "[David said: This is the House of the LORD the God] and this is the altar of sacrifices (*mizbah le-'olah*) for Israel" [1 Chronicles 22:1].[5]

Maimonides then goes on to provide the prehistory of the altar, engaging with Midrashim, something quite out of character for Maimonides, who usually adheres strictly to the *halakhah* without romanticizing about the past.

...and on the altar Isaac our Father was bound, as it says: "Go to the land of Moriah [Genesis 22:2], and it says, "Solomon built the Temple on Mount Moriah" [1 Kings 6:14 and 2 Chronicles 3:1].

And it is a common tradition that the place that David[6] and Solomon built the altar in the field of Araunah, is the [very] place where Abraham built the altar and bound upon it Isaac; and it is the place where Noah built [an altar] when he went out from the Ark; and it is the altar upon which Cain and Abel sacrificed; and upon it Adam sacrificed when he was just created; and from there he was created. Said the Sages: Adam was created from the place of his atonement.[7]

The statement of Rav, "Bezalel knew [how] to combine the letters with which heaven and earth were created," lacks context. To what was Rav referring? In order to craft all the articles of the Tabernacle, did Bezalel really require esoteric knowledge; did he truly need to know the building blocks of God's creation?[8] Certainly, he would have needed to be familiar with the basics of design; he would have had to master the wisdom of architecture, but "combining the letters with which heaven and earth were created"? This is too much! Was Rav engaging in exaggeration, in hyperbole?

I believe that Maimonides has provided the key which will at once unlock the mystery of the verses in Chronicles and afford context to Rav's enigmatic statement.

Moses, "the servant of the LORD," is credited with responsibility for making the entire Tabernacle, with one notable exception—the altar of bronze. That was simply beyond his ken. To make that altar there was required one who "knew [how] to combine the letters with which heaven and earth were created." As Maimonides explained so eloquently, that altar reaches back in time to the very creation of man. Man's heartstrings are tied to that altar. The altar is part and parcel of man's existential condition. This in a nutshell is the human condition. Man is prone to sin and is in need of expiation. "Man was created from the place of his atonement." Which is to say that the altar is the very fabric from which man was cut. What the Sages are conveying to us is that the altar is the *ground* of man's being. Inherent in man is the potential for renewal, reinvention, and recreation.[9]

Ki Tissa

Moses is the "servant of the LORD," but that still does not give him the requisite insight into man's soul; into man's weakness and strength; into man's sinfulness and power of return. For that, one needs to know the prehistory of man, the mystery of man's creation. Only a Bezalel, who "knew the combination of the letters with which heaven and earth were created," was capable of crafting the altar.[10]

As for Rashi's comment that the letters were taught in *Sefer Yetsirah* (the *Book of Creation*). Rashi explains elsewhere how it was possible for the Talmudic sage Rava to create a man (albeit a man lacking the power of speech):

> By *Sefer Yetsirah* they learned the combination of the letters (*tseiruf otiyot*) of the Name.[11]

The same knowledge that could go into the creation of man, was the knowledge that informed Bezalel's fashioning of the altar of bronze.[12]

---

[1] 2 Chronicles 1:3.
[2] 2 Chronicles 1:5.
   In Exodus 29:44 the Tent of Meeting and the altar are presented as two distinct entities.
   In the blessing recited after partaking of the seven species by which the Land of Israel was praised (*berakhah me-'eyn shalosh*) we ask the LORD to

have mercy upon the altar and the Temple (*"ve-'al mizbehekha ve-'al heikhalekha"*). Again, two distinct entities.

³ Indeed, in the Talmud (*b. Zevahim* 59b), the altar of bronze is referred to as the "altar that Moses made" (in opposition to the altar of stones made by Solomon that replaced it).

Rabbi Moshe Maimon *shelit"a* graciously shared with me his extensive footnotes to his forthcoming edition of Rabbi Abraham Maimonides' commentary to the Book of Exodus. In Exodus 25:10, 11, Rabbi Maimon will discuss at some length the problem of *shelihut* (agency) in regard to the construction of the Tabernacle, based on the commentaries of Rabbi Abraham Ibn Ezra, Rabbi Abraham Maimonides, Nahmanides, and Rabbi Hayyim ibn 'Attar (*"'Or ha-Hayyim ha-Kadosh"*).

See also *b. Yoma* 3b, Rashi s.v. *bi-zeman she-hen 'osin retsono shel makom*, and Maharasha ad loc.; and the recently published novellae of *Sha'agat Aryeh* to *Parashat Terumah*, in *Arazim* 5 (Jerusalem, 2019), p. 50.

⁴ The dedication of the altar (*hanukkat ha-mizbe'ah*) in the Tabernacle is mentioned in Numbers 7:10, 11, 84, 88; the dedication of the altar (*hanukkat ha-mizbe'ah*) in Solomon's Temple in 2 Chronicles 7:9.

Later, in the post-Biblical era, the altar looms large in the saga of Hanukkah, and its dedication (*hanukkat ha-mizbe'ah*) gives the festival its name. See 1 Maccabees 4:59; the *scholion* to *Megillat Ta'anit*; Rashi, *Megillah* 30b, s.v. *be-Hanukkah ba-Nesi'im*; Rabbi Isaac 'Or Zaru'a of Vienna, *'Or Zaru'a*, part 2 (Zhitomir, 1862), *Hilkhot Hanukkah*, chap. 321; and Rabbi Shelomo Yosef Zevin, *Ha-Mo'adim ba-Halakhah* (Tel-Aviv: Abraham Zioni, n.d.), p. 161.

For Maimonides' remarks concerning the dedication of the altar (*hanukkat ha-mizbe'ah*) in the Third Temple, see *MT*, *Hil. Ma'aseh ha-Korbanot* 2:14.

The first stanza of the immensely popular medieval hymn *Ma'oz Tsur* (translated into English as "Rock of Ages") ends on the note of dedicating the future altar: *"Az egmor be-shir mizmor hanukkat ha-mizbe'ah."* See Rabbi Joseph Baer Soloveitchik's halakhic interpretation of those words, in *Harerei Kedem*, ed. Rabbi Mikhel Zalman Shurkin, vol. 1 (Jerusalem, 2000), p. 305.

⁵ Maimonides, *MT*, *Hil. Beit ha-Behirah* 2:1. Maimonides quotes the verse earlier as well, in *Hil. Beit ha-Behirah* 1:3.

See the incisive remarks of Rabbi Yitzhak Ze'ev Halevi Soloveitchik in a letter published at the conclusion of *Hiddushei Maran RYZ Halevi* (Jerusalem, 1998), 81a-b. The letter is datelined "12 Adar 5693 [i.e., 1933]." And see Rabbi Mordechai Ilan, *Torat ha-Kodesh*, vol. 2 (B'nei Berak, 1969), chap. 11, para. 2 (54a-b).

⁶ Regarding the role that David played in "building" the place of the altar, see the explanation of Rabbi Isaac Hutner, in *Reshimot Lev*, ed. Rabbi Leib Rutta, vol. 2 (Brooklyn, 2000), *Sukkot* 5735, *"Ushpiza de-Yosef ha-Tsaddik"* (pp. 150-152).

⁷ *Genesis Rabbah* 14:8; *y. Nazir* 7:2. *Hil. Beit ha-Behirah* 2:1, 2.

Rabbi Aharon Lichtenstein once observed that Maimonides and Nahmanides disagree as to which is the essential element of the Temple. For Maimonides, it is clearly the altar. For Nahmanides, on the other hand, the focal point of the Temple is—the ark. See Nahmanides' commentary, beginning *Terumah* (Exodus 25:1; Chavel edition, pp. 553-554) and his animadversion to Maimonides' *Sefer ha-Mitsvot*, positive commandment 33. There, Nahmanides states his opinion that the making of the ark should be reckoned as a

KI TISSA

separate commandment, apart from the commandment to build the Temple (Maimonides' positive commandment 20).

Earlier, RABaD of Posquières questioned why Maimonides did not count building the altar as a separate commandment. See *Hasagot ha-RABaD le-Mishneh Torah*, ed. Bezalel Naor (Jerusalem, 1985), *Minyan ha-Mitsvot*, positive commandment 20 (p. 7).

Recently, Rabbi Benjamin Zeilberger showed that there are instances where Maimonides writes *"bi-fnei ha-bayit"* ("in the presence of the Temple") when he actually refers to the existence of the altar. The author assumes that this peculiar usage derives from Maimonides' reckoning the altar as essential to the Temple. See *Nahalat Binyamin: Bikkurim* (Jerusalem, 2016), chap. 37 (ff. 100-103).

[8] Rabbi Moses Schreiber (*"Hatam Sofer"*) understood that by uttering the *tseiruf otiyot* (permutations of the letters) Bezalel was able to make the vessels in no time. See *Torat Moshe*, ed. Shim'on Sofer (Pressburg, 1906), *Vayyakhel*, s.v. *Bezalel*, 90c-d.

[9] It might be noteworthy that Rabbi Yosé (*b. Zevahim* 59b) personifies the original altar of bronze (later replaced by Solomon with an altar of stones) as a "dwarf" (*nanas*). Certainly, this is merely a figure of speech, as explained by Rashi *ad locum*. However, on a deeper level, it might bespeak the "humanity" of the altar.

For another "humanizing" statement concerning the altar, see *b. Gittin* 90b: "Rabbi El'azar said: Whoever divorces his first wife, even the altar sheds tears for him."

[10] This disparity between Moses and Bezalel, whereby Bezalel displays greater familiarity with the common experience of man, is borne out in the dialogue between Moses and Bezalel reported in the passage immediately preceding in the Talmud:

> Said Rabbi Samuel bar Nahmani in the name of Rabbi Jonathan: Bezalel was named so on account of his wisdom.
>
> At the time that the Holy One, blessed be He, said to Moses, Go tell Bezalel, make for Me a tabernacle, ark and vessels, Moses went and reversed the order, and said to him, Make an ark, vessels and tabernacle.
>
> Bezalel said to him: Moses our Teacher, it is customary that a man builds a house and afterwards brings inside the vessels. But you say, Make Me an ark, vessels and tabernacle. Where should I bring the vessels that I make? Perhaps the Holy One, blessed be he, said to you, Make a tabernacle, ark and vessels.
>
> Moses said to Bezalel: Perhaps you were in the shadow of God (*be-tsel El*) and [that is how] you knew.
>
> (*b. Berakhot* 55a)

An ingenious explanation of the dialogue between Moses and Bezalel (based on *Meshekh Hokhmah*, *Terumah*, s.v. *ve-khen ta'asu*) was put forth by Rabbi David Havlin, *Ve-Nitsdak Kodesh* (Jerusalem, 1981), pp. 282-284.

[11] Rashi, *Sanhedrin* 65b, s.v. *bara gavra*.

See further Ephraim Kanarfogel, "Rashi's Awareness of Jewish Mystical

Literature and Traditions," in *Raschi und seine Erbe*, ed. Krochmalnik, Liss and Reichman (Heidelberg: Hochschule für Jüdische Studien, 2007), pp. 23-34.

[12] My dear friend Rabbi Yisrael Herczeg, *shelit"a*, who has published extensively on Rashi, finds possible support for the "prehistoric" or "supernatural" nature of the altar in the precise wording of the Mishnah, *Middot* 3:4: "Since iron was created (*nivra*) to shorten the days of man, and the altar was created (*nivra*) to lengthen the days of man, it is unlawful that that which shortens should be lifted against that which lengthens." Usually, the word *"bara"* (created) is reserved for the divine or supernatural. (Cf. *b. Kiddushin* 30b: "I created [*barati*] the evil inclination, and I created [*barati*] the Torah as its antidote.") See Nahmanides, Genesis 1:1, s.v. *Bereshit* (Chavel ed., p. 12); and Genesis 1:21, s.v. *Vayyivra Elohim et ha-taninim ha-gedolim* (Chavel ed., p. 26).

Rashi quotes the Mishnah *Middot* in his commentary to Exodus 20:22. Maimonides (*Guide* III, 45; Pines edition, p. 578) quotes the tail end: "It is unlawful that that which shortens should be lifted against that which lengthens."

Vayyakhel-Pekudei
Nahmanides on the Tabernacle

A major portion of the book of Exodus is taken up by a painstakingly detailed description of the construction of the Tabernacle (*Mishkan*) in the desert. The magnificent architecture has come to be associated with the name of Bezalel, the chief craftsman or artisan, the mastermind in charge of the design, lo, the "brains" of the operation.

Yet the question remains: Why should the Torah lavish so much attention upon the layout of this prototypical temple? Moses is not Frank Lloyd Wright. Whatever the Torah of Moses is (and that is open to some debate), it is not a manual of architecture.

I believe that a solution to this vexatious problem may lie in the famous words of Nahmanides' Introduction to the Book of Exodus:

> The text completed the Book of Genesis, which is the book of the creation of the world and the creation of all the creatures, and the events of the Patriarchs, which are sort of the creation for their seed, for all their events are illustrations, alluding to all that will befall them in the future.
>
> And after having completed the creation, [the text] commenced another book concerning the deed that proceeds from those allusions. The Book of Exodus is devoted to the first exile that was explicitly decreed, and upon the

redemption from it. Therefore it begins with the names of those who descended to Egypt, and their number, though that had been written earlier [in the Book of Genesis], for their descent there is the beginning of the exile, from whence it commenced.

Now the exile is not terminated until the day of their return to their place and to the level of their forefathers. When they went out of Egypt, though they emerged from the house of bondage, they would yet be considered exiles, for they were in a foreign land, straying in the desert. When they arrived at Mount Sinai, and made the Tabernacle, whereby the Holy One, blessed be He, restored His divine presence to their midst, then they returned to the level of their forefathers, upon whose tents rested the divine mystery, they [i.e., the forefathers] being the Chariot [of God]. *And then they were considered redeemed (ve-'az nehshavu ge'ulim).* Therefore this book concludes with the completion of the Tabernacle and the glory of the Lord filling it perpetually.[1]

The sentence that I have seen fit to italicize is a bold statement indeed. It would be a bold statement coming from any Jew, but all the more so from the pen of Nahmanides! Many years ago, the late *Rosh Yeshivah* of Ponevezh in B'nei Berak, the great Torah sage Rabbi El'azar Menahem Man Shach aroused the ire of many when he somewhat minimized the importance of the State of Israel by stating the rather obvious fact that the Jewish People experienced nationhood before ever arriving in the Land. He did not invoke the passage in Nahmanides' commentary cited above. Nahmanides' statement is perhaps even more daring than that of the Ponevezh Rosh Yeshivah: "And then they were considered redeemed!" Not having stepped foot on the holy soil of the Land of Israel, the People were already reckoned redeemed by virtue of the fact that they had regained their former spiritual height, inasmuch as the divine presence permeated the Tabernacle.

This statement, which seems to call into question the absolute necessity of dwelling in the Land, is all the more surprising having been uttered by none other than Nahmanides. Anyone at all familiar with Nahmanides, knows that among all the *Rishonim* or medieval giants, he stands out in his declaration of the centrality of the Land of Israel to Judaism. It is Nahmanides who writes at great length in his commentary to the Pentateuch that essentially the performance of the commandments (all the commandments, not just *mitsvot ha-teluyot ba-arets*, such as the various agricultural laws) pivots on the Land of Israel. He cites the *Sifré* ('*Ekev*) to the effect that in performing commandments outside the Land, we are merely going through the motions, so that these observances not be forgotten.[2] It is also Nahmanides who (in his glosses to Maimonides' *Book of the Commandments*) counts dwelling in the Land of Israel as a positive commandment, trailing off on the note that "dwelling in the Land of Israel is equal to all the commandments."[3] Yet it is this same Nahmanides who issues our curious statement: "And *then* they were considered redeemed (*ve-'az nehshavu ge'ulim*)."

Torah

I believe that it is *because* Nahmanides views the Land of Israel to be central to Judaism, that he is forced to conclude that the Tabernacle is, in so many words, a virtual Erets Yisrael. (In Hebrew, this logic is formulated as *"ve-hi ha-notenet."*) Nahmanides would have been struck by a glaring omission from the Five Books of Moses: the Land of Israel. When the Five Books conclude, the People are yet outside the Land. Conceptually this is unthinkable. The solution? The Tabernacle in the desert constitutes a virtual Land of Israel. And this may be the solution to our original conundrum.

The Talmud states: "Had Israel not sinned, they would have been given only the Five Books of Moses and the Book of Joshua, because it [i.e., the Book of Joshua] is the value of the Land of Israel *('erkah shel Erets Yisrael)*."[4] All the remaining books of the Bible, the Prophets and Writings (*Nevi'im u-Ketuvim*) are nonessential. The Five Books of Moses and the Book of Joshua are of the essence. But within the very Five Books of Moses there resides a virtual Book of Joshua that, short of actual entry into the Land of Israel, assumes the value of the Land of Israel (*'erkah shel Erets Yisrael*), namely the portion of the Book of Exodus devoted to the work of the Tabernacle. And just as the Book of Joshua will detail ever so lovingly the geography of the Land of Israel, so our section of the Torah will sumptuously, lavishly detail the contours of this Land before the Land: the *Mishkan* or Tabernacle in the Wilderness.

[1] A reference to Exodus 40:34-35.
[2] See Nahmanides, Leviticus 18:25 (Chavel ed., pp. 109-112). See also Nahmanides' comments to Genesis 24:3 (Chavel ed., p. 134); Genesis 26:5 (Chavel ed., p. 150); and Deuteronomy 11:18 (Chavel ed., p. 394).
[3] See Positive Commandment 4 according to the opinion of Nahmanides. In that instance, Nahmanides quotes the *Sifré* (*Re'eh*, 80). In his commentary to Leviticus 18:25 (Chavel ed., p. 111), in addition to the *Sifré*, Nahmanides sources the statement, "Dwelling in the Land of Israel is equal to all the commandments," in the *Tosefta*, *'Avodah Zarah* (chap. 4; Zuckermandel ed., p. 466).
[4] *b. Nedarim* 22b. The commentators (Pseudo-Rashi, Rabbeinu Asher, Rabbeinu Nissim) explain that the Book of Joshua provides the cities and the borders of the territories of the tribes of Israel.

❧ II ❧

TALMUD

The Head Movements of *Shema‘*
(*b. Berakhot* 13b)

The most important utterance in Judaism is the *Shema‘*: *"Shema‘ Yisrael Adonai Eloheinu Adonai ehad."* ("Hear O Israel, the Lord our God, the Lord is one.")[1] This declaration of the absolute unity of God is the cornerstone of our faith. By Biblical mandate, a Jew recites the *Shema‘* twice daily, *"be-shokhbekha u-ve-kumekha"* ("when you lie down and when you rise up").[2]

All of the above is quite famous. What remains today a little known fact is that once upon a time this recitation was accompanied by head movements to the four directions, and up and down. This practice is recorded both in the *Ge'onim* (post-Talmudic Babylonian sages) and the *Rishonim* (medieval European sages).[3] The basis for this observance is the following statement in the Talmud:

> Symmachus says: "Whoever prolongs the word *'ehad'* ('one'), his days and years are prolonged."
>
> Said Rav Aha bar Ya‘akov: "And [specifically] the letter *dalet* [of *'ehad'*]."
>
> Said Rav Ashi: "Provided he does not speed up the letter *het* [of *'ehad'*]."
>
> Rav Yirmiyah was sitting before R. [Hiyya bar Abba]. He saw that he was prolonging overly much. He said to

him: "Once you have proclaimed Him king above and below, and to the four winds of heaven, you need not any further."[4]

Rashi, the eleventh-century exegete of Troyes, France, comments: "**Proclaimed Him king above, etc.** – You have prolonged the amount [of time] necessary to think in your heart that the Lord is one in heaven and on earth and its four directions."

This is a disembodied approach; no mention in Rashi of actual body movements. The visualization of heaven and earth and the four cardinal points is purely mental.

However, if one consults the commentary of Rabbi Menahem ha-Me'iri of Perpignan, Provence (1249-1315?), one finds an added dimension: "The amount of lengthening [the letter] *dalet* is that required to picture in the heart that He, blessed be He, rules over heaven and earth and the four winds of the world. And for this reason, it is customary to tilt the head and move it to these sides. Nevertheless, if one prefers not to tilt the head, one need not, because the thing depends not on the tilting of the head and its movements, but rather upon the feeling of the heart."[5]

Me'iri revisits this theme in his commentary to Tractate *Sukkah* when discussing the *na'anu'im* or waving of the *lulav* (palm frond) during the *Sukkot* festival. There, he opines that both in regard to the movement of the *lulav* during the recitation of *Hallel* and the movement of the head during *Shema'*, only a to-and-fro and up-and-down movement is called for (as opposed to the four directions, and up and down): "Even that which they said. . .to prolong [the word] *'ehad'* ('one') sufficiently to proclaim Him king above and below and in the four winds of the world, even this necessitates only a movement to two directions, and below and above . . . Furthermore, some say that in *'ehad'* no movement is necessary, only picturing in the heart, as we explained in its place."[6]

Neither is Me'iri the only Provencal commentator to bear witness to the practice of head movements. His contemporary Rabbi David ben Levi of Narbonne writes: "**How long? Long enough to proclaim Him king, etc.** – Some interpret that one proclaims Him king by moving one's head. And so interpreted Rabbeinu Hai, of blessed memory."[7]

In Provence, where we find most evidence of the head movements, there were some who found the practice ludicrous (*huka ve-itlula*).[8] Perhaps these authorities took exception not so much to the movements themselves, as to the fact that as often happens in the case of rituals, the simple folk focus on the externals rather than on the inner awareness which is the essence.[9]

The German codifier Rabbi Jacob ben Asher (d. Toledo, Spain 1343) defended the practice of the head movements accompanying *Shema'*:

> One must prolong the *dalet* of "*ehad*" the amount [of time] necessary to think in one's heart that the Holy One, blessed be He, is unique in His world, above and below, and in the four winds of the world. There are some accustomed to tilt the head according to the thought, above and below, and to the four directions. Some object to the practice because of the statement of the Rabbis, "He who recites *Shema'* should not gesticulate with his

eyes or lips."[10] My father, of blessed memory, used to say that one need not heed [their words], for there, the gesticulations are for an extraneous purpose, and interrupt the concentration, but here, the gesture is a requisite of the concentration and brings it about (*tsorekh ha-kavvanah ve-goremet otah*)."[11]

Rabbi Joshua Boaz Baruch (Italy, d. 1557) offers a very graphic description of the head movements of *Shema'*:

> This is the amount [of time] to prolong the word *ehad*: one third in the letter *het* and two thirds in the letter *dalet*. How does one proclaim the kingship? Up and down during the *het*, and in the four directions during the *dalet*.[12] And one concentrates while moving the head up and down; to the east and to the west, to the north and to the south....[13]

One can only speculate what happened to these head movements. Whereas the movements of the *lulav* or palm frond continue in full force to this day, wherever Jews are found, we are not aware of any community that has retained the custom of moving the head during *Shema'*, though as we have seen, it was once widespread in communities as diverse as Babel (today Iraq), Provence, Spain and Italy.[14]

Perhaps these head movements of *Shema'* are a "*mitsvah yetomah*" ("orphan *mitsvah*") due for revival.[15]

---

[1] Deuteronomy 6:4.
[2] Deuteronomy 6:7.
[3] These head movements of the *Shema'* are not to be confused with those

employed in the so-called school of "Prophetic Kabbalah" founded by Abraham Abulafia (1240-c.1291), although it is possible that Abulafia was inspired in this respect by the earlier tradition surrounding the *Shema'*. Prof. Gershom Scholem was struck by the similarity between the Abulafian technique (especially the technique of breathing) and Indian Yogic practices. It is unlikely that Scholem was unaware of the Judaic practice surrounding *Shema'*. Perhaps Scholem regarded even this practice, stretching back at least as far as Rav Hai Gaon, as influenced by Yogic or Sufic tradition. See Gershom G. Scholem, *Major Trends in Jewish Mysticism* (New York: Schocken, 1971), pp. 139, 144; Aryeh Kaplan, *Meditation and Kabbalah* (York Beach, Maine: Samuel Weiser, 1985), pp. 55-114.

4 *b. Berakhot* 13b. The words "Hiyya bar Abba" are bracketed in the standard Vilna edition. In the parallel discussion in *Talmud Yerushalmi, Berakhot* 2:1, rather than R. Hiyya bar Abba, it is Ze'ira who apprises Rav Yirmiyah that he needn't overly prolong the recitation. R. Aryeh Leib Yellin (*Yefeh 'Einayim*) suggests that the text of the Bavli be emended to "R. Zeira" to conform to the *Yerushalmi*.

5 Rabbi Menahem ben Shelomo ha-Me'iri, *Beit ha-Behirah, Berakhot*, ed. Shmuel Dikman (Jerusalem: Makhon ha-Talmud ha-Yisraeli, 1965), *Berakhot* 13b (p. 42).

6 Rabbi Menahem ben Shelomo ha-Me'ri, *Beit ha-Behirah, Sukkah*, ed. Avraham Liss (Jerusalem: Makhon ha-Talmud ha-Yisraeli, 1966), *Sukkah* 37b (p. 133).

7 Rabbi David ben Levi of Narbonne, *Sefer ha-Mikhtam*, in *Ginzei Rishonim / Berakhot*, ed. Moshe Hershler (Jerusalem: Makhon ha-Talmud ha-Yisraeli, 1967), p. 28. This comment of Rabbeinu Hai ben Sherira Gaon (939-1038) first crops up in the *Sefer ha-Eshkol* of Rabbi Abraham ben Isaac, Av-Beit-Din of Narbonne (d. 1158). See *Sefer ha-Eshkol*, ed. Shalom Albeck, p. 14; included in *Otsar ha-Ge'onim*, ed. B.M. Lewin, vol. 1, *Berakhot* (Haifa, 1928), *Peirushim*, p. 13. Cf. Rabbi Nathan ben Yehiel of Rome, *'Arukh*, s.v. *bar pahatei*.

8 *Sefer ha-Mikhtam*, loc. cit.; Rabbi Asher of Lunel, *Orhot Hayyim*, chap. 18.

9 For example, Rabbi Hayyim El'azar Spira of Munkatch (Mukachevo) explained the custom of reciting the verse *Atah hor'eita la-da'at* ("Unto you it was shown, that you might know, that the Lord is the God; there is none else besides Him") (Deuteronomy 4:35) on *Simhat Torah* at the opening of the Ark before commencing the *hakafot* or circumambulations with the Torah scroll in hand, as an antidote to any perverse notions that might creep into the common mind. By declaring the absolute unity of God, we stave off any misguided tendency to deify the Torah. See Rabbi Hayyim El'azar Spira, *Sha'ar Yissaskhar 'al Mo'adim* (Brooklyn, NY, 1992), Part Two, *Ma'amrei Hodesh Tishri, Ma'amar Zeman Simhateinu*, par. 4 (408b). Cf. Rabbi Meir Simhah Cohen of Dvinsk, *Meshekh Hokhmah* (Riga, 1927), Exodus 32:19, who explains that Moses smashed the Tablets of the Law to prevent their deification by the worshippers of the Golden Calf.

10 *b. Yoma* 19b. There, included in the prohibition is gesticulating with the finger(s).

11 Rabbi Jacob ben Asher, *Tur, Orah Hayyim*, chap. 61. The *Tur*'s statement, "There are some accustomed to tilt the head according to the thought, above and below, and to the four directions," is quoted in Rabbi Joseph Karo, *Shulhan 'Arukh* 61:6. See *Mishnah Berurah* there, quoting *'Ateret Zekenim*. And

see now my remarks in *The Koren Rav Kook Siddur* (Jerusalem, 2017), p. 155, note 19.

[12] The Hebrew letters also signify numbers. Thus, *ḥet* has the numerical value of 8; *dalet*, the numerical value of 4. The head movements up and down allude to the seven heavens and earth, a total of eight. It is appropriate that they occur during recitation of the letter *ḥet*. The movements in the four directions of the compass occur during the recitation of the letter *dalet*.

On the practical level, one may question how it is possible to prolong the sound of the letter *dalet* (twice as long as the letter *ḥet*!) when the consonant *dalet* is a stop or plosive. The question is based on ignorance of the correct pronunciation of the Hebrew letters. In the Ashkenazic community, the differentiation between *dalet degushah* (hard *dalet*, indicated by the dot or *dagesh* sign) and *dalet rafah* (soft *dalet*, lacking the *dagesh* or dot) was lost. In the Oriental communities, this tradition was maintained. In truth, only the hard *dalet* has the "d" sound; the soft *dalet* is pronounced "th" as in the English word "the." In phonetics, such a sound is referred to as a "continuant," as opposed to a "stop" or "plosive." As the *dalet* of *ehad* is soft, the word is properly pronounced "ehath." Adhering to these basic rules of the Hebrew language, the *dalet* of *ehad* may certainly be drawn out. See Rabbi Nahum L. Rabinovitch, *Yad Peshutah* (Jerusalem, 1984), *Hil. Keri'at Shema* 2:9 (p. 64). For the record, there were several Ashkenazic *gedolim* who were sensitive to the refinements of Hebrew pronunciation, as practiced by the Oriental communities. In the previous generation, Rabbis Joseph Elijah Henkin and Jacob Kamenecki expressed such concerns, to name but two.

[13] Rabbi Joshua Boaz Baruch, *Shiltei ha-Gibborim* to *Mordekhai, Berakhot* (Vilna ed., 46a).

[14] It was pointed out to me that the late Lubavitcher Rebbe, Rabbi Menahem Mendel Schneerson, practiced the head movements of *Shema'*, but this remained the practice of an individual. It was not the practice of the Lubavitch community.

It should also be mentioned that the Piaseczna Rebbe, Rabbi Kalonymos Kalmish Shapira—who led his flock in the Warsaw Ghetto and was martyred in the Holocaust—advocated these head movements. See his *Hakhsharat ha-Avrekhim* (Jerusalem: Feldheim, 2001), chap. 14 (p. 169).

[15] Rabbi Jacob Moses Harlap, the eminent disciple of Rav Kook, wrote that the revival of *mitsvot* that have fallen into desuetude is a cure for the malady of our generation of *neshamot she-be-'olam ha-tohu* (souls of the World of Chaos), whose vessel is too narrow to contain the great light due to penetrate it. This thought is expressed in a letter Rabbi Harlap wrote in 1946 upon the occasion of the renewed *"Hakhel"* ceremony. Published as an appendix to Rabbi J.M. Harlap, *Mei Marom*, vol. 5 (*Nimmukei ha-Mikra'ot*) (Jerusalem, 1981). Cf. the essay entitled *"Ha-Neshamot shel 'Olam ha-Tohu"* ("The Souls of the World of Chaos") in Rabbi Abraham Isaac Hakohen Kook, *Orot* (Jerusalem, 1950), pp. 121-123.

Postscript: After my article appeared in print, Eliezer Brodt brought to my attention the earlier article by Eric Zimmer. See Yitzhak Zimmer, *"Tenuhot u-tenu'ot ha-guf bi-she'at Keri'at Shema',"* *Asufot* 8 (1994), pp. 359-362.

The Carnal Kippur
(*b. Yoma* 19b-20a)

The important people of Jerusalem would not sleep the entire night [of Yom Kippur] so that the High Priest might hear the noise and not be overcome by slumber.

It was taught in a *beraita*:

Abba Shaul said: "Even outside of Jerusalem they would do so [as a] commemoration of the Temple (*zekher la-mikdash*), but it led to sexual frivolity between men and women."

Said Abaye, or alternatively Rav Nahman bar Yitzhak: "Interpret that as referring to Neharde'a, for Elijah [the Prophet] said to Rav Yehudah, the brother of Rav Sala Hasida, 'You ask why Messiah does not come. Today is Yom Kippur [the Day of Atonement] and several virgins were deflowered in Neharde'a!' [Rav Yehudah] asked him [i.e., Elijah]: 'What does the Holy One, blessed be He, say [about that]?' [Elijah] responded to him: 'Sin crouches at the door' [Genesis 4:7]."

(*b. Yoma* 19b-20a)

Rabbi Barukh Halevi Epstein of Pinsk, author of the immensely popular Torah commentary, *Torah Temimah*, wondered aloud why we find such a proliferation of forbidden sexual relations on the most solemn day of the year, *Yom Kippur*, the Day of Atonement.[1] These do not seem to be isolated instances. Beyond the scandalous situation in Neharde'a recorded in the passage above, a pattern emerges across the tomes of Talmud.

In Tractate *Sotah*, one of the justifications given for Elisha the Prophet cursing the lads who mocked him (which resulted in forty-two of their number being mauled to death by bears),[2] was the fact that "he saw that all of them had been conceived by their mothers on Yom Kippur."[3] (For whatever reason, this particular passage in the Talmud is missing from Rabbi Epstein's roster.)

In these two cases (the maidens of Neharde'a, and the mothers who conceived Elisha's detractors) we may presume that the relations themselves would have been permitted another day of the year.[4] The only prohibition transgressed was having conjugal relations on Yom Kippur. There is discussion in the *rishonim* (medieval authorities) as to the nature of the prohibition, whether it be of Pentateuchal or rabbinic origin. (There are authorities who hold that only eating and drinking on Yom Kippur are prohibited by Torah, while the other prohibitions of washing, anointing with oil, wearing shoes and sexual relations are merely rabbinic.)[5] Whether the prohibition is technically *de-'oraita* or *de-rabbanan*, is not the issue here. Even if one should opine that relations on the holy day are a later rabbinic prohibition, the very fact that a Jew would engage in carnal relations on the Day of Atonement was considered heinous beyond belief.[6]

The Carnal Kippur

The next two instances are cases of intrinsically forbidden relations that were entered into on Yom Kippur. In Tractate *Gittin* it is told that there were found in Kefar Sekhanya of Egypt a father and son who had relations with a betrothed young woman (*na'arah me'orasah*) on Yom Kippur. They were promptly brought up in court (*beit din*) and stoned.[7]

Similarly in Tractate *Bava Metsi'a*, when Rabbi El'azar, son of the famous Rabbi Shim'on ben Yohai, suspected a launderer of wrongdoing, it was later confirmed that the launderer and his son had relations with a betrothed young woman (*na'arah me'orasah*) on Yom Kippur. (In that case, the Roman authorities hung the launderer.)[8]

Rabbi Epstein speculated that the common folk fell prey to sexual temptation because of the ceremony that took place every year on Yom Kippur whereby the daughters of Jerusalem, decked in finery, would dance in a circle and call out to the young men to choose a mate.[9] To back up his supposition, Rabbi Epstein adduces the Torah reading of *'Arayot* (the forbidden incestuous relations in Leviticus 18) on the afternoon of Yom Kippur.[10] It is assumed that this particular portion was read as an advisory to prevent the sexual commingling that might otherwise be aroused by the spectacle of the young maidens' dance circle.[11]

Though seemingly plausible, Rabbi Epstein's solution presents several problems. It seems from the Mishnah (end *Ta'anit*) that the dancing of the young eligible maidens was restricted in both space and time. Spatially, it would not have exceeded the environs of

Jerusalem. Temporally, this celebration probably did not persist after the destruction of the Temple.

The incident concerning Elisha the Prophet took place *en route* from Jericho to Beth-El.[12] Though one cannot say with any certainty where the louts were conceived, we may safely assume that their parents were not present at the festivities in Jerusalem on Yom Kippur. Jeroboam, founder of the Northern Kingdom of Israel, had erected barriers preventing the populace from making the pilgrimage to the Temple in Jerusalem.[13] In order to divert their devotion, he erected two pagan temples in Beth-El and Dan.[14] (Furthermore, Jeroboam replaced the Levitical priests with commoners, and the Festival of Booths with an invented holiday a month later.)[15] As a result of the thoroughgoing alienation of the Israelites from the Judahites, it is most unlikely that the mothers of the forty-two lads were present on Yom Kippur in Jerusalem.

The deflowering of maidens in Neharde'a occurred in distant Babylonia; it also postdated the destruction of the Temple.

The incident in Kefar Sekhanya of Egypt involving the rape of a betrothed woman, might very well have taken place prior to the destruction of the Temple.[16] Yet, as difficult as it is to determine the exact location of *"Kefar Sekhanya shel Mitsrayim,"*[17] it certainly was not within the bounds of Jerusalem.

As for Rabbi El'azar ben Shim'on, he lived in the second century C.E., well after the destruction of the Temple. (He was a contemporary of Rabbi Judah the Prince.)[18]

Thus, pinning the numerous sexual offenses committed on Yom Kippur (scattered throughout the Talmud) on this festivity of the dance of the daughters of Jerusalem, seems far-fetched.[19] We must search for some more essential component of Yom Kippur that excites the erotic imagination.

The highpoint, the crescendo, if you would have it, the essence, of Yom Kippur is the entry of the High Priest into the *Kodesh Kodashim*, the *Sanctum Sanctorum*, the Holy of Holies, and the burning of incense before the Ark of the LORD, upon whose lid were ensconced the two Cherubim. (In the Second Temple, in the absence of the Ark, the High Priest would offer the incense in that exact place where the Ark was once located.)[20]

The Cherubim were locked in a loving, physical embrace. In the glory days of the Temple, the curtain would be rolled aside revealing the Cherubim wrapped in each other's wings, an expression of the Omnipresent's love for the nation of Israel. And at the time of the Temple's destruction, the pagan invaders held those same Cherubim up to ridicule, finding ludicrous Israel's veneration of this erotic representation. "All who honored her debased her because they have seen her nakedness" (Lamentations 1:8).[21]

Long after the destruction of the Temple, in all the lands of their dispersion, Jews would continue to relate—and relive—on Yom Kippur the High Priest's encounter with the Cherubim. The *Mishnah* mandated the reading of that portion in Leviticus 16.[22] Later, in the Amoraic period, the *Seder 'Avodah* (Order of the Service), a detailed account of the High Priest's ministrations in the Temple on that day, was integrated into the synagogue service.[23]

The primal energy unleashed in the popular imagination by conjuring up the image of the Cherubim could—and did on occasion—go awry. Children could be conceived in sin on the Day of Atonement, in total disregard for the sanctity of the day (in addition to whatever formal prohibition was infracted in so doing, be it biblical or rabbinic). And, horror of horrors, a betrothed woman might be raped on that day.

On the bright side, every Jew identifies with the High Priest on Yom Kippur.[24] The psychic identification is stronger in some than in others. When reciting the *Seder 'Avodah*, the *"Apter Rov,"* Rabbi Abraham Joshua Heschel of Opatów, went so far as to substitute for "And so *he* would say" (*"Ve-kakh* hayah *'omer"*)—"And so *I* would say" (*"Ve-kakh* hayiti *'omer"*).[25]

---

[1] Rabbi Barukh Halevi Epstein, *Torah Temimah* (Vilna: Romm, 1902), Genesis 4:7 (par. 10).

[2] 2Kings 2:24.

[3] *b. Sotah* 46b. The statement was authored by Samuel. In Lurianic Kabbalah much thought was given to this passage of the Talmud. See Rabbi Hayyim Vital, *Sha'ar ha-Gilgulim* (Jerusalem: Keren Hotsa'at Sifrei Rabbanei Bavel, 1990), *hakdamah* 32 (p. 251); idem, *Likkutei Torah* (Vilna, 1880; photo offset Jerusalem, 1972), 2Kings, chap. 2 (114a), s.v. *'aleh kere'ah*; *Sefer ha-Likkutim* (Jerusalem, 1913), 2Kings, chap. 2 (78b-c); Rabbi Samuel Laniado (Venice, 1603), *Keli Yakar*, 2Kings 2:24, quoting Rabbi Isaac Luria.

[4] It seems that the term *"mamzerim"* ("bastards") in *Likkutei Torah* (see the previous note) in regard to the forty-two lads is used colloquially. Similarly, Maimonides explains in the *Epistle to Yemen* that *"mamzer"* in regard to Jesus of Nazareth is a loose rather than legal term.

[5] The medieval authorities in each camp are listed by Rabbi Israel Meir Kagan in the *Sha'ar ha-Tsiyun* to *Mishnah Berurah*, Rabbi Kagan's commentary to Rabbi Joseph Karo, *Shulhan 'Arukh*, *Orah Hayyim* 611:2.

[6] For the sake of comparison, there exists a controversy whether the obligation to recite a blessing before learning Torah (*Birkat ha-Torah*) originates in the Torah or is merely a later rabbinic duty. Nahmanides in his animadversions to Maimonides' *Book of Commandments* lists *Birkat ha-Torah* as positive commandment 15. (Whether Maimonides regarded *Birkat ha-Torah* as a rabbinic obligation, or was loath to enumerate it as a separate commandment for technical reasons, remains a moot point.) In *b. Nedarim* 81a the Talmud (interpret-

ing Jeremiah 9:11) states that the Land of Israel was lost because Jews did not recite *Birkat ha-Torah* before studying Torah. Rabbi Aryeh Leib Günzburg of Minsk and Metz reasoned that since this terrible punishment was visited on the nation of Israel, perforce the obligation of *Birkat ha-Torah* dates back to the Torah; it is inconceivable that failure to perform a rabbinic duty would have warranted the destruction. See *Sha'agat Aryeh*, end chap. 24. However, one may argue that the *Sha'agat Aryeh*'s supposed proof is inconclusive. It is highly conceivable that though the obligation to recite the blessing is rabbinic, failure to do so represented a flagrant disregard for the sanctity of Torah learning. The terrible devastation was brought about for the disrespect to Torah. (See Rabbi Abraham Danzig's rejoinder to *Peri Hadash*, in *Nishmat Adam*, notes to *Hayyei Adam*, *kelal* 9, note 1.) By the same token, though perhaps technically a rabbinic infraction, sexual relations on the Day of Atonement were evidently viewed by the sages as unpardonable disrespect for the sanctity of the day.

[7] *b. Gittin* 57a.

[8] *b. Bava Metsi'a* 83b. The Tosafists raised the question why the launderer was hung and not stoned as befits one who has relations with another man's fiancée. (The Talmud states that even after capital punishment was abolished with the destruction of the Temple in Jerusalem, through divine supervision it will come about that the criminal receives his due punishment. For example, one who deserves the punishment of lapidation will fall off the rooftop to his death.) Various solutions were offered. See *Tosafot*, *Ketubot* 30b, s.v. *din arba' mitot lo batlu*; *Sotah* 8b, s.v. *mi she-nithayyev sekilah*; and *Sanhedrin* 37b, s.v. *mi-yom she-harav beit ha-mikdash*.

[9] *m. Ta'anit* 4:8.

[10] *b. Megillah* 31a.

[11] *Tosafot* ibid. s.v. *be-minhah korin ba-'arayot*.

[12] 2 Kings 2:23.

[13] According to the Rabbis, unrestricted passage to the Temple in Jerusalem was first allowed in the reign of Hosea ben Elah. See *y. Ta'anit* 4:7; and *b. Ta'anit* 28a, 30b-31a.

[14] Malbim offers that the lads, who had been raised in Beit-El, the seat of the calf worship (instituted by Jeroboam), were disdainful of the prophets of the LORD. For this reason, in order to extirpate idolatry from the midst of the nation, Elisha dealt with the lads in such a harsh manner. See Rabbi Meir Leibush Malbim, *Lev Melakhim*, 2Kings 2:23.

[15] 1Kings 12:26-33.

[16] See Rabbi Samuel Edels (MaHaRaShA), *Hiddushei Aggadot*, *Gittin* 57a, s.v. *u-mats'u av u-beno she-ba'u 'al na'arah me'orasah*. Maharasha arrived at this conclusion based on the mention of Bava ben Buta who lived in the period of Herod's Temple (see *b. Bava Batra* 3b-4a).

One might have concluded the same based on the fact that capital punishment was meted out by the *Beit Din*. Capital punishment ceased forty years before the destruction of the Second Temple (*b. Sanhedrin* 41a, *'Avodah Zarah* 8b; Maimonides, *Hil. Sanhedrin* 14:13). Although one might counter that this was a *hora'at sha'*ah, or extreme *ad hoc* measure on the part of the court. *Tosafot* (*Sanhedrin* 37b, s.v. *mi-yom she-harav beit ha-mikdash*; *'Avodah Zarah* 8b, s.v. *'ela she-lo danu dinei nefashot*) posited that right up to the destruction of the Temple, if the Sanhedrin saw that it was a requisite of the hour (*tsorekh sha'ah*) they would once again take up their residence in the *Lishkat ha-Gazit* (Chamber of Hewn Stone) and adjudicate capital punishment. But even after the destruction of the Temple, on rare occasions, the *Beit Din* might resort to capital punishment "to make a fence around the Torah." These extrajudicial punitive measures come under the rubric of *"Beit Din makkin ve-'onshin she-lo min ha-din"* (b. *Sanhedrin* 46a). See Maimonides, *Hil. Sanhedrin* 24:4. (The caveat in the margin of some printed editions of *Mishneh Torah*—"These laws applied when the Temple existed"—is pure apologetics added to appease the Tsarist censor.) See Rabbi Isaac ben Sheshet Perfet, *She'elot u-Teshuvot RIVaSh*, no. 234; Rabbi Joseph Karo, *Shulhan 'Arukh, Hoshen Mishpat* 2:1; Rabbi Jacob Moses Harlap, *Beit Zevul*, Part Six (Jerusalem, 1966), chap. 11 (p. 50); and Rabbi Abraham Aaron Price, *Sefer Hasidim* with commentary *"Mishnat Avraham,"* vol. 1 (Toronto, 1955), chap. 172 (93b-94a). (The responsum attributed to Rabbi Solomon ben Abraham ibn Adret [RaShBA] in Saul Berlin's spurious collection *Besamim Rosh*, no. 192, is an obvious forgery, as was observed by Rabbi Price's own teacher, Rabbi Abraham Bornstein of Sochatchov.) See further Rabbi Hayyim Soloveitchik's fascinating study of Maimonides' concept of *"makkat mardut"* (*Hil. Hamets u-Matsah* 6:12) as a possible extension of the principle of *"Beit Din makkin ve-'onshin she-lo min ha-din"*; in *Hiddushei ha-GRaH he-Hadash*, vol 3 (stencil, Jerusalem, 1967), *"Kefiyah 'al ha-Mitsvot"* (p. 59).

[17] See Rabbi Judah Löw (Maharal) of Prague, *Hiddushei Aggadot, Gittin* 57a, s.v. *Rav Minyumi bar Hilkiyah*; and idem, *Netsah Yisrael*, end chap. 6. Based on the text of the Talmud, Maharal is undecided whether Kefar Sekhanya shel Mitsrayim was one of the villages that comprised the legendary Tur Malka (Aramaic) or Har ha-Melekh (Hebrew), which was the heartland of Israel. (Why it was designated "of Egypt" remains unresolved. One speculates that perhaps it had been settled by Egyptians.)

There is a school of opinion that the village was actually located in Egypt. Admittedly, it is strange that Bava ben Buta should turn up in Egypt. (See the previous note.) On the other hand, capital punishment could be dealt out by a Sanhedrin of twenty-three judges in Egypt (as long as capital punishment was still being dealt out by the Sanhedrin in the Land of Israel). See Maimonides, *Hil. Sanhedrin* 14:14.

[18] b. *Bava Metsi'a* 84b.

[19] The *Mishnah* (end *Ta'anit*) that tells us of the daughters of Jerusalem's dance circle, trails off with the verse from Song of Songs 3:11: "Go forth, daughters of Zion, and gaze upon King Solomon, upon the crown with which his mother crowned him on the day of his wedding, and on the day of the gladness of his heart." The *Mishnah* concludes: "'On the day of his wedding'—this refers to the giving of the Torah; 'and on the day of the gladness of his heart'—this refers to the building of the Temple." Pseudo-Rashi (*Ta'anit* 26b) clues us in that "King Solomon" (*"Melekh Shelomo"*) in this context is none other than the Almighty ("the King who possesses peace"). "The giving of the Torah," explains Pseudo-Rashi, refers to Yom Kippur, when the second tablets were given to Moses on Mount Sinai. Other commentators (see, e.g., Bertinuro) add that "the building of the Temple," meaning its dedication by King Solomon, also took place on Yom Kippur. See 1 Kings 8:65 and b. *Mo'ed Katan* 9a;

and the lengthy discussion in Rabbi Bezalel ha-Kohen of Vilna, Responsa *Reshit Bikkurim* (Vilna, 1869; photo offset Jerusalem, 1969), Part Two, no. 4 (f. 123).

Yet neither of these historical events in and of themselves (*sans* the actual dancing of the daughters of Zion) would account for the sexual improprieties committed on Yom Kippur.

[20] *b. Yoma* 52b.

[21] *b. Yoma* 54.

[22] *m. Megillah* 3:5.

[23] See Rashi, *Yoma* 36b, s.v. *ha-hu de-nahit*. Rashi explains that this is a vicarious form of sacrifice in fulfillment of the verse, "We will pay [instead of] bulls [the offering of] our lips" (Hosea 14:3). Though initially customs differed in which prayer of the day to recite the *Seder 'Avodah*, eventually the custom prevailed to recite it in *Musaf* (the Additional Service). For a halakhic justification of the prevalent custom, see Rabbi Yosef Dov ha-Levi Soloveitchik, *Kuntres be-'Inyan 'Avodat Yom ha-Kippurim*, ed. Rabbi Aharon Lichtenstein (Jerusalem, 1986), *Yoma* 36b (pp. 30-31).

[24] In *b. Yoma* 52a, Rashi takes at face value the statement in defense of Rabbi Yosé's position, "Beloved are Israel for Scripture did not require them to engage an emissary (*shali'ah*)." The statement was intended by the Talmud to explain the High Priest's ability to behold directly the Holy of Holies. Rashi spells out that each and every Israelite prays on his own behalf, thus their emissary [the High Priest] may enter the Holy of Holies directly (without meandering). Rashi's interpretation was later rejected by *Tosafot Yeshanim* and Rabbi Yom Tov ben Abraham Asevilli (RITBA) for the earlier interpretation of Rabbeinu Hananel which was found more cogent. Nonetheless, when taken at face value, the rationale of Rabbi Yosé bespeaks a democratization. See further Rabbi Yosef Hayyim of Baghdad, *Ben Yehoyada'*, and idem, *Benayahu*, *Yoma* 52a.

[25] Legend has it that the Apter Rov believed himself to be a reincarnation (*gilgul*) of the High Priest.

A Meditation on *Masekhet Megillah*

(*b. MEGILLAH* 5b-6b)

THANKS TO THREE LIBERATED *LITVAKS*:
RABBI ZADOK HAKOHEN, EMMANUEL LEVINAS,
AND M. SHOSHANI

This Talmudic study will employ a unique methodology that rests upon several suppositions. These ground assumptions should be enunciated at the onset.

First, we have the notion of the Hasidic master Rabbi Zadok Hakohen Rabinowitz (1823-1900) that the aggadic portion of any given tractate must somehow be conceptually integrated within the overall halakhic theme of that tractate.[1] This was a teaching that Rabbi Zadok received from his master, Rabbi Mordechai Yosef Leiner of Izbica (author of *Mei ha-Shilo'ah*).[2] Spread throughout the voluminous corpus of Rabbi Zadok's published *oeuvre*,[3] there abound numerous examples where this hermeneutic principle is applied. Thus, Rabbi Zadok explains the fact that the *aggadah* concerning the giving of the Torah on Mount Sinai is contained in Tractate *Shabbat*;[4] and that concerning the manna in the desert in Tractate *Yoma*.[5] The appearance in Tractate *Gittin* of both the legends of the destruction of the Temple (in chapter five) and the legends of King Solomon (in chapter seven), prompts Rabbi Zadok to link both cycles of legends to the theme of divorce.[6] Likewise,

Rabbi Zadok discusses the relevance of the levels of spiritual attainment culminating in prophecy, to Tractate *'Avodah Zarah*.[7] Finally, Rabbi Zadok explains why the saying, "Let the grape cluster pray on behalf of the [surrounding] leaves, because if not for the leaves, the cluster could not survive [the elements]," occurs in the seventh chapter of Tractate *Hullin* which discusses the sciatic nerve (*gid ha-nasheh*).[8]

Another light we shall train on our discussion is that gleaned from the writings of the French existentialist writer Emmanuel Levinas (1906-1995).[9] Levinas, while possessing nothing near Rabbi Zadok's expertise in Talmud, was able, nonetheless, to develop a novel method of viewing *aggadeta*. For Levinas, an aggadic discussion in the Talmud is a coherent literary unit, carefully crafted and pregnant with overarching philosophic significance, rather than a rambling array of random rabbinic sayings.

Bref! Let us commence our *étude*. The *sugyah* we shall analyze is found in Tractate *Megillah* 5b-6b. The departure point of the *Gemara*'s discussion is the halakhic status of the city of Tiberias. We are told that the *tanna* Hezekiah read the *Megillah* in Tiberias on both the fourteenth and the fifteenth of Adar because he was in doubt whether Tiberias qualifies as "a walled city from the days of Joshua bin Nun," or not. (Only in such cities is the *Megillah* read on the fifteenth; unwalled cities read on the fourteenth.) The *Gemara* quickly clarifies that the doubt arose in Hezekiah's mind due to the fact that one of the walls of the city consists of the natural sea-wall. (On one side, Tiberias abuts the Sea of Galilee.)

From moorings in this rather succinct legal discussion, the *Gemara* launches into a protracted excursus concerning the history of Tiberias and the various names of the city, ancient and contemporary. Somewhere along the way, Tiberias trails off in the distance and the imperial city of Romes comes into sharp focus: "Said 'Ulla: 'Italy of Ionia (*Italia shel Yavan*). This is the great city of Rome.'"[10] The entire discussion ends on this note:

> Its [i.e., Rome's] area is three hundred parasangs by three hundred parasangs. There are in it three hundred and sixty-five markets corresponding to the days of the solar year;[11] the least of them is [the market] of the poultry dealers, with an area of sixteen *mil* by sixteen *mil*....There are three thousand baths, and five hundred chimneys taller than the city wall.[12] One side of it [i.e., Rome] is the sea,[13] and one side is mountains and hills; one side is a wall of iron, and one side is sand and pebbles.

One need not be especially astute to observe that Hezekiah's treatment of Tiberias, which borders the sea on one side,[14] and 'Ulla's description of Rome as bordering the sea on one side, are the two bookends of our *sugyah*. At this point, we need to ask two questions: First (à la Levinas), what is the philosophic significance of juxtaposing these two cities? Second (à la Rabbi

Zadok), how does this tale of two cities pertain to the general theme of Tractate *Megillah*?

※❦※

Let us preface our remarks by establishing that historically, the events outlined in *Megillat Esther* signal that the Jewish People has hereby entered a new phase of its existence: the Age of Empire. For the first time in our history, we found ourselves citizens of an empire. Esther's very first verse sets the tone: "And it came to pass in the days of Ahashverosh, the same Ahashverosh who reigned from India even unto Ethiopia, over a hundred and twenty and seven provinces." Of great significance in this regard, is the Midrash which speaks of Ahashverosh as a *cosmocrat*.[15] From a provincial nation, the Jews were transformed practically overnight into cosmopolitans. They were exposed to a much larger political reality than ever they experienced.

The *Halakhah* which defined a walled city as one "walled from the days of Joshua bin Nun," was designed to compensate for the fact that the Land of Israel was desolate at the time Purim was declared a festival. In order to accord the cities of the Land of Israel the same importance and status as that of Shushan, Persia's capital, the determination was made retroactive to the days of Joshua bin Nun, regardless of the city's present decrepit state. Thus, the honor of the Land of Israel was preserved.[16]

However, the *tikkun*, the enactment of that era, was of little practical avail at a later stage of our national history. It may have

A Meditation on *Masekhet Megillah*

sufficed when Israel was presented with the reality of Persian Empire. But all too soon, Persian Empire was replaced by Roman Empire. No longer was Jerusalem the center of Jewish life in the Land of Israel. By the time our Talmudic discussion takes place, Tiberias had become the center. It was there that the national leader Rabbi Judah the Prince resided.[17] There the Sanhedrin sat in session.[18] It has been quipped that *"Talmud Yerushalmi"* ("Jerusalem Talmud") is a misnomer. This Talmud of the West (*Talmuda di-B'nei Ma'arava*) should more properly be called *"Talmud Tiveryani"* ("Tiberian Talmud"). Tiberias' walls were examined from the perspective of the *Megillah* and found wanting. The city of Tiberias is not so much an insular reality as a semipermeable membrane. The sea comes lapping at its shore. The sea, symbolic of the external, threatens to invade at a moment's notice.

Furthermore, the very name of the city is not truly Jewish. It was named in honor of the Roman Emperor Tiberius.[19] How proud Jews must have choked over the name "Tiveryah." Little wonder then that our *Gemara* goes to great lengths to prove that the true name of the city is the Biblical "Rakat."[20] And Tiveryah? Various suggestions are proffered. "It sits in the navel (*tabor*) of the Land of Israel."[21] Alternatively, "Its vision is goodly (*tovah re'iyatah*)."[22]

The ones to feel most acutely this new world order impinging upon them were the members of the tribe of Zevulun. The inheritance of Zevulun was the coastal strip running roughly from the "Ladders of Tyre" south to Haifa.[23] "Said Zevulun before the Holy One, blessed be He: 'Master of the Universe, to my brothers you gave fields and vineyards, and to me you gave mountains and hills;

to my brothers you gave lands, and to me you gave seas and rivers.'"[24]

The entire discussion in the Talmud is an attempt to come to terms with the encroaching reality of the Roman Empire, or, if you would have it, of Western Civilization.[25] The "men of Ionia" (*anshei yavan*) emerge from the sea.[26] The sea comes to be symbolic of all that is threatening in the outside world; all that would impugn and undermine the *kedushat 'arei homah*, the sanctity of the walled cities of the Land of Israel. Tiberias shares the same layout as Rome. Its one side is open to the sea. This is the nature of the New World Order. There is no insulation.

What comfort does the Holy One, blessed be He, hold out to Zevulun?

> He said to him: "All will have need of you on account of *hilazon.*"
>
> As it says: "The nations are gathered to the mountain....[in order to acquire] the treasures hidden in the sand (*sefunei temunei hol*)."[27]
>
> Rav Yosef taught: "*Sefunei*" refers to *hilazon*...."*hol*" refers to *zekhukhit levanah*.[28]

From the *hilazon*, a murex snail, was derived the sky-blue color of *tekhelet*. From the *hol*, the sand itself, was produced *zekhukhit levanah*,[29] literally "white glass." Both these commodities were exceptionally rare.[30]

A Meditation on *Masekhet Megillah*

That which *tekhelet* and *zekhukhit levanah* share in common is their visionary quality.

"*Tekhelet* resembles the sea; and the sea resembles the sky; and the sky resembles the Throne of Glory."[31] Placed on the four corners of the garment, the thread of blue represents a breakthrough in awareness. A consciousness previously hemmed in, is shown a larger horizon. To the eye, the sea and the sky appear infinite. Thus, *tekhelet* is a portal to the boundless and unlimited.

Likewise, *zekhukhit levanah*, translucent glass, assumed mythic proportions. "With the destruction of the Temple, white glass became extinct."[32]

The merchant marine, Zevulun, has lost the connection to the land, to the fields and vineyards. An irreplaceable loss is felt. There is great sadness on this account. However, the Holy One, blessed be He, points out to Zevulun that in leaving behind the boundaries of land, he has opened himself to a different type of blessing. Though poor in land, he is rich in vision. Though they will never possess anything as tangible or as permanent as land; though their fortunes are as fleeting and shifting as the sands and the sea, the men of Zevulun are privy to rare vision.

---

[1] See Sarah Friedland-Ben Arza, "Shekhenut ve-korat gag—'al shnei 'ekronot darshanut tsuraniyim be-kitvei R' Zadok Hakohen mi-Lublin," in *Me'at la-Zaddik*, ed. Gershon Kitsis (Jerusalem, 2000), pp. 276-281.

Rabbi Yeruham Leiner, the Radzyner Rebbe of Brooklyn, wrote that this fundamental was to be found earlier in Maimonides' introduction to his *Commentary to the Mishnah* (Kafah edition, p. 19): "And the fourth [objective], homilies that fit into the content matter of each chapter." See Rabbi Yeruham Leiner, *Tif'eret Yeruham* (Brooklyn, NY, 1967), *Shabbat Hazon* (pp. 95-96).

(Rabbi Yeruham Leiner himself makes use of the methodology in explaining the placement of Rabbi Yohanan's statement regarding the Oral Law in Tractate *Gittin* [60b]. The Oral Law gained ascendancy after the destruction of the Temple.)

[2] See Rabbi Zadok Hakohen Rabinowitz, *Yisrael Kedoshim* (Lublin, 1928), 24b; *Komets ha-Minhah* (Lublin, 1939), 37a; Rabbi Yeruham Leiner loc. cit. (It is known that whenever Rabbi Zadok writes simply, *"Shama'ti"* ["I heard"] or *"Kibbalti"* ["I received"], the reference is to his master, the Rebbe of Izbica, Rabbi Mordechai Yosef Leiner; see Rabbi Yeruham Leiner, op. cit. pp. 160-161, recalling a conversation between his father, Rabbi Avraham Yehoshu'a Heschel Leiner, and Rabbi Zadok.)

In *Iggeret ha-Kodesh*, a personal letter sent to the companion of his youth who since emigrated to Manchester, England, Rabbi Zadok explains why the passage in praise of Erets Yisrael occurs at the conclusion of Tractate *Ketubot*. The letter is appended to Rabbi Zadok Hakohen of Lublin, *Poked 'Akarim* (Piotrków, 1922), 28b.

Sarah Friedland-Ben Arza speculates that the methodology goes back a generation earlier to the teacher of Rabbi Mordechai Yosef, Rabbi Simhah Bunem of Pshiskha. See Yisrael Berger, *Simhat Yisrael* (Piotrków, 1910), *Torat Simhah*, par. 156 (46b); quoted in Friedland-Ben Arza, p. 274.

Rabbi Mordechai Yosef's son, Rabbi Ya'akov Leiner of Izbica-Radzyn, employs this methodology to explain the occurrence of the chapter *"Makom she-Nahagu"* (which deals with differing customs of various communities) in Tractate *Pesahim*. He justifies this situation based on the etymology of the word *"matsah,"* strife or disagreement. See Rabbi Ya'akov Leiner, *Seder Haggadah shel Pesah 'im Sefer ha-Zemanim* (Jerusalem, 2010), s.v. *'o yahazek be-ma'uzi* [Isaiah 27:5], 94a. (It appears as a comment on the passage in the Haggadah, *"Matsah zo."*)

[3] As is well known, the published works are but a fraction of Rabbi Zadok's total literary output. The late librarian of the Mendel Gottesman Library of Yeshiva University, Rabbi Jacob B. Mandelbaum, shared with this writer (BN) that sometime before World War Two he visited the *beit midrash* of Rabbi Zadok in Lublin. On that occasion, the Hasidim pointed out to Rabbi Mandelbaum the *"aron"* or chest containing the manuscripts of the deceased Rabbi Zadok. It is presumed that all those writings were lost in the Holocaust.

See also Rabbi Yeruham Leiner's account of his visit to Rabbi Zadok's *beit midrash* together with the Rabbi of Lublin, Elijah Klatzkin; *Tif'eret Yeruham*, p. 158.

[4] *Peri Zaddik*, vol. 2 (Lublin, 1907), *Yitro* 1 (42a); *Peri Zaddik*, vol. 5 (Lublin, 1934), *Erev Yom Kippur* 5 (109a-b).

[5] *Peri Zaddik*, vol. 5, *Erev Yom Kippur* (109a-b); *Peri Zaddik*, vol. 1 (Lublin, 1901), *Kuntres Kedushat Shabbat*, ma'amar 7 (23c). Cf. Rabbi Mordechai Yosef Leiner of Izbica, *Mei ha-Shilo'ah*, Part Two (Lublin, 1922), *Likkutei ha-Shas, Masekhet Yoma* (59a). Friedland-Ben Arza expresses doubts whether the juxtaposition of the manna to Tractate *Yoma* as expressed by Rabbi Mordechai Yosef is truly an instance of the general methodology conveyed to Rabbi Zadok; Friedland-Ben Arza, p. 278, n. 38.

[6] *Peri Zaddik*, vol. 5, *Erev Yom Kippur* 5 (109b); *Peri Zaddik*, vol. 1, *Kuntres Kedushat Shabbat*, ma'amar 3 (6d).

[7] *Yisrael Kedoshim*, 24b. In *Yisrael Kedoshim* 32d-33a, Rabbi Zadok explains why the *beraita* of Rabbi Pinhas ben Yair was appended at the conclusion of Tractate *Sotah*.

[8] *Komets ha-Minhah*, 37a. For *"Perek Gid ha-Nasheh* (91)," read *"Perek Gid ha-Nasheh* (92a)."

[9] See Emmanuel Levinas, *Difficile liberté: Essais sur le Judaïsme* (Paris, 1963) ; *Quatre lectures talmudiques* (Paris, 1968); *Du sacré au saint: Cinq lectures talmudiques* (Paris, 1977); *L'Au-delà du verset: Lectures et discours talmudiques* (Paris, 1982).

According to Levinas, he was inspired in this new reading of Talmudic texts by his master, the enigmatic, peripatetic teacher Monsieur Shoshani, who, also taught André Neher (Chairman of Judaic Studies at the University of Strasbourg) and the writer Elie Wiesel. This indebtedness to Shoshani is formally acknowledged by Levinas in his introduction to *Quatre lecture talmudiques*, p. 22. There, Levinas confides that he has just learned of his master's passing in South America. Shoshani is buried in Montevideo, Uruguay, where he spent the final years of his life. One of his disciples in this final phase was the young Shalom Rosenberg, who went on to become a professor of philosophy at Hebrew University in Jerusalem. See *Darkhei Shalom* (Shalom Rosenberg *Festschrift*), ed. Benjamin Ish-Shalom (Jerusalem, 2007).

The elusive Shoshani's total command of Talmud, as well as his panache, are legendary. Neher shared with the present writer (BN) the following anecdote. Neher's father engaged Shoshani to teach his son Talmud. At their first session together, they were to commence study of Tractate *Beitsah*. Shoshani offered his new student a choice. They could devote the lesson to the first page of the tractate, or alternatively, they could encompass the entire tractate in one lesson!

Shoshani's life remains shrouded in mystery. I am told, however, that he was a *Litvak* (a native of Lithuania). Rabbi Zadok Hakohen hailed from Kreisberg (Krustpils) in the Courland region of Latvia; Levinas was a native of Kovno (Kaunas), Lithuania. Hence, my appreciation.

[10] *b. Megillah* 6b. 'Ulla's statement is missing in censored editions of the Talmud. Evidently, the Churchmen perceived this otherwise innocuous statement regarding the layout of ancient Rome as being somehow a veiled criticism of the Vatican.

[11] Israel reckons time by the lunar year; the nations by the solar year. See *b. Sukkah* 29a.

Inter alia, the name "Alexander" spelled in Hebrew characters has the numerical value of 365.

[12] Rashi comments that the smoke stacks' importance consisted in the fact that being taller than the walled city, they did not deposit soot on the wall.

[13] Is this perhaps an allusion to the Tiber River?

[14] One cannot help but notice the parallel between the *tanna* Hezekiah and his namesake King Hezekiah, who fortified the walls of Jerusalem, which were about to be stormed by the invading army of Sancherib, King of Assyria. See 2 Chronicles 32:5.

[15] *Esther Rabbah* 1:12. The Midrash employs the Greek loanword *cosmocrator* (κοσμοκράτωρ).

[16] *y. Megillah* 1:1; Maimonides, *Commentary to the Mishnah, Megillah* 1:1

(Kafah edition, p. 228); idem, *MT, Hil. Megillah* 1:5.
[17] See *b. Megillah* 5b.
[18] See *b. Rosh Hashanah* 31; Maimonides, *MT, Hil. Sanhedrin* 14:12.
[19] See the glosses of Rabbi Jacob Emden and Rabbi Samuel Strashun, *Megillah* 6a.
[20] See Joshua 19:35.
[21] *b. Megillah* 6a.
[22] Ibid.
[23] See *b. Shabbat* 26a.
[24] *b. Megillah* 6a.
[25] Israel first encountered Western Civilization in the person of Alexander the Macedonian (i.e., Alexander the Great) at the time of his conquest of *Erets Yisrael*. See *b. Yoma* 69a, and see above note 11.
[26] Rashi (*Megillah* 6b) comments on the words of 'Ulla, *"Italia shel Yavan"*: "A great city that arose because of the sin of [King] Manasseh, for at the very hour that he placed a graven image in the Temple, [the angel] Gabriel went down and stuck a reed in the sea, upon which amassed land, whereupon was built *Italia shel Yavan* [i.e., the city of Rome]." However, in the Talmud, this calamity is linked to the sin of Solomon wedding the daughter of Pharaoh; and to the sin of Jeroboam erecting two golden calves, one in Bethel, and one in Dan. See *b. Shabbat* 56b and *Sanhedrin* 21b.
[27] Deuteronomy 33:19.
[28] *b. Megillah* 6a.
[29] See Rashi, s.v. *zekhukhit levanah*.
[30] For the rarity of *tekhelet*, see *Sifré, Berakhah* (Deuteronomy 33:19), and *b. Menahot* 44a. Regarding the rarity of *zekhukhit levanah*, see *b. Sotah* 48a; and *Tosafot, Bava Metsi'a* 29b, s.v. *bi-zekhukhit levanah*.
[31] *b. Sotah* 17a; *Menahot* 43b.
[32] *b. Sotah* 48a.

First Fruits and the Talmudic View of Capital: An *Essai* in the Philosophy of *Halakhah*

(b. GITTIN 47b)

The Torah commanded that the first fruits (*bikkurim*) be placed in a basket and brought to the site of the future Temple. There, the basket is presented to the *kohen* or priest and the owner recites a lengthy narrative (*mikra bikkurim*) which recounts the collective history of the People of Israel. The narrative commences with the tribulations of Jacob in Laban's house, continues with the descent to and bondage in Egypt, proceeds to the wondrous Exodus from Egypt, and concludes with the arrival in this "land flowing with milk and honey."[1] The last line, in an abrupt update, switches to first person singular: "And now, behold, I have brought the first fruit of the land that You have given me, O LORD."[2]

According to the *Mishnah*, the bringing of the first fruits to the Temple Mount in Jerusalem would commence on the festival of *Shavu'ot* and continue until *Sukkot*. (The actual bringing could continue until *Hanukkah*, but after *Sukkot* the accompanying narrative would no longer be recited.)[3]

In his *Guide*, Maimonides spells out the rationale of this Biblical commandment:

As for the reading on the occasion of the offering of first fruits, it also is conducive to the moral quality of humility, for it is carried out by him who carries the basket on his shoulders. It contains an acknowledgment of God's beneficence and bountifulness, so that man should know that it is a part of the divine worship that man should remember states of distress at a time when he prospers. This purpose is frequently affirmed in the Torah: *And you shall remember that you were a servant*, and so on.[4] For there was a fear of the moral qualities that are generally acquired by all those who are brought up in prosperity—I mean conceit, vanity, and neglect of the correct opinions: *Lest when you have eaten and are satisfied, and houses*, and so on.[5] And it says: *But Jeshurun waxed fat, and kicked*, and so on.[6] It is because of this apprehension that the commandment has been given to carry out a reading every year before Him, may He be exalted, and in presence of His Indwelling, on the occasion of the offering of first fruits.[7]

Hoping not to sound clichéd, this is a lesson in humility. In fact, Maimonides, in an interesting twist of language, refers to this narrative as *"viddui"* or confession.[8]

※

With this introduction in mind, my aim is to examine one unit of the many laws of *bikkurim* as laid out in the Talmud. This single

BIKKURIM: FIRST FRUITS

halakhah may very well serve as a microcosm of a "philosophy" of *bikkurim*.

In Tractate *Gittin* 47b, we read:

> If a man was coming on the way [to Jerusalem] and the first fruits of his wife were in his hand, and he heard that his wife died—he brings [the first fruits] and recites [the narrative].
>
> Only if she died [does he recite the narrative]?[9]
>
> The law would be the same if she did not die, but it is necessary to stipulate that the law obtains even if she dies, for I might have assumed that in such a case we should decree [that the husband not recite the narrative] because of the principle enunciated by Rabbi Yosé bar Hanina, who said:
>
> [If the owner of the land] harvested them and sent them with an emissary, and the emissary died on the way [to Jerusalem]—the owner brings, but does not recite, for it says: "You shall take" (*ve-lakahta*) and "You shall bring" (*ve-heveta*).[10] [One does not recite] unless the taking (*lekihah*)[11] and bringing (*hava'ah*) are done by one person.
>
> [Therefore,] we are apprised [that there is no decree disqualifying the husband from reciting if his wife died].

Rabbi Yosé bar Hanina taught that when it comes to the recitation of *mikra bikkurim* there can be no division of labor. The "taking" and "bringing" of the first fruits can be done by two people, but in such a scenario, upon arrival at the Temple, the owner will not be able to recite the narrative. *Mikra bikkurim* is contingent upon the harvesting and conveyance being executed by one and the same person.

One is left wondering: Why would we have entertained the thought of comparing the two vastly different scenarios? Who would ever make an analogy between the case of the husband *en route* discovering that his wife died and Rabbi Yosé bar Hanina's case of the emissary dying *en route*?

Rashi explains that his wife's death has altered the husband's relation to her real estate. While yet she lived he had merely the usufruct (*kinyan peirot*).[12] With her death, as her heir, he now has full possession of the land (*kinyan ha-guf*). One might have thought that his new socioeconomic status has transformed the husband into a new man, so to speak. Whereas previously, in a sense he was bringing his wife's *bikkurim* as her surrogate or *shali'ah*, he is now transformed into the owner or *ba'alim*.[13]

By outer appearances, it is as if the emissary died *en route* and has been replaced with the owner himself. Thus, one might have deemed this case analogous to that of Rabbi Yosé bar Hanina, where the emissary actually, physically died *en route* and the bringing of the *bikkurim* was completed by the owner.

For some reason not made explicit in the Talmud, the analogy breaks down. Therefore, no *gezerah* or decree precluding the husband from reciting *mikra bikkurim* was ever issued. Where does the analogy founder? Perhaps the point is that it beggars belief that an upward turn in financial status would turn one into another person altogether; that the original version and the wealthier version would be for all intents and purposes "two bodies" (*trei gufei*).[14]

Mikra bikkurim requires continuity from the harvesting of the fruits until their arrival at the Temple. The *lekihah* and *hava'ah* must be done by one and the same person. The physical death of the *shali'ah* shatters the unity. An uptick in terms of ownership of the parcel of land does not.

※ ※

A Talmudic genius who delved deeply into the relation between personhood and capital was Rabbi Joseph Rosen (1858-1936), the famed Rogatchover Gaon.[15] One of his points of departure is the statement that occurs several times in the Talmud: "Since if one should desire to relinquish ownership of his possessions and become a poor man, it would be fitting for him, now too it is fitting for him."[16]

One context where this principle of potentiality is applied is that of *demai*. *Demai* is produce which may or may not have been tithed. Most common folk do tithe, but then there is the minority who do not. The ruling is that only the poor are allowed to consume *demai*; the wealthy may not.[17] Now what is the *halakhah* if the first night of Passover a rich man eats *matsah* of *demai*? Does he fulfill the commandment of eating *matsah*? The answer is affirmative. Though in actuality he is a wealthy man, in potential he is a poor man, for he can always divest himself of his assets.[18]

There is continuity of personality. Rich and poor are not two bodies (*trei gufei*). Loss of possessions does not transform one into a different person. Essentially, one remains the same person. This is the opposite of the scenario of *bikkurim* discussed earlier. There the individual's financial status improved. The principle remains the same. Altered economic status does not result in discontinuity of personality. The integrity of personhood is uncompromised.

The Rogatchover is famous for applying to the study of Talmud philosophic categories of thought gleaned from Maimonides' *Guide of the Perplexed*. In regard to the potential transformation from "riches to rags," the Rogatchover writes: "The issue is whether this is an attribute of the body or an external cause...And so wrote *Rabbeinu* [i.e., Maimonides] in the *Moreh* that every change comes from elsewhere, not from the essence...Perforce, this is not an essential change."[19]

The method by which this East European rabbi harnesses Aristotelian modalities obtained by way of Maimonides' *Guide* to the study of Talmudic jurisprudence might bring a smirk to the face of a cynic. Nonetheless, the Rogatchover's point is well taken. Capital is not the essence of the human being but rather external; it belongs to the material (*homer*) as opposed to the formal realm (*tsurah*).

※

A Talmudic genius in the same league as the Rogatchover, of the generation preceding him, was Rabbi Zadok Hakohen Rabinowitz of Lublin (1823-1900).[20] In his seminal work, *Tsidkat ha-Tsaddik*, he wrote:

> "Whatever is a possession (*kinyan*) of man—his wife and children, manservant and maid, ox and donkey, tent and silver and gold, and all that is his—all is from the root of his soul."[21]

This is a mystical vision of the interconnectedness of the various elements of reality. Such empathic thinking could lead to enhanced concern for ecology and the environment. It could sensitize one to social justice and animal welfare.

But the keyword in Rabbi Zadok's pronouncement is *"kinyan."* Rabbi Zadok came to the Hasidic court of Izhbitsa (Polish, Izbica) from the Talmudic stronghold of *Lita*. It is as if he brought with him the Talmudic terminology. Thus, the *"torat ha-kinyanim"* (theory of possessions or acquistions) of Talmudic analysis was married to the mysticism of the Baʻal Shem Tov.

Rabbi Zadok is fascinated by the way in which a man's moral standing impacts upon that of his children, his wife, and even his beast (as is the case regarding the donkey of Rabbi Pinhas ben Yair[22]). All are from the "root of his soul" (*mi-shoresh nafsho*). Once again, we have an accomplished Talmudist (albeit turned Hasidic master) exploring the borders of selfhood, probing the relation between man and his acquisitions, and arriving at a notion of possessions as extensions of one's personality.

Is it pure coincidence that Rabbi Zadok penned those lines in 1848,[23] the very year in which Karl Marx issued his *Communist Manifesto*? Did the same *Zeitgeist* waft into the Hasidic study hall of Izhbitsa and the secret society of The League of the Just in Brussels? The sound waves of the *"bat kol"* certainly registered differently in the consciousness of the two men.[24]

Marx would go on to publish these lines:

> "The mode of production of material life determines the social, political and intellectual life process in general. It is not the consciousness of men that determines their being, but, on the contrary, their social being that determines their consciousness."[25]

Marx observed how in the Industrial Era the alienation of the laborers from their products resulted in their alienation (*Entfremdung*).

Rabbi Zadok's stance is diametrically opposed to that of Marx. Where Marx has capital defining personality, Rabbi Zadok has a romantic notion of the "root of the soul" impacting upon *"kinyanim."*

Bikkurim: First Fruits

The moral lesson of *Bikkurim* is that one's material bounty is a divine gift. Material possessions are not essential to, nor do they define one's personality. This assertion was buttressed by the Rogatchover with proofs from the *Guide*. Two contemporaries, Rabbi Zadok Hakohen of Lublin and Karl Marx, expressed opposite ideas concerning the relation of man to his possessions. Whereas for Rabbi Zadok they may be extensions (but never the essence of self), for Marx, capital defines man.

---

[1] Deuteronomy 26:9.
[2] Deuteronomy 26:10.
[3] *m. Bikkurim* 1:6, 10.
[4] Deuteronomy 5:15; 16:12.
[5] Deuteronomy 8:12.
[6] Deuteronomy 32:15.
[7] Moses Maimonides, *The Guide of the Perplexed*, transl. Shlomo Pines (Chicago: University of Chicago Press, 1964), III, 39 (pp. 551-552).
[8] Maimonides, *MT, Hil. Bikkurim* 4:1 and earlier 3:10. Cf. Rabbi Nissim ben Reuben of Gerona's commentary to Alfasi, *Megillah* (7a in foliation of Alfasi): *"Viddui Bikkurim."* Finally, see Rabbi Aryeh Leib Ginsburg, *Turei Even, Megillah* 20b; and Rabbi Joseph Babad, *Minhat Hinnukh*, commandment 606, par. 1.
   One is tempted to source Maimonides' expression *"Viddui Bikkurim"* in *m. Bikkurim* 2:2, however upon closer inspection one discovers that Maimonides, following the *Yerushalmi*, understood the reference there to *Viddui Ma'aser*. See Maimonides' *Commentary to the Mishnah*, ibid. (Kafah ed., p. 265); *MT, Hil. Ma'aser Sheni* 11:14, and *Kesef Mishneh* and Rabbi David ibn Abi Zimra (RaDBaZ) ad loc.
   Unlike the *Yerushalmi*, Rashi (*Yevamot* 73a) and Rabbeinu Ovadiah Bertinuro interpret *"Viddui Bikkurim"* in that *mishnah* as referring to *Mikra Bikkurim*. For a clarification of Rashi's comment, see Rabbi Yehudah Gershuni, *"Be-'Inyan Keri'at Bikkurim,"* in *Kovets Ma'amarim*, included in *Shitah Mekubetset 'al Masekhet Pesahim* (New York, 1966), pp. 145-147.
[9] In *Talmud Yerushalmi*, Rabbi Shim'on ben Lakish is truly of the opinion that only after the wife's death may her husband, as heir, recite *mikra bikkurim*. See *y. Bikkurim* 1:5 and *Ketubot* 8:5; and Rabbi Samson of Sens, *Bikkurim* 1:5.
[10] The exact word *ve-heveta* does not occur in Scripture. See RaShBaM, *Bava Batra* 81b, s.v. *ve-lakahta ve-heveta*.
[11] The two brothers Rabbi Samuel ben Meir (RaShBaM) and Rabbi Jacob ben Meir (Rabbeinu Tam) disagreed as to the definition of *lekihah*. Rashbam

equated it with *"betsirah"* or harvesting, and Rabbeinu Tam understood it as "removal from the house." See *Tosafot, Gittin* 47b, s.v. *betsaran.*

[12] The land entered the marriage as *"nikhsei melug."*

[13] See commentary of Rabbeinu Menahem ha-Me'iri, *Gittin* 47b.

[14] See Rashi, *Temurah* 20a, s.v. *trei gufei ninhu,* and *Tosafot,* ibid., s.v. *hanei trei gufei.*

[15] See Rabbi Menahem Mendel Kasher, *Mef'ane'ah Tsefunot* (New York, 1959), 6:6, *"'Ani ve-'Ashir"* (pp. 147-149); and Rabbi Moshe Shelomo Kasher, *Ha-Ga'on ha-Rogatchovi ve-Talmudo* (Jerusalem, 1958), pp. 49-52 (*"'Ani ve-'Ashir"*).

[16] In *b. Bava Metsi'a* 9b, in regard to *pe'ah,* this is typified as a *"mi-go."* In regard to *demai,* the *terminus technicus "mi-go"* interchanges with *"keivan."* (See below note 18.)

[17] *m. Demai* 3:1.

[18] *b. Pesahim* 35b. See also *Berakhot* 47a; *Shabbat* 127b; *'Eruvin* 31a; and *Sukkah* 35b.

[19] *Tsafnat P'ane'ah, Mahadura Tinyana* (Dvinsk, 1930), 73c (p. 146). Though in this particular instance the Rogatchover did not provide the exact reference in Maimonides' *Guide,* by cross-referencing to other passages in the Gaon's writings, Rabbi Kasher was able to find the Rogatchover's two sources in the *Guide*:

"All bodies subject to generation and corruption are attained by corruption only because of their matter; with regards to form and with respect to the latter's essence, they are not attained by corruption, but are permanent." (Moses Maimonides, *Guide of the Perplexed* III, 8 [Pines transl. p. 430])

"Everything that passes from potentiality to actuality has something other than itself that causes it to pass, and this cause is of necessity outside that thing." (*Guide* II, eighteenth premise [Pines transl. p. 238])

See Rabbi M.M. Kasher, *Mef'ane'ah Tsefunot* (New York, 1959), 6:6:5 (p. 148) and 14:4:1, 2 (p. 221). The exact references to the *Guide* are supplied in *Tsafnat P'ane'ah, Kuntres Hashlamah* (Warsaw, 1909), pp. 3 and 26.

[20] See the account of the meeting of Rabbi Joseph Rosen of Denenburg (later Dvinsk, today Daugavpils, Latvia) and Rabbi Zadok, in the short biographical sketch that prefaces *Sihat Mal'akhei ha-Sharet* (Lublin, 1927).

[21] *Tsidkat ha-Tsaddik* (Lublin, 1902), chap. 86.

[22] *b. Hullin* 7.

[23] See Rabbi Gershon Kitsis' bibliography of the writings of Rabbi Zadok in *Me'at la-Zaddik,* ed. Kitsis (Jerusalem, 2000), p. 346.

[24] Rabbi Zadok expounded his theory of the *bat kol* or *"kala de-hadra"* (*Zohar*), whereby a divine idea enters the world and is immediately refracted through the consciousness of various peoples and individuals, yielding some astonishingly different interpretations. See *Dover Zedek* (Piotrków, 1911), 71d-72c; English translation in Bezalel Naor, *Lights of Prophecy* (New York: Union of Orthodox Jewish Congregations of America, 1990), pp. 38-41.

[25] *The Portable Karl Marx,* ed. Eugene Kamenka (New York: Penguin, 1983), pp. 159-160.

Mindfulness and the Cities of Refuge[1]

(b. MAKKOT 10a)

BACKGROUND

The Torah provided cities of refuge for the unintentional manslayer. Simply, the purpose of these cities was to afford the blameless homicide protection from a kinsman of the deceased seeking to avenge his blood. There were six of these "cities of refuge" (*'arei miklat*), three in Transjordan designated by Moses, and three in the Land of Canaan designated later by Joshua, Moses' successor. In addition, there were forty-two cities of the Levites (*'arei ha-leviyim* or *'arei migrash*) that doubled as sanctuary cities.[2]

How far back in time did this unique institution extend? How long did it persist? What are the prospects for the future?

According to the Talmud, already in the Sinai desert the unintentional murderer would relocate to the Camp of the Levites.[3] This would be the earliest example, the *terminus a quo*.

At the other end, the *terminus ad quem*, the forty-two *'arei migrash* of the Levites were defunct in the Second Temple Era. In the words of the *Tosefta*: "From the [time of the] destruction of the First Temple, the Kingdom of the House of David ceased, the Urim and Thummim ceased, and the cities of the Levites (*'arei migrash*) stopped."[4] Nonetheless, it seems plausible that the six cities of refuge continued to service homicidal exiles in the Second Temple Era, even though the forty-two cities of the Levites ceased.[5]

Toward the future, the Torah enjoins us to eventually add another three cities of refuge to the original six, bringing the total up to nine cities.[6] According to Maimonides, the additional three cities will be located in the former territory of the Kenite, the Kenizite and the Kadmonite.[7] Maimonides goes so far as to adduce proof for the Messianic Era from this futuristic commandment of the Torah: "Even in regard to the cities of refuge it says: 'If the LORD should expand your boundary…you shall add for yourself another three cities in addition to these three.' And this thing never came about, and the LORD did not command for naught."[8]

THE SIX AND THE FORTY-TWO

The Talmud establishes differences between the six cities of refuge and the forty-two cities of the Levites. According to the Mishnah (in the opinion of Rabbi Judah), in the six cities, the fugitive dwelled rent-free; in the forty-two cities, he would have to pay rent to the Levites.[9]

Beyond this, the third-century Babylonian *amora* Abbaye delivered another differential: The six cities of refuge absorb the exile with or without his knowledge (*bein le-da'at, bein she-lo le-da'at*); the forty-cities of the Levites absorb the exile only if he be conscious at the time of entry.[10]

DEFINING "MINDFULNESS"

This entire topic of "mindfulness" in regard to the sanctuary cities is most intriguing. What sort of mindfulness (or lack thereof) does Abbaye refer to?

Rabbi Shelomo Yitzhaki (RaShI) understands by this that one has in mind to be absorbed in the city; conversely, lack of mindfulness is defined by RaShI as unawareness that the city has the ability to aborb the manslaughterer.

Rabbi Yom Tov ben Abraham Asevilli (RITBA) offers two alternatives. Either *"da'at"* refers to waking consciousness as opposed to the sleeping state; or it refers to cognizance of the city's privileged status:

> **Unwittingly**—i.e., for example, he entered asleep on another's shoulders or on the back of a beast; or he did not know that it is a city of refuge.[11]

At this juncture, one asks: Why is the element of mindfulness necessary in order for the exile to be absorbed within the city of refuge? The literature of the *Aharonim* (late rabbinic authorities) contains three responses to this question. We shall term these approaches: the juridical or procedural; the proprietary; and the expiatory.

JURIDICAL OR PROCEDURAL

Rabbi Yitzhak Hayes of Brody[12] believed that mindfulness (or lack thereof) comes about in the following manner.

Talmud

When a murder has been committed, the perpetrator is immediately bundled off to one of the six cities of refuge. Afterward, he must stand trial in the city where the murder took place. At the conclusion of the trial there are three possibilities. Either the court will find him guilty of intentional murder, in which case he will be executed; or he will be exonerated, in which case he will be set free; or the court will find that the murder was committed unintentionally, whereupon he will be escorted (once again) to a city of refuge.[13]

The author assumes that the first time the murderer is exiled, it can only be to one of the six cities, not to one of the forty-two cities.[14] Thus does he understand Abbaye's differential between the six and the forty-two cities. The entry into the six cities can be either with the knowledge that he is banished there or without that knowledge (because the court has yet to decide his fate), depending on whether he is entering the city for the first or second time. However, in regard to the forty-two cities, he must know that the court has decided that he dwell there.

PROPRIETARY

Rabbi Jacob Ettlinger[15] connects our law to the law of possession known as *"kinyan hatser,"* whereby one's courtyard acquires possessions that enter it even without the knowledge of the owner of the courtyard.[16] Relying on the interpretation "'for you'—for all your needs" (*"'lakhem'—le-khol tsorkheikhem"*),[17] which applies to the six cities but not to the forty-two cities, Rabbi Ettlinger posits that in the six cities the manslayers have proprietary rights so that their taking up dwelling there may occur unconsciously, as opposed to the forty-two cities where the Levites (not the manslayers) are in complete possession, necessitating consciousness upon the part of the newly arrived tenant.[18]

EXPIATORY

The famed Rogatchover Gaon, Rabbi Joseph Rosen, in his notes to Tractate *Makkot*, clarified that exile to the city of refuge serves two purposes.[19] Simply, it provides protection (*haganah*) against an avenger. Beyond that, it achieves atonement (*kaparah*) for having shed blood.[20] In this respect, it acts much as a sacrifice brought to the Temple. And a sacrifice expiates only with the owner's knowledge.[21] (Curiously, the Gaon left unexplained why consciousness is not required to attain atonement in the six cities.)

I would like to suggest a fourth explanation of *"da'at"* or mindfulness, albeit not taken from the realm of *halakhah* but from the realm of *aggadah*.

AGGADAH

According to the Talmud, the "portion of murderers" (*parashat rotzhim*)[22] is predicated on the principle of divine providence:

> Rabbi Shim'on ben Lakish opened his homily for this portion from here: "And if a man lie not in wait, but God caused it to come to his hand" [Exodus 21:13].

This is what is referred to by the verse, "As the proverb of the ancient says: 'Out of the wicked comes forth wickedness'" [1 Samuel 24:13].

To what does the verse refer? To two people who committed murder. One killed unintentionally; the other killed intentionally. In neither case are there witnesses. The Holy One, blessed be He, invites them to the same inn. The one who killed intentionally sits under the ladder, and the one who killed unintentionally descends the ladder and falls upon him and kills him. The one who killed intentionally, is killed; and the one who killed unintentionally is exiled [to a city of refuge].[23]

We have discussed the fact that exile expiates. How exactly does the expiation come about? It is possible that the physical and emotional hardship of displacement removes the stain of having shed blood.[24] But perhaps more than that is required. Perhaps exile to the city of refuge represents a process of reeducation.[25] One must reach the state of mindfulness that Rabbi Shim'on ben Lakish deemed the appropriate overture to the "portion of the murderers": the realization that the Creator orchestrates an ineluctable chain of causality. No deed goes unpunished. Maimonides in his philosophic work, *Guide of the Perplexed*, will refer to this principle as "divine providence."[26] Perhaps this awareness is part and parcel of the *da'at* necessary for absorption into the sanctuary city. But why is it required in the forty-two cities and not in the six cities? Admittedly, this is a difficult question to answer.

The Cities of Refuge

We need to retrace the development of the six cities. Though they would first become operational (which is to say, ready to receive fugitives) only during Joshua's reign,[27] the first three cities in Transjordan were already established by Moses. Moses reasoned: "Since a commandment (*mitsvah*) has come into my hand, I shall fulfill it."[28]

As altruistic and noble as his intentions were, Moses was not a totally disinterested party to the establishment of the cities of refuge. Having himself killed the Egyptian and been forced to flee thereafter to Midian, Moses was certainly capable of empathizing with the plight of the manslayer. In the words of the Midrash: "One who has eaten from the cauldron knows the taste of the dish."[29] Moses is said to have put his soul into the cities of refuge.[30] They are listed as one of the three things that Moses put his soul into and which were called by his name: Torah, Israel and the cities of refuge.[31] Finally, upon the establishment of the cities of refuge, Moses burst out in song as he did at the splitting of the Reed Sea.[32]

To answer our question of why the forty-two cities require *da'at* but not the six cities, this may result from the fact that Moses invested himself in the six cities, and thus they remain imbued with his *da'at*, his consciousness, his awareness.[33] For this reason, the fugitive who enters into one of these cities need not be mindful in order to be absorbed there. His individual consciousness is unnecessary; these cities are forever stamped with the collective consciousness of Moses. On the other hand, should the individual wish to be absorbed in one of the forty-two cities—which in no way were established by Moses—he must activate his own individual *da'at*.³⁴

When confronted with the conundrum of why three additional cities of refuge will be required in the Messianic Era when mankind's base instinct for revenge will have been extirpated, Rabbi Joseph Babad of Tarnopol wrote that this is simply a *"gezeirat hakatuv,"* a divine decree, without practical application.³⁵ I humbly submit that those cities will stand as a symbol of *"da'at,"* a mindfulness of the exquisite workings of divine supervision, an awareness that will most certainly be enhanced and augmented in the Days of Messiah. In the concluding words of Maimonides:

> And the occupation of the entire world will be only to know the LORD. Therefore, they will be great sages, knowing the deep, hidden matters. And they will comprehend the knowledge of their Creator as much as is humanly possible, as it says: "For the earth shall be full of the knowledge of God as the waters cover the sea [Isaiah 11:9]."³⁶

---

[1] Some of the materials for this essay first appeared in the chapter *"Ha-Utopia ha-'Ivrit* ("The Hebrew Utopia") in my book *Avirin* (Jerusalem: Zur-Ot, 1980), pp. 97-101.

[2] See Exodus 21:13; Numbers, chap. 35; Deuteronomy 4:41-43, 19:1-13; Joshua, chap. 21; *t. Makkot* 3:1-2 (Zuckermandel edition, p. 440).

The Cities of Refuge

[3] *b. Makkot* 11b.

[4] *Tosefta, Sotah* 13:3 (Lieberman edition, p. 230); *b. Sotah* 48b.

Saul Lieberman speculates that there is a causal relation between the cessation of the Davidic dynasty and the Urim and Thummim, on the one hand, and the disruption of the Levitic cities, on the other. See S. Lieberman, *Tosefta ki-Fshutah* (Commentary), Part VIII (*Nashim*) (Philadelphia: JTSA, 1973), p. 735, lines 37-39. See earlier Rabbi Meir Simhah Ha-Kohen, *Meshekh Hokhmah, Mas'ei,* s.v. *shesh 'arei miklat.* (Note however that in the Bavli the order is reversed.)

[5] See *Meshekh Hokhmah,* loc. cit.; Rabbi Joseph Rosen, *Tsaphnat P'ane'ah,* ed. Rabbi M.M. Kasher, vol. 4 (Numbers) (Jerusalem, 1962), *Mas'ei,* Numbers 35:11 (p. 309) and Numbers 35:29 (p. 314); and Rabbi Hayyim Kanievsky, *Kiryat Melekh, Hil. Rotse'ah* 8:1.

[6] Deuteronomy 19:9; *t. Makkot* 3:10 (Zuckermandel edition, p. 441); *y. Makkot* 2:6.

[7] Maimonides, *Hil. Rotse'ah* 8:4. The source for Maimonides' statement remains elusive. See Rabbi Joseph Babad, *Minhat Hinukh* (to *Sefer ha-Hinukh*), commandment 520. Rabbi Hayyim Kanievsky jotted down as a possible source *Midrash Tanna'im,* Deuteronomy 19:9, adding judiciously: "I do not know whether it is possible to rely on him" (*Kiryat Melekh, Hil. Rotse'ah* 8:4). The reference is to Rabbi David Zevi Hoffman's production, *Midrash Tanna'im* to the Book of Deuteronomy (Berlin, 1908), p. 114. Rabbi Kanievsky was wise to express misgivings. By now, it is well known that Rabbi David Adani's *Midrash ha-Gadol,* from which Hoffman culled, is largely a regurgitation of Maimonides' code, hardly a source for his rulings.

It is possible that since the *Sifré* (quoted in Rashi) interpreted the expansion of the boundary in Deuteronomy 19:8 to refer to the land of the Kenite, the Kenizite and the Kadmonite, Maimonides assumed that the three additional cities commanded in the following verse were to be established in that same territory.

As for the identity of the three nations, the Kenite, the Kenizite, and the Kadmonite, see Rashi, Genesis 15:19, as well as the various opinions in *y. Shevi'it* 6:1, *Kiddushin* 1:8; *Genesis Rabbah* 44:23; and *b. Bava Batra* 56a.

[8] Maimonides, *Hil. Melakhim* 11:2.

Starting with the medieval Ashkenazic compilation *Sefer Hasidim,* many have puzzled over the seemingly irreconcilable contradiction between Moses' call for three more additional cities of refuge and Isaiah's halcyon portrayal of the Messianic Era (which Maimonides quotes at the beginning of the next chapter of *Hil. Melakhim*): "The wolf shall dwell with the lamb, and the leopard shall lie down with the kid" (Isaiah 11:6). To quote Deuteronomy 19:6, the city of refuge is provided "lest the avenger of blood pursue the manslayer, *while his heart is hot* (*ki yeham levavo*), and overtake him, because the way is long, and smite him mortally; whereas he was not deserving of death, inasmuch as he did not hate him in time past." This seems a most unlikely eventuality once mankind has been mollified. (Maimonides explains there that Isaiah's prophecy is not to be taken literally, rather it is a fable designed to convey "that Israel will dwell securely with the wicked of the world who are compared to the wolf and the leopard.")

Sefer Hasidim's solution is that in addition to providing protection for the unintentional murderer (which will be unnecessary in the Days of Messiah), exile is also a form of expiation (*kaparah*) for having inadvertently shed blood (on a par with sacrifices). (Cf. the remarks of the Rogatchover at note 19.) This segment is found in the Parma manuscript of *Sefer Hasidim*, which was the basis for Wistinetzki's edition (and later for Rabbi Abraham A. Price of Toronto's multivolume edition with commentary *"Mishnat Avraham"*). It is not found in the corresponding chapter of the Bologna edition of *Sefer Hasidim*, which is the basis of Rabbi Reuven Margaliyot's edition. See *Sefer Hasidim*, ed. Jehuda Wistinetzki (Berlin: Mekitsei Nirdamim, 1893), chap. 1054 (pp. 266-267); Rabbi A.A. Price, *Sefer Hasidim* with commentary *Mishnat Avraham*, vol. 2 (New York, 1960), chap. 1054 (pp. 212-213). Cf. *Sefer Hasidim*, ed. Reuven Margaliyot (Jerusalem: Mossad Harav Kook, 1957), chap. 368 (p. 271).

For others who grappled with this problem, see Rabbi Hayyim Vital, *Likkutei Torah* (Vilna, 1880), *Shofetim*, s.v. *ve-'im yarhiv Hashem* (103a-104a); transcribed in Rabbi Isaiah Halevi Horowitz, *Shnei Luhot ha-Berit* (Amsterdam, 1648), end *Beit David* (f. 24); Rabbi David Pardo, *Maskil le-David* (super-commentary to Rashi) (Venice, 1760), Deuteronomy 19:8; Rabbi Judah Alkalay, *Minhat Yehudah* (1843), chap. 31 (17b-18a), quoting *Shnei Luhot ha-Berit*; Rabbi Abraham Tsevi Margaliyot, *Keren 'Orah* (Jerusalem, 1986), *Shofetim*, s.v. *ve-'im yarhiv Hashem* (pp. 280-281); Rabbi Samuel Bornstein of Sochatchov, *Shem mi-Shmuel* (Jerusalem, 1974), *Shofetim* 5676, s.v. *ve-'im yarhiv Hashem* (pp. 123-126); Rabbi Meir Simhah ha-Kohen, *Meshekh Hokhmah* (Riga, 1927), *Shofetim*, s.v. *ve-'im yarhiv* (183a) (a rehashing of Rabbi Hayyim Vital, *Likkutei Torah*); Rabbi Abraham Isaac Hakohen Kook, *'Ets Hadar ha-Shalem*, ed. Judah Zoldan (Jerusalem, 1986), Introduction (*"Rosh Amir"*), pp. 12-13; Rabbi M.M. Schneerson, *Likkutei Sihot* (Yiddish), vol. 24 (Israel, 2006), *Shofetim* (2), pp. 107-114.

Most interesting is the conclusion of Rabbi Joseph Babad, *Minhat Hinukh*, commandment 520, that in truth, the cities of refuge will serve no practical purpose in the future, once mankind has been purged of its homicidal tendencies. The cities of refuge will be designated simply as a divine decree (*gezeirat ha-katuv*). We will have more to say in this regard at the conclusion of our essay.

[9] *m. Makkot* 2:8; *b. Makkot* 13a. So in the reconstruction of Rava. (Rav Kahana reconstructed Rabbi Judah's opinion differently, whereby even in the six cities the fugitives must pay rent to the Levites.)

[10] *b. Makkot* 10a.

Rabbi Samuel Strashun (RaShaSh) and Rabbi Yitzhak Hayes (*Si'ah Yitzhak*) conjectured that Abbaye provided this differential in accordance with the dissenting opinion of Rabbi Meir in the Mishnah (*Makkot* 2:8) that there is no difference between the six cities and the forty-two cities in regard to rent. (Even in the forty-two cities the fugitive resides rent-free.) According to the opinion of Rabbi Judah, Abbaye's differential would have been superfluous. See Rava's reconstruction (as opposed to Rav Kahana's reconstruction) of Rabbi Judah and Rabbi Meir's opinions in *b. Makkot* 13a.

[11] *Hiddushei ha-RITBA*, *Makkot* 10a.

[12] Rabbi Yitzhak Hayes, *Si'ah Yitzhak* (Podgorze, 1900), *Makkot* 10a, s.v. *ve-tu leka*.

The Cities of Refuge

13 *m. Makkot* 2:6; *b. Makkot* 9b; Maimonides, *Hil. Rotse'ah* 5:7.

14 Rabbi Yitzhak Arieli (evidently unaware of the *Si'ah Yitzhak*'s remarks) concluded just the opposite that the initial exile (before the court's determination of status) need not be to one of the six cities of refuge; it may also be to one of the forty-two Levitic cities. See Rabbi Yitzhak Arieli, *'Eynayim le-Mishpat*, Tractate *Makkot* (Jerusalem: Mossad Harav Kook, 1959), *Makkot* 9b, s.v. *ba-tehillah ehad shogeg* (67b).

One may deduce that Rabbi Arieli is correct from the final words of the *Mishnah* (*Makkot* 2:6): "One who was sentenced to exile, they return him to his place, for it says, 'The congregation shall return him to his city of refuge, whither he fled' [Numbers 35:25]." If, on the other hand, one assumes (as does Rabbi Hayes) that the initial exile must never be to the forty-cities but only to the six cities, how then does the unintentional murderer ever end up in one of the forty-two cities? According to the *Mishnah*, after judgment, he will always be escorted back to one of the original six cities!

15 Rabbi Jacob Ettlinger, *'Arukh la-Ner*, *Makkot* 10a, s.v. *ve-tu leka*.

16 "A man's courtyard acquires for him without his knowledge" ("*Hatsero shel adam konah lo she-lo mi-da'ato*") (*b. Bava Metsi'a* 11a; Maimonides, *Hil. Gezeilah va-Aveidah* 17:8; *Hil. Zekhiyah u-Matanah* 4:8).

17 "The cities shall be *for you* a refuge from an avenger" (Numbers 35:12). See *b. Makkot* 13a. RaShI ibid. (s.v. *lakhem*) explains that this statement was addressed to the manslayers.

18 This novel approach of Rabbi Ettlinger will be difficult to maintain if one assumes (as did Rabbi Samuel Strashun, see above note 10) that Abbaye's differential was supplied to compensate for Rabbi Meir's non-differentiation between the six and the forty-two cities. In Rabbi Meir's reckoning, "for all your needs" ("*le-khol tsorkheikhem*") applies to the forty-two cities as well. Only in Rabbi Yehudah's reckoning is "for all your needs" restricted to the six cities. See *b. Makkot* 13a.

On the other hand, one might find support for Rabbi Ettlinger's explanation in Maimonides' grouping of the laws in *Hil. Rotse'ah* 8:11. From Maimonides' juxtaposition of the two differentials between the six and the forty-two cities—namely, the requirement of consciousness and the requirement to pay rent to the Levites—one may argue that Maimonides understood that they derive from the same principle. But this is inconclusive.

19 Rabbi Joseph Rosen, *Tsaphnat P'ane'ah*, Tractate *Makkot*, ed. Rabbi M.M. Kasher (New York: Shulsinger Bros., 1959), *Makkot* 10a, s.v. *halalu koletot* (f.28). Cf. Rabbi Meir Simhah ha-Kohen, *'Or Same'ah*, *Hil. Rotse'ah*, 6:12.

20 One should not be misled by the wording of the Talmud's rhetorical question, "Does exile atone? It is the death of the [high] priest that atones!" (*b. Makkot* 11b). The Talmud is not denying the expiatory value of exile, rather it refers to the atonement that allows the manslayer to leave the city of refuge and return to his former life. See *Tosafot* and RITBA, ad loc., s.v. *midei galut ka mekhaperah*; and Rabbi Jacob Ettlinger, *'Arukh la-Ner*, ad loc., s.v. *mitat kohen hi di-mekhaperah*.

Truly, there are numerous proofs to the expiatory value of exile. The Rogatchover jotted down, almost at random, *b. Makkot* 2b ["...*lo liglei ki heikhi de-lo teheveh leh kaparah...liglu ki heikhi de-lehevei lehu kaparah*"]; [*Tosafot*] *Makkot* 9a [s.v. *amar leh*]. See also RaShI, *Makkot* 8b, s.v. *le-Rabbi*

Shim'on de-amar; RaShI, *'Arakhin* 6b, s.v. *mitot kalot*; and Maimonides, *Hil. Rotse'ah* 6:4: "Since his sin is severe, exile does not atone for him."

For an extensive discussion of the topic (including the opinion of Rabbi Jonathan of Lunel, *Makkot*, who seems to minimize the expiatory value of exile), see Rabbi Yisrael Herczeg, *Keren David, Makkot* (Jerusalem, 1982), "Kaparah de-Galut," pp. 90-94.

Rabbi Isaac Hutner wrote that only the second exile to the city of refuge, after sentencing (*gemar din*), is an "expiatory exile" (*"galut shel kaparah"*), as opposed to the initial exile to the city of refuge (before sentencing), which is an exile designed merely to rescue the homicide from the avenger (*"galut shel hatsalah"*). See Rabbi Isaac Hutner, *Sefer ha-Zikaron le-Maran Ba'al Pahad Yitzhak*, ed. Rabbi Yonatan David (Brooklyn, NY, 2014), p. 277.

[21] *b. 'Arakhin* 21.

It occurs to the writer (BN) that atonement by exile (*galut*) should be comparable to atonement by tribulations (*yissurim*). In the latter regard, we have the statement, "Just as a guilt-offering must be with knowledge, so tribulations must be with knowledge" (*b. Berakhot* 5a). ("*Mah asham le-da'at, af yissurim le-da'at.*) In context, the statement refers to accepting willingly the tribulations sent one's way.

[22] RaShI, *Makkhot* 10b, s.v. *patah leh pitha*. The term *"parashat rotzhim"* occurs earlier in *b. Makkot*, end 10b. Cf. *Deuteronomy Rabbah* 2:29: *"parashat rotse'ah."*

[23] *b. Makkot* 10b. RaShI, Exodus 21:13 has a fuller version.

[24] The anonymous author of *Sefer ha-Hinukh* (commandment 410) describes in most graphic terms the ordeal of exile: "It is worthy for one who has killed, even unintentionally—since such a great calamity came about through him—to suffer on that account the pain of exile, which is almost equal to the pain of death, inasmuch as man is separated from his friends and birthplace, and dwells all his days with strangers."

[25] This may be the key to understanding why the manslayer must take up residence in the city of Levites. See anonymous, *Sefer ha-Hinukh*, commandment 408. The Levites were the teachers of Torah to Israel (Deuteronomy 33:10).

[26] Moses Maimonides, *Guide of the Perplexed* III, 17 (Pines translation, p. 471). The Judeo-Arabic term is: *al-'inaya al-ilahiyya*. Ibn Tibbon translates: *Hashgahah Elohit*. Al-Harizi translates: *Shemirah Elohit*. See *Moreh ha-Nevukhim*, transl. Judah al-Harizi (Tel-Aviv: Mossad Harav Kook, n.d.), vol. 2, p. 676. And see Schwarz edition of *Moreh Nevukhim* I, 27 (p. 64, n. 3).

[27] *m. Makkot* 2:4; *b. Makkot* 9b.

[28] *b. Makkot* 10a; Maimonides, *Hil. Rotse'ah* 8:3. See also *Deuteronomy Rabbah* 2:26-27.

In his *Commentary to the Mishnah*, Maimonides refers to this as "half of a (positive) commandment." See *Commentary to the Mishnah*, *Avot* 4:1 (Kafah edition, p. 286). (See also Rabbi Obadiah Seforno, Deuteronomy 4:41.)

There may be halakhic ramifications of this statement. A practical application would be the desirability of eating half an olive-size (*ke-zayit*) of *matsah* on the night of the fifteenth of Nissan, when a whole olive-size is unavailable. See Rabbi Meir Dan Plotski, *Keli Hemdah* (Piotrków, 1906), *Pekudei*, 162d-163a; Rabbi Judah Rosanes, *Mishneh le-Melekh*, *Hil. Hamets u-Matsah*

1:7; Rabbi Yom Tov Algaze, commentary to Nahmanides' *Hil. Hallah* (published end Tractate *Bekhorot* in the Vilna edition of the Talmud), 34d-35a; idem, *Tosefet de-Rabbanan* in *Kehillat Ya'akov* (Saloniki, 1786), s.v. *hatsi shi'ur* (36c); Rabbi Hayyim Mordechai Margaliyot, *Sha'arei Teshuvah* to *Shulhan 'Arukh*, *Orah Hayyim* 475:6; Rabbi Ezekiel Landau, *Doresh le-Zion*, *derush* 1 (note of author's son, Rabbi Samuel Landau); Rabbi Moses Schreiber, Responsa *Hatam Sofer*, *Orah Hayyim*, nos. 49, 140; *MaHaRaTs Hayyot*, *Yoma* 39a; Rabbi Yosef Dov Baer ha-Levi Soloveitchik (of Brisk); Responsa *Beit Halevi*, Part 1, chap. 2, par. 7; Part 3, chap. 51, par. 3, 4; Rabbi Yosef Dov ha-Levi Soloveitchik (of Boston), *Reshimot Shi'urim*, Tractates *Shavu'ot—Nedarim*, Part 1, ed. Rabbi H. Reichman (Union City, NJ, 1993), *Shavu'ot* 21b (p. 36, column a); Rabbi Moshe Dov Baer Rivkin, *Tif'eret Zion* (New York, 1975), chap. 2, par. 54-57 (pp. 52-54), chap. 3 (pp. 62-72); Rabbi Isaac Hutner, *Sefer ha-Zikaron le-Maran Ba'al Pahad Yitzhak*, p. 147.

Although one might argue that the analogy of three out of six cities to a "*hatsi shi'ur*" ("half a measure") is a poor analogy. Those who militate for eating even half an olive-size of *matsah*, take the premise of Rabbi Yohanan (*b. Yoma* 74a), "half a measurement is prohibited by the Torah" ("*hatsi shi'ur assur min ha-Torah*"), and attempt to apply it to the opposite scenario of half the measurement required to fulfill a positive commandment. It may be difficult to conceptualize three out of six cities as "half a measurement," if only for the reason that the three cities in Transjordan absorb fugitives only once the three cities in the Land of Israel proper have been set aside. See *Keli Hemdah*, *Pekudei*, 164a. Cf. Rabbi Menahem ha-Me'iri's distinction between half a measurement and half a *melakhah* (forbidden labor on Sabbath); quoted in Rabbi Menahem Ziemba, *Tots'ot Hayyim* (Warsaw, 1921; photo offset Brooklyn, 1976), chap. 8, par. 1 (36a).

[29] *Midrash Debarim Rabbah* (from Oxford ms.), ed. Saul Lieberman (Jerusalem, 1940), p. 59. (With slight variation in the standard edition of *Deuteronomy Rabbah* 2:29.) Rabbi Menahem Kasher collected the various versions of the *midrash* in *Torah Sheleimah*, vol. 9 (New York, 1944), Exodus 2:15 (p. 89, par. 129).

[30] *Deuteronomy Rabbah* 2:29.

[31] *Midrash Debarim Rabbah*, ed. Lieberman, p. 60.

[32] *Deuteronomy Rabbah* 2:29; *Midrash Debarim Rabbah*, ed. Lieberman, p. 59. The Midrash juxtaposes "*Az yashir Moshe*" ("Then Moses sang") of the Song at the Sea (Exodus 15:1) to "*Az yavdil Moshe*" in Deuteronomy 4:41.

There is yet another *midrash* which declares: "Moses' business (*prakmatya*) is always conducted with '*az*' ('then')." See *Yalkut Shim'oni*, *Shemot*, *remez* 174 (Exodus 4:26); and Rabbi Isaac Hutner's explanation of the *midrash* in *Ma'amrei Pahad Yitzhak: Sha'ar Hodesh ha-Aviv/Pesah* (Brooklyn, NY, 2017), 53:13 (p. 196).

In Lurianic Kabbalah, the promise of a place of refuge is addressed personally to Moses, whose soul is in need of correction. A hint is contained in the last word of the verse in Exodus 21:13: "And if a man lie not in wait, but God caused it to come to his hand; then I will appoint for *you* (*lekha*) a place that he may flee there (*shamah*)." By metathesis, *shamah* becomes *Moshe*. Rabbi Hayyim Vital, *Likkutei Torah* (Vilna, 1880), *Shofetim*, s.v. *ve-'im yarhiv Hashem* (103a). Cf. *b. Makkot* 12b where *lekha* is interpreted to refer personally to Moses. According to RaShI (s.v. *ve-samti lekha be-hayyekha*), Moses was thereby promised that during his lifetime he would merit the *mitsvah* of establishing the three cities [of refuge].

In *Sha'ar ha-Mitsvot*, in addition, the word *shamah* in Deuteronomy 19:3 is metathesized to *Moshe*. "Moses was obligated to go into exile and therefore he was eager to set up cities of refuge in Transjordan...as the Rabbis wrote, and the reason is that by setting them aside, his exile was already atoned for, and this is hinted to by [the words] 'to flee there (*shamah*) every manslayer,' the letters of *Moshe*, who slayed his companion Cain unintentionally" (Rabbi Hayyim Vital, *Sha'ar ha-Mitsvot* [Jerusalem, 1905], *Shofetim, mitsvat 'arei miklat*, 53b).

According to the Kabbalah, the Egyptian slain by Moses was a reincarnation of Cain; see earlier Rabbi Menahem Ziyoni, *Sefer Ziyoni*, beginning *Korah*. (And in a complete role reversal, Moses, the slayer, was a reincarnation of Abel. According to *Tikkunei Zohar*, the three letters of *Moshe* are initials of his three reincarnations in reverse order: Moshe, Sheth, Hevel. See *Tikkunei Zohar, tikkun* 69 [Margaliyot edition, f. 117].)

Rabbi Kasher dealt with the differing accounts whether Moses slayed the Egyptian deliberately or unintentionally. See *Torah Sheleimah*, vol. 9, pp. 89-90, par. 129.

It is apparent that Rabbi Isaac Luria's remarks concerning Moses' slaying of the Egyptian could not possibly have been uttered in a halakhic vein. The unintentional murder of a gentile does not warrant exile. See Maimonides, *Hil. Rotse'ah* 5:3, 4; *Hil. Melakhim* 10:1. (Although one might argue that perhaps the law was different before the giving of the Torah.)

[33] Rabbi Meir Dan Plotski wrote that since the cities of refuge were initially invested with the power of Moses (*"koho shel Moshe"*), the leader of Israel, they endure for eternity. Rabbi Plotski's assertion that they are called by the name of Moses was stated in *Midrash Debarim Rabbah* (see above note 31). See *Keli Hemdah, Pekudei*, 164a-b.

By the way, *Keli Hemdah* was a favorite of Rav Kook who was reputed to have studied it on *Shabbat* in conjunction with the Torah portion of the week.

Coincidentally, in Kabbalah, Moses is equated with the *sefirah* of *Da'at*. The maxim goes: *"Ya'akov mi-le-var, Moshe mi-le-go."* "Jacob on the outside (i.e., the *sefirah* of *Tif'eret*), Moses on the inside (i.e., the *sefirah* of *Da'at*)." See *Tikkunei Zohar, tikkun* 13 (Margaliyot edition, 29a); Rabbi Abraham Azulai, *Hesed le-Avraham* (Amsterdam, 1685), *ma'yan* 3 (*'Eyn ha-Arets*), *nahar* 3 (29b); Rabbi Kalonymos Kalman Epstein, *Ma'or va-Shemesh, Pinhas*, s.v. *va-tikravnah benot Zelophehad* (Numbers 27:1).

[34] Cf. Rabbi Joseph Hayyim of Baghdad, *Ben Yehoyada', Makkot* 10a. The great kabbalist likens the three (!) cities to the three obligatory prayers (*tefillot hovah*) of morning, afternoon and evening, and the forty-two cities to voluntary prayers (*tefillot nedavah*). As opposed to the obligatory prayers, where one may rely on the *"da'at beit din,"* on the mindfulness of the Men of the Great Assembly who founded the prayers, in the case of voluntary prayers one must exercise one's individual intentionality or *kavvanah*. However, Rabbi Joseph Hayyim (known as the *"Ben Ish Hai"*) leaves Moses out. To our thinking, Moses is crucial to the discussion.

[35] Rabbi Joseph Babad, *Minhat Hinukh* (commentary on anonymous *Sefer ha-*

Hinukh), commandment 520.

[36] Maimonides, *Hil. Melakhim* 12:5.

In Kabbalistic symbology, the three nations of the Kenite, Kenizite and Kadmonite parallel the three highest *sefirot* of *Keter*, *Hokhmah* and *Binah*, as opposed to the seven Canaanite nations which correspond to the seven lower *sefirot*. See Rabbi Hayyim Vital, *Likkutei Torah* (Vilna, 1880), *Lekh Lekha*, s.v. *et ha-keni ve-et ha-kenizi* (25b). Alternatively the Kenite, Kenizite and Kadmonite correspond to *Hokhmah*, *Binah* and *Da'at* (Wisdom, Understanding and Knowledge). That the future three cities are to be established in the territory of the Kenite, Kenizite and Kadmonite, bespeaks a new, more elevated consciousness. See Rabbi Abraham Azulai, *Hesed le-Avraham* (Amsterdam, 1685), *ma'yan* 3 (*'Eyn ha-Arets*), *nahar* 3 (29a-b). Equating the Kenite, Kenizite and Kadmonite with the land of Sihon and 'Og, Rabbi Azulai suggests that perhaps for this reason, Moses—synonymous with the *sefirah* of *Da'at*—is buried there. See also Rabbi Samuel Bornstein of Sochatchov, *Shem mi-Shmuel* (Jerusalem, 1974), *Shofetim* 5676, s.v. *ve-'im yarhiv Hashem* (pp. 124-125).

Moses Enters the Divine Superconscious

(*b. MENAHOT* 29b)

Said Rav Yehudah in the name of Rav:

At the time that Moses ascended on high, he found the Holy One, blessed be He, sitting and affixing crownlets to the letters [of the Torah].

Moses said to Him: "Master of the Universe, Who is holding You up?"

[Rashi: **Who is holding You up?**—What You have written, that You must add on crownlets?]

He said to Moses: "In the future at the end of several generations, there will be a man by the name of Akiva son of Joseph, who will interpret upon each and every "thorn" (or crownlet) mounds upon mounds of *halakhot* (laws)."

Moses said to Him: "Master of the Universe, show him to me."

He said to Moses: "Turn around."

Moses went and sat at the end of eight rows [in the lecture hall of Rabbi Akiva] and did not know what Rabbi Akiva was saying.

Moses' strength weakened.

When Rabbi Akiva arrived at a certain matter, his students challenged him: "Rabbi, what is your source for this?"

Rabbi Akiva said to them: "It is a law to Moses from Sinai."

Moses was reassured.

Moses returned to the Holy One, blessed be He. Moses said to Him: "Master of the Universe, You have such a man and yet You give the Torah through me?"

He said to Moses: "Keep silent! So did it arise in thought before Me."

Moses said to Him: "Master of the Universe, you have shown me his Torah. Show me his reward."

He said to Moses: "Turn around."

Moses turned around. He saw them weighing Rabbi Akiva's flesh in the butchery.

Moses said to Him: "Master of the Universe, this is the Torah and this is its reward?"

He said to Moses: "Keep silent! So did it arise in thought before Me."

(b. Menahot 29b)

This charming legend of the Talmud is quite famous. It is often cited to demonstrate that the Torah, rather than being suspended and frozen in time, continues to grow and develop over the generations. This is borne out by the ironical, almost comical situation wherein Moses, the Lawgiver himself, is incapable of following the discourse of the later sage of the Mishnaic era, Rabbi Akiva. (Up to this point, the Karaites—or *"B'nei ha-Mikra,"* as they referred to themselves—who rejected the Talmud of the so-called "Rabbanites," would have had a field day with this *aggadah!*) Just when we begin to harbor the suspicion that Talmudic Judaism has wrenched loose of its Biblical moorings, we (like Moses) are reassured by Rabbi Akiva's citing the "law to Moses from Sinai."

It is important to remember in this regard that Rabbi Akiva is not just one of many Talmudic sages. In a sense, Rabbi Akiva is the father of the entire rabbinic enterprise. "The anonymous *Mishnah* is Rabbi Meir; the anonymous *Tosefta* is Rabbi Nehemiah; the anonymous *Sifra* is Rabbi Judah; the anonymous *Sifré* is Rabbi Simeon—and all of them are in accordance with [the teaching received from] Rabbi Akiva."[1]

If we were to adopt the three dimensions of *The Book of Creation* (*Sefer Yetsirah*), the story is about Moses transcending space, time and soul.

Spatially, or graphically,[2] Moses is going beyond the bounds of the letters. The "crownlets" or "thorns" protrude above the letters.

Temporally, Moses is transported several generations into the future. That he is seated at the end of eight rows in Rabbi Akiva's lecture hall, may conjure up the final eight verses of the Torah that follow the death of Moses. (The sages were divided who wrote those eight verses from "Moses died." According to one opinion they were written by Joshua, Moses' successor. According to the other opinion, Moses wrote them, albeit tearfully.)[3] Those eight ending verses of the Torah are post-Mosaic. Thus, the number eight conveys the sense that Moses, accepting (however reluctantly) his own finitude, enters the post-Mosaic period.[4]

Finally, and this is most significant, granted this awesome vision, Moses enters a dimension of *soul* that transcends our normal reality.

The portal to this transcendental reality is provided by way of the crownlets upon the letters. There is something dark and foreboding about those crownlets. Perhaps for that reason, they are alternately referred to as "thorns."

The Rabbis interpreted homiletically the verse in Songs of Songs 5:11:

> "*Kevutsotav taltalim.*" "His locks are curls."
> Said Rav Hisda in the name of Mar 'Ukva:
> This teaches that it is possible to interpret upon each and every *kots* (thorn) *tilei tilim* (mounds upon mounds) of laws.
> "*Shehorot ka-'orev.*" "Black as the raven."
> Who has this ability?
> One who pores over them morning and evening in the study hall.
> [Rashi: **Morning and evening**—*shehorot* related to *shaharit* (morning) and *'orev* related to *'arvit* (evening).]
> Rabbah said: One who blackens his face [i.e., fasting] over them as a raven.[5]
> Rava said: One who makes himself cruel to his children and household as a raven.
> [Rashi: A raven is cruel towards its fledglings....]
>
> (*b. 'Eruvin* 21b–22a)

The ability to unlock the treasures contained in the "thorns" is made contingent upon cruelty and inhumanity toward oneself and toward the members of one's household, to wit one's own child. In the latter regard, the Talmud tells an anecdote concerning one Rav Ada bar Matnah, who on his way out to the study hall, was asked by his wife what to feed his baby. The sage responded with a rhetorical flourish: "Have the legumes from the swamp been exhausted?"[6] Speak of the iron discipline of the scholar!

Thus there is a darkness to this realm. And a silence too. While the letters produce sounds, the crownlets hinged to their tops are mute.

One begins to suspect that more than *halakhot*, readily definable legal prescriptions, will issue from these "thorns."[7] The thorniest, most vexatious problems of existence are associated with these thorns. By stepping through this portal, Moses will be exposed to the full intensity of the problem of evil.

Please note that in Kabbalah, the ten levels that correspond to the ten *sefirot* of holiness, are not termed "the ten *sefirot* of impurity," but rather the "ten *crowns* of impurity" (*'eser kitrin di-mesa'avuta*).

Moses will be assailed by the infernal blast of injustice at two junctures of Rabbi Akiva's biography. First, it will strike Moses as grossly unfair that Rabbi Akiva, who appears much more talented than Moses as an interpreter of the Law, is not chosen to be the Lawgiver. "You have such a man and yet You give the Torah through me?" Second, Moses is horrified to witness the ignominious end of Rabbi Akiva.

The fate that awaits Rabbi Akiva violates even the minimal code of morality that the nations of the world chose to observe:

'Ulla said: These are thirty commandments that the sons of Noah accepted upon themselves, though they observe but three....One, that they do not weigh [human] flesh in the butchery....[8]

If you would have it, this was the Geneva Convention of the day. Yet, Moses was witness to the spectacle of Rabbi Akiva's flesh being weighed in the butcher shop. Horrified, he cried out: "This is the Torah—a Torah so sublime that even I, Moses, cannot understand it—and this—this most degrading of deaths—is its reward?"

To both questions (of Rabbi Akiva not receiving the honor of bestowing the Torah on Mount Sinai, and of his being dishonored in death), Moses received the sharp rebuke:

> "Keep silent! So did it arise in thought before Me."

In the Hebrew, the divine response of *"Shetok! Kakh 'alah be-mahshavah"* lends itself to another reading:

> "Keep silent! So did he (i.e., Rabbi Akiva) arise in thought before Me."

Through silence (*shetikah*), Rabbi Akiva was able to reach the level of thought (*mahshavah*)—symbolized by the crownlets—which is beyond the level of speech (*dibbur*), contained in the letters of the Torah.[9]

The Divine Superconscious

When Moses first encounters God, he is puzzled by His action (or lack thereof). The Hebrew question to God reads: *"Mi me'akkev 'al yadekha?"* Literally, "Who is holding You up?" In other words, "What is holding you back?" The keyword is *"me'akkev"* ("holding up" or "halting"). Moses discovers the Holy One, blessed be He, "sitting" (*yoshev*). In Biblical Hebrew, *"yeshivah"* (sitting) has another sense as well. To quote the famous Rashi: *"Ein yeshivah ela leshon 'akavah."* "Sitting is but an expression for halting."[10]

Let us get the picture. The Holy One, blessed be He, is, as it were, suffering from some form of writer's block. For some inexplicable reason (which Moses will attempt to fathom) the divine writing process has been arrested, has ground to a halt. As writers are wont to do when they are temporarily blocked, the Almighty takes to embellishing and ornamenting the letters that He has already written—what we would refer to colloquially as "doodling." Now, as any astute psychologist will tell you, the distracted scribblings of the writer are not without significance. The offhanded jottings may in fact issue from a deeper level of consciousness than the text itself. As it will turn out, these "superscripts" on the letters of the Torah represent the divine superconscious.[11] The crownlets on the letters are, so to speak, the "rabbit hole" through which Moses will enter another reality.

According to the Sages, Moses was profoundly disturbed by the problem of theodicy, or as they expressed it: *"Tsaddik ve-ra' lo"* ("a righteous man who suffers evil").[12] In our contemporary parlance:

"Why do bad things happen to good people?" (Although in the rabbinic understanding, Moses was equally perturbed by the converse scenario of *"Rasha' ve-tov lo"* ["a wicked man who enjoys good"].) How fitting that according to one opinion it was none other than Moses who authored the Book of Job, that book of the Bible devoted entirely to the problem of the righteous suffering.[13]

Note that the vision beheld by Moses is not what we would expect, namely the scene of Rabbi Akiva's tragic death, the Romans flaying Rabbi Akiva's flesh with iron combs, literally skinning him alive for his dogged determination to teach Torah in public despite imperial decree,[14] but a belated *post mortem* scene, almost a postscript, in which Rabbi Akiva's flesh is being weighed (one presumes for sale) in the abattoir. This shift should give us pause for thought.

This dilemma, and the previous dilemma ("You have such a man and yet You give the Torah through me?"), both visions being the fulfillment of the request "Show me," lead one to suspect that our *aggadah* is a rabbinic paraphrase of the exchange in the Pentateuch whereby Moses asks of the LORD, "Show me please Your glory," and the divine response was, "You shall see My back (*ahorai*), but My face shall not be seen."[15]

Each time that Moses in our legend makes the request "Show me," he is subsequently instructed, *"Hazor la-ahorekha"* ("Turn back" or "Turn around"). Maharal of Prague astutely observes that in Hebrew the word for the posterior of the body (*"ahor"*) comes remarkably close to the word for the posterior in time (*"ahar"*). When Moses is told to turn around in space, he is truly being directed to view the generations that will follow him in time.[16]

THE DIVINE SUPERCONSCIOUS

Maharal was not the first to play with the Hebrew word *"ahor."* He was preceded several centuries by Moses Maimonides:

> Back (*ahor*) is an equivocal term. It is a term denoting the back....Sometimes it is used as an adverb of time in the sense of: after.[17]

When God responded to Moses' request of "Show me please Your glory" (*"Har'eni na et kevodekha"*) by saying, "You shall see My back" (*"ve-ra'ita et ahorai"*), He may in fact have been saying "You shall see that which follows Me (in time)."[18]

What was Moses seeking when he asked to see the *kavod*, the glory of God? Maimonides understood that Moses sought to know "His essence and true reality."[19]

In our *aggadah* as well, Moses is asking to be shown something. I will take the liberty of positing a phantom subtext in which Moses is indeed requesting to be shown the *kavod*, the glory of God, but specifically as it translates into the honor of the Torah, *kevod ha-Torah*. And upon request, Moses is directed to the succeeding generations (posterior in time, as Maharal explains). But where Moses expects to find the greatest honor of Torah (*kevod ha-Torah*), he witnesses instead the worst sort of dishonor, the most inglorious end of Rabbi Akiva, the greatest Torah scholar of all time.[20]

(That Rabbi Akiva was not singled out for the honor of Lawgiver, though cause for perplexity and wonderment, cannot compare to the sheer brutishness of human flesh being sold on the butcher's block.)

The weighing of human flesh for sale on the butcher's block is the ultimate lack of honor or respect for the dead (*"kevod ha-met"*); this is the most extreme example of *"nivvul ha-met"* ("disgracing the dead").

In truth, the very portal through which Moses enters this other reality—the *keter*, the "crown" or "crownlet"—is riddled with paradox. On the one hand, the crown is the symbol of majesty. But this crown is also referred to as a "thorn" (*kots*). The one man (Akiva son of Joseph) destined "to seek out" (*lidrosh*) the thorns that reside atop the letters of the Torah, will suffer excruciating pain and unimaginable indignity.

And in so doing, he ascended in thought before Me. *Kakh 'alah be-mahshavah lefanai.*

---

[1] *b. Sanhedrin* 86a.

[2] A reasonable assumption is that the "three books: text, number and narrative" (*"sefer, sefar ve-sippur"*) which serve as the introduction to *Sefer Yetsirah* (*The Book of Creation*), correspond to the three dimensions of "space, time and soul" (*"'olam, shanah, nefesh"*) later articulated therein. By virtue of this correspondence, space lines up with text, time with mathematics, and soul with narrative. See Aryeh Kaplan, *Sefer Yetzirah: The Book of Creation* (York Beach, Maine, 1997), pp. 19-22. Perhaps on another occasion I will yet have the opportunity to spin out the implications of this last correspondence (soul/narrative).

[3] *b. Bava Batra* 15a; *Menahot* 30a.

[4] I have adopted the reading of the Venice and Vilna editions of the Talmud. In the Salonikan *'Eyn Ya'akov*, there is found a variant reading of "eighteen rows" rather than "eight rows." Rabbi Azriel of Gerona also reads "eighteen rows"; see *Commentary on Talmudic Aggadoth by Rabbi Azriel of Gerona* (Hebrew), ed. Isaiah Tishby (Jerusalem: Magnes, 1982), 49b in foliation of the manuscript (pp. 160-161).

5 See Rabbi Samuel Edels, *Hiddushei Aggadot MaHaRaShA*.
6 *b. 'Eruvin* 22a.
7 See Rabbi Samuel Edels, *Hiddushei Aggadot MaHaRaShA*, *'Eruvin* 21b, s.v. *'al kol kots*.
8 *b. Hullin* 92.
9 For Kabbalistic and Hasidic interpretations of the keyword *mahshavah*, see Rabbi Hayyim Vital, *'Ets Hayyim* 50:5; Nathan of Gaza, *Sefer ha-Beri'ah*, ed. Leor Holzer (Jerusalem: Holzer, 2019), p. 343; Rabbi Dov Baer of Mezritch, *'Or Torah*, ed. Rabbi Isaiah Dinowitz, *Ki Tetsei*, end s.v. *Shalle'ah teshallah* (par. 175); Rabbi Nahman of Breslov, *Likkutei Moharan* I, 64:3; and Rabbi Shneur Zalman of Liadi, *Likkutei Torah, Behukkotai*, s.v. *'Im be-hukotai telekhu* (46c). See also Rabbi Isaac Hutner, *Pahad Yitzhak: Rosh Hashanah* (New York, NY, 2003), *Kuntres ha-Hesed, ma'amar* 4, chap. 3, par. 11-13 (pp. 53-56), referencing the Commentary of the Vilna Gaon to *Sifra di-Tseni'uta* (Vilna and Horadna, 1820), chap. 1, s.v. *mashgihin 'apin be-'apin* (3c-d); Rabbi Israel Elijah Weintraub, *Nefesh Eliyahu 'al Sifra di-Tseni'uta 'im Be'ur ha-GRA* (n.p., n.d. [2012]), p. 432.
10 Rashi, Leviticus 12:4.
11 In Kabbalah, there is an equation of the *"ziyunim"* (crownlets) with *mohin* (brains). See the Commentary of the Vilna Gaon to *Sifra di-Tseni'uta*, chap. 1, s.v. *ve-ziyuneihon lo ishtak-hu* (4b) and the gloss thereto.
12 *b. Berakhot* 7a.
13 *b. Bava Batra* 14b-15a.
14 *b. Berakhot* 61b.
15 Exodus 33, verses 18 and 23.
16 Rabbi Judah Löw (Maharal), *Tif'eret Yisrael*, chap. 63.
17 Moses Maimonides, *The Guide of the Perplexed* I, 38 (Pines translation, p. 87).
18 See *Guide*, ibid., and the commentary of Abravanel who maintains that Maimonides interprets the keyword *"ahorai"* both temporally and in terms of *imitatio Dei*.
19 Moses Maimonides, *The Guide of the Perplexed* I, beginning chap. 54 (Pines translation, p. 123), and chap. 64 (Pines translation, p. 156).
20 See *m. Sotah* 9:15: "From the time that Rabbi Akiva died, the honor of the Torah (*kevod ha-Torah*) was nullified." Rashi (*Sotah* 49a) explains "that [Rabbi Akiva] would put his heart to interpret all the thorns (*kol kots ve-kots*) of each letter ... and this is great honor for the Torah that nothing in it is in vain."

III

CHRISTIANITY AND ISLAM

JUDAISM'S STRUGGLE WITH SUPERSESSIONISM

The Theological Boldness of Nahmanides: Israel's Reaffirmation of Vows

If one reads the narrative of the giving of the Torah on Mount Sinai purely through the Biblical lens, unaided by Rabbinic commentary, the acceptance of the Torah on the part of Israel appears to be totally volitional. The shorter version of Israel's formal acceptance reads: "The entire people responded together and said, 'All that the Lord has spoken we shall do.'"[1] The longer, more famous version reads: "They said, 'All that the Lord has spoken we shall do and we shall hearken [to].'"[2] In Hebrew, *"Na'aseh ve-nishma'."*

Comes the Talmud and injects an unforeseen element of coercion:

> "They stood at the bottom of the mountain."[3]
>
> Said Rav Avdimi bar Hama bar Hasa: [This] teaches that the Holy One, blessed be He, held the mountain over them as a vat and said to them, "If you accept the Torah, good, and if not, there will be your burial [place]."
>
> Said Rav Aha bar Ya'akov: From here there is a great protest (i.e., grounds for annulment) of the Torah.
>
> Said Rava: Nonetheless, later they accepted it in the days of Ahashverosh, for it is written, "The Jews fulfilled

and accepted."[4] They fulfilled that which they already accepted.[5]

Rashi, the all-time great Talmudic commentator, adopts a relatively conservative posture. Commenting on the words *"moda'a raba"* ("great protest"), Rashi writes: "Should He summon them for judgment [saying], 'Why have you not fulfilled that which you have accepted upon yourselves,' they have an answer, that they accepted it under coercion."

Evidently Rashi found it inconceivable that at any time in Jewish history there actually took place an annulment of the Torah on the grounds that it had been accepted at Sinai under duress. At most, this was a theoretical argument that was never utilized.

Nahmanides' comment on this passage in the Talmud is by comparison so bold as to make one shudder. He writes:

> It seems to me that though from the onset they had grounds for annulment, nonetheless He gave the Land to them only in order that they fulfill the Torah, as is explicit in the Torah in several passages, and it is written, "He gave them lands of nations and the toil of peoples they inherited, in order that they keep His statutes and guard His laws."[6] And they themselves did not object in the least and put up no protest, but willingly proclaimed, "All that the Lord has spoken we shall do and we shall hearken [to]." Therefore, when they transgressed the Torah, He exiled them from the land. Once they were exiled, they did pro-

The Boldness of Nahmanides

test the thing, for it is written, "That which arises in your spirit shall not come to pass, that which you say, 'We shall be as the nations, as the families of the lands, to serve wood and stone.'"[7] And as we say in the *Aggadah*: "Ezekiel our teacher, a slave sold by his master, does he [i.e., the master] have any [claim] on him?" Therefore, when they entered the land a second time in the days of Ezra, they took upon themselves to accept it willingly, so that there could be no further rejection.[8] And this coincided with the days of Ahashverosh, whereupon [God] took them out from death to life.[9] And this was more beloved to them than the redemption from Egypt.[10]

For Nahmanides, unlike Rashi, the argument that the Torah had originally been accepted under duress did not remain theoretical, but was actually presented in the gap between the destruction of the First Temple and the subsequent exile from the land, and the return to the land in the days of Ezra. For those seventy years of Babylonian captivity there was, if we understand Nahmanides correctly, an actual abrogation of the treaty between God and the Jewish nation whereby the nation was duty-bound to keep the commandments of the Torah.

What is all the more remarkable in this Talmudic exegesis is the man who authored it. None other than Moses Nahmanides (1194-1270), who was locked in mortal combat with the all-powerful Catholic Church! Christianity is famous (or infamous) for its supersessionist theology, whereby the historic people of Israel is supplanted by *"Verus Israel,"* the "True Israel," and the Old Covenant is replaced with the New Covenant. In Barcelona in the year 1263, Nahmanides would engage in a religious disputation with an apostate Jew by the name of Pablo Christiani. In that disputation, Nahmanides would valiantly parry against the claims of the dominant religion. Objectively speaking, I am not prepared to offer the exact or even approximate date in which Nahmanides composed his commentary to Tractate *Shabbat*. Be that as it may, it is simply not possible that any time in his literary career Nahmanides was oblivious to the claim made by Pauline Christianity that the covenant made with Israel at Sinai had been abrogated with the arrival of Jesus.[11]

And yet it is just Nahmanides, living as he did in a Catholic monarchy bent on the conversion of its Jewish inhabitants, who dared to interpret our passage of the Talmud in such a bold and daring manner. This should give us pause for thought.

Is it possible that Nahmanides understood the passage in the Talmud to have been conceived in a polemic vein, as a sort of refutation of the claims of Christianity? Did Nahmanides believe that Rava's retort was designed to serve as a *"teshuvat ha-minim"* or *"teshuvat ha-Notsrim"*?[12] Assuming that we are on the right track, the counterargument to Christianity would work in the same way that in 1796 Edward Jenner saved the English population from smallpox with "vaccine" (from cowpox), or that a century later in 1895 Albert Calmette developed an antivenom for the treatment of snakebite by injecting a small amount of snake venom into an animal (horse or sheep) and harvesting the antibodies from the animal's blood. In Aramaic, this strategy is referred to as *"Leshaduyé beh narga mineh u-veh."*[13] By introjecting the concept of abrogation of the covenant and revealing that the very breaking of the vows had indeed been followed by a renewal of the vows (to borrow from the nuptial terminology deemed by the Rabbis appropriate for the covenant at Sinai),[14] Paul (a.k.a. Saul of Tarsus) would have been discomfited.

AFTERWORD

Nahmanides' internalization of Christianity's critique of Judaism may evidence itself in yet another crucial respect: his bold assertion that the commandments of the Torah truly pertain only in the Land of Israel and that outside the Land we are only "going through the motions," so to speak.[15] It is possible that this too—and here one merely speculates—is Nahmanides' response to the Christian allegorization of the commandments.

One invokes in this regard the authority of Maimonides, *MT, Hilkhot Melakhim* 11:8:

> The entire world has already been filled with the words of the Messiah, and the words of the Torah, and the words of the commandments, and these words spread to distant isles and among numerous peoples of uncircumcised heart; and they debate these words and the commandments of the Torah. These say, these commandments were true [i.e., to be taken literally], but they are already nullified at this time, for they did not apply for generations [to come]. And those say, they contain hidden meanings, and they are not literal, and the Messiah [i.e., Jesus] has already arrived and revealed their hidden meanings.

Nahmanides quotes approvingly this passage from Maimonides in his sermon, *"Torat Hashem Temimah,"*[16] so it is not unreasonable to assume that it impacted upon his consciousness with far-reaching theological results.

The Boldness of Nahmanides

Christianity comes at Judaism with two distinct complaints, both duly noted by Maimonides. In one narrative, the commandments, once intended to be construed literally, are no longer in effect.[17] In the second narrative, the Jews misinterpreted the commandments, taking them at face value, when they were meant allegorically; their true allegorical content awaited the coming of the Messiah. The common denominator of the two complaints is that with the advent of Christianity, literal adherence to the commandments of the Torah is rendered anachronistic and thus unwarranted.

Nahmanides, it seems, responds to this "hollowing" of the commandments by attributing the phenomenon not to an event in time—namely the coming of Christianity's Messiah—but to an event in space: exile from the Land of Israel, which is the proper domain of the commandments of the Torah. Within the boundaries of the Land, the commandments retain their full efficacy to this very day.

---

[1] Exodus 19:8. Cf. Exodus 24:3: "The entire people responded [in] a single voice and said, 'All the things that the Lord has spoken we shall do.'"
[2] Exodus 24:7.
[3] Exodus 19:17.
[4] Esther 9:27.
[5] b. *Shabbat* 88a.
[6] Psalms 105:44, 45.
[7] Ezekiel 20:32.
[8] See Nehemiah chap. 10 regarding the "treaty" (*"amanah"*)—or to use our nuptial terminology, "reaffirmation of vows"—that was struck in the days of Ezra and Nehemiah. *Inter alia*, based on the passage in Nehemiah, Rabbi Joseph Dov Baer ha-Levi Soloveitchik of Brisk posited that nowadays *Shemittah* (observance of the Sabbatical Year) must be considered *"divrei kabbalah,"* a halakhic status which carries more weight than a rabbinic ordinance (*"de-*

rabbanan"). This novel thesis was refuted by Rabbi Abraham Isaac Hakohen Kook in his work devoted to the laws of *Shemittah*. See Rabbi Joseph Dov Baer ha-Levi Soloveitchik, *She'elot u-Teshuvot Beit Halevi*, Pt. III (Warsaw, 1890), no. 1, chap. 6, par. 2; Rabbi Abraham Isaac Hakohen Kook, *Shabbat ha-Arets* (Jerusalem, 1910), Introduction, chap. 8.

[9] *b. Megillah* 14a.

[10] *Hiddushei ha-RaMBaN, Shabbat* 88a.

[11] Some years ago, Rabbi Moshe Rosenwasser examined several passages in Nahmanides' commentary to the Pentateuch against the backdrop of Christian theology. See Moshe Yehudah Rosenwasser, *"Peirush ha-RaMBaN 'al ha-Torah le-'or ha-'imut 'im ha-Notsrut," HaMa'ayan* 47:2 (Tevet 5767), pp. 19-32.

[12] One is tempted to link this statement of Rava ("Nonetheless, later they accepted it in the days of Ahashverosh, for it is written, 'The Jews fulfilled and accepted.' They fulfilled that which they already accepted") with the subsequent dialogue between Rava and an anonymous sectarian who held Israel up to ridicule "for having put their mouths before their ears" at Sinai. The sectarian's point was that Israel were hasty in committing to accepting the Torah before deliberating whether they would in fact be capable of keeping to their commitment. (See *Shabbat* 88.) Though the identity of the sectarian is not disclosed, this attempt to impugn or somehow vitiate the Sinaitic covenant may reflect a Christian supersessionist agenda.

(As convenient as it is to link the two statements of Rava, a monkey wrench is thrown our way by the reading of the BaH [initials of *Bayit Hadash*, i.e., Rabbi Joel Sirkes] in the first instance: "Rabbah" rather than "Rava.")

An obvious question arises: Why would Rava, living in Babylonia, dialogue with a Christian concerning the covenant at Sinai? This question was already posed by Richard Kalmin. He points out that the interaction between Rava and a heretic (*min*) in *Shabbat* 88a-b is one of only two cases recorded in the Babylonian Talmud where there is interaction between a Babylonian rabbi and a heretic. Kalmin offers two possible solutions: 1) Later Babylonian Amora'im such as Rava are frequently depicted as behaving in accordance with Palestinian models. 2) The name "Rava" is frequently confused with the name "R. Abba." There were apparently several Amora'im named R. Abba, and all of their statements, as far as we can determine, derive from Palestine. It is possible, therefore, that even this narrative depicts a dialogue between a heretic and a rabbi in Palestine. Kalmin points out in this regard, that this very jab at a "rash nation who put their mouths before their ears" was directed by a sectarian at Rabbi Zeira immediately upon arrival in Erets Israel (see *b. Ketubot* 112a). See Richard Kalmin, *Jewish Babylonia between Persia and Roman Palestine* (Oxford University Press, 2006), pp. 100; 223, note 59.

[13] See *b. Sanhedrin* 39b.

[14] See *m. Ta'anit* 4:8: "'On His wedding day'—This refers to the Giving of the Torah." See also Rashi, Exodus 34:1, quoting *Midrash Tanhuma, Ki Tissa* 30.

[15] Rabbeinu Moshe ben Nahman, *Peirushei ha-Torah*, ed. C.B. Chavel, 2 vols. (Jerusalem: Mossad Harav Kook, 1969), Genesis 24:3 (p. 134); 26:5 (p. 150); Leviticus 18:25 (pp. 109-112); Deuteronomy 11:18 (p. 394).

(My friend Ya'akov Rosenberg has pointed out to me in this connection Nahmanides' remarks to Deuteronomy 23:16.)

[16] In *Kitvei Rabbeinu Moshe ben Nahman*, ed. C.B. Chavel, vol. 1 (Jerusalem: Mossad Harav Kook, 1968), p. 144.

Lea Naomi Vogelmann-Goldfeld discussed the slight variations of Nahmanides' version of the text of Maimonides; see Lea Naomi Goldfeld, "*Hilkhot Melakhim u-Milhamot u-Melekh ha-Mashiah*," *Sinai* 96 (1985), pp. 67-79.

[17] This notion of the abrogation of the law is common to Islam as well, where it goes by the Arabic name of *"naskh."* See Rabbi Solomon ben Abraham ibn Adret (RaShBA), *Ma'amar 'al Yishmael*, ed. Bezalel Naor (Spring Valley, NY: Orot, 2008), *Avant-Propos*, p. 7.

From Deicide to Calf-Worship:
Islam and Judaism

*"There is no generation that does not take
an ounce of the deed of the Calf."*
(*Midrash Rabbah*)

Or as the great French Bible commentator, Rashi, paraphrased the words of the Midrash: "There is no calamity that befalls Israel that is not partial payment for the sin of the Calf."[1] To what were the sages of Israel alluding? Was this perhaps an overstatement, an example of the Sages engaging in hyperbole?

Judaism gave birth to two daughter religions: Christianity and Islam. Both daughters developed supersessionist theologies, whereby the once Chosen People, with their rejection of Jesus and later Muhammad, were left back in time, an unredeemed, if not damned nation.[2] In the words of the twentieth-century thinker Rav Kook, it was the case of "the daughter who bites her mother's breast."[3]

Christianity held the Jewish People accountable for the crime of deicide. Having coopted the Jew, Jesus of Nazareth, and deified him, the Church then accused the Jews of being responsible for his crucifixion. Put crudely, the Jews were a nation of "Christ-killers."

Islam, on the other hand, did not hold the Jews responsible for Jesus' death. The Jews were absolved of any complicity in his execution by the Romans, simply because Jesus never died!

> And for their saying, "We slew the Messiah, Jesus son of Mary, the messenger of God"—though they did not slay him; nor did they crucify him, but it appeared so unto them. Those who differ concerning him are in doubt thereof. They have no knowledge of it, but follow only conjecture; they slew him not for certain.
> But God raised him up unto Himself.[4]

Islam came at Judaism with a much older complaint.[5] Time and time again, the *Quran* (2:92-93; 4:153; 7:150-152; 20:85-97) levels the accusation that while Moses was up on Mount Sinai, down below the Children of Israel worshipped the Golden Calf:

> And indeed Moses brought you clear proofs, but then you took up the calf while he was away, and you were wrongdoers.
> And when We made a covenant with you, and raised the Mount over you [saying], "Take hold of what We have given you with strength, and listen!" They said [instead], "We hear, and disobey," and they were made to drink the calf into their hearts because of their disbelief.[6]

As scholars from Abraham Geiger to Abraham Katsh have documented, the *Quran* is informed not only by the Torah *per se*, but also by Midrash. In three other passages (2:63; 4:154; 7:171), the *Quran* states that Mount Sinai was raised over the Children of Israel at the time of the establishment of the covenant. The last passage is most graphic: "And when We lifted the mountain above them, *as if it were a canopy* [italics mine—BN], and they thought it would fall upon them." This is clearly a reiteration of the famous *aggadah* recorded in the Babylonian Talmud:

> The Holy One, blessed be He, held the mountain over them as a vat, and said to them: "If you accept the Torah, good, and if not, there will be your burial [place]."[7]

In a rather obvious parody, the Quran replaces the Israelites' declaration of unconditional acceptance, "We shall do and obey" ("*Na'aseh ve-Nishma'*"),[8] with a brazen, "in your face" rejection: "We hear, and disobey."

> Among those who are Jews, are those who distort the meaning of the word, and say, "We hear and disobey." ... And had they said, "We hear and obey," it would have been better for them and more proper.[9]

In *Surah* 20, the Israelites shift the blame for fashioning the Calf to an anonymous "Samaritan" (*al-Samiri*):

> They said, "We did not fail our tryst with you of our own will, but we were laden with the burden of the people's ornaments. So we cast them [into the fire], and thus did the Samaritan throw."
>
> Then he brought forth for them a calf that lowed, and they said, "This is your god..."[10]

Scholars have long puzzled over the identity of *"al-Samiri."* Geiger thought Samiri might be a corruption of Samael (or Satan) who entered into the calf,[11] or that somehow Micah of Judges 17 was confused with Samiri.[12] One ventures a guess that the Egyptian magicians Jannes and Jambres of Rabbinic legend,[13] have been fused together into the anonymous Samaritan. A.S. Yahuda suggested that the Quran conflated the stories of the Golden Calf in the desert and the two golden calves later erected by Jeroboam in Bethel and Dan.[14] Jeroboam, King of the Northern Kingdom of Samaria, was technically "the Samaritan."[15]

A few verses later, "the Samaritan" reveals by what magic he was able to conjure up the Calf:

> So I took a handful [of dust] from the footsteps of the messenger, and I cast it.[16]

"The messenger" *(al-rasul)* in this context is none other than Moses. By some stretch of the imagination, we hear the strains of the Midrash:

[Aaron] threw [the earrings] to the fire, and there came along the magicians and performed their magic.

Some say, it was Micah.... He took the plate upon which Moses wrote "Rise up, O Ox," when he raised the sarcophagus of Joseph [from the Nile]. Micah threw it into the furnace among the earrings, and the calf hopped out lowing.[17]

Saul Lieberman did not let even "a handful of dust" slip through his deft hands. He found an obscure Midrash to Song of Songs which reads:

When [the Children of Israel] passed through the Sea, Micah beheld the Celestial Chariot and took from the dust that is under the Ox, and put it away for the right time.[18]

Moses burnt the Golden Calf, reduced it to ash and cast the ashes into the water.[19] The Israelites were then forced to drink it down.[20]

In the Islamic view, the Calf-worshippers' sin was the most dangerous of all offenses, that of *shirq*, idolatry. "And those who took up the calf, anger from their Lord shall seize them, and abasement in the life of this world."[21] In this new narrative, the Jews were no longer "Christ-killers" but "Calf-worshippers."[22]

The odious insult shows up in the most unlikely of places. Scholars have long debated the age and provenance of the *Heikhalot* literature, a genre that describes mystical ascents to heaven. Nineteenth-century German scholars Heinrich Graetz and Phillip Bloch assumed that these Jewish mystics were active in the Geonic period and influenced by Muslim mystics. Scholem, the *"Buchhalter"* or "Accountant" of Kabbalah, set research back in this respect when, perhaps naively, he thought the material to be older than it actually is, supposing that it preserves authentic second-century Tannaitic tradition.[23] Today, scholarly opinion has come almost full circle, with the consensus being that the works of the *Heikhalot* were edited in Babylonia as late as Geonic times. In a passage of the *Heikhalot* that Scholem banked on for his early dating, we read:

> And at the gate of the sixth palace it seemed as though hundreds of thousands and millions of waves of water stormed against him, and yet there was not a drop of water, only the ethereal glitter of the marble plates with which the palace was tessellated. But he was standing in front of the angels and when he asked: "What is the meaning of these waters," they began to stone him and said: "Wretch, do you not see it with your own eyes? *Are you perhaps a descendant of those who kissed the Golden Calf* [italics mine—BN], and are you unworthy to see the King in his beauty?"[24]

ISLAM AND JUDAISM

This defamation of Jewish character was placed in the mouth of the King of Khazaria by the medieval Spanish poet and philosopher (or perhaps "anti-philosopher" is the more apt term) Judah Halevi:

> Take care, O Rabbi, lest too great indulgence in the description of the superiority of your people make them not unbearable, causing you to overlook what is known of their disobedience in spite of the Revelation. *I have heard that in the midst of it they made a calf and worshipped it.* [Italics mine—BN.][25]

The Rabbi (a fictitious rabbi whom later generations would gullibly identify as "Rabbi Isaac Sangeri,"[26] *sanegor* being the Hebrew word for "defense lawyer") then goes to great lengths to try to minimize the guilt of the Golden Calf.[27]

Judah Halevi's *Book of Kuzari* is subtitled *The Book of Refutation and Demonstration in Defense of the Despised Religion (Kitab al-radd wa'l-dalil fi'l-din al-dhalil)*. The "despised religion" is of course Judaism. Halevi was defending his faith against the onslaught of Islam. He argues that there were mitigating circumstances. What to the untrained eye might appear as outright idolatry, was in fact, an attempt to provide a medium upon which the divine presence might rest. Thus, the calf was not substantially different from the cherubim over the ark—with one notable exception. The gold cherubim were divinely enjoined, while the gold calf was a case of the Israelites "taking the bull by the horns" (pun intended) and acting purely on their own initiative.

Halevi's argument strikes the modern reader as clever rather than convincing. Be that as it may, Halevi's theory cast a long shadow, entering, if you would have it, the "collective unconscious" of the Jewish People. In 1884, the brilliant, irascible Rabbi of Brisk, Joseph Baer Soloveitchik, would essentially rehash the *Kuzari*'s defense, adding in brackets:

> It is possible that something similar is found written in a book. However, I have not seen all this, and on my own cognizance I write so.[28]

---

[1] Rashi, Exodus 32:34.

[2] It is interesting to study the differing ways the "daughters" appropriated the mother religion's Scriptures. *Midrash Tanhuma* noted already that the Church, by coming into possession of the Bible in translation, was able to make the audacious claim, "We are Israel!" (*"Anu Yisrael!"*). See *Midrash Tanhuma, Ki Tissa*, 34. Cf. *Exodus Rabbah* 47:1; quoted in *Tosafot, Gittin* 60b, s.v. *atmuhei ka metamah*. (The Rabbis took comfort in the fact that the inviolable nature of the Oral Law would forever safeguard Israel's claim to chosenness.)

In a halakhic responsum concerning the permissibility of teaching Torah to non-Jews, Maimonides differentiated between Christians and Muslims. He ruled that one may teach the Torah to Christians because they do not corrupt the text, although, on occasion, they pervert the meaning of the Scripture. Muslims, on the other hand, accuse the Jews of having altered the original text of the Torah. (In Islam, this is the doctrine of *tahrif* [*al-nass*] or *tabdil*.) See *Teshuvot ha-Rambam*, ed. Joshua Blau, vol. 1 (Jerusalem: Mekize Nirdamim, 1957), no. 149 (pp. 284-285). See also Maimonides' *Epistle to Yemen* (Shilat ed., p. 131); and Abraham Maimonides' commentary to Gen. 21:10. Later, Rabbi Solomon ben Abraham (RaShBA) of Barcelona would devote an entire work to refuting Ibn Hazm's assault on the integrity of the Torah; see Rabbi Solomon ben Abraham ibn Adret, *Ma'amar 'al Yishmael*, ed. Bezalel Naor (Spring Valley, NY: Orot, 2008).

The great Lithuanian kabbalist, Rabbi Isaac Haver, interpreted the wound to Jacob's thigh (Genesis 32:25) as the usurpation by Esau (or Edom) of the Prophets (symbolized in Kabbalah by the thighs), specifically the Later Prophets. The allusion to Christianity's misappropriation of Isaiah, chapter 53 ("the Suffering Servant"), is quite transparent. In that same passage, the kabbalist speaks of "the two known heads of the *Sitra Ahera* (Other Side) who derived heresy from the words of the Torah," an allusion to Ishmael (Islam) and Esau (Christianity). See Rabbi Yitzhak Eizik Haver (Wildman), *Pithei She'arim* (Warsaw, 1888; photo offset Tel-Aviv: Sinai, 1964), Part 1, *Netiv 'Olam ha-Tikkun*, chap. 22 (76a). The works of Rabbi Isaac Haver's teacher, Rabbi Menahem Mendel of Shklov—some of which were published only recently—are chock-full of references to the two so-called "daughter religions."

[3] *Iggerot ha-RAYaH*, vol. 1, second edition (Jerusalem: Mossad Harav Kook, 1962), Letter 176 (p. 226). Rav Kook was referring to Christianity.

[4] *The Study Quran: A New Translation and Commentary*, ed. Seyyed Hossein Nasr (New York: HarperOne, 2015), 4:157-158.

[5] This is not to say that Christianity "absolved" the Jews of the sin of having worshiped the Golden Calf, but in the Patristic literature this crime certainly paled in comparison with the more recent charge of deicide. For a sampler of early Christian literature that throws up to the Jews the sin of the Golden Calf, see now Joel S. Baden, *The Book of Exodus: A Biography* (Princeton, NJ: Princeton University Press, 2019), pp. 116-122.

[6] Quran 2:92-93.

[7] *b. Shabbat* 88a.

[8] Exodus 24:7. Traditionally, Jews prided themselves on the fact that at Sinai they accepted to obey the Torah without hesitation. See, e.g., Rava's interaction with an anonymous heretic in *b. Shabbat* 88a.

[9] Quran 4:46. See David Nirenberg, *Anti-Judaism: The Western Tradition* (New York: W.W. Norton, 2013), pp. 139-140.

[10] Quran 20:87-88.

[11] See *Pirke de-Rabbi Eliezer*, transl. Gerald Friedlander (New York: Sepher-Hermon, 1981), chap. 45 (p. 355).

[12] See Rashi, *Sanhedrin* 101b and 103b.

[13] See *Midrash Tanhuma, Ki Tissa*, 19. Jannes and Jambres are the Greek form of their names. (See also Targum Pseudo-Jonathan to Exodus 1:15, Exodus 7:11, and Numbers 22:22.) In *b. Menahot* 85a their names are given Semitic form: Yohana and Mamre.

[14] 1 Kings 12:28-29.

[15] A.S. Yahuda, "A Contribution to Qur'an and Hadith Interpretation," *Ignace Goldziher Memorial Volume*, Part I, ed. Samuel Löwinger and Joseph Somogyi (Budapest, 1948), pp. 286-287.

[16] Quran 20:96.

[17] *Midrash Tanhuma, Ki Tissa*, 19.

[18] *Midreshei Teiman*, ed. Lieberman (Jerusalem, 1940), pp. 17-18.

[19] Quran 20:97. Cf. Exodus 32:20, Deut. 9:21.

[20] Quran 2:93. Cf. Exodus 32:20.

[21] Quran 7:152.

[22] See *Numbers Rabbah* 27:8: "The nations of the world take Israel to task, saying to them: 'You made the Calf.'"

[23] Gershom G. Scholem, *Major Trends in Jewish Mysticism* (New York: Schocken, 1971), pp. 52-53.

See more recently Ronald C. Kiener, "Jewish Mysticism in the Lands of the Ishmaelites: A Re-Orientation," in *The Convergence of Judaism and Islam: Religious, Scientific, and Cultural Dimensions*, ed. Michael M. Laskier and Yaacov Lev (Gainesville: University Press of Florida, 2011), pp. 148-151.

[24] *Major Trends in Jewish Mysticism*, p. 53. One may now check the minor *variae lectionis* in Peter Schäfer, *Synopse zur Hekhalot-Literatur* (Tübingen 1981), 259§ (p. 116) and 408§ (p. 172).

[25] Judah Halevi, *Book of Kuzari*, transl. Hartwig Hirschfeld (New York: Pardes, 1946), I, 92 (p. 56).

[26] See Nahmanides, *"Torat Hashem Temimah,"* in *Kitvei Rabbeinu Moshe ben Nahman*, ed. C.B. Chavel, vol. 1 (Jerusalem: Mossad Harav Kook, 1968), p. 151.

[27] *Book of Kuzari* I, 97 (pp. 59-62).

[28] Rabbi Joseph Dov Baer ha-Levi Soloveitchik, *Beit Halevi* (Warsaw, 1884), *Ki Tissa*, 27b.

The Cain-Korah-Christianity Connection

In a *pensée* written in St. Gallen, Switzerland, during Rav Kook's exile there during World War One (and later published in his seminal work, *Orot*), the Rav drew parallels between Korah, who led a mutiny against Moses in the desert, and Cain, whose sacrifice was spurned by God, and who subsequently murdered his brother Abel. As if that is not enough, Rav Kook then goes on to typify Christianity as embodying elements of both Cain and Korah.[1]

Attempting to solve the mystery of why Cain's sacrifice was rejected while Abel's was accepted, Rav Kook posits that Cain's murderous nature, which later became manifest, was already latent at the time he brought his offering. Thus, Cain comes to symbolize a false religiosity that is hypocritical; a professed piety that is but a cover-up for homicidal tendencies. So much for Cain.

Korah's assault upon the Torah of Moses takes the form of democratization of the spiritual realm; Korah attempts to create a "level playing field," whereby all Israel are endowed with equal aptitude for sanctity. His clarion call is: "All the congregation are holy, every one of them, and the LORD is in their midst, so why do you lift yourselves above the assembly of the LORD?"[2]

Rav Kook identifies both of these shortcomings in Christianity. In common with Cain, the Church has a history of murder, while at the same time offering sacraments. And Christianity's assault upon Israel's chosenness, and levelling of diversity and difference, harks back to Korah's rebellion against Moses' and Aaron's chosenness.

The entire *pensée*—the juxtaposition of Korah to Cain, and that of both of them to Christianity—is baffling, to say the least.

It is well known by now that many of Rav Kook's reflections have their basis in Kabbalah. While I would not go to the extreme of lining up Rav Kook's writings word for word with the Kabbalistic lexicon (as did Yosef Avivi in his recent four-volume work, *Kabbalat ha-RAYaH*), it is impossible to deny that the present *pensée* was intended to hang ideational flesh on a kabbalistic code.

Rabbi Menahem Ziyyoni is an obscure kabbalist who resided in Speyer, Germany, in the fifteenth century. His commentary on the Pentateuch was published in Cremona in 1559. At the beginning of *Korah*, Ziyyoni hints to an earlier Kabbalistic notion (made famous by *Tikkunei Zohar*) that Moses was a reincarnation of Abel,[3] and the Egyptian slain by Moses was none other than Cain redux. To quote Ziyyoni: "The slain slays his slayer" (*"he-harug horeg et horego"*). Ziyyoni then throws in (again in cryptic fashion) that Korah being swallowed by the earth was punishment measure for measure for the blood of Abel crying out from the earth. (In other words, Korah was a reincarnation of the slayer Cain.) Finally, Ziyyoni riddles: "Investigate thoroughly Korah, make the sign of the cross (*sheti ve-'erev*, or warp and woof), and you will find a wondrous mystery."

The mystery is that Jesus of Nazareth was a reincarnation of Korah (who, in turn, was a reincarnation of Cain). This mystical model of the three incarnations of Cain, Korah and Jesus provided Rav Kook with food for theological thought.

How was Rav Kook able to break Ziyyoni's code? It is possible that the allusion to the "cross" was sufficient for Rav Kook to solve the puzzle.

But it is also possible that Rav Kook was helped by Rabbi Naftali Bachrach's work, *'Emek ha-Melekh* (Amsterdam, 1648), which enjoyed great popularity among East European kabbalists, despite its many detractors. (Rav Kook's mentor in Kabbalah, Rabbi Shelomo Eliashov recommended *'Emek ha-Melekh* in his work *Hakdamot u-She'arim*.)[4] Bachrach lifts the veil off Ziyyoni's mystery.

> That man (*oto ha-ish*, i.e., Jesus), condemned to boiling excrement,[5] is the last limit of the impurity of Cain.... He is hinted at in the word *"Kayin,"* which is initials *Korah-Yeshu-Notsri*.[6] And in this regard Ziyyoni stated: "Investigate thoroughly Korah and you will find *sheti ve-'erev* (the sign of the cross)."[7] He did not mention him [i.e., Jesus of Nazareth] by name because of the danger [of Church censorship]. The expression "investigate thoroughly" is meant to convey: "Investigate all his reincarnations."[8]

---

[1] See *Shemonah Kevatsim* 7:45; and *Orot, Yisrael u-Tehiyato*, chap. 15.
[2] Numbers 16:3.
[3] *Tikkunei Zohar, tikkun* 69.
[4] See Rabbi Shelomo Eliashov, *Hakdamot u-She'arim* (Piotrkow, 1909), 59b.
[5] *b. Gittin* 57a.
[6] The words *Yeshu Notsri* are encoded by Bachrach in ATBaSh.

[7] The words *sheti ve-'erev* are encoded by Bachrach in ATBaSh.
[8] Rabbi Naphtali Bachrach, *'Emek ha-Melekh* (Amsterdam, 1648), *Sha'ar 'Olam ha-Tohu* (20d).

See also Rabbi Samson of Ostropolia, quoted in Rabbi Avraham Ya'akov Bombach, *Nitsutsei Shimshon* (2013), *Korah*, pp. 172-174; Rabbi Mordechai Spielman, *Tif'eret Tsevi* (on *Zohar*), vol. 5 (Brooklyn, 1999), p. 241 (left column); and Spielman's letter concerning Ziyyoni, in Melekh Shapiro, *Iggerot Malkhei Rabbanan* (Scranton, 5779/2019), chap. 163 (pp. 346-347).

(The quote from Rabbi Samson of Ostropolia is found in a manuscript of Rabbi Tsevi Hirsch Hurwitz, author of the commentary *Aspaklaryah ha-Me'irah* on the *Zohar*.)

IV

MAIMONIDES

The Religious Phenomenology of Maimonides

Over the years, many have expressed the desideratum of a Jewish analog to *The Varieties of Religious Experience* (1902) by Harvard philosopher cum psychologist William James. It seems that the first to voice this need was the religious thinker and mystic, Hillel Zeitlin.[1] In a monograph entitled *Be-Hevyon ha-Neshamah (In the Hiding Place of the Soul)*,[2] Zeitlin bemoaned the fact that James had restricted his study to Christianity and almost totally neglected Judaism.[3] In the ensuing pages, Zeitlin sought to remedy this situation, becoming in the words of Jonathan Meir, "the Jewish James."[4]

There are those who are convinced that in its own way, Hasidism—the East European Jewish mysticism whose roots lie in the teachings of the eighteenth-century Podolian wonderworker Israel Ba'al Shem—answers this need, especially in its more analytic school of HaBaD. On at least one occasion, the present writer heard from the late Zalman Schachter-Shalomi that HaBaD provides a wonderful language of religious experience.[5]

I am about to propose that in truth, much before HaBaD, an eloquent, if subtle, religious phenomenology was crouching right under our eyes in the work of—Maimonides. Moses Maimonides (1138-1204) has the almost unimaginable distinction of wearing two crowns on his head: He is at once the greatest Jewish philosopher and the greatest Jewish legalist of all time. If you would have it, Maimonides' religious phenomenology is located where one would least expect it. Not in the philosophic masterpiece *Guide of the Perplexed*,[6] but tucked away in the nooks and crannies of the monumental code of law, *Mishneh Torah*.

I shall point out two passages in particular that lend themselves to phenomenological analysis.

> This God, honored and revered, it is a commandment to love Him and fear from Him, as it is said, "You shall love the LORD, your God,"[7] and it is said, "The LORD, your God, you shall fear."[8]
>
> And what is the way to the love of Him and the fear of Him?
>
> At the hour that a man contemplates His great and wondrous works and creatures, and from them obtains a glimpse of His wisdom which is incomparable and infinite, he will straightaway love Him, praise Him, glorify Him, and desire with an exceeding desire to know His great name, even as David said, "My soul thirsts for God, for the living God."[9]
>
> And when he ponders these very matters, he will straightaway recoil and be frightened, and realize that he is a small creature, lowly and obscure, endowed with slight and slender intelligence, standing in the presence of Him who is perfect in knowledge. And so David said, "When I

consider Your heavens, the work of Your fingers—what is man that You are mindful of him?"[10]

Maimonides has described an experience of great psychological impact. He could not have done a more splendid job of conveying all the key elements, all the essential ingredients that we have come to associate with Rudolf Otto's groundbreaking work *Das Heilige* (terribly mistranslated as *The Idea of the Holy*). The Wholly Other is at the same time both [*mysterium*] *tremendum* and *fascinans*. One is attracted, fascinated, even as one recoils in fear, terrified. For Maimonides, the aspect of *fascinans* is the motive of love (*ahavah*); the dimension of *tremendum* generates fear (*yir'ah*).

The student of Maimonides is forever in search of sources. In the overwhelming majority of cases, Maimonides did not write in an historical vacuum. There were antecedents galore in Talmudic or post-Talmudic literature. Almost a half century ago, I suggested as a source for the aforementioned passage the anonymous *Sefer Yetsirah* (*Book of Creation*).[11] The book, whose origin remains to this day a mystery, enjoyed immense popularity among Spanish Jewry, as attested to by the commentaries penned by Maimonides' predecessors Rabbi Judah ben Barzillai (Albargeloni) and Rabbi Judah Halevi.[12] And earlier, the man who is credited as being the father of Jewish philosophy, Sa'adyah Gaon, wrote his commentary to *Sefer Yetsirah*.[13] Never once does Maimonides mention *Sefer Yetsirah* by name, but given the intellectual milieu in which he was raised, it is most improbable that he was not familiar with its contents.

Not too far along in *Sefer Yetsirah*, we read:

> Ten *Sefirot* of Nothingness.
> Bridle your mouth from speaking
> and your heart from thinking.
> And if your heart runs,
> return to the place.
> It is therefore written,
> "The *Hayyot* running and returning."[14]
> Regarding this a covenant was made.[15]

The anonymous author of *Sefer Yetsirah* has done something quite remarkable. He has taken the image of *"ratso va-shov"* ("running and returning") reserved for the *Hayyot* seen in Ezekiel's prophetic vision and transformed it into a trope for the mystic's own encounter with the divine. This to-and-fro motion, this dialectical movement has been appropriated from the world of the angels and applied to the realm of human experience. (Later the term *"ratso va-shov"* will become a mainstay of Hasidic thought.) Short of actually quoting the verse at the beginning of Ezekiel, Maimonides has done everything possible to conjure up in a most graphic manner the magnetic pull of the divine followed by the inevitable recoil.

Add to this the context in which Maimonides shares this experience. It is his preamble to *Ma'aseh Merkavah* (the Work of the Chariot) and *Ma'aseh Bereshit* (the Work of Genesis). Those matters will go on for the next three chapters of *Hilkhot Yesodei ha-*

Torah (chaps. 2-4). In fact, the love-fear dyad bookends the entire discussion. Summing up the discourse of *Ma'aseh Bereshit* and *Ma'aseh Merkavah*, Maimonides writes once again:

> When a man reflects on these things, studies all these created beings, from the angels and spheres down to human beings and so on, and realizes the Divine Wisdom manifested in them all, his love for the Place (*ha-Makom*) will increase,[16] his soul will thirst, his very flesh will yearn, to love the Place, blessed be He. And he will fear and be frightened on account of his lowliness, his poverty and his insignificance, when he compares himself to any one of the great and holy bodies; still more [when he compares himself] to any one of the pure forms that are incorporeal and have never had association with corporeal substance. He will then find himself a vessel full of shame and reproach, empty and deficient.[17]

Is it pure coincidence that this same dialectic is emblazoned on the doorpost to *Sefer Yetsirah*, the *Book of Creation*, a work which, as its name indicates, is devoted to *Ma'aseh Bereshit*?

> Man must be careful concerning the *mezuzah*, because it is obligatory upon all constantly, and whenever he enters and exits he will encounter the unity of the name of the Holy

One, blessed be He, and remember His love, and be aroused from his slumber and his erring in the vanities of the time, and will know that there is nothing that stands for eternity but the knowledge of the Rock of the World, and immediately he regains his consciousness and goes on the ways of righteousness.

The early Sages said[18]: Whoever has phylacteries on his head and arm, and fringes on his garment, and a *mezuzah* at his entrance—is assured that he will not sin, for he has numerous reminders. And these are the "angels" that save him from sinning, for it says: "The angel of the LORD camps round about those who fear Him, and saves them."[19]

(MT, Hil. Tefillin u-Mezuzah ve-Sefer Torah 6:13)

Several of the motifs briefly touched upon in this *halakhah* are familiar to us from other earlier passages in Mishneh Torah. The part about waking up from one's spiritual slumber and renouncing the "vanities of the time" (*"havlei ha-zeman"*) reiterates Maimonides' famous symbolism of blowing the *shofar* (Hil. Teshuvah 3:4). Likewise, we are treated to a brief review of Maimonides' theory of the immortality of the soul, elaborated upon in Hil. Teshuvah 8:2-3. It is only the knowledge of the Creator that will survive in the World to Come.

What is specific to the *mezuzah* is "the unity of the name of the Holy One, blessed be He" and "His love." A fuller version of the essential ingredients of the *mezuzah* is provided earlier in Hilkhot Mezuzah: "the unity of the name of the Holy One, blessed be He, and His love, and His service."[20] These three components (unity, love, service) are direct quotes from the two paragraphs contained in the *mezuzah*, *Shema'* and *Ve-Hayah 'im shamo'a*.[21] The first verse of *Shema'* is a statement of the unity of the LORD.[22] The second verse enjoins: "And you shall love the LORD your God with all your heart and with all your soul, and with all your means."[23] The first verse of *Ve-Hayah 'im shamo'a* would ask of us "to love the LORD your God and to serve Him with all your heart and with all your soul."[24]

Maimonides groups together in one unit the laws of *Tefillin*, *Mezuzah* and *Sefer Torah*. At the conclusion of these laws, he writes:

> Whoever sits before a Torah scroll, should sit with gravitas (*koved rosh*) and awe and fear, for it is the faithful witness to all the inhabitants of the world, as it says, "and it will be there against you as a witness."[25] And he should honor it to his ability. The early Sages said[26]: "Whosoever desecrates the Torah, his body shall be desecrated by people; and whosoever honors the Torah, his body shall be honored by people.[27]

One is struck by the radically dissimilar affect evoked by these sacred scripts. Whereas the *mezuzah* speaks to love, the *Sefer Torah* speaks to fear. Let us probe these emotions. Why can't the *mezuzah* trigger fear? Why can't the *Sefer Torah* move us to love the LORD?

If we focus on the texts associated with the ritual objects, the element of fear does not occur in the two paragraphs of the *mezuzah*, whereas love is repeated in both. When it comes to the *Sefer Torah*, on the other hand, Maimonides has chosen the verse from Deuteronomy, "and it will be there against you as a witness," as its signature motif. Thus, the *Sefer Torah* creates a solemn atmosphere designed to instill fear. But, one counters, cannot the *mezuzah* produce a similar solemnity? Though it be only a *derash*, the large letters of the first verse of *Shema'*—the *'ayin* of *Shema'* and the *dalet* of *Ehad*—form the word *'Ed* (witness).[28]

Something else is bothersome about Maimonides' depiction of the scene of the *Sefer Torah*. Why must the affect that Maimonides attributes to the *Sefer Torah* be reserved for the seated position? Earlier, Maimonides enjoined one who beholds the *Sefer Torah* in movement to stand in its presence.[29] In that instance, Maimonides addressed none of the emotions. The proper attitude and frame of mind was delayed by Maimonides until he discussed sitting in the presence of the *Sefer Torah*. Why?

Let us now segue to *Hilkhot Shabbat* of Maimonides. The language that he employs there is highly reminiscent of the passage regarding the *Sefer Torah*:

> What is honor (*kibbud*)? This is what the Sages said that it is incumbent upon man to wash his face, hands and feet in hot water on the Eve of the Sabbath because of the honor of the Sabbath. And he wraps himself in a fringed garment (*tsitsit*) and sits with gravitas (*koved rosh*), awaiting recep-

tion of the face of the Sabbath, as if he is going out to meet the King. And the early Sages would gather their disciples on the Eve of the Sabbath, wrap themselves up and say: "Let us go out to meet Sabbath the King."[30]

The common denominator is that both in the presence of the *Sefer Torah* and the approaching Sabbath, one "sits with gravitas" (*yoshev be-koved rosh*). Sitting is conducive to meditation. It seems that "on the go" it is certainly difficult, if not well-nigh impossible, to enter this state of mindfulness. Thus, the *mezuzah* and the "*Sefer Torah ke-she-hu mehalekh*" ("walking *Sefer Torah*")[31] do not occasion this peculiar gravitas.

Normally, one does not sit opposite the *mezuzah* reflecting on its contents. As Maimonides put it, one's interaction with the *mezuzah* is "whenever one enters and exits."[32] But what if one *were* to sit opposite the *mezuzah* the way one sits opposite the *Sefer Torah*? Why doesn't Maimonides entertain that possibility?

It is possible that there is yet another touchstone here. The gravitas that Maimonides describes can only occur vis-à-vis an external presence; only when confronted with the wholly other. This is so in the case of the *Sefer Torah*. It is especially so in the case of the Sabbath which has been personified as a King. The *mezuzah*, on the other hand, has been internalized; it has become an extension of man's self. Just as the "*tefillin* on his head and arm, and *tsitsit* on his garment," so too the "*mezuzah* at his entrance" has been absorbed within his extended self.[33] There is a well-known saying: "Familiarity breeds contempt."³⁴ Granted the *mezuzah* acts as a "guardian angel" staving off sin, but it is too close to evoke fear.

There is only one man in Israel who enjoys this closeness with the *Sefer Torah*. That is the King of Israel. In addition to the *Sefer Torah* that every Jew must write, the King is obligated to write a second *Sefer Torah*. Concerning that additional Torah scroll, Maimonides writes:

> It shall be with him always. If he should go to war, this *Sefer Torah* is with him; if he should enter in, it is with him; if he should sit in judgment, it is with him; if he should recline, it is opposite him, for it says, "It shall be with him and he shall read in it all the days of his life."³⁵
>
> It shall depart from him only at night or when he enters the bathhouse or the lavatory or to sleep in his bed.³⁶

If our psychological perception of the *Sefer Torah* is correct, then we should observe a difference in the way the King relates to the *Sefer Torah*. Its utter proximity should engender love. It is possible that exactly this attitude of love was alluded to by the Aramaic Targum. The verse in Psalms 45:10 reads:

> Kings' daughters are among your favorites; at your right hand stands a concubine in gold of Ophir.

The Targum paraphrases the verse thus:

> Principalities come to receive your face and render you homage at the time the *Sefer Torah* is ready[37] at your right side written in pure gold from Ophir.

Perhaps we are reading too much into the Targum, but its image of the *Sefer Torah* as a royal concubine (*shegal*) suggests a level of intimacy reserved for the King alone in view of his unique halakhic status.[38] Gone is the *distance* that characterizes the common Jew's relation to the *Sefer Torah*. In its stead, there develops a unique relation of *love*.

Undoubtedly, the best solution to the differing postures vis-à-vis the *mezuzah* and the *Sefer Torah* is that provided by Maimonides himself in the guidelines that he laid down in the penultimate chapters of the later work, *Guide of the Perplexed*. There, the Great Eagle will sum up in remarkably terse language his entire outlook on the Torah and the commandments:

> For these two ends, namely *love* and *fear*, are achieved through two things: *love* through the opinions taught by the Law, which include the apprehension of His being as He, may He be exalted, is in truth; while *fear* is achieved

by means of all actions prescribed by the Law, as we have explained. Understand this summary.[39]

This then is the crux of the issue. When it comes to the *mezuzah*, we contemplate the *de'ot*, the teaching contained therein, which is *"yihud shemo shel Ha-Kadosh Barukh Hu,"*[40] "the unity of the name of the Holy One, blessed be He."[41] This in turn engenders *"ahavato"* ("His love"),[42] and finally *"'avodato"* ("His service").[43] Were we to reflect upon the theological truths contained in the Torah scroll, then it too might evoke the love response. But that is not the case. We are directed not to "the opinions of the Torah," the *"de'ot ha-Torah,"* but to the "actions of the Torah," the *"ma'asei ha-Torah."* Our focus is upon the *Sefer Torah* as a symbol of authority commanding gravitas, awe and fear. This all-encompassing perception of the *Sefer Torah* as awe-inspiring was given eloquent expression in that passage of the *Guide*:

> He, may He be exalted, has explained that the end of the actions prescribed by the whole Law is to bring about the passion of which it is correct that it be brought about, as we have demonstrated in this chapter for the benefit of those who know the true realities. I refer to the fear of Him, may He be exalted, and the awe before His command. It says: *If thou wilt not take care to observe all the words of this Law that are written in this book, that thou mayest fear this glorious and fearful Name, the LORD thy God.*[44] Consider how it is explicitly stated for your benefit

that the intention of *all the words of this Law* is one end, namely, *that thou mayest fear the Name*, and so on.[45]

---

[1] See the recent anthology *Hasidic Spirituality for a New Era: The Religious Writings of Hillel Zeitlin*, ed. Arthur Green (Paulist Press: Mahwah, NJ, 2012).

[2] Published in the journal *Netivot*, vol. 1 (Warsaw: Ahisefer, 1913), pp. 205-235. Jonathan Meir publicized Zeitlin's Jamesian tract in his lecture "Hillel Zeitlin, William James and Hasidism," delivered March 7, 2016 at "Life as a Dialogue," International Conference in Honor of Ephraim Meir, Bar Ilan University.

[3] *"Be-Hevyon ha-Neshamah,"* pp. 208-209. James' token foray into the Jewish tradition is a symbolic survey of the Hebrew prophets followed by a reference to the Alexandrian Jewish philosopher, Philo. See William James, *The Varieties of Religious Experience* (New York, 1929), pp. 469-471.

[4] In the video of Prof. Meir's lecture at 19:57. Available on Youtube: https://www.youtube.com/watch?v=h2TKkSbwcsA

[5] Perhaps it is no coincidence that Hillel Zeitlin was raised in a HaBaD milieu. In his youth, the rabbi of his hometown of Korma, Rabbi Zalman Duchman, exposed him to the spiritual legacy of the great expositor of HaBaD Hasidism, Rabbi Eizik Epstein of Homel. Duchman was an eminent disciple of Rabbi Eizik Homler. (Rabbi E.E. Dessler was introduced to HaBaD thought in his youth, spent in Homel, by Rabbi Zalman's brother, Rabbi Mordechai Yoel Duchman, also an eminent disciple of Rabbi Eizik Homler.) See Bezalel Naor, *Mahol la-Tsaddikim* (Jerusalem and Monsey, 2015), p. 113.
HaBaD is well represented in Zeitlin's aforementioned tract, *Be-Hevyon ha-Neshamah*. On p. 211 there is an unattributed quote from *Tanya* (I, 2, note; II, 9, note). And in note 3 on p. 226 we find an explicit reference to the *"Siddur of the Rabbi of Liadi, He'arah le-Tikkun Hatsot."*

[6] In no way do I intend thereby to minimize the value of the experiential tenor of the fifty-first chapter of Part Three of the *Guide*, which deservedly earned the appellation *"Perek ha-Mitboded"* ("The Chapter of the Contemplative").

[7] Deuteronomy 6:5.

[8] Deuteronomy 6:13.

[9] Psalms 42:3.

[10] Psalms 8:4-5; Maimonides, *Mishneh Torah, Hil. Yesodei ha-Torah* 2:1-2. In general, I have followed Hyamson's translation with slight deviations. See Maimonides, *Mishneh Torah: The Book of Knowledge*, transl. Moses Hyamson (Jerusalem: Feldheim, 1971), page 35b.

[11] I put forth the suggestion in a self-published monograph on Maimonides' *Sefer ha-Madda'*, entitled *Lev Atsal* (5733/1973), pp. 35-36. By metathesis, the title alludes to the author's name, Betsalel.

I met with Rabbi Abraham Joshua Heschel in 1972 (the last year of Heschel's life), at which time I proposed *Sefer Yetsirah* as the source for the passage in Maimonides. Heschel's enigmatic response—to read his article in the *Louis Ginzberg Jubilee Volume*, "Did Maimonides Believe That He Attained Prophecy?" (Hebrew)—has left me wondering to this day what Heschel meant to convey thereby.

I imagine that Heschel, while not responding directly to my suggestion that *Sefer Yetsirah* was the source, was countering that Maimonides' source was not textual at all but rather experiential, rooted in Maimonides' own prophetic or near-prophetic experience. Somewhat reminiscent of the Hasidic master Rabbi Zusha of Anipoli's response when asked how he knew an obscure passage in the *Talmud Yerushalmi*: "Truly, I did not know of this passage in the *Yerushalmi*, but the same source from which the *Yerushalmi* derived this, was revealed to me" (Mendel Zitrin, *Shivhei Tsaddikim*, Warsaw, 1884, pp. 30-31).

Earlier, Zeitlin (op. cit., pp. 224-225) assumed that Maimonides was describing his own personal experience of the divinity, and was impressed with the simplicity and candor by which Maimonides brings together the two opposite emotions of love and fear. Over several pages (220-227), Zeitlin documents Jewish sources about the fusion of positive and negative affect that occurs in the encounter with the divine.

While Rabbi Joseph Baer Soloveitchik certainly juxtaposed the contents of the second chapter of *Hilkhot Yesodei ha-Torah* to the concept of *"ratso va-shov"* (which figures prominently in HaBaD Hasidic philosophy for which Rabbi Soloveitchik had a penchant), Rabbi Soloveitchik stopped short of boldly suggesting that *Sefer Yetsirah* served as the source for Maimonides' description of the experience. See Rabbi Joseph B. Soloveitchik, *And From There You Shall Seek*, transl. Naomi Goldblum (Jersey City, 2008), pp. 69-71. (This is a translation of the Hebrew essay *"U-Vikkashtem mi-Sham,"* which did not appear in print until 1978, when Rabbi Soloveitchik published it in the rabbinic journal *Hadarom*.)

In *And From There You Shall Seek*, p. 174, n. 12, Rabbi Soloveitchik refers the reader to Rabbi Shneur Zalman's *Likkutei Torah, Parashat Hukkat*. (See ibid., s.v. *Zot Hukkat ha-Torah* [56b].) For the record, the equation of *"ratso"* with the human emotion of love, and *"shov"* with fear, originated with Rabbi Shneur Zalman's master, Rabbi Dov Baer of Mezritch. See idem, *'Or Torah* (Korets, 1804), *Ha'azinu*.

Rabbi Soloveitchik's fondness for *Likkutei Torah* is famous. His groundbreaking essay, *"Ish ha-Halakhah,"* is chock-full of references to *Likkutei Torah*. (See Rabbi Joseph Dov Soloveitchik, *"Ish ha-Halakhah," Talpiyot* 1:3-4 [5704-5/1944], pp. 682-685, 690.) Rabbi Soloveitchik once confided to a Lubavitcher Hasid, Rabbi Jacob Israel Zuber of Boston, that he knows *Likkutei Torah* by heart (*"oisvenig"*). (Told to the writer by the late Rabbi David Edelman of Springfield, Mass., son-in-law of Rabbi Zuber.)

Further along in that lengthy note in *And From There You Shall Seek* (p. 175), Rabbi Soloveitchik speculates that it was Bahya ibn Pakuda's *Duties of the Heart* (Gate 10: The Gate of Love of God, chap. 1) that inspired Maimonides' conception of the dialectic nature of love and fear of God. (His son, Abraham Maimonides, referenced Bahya's *Sha'ar ha-Perishut* in his own *Sha'ar ha-Perishut*. See Abraham Maimonides, *Ha-Maspik le-'Ovdei Hashem* [*Kitab Kifayah al-'Abidin*], transl. Yosef Dori, Jerusalem 1973, p. 121.) Recently, Diana Lobel wrote that Maimonides' coupling of love and fear may have been inspired by Bahya (*Duties of the Heart* X, 6). See Diana Lobel, *A Sufi-Jewish Dialogue: Philosophy and Mysticism in Bahya Ibn Paquda's* Duties of the Heart (Philadelphia: University of Pennsylvania Press, 2007), pp. 236-237. Yet, in both the chapter cited by Rabbi Soloveitchik and that cited by

Lobel, the progression is from fear to love, which is the opposite of Maimonides' movement from fear to love.

See now the parallel discussion in Lawrence J. Kaplan, *Maimonides—Between Philosophy and Halakhah: Rabbi Joseph B. Soloveitchik's Lectures on the* Guide of the Perplexed (Jerusalem, 2016), pp. 219-235.

Finally, see Y. Tzvi Langermann's remarks regarding Maimonides and *Sefer Yetsirah* in his article "On Some Passages Attributed to Maimonides" (Hebrew) in *Me'ah She'arim: Studies in Medieval Jewish Spiritual Life in Memory of Isadore Twersky*, ed. Fleischer, Blidstein, Horowitz, and Septimus (Jerusalem, 2001), pp. 224-227.

[12] See *Kuzari* IV, 25-27 (Hirschfeld transl. pp. 201-212).

[13] Many a student of Maimonides has been perplexed by the Master's virtual silence in regard to Sa'adyah. The one outright reference to Sa'adyah catches the man at his worst moment: calculating the End. (See *Iggeret Teiman*, in Rabbeinu Moshe ben Maimon, *Iggerot*, ed. Kafah [Jerusalem: Mossad Harav Kook, 1994], p. 40.) And though Maimonides defends Sa'adyah on that occasion, chalking up the deplorable exercise to extenuating circumstances (ibid. pp. 41-42), one might have imagined that Maimonides—who invokes ever so many philosophers in his literary *oeuvre*—would somewhere mention Sa'adyah's name in some more salutary connection.

Although hardly explicit, many scholars assume that Maimonides' derogation in the sixth chapter of the *Shemonah Perakim* of "some of the later wise men who came down with the illness of the *Mutakallimun*" is an oblique reference to Sa'adyah. See Maimonides, *Commentary to the Mishnah*, ed. Kafah (Jerusalem: Mossad Harav Kook, 1963), *Seder Nezikin*, p. 258.

Into the next generation, Abraham Maimonides' Commentary to the Pentateuch is replete with citations from Sa'adyah's Bible commentaries. One assumes that the father Moses Maimonides also approved of Sa'adyah's exegesis, while perhaps distancing himself from Sa'adyah's philosophy.

[14] Ezekiel 1:14.

[15] *Sefer Yetzirah: The Book of Creation*, transl. Aryeh Kaplan (York Beach, ME: Samuel Weiser, 1997), 1:8 (p. 66).

[16] *Ha-Makom* (the Place) is a rabbinic term for the deity. As the Rabbis said: "He is the place of the world, and the world is not His place" (*Genesis Rabbah* 68:9). *Ha-Makom* is usually translated into English as "the Omnipresent."

[17] *Hil. Yesodei ha-Torah* 4:12; Hyamson translation, page 39b (with slight deviations).

[18] *b. Menahot* 43b.

[19] Psalms 34:8.

[20] *Hil. Tefillin u-Mezuzah ve-Sefer Torah* 5:4.

[21] Deuteronomy 6:4-9; 11:13-21.

[22] Deuteronomy 6:4.

[23] Deuteronomy 6:5.

[24] Deuteronomy 11:13.

[25] Deuteronomy 31:26.

[26] *m. Avot* 4:8. See Maimonides' commentary there (Kafah ed., p. 291). Rabbi Nahum Rabinovitch wrote that Maimonides deliberately reversed the order of the *Mishnah* to end these *halakhot* on a salutary note. See *Yad Peshutah* (Jerusalem, 1984), end *Hil. Tefillin u-Mezuzah ve-Sefer Torah* (p. 790). However,

this reversal on Maimonides' part occurs also in *Hil. Sanhedrin* 24:9, which is not the conclusion of an entire section of *Mishneh Torah* but only a chapter.

[27] *Hil. Tefillin u-Mezuzah ve-Sefer Torah* 10:11.
[28] See *Ba'al ha-Turim* and *Keli Yakar* to Deuteronomy 6:4.
[29] *Hil. Tefillin u-Mezuzah ve-Sefer Torah* 10:9.
[30] *Hil. Shabbat* 30:2. Cf. *Hil. Sanhedrin* 3:7.
[31] *Hil. Tefillin u-Mezuzah ve-Sefer Torah* 10:9.
[32] *Hil. Tefillin u-Mezuzah ve-Sefer Torah* 6:13.
[33] *Hil. Tefillin u-Mezuzah ve-Sefer Torah* 6:13.
[34] The *Talmud Yerushalmi* alluded to this truism: "Do out of love and do out of fear....Do out of fear, so that if you come to kick, know that you fear, and one who fears, does not kick" (*y. Berakhot* 9:5).
[35] Deuteronomy 17:19; *Hil. Tefillin u-Mezuzah ve-Sefer Torah* 7:2.
[36] *Hil. Tefillin u-Mezuzah ve-Sefer Torah* 7:3. Maimonides repeats these laws in *Hil. Melakhim* 3:1.
[37] *Di-me'atar* is obviously a copyist's error. The Targum should read *di-me'atad*.
[38] For Maimonides' understanding of the term *"shegal"* within the context of Psalms 45:10, see *Guide of the Perplexed* III, end chap. 8. Cf. Ibn Ezra's commentary to Psalms.

In *b. Rosh Hashanah* 4a the "prophecy" is interpreted thus: "As a reward for the Torah being beloved to Israel as a concubine is to the nations, you shall merit the gold of Ophir."

The *Gemara* uses the term *"navi"* loosely, for the Book of Psalms is not considered full-blown prophecy, rather *ru'ah ha-kodesh*. See Maimonides, *Guide of the Perplexed* II, 45 (the second degree). Neither are the sons of Korah reckoned among the prophets. See the gloss of Rabbi Tsevi Hirsch Chajes (*MaHaRaTs Hayyot*) to *Rosh Hashanah* 4a; and Rabbi Reuven Margaliyot, *Nitsutsei 'Or* (Jerusalem: Mossad Harav Kook, 2002), ad loc. The offending phrase containing *"navi"* is not found in some manuscripts of the Talmud; see Rabbi Raphael Nathan Nata Rabbinowicz, *Dikdukei Soferim, Rosh Hashanah* (Munich, 1872).

[39] *Guide of the Perplexed* III, end chap. 52; Pines translation, p. 630. (The italics occur in Pines' translation.)
[40] *Hil. Tefillin u-Mezuzah ve-Sefer Torah* 5:4 and 6:13.
[41] A sentence earlier in that passage of the *Guide*, Maimonides writes:
> As for the opinions that the *Torah* teaches us—namely, the apprehension of His being and His unity, may He be exalted—these opinions teach us *love*, as we have explained several times.
> (Pines translation, p. 630; italics in Pines' translation).

[42] *Hil. Tefillin u-Mezuzah ve-Sefer Torah* 5:4 and 6:13.
[43] *Hil. Tefillin u-Mezuzah ve-Sefer Torah* 5:4. Cf. *Guide* III, 51:
> The *Torah* has made it clear that this last worship to which we have drawn attention in this chapter can only be engaged in after apprehension has been achieved; it says: *To love the Lord your God, and to serve Him with all your heart and with all your soul* [Deuteronomy 11:13]. Now we have made it clear several times that love is proportionate to apprehension. After *love* comes this worship to which attention has also been drawn by [the Sages], may their memory be blessed, who said: *This is the worship in the heart*. In my opinion it consists in set-

ting thought to work on the first intelligible and in devoting oneself exclusively to this as far as this is within one's capacity.

(Pines translation, p. 621; italics in Pines' translation)

[44] Deuteronomy 28:58.
[45] Pines translation, p. 630; italics in Pines' translation.

When Rambam Met the Izhbitser Rebbe: Response to a Straussian Reading of *Hilkhot Teshuvah*

The renowned German Jewish scholar Leo Strauss revolutionized intellectual history when he published in 1952 his book *Persecution and the Art of Writing*. Strauss made the bold claim that some of our great authors wrote on two levels within the same work. For the masses, they wrote on the exoteric level, but they tucked away another, esoteric level available only to the cognoscenti, and it is the latter level that contains their true opinion. The three paradigms Strauss provided are three of Judaism's greatest thinkers: Judah Halevi, Maimonides, and Spinoza.

A decade later, in 1963, the University of Chicago Press published an edition of Maimonides' *The Guide of the Perplexed* containing Shlomo Pines' English translation of the Arabic, and a sprawling introductory essay by Strauss, "How To Begin To Study *The Guide of the Perplexed*," employing his hermeneutic. As this edition became the standard English edition of *The Guide*, it certainly contributed to the mainstreaming of Strauss' ideas.

Forty years after the appearance of Strauss' seminal work, another Maimonidean scholar, Bezalel Safran, offered an application of Strauss' method to Maimonides' halakhic work, *Mishneh Torah*. Safran's article, "Maimonides on Free Will, Determinism and Esotericism,"[1] attempts to demonstrate that not only in the philosophic work, *Guide of the Perplexed*, did Maimonides write for two very different audiences, but in the *Commentary to the Mishnah* and in *Mishneh Torah* as well.[2]

The departure point for the discussion is the perhaps enigmatic passage in *Mishneh Torah, Hilkhot Teshuvah* (Laws of Return) 6:4, which dwells on King David's guilt-ridden spiritual struggle with sin. The paragraph reads (in Safran's translation):

> And concerning this matter the righteous ones and the prophets ask in their prayer from God to aid them on the Way of Truth, as David had said (Psalms 86:21), "Teach me Your way, O God, I shall walk in Your truth," that is to say, let not my sins prevent me [from attaining] the Way of Truth, through which I will know Your way and the unity of Your name. And also that which [David] said (Psalm 51:14), "And a generous spirit will support me," that is to say, let my spirit do its desire, and let not my sins cause me to be prevented from repentance; rather, may freedom of the will be in my hand [may it be within my grasp to do repentance] until I return [to the Way of Truth] and shall understand and know the Way of Truth. And in this way [are to be interpreted] all that resemble these verses.[3]

Safran argues that this paragraph flies in the face of the preceding paragraph. Whereas what precedes forcefully argues for free will, this paragraph—when decoded by utilizing Straussian cryptology—sends the exact opposite message of determinism. But again, argues Safran, that true opinion of Maimonides is privileged information reserved for the elite, of which there were very few, even among Maimonides' rabbinic peers.[4]

Safran puzzles over the fact that three times in the single paragraph of *Hil. Teshuvah* 6:4 Maimonides repeats the term *"derekh ha-emet"* (the Way of Truth). For Safran, this is more than just a *terminus technicus*; this is the proverbial smoking gun. "The Way of Truth" is a term loaded with esoteric significance.

After noting the term's earlier appearance in *Hil. 'Avodah Zarah* 1:3, Safran traces it back to its Biblical root in Genesis 24:48, where Abraham's servant Eliezer expresses gratitude to God "who guided me on a Way of Truth (*derekh emet*) to take the daughter of my master's brother for his son."[5] And just as in the context of Rebekah's marriage to Isaac, the gist is clearly deterministic, so too in Maimonides's lexicon, the "Way of Truth" harbors an esoteric truth, whereby the patina of man's free will is peeled away to reveal the reality of divine preordination and predestination.

This is the secret message that Safran has unpacked from the passage in *Hilkhot Teshuvah*: King David was praying for some sort of epiphany by which there would be revealed to him that his sin with Bathsheba was in reality engineered from Above, and that he was, so to speak, merely a pawn on a divine chessboard.[6]

The author of the article finds confirmation for his theory that in truth Maimonides subscribes to determinism, in a self-declaredly esoteric passage in the earlier *Commentary to the Mishnah, Rosh Hashanah* 1:2. There, Maimonides writes concerning the judgment meted out to earth's inhabitants on the New Year:

The exoteric aspect of this Mishnaic statement is spelled out as you will see. The esoteric dimension, however, its meaning is indubitably very difficult.[7]

There too, Safran assumes that Maimonides alludes to his deterministic theory, in direct opposition to what he writes elsewhere in his *Commentary to the Mishnah*. The entire final chapter of the *Shemonah Perakim* (Eight Chapters), Maimonides' introduction to *Avot*, champions man's free will.

By the time Safran concludes his study of Maimonides, the reader is nudged to the realization that Maimonides' true opinion is not so far removed from (though not identical with) the philosophy of Rabbi Mordecai Joseph Leiner (the Rebbe of Izbica), famously typecast by Joseph Weiss as "religious determinism."[8]

Let us attempt to deconstruct Safran's argument and offer a counter-interpretation of the Maimonidean texts.

First, while in principle I do not find objectionable Safran's method of searching for Biblical precedent to Maimonides' lexicology, I do find it highly unlikely that a term as generic and sweeping as "the Way of Truth" must be reduced to the rather unique situation of Eliezer's experience in searching for a spouse to suit Isaac.[9]

Besides the impracticality of subordinating every occurrence of the term "the Way of Truth" in Maimonides' *oeuvre* to Eliezer's narrative,[10] it just so happens that Maimonides penned a responsum in which he disabuses the questioner of the notion that marriages are divinely preordained. The upshot of Maimonides' response is that in general, matches are not made in heaven but on earth; only in isolated instances is there divine orchestration. (Though one may wish to argue that in Maimonides' estimation his addressee, Obadiah the Proselyte, was not worthy of being privy to Maimonides' true opinion on the matter, the effusive praise that Maimonides heaps upon his correspondent would seem to indicate otherwise.)

So germane is this responsum to our discussion that it bears reproduction here (in my English translation):

> Question: Regarding [the statement] "All is in the hands of heaven except for the fear of heaven."[11]

> Answer: Regarding that which you said, that all of mankind's deeds are not decreed beforehand by the Creator. That is the impeccable truth, and therefore reward is given if one goes on a good way, and punishment is exacted if one goes on a bad way. All mankind's deeds come under the rubric of "fear of heaven," for in the final analysis, all mankind's deeds produce either [fulfillment of] a commandment or a sin. When the Rabbis, of blessed memory, said, "All is in the hands of heaven," [they were referring to] the natural order of the world, such as species of trees and wildlife, and the science of the heavenly spheres, and the

angels. We have already expanded on this subject in the commentary to Tractate *Avot*,[12] and brought proofs. Also at the beginning of the magnum opus which we composed of all the commandments.[13]

Whoever leaves behind the things we explained, that are constructed upon the foundations of the world, and sets out to seek in a *haggadah* or *midrash*, or in the words of one of the Ge'onim, of blessed memory, a single word that would refute our words, words of knowledge and understanding—is committing suicide, and what he has wreaked to himself is sufficient [punishment].

This [saying] that your Rabbi quoted to you, "[A heavenly voice goes out, saying:] 'The daughter of so-and-so [is destined to be wed] to so-and-so.'"[14] If it applies universally to all, and is to be taken literally, then why does it state in the Torah, "[Who is the man who has betrothed a woman and not married her? Let him go and return to his house,] lest he die in battle and another man marry her"?[15] Is there in the world a rational person who would entertain doubt in this matter after what is written in the Torah? Rather it is worthy for one who is understanding and whose heart is prepared to adopt the Way of Truth (*derekh ha-emet*),[16] that he make this matter explicit in the Torah the fundament and the foundation, so that the building not collapse and the tent-peg not come loose. And if one finds a verse in the Prophets or a maxim of the Rabbis, of blessed memory, that assails this fundament and tears down this premise, let one seek out with the mind's eye until one has understood the words of the prophet or the sage. If their words are found compatible with that made explicit in the Torah, good! And if not, let one say that: "I do not know the words of this prophet or this sage. They are esoteric and not literal."

That which the sage said, "The daughter of so-and-so [is destined to be wed] to so-and-so," refers to the way of reward or the way of punishment. If this man or this woman performed a commandment for which the proper reward is a harmonious marriage, then the Holy One, blessed be He, matches them together. And by the same token, if their due punishment is an acrimonious marriage, He matches them. This is akin to the saying of the Rabbis, of blessed memory: "If there be but one *mamzer* (male bastard) at one end of the world, and but one *mamzeret* (female bastard) at the other end of the world, the Holy One, blessed be He, brings them together and matches them."[17] This does not apply universally to all, rather to those deserving of reward or punishment, as is just in the eyes of God.

All these matters are built upon what we explained in the *Commentary to the Mishnah, Avot*, as you understood. You are a great wise man and you have an understanding heart by which you understood the things and knew the straight way.

Moses ben Maimon, of blessed memory[18]

It would be difficult to imagine that Maimonides was posturing in this responsum, while truly subscribing to a determinist philosophy. The responsum is a forthright presentation of Maimonides' firm belief in free will as opposed to predestination. It sums up what has been elucidated previously in the *Commentary to the Mishnah* and *Mishneh Torah*. As for the recipient's intellectual acumen, Maimonides closes by saying: "You are a great wise man and you have an understanding heart by which you understood the things and knew the straight way."

And then there is the passage in the *Commentary to the Mishnah, Rosh Hashanah*, which alludes to some esoterica. Safran believes that the allusion is to a theory of determinism. However, it is much more likely that the issue at stake is not determinism versus free will, but general divine supervision (*hashgahah kelalit*) versus individual divine supervision (*hashgahah peratit*).[19]

The verse from *Psalms* 33:15 adduced by the *Mishnah*, "Who forms together their heart; Who understands all their deeds," follows on the heels of the previous verse: "From the place of His habitation He supervised (*hishgi'ah*) all the inhabitants of the earth." And our own verse of *Psalms* 33:15 is quoted by Maimonides in the *Guide* III, 17 in his discussion of this very issue of individual divine providence (see Pines ed., p. 472).

One might counter that unlike the doctrine of determinism, there is nothing esoteric about the doctrine of *hashgahah peratit* or individual providence. Not so fast! What Maimonides dispenses in the very next chapter of the *Guide* (III, 18) eminently qualifies as "esoterica." I am referring to Maimonides' belief that there are degrees of providence commensurate with how intently one focuses one's mind on the divine. Those whose intellects are riveted to the divine, merit more divine supervision; those easily distracted, receive less divine attention. How do I know that Maimonides considers this topic esoteric? He says so explicitly:

> A most extraordinary speculation has occurred to me just now through which doubts may be dispelled and *divine secrets*[20] revealed. We have already explained in the chapters concerning providence[21] that providence watches over everyone endowed with intellect proportionately to the measure of his intellect. Thus providence always watches over an individual endowed with perfect apprehension, whose intellect never ceases from being occupied with God. On the other hand, an individual endowed with perfect apprehension, whose thought sometimes for a certain time is emptied of God, is watched over by providence only during the time when he thinks of God; providence withdraws from him during the time when he is occupied with something else.[22]

Let us summarize our findings.

Safran suggests that the paragraph in *Hilkhot Teshuvah* 6:4 possesses an esoteric meaning: David is aspiring to a level of esoteric knowledge, to an epiphany, whereby it will be revealed to him that his misdeeds were movements in a divine symphony. But it is possible that there is nothing esoteric about this paragraph at all. David prays that on account of his grievous misdeeds he not be barred from the Way of Return (*Teshuvah*), as were some of the most vile miscreants in human history discussed in the previous *halakhah* (the prime example being the Pharaoh of the Exodus). This is the straightforward reading of the *halakhah*.

Whatever "the Way of Truth" signifies for Maimonides, we shall not find the answer in the peroration of Eliezer servant of Abraham. Maimonides' opening categorical statement—"Free will is bestowed on every human being. If one desires to turn towards the good way and be righteous, he is at liberty to do so; and if one wishes to turn towards the evil way and be wicked, he is at liberty to do so."[23]—was never intended as a useful, provisional belief to be discarded upon attaining philosophic maturity. And it is well-nigh inconceivable that Maimonides—like later the Izhbitser Rebbe—was a religious determinist.

---

[1] Published in *Porat Yosef: Studies Presented to Rabbi Dr. Joseph Safran*, ed. Bezalel Safran and Eliyahu Safran (Hoboken, New Jersey: Ktav, 1992), pp. 111-128.

[2] Actually, Strauss had already extended his method to *Mishneh Torah*. See L. Strauss, "Notes on Maimonides' *Book of Knowledge*," in *Studies in Mysticism and Religion Presented to Gershom G. Scholem* (Jerusalem, 1967), pp. 269-283. Safran credits Prof. Arthur Hyman with reminding him of this article, "a pioneering mode of esoteric reading of *Mishneh Torah*" (Safran, p. 127, n. 27).

[3] Safran, p. 112.

[4] After positing that the two *halakhot* (*Hil. Teshuvah* 6:3 and 6:4) are contradictory (a supposition that I reject), Safran chalks up the contradiction to Maimonides' "seventh cause" in the Introduction to *The Guide of the Perplexed*: "In speaking about very obscure matters it is necessary to conceal some parts and to disclose others . . . In such cases the vulgar must in no way

be aware of the contradiction; the author accordingly uses some device to conceal it by all means" (Pines ed., p. 18). Maimonides goes on to say: "Divergences that are to be found in this Treatise are due to the fifth cause and the seventh" (ibid., p. 20).

*

I find it surprising that none of our great savants has pointed out the rather obvious similarity between Maimonides' stated method in the Introduction to the *Guide* and Aristotle's response to his disciple Alexander, as recorded by the Greek historian Plutarch.

Maimonides was hard put to justify his publishing the secrets of the Account of the Beginning (*Ma'aseh Bereshit*):

> For you know the saying of [the Sages], *may their memory be blessed: The Account of the Beginning ought not to be taught in the presence of two.* Now if someone explained all those matters in a book, he in effect would be *teaching* them to thousands. (Pines transl., p. 7)

In order to obviate this prohibition of the Sages, Maimonides adopted a stratagem of engaging in deliberate obfuscation. (See Strauss' introduction, pp. xiv-xv.)

We read that when Alexander learned that his master Aristotle had published certain treatises on recondite matters hitherto transmitted by the philosophers to only a select few, he wrote Aristotle a brusque letter upbraiding him for sharing these secret teachings with the common man. To which Aristotle apologized, "by saying that the doctrines of which he spoke were *both published and not published* (και εκδεδομενων και μη εκδεδομενων); for in truth, his treatise on metaphysics is of no use for those who would either teach or learn the science, but is written as a memorandum for those already trained therein." See Plutarch, *Plutarch's Lives*, with translation by Bernadotte Perrin (Cambridge, MA: Harvard University Press, 1919), *Alexander* 7.3-5.

[5] Though nowhere in the story (Genesis 24) is the servant of Abraham named "Eliezer," I follow Maimonides' lead in *Hilkhot 'Avodah Zarah* 11:4 where the protagonist of the story is referred to as *"Eliezer 'eved Avraham"* ("Eliezer servant of Abraham").

[6] See *b. 'Avodah Zarah* 4b-5a. Rashi (ibid., s.v. *lomar lekha*) writes: "It was the decree of the King" (*"Gezeirat melekh hi"*). Quoted by Safran, p. 124, n. 17.

Safran's reading of the *halakhah* in Maimonides is most reminiscent of a passage in the writings of Rabbi Zadok Hakohen [Rabinowitz] of Lublin: "The main Return (*Teshuvah*) is [not accomplished] until the Lord will enlighten his eyes, [whereby] the sins become merits, which is to say, that he will recognize and understand that whatever sin he committed was also the will of the Lord, blessed be He ..." (*Tsidkat ha-Tsaddik* [Lublin, 1913], par. 40 [6a]).

For a discussion of Rabbi Zadok's determinism as well as that of Rav Kook, see my article, "'*Zedonot na'asot ke-zakhuyot*' *be-mishnato shel Harav Kuk*" ("'Sins Become as Merits' in the Philosophy of Rav Kook"), in *'Ofer ha-Ayyalim: Sefer Zikaron le-ha-Kadosh 'Ofer Eliyahu Cohen*, ed. Dani Kokhav (Koch) (Jerusalem, 1994), pp. 299-312.

[7] Safran's English translation (pp. 119-120), based on Kafah's Hebrew translation from the Arabic, in his edition of *Mishnah 'im Peirush Rabbeinu Moshe ben Maimon* (Jerusalem, 1965).

[8] See Safran, p. 125, n. 21. In that same endnote, "another great determinist, Hasdai Crescas" is referenced.

[9] When I read Rabbi Abraham Maimonides' commentary to the story of Abraham's servant and Rebekah, at first blush it seemed to confirm Safran's contention that "the Way of Truth" is at the very least a *terminus technicus* in the Maimonidean lexicon of both father and son. In his commentary to Genesis 24:7, s.v. *mal'akho*, Rabbi Abraham Maimonides writes:

> Praised be the One who has guided us in the Way of Truth (*be-derekh ha-emet*) to every correct and fine reason, whose end is beyond our intellect, by opening [for us] a gate to what is written in the Torah.
> (*Peirush Rabbeinu Avraham ben ha-Rambam 'al Bereshit u-Shemot*, ed. Wiesenberg [London: L. Honig & Sons, 1958], p. 54)

One who reads the Hebrew translation might think that Rabbi Abraham Maimonides embedded the Hebrew words *"be-derekh ha-emet"* in his Judeo-Arabic statement (especially because of its close proximity to Abraham's servant's utterance some verses later). However, if one consults the Judeo-Arabic (provided in that edition), one is in for a surprise. The phrase "in the Way of Truth" simply does not occur! In the Judeo-Arabic (f.14r. of the Oxford ms.; p. 55 of the London edition) the phrase reads *tout court*:

פסבחאן מן ארשדנא לכל מעני צחיח דקיק....

This would translate as: "Praised be the One who has guided us to every correct, fine reason...."

This was confirmed for me by my dear friend Rabbi Moshe Maimon, who is in the process of preparing for publication a new Hebrew translation of Abraham Maimonides' commentary to the Pentateuch. (The Oxford manuscript, Huntington 166, is a unicum.)

Evidently, the translator (according to the introduction of the publisher, Rabbi Solomon Sasoon, the Book of Genesis was translated by Hakham Yosef ben Salah Dori, and the Book of Exodus by Rabbi Efraim Yehudah Wiesenberg) took the literary license of adding the flourish *"be-derekh ha-emet"* (the Way of Truth) to Rabbi Abraham Maimonides' statement of gratitude, perhaps in emulation of Abraham's servant's peroration a few verses later.

[10] Unnoted by Safran, the term *"derekh ha-emet"* ("the Way of Truth") occurs also in *Hilkhot 'Avodah Zarah* 1:3 (three times) and *Hilkhot Teshuvah* 4:2.

[11] b. *Berakhot* 33b, *Megillah* 25a, *Niddah* 16b.

[12] Maimonides' Introduction to Tractate *Avot*, *Shemonah Perakim* (Eight Chapters), chap. 8, and *Avot* 1:13 (Kafah ed., p. 271), 3:18, 19 (Kafah ed., pp. 284-285), and 4:28 (Kafah ed., p. 295).

[13] While the editor Joshua Blau is certainly correct that the reference is to *Mishneh Torah* and not *Sefer ha-Mitsvot*, he mistakenly directs the reader to the beginning of *Hil. De'ot*, while the proper address is chapters 5-6 of *Hilkhot Teshuvah*. See Yitzhak Shilat (Greenspan), *Iggerot ha-Rambam*, vol. 1 (Jerusalem, 1995), p. 236, n. 15.

[14] b. *Sotah* 2a; *Mo'ed Katan* 18b.

[15] Deuteronomy 20:7.

In the final chapter of *Shemonah Perakim* (Kafah ed., p. 262), Maimonides marshals a different proof that marrying a certain woman cannot be divinely ordained but must rather be a matter of choice: Marriage is a *mitsvah* and God does not preordain that one perform a commandment. Cf. *Sefer ha-*

Mitsvot, positive commandment 213; *Mishneh Torah, Hilkhot Ishut* 1:1-2; and Abraham Maimonides' responsum in *Birkat Avraham*, ed. Baer Goldberg (Lyck, 1859), no. 44. (However, Rabbeinu Asher disagrees with Maimonides. For Rabbeinu Asher, only procreation [*periyah u-reviyah*] is a *mitsvah*; marriage per se is not a *mitsvah*. See Rabbeinu Asher, *Ketubot* 1:12 [corresponding to *b. Ketubot* 7b].)

[16] Yitzhak Shilat is convinced that unlike the vast majority of Maimonides' responsa which were penned in Arabic, the responsa to Obadiah the Proselyte were written in Hebrew. Assuming that Shilat is correct in his pronouncement, and the term *"derekh ha-emet"* in our responsum is Maimonides' own language and not a translation, we are certainly justified in making capital of the expression. Clearly, within the context of the responsum, "the Way of Truth" lies on the side of free will and not on the side of causality. See Yitzhak Shilat, *Iggerot ha-Rambam*, vol. 1, p. 231.

[17] *y. Kiddushin* 3:12; *Genesis Rabbah* 65:2.

[18] *Teshuvot ha-Rambam*, ed. Joshua Blau, vol. 2 (Jerusalem: Mekitzei Nirdamim, 1960), no. 436 (pp. 714-716).

[19] See Rabbi Yom Tov Lipmann Heller, *Tosefot Yom Tov* to *Rosh Hashanah* 1:2, and Rabbi Samuel Edels, *Hiddushei Aggadot*, *Rosh Hashanah* 18a, s.v. *kema'alot Beit Horon*.

[20] The Hebrew translators (Ibn Tibbon, al-Harizi, Kafah, Schwarz) render this: "*sodot elohiyim*."

[21] *Guide* III, chaps. 17 and 18.

[22] Moses Maimonides, *The Guide of the Perplexed* III, 51 (Pines ed., pp. 624-625). Various commentators of the *Guide* grapple with the problem of why the rehashing of this doctrine in chapter 51 is considered by Maimonides more wonderful than its earlier presentation in the *"Pirkei ha-Hashgahah"* (i.e., chapters 17-18). See, e.g., Kafah's translation of *Moreh ha-Nevukhim* (Jerusalem: Mossad Harav Kook, 1977), p. 408, n. 75.

One notes with interest that Nahmanides, the great medieval representative of the kabbalistic tradition, quotes approvingly this novel doctrine of the *Guide*. See Nahmanides' commentary to Job 36:7; in *Kitvei Rabbeinu Moshe ben Nahman*, ed. C.B. Chavel (Jerusalem: Mossad Harav Kook, 1968), vol. 1, pp. 108-109; and in the new *Sefer Iyov 'im Peirush ha-Ramban*, ed. Yehudah Leib Friedman (Israel: Feldheim, 2018), pp. 451-458.

[23] Maimonides, *Hilkhot Teshuvah* 5:1 (Moses Hyamson translation).

V

KABBALAH

The Orality of *Shir ha-Shirim* and of *Tikkunei Zohar*

Without doubt, the most widely known passage of *Tikkunei Zohar*, an early fourteenth-century composition, is the Introduction, *"Patah Eliyahu"* ("Elijah opened"). Its popularity is attested to by the fact that it is printed in numerous *siddurim* (prayer books) of the Sephardic and Hasidic communities, upon whose liturgy Kabbalah has had the most impact.[1]

The Introduction provides an embodiment of the ten *sefirot* or divine attributes, working its way down the divine frame, as it were, coordinating various limbs of the body with their corresponding *sefirot*:

> *Hesed* (Kindness) is the right arm;
> *Gevurah* (Power) is the left arm;
> *Tif'eret* (Splendor) is the torso;
> *Netsah* (Eternity) and *Hod* (Glory) are the two thighs;
> *Yesod* (Foundation) is the end of the torso, the symbol of the sacred covenant;[2]
> *Malkhut* (Kingship) is the mouth, which we refer to as the Oral Torah.
> *Hokhmah* (Wisdom) is the brain...
> *Binah* (Understanding) is the heart...

Keter 'Elyon (Supreme Crown) is the crown of kingship.³

What is otherwise an orderly downward articulation of the limbs, abruptly shifts direction at *Malkhut*, whereupon we jump back up to the mouth. Many a reader has been perplexed by this anomaly.⁴

It is widely held by scholars that the Jewish mystical literature that comes under the rubric of *Shi'ur Komah* (Body of God) has its origins in *Shir ha-Shirim*, Song of Songs.⁵

Song of Songs contains several catalogs in sequence of segments of the male or female body. These catalogs of body parts have come to be known in scholarly studies of the Song by the technical term *wasf*, an Arabic word meaning "description." (*Wasfs* are common in modern Arabic poetry.)⁶

There are four *wasfs* in Song of Songs. Three describe the body of Shulamith (Song of Songs 4:1-5; 6:4-7; 7:1-6); one describes that of Shelomo (Song of Songs 5:10-16). The first three proceed from top down. The fourth works its way up from the feet of Shulamith. (As it begins by calling Shulamith to dance, the focus initially is upon her feet.)

If we pay close attention to the *wasf* of the *dod*, the male lover, we should notice a peculiarity:

"I adjure you, O daughters of Jerusalem, if you find my beloved, what will you tell him? That I am lovesick."

"In what way is your beloved more than another beloved, O fairest among women? In what way is your beloved more than another beloved, that you have adjured us so?"

"My beloved is shining white and ruddy, prominent among ten thousand.

His head is purest gold; his locks are curls, black as the raven.

His eyes are like doves by the brooks of water; bathing in milk, dwelling by a pool.

His cheeks are as a bed of spice, towers of perfumes; his lips are lilies, dripping flowing myrrh.

His arms are rods of gold inset with beryl; his belly polished ivory overlaid with sapphires.

His thighs are pillars of marble, set upon sockets of gold; his look like Lebanon, choice as the cedars.

His mouth (*hiko*) is sweet, and all of him is delight.

This is my beloved and this is my friend, O daughters of Jerusalem."

(Song of Songs 5:8-16)

As one can readily see, the *wasf* proceeds in orderly fashion from the head, down through the arms, the belly and the thighs, to—the mouth? At *"hiko"* (literally, "his palate") the flow chart has abruptly reversed direction.

Bible scholar Robert Alter provides an answer:

> The reversion to the mouth does not really violate the vertical movement of the poem downward because it is a kind of summary at the end: the beloved, having canvassed her lover's beauty from head to foot, returns to the physical site of those kisses that epitomize physical intimacy with him and give her such gratification.[7]

Be that as it may. Whatever the explanation for the reversal of direction, one thing is certain: *Patah Eliyahu* of *Tikkunei Zohar* has patterned itself after the *wasf* of *Shir ha-Shirim*, jumping from the lower portion of the male anatomy to the mouth. And from this mouth, proceeds the (Oral) Torah, in conformity to the Targum's rendition of *"hiko mamtakim"* ("his mouth is sweet"):

Milei morigoi metikan ke-duvsha.
The words of His palate are sweet like honey.[8]

---

[1] *"Patah Eliyahu"* is generally printed in the beginning of the *siddur* before the commencement of the Morning Prayer. An exception is the *siddur* of Rabbi Shneur Zalman of Liadi (known in Lubavitch as the *Siddur 'im DA"H*, or colloquially as the *"Alter Rebbe's Siddur"*) where it precedes the Afternoon Service on the Eve of the Sabbath.

[2] I.e., the phallus.

[3] *Siddur Eitz Chaim: The Complete Artscroll Siddur (Nusach Sefard)*, transl. Rabbi Nosson Scherman (Brooklyn, NY: Mesorah Publications, 1985), pp. 11, 13.

In the Kabbalistic tradition, the *"shalosh rishonot"* (first three *sefirot* of *Keter, Hokhmah* and *Binah*) and the *"sheva' tahtonot"* (seven lower *sefirot* of *Hesed, Gevurah, Tif'eret, Netsah, Hod, Yesod* and *Malkhut*) are treated as two

discrete units. In this study, our focus is strictly upon the *"sheva' tahtonot."*
[4] Rabbi Isaac Hutner, Rosh Yeshivah of Metivta Rabbeinu Chaim Berlin, was forced to conclude that *Tikkunei Zohar* employs *peh* (mouth) in this context as an oblique reference to the lower female anatomy. (Quoted in Rabbi Israel Elijah Weintraub, *Nefesh Eliyahu: Hakdamot u-She'arim* [n.p., 2002], Letter 19 [p. 69].) See Proverbs 30:20: "So is the way of an adulterous woman: She ate, and wiped her *mouth (u-mahatah fihah).*" An extension of this euphemism would be the Mishnaic locution *"ra'uha medaberet"* ("they saw her *speaking*") (*m. Ketubot* 1:8). See the Talmud's explanation of Rav Asi's opinion in *b. Ketubot* 13a. In *y. Ketubot* 1:8 there exists but the single opinion that *"medaberet"* refers to sexual intercourse and that Rabbi (i.e., Rabbi Judah the Prince), editor of the *Mishnah*, employed a euphemism (*"lashon naki"*). (One should also note that the Yerushalmi does not reference the verse in Proverbs. Though the commentaries *Korban ha-'Edah* and *P'nei Moshe*, influenced by the Bavli, invoke that verse, there is no indication that the Yerushalmi is of a like mind.) See also *b. Menahot* 88a and Rashi ad loc., s.v. *peh she-le-matah*.

Though the solution offered is certainly ingenious, it is problematic, to say the least. Taken at face value, it would posit an androgynous body of God. That objection might be overcome by assuming that *Tikkunei Zohar* is imaging the body of *Adam Kadmon* before the mythic *"nesirah"* (splitting) and the emergence of woman as a separate body, a distinct entity apart from man.

See the earlier *Sefer ha-Bahir* (referred to by Nahmanides in his commentary to the Pentateuch as *"Midrash Rabbi Nehunyah ben Hakanah"*):

> The Holy One, blessed be He, has seven holy forms, and they all have [something] corresponding in man, for it says, "In the image of God He created him" [Genesis 1:27]. And these are: the right and left thigh; the right and left hand; the torso, and the *berit* (covenant). All told six.
> But you said, "Seven"?
> It is seven with his wife, as it is written, "And they shall become one flesh" [Genesis 2:24].
> But she was taken from his side (*mi-tsal'otav*), as it is written, "He took one of his sides (*mi-tsal'otav*)" [Genesis 2:21]. Does he have a *tsela'* (side)? Yes, as the Targum translates, *"U-le-tsela' ha-mishkan"* [Exodus 26:20]: *"Ve-li-setar mashkena"* ("And for the side of the Tabernacle").
> (*Sefer ha-Bahir*, Amsterdam 1651, facsimile edition in *The Book Bahir*, ed. Daniel Abrams [Los Angeles: Cherub Press, 1994], p. 281)

The description of the anatomy of the male (two thighs, two hands, torso and "covenant") lines up with that of *Tikkunei Zohar*—with the exception of the "mouth." This is also the reading of the *Bahir* preserved in the *Hashmatot* printed at the conclusion of Rabbi Reuven Margaliyot's edition of *Zohar* I, 264b (chap. 38) and in the *"Hiddushei ha-Bahir"* printed in the Cremona 1558 edition of *Zohar* I, 32a-b (facsimile in Daniel Abram's edition of *Bahir*, p. 246).

For *variae lectiones* (that will not tally with *Tikkunei Zohar's* configuration), see *Sefer ha-Bahir*, Margaliyot edition, par. 172 (p. 75, note 3); and Abrams edition, par. 116 (pp. 200-201, based on Munich manuscript with variants of Vatican ms.). See further Abrams ed., p. 42 (for variants of Moscow mss. and JTSA ms.).

Assuming that Rabbi Hutner is correct in translating *"peh"* in *Tikkunei Zohar* as the feminine orifice, we might say that whereas *Sefer ha-Bahir* imaged *Adam Kadmon* after the splitting of man and woman into two bodies, *Tikkunei Zohar* addressed the original androgynous configuration.

Putting that grievance aside, we would still be hard-pressed to account for the correlation of this orifice (the *peh she-le-matah*, as opposed to the *peh she-le-ma'alah*) with the Oral Law (*Torah she-be-'al peh*). That, it seems to me, is a more basic objection.

Par contre, Rabbi Weintraub (*Nefesh Eliyahu*, Letters, pp. 70-71) upheld the simple understanding that the mouth referred to in *Tikkunei Zohar* is in the head, not the lower extremity. He furthermore endorsed the explanation of Rabbi Shneur Zalman of Liadi, *Torah 'Or* (Brooklyn: Kehot, 1972), *Ki Tissa*, 111c-d, based on the verse in Ecclesiastes 8:4: *"devar melekh shilton"* ("the king's word [is] power"). See *Nefesh Eliyahu*, Letters, pp. 69, 71.

[5] Scholem writes:

> The fragment in question [i.e., *Shi'ur Komah*], of which several different texts are extant, describes the "body" of the Creator, in close analogy to the description of the body of the beloved one in the fifth chapter of the "Song of Solomon," giving enormous figures for the length of each organ.
> (Gershom G. Scholem, *Major Trends in Jewish Mysticism* [New York: Schocken Books, 1971], pp. 63-64)

See further Gershom Scholem, *On the Mystical Shape of the Godhead* (New York: Schocken Books, 1991), pp. 22-23, 30-33; idem, *Origins of the Kabbalah* (Princeton University Press, 1990), pp. 20-21; idem, *Jewish Gnosticism, Merkabah Mysticism and Talmudic Tradition* (New York, 1965), pp. 38-40; Saul Lieberman, *Midreshei Teiman* (Jerusalem, 1940), pp. 13-17; idem, "Mishnat Shir ha-Shirim," Appendix D to Scholem, *Jewish Gnosticism, Merkabah Mysticism and Talmudic Tradition*, pp. 118-126; Arthur Green, "The Song of Songs in Early Jewish Mysticism," in *The Song of Songs: Modern Critical Interpretations*, ed. Harold Bloom (New York: Chelsea House Publishers, 1988), pp. 143-145.

See however Boyarin's refutation of his teacher Lieberman; Daniel Boyarin, "Two Introductions to the Midrash on the Song of Songs" (Hebrew), *Tarbiz* 56:4 (1987), pp. 492-500.

[6] See Marcia Falk, "The *Wasf*," in *The Song of Songs: Modern Critical Interpretations*, 67ff.

[7] *The Hebrew Bible*, vol. 3: The Writings/*Ketuvim*, transl. with commentary, Robert Alter (New York: W.W. Norton & Company, 2019), p. 605, n. 16.

[8] Song of Songs 5:16.

The Anonymous Author of *Tikkunei Zohar* and *Ra'ya Mehemna*: An Antinomian or a Radical Maimonidean?

Today, it is an accepted fact in scholarly circles that *Tikkunei Zohar* and *Ra'ya Mehemna* form a single unit that postdates the main body of *Zohar*.[1] More than one reader has been scandalized by statements in *Tikkunei Zohar* and *Ra'ya Mehemna* likening the *Mishnah* to a *shifhah* or maidservant.[2] Predictably, in response, there grew an apologetic literature that attempts to justify how such shocking statements are compatible with normative Halakhah.[3]

One cannot rule out altogether the assertion by various secular historians that these pejorative statements betray an antinomian streak,[4] though to be certain, such statements of *Tikkunei Zohar* and *Ra'ya Mehemna* are not situated in the present but deferred to the future. With this proviso, they are no more "antinomian" than the statement of Rav Yosef in the Talmud: "*Mitsvot* (commandments) are nullified in the future."[5]

I wish to present a hitherto unexplored possibility. It seems likely that the anonymous author of *Tikkunei Zohar* and *Ra'ya Mehemna* (which surfaced in Spain in the first decades of the fourteenth century)[6] was not so much an antinomian as a radical Maimonidean. It is in this light that we should understand negative statements issuing from the author regarding the study of *Mishnah* or those comparing the various Talmudic exercises and mental gymnastics to the backbreaking labor to which the Children of Israel were subjected in Egyptian exile.[7] These do not spring from an anti-halakhic mindset but rather from taking at face value Maimonides' syllabus as laid out in his introduction to *Mishneh Torah*:

> Hence, I have entitled this work *Mishneh Torah* (Review of the Law), for the reason that a person, who first reads the Written Law and then this [compilation], will know from it the whole of the Oral Law, *without having need to read any other book between them* [italics mine—BN].

We should be asking ourselves: Are there any historical grounds to assert that in Spain in the early 1300s there were halakhic Jews who openly—we should add, brazenly—promulgated the Maimonidean curriculum to the exclusion of Talmudic studies and the concomitant exercise of *pilpul*?

I offer the words of Joseph Ibn Kaspi:

> Therefore my rabbis, listen to me and God will listen to you! I see that it is the intention of those among you who engage in *Gemara*, novellae and opinions (*shitot*),[8] to know proofs for the practical commandments, for you are not satisfied with the tradition from *Mishneh Torah* composed by Rabbeinu Moshe [i.e., Maimonides], though he said: *"And one shall have no need of any other book between them* [Italics mine—BN]."

Here is an example. *Ha-Rav ha-Moreh* [i.e., Maimonides] wrote in his laws: "A *sukkah* that is higher than twenty *ammah* is invalid."⁹ Yet you despair and are without comfort until you know whether the reason is because "the eye does not rest upon it," or because "one is not sitting in the shade of the *sekhakh* (overhead boughs) but of the walls," or because "the *sukkah* must be a temporary dwelling," as written in the *Gemara*.¹⁰ Even this will not satisfy the very punctilious (*mehadrin min ha-mehadrin*) until they have added problems and opinions (*shitot*)¹¹: "If you should say," "one may say," etc.

Truly, I admit that this is good, but why is the knowledge of proofs an obligation in regard to practical commandments, while not [even] an option,¹² but an outright prohibition when it comes to commandments of the heart? What sin has been committed by these four commandments of the heart (that I mentioned) that you do not treat them in the same manner but are satisfied by a weak tradition of few words, wanting comprehension?¹³

Who was Joseph Ibn Kaspi? Born either in Arles, Provence or Argentière, Languedoc,¹⁴ around the year 1280, he passed in 1345 on the island of Majorca. His was a peripatetic life. The first period of his life was spent in the south of France. Later he gravitated to Barcelona, where his married son, David, resided. At approximately age thirty-five he travelled to Egypt for several months,¹⁵ hoping to acquire there the intellectual legacy of Maimonides from the

Master's fourth and fifth generation descendants but was sorely disappointed in this respect. He even entertained the thought of traveling to Fez, Morocco in search of wisdom,[16] but that particular journey never materialized.

Ibn Kaspi's reputation is that of an ultra-rationalist. His naturalistic explanations of events in the Bible far exceed even those of Maimonides; for that reason his opinions were marginalized. Though there is an abundance of manuscripts, it was only in the nineteenth century that Ibn Kaspi's works were published from manuscript. (A few still remain in manuscript.)[17] To this day, his interpretations have yet to "mainstream."

My juxtaposing the Maimonidean enthusiast Joseph ibn Kaspi to the anonymous author of the kabbalistic works known as *Ra'ya Mehemna* and *Tikkunei Zohar* may strike the reader of this *essai* as bizarre. Besides their contemporaneity, what basis is there for this juxtaposition?

Geographically, there are certainly grounds for relating the two authors to one another. Though separated by the Pyrenees, there was much traffic, intellectual and otherwise between Provence and Northern Spain. Some of the greatest families of Provencal scholars originated in Spain: the Kimhis, Joseph and his son David, who excelled as grammarians and Bible exegetes; and the Tibbonides, Judah and his son Samuel, who were the premier translators of classic philosophic works from Judeo-Arabic to Hebrew. And the traffic was two-way. Prominent Provencal families wended their way to Sefarad. The halakhist Rabbi Zerahyah Halevi (*"Ba'al ha-Ma'or"*), a native of Gerona, established his career in Narbonne, only to return to Gerona at the end of his days. (His great-grandson was the Talmudist Rabbi Aharon Halevi of Barcelona.)[18] Ibn Kaspi is an example of a Provencal scholar who relocated to Catalonia: Barcelona, and eventually, the Balearic isle of Majorca. Thus, there could easily have been a sharing of ideas between southern France and northern Spain.[19]

In terms of mindset, the border between rationalist philosophy and kabbalah was especially porous at this time. Whoever authored *Ra'ya Mehemna* and *Tikkunei Zohar*, carried with him much Maimonidean baggage. Linguistically, it is apparent to any student of the *Ra'ya Mehemna* and *Tikkunim* that they are rife with the philosophic jargon made popular by the Tibbonides' translations from Judeo-Arabic.[20] And let us not forget that the very backbone of *Ra'ya Mehemna* is an enumeration of the commandments à la Maimonides' *Sefer ha-Mitsvot*. (Rabbi Reuven Margaliyot isolated these commandments and presented them in orderly fashion in the introduction to his edition of the *Zohar*.)

When we put it all together it makes perfect sense. As shocking as some of its bold statements may be, the literary oeuvre of *Ra'ya Mehemna* and *Tikkunei Zohar* cannot be construed as issuing from the mind of an antinomian. An antinomian would not go to the bother of constructing a Book of Commandments after a fashion. Rather, I maintain that the downgrading of the study of Talmud in general, and *Mishnah* in particular, should be attributed to a radical adoption of Maimonides' curriculum of studies, whereby his halakhic magnum opus *Mishneh Torah* has superseded the study of *Mishnah* and *Gemara*.

In this respect, Maimonides' devotees in Provence and Spain ventured beyond the Master himself. Maimonides penned a convincing letter to Rabbi Pinhas, the *Dayyan* (Justice) of Alexandria,[21] that regardless of what he wrote in the introduction to *Mishneh Torah*, the traditional study of the Talmudic tractates (albeit as summarized in Alfasi's *Halakhot*) continues unabated in his *beit midrash*.[22] The curriculum that Maimonides once proposed remained an abstraction. It seems that Egyptian Jewry was not overly receptive to this innovation. Only well over a century later, did this great intellectual experiment of Maimonides, *Mishneh Torah*, a hivemind of *halakhah*,[23] designed to replace the "dialectics of Abayye and Rava," find foot soldiers in the likes of Ibn Kaspi and the anonymous author of *Ra'ya Mehemna* and *Tikkunei Zohar*. They launched their campaign from the soil of Provence and Spain.

Our thesis does not ride on the reputation of Joseph ibn Kaspi. Ibn Kaspi's statement is perhaps the most outspoken and provocative call for adoption of Maimonides' *Mishneh Torah* as a way of bypassing Talmudic studies, yet there are other testimonies (from the least expected quarter) that the exclusive study of *Mishneh Torah* was starting to gain traction in medieval Spain.

The great halakhist Rabbi Asher ben Yehiel (ROSh) emigrated from Germany to Spain at the turn of the fourteenth century and eventually emerged as the Rabbi of Toledo, Castile, where he left his stamp on the shape of Castilian *Halakhah*.[24] Evidently, Rabbi

Antinomian or Radical Maimonidean?

Asher had cause to fulminate against authorities who decided questions of practical *Halakhah* based solely on the rulings of *Mishneh Torah* without recourse to Talmud.

Rabbi Asher writes:

> I heard from a great man in Barcelona who was eminently familiar with three orders [of the Talmud, i.e., *Mo'ed*, *Nashim* and *Nezikin*]. He said: "I am amazed at people who have not studied *Gemara* and adjudicate based on their reading in the books of Maimonides, of blessed memory, believing that they understand them. I know myself, when it comes to the three orders that I studied, I am able to understand when I read Maimonides' books. However, his books that are based on *Kodashim* and *Zera'im*—I do not understand at all. And I know that it is that way for them regarding all his books!"[25]

※※※

Rabbi Yahya Kafah (1850-1931) was not wide of the mark when he asserted that those statements in Zoharic literature that undercut the Talmud (comprised of *Mishnah* and *Gemara*) were designed to enhance the prestige of the Kabbalah.[26] (By the same token, one may safely say that Ibn Kaspi's desire to streamline the study of *Halakhah*, stemmed from his valorization of Philosophy.)

Logically, our next question should be: What was Maimonides' own stake in proposing that his compendium *Mishneh Torah* take the place of protracted Talmudic studies? Maimonides provides a simple answer to this question in his introduction to *Mishneh Torah*:

> At this time, severe vicissitudes prevail, and all feel the pressure of hard times. The wisdom of our wise men has disappeared; the understanding of our prudent men is hidden. Hence, the commentaries of the Geonim and their compilations of laws and responses, which they took care to make clear, have in our times become hard to understand so that only a few individuals properly comprehend them. Needless to add that such is the case in regard to the Talmud itself—the Babylonian as well as the Palestinian—the *Sifra*, the *Sifre* and the *Tosefta*, all of which works require a broad mind, a wise soul and lengthy time, and then one can know from them the correct practice as to what is forbidden or permitted, and the other rules of the Torah.
>
> On these grounds, I, Moses the son of Rabbi Maimon the Sefardi, bestirred myself....[27]

While perhaps not the ideal curriculum, the exigencies of the time demanded the production of a bold new work on the order of *Mishneh Torah* that would preserve the practice of *Halakhah* for the masses ill-equipped to make their way through the labyrinthine discussions of the Talmud or even the decisions of the Gaonica (originally intended to clarify the canons of Jewish Law).

Antinomian or Radical Maimonidean?

But was there perhaps another purpose of *Mishneh Torah* that Maimonides kept to himself and was not willing to divulge in writing? In *Hilkhot Talmud Torah* (Laws of the Study of Torah), Maimonides would proceed to sketch the traditional trivium of *Mikra* (Bible), *Mishnah* and *Talmud*, [28]such that *Pardes* (the esoteric teachings of Judaism) comes under the rubric of *"Talmud"*[29]; and that furthermore, the mature scholar who has covered the requisite literature and is thus no longer bound by the daily trivium, "will devote all his days exclusively to *Talmud*, according to the breadth of his mind and the composure of his intellect."[30]

Was the condensing of Talmud into *Mishneh Torah* Maimonides' master plan to free time for the study of *Pardes* or esoterica? Should that prove true, then Ibn Kaspi's interest,[31] and *mutatis mutandis* that of the *Tikkunei Zohar* and *Ra'ya Mehemna*, was not so very different from that of *ha-Rav ha-Moreh*.[32]

---

[1] This fact was recognized two and a half centuries ago by the discerning eye of Rabbi Jacob Emden. See Emden's *Mitpahat Sefarim*, Altona 1768, Part 1, chap. 3 (6b); chaps. 6-7 (16b-17b); Lvov 1870, pp. 12, 37-39.

 Whereas *Zohar* itself has come to be associated with the name of Rabbi Moses de Leon, no single name surfaces in regard to *Tikkunei Zohar* and *Ra'ya Mehemna* (though there are some who would attribute the latter to a yet unidentified disciple of De Leon). Moshe Idel toyed with the idea that Rabbi Menahem Recanati authored *Tikkunei Zohar* and *Ra'ya Mehemna* but found this hypothesis untenable. See Moshe Idel, *R. Menahem Recanati ha-Mekubal*, vol. 1 (Jerusalem and Tel-Aviv: Schocken, 1998), pp. 108-110.

 It should be mentioned in passing that even in regard to the authorship of the *Zohar* there has been a sea change in scholarly thinking. Unlike Scholem, who was convinced that the single author of the *Zohar* was Rabbi Moses de Leon, current thinking (spearheaded by Yehuda Liebes) rejects this notion of single authorship and assumes the *Zohar* to be a collaborative or composite work on the part of a mystic fraternity or *haburah*.

[2] See *Zohar* I, 27b. This is actually a segment of *Tikkunei Zohar* that the Italian

printers in 1558 mistakenly embedded in *Zohar*. See Editor Daniel Matt's note to the Pritzker edition of the *Zohar*, vol. 1 (Stanford, California: Stanford University Press, 2004), p. 170, note 499. See also the Introduction to *Tikkunei Zohar* (Vilna, 1867), 15b, and gloss of the Vilna Gaon, s.v. *shalta shifhah*.

And see the *Tikkunim* appended to *Tikkunei Zohar* (Margaliyot ed.), tikkun 9 (147a).

By the same token, there are passages where the *Mishnah* is related to Metatron, the *"'eved"* (male servant). See e.g. *Ra'ya Mehemna* in *Zohar* III, 29b; and *The Hebrew Writings of the Author of* Tiqqunei Zohar *and* Ra'aya Mehemna (Hebrew), ed. Efraim Gottlieb (Jerusalem: The Israel Academy of Sciences and Humanities, 2003), p. 1, line 3.

Moshe Idel has demonstrated that this motif whereby the *Mishnah* is juxtaposed to Metatron is to be found in the obscure work of Rabbi Abraham Esquira, *Yesod 'Olam* (Ms. Moscow, *Günzburg* 607, 80a-b). See Idel's introduction to *The Hebrew Writings of the Author of* Tiqqunei Zohar *and* Ra'aya Mehemna, pp. 23-24, 27-28. Inter alia, Esquira's text makes mention of "six hundred orders of *Mishnah*." This is a reference to *b. Hagigah* 14a. See Rashi there, s.v. *shesh me'ot sidrei Mishnah*. Thus, p. 23, n. 76 of Idel's introduction is in need of correction. By the same token, Esquira's "seven hundred orders of confusion" (*"shesh me'ot sidrei bilbulim"*) is a parody of the "seven hundred orders of *Mishnah*" in *b. Hagigah* 14a. See Idel, ibid. p. 28, n. 105. (Concerning the seven hundred orders of *Mishnah*, see Rabbi Reuven Margaliyot, *Shem 'Olam* [Jerusalem: Mossad Harav Kook, 1989], Introduction, p. 35; and idem, *Yesod ha-Mishnah va-'Arikhatah* [Lwów, 1933], p. 29.)

Concerning the juxtaposition of the six-lettered Metatron, the servant, to the six days of the work week, see the Vilna Gaon's gloss to *Tikkunei Zohar* (Vilna, 1867), *tikkun* 18 (33b), s.v. *be-gin de-Metatron*. There is precedent in a *Teshuvat ha-Ge'onim* (Gaonic responsum) for restricting the activity of the angelic realm to the six days of the week and reserving the seventh Sabbath day for Israel's sphere of influence. See *Tosafot, Sanhedrin* 37b, s.v. *mi-kenaf ha-'arets zemirot shama'nu*; and Rabbi Reuven Margaliyot, *Margaliyot ha-Yam* ad locum, and idem, *Nitsutsei Zohar* to *Ra'ya Mehemna* in *Zohar* III, 93a, n. 2.

Later, in sixteenth-century Safed, Rabbi Isaac Luria advised reserving the Sabbath day for the exclusive study of Kabbalah ("as was the custom of the early ones"), while relegating the study of *Halakhah* to the six work days. This is hinted to in the two verses, *"Hishtahavu la-Hashem be-hadrat kodesh"* (whose initials when reversed form the word "Kabbalah") (Psalms 96:9; 1 Chronicles 16:29) and *"Hari'u la-Hashem kol ha-'arets"* (initials "Halakhah") (Psalms 98:4; 100:1). See Rabbi Hayyim Vital, *Peri 'Ets Hayyim* (Dubrovna, 1804), *Sha'ar ha-Shabbat*, chap. 21 (103c); Rabbi Jacob Tsemah, *Nagid u-Metsaveh* (Lublin, 1881), 25b. And see *Peri 'Ets Hayyim, Sha'ar Hanhagat ha-Limmud*, s.v. *kavvanat keri'at ha-Mishnah* (85a): "Know that the *Mishnah* is Metatron in *Yetsirah*..."

In the *Ra'ya Mehemna* in *Zohar* III, 279b, the *Mishnah* is referred to as the *"shifhah...*the female of the *'eved, na'ar* ("lad"). "*Na'ar*" or "lad" is yet another epithet for Metatron; see *b. Yevamot* 16b (based on Psalms 37:25), and *Tosafot* ad loc., s.v. *pasuk zeh sar ha-'olam amaro*. Just as Metatron is referred to as *"'eved,"* "for his name is like that of his Master" (*b. Sanhedrin* 38b). Both *Metatron* and *Shaddai* have the numerical value of 314. (In *Ra'ya Mehemna* in

Zohar III, 82b it is spelled out that "Metatron is a good servant, a faithful servant to his Master.")

In *Ra'ya Mehemna*, in *Zohar* III, 276a, three of the most difficult tractates of the *Mishnah*, *'Eruvin, Niddah and Yevamot*, are singled out for derision, as they are assigned the acronym *'Ani* (poor man). The Vilna Gaon points out that the derogation of the rabbis, students of the *Mishnah*, is not absolute, but only relative to the *"ba'alei kabbalah"* ("masters of the Kabbalah"). See *Yahel 'Or*, ed. Naftali Hertz Halevi (Vilna, 1882), *Tetsei*, 276a, s.v. *ve-i teima*.

Earlier in that passage *(Zohar* 275b) we have the underhanded compliment, *"Hakham Mufle Ve-Rav Rabbanan"* ("Outstanding Sage and Rabbi of Rabbis"), whose initials spell the word *"hamor"* (jackass). (This cynical remark found its way into the modern mystery novel by Richard Zimler, *The Last Kabbalist of Lisbon* [Woodstock, NY: The Overlook Press, 1998], p. 44.)

One who found absolutely outrageous the labeling of the *Mishnah* as a *"shifhah,"* was the Chief Rabbi of Sana'a, Yemen, Rabbi Yahya ben Shelomo (Sliman) Kafah (1850-1931). See his *'Amal u-Re'ut Ru'ah va-Haramot u-Teshuvatam* (Tel-Aviv, 1914; limited facsimile edition Jerusalem 1976), p. 12. Available at hebrewbooks.org.

'Amal u-Re'ut Ru'ah va-Haramot u-Teshuvatam is Rabbi Kafah's rejoinder to the bans placed upon him by the various *batei din* (courts) of Jerusalem—Ashkenazic, Hasidic and Sefardic. It struck Rabbi Kafah as highly ironic that he, a staunch defender of Talmudic Judaism, was placed under the ban, while the *Zohar*, with its numerous derisions of Talmud and its students, was upheld and, what is more, sanctified. Ibid. p. 14.

The constraints of space do not allow us to explore the controversy regarding the *Zohar* that erupted in Yemen in the early part of the twentieth century between Rabbi Kafah and his disciples, the self-styled *Darda'im*, on the one hand, and their opponents, to whom they referred as *'Ikkeshim*. (The first label is based on the Midrashic pun on Darda' [1 Kings 5:11] as *Dor De'ah*, "a generation of knowledge"; the second comes from Deuteronomy 32:5, *"dor 'ikkesh u-fetaltol,"* "a perverse and twisted generation.") At the instigation of his critics, Rabbi Kafah was jailed on more than one occasion by the Muslim authorities. (Rabbi Kafah alludes to this in *'Amal u-Re'ut Ru'ah va-Haramot u-Teshuvatam*, p. 14.)

The man who acted as a peacemaker between the warring factions was none other than Rabbi Abraham Isaac Hakohen Kook. While upholding Rabbi Kafah's status as an unusual Torah scholar, Rabbi Kook conveyed to him that he had erred in taking literally passages that were intended to be understood metaphorically. See *Iggerot ha-RAYaH*, vol. 2, ed. RZYH Kook (Jerusalem: Mossad Harav Kook 1961), no. 626 (pp. 247-248); *Haskamot ha-RAYaH*, ed. Y.M. Yismah and B.Z Kahana (Jerusalem, 1988), no. 41 (pp. 46-47); *Ma'amrei ha-RAYaH*, vol. 2, ed. Rabbi Elisha Aviner (Langenauer) (Jerusalem, 1984), pp. 518-521. An incomplete variant of the letter in *Haskamot ha-RAYaH* was published by Rabbi Moshe Zuriel, *Otserot ha-Rayah*, vol. 1 (Rishon LeZion, 2002), no. 76 (p. 447). See further Rabbi Tsevi Yehudah Hakohen Kook, *Li-Sheloshah be-Ellul* I (Jerusalem, 1938; photo offset Jerusalem, 1978), par. 107 (p. 46).

For Rav Kook's involvement with the Yemenite community and his facilitating their *'aliyah* at the beginning of the twentieth century, see ibid. par. 42

(p. 21); and recently Ben Zion Rosenfeld, *"Yahaso shel ha-RAYaH Kook le-Hakhmei ha-Mizrah bi-Tekufat Yaffo 5664-5674 (1904-1914)"* ["HaRav Avraham Isaac HaCohen Kook and his Attitude Regarding the Sephardi Sages During His Stay in Jaffa 5664–5674 (1904–1914)"], *Libi ba-Mizrah (My Heart Is in the East)* 1(2019), pp. 287-290.

3 See Rabbi Hayyim Vital, introduction to *Sha'ar ha-Hakdamot* (printed as an introduction to the standard editions of *'Ets Hayyim*); Rabbi Shneur Zalman of Liadi, *Iggeret ha-Kodesh* (fourth section of *Tanya*), chap. 26 (especially 143a). And see Rabbi Dov Baer Shneuri, *Be'urei ha-Zohar* (Brooklyn, NY: Kehot, 2015), *Bereshit* (to *Zohar* I, 27b), 5a-8d.

4 Heinrich Graetz, *History of the Jews*, cited in Gershom G. Scholem, "The Meaning of the Torah in Jewish Mysticism," in idem, *On the Kabbalah and Its Symbolism* (New York: Schocken Books, 1970), p. 70, n. 1.

5 *b. Niddah* 61b.

Contra Graetz, Scholem, referring to "the ambiguity of certain statements about the hierarchical order of the Bible, the *Mishnah*, the Talmud, and the Kabbalah, which are frequent in the *Ra'ya Mehemna* and the *Tikkunim*, and which have baffled not a few readers of these texts," states categorically: "It would be a mistake to term these passages antinomistic or anti-Talmudic" (op. cit., p. 70). Rather, to describe the peculiar posture of the *Ra'ya Mehemna* and the *Tikkunim*, Scholem coins the term "utopian antinomianism" or "antinomian utopia" (op. cit., pp. 80, 82).

Other secular scholars who objected to Graetz's judgment concerning the controversial passages in the *Zohar* (or to be more precise, *Tikkunei Zohar*) were Bernfeld and Zinberg. See Heinrich Graetz, *Geschichte der Juden*, 7, *Beilage* 12; Shim'on Bernfeld, *Da'at Elohim*, Part 1 (Warsaw, 1897), pp. 396-397, note 1; Israel Zinberg, *A History of Jewish Literature*, vol. 3, transl. Bernard Martin (Cleveland: The Press of Case Western Reserve University, 1973), pp. 55-56.

See further Efraim Gottlieb, *Mehkarim be-Sifrut ha-Kabbalah*, ed. Joseph Hecker (Tel-Aviv, 1976), pp. 545-550; and Moshe Idel, *R' Menahem Recanati ha-Mekubal*, p. 110.

6 Scholem and Idel would date *Tikkunei Zohar* and *Ra'ya Mehemna* as early as the end of the thirteenth century (bringing the work in contact with Rabbi Moses de Leon). See Idel's introduction to *The Hebrew Writings of the Author of* Tiqqunei Zohar *and* Ra'aya Mehemna, pp. 10, 25-26, 29. Tishby established the years 1312-1313 as the *terminus ad quem* for the composition of *Tikkunei Zohar* based on its Messianic expectations for those years. Cited in Idel, ibid. p. 10, n. 7. See also p. 23. Idel, relying on Liebes, would make the *terminus ad quem* a year earlier, 1311. (Ibid.)

7 See *Zohar* I, 27a:

> They embittered their lives with hard labor (*'avodah kashah*)—with *kushya* (difficulty);
> with mortar (*homer*)—with *kal ve-homer* (*a fortiori*);
> and with bricks (*levenim*)—with *libbun hilkheta* (clarification of the law); and with all [manner of] labor in the field—this is *Beraita;*
> all their labor—this is *Mishnah*.

Though mistakenly embedded by the Italian printers back in 1558 in the text of the *Zohar*, this is actually a segment from the later work *Tikkunei Zohar*. See above note 2.

This same anachronistic interpretation of the verse in Exodus 1:14 is found (with slight variations) in the *Ra'ya Mehemna*, again embedded in *Zohar* III, 153a, 229b (though in this case explicitly identified as *Ra'ya Mehemna*). See also *Tikkunei Zohar, tikkun* 21 (Margaliyot ed., 44a); the additional *Tikkunim* appended to *Tikkunei Zohar, tikkun* 9 (147a); and the *Tikkunim* appended to *Zohar Hadash* (Margaliyot ed.), 97d (where the end of the verse is interpreted, *"be-pharekh—da pirkha"*), 98b, 99b.

And see now, *The Hebrew Writings of the Author of* Tiqqunei Zohar *and* Ra'aya Mehemna (Hebrew), ed. Efraim Gottlieb and Moshe Idel (Jerusalem: The Israel Academy of Sciences and Humanities, 2003), pp. 39-40.

This degradation of Talmudic hermeneutic was duly noted by Rabbi Kafah (see above note 2). Kafah believed that the not so hidden agenda of the anonymous writer was to promote the study of Kabbalah at the expense of the study of Talmud. See *'Amal u-Re'ut Ru'ah va-Haramot u-Teshuvatam*, p. 12: "The entire purpose of the author of the *Zohar* is to cause the *Mishnah* and the Talmud to be forgotten from Israel, to stop up the mouth of the well of living waters from which flow the ways of the Oral Law, and have them occupy themselves with his new Torah."

[8] The primary meaning of the Hebrew word *shitah* is a "line"; hence, a line of thought. For its derivative usage in medieval rabbinical literature, see Mordechai Breuer, *'Ohalei Torah* (Jerusalem: Shazar Center, 2004), pp. 109, 510; Ya'akov Spiegel, *'Ammudim be-Toledot ha-Sefer ha-'Ivri*, vol. 2 (Ramat Gan: Bar Ilan, 2005), p. 442; and lately, Hayyim Eliezer Ashkenazi, "Heker ve-'Iyun be-Sifrei Rishonim (4)," *Yeshurun*, vol. 40 (Nisan 5779), p. 930, n. 7.

In the London Beth Din Ms. 40 (designated in the microfilm collection of the National Library of Israel, F4708), f.30, this word reads *"mishnayot,"* rather than *shitot*, but the reading is unlikely, to say the least. Cf. below n. 11.

[9] Maimonides, *MT, Hil. Sukkah* 4:1.

[10] The three opinions are found in *b. Sukkah* 2a.

[11] In the London Beth Din manuscript, for *"shitot"* there occurs the grotesquerie *"shtuyot"* (foolishness).

[12] The London Beth Din manuscript has the superior reading, *"<u>eino</u> reshut o makom patur."*

[13] Joseph ben Abba Mari ibn Kaspi, *Sefer ha-Mussar/Yoreh De'ah*, chap. 15.

The "four commandments of the heart" are: belief in God; belief in His unity; love of God; and fear of God.

Ibn Kaspi's *Sefer ha-Mussar* was published in a couple of collections: Eliezer Ashkenazi of Tunis' *Ta'am Zekenim* (Frankfurt am Main, 1854); and Isaac Last's *'Asarah Klei Kesef* (Pressburg, 1903). Our particular chapter (15) appeared earlier in the introduction to Ibn Kaspi's *'Ammudei Kesef u-Maskiyot Kesef*, ed. Salomo Werbluner (Frankfurt am Main, 1848), p. xv. In *Ta'am Zekenim* our quote appears on 53a; in *'Asarah Klei Kesef* on p. 70.

Sefer ha-Mussar was written for Ibn Kaspi's twelve year old son, Shelomo, residing in Tarascon (Provence). According to the colophon, it was completed in 1332 in Valencia (Catalonia).

[14] Moshe Kahan is of the opinion that Joseph himself was born in Arles, and that it was his ancestors who hailed from Argentière (hence the Hebrew surname

Kaspi). See M. Kahan, "Joseph ibn Kaspi—From Arles to Majorca," *Iberia Judaica* VIII (2016), pp. 181-192.

[15] Kahan dates the journey between the years 1313-1315, and writes that Ibn Kaspi stayed in Egypt for about five months. Op. cit. p. 182.

In *Mishneh Kesef* I, ed. Isaac Last (Pressburg, 1905; photo offset Jerusalem, 1970), chap. 14 (pp. 18-19), Ibn Kaspi writes that about two years ago, at approximately age thirty-five, he went down to Egypt. The colophon of the book (p. 168) is datelined Arles, 1317, which would mean that the Egyptian expedition took place about the year 1315.

In *Sefer ha-Mussar*, which according to the colophon was completed in Valencia in 1332, we receive a slightly different picture. In the introduction, Ibn Kaspi writes that twenty years previous he wandered to Egypt; the total trip, from beginning to end, lasted five months. If we take him at his word, the trip to Egypt was in 1312. What is clear is that the actual sojourn in Egypt was less than five months.

[16] Introduction to *Sefer ha-Mussar*. In chap. 15, Ibn Kaspi spells out his fascination with Fez: "The Jews find repulsive and abandon today the *Guide*...the Christians respect and exalt it, and have translated it [to Latin]. All the more so the Ishmaelites; *in Fez* [italics mine—BN] and other lands, they established study-houses to learn the *Guide* from the mouth of Jewish scribes."

[17] See the exhaustive bibliography in the introduction to Joseph Ibn Kaspi, *Shulhan Kesef*, ed. Hannah Kasher (Jerusalem: Ben-Zvi Institute, 1996).

[18] See Israel Ta-Shma, *Rabbi Zerahyah Halevi (Ba'al ha-Ma'or) u-B'nei Hugo* (Jerusalem: Mossad Harav Kook, 1992), pp. 2, 16; Hayyim Eliezer Ashkenazi, "Heker ve-'Iyun be-Sifrei Rishonim (4)," p. 933, n. 17.

[19] Though scholars assume a Castilian—rather than a Catalonian—provenance for *Tikkunei Zohar* and *Ra'ya Mehemna*, I do not see that as a major obstacle. Surely, the main flow of traffic was between Provence in the south of France and Catalonia in the north of Spain, but for Jews, *Sefarad* was an overarching unity, no matter the local kingdoms into which it was fragmented. Thus, in 1305, the Rabbi of Barcelona, Catalonia, Rabbi Solomon ben Abraham ibn Adret (RaShBA) was able to place a newly arrived German émigré, Rabbi Asher ben Yehiel (ROSh) in the rabbinate of Toledo, Castile. (See Avraham Hayyim Freimann, *Ha-Rosh ve-Tse'etsa'av*, transl. Menahem Eldar [Jerusalem: Mossad Harav Kook, 1986], pp. 28-29.)

Sometimes, within a single family one finds both strands of Kabbalah, Castilian and Catalonian. Isaac ibn Sahula, native of Guadalajara, Castile, author of the bestiary *Meshal ha-Kadmoni* (1281), as well as a kabbalistic commentary to Song of Songs, was a disciple of Rabbi Moses of Burgos, as well as an assumed associate of Rabbi Moses de Leon. (The first reference to the *Midrash ha-Ne'elam*, an early stratum of the Zoharic literature, is found in Ibn Sahula's *Meshal ha-Kadmoni*.) His brother, Meir ibn Sahula, on the other hand, prided himself on his Catalonian and Provencal pedigree, being a disciple of "Rabbi Joshua ibn Shu'aib and of Rabbi Solomon ben Abraham ibn Adret (RaShBA), who received from Nahmanides, who in turn received from Rabbi Isaac the Blind, son of Rabad of Posquières, who in turn received from Elijah the Prophet." So writes Meir ibn Sahula at the conclusion to his commentary on the *Bahir*, "'Or ha-Ganuz."

(Yehuda Liebes speculated that the especially acerbic remarks that pre-

Antinomian or Radical Maimonidean?

cede this peroration are directed against recent developments in Castilian Kabbalah, namely the *Zohar*. See Y. Liebes, *Studies in the Zohar* [Albany: State University of New York Press, 1993], pp. 168-169, n. 50. However, in all fairness, the description of those "who expound books and books of the nations, and transcribe therein their gods, and call them 'Secrets of the Torah' [*Sitrei Torah*]," sounds more like an attack on Maimonides and his followers who construe Aristotelian philosophy as *Sitrei Torah*, than an assault upon the *Zohar*. At the end of his lengthy footnote, Liebes conceded this distinct possibility.)

Thus, the division of Spanish Kabbalah into discrete units of Castilian versus Catalonian traditions need not prejudice us against the possibility of penetrations and influences that defy this dyadic model. One needs to complexify the general picture of Spanish Kabbalah in order to appreciate the multiplicity of forces at work. Binaries are helpful as historic guidelines but they can never do justice to the complexity of lived reality.

※※

It has been brought to my attention that there are scholars who argue that Nahmanides, a Catalonian, did not view himself as a Sefaradi. Their assertion is based on the fact that Nahmanides in his commentaries to the Talmud refers to Maimonides as "Rabbi Moshe ha-Sefaradi." From this, they infer that Nahmanides himself did not regard himself as Sefaradi. These scholars would do well to read the epistle that Nahmanides wrote to his countrymen at the height of the Maimonidean controversy. First, he addresses them generically as *"Darei Yerushalayim asher bi-Sefarad"* ("dwellers of Jerusalem who are in Sefarad"), adapted from the verse in Obadiah 1:20. In the next line, he breaks them down into *"Nesi'ei Aragon, 'atsilei Navarra ve-sarei Castilia"* ("Princes of Aragon, nobles of Navarre and ministers of Castile"). Nahmanides' own Catalonia was under Aragonese rule at that time. See C.B. Chavel, *Kitvei Rabbeinu Moshe ben Nahman*, vol. 1 (Jerusalem: Mossad Harav Kook, 1968), Epistle 1, p. 331.

[20] Tishby collected some of these Tibbonide neologisms, starting with *"nefesh ha-sikhlit"* or "intellectual soul" (*Ra'ya Mehemna* in *Zohar* III, 29b). See Isaiah Tishby, *Mishnat ha-Zohar*, vol. 1, 2nd printing with corrections (Jerusalem: Mossad Bialik, 1949), pp. 77-78.

One can well appreciate how the Chief Rabbi of Sana'a, Yemen, Yahya ben Shelomo Kafah, a most outspoken opponent of the *Zohar*, typified its author as "the philosopher, author of the Zohar" (*"ha-philosoph, mehabber ha-Zohar"*). See his *'Amal u-Re'ut Ru'ah va-Haramot u-Teshuvatam*, pp. 12-16.

Besides the obvious use of Maimonidean terminology, there is the subtle copying of categories. An example would be the way in which the author of *Tikkunei Zohar* patterned his *"hamesh minim"* ("five species" or "five sects") of the *'Erev Rav* (Mixed Multitude) after Maimonides' *"hamishah minim"* ("five sectarians"). The passage from *Tikkunei Zohar* was incorporated by the printers in *Zohar* I, 25a. (The note in *Derekh Emet* alerts the reader that the material correlates to *Tikkunei Zohar, tikkun* 50. In the new Pritzker edition of the *Zohar*, the passage from *Tikkunei Zohar* has been removed.) Maimonides' *"hamishah minim"* are found in *MT, Hil. Teshuvah* 3:7. This is just a random sample of the pervasive influence of Maimonides on the author of *Tikkunei Zohar* and *Ra'ya Mehemna*.

Cf. the direct quote from Maimonides, *Hil. Teshuvah* 3:6 in Isaac ibn Sahula's *Meshal ha-Kadmoni* (Venice, 1546), *Sha'ar ha-Rishon* (10a), s.v. *va-yo'el ha-tsevi le-va'er*. And see now Sarah Offenberg, "On Heresy and Polemics in Two Proverbs in *Meshal Haqadmoni*" (Hebrew), *Jewish Thought* 1 (2019), pp. 64-65. Recently, Hartley Lachter has attempted to demonstrate that the general tenor of *Meshal ha-Kadmoni* is esoteric; see H. Lachter, "Spreading Secrets: Kabbalah and Esotericism in Isaac ibn Sahula's *Meshal ha-Kadmoni*," *Jewish Quarterly Review*, Vol. 100, No. 1 (Winter 2010), pp. 111-138.

[21] It should be noted, for whatever it is worth, that Pinhas ben Meshullam was a Provencal rabbi who took up the post of *Dayyan* of Alexandria, Egypt. It would be pure conjecture on my part to posit that his critique of Maimonides reflected the way in which *Mishneh Torah* had been received in Provence. It is equally possible that Rabbi Pinhas' critique was not based on actual observation of the Provencal reception of *Mishneh Torah*.

[22] See *Iggerot ha-Rambam*, ed. Yitzhak Shilat, vol. 2 (Jerusalem, 1988), pp. 438-439; quoted in Bezalel Naor, *The Limit of Intellectual Freedom: The Letters of Rav Kook* (Spring Valley, NY: Orot, 2011), pp. 297-298.

Modern scholars debate whether Maimonides' reply to Rabbi Pinhas was forthright or disingenuous. While Maimonidean authority Isadore Twersky accepts the response at face value, others, such as Samuel David Luzzatto and recently Shamma Friedman, are skeptical and suspect Maimonides of posturing. See Shamma Yehudah Friedman, *"Ha-Rambam ve-ha-Talmud," Dinei Yisrael*, 26-27 (5769-5770), pp. 228-230, 233-234.

[23] The term "hivemind" referred originally to the coordinated behavior of a colony of insects (bees or ants) which to an outside observer, appears the workings of a single mind. In the age of the Internet, it refers to the collectivity of the users who function as a single mind in expressing their thoughts and opinions. This is, in effect, what Maimonides created in *Mishneh Torah*. As he stated it so eloquently in the introduction to that work:

> I...intently studied all these works, with the view of putting together the results obtained from them in regard to what is forbidden or permitted, clean or unclean, and the other rules of the Torah—all in plain language and terse style, so that thus the entire Oral Law might become systematically known to all, without citing difficulties and solutions or differences of view, *one person saying so, and another something else* [italics mine—BN]—but consisting of statements, clear and convincing, and in accordance with the conclusions drawn from all these compilations and commentaries that have appeared from the time of *Rabbeinu ha-Kadosh* [i.e., Rabbi Judah the Prince] to the present, so that all the rules shall be accessible to young and old, whether these appertain to the (Pentateuchal) precepts or to the institutions established by the sages and prophets, so that no other work should be needed for ascertaining any of the laws of Israel, but

that this work might serve as a compendium of the entire Oral Law....
(Moses Hyamson translation with correction)

[24] See A.H. Freimann, *Ha-ROSh ve-Tse'etsa'av*, chap. 4 (pp. 32-41).
[25] *She'elot u-Teshuvot ha-ROSh* 31:9; quoted in Bezalel Naor, *The Limit of Intellectual Freedom*, pp. 300-301.
[26] Rabbi Yahya Kafah, *'Amal u-Re'ut Ru'ah*, p. 12.
[27] Translation of Moses Hyamson with slight alterations.
[28] *b. Kiddushin* 30a. See *Tosafot* there, s.v. *lo tserikha le-yomei*.
[29] *MT, Hil. Talmud Torah* 1:11.
[30] Ibid. 1:12.
[31] In *Sefer ha-Mussar*, chap. 10, Ibn Kaspi lays out a study plan for his twelve year old son, Shelomo. He advises Shelomo to spend the next two years studying Bible and Talmud. From fourteen to sixteen, he should turn his attention to ethics: Proverbs, Ecclesiastes, *Avot* with the commentary and introduction of Maimonides, *Hilkhot De'ot* of *Sefer ha-Madda'*, as well as Aristotle's *Nicomachean Ethics*. Starting at age sixteen, for the next two years, he should tackle the halakhic codes of Alfasi, Rabbi Moses of Coucy [i.e., *Sefer Mitsvot Gadol* or SeMaG] and Maimonides, and pursue the study of logic. At age eighteen, he would be well advised to study natural science for two years. Finally, at age twenty, Shelomo should commence studying Aristotle's *Metaphysics* and Maimonides' *Guide*. (He is also advised to take a wife at that time.)
[32] See Maimonides' famous parable of the King's palace in *Guide of the Perplexed* III, 51.

Kabbalah—Escape from Reality or Affirmation of Life?

A RESPONSE TO LIPPMAN BODOFF, "JEWISH MYSTICISM: MEDIEVAL ROOTS, CONTEMPORARY DANGERS AND PROSPECTIVE CHALLENGES"[1]

Lipmann Bodoff's bold new credo is packed into the following explosive statement:

> I believe, therefore, that the new ascetic-mystical spirituality of Ashkenazi Jewry arose not as an inevitable organic development from within rabbinic culture, but as a result of on-going Christian persecution and pressure, and a resulting sense of vulnerability and hopelessness of any redemption through history. If so, the progeny of that historical trauma, represented in Jewish mystical movements and their many forms of escapist, separatist, anti-rationalist, esoteric, and ascetic religiosity, which have engulfed Judaism in the last one thousand years, culminating in Hasidim for the past two hundred and fifty years, is subject to reexamination and question in the radically new situation of Jews and Judaism in the twenty-first century... Today's scholars have a right and even a duty to consider whether at least some of these ascetic and mystical ideas and practices, having arisen as responses to historical trau-

ma, may no longer be relevant, and may perhaps even be dangerous to Judaism today.

Without doubt, Lipmann Bodoff's article is one of the most original essays to enter public Jewish discourse in the past several years. Whether one subscribes to its historic thesis and contemporary ramifications or not (and the present writer has serious reservations in both regards), Bodoff's article is a must-read for any committed student of Kabbalah. Having said that, let me proceed to my response to Bodoff's analysis of Jewish Mysticism.

What is most refreshing to a student of Jewish Mysticism or Kabbalah who reads Bodoff's article is the shifting of focus from Provence to *Ashkenaz*. Since the meteoric appearance of Gershom Scholem's *Das Buch Bahir* in Leipzig in 1923, academic students of Kabbalah have been primed that the esoteric wisdom originated in Provence. Mr. Bodoff has moved the cradle of Kabbalah from the sunny Mediterranean clime of Provence to the dark, dour surroundings of the German Rhineland. In so doing, the essayist has effected not only a geographic shift but a major shift in terms of worldview.

What, the reader may ask, is refreshing about this perspective? Well, for one, if pursued properly, it would acknowledge the influence of the *Hasidei Ashkenaz*, those Rhenish pietists, on the development of the *Zohar*. True, the *Zohar* (not undeservedly referred to on occasion as "the Bible of Jewish Mysticism"), which surfaces in Castile at the end of the thirteenth century, is deeply indebted to the earlier *Bahir*, but it might appear that traces of Rabbi El'azar of Worm's angelology are to be found in the *Zohar*.[2] (I offer the *Roke'ah*'s angelology as merely one of the influences of *Ashkenaz* upon the *Zohar*'s mysticism.)[3]

And by the way, there are now scholars who contend that Scholem got the *Bahir* wrong when he conceived it as a Provencal creation. Of late, we are told that the *Bahir* too has its roots in *Ashkenaz*.[4] So, Bodoff has hit the mark in repositioning the origins of the Kabbalah.

What comes next is highly tendentious, to say the least. Bodoff would have us believe that Jewish Mysticism as it developed in the Rhineland was a direct response to the Crusades and the concomitant martyrdom that befell entire Jewish communities. Their plight is narrated in the *kinot* or elegies that Ashkenazic Jewry recite to this day on the fast of the Ninth of Av. Who has not been touched to the core by the account of the decimation of the once proud communities of Speyers, Worms and Mayence? And in the spiritual laboratory of Ashkenazic Jewry's limitless suffering was spawned the bacillus of—Kabbalah. (I use the term "bacillus" borrowed from the field of Biology to convey the tenor of Bodoff's perception of Jewish Mysticism, which is remarkably similar to that of the Jewish historian Heinrich Graetz. Had Bodoff written in German rather than English, I am convinced that we would have been treated to Graetz's vintage term of *"Schwärmerei"* as a depiction of Kabbalah.)

The problem with this original thesis is the same problem that critics point out in Scholem's much vaunted thesis that Lurianic Kabbalah was a response to the Spanish Expulsion of 1492. While at first blush there might be something attractive about imagining Luria's "shattering of the vessels" and the cosmic exile of the sparks that ensued, as a trope for the catastrophe that befell Iberian Jewry—the facts do not support this notion. For starters, Isaac Luria was an Ashkenazic Jew born and bred in Egypt.[5] Though Safed, where he spent the last two years of his short life, was populated by Sephardic Jews whose spoken language was Castilian, it does not strike one as convincing that Luria himself would be so moved by the traumatization of Spanish-Portuguese Jewry as to apotheosize their collective experience. He might be duly sympathetic to their ordeal, but that he would develop a cosmogony based on that historic event, beggars the imagination.[6]

Now Mr. Bodoff tells us that the mysticism of the Pietists of Ashkenaz (*Hasidei Ashkenaz*) was a response to the pillaging and rapine of the Rhenish Jewish communities during the Crusades. Though this thesis does not suffer from the same weakness as that of Prof. Scholem, whereby an Ashkenazic Jew takes up the litany of Sephardic Jewry, it does suffer from another major weakness (which in all fairness, Bodoff is sensitive to), namely that of dating. The major catastrophe of the Crusades is centered on the year 1096, while Ashkenazic mysticism reaches its crescendo in Rabbi El'azar of Worms (circa 1176-1238), a full century later. (Scholem's dates tend to be a tad tighter, with Luria [1534-1572] dying but eighty years after the Expulsion of 1492.)

Bodoff's rejoinder might have been that the historic consciousness of those tragic events of 1096 was a palpable reality for the likes of the author of the *Roke'ah*. On the night of 22 Kislev, 1196, Rabbi

Escape or Affirmation?

El'azar was busy composing his commentary on the Book of Genesis, when two men (possibly Crusaders) entered his home and killed his wife Dulce and daughters Belette and Hannah, and wounded his son Jacob. (The elegy *"Tsiyon, halo tish'ali li-shelom 'aluvayikh"* is attributed to Rabbi El'azar of Worms.)

Instead, Bodoff parries by positing something like the collective unconscious of Ashkenazic Jewry:

> I believe the evidence supports the powerful impact of external causes. From the facts developed by Chazan, Soloveitchik and Kanarfogel, it appears that a milder form of asceticism and esotericism developed before the First Crusade in response to a milder Christian hostility at that earlier time, and a more radical Jewish response developed after it – and continued to do so in various forms in the face of new developments and an ever more pervasive, insistent and continuing Christian hostility to Jewry in its Diaspora environment. Therefore, any attempt to discount outside influences as a cause of Jewish mysticism simultaneously ignores not only the psychological mechanism of mystical responses, but that sense of continuing threat and vulnerability created by a triumphant, powerful, zealous, and hostile Christianity during virtually all of the last thousand years. Moreover, looking for *immediate* cause-and-effect manifestations reflects a too rigid and fragmented understanding and expectation regarding the nature of mystical responses, and – in particular – the pervasive and

continuing nature of Christian threats and pressures on Jewry, and the Jewish responses to it. Sometimes the impetus to a mystical or messianic response may even be an event that provides hope that an apocalyptic end to history is imminent. But, that, too, is in no way inconsistent with the paradigm I have described. Psychoanalytic studies have shown that mysticism is a psychologically based response to a perceived threat to one's identity, presented by the abyss between the real and the ideal in the world, and can lie dormant for a prolonged period.

In an endnote we are told:

A traumatic external cause may also induce a mystical effect that is not immediate, but survives, "underground" as it were, for a long period, emerging when circumstances are propitious.

All of this is but preparation for Bodoff's central argument and that is that mysticism in general, and Jewish mysticism in particular, poses an escape from reality. Rather than being life-affirming, it is life-negating. This is not the first time that we hear this complaint from a Jewish thinker. Rabbi J.B. Soloveitchik in his study *"Ish ha-Halakhah"* (first published in *Talpiyot* in 1944) contrasted the mystic (specifically the adherent to HaBaD Hasidism, to which Rabbi Soloveitchik was exposed in youth), with his otherworldly pining and his perception of the *Shekhinah* as being in exile in this

Escape or Affirmation?

world, to the halakhist, blessed with a robust, healthy, this-worldly outlook. (So goes Rabbi Soloveitchik's typology.)

The complaint is certainly a valid complaint. Even a kabbalist such as Rav Kook observed that there are those who engage in Jewish mysticism as an escape from reality. But Kabbalah needn't be a rejection of everyday life and a retreat to the cave.

Bodoff is familiar with the writings of Martin Buber. (There is very little in the way of Judaic literature that Bodoff is not aware of.) He knows that Buber proposed a "Neo-Hasidism," which would be very much a celebration of life. In Buber's book *Ich und Du* (mistranslated into English as *I and Thou*, when *I and You* would have been the correct translation), the *Shekhinah* is precisely the Presence in every aspect of living. Rather than being a *"Shekhinta be-galuta,"* an exiled *Shekhinah*, it is the very here-and-now. Bodoff ends up (as so many others before him, whether they be Hasidim of the old school, or academicians such as Scholem) trashing Buber's reading of Hasidism as wide of the mark, if not downright unlawful.[7]

The truth be told, Buber was a genius at starting the conversation between the sacred and the secular. By effecting the interpenetration of the two, Jewish mysticism becomes pronouncedly this-worldly. I am not convinced that Buber got the immanentalism of the Ba'al Shem Tov so very wrong.

Another master at setting up the meeting of *kodesh ve-hol*, the holy and the profane, was Rabbi Abraham Isaac Hakohen Kook. (While not a disciple, Buber was certainly a great admirer of Rav Kook.)[8] Rav Kook's Kabbalah is a celebration of life, of the incarnate, of flesh and blood. There is nothing spectral or spooky about it. In Rav Kook's vision, not only would a deeper understanding of Kabbalah not undermine the Jews' return to a landed existence and to normalcy, but rather (drawing on the prediction of the *Ra'ya Mehemna*), "With this composition of yours, which is the *Book of Splendor (Sefer ha-Zohar)*...they shall emerge from exile with mercy."[9]

> A mass whose hearts have been touched by the Lord, of this divine camp, will be the power that establishes the foundation of the salvation, the power that gives grace, the light of life and the pride of greatness to the entire *élan vital* of the national renascence in the Land of Israel. The *Book of Splendor (Zohar)* that breaks new ways, making a way in the desert, a road in the wilderness, it and all its crop are ready to open doors of redemption. "Since Israel are destined to taste of the Tree of Life which is the *Book of Splendor (Zohar)*, they shall emerge from exile with mercy" [*Zohar* III, 124b].[10]

While deploring delving into mysticism before one has paid one's dues to the revealed Torah, Rav Kook maintains that the exoteric and the esoteric are best conceived as two sides of the coin of reality. They complement and enhance one another.

> The schism between the esoteric and exoteric comes about always due to the lack of wholeness of both ele-

ments. The exoteric that is restricted to its borders, which does not long for its source and root, will feel a certain antipathy to the esoteric, which cares to know no restriction or limitation. Lack of preparation for the hidden, jumping into it only because of a weakness of inner appetite, coupled with sloppiness and impracticality, causes the form of the esoteric to be distorted. Only unrealism, weak vitality, and lack of ability to grasp the living world, its deeds, movements, events, and charming currents, full of majesty and strength, cause immersion in the depth of the esoteric despite lack of preparation. But neither can exist exclusive of the other; life cannot be established on only one side of the global and Torah coin.[11]

Drawing on Maimonides' prescription that one first fill one's belly with bread and meat before venturing into the speculative orchard (*Pardes*),[12] Rav Kook explains that "filling the belly" extends to all healthy aspects of life. These are the grounding necessary prior to ascent to the more rarefied levels of human existence:

> The germ of the esoteric is ready, but it will be successfully actualized only after the full preparation of the exoteric. Filling the belly with "bread, meat and wine" must precede the "stroll in paradise." "Filling the belly" in its full sense includes within it also knowledge of the world and life, ethical and character development, strength of will

and recognition of human value, and all the good, aesthetic, and orderly in existence that comes from an education good and proper in all its facets, which joins together with all that is aroused to life and freshness, in all areas: man and nation, literature and life, secular and holy and holy-of-holies. The demand of the esoteric, which is filled when its time comes, is a firm demand, which brings the liberating word, which frees the great Israelite saying from the prison of its muteness. It renews firm life, it arouses the spirit of strength in the absolute holiness, which is much simpler and more natural than anything secular and mundane, and yet retains its loftiness and glory.[13]

Authentic Jewish mysticism comes not to escape but rather to enhance reality. Rav Kook is very clear about this, and indeed he revisits this theme on innumerable occasions in his vast literary oeuvre. I think that this point might best be illustrated by juxtaposing momentarily to the field of music.

Who of us has not felt at one significant moment or another the reality at hand enhanced by the accompaniment of music? Whether it was a life-cycle event such as a wedding or funeral, a picturesque scene, or a passage in a book, one felt a quickening, an enlargement, a maximizing, on account of the music playing in the background. Now for some, music might be attractive as an escape from reality, as a way of "tuning out" everyday life with its many challenges. And there is no denying that from an innocent attraction, music might turn into a deadly addiction. (Youth in particular are susceptible to this siren call.) But would the thought arise in the mind of any sane human to therefore declare a "jihad" against music? Music, the invention of the Biblical figure Yuval, is one of the features that ennoble our being. How impoverished would our civilization be without fine music!

By the same token, I think it fair to say that Jewish mysticism in the hands of an ethical genius such as a Rav Kook or an Abraham Joshua Heschel, enriches rather than impoverishes, invigorates rather than vitiates our existence.

Bodoff's response to my summoning of the spirit of Rav Kook (to whom he is sympathetic),[14] would be that the man was not a *homo mysticus*, but rather a poet![15]

---

[1] Available at: http://www.edah.org/backend/coldfusion/search/document.cfm?title=Jewish+Mysticism:+Medieval+Roots,+Contemporary+Dangers+and+Prospective+Challenges&hyperlink=Bodoff3_1.htm&type=JournalArticle&category=Orthodoxy+and+Modernity&authortitle&firstname=Lippman&lastname=Bodoff&pubsource=not+available&authorid=531&pdfattachment=Bodoff3_1.pdf

[2] I make this bold assertion fully cognizant of the earlier layer of *Heikhalot* literature that undergirds most of the works of Rabbi El'azar of Worms. See Isaiah Tishby, *Commentary on Talmudic Aggadoth by Rabbi Azriel of Gerona* (Jerusalem: Magnes, 1982), p. 38. The correlation of the angelology of the *Zohar* to that of Rabbi El'azar of Worms might be made easier if in Rabbi Reuven Margaliyot's encyclopedia *Mal'akhei 'Elyon* the obsolete references to *Sefer Raziel ha-Mal'akh* (Amsterdam, 1701) were updated to *Sodei Razayya* by Rabbi El'azar of Worms. For a survey of *Sodei Razayya*, see Joseph Dan, *History of Jewish Mysticism and Esotericism: The Middle Ages*, vol. 6 (Jerusalem: Zalman Shazar Center for Jewish History, 2011), pp. 493-558.

Moshe Idel writes (perhaps tentatively) that the angelology of *Ashkenaz* that made its way southward to *Sefarad*, was not that of *Hasidei Ashkenaz*, but that of a rather obscure figure, Rabbi Nehemiah ben Solomon of Erfurt (Rabbi Tröstlin the Prophet), a younger contemporary of Rabbi El'azar of Worms. See M. Idel, *The Angelic World: Apotheosis and Theophany* (Hebrew) (Tel-Aviv: Yedioth Ahronoth, 2008). Idel identified material of Rabbi Nehemiah in *Sefer*

Raziel; see *The Angelic World*, p. 147. (Thanks to Yosef Yitzhak Lifshitz who brought Idel's work on angelology to my attention.)

Elsewhere, I noted a striking similarity between *"Hilkhot ha-Kissei"* of Rabbi El'azar of Worms and Rabbi Ezra of Gerona's Commentary to Song of Songs 3:10. Cf. *Sodei Razayya* II, ed. Aaron Eisenbach (Jerusalem, 2004), pp. 33, 37 to *Kitvei Ramban*, ed. C.B. Chavel, vol. 2 (Jerusalem: Mossad Harav Kook, 1968), p. 494, s.v. *merkavo argaman*. See *Hassagot ha-Rabad le-Mishneh Torah*, ed. Bezalel Naor (Jerusalem, 1985), Intro., pp. 23-24, n. 5.

[3] Israel Ta-Shma was convinced that there are residues of Ashkenazic *halakhah* in the *Zohar*; see I. Ta-Shma, *Ha-Nigleh she-ba-Nistar* (Tel Aviv, 1995).

More recently, Moshe Idel has briefly sketched the profound influence the *Hasidei Ashkenaz* or Rhineland Pietists (specifically Rabbi El'azar of Worms) exerted upon the development of Spanish Kabbalah. See Idel's Introduction to *The Hebrew Writings of the Author of* Tiqqunei Zohar *and* Ra'aya Mehemna (Hebrew), ed. Efraim Gottlieb (Jerusalem, 2003), pp. 12-15.

One cannot be but impressed—as was Idel—by the deferential tone assumed by the leader of Catalonian Jewry in the second half of the thirteenth century, Rabbi Solomon ben Abraham Ibn Adret (RaShBA), when referring to the spiritual prowess of the German Jewish mystics. How ironic that in the very responsum to the Jewish community of Avila (*She'elot u-Teshuvot RaShBA*, Part 1, no. 548) that impugns the so-called "Prophet of Avila," RaShBa lauds the extrasensory accomplishments of Abraham of Cologne (who reportedly acted as a medium for Elijah the Prophet). That the acknowledged leader of Spanish Jewry, in the very process of debunking his own countrymen's forays into the *terra incognita* of preterrational consciousness, would so romanticize the prophetic ability of Ashkenazic Jewry, is indeed remarkable. By the same token, while speaking *ad hominem*, the fact that RaShBA sponsored Rabbeinu Asher ben Yehiel (ROSh), a German refugee rabbi (disciple of Rabbi Meir of Rothenburg), to assume the rabbinate of Toledo, also bespeaks enormous respect for the *Hakhmei Ashkenaz*. See A.H. Freimann, *Ha-ROSh, Rabbeinu Asher ben Rabbi Yehiel ve-Tse'etsa'av* (Jerusalem: Mossad Harav Kook, 1986), pp. 28, 158.

Inter alia, in a recent newspaper interview, Haym Soloveitchik observed that generally, halakhic texts moved from North to South, from *Ashkenaz* to *Sefarad*, and not *vice versa*. The one notable exception was Maimonides' code meriting *Hagahot Maimoniyot*, the glosses penned by a disciple of Rabbi Meir (MaHaRaM) of Rothenburg.

> In the volume that already appeared [= *Collected Essays*, Vol. 1], I address the "one way street" that you mention. For example, the Rosh moved from Germany to Spain in the beginning of the fourteenth century. His *Pesakim* and the *Tur*, the work of his son, made their way swiftly to *Ashkenaz*, but the *Hiddushei HaRamban* or those of the *Rashba* never did. The same caravans or boats which brought the *Piskei HaRosh* to Cologne, could have brought the *Hiddushei HaRashba*, had people in Germany been interested in them. Apparently, they weren't.
>
> ("Interview with Professor Haym Soloveitchik by Rabbi Yair Hoffman," *Five Towns Jewish Times*, Wednesday, January 8th, 2014)

Available at: http://www.theyeshivaworld.com/news/headlines-breaking-stories/209453/interview-with-professor-haym-soloveitchik-by-rabbi-yair-hoffman.html

Summing up, we see emerging a pattern whereby in both the exoteric and esoteric realms, for some yet unexplained reason, the *Hakhmei Sefarad* adopted what one might term a reverential attitude toward the *Hakhmei Ashkenaz*.

[4] Daniel Abrams "argued for the Ashkenazi composition of the *Bahir* (outside of the German Pietist circles)" (Daniel Abrams, *The Book Bahir: An Edition Based on the Earliest Manuscripts* [Los Angeles: Cherub, 1994], p. *13).

[5] Though it seems that Rabbi Moshe Schreiber erred when he wrote that Luria was a Sephardi, his point concerning the Lurianic *kavvanot* or mystical intentions is well taken. The reason that Luria loaded his *kavvanot* onto the Sephardic rite (*Nusah Sepharad*) was because that was the prayer book in use in Safed in his day. Had Luria transmitted his teachings in an Ashkenazic milieu, he undoubtedly would have adapted the *kavvanot* to the Ashkenazic rite (*Nusah Ashkenaz*). See *She'elot u-Teshuvot Hatam Sofer*, Orah Hayyim 15(2).

[6] See Moshe Idel, *Kabbalah: New Perspectives* (New Haven: Yale University Press, 1988), p. 265.

[7] See Bodoff, note 65:

> While Buber sought to portray Hasidism as changing Lurianic kabbalah's anti-worldly approach, the better view of scholars is that he was incorrect; see Jerome Gellman, "Buber's Blunder" [= "Buber's Blunder: Buber's Replies to Scholem and Schatz-Uffenheimer," *Modern Judaism*, February 2000], pp. 20-40. Buber's romanticized view, which has proved attractive to many, is discussed in Joseph Dan, "A Bow to Frumkinian Hasidism," *Modern Judaism*, May 1991, pp. 175-194.

[8] In Buber's book, *Bein 'Am le-Artso* (Jerusalem: Schocken, 1944), which grew out of a series of lectures on the history of Zionism, a chapter is devoted to Rav Kook. The chapter is entitled aptly enough: "*Hiddush ha-Kedushah*" ("The Renewal of Holiness"). In the introduction, the author writes that the volume was inspired by meetings with two men: A.D. Gordon and Rav Kook. Buber met the latter in Jerusalem in 1927. For an analysis of the aforementioned chapter, see Paulina Sarah Sklarevski, "*Hiddush ha-Kedushah: Ha-RAYaH Kook bi-re'i tefisat ha-tsiyonut shel Buber be-sefer 'Bein 'Am le-Artso,'*" (Term Paper, Jerusalem: Hebrew University, July 31, 2013). Available at www.academia.edu. Buber's book has been brought out in English translation under the title *On Zion: The History of an Idea* (Syracuse: Syracuse University Press, 1997).

[9] *Zohar* III, 124b.

[10] Rabbi Abraham Isaac Hakohen Kook, *Orot* (Jerusalem, 1920), *Orot ha-Tehiyah* (Lights of Renascence), end chap. 57; idem, *Orot*, transl. Bezalel Naor (Jerusalem: Maggid, 2015), p. 395.

[11] Ibid., beginning chap. 60 (p. 401).

[12] Maimonides, *Hil. Yesodei ha-Torah* 4:13.

[13] *Orot ha-Tehiyah*, end chap. 60 (pp. 401-403).

[14] Bodoff's final sentence (Appendix 13) reads:

> Rav Kook offers the strongest and simplest argument for secular activities, dispensing with kabbalistic ideas of mystical exegesis, sefirotic emanations, and the intricate structure of mystical ritual activity. For him, spirituality is the *result* of using the tools of modern culture to guide the historical, earthly process of redemption; it is not achieved by casting off corporeality or by the negation of the self; see Eliezer Schweid, "Prophetic Mysticism in Twentieth-Century Jewish Thought," *Modern Judaism*, May 1994, pp. 166-169.

[15] Bodoff writes in note 52:

> Marvin Fox applied a kind of hybrid analysis, similar to my own in some respects, in concluding that Rav Kook was – a poet! See his "Rav Kook: Neither Philosopher nor Kabbalist," *Rabbi Abraham Isaac Kook and Jewish Spirituality*, ed. David Shatz and Lawrence Kaplan (New York: NYU Press, 1995), pp. 78-87.

VI

HASIDISM

Rabbi Nahman's *Shir Na'im* as a Reply to Maimonides

Rabbi David Sears has written a groundbreaking study comparing Rabbi Nahman of Breslov's poem *Shir Na'im* to—among other referents—the medieval poem *Akdamut* recited in the synagogue on the festival of *Shavu'ot*. To my thinking, it would be valuable to compare the poem to Maimonides' *Hilkhot Yesodei ha-Torah* (Laws of the Fundamentals of the Torah). At this juncture, one might ask from whence sprouts such a "heretical" thought to compare a poem of Rabbi Nahman, famous for his opposition to philosophy,[1] to *Hilkhot Yesodei ha-Torah*, which—as the remainder of *Sefer ha-Madda'* (the *Book of Knowledge*), a classic of Maimonidean thought—aroused the ire of the anti-Maimonideans in France and other lands?

The answer to this question is the keyword "Necessary Existent" ("*nimtsa ha-mehuyyav*").[2] Elsewhere I have elaborated on the opposition this uniquely Maimonidean coinage for the deity encountered in kabbalistic circles, to the point that it was condemned in both the "study house of the Gaon Rabbi Elijah" (i.e., the Vilna Gaon) and the "study house of the Gaon Rabbi Zalman" (i.e., Rabbi Shneur Zalman of Liadi, author of *Tanya*).[3] And lo and behold, in the writings of none other than one of the outstanding opponents of Maimonides' philosophy—Rabbi Nahman of Breslov—we find this very term spelled out "black on white"!

A probable explanation for this enigma is that Rabbi Nahman's overall opposition to Maimonides' philosophy did not preclude his drawing from Maimonides a term that he deemed faithful to Torah.[4] I might point out that Rabbi Nahman's contemporary, the Gaon of Vilna, who was equally adverse to philosophy in general and Maimonides' philosophy in particular, nevertheless adopted certain philosophic terms in his writings.[5]

If we pursue our assumption that *Shir Na'im*, printed at the beginning of *Likkutei MOHaRaN* as a sort of preamble to that work, is Rabbi Nahman's response to *Hilkhot Yesodei ha-Torah*, the overture to Maimonides' magnum opus *Mishneh Torah*, we will find the parallels between the two prolegomena simply astounding.

Shir Na'im opens with the veracity of the Torah, the theophany on Mount Sinai, and Moses' abstinence—themes that Maimonides treats at great length in *Hilkhot Yesodei ha-Torah* (7:6 and chap. 8).

Rabbi Nahman goes on to pit his kabbalistic cosmology against Maimonides' Aristotelian cosmology. Thus, Rabbi Nahman surveys souls hewn from the Throne of Glory, angels, earth and the surrounding spheres. Compare *Hilkhot Yesodei ha-Torah* 4:8, 9 (the soul); 2:3-8 (angels); 3:10-4:7 (earth); and 3:1-9 (the spheres).

Rabbi Nahman includes in his cosmology demons and sorcerers (which abound in the Talmud)—a frontal assault on Maimonides, who banished demons to the realm of unreality.[6]

Prophecy is one of the major themes of *Hilkhot Yesodei ha-Torah* (chap. 7). Rabbi Nahman's concluding stanza—"A prophet whose heart is endowed with wisdom....Contemplating this is conducive to knowledge of the Creator Who forms all things"—

could easily reflect Maimonides' portrayal of the quest for prophecy, "to comprehend the pure and holy forms, and contemplate the entire wisdom of the Holy One, blessed be He, from the first form to the center of the earth, gleaning from them His greatness" (*Hilkhot Yesodei ha-Torah* 7:1).

However, once again, the reader is in for a surprise. Whereas in Maimonides' system, contemplation of nature leads to discovery of the great wisdom of the Creator, in Rabbi Nahman's setup, inspired by the Kabbalah, it is meditation upon the structure and dimensions of the human body that grants the wise man who aspires to prophecy an inkling of the grandeur of the *Macroanthropus*.

The mature Maimonides would have no truck with this notion of the *Shi'ur Komah* (the "Body" of the Creator). In a famous responsum, Maimonides writes that the notion smacks of idolatry, while dismissing the supposedly ancient book by that name, which is the source of this idea, as "the work of one of the Byzantine preachers."[7]

Rabbi Nahman no doubt took with the greatest earnestness the saying attributed to Rabbi Ishmael in that work, "Whoever knows the measurement (*shi'ur*) of the Creator is assured the World to Come." Rabbi Nahman might well have concluded as did the anonymous author of *Ma'arekhet ha-Elohut*:

> Now that you know the structure of the human form (*binyan tsurat ha-adam*), you can be enlightened—if you received from mouth to mouth—[as to] the veracity of the vision seen by the prophets. Our rabbis, of blessed

memory, referred to that vision as *shi'ur komah* (the "Body of the Creator")....This is the secret of "Whoever knows the measurement (*shi'ur*) of the Creator...." In this regard, the verse states, "Let us make man in Our image, in Our likeness" [Genesis 1:26]. And in regard to that vision it was said, "And by the hand of the prophets I have appeared in simulacra" [Hosea 12:11].[8]

This is not to say that Rabbi Nahman would tolerate corporealization of the deity (*hagshamat elohut*). In fact, in Rabbi Nahman's conception of spiritual growth, one evolves to ever more rarefied perceptions of the divinity. "We find that based on his present perception, his previous perception is certainly reckoned a corporealization. It follows that he must repent of his previous perception, for his having corporealized the exalted divinity."[9]

But neither did Rabbi Nahman shrink for this reason from anthropomorphic figures of speech in regard to divinity. Perhaps the following pensée of a later kabbalist would approximate Rabbi Nahman's attitude:

> The fear that some have of the corporeal tropes (*meshalim*) contained in the mysteries of Torah, is a foolish fear (*yir'ah shel shetut*). We know for a fact that all these [tropes] do not damage in the least the luminous foundation of pure belief in one God, blessed be He; rather, they add to our understanding light and lucidity, and [provide] adaptability to the divine light.[10]

POSTSCRIPT

In 1985, Rabbi Nathan Tsevi Kenig published in Jerusalem an edition of *Likkutei MOHaRaN* to which he appended variants found in Rabbi Nathan Sternhartz's own manuscript of the work. (One recalls that Rabbi Nathan was Rabbi Nahman's *sofer* or scribe. With the exception of a few pieces in Rabbi Nahman's own hand, the vast majority of the text of *Likkutei MOHaRaN* consists of Rabbi Nathan's transcripts of Rabbi Nahman's teachings.)

In *Likkutei MOHaRaN* I, 112 we read:

> Behold, *it is known* that there are three worlds: the world of the angels; and the spheres; and the physical.

Now in Rabbi Nathan's autograph the sentence reads as follows:

> Behold, *Rambam z"l* [Maimonides, of blessed memory] *wrote* that there are three worlds: the world of the angels; and the spheres; and the physical.

Clearly, the reference is to *MT, Hilkhot Yesodei ha-Torah* 2:3 ff. Why the reference to Maimonides was left out of the printed version of the work remains a mystery. At any rate, this discovery strengthens my hand that Rabbi Nahman was eminently familiar with the cosmology of *Hilkhot Yesodei ha-Torah*. (On at least this one occasion he actually referenced it in a discourse.) It is my contention that it so exercised him that he composed *Shir Na'im* as a foil for the cosmology of Rambam's *Hilkhot Yesodei ha-Torah*.

¹ Should it turn out that the anonymous anti-philosophical tract *Kin'at Hashem Tseva'ot* was not written by Rabbi Nathan Sternhartz of Nemirov and Breslov, Rabbi Nahman's most intimate disciple, this would not detract in the least from my contention. Rabbi Nahman's opposition to *hakirah*, philosophical speculation in general, and Maimonides' philosophy in particular, is a matter of public knowledge. For starters, see Rabbi Nathan Sternhartz, *Sihot ha-RaN* (B'nei Berak, 1976), par. 32, 40, 81, 102 (end), 217, 219; idem, *Hayyei MOHaRaN* (Jerusalem: Keren R. Israel Dov Odesser, n.d.), pp. 214-215 (par. 24); 408-420 (especially par. 1, 2, 5 where Maimonides' *Hilkhot Yesodei ha-Torah* and *Guide of the Perplexed* are singled out for mention). There is a Lurianic tradition that the root of the soul of Maimonides is the left corner of the beard of *Ze'ir Anpin*, and the root of Nahmanides' soul the right corner. See Rabbi Hayyim Joseph David Azulai, *Shem ha-Gedolim*, s.v. *Rambam* and *Ramban*. So basic was Rabbi Nahman's antipathy to Maimonides' philosophy that he called into question whether this tradition truly originates with Rabbi Isaac Luria. Likewise, Rabbi Nahman once related a dream in which he remonstrated with Maimonides for writing such things (i.e., philosophy). Both anecdotes were deleted from the printed version of *Hayyei MOHaRaN* and are to be found in an appendix (*"Hashmatot"*) to *Kuntres Yemei ha-Tela'ot*.

² Cf. *Likkutei MOHaRaN* I, 52: "*mehuyyav ha-metsi'ut.*"

Rav Kook, of a like mind, wrote: "It is impossible to attribute positive [attribution] vis-à-vis *Ein Sof* except in relation to the essential being that we call 'Necessary Existence' ('*mehuyyav ha-metsi'ut*'), and even this we permit ourselves to express with difficulty" (Notes to *Hezyonei Amatsyahu*, in Rabbi Moshe Yehiel Zuriel, *Otserot ha-RAYaH*, vol. 2 [Tel-Aviv, 1988], pp. 1035-1036). See also Rabbi Mordechai Gimpel Barg's notes of Rav Kook's lectures on the *Book of Kuzari*, in *Ma'amrei ha-RAYaH*, vol. 2, ed. Rabbi Elisha Aviner (Langenauer) (Jerusalem, 1984), p. 488, end chap. 3: "The true philosophy comes to remove and negate coarse human positive [attribution] that clouds the divine content, thereby clearing space for the true positive [attribution] that is *the necessary (ha-mehuyyav).*"

³ Maimonides, *MT, Hil. Yesodei ha-Torah* 1:1-5; idem, *Guide of the Perplexed* I, 52(4) and I, 57. *Par contre*, *Likkutim* published at the end of *Be'ur ha-GRA* to *Sifra di-Tseni'uta*; and Rabbi Yitzhak Eizik Halevi Epstein of Homel, *Hannah Ariel* (Berdichev, 5672/1912), *Toledot*, 43b. See Bezalel Naor, "Rav Kook and Emmanuel Levinas on the 'Non-Existence' of God," *Orot: A Multidisciplinary Journal of Judaism*, vol. 1 (5751/1991), pp. 1-11 (reprinted in Bezalel Naor, *From a Kabbalist's Diary: Collected Essays* [Spring Valley, NY: Orot, 5765/2005], pp. 75-90).

⁴ Rabbi Tsevi Yehudah Hakohen Kook was distressed by a certain article in which the author let drop that Rabbi Nahman of Breslov "was not a philosopher." Rabbi Tsevi Yehudah lodged the following protest:

> The description "was not a philosopher" is out of place, because by its negation it would take away from the described [Rabbi Nahman] original thought of any value. The truth is that even in his negation of philosophy and his laying stress upon *naïveté* and simplicity, there is deep thought possessing sacred originality. By the same token, the philosophy of Rabbi Yehudah Halevi in the *Book of Kuzari* has been typified as "the philosophy of anti-philosophy."
> (Rabbi Tsevi Yehudah Hakohen Kook, *Li-Netivot Yisrael*, vol. 2 [Jerusalem, 5739/1979], pp. 214-215)

Elsewhere (in a eulogy for the martyred writer Hillel Zeitlin, who authored a biography of Rabbi Nahman), Rabbi Tsevi Yehudah refers to Rabbi Nahman of Breslov as "the great man, exceptional in the....thought of divine *devekut* (cleaving)." Ibid. p. 25.

I might add that an authority of the stature of the *SheLaH ha-Kadosh* saw no contradiction between the Maimonidean term *"mehuyyav ha-metsi'ut"* and the kabbalists' term *Ein Sof*. See Rabbi Isaiah Halevi Horowitz, *Siddur ha-SheLaH*, vol. 1 (Jerusalem: Ahavat Shalom, 1998), p. 133, s.v. *nimtsa ve-ein 'et el metsi'uto*. Likewise, Rabbi Baruch of Kosov, *'Ammud ha-'Avodah* (Czernowitz, 1863), 86d. Neither did Rabbi Pinhas Elijah Hurwitz of Vilna hesitate to refer to the deity as *"mehuyyav ha-metsi'ut."* See Hurwitz, *Sefer ha-Berit*, Part 1 (Brünn, 1797), 20:15 (109a-110a).

[5] See *Be'ur ha-GRA* to *Yoreh De'ah* 179:6 where the Gaon twice excoriates "accursed philosophy." The word "accursed" was censored by the *maskilim* ("enlightened ones") who ran the Vilna press. See Rabbi Joshua Heschel Levin, *'Aliyot Eliyahu* (Jerusalem, 5749/1989), pp. 43-45. In *Be'ur ha-GRA* to *Yoreh De'ah* 246:4 the Gaon lambastes both Maimonides and Rabbi Moses Isserles, who authored the philosophic work *Torat ha-'Olah*. On the other hand, one need only peruse *Be'ur ha-GRA* to Proverbs to see how chock-full it is with philosophic jargon. (Though one might counter that the work was not written by the Gaon, rather by his disciple Rabbi Menahem Mendel of Shklov.) According to his biographer, the Gaon "was expert in philosophy and remarked that he extracted from it two good things...." *'Aliyot Eliyahu*, p. 79. See the recent discussion by Allan Brill, "Auxiliary to *Hokhmah*: The Writings of the Vilna Gaon and Philosophical Terminology" in *The Vilna Gaon and His Disciples*, ed. Hallamish, Rivlin, and Shuchat (Ramat Gan: Bar-Ilan University Press, 2003), pp. 9-37. Earlier, see Meyer Waxman, *"Ha-Gaon mi-Vilna"* in *Sefer ha-Shanah li-Yehudei Amerika*, vols. X-XI (1949), pp. 346-347.

[6] See *Be'ur ha-GRA* to *Yoreh De'ah* 179:6; Rabbi Yitzhak Arieli, *'Eynayim le-Mishpat: Bava Batra*, Part Two (Jerusalem, 1975), *Bava Batra* 109b (pp. 55-56); Bezalel Naor, *Hassagot ha-RABaD le-Mishneh Torah* (Jerusalem, 1985), *Hil. Tefillah* 7:8 (pp. 84-85); Jacob Levinger, *Maimonides' Techniques of Codification: A Study in the Method of Mishneh Torah* (Hebrew)(Jerusalem: Magnes, 1965), pp. 151-152; Marc B. Shapiro, *Studies in Maimonides and His Interpreters* (Scranton, PA: University of Scranton Press, 2008), pp. 95-150 ("Maimonidean Halakhah and Superstition").

Maimonides does not discuss sorcery in *Hilkhot Yesodei ha-Torah* but later in *Sefer ha-Madda'*, in *Hilkhot 'Avodah Zarah*. There, he sums up the discussion by belittling those credulous enough to be beguiled by the practitioners of magic. (See *Hil. 'Avodah Zarah* 11:16.) At the opposite extreme, Nahmanides, the great representative of the kabbalistic tradition, takes rationalist philosophers to task on this account. The mystic believes that necromancers possess true powers. See Nahmanides, *Commentary to the Pentateuch*, ed. C.B. Chavel, vol. 2 (Jerusalem: Mossad Harav Kook, 1969), Deuteronomy 18:9 (p. 427, n. 92); and idem, *"Torat Hashem Temimah"* in *Kitvei Rabbeinu Moshe ben Nahman*, ed. C.B. Chavel, vol. 1 (Jerusalem: Mossad Harav Kook, 1968), p. 149. In the latter work, Nahmanides singles out for criticism Rabbi Abraham ibn Ezra, who in his commentary (Lev. 19:31) expressed disbelief in the truth of magic.

The controversy between Ibn Ezra and Maimonides on the one hand, and Nahmanides on the other, revolves around the question why the Torah forbade such practices. Is it because they are false (Ibn Ezra and Maimonides), or because they are true—and diabolical (Nahmanides)?

[7] *Teshuvot ha-Rambam* (Freimann ed., no. 373; Blau ed., no. 117). The Judeo-Arabic designation *"al-Rum"* is best translated for our purposes as "Byzantine."

In his *Commentary to the Mishnah*, written while he was yet a young man (in his twenties), Maimonides seems to have approved of *Shi'ur Komah*, but he later revised the *Commentary*, striking out that passage. See Maimonides, *Commentary to the Mishnah*, ed. Kafah, *Seder Nezikin* (Jerusalem: Mossad Harav Kook, 1963), Introduction to *Perek Helek*, the sixth fundamental, p. 142, note 42. (Evidently, in his youth, Maimonides thought that *Shi'ur Komah* could be interpreted figuratively, perhaps following the lead of Rabbi Abraham Ibn Ezra in his commentary to Song of Songs. For later figurative interpretations of *Shi'ur Komah*, see Moshe Idel, "The Kabbalah in Byzantium—Preliminary Remarks," in *Jews in Byzantium: Dialectics of Minority and Majority Cultures*, ed. Robert Bonfil [Leiden: Brill, 2012], pp. 689-690.)

Concerning the words *"Shi'ur Komah"* in the *Commentary to the Mishnah* and the failure of some Yemenite sages to comprehend them, see *She'elot R. Hoter ben Shelomo*, ed. Kafah (Jerusalem, 2001), pp. 175-176, 201-204, 235-238.

Saul Lieberman detected that even in *Mishneh Torah* Maimonides made halakhic use of anatomical knowledge gleaned from *Shi'ur Komah*. See S. Lieberman, *Sheki'in* (Jerusalem, 1939), p. 12; and Lieberman's letter to Louis Ginzberg, in Marc B. Shapiro, *Saul Lieberman and the Orthodox* (Scranton: University of Scranton Press, 2006), p. 16.

See further *Hassagot ha-RABaD le-Mishneh Torah*, ed. Bezalel Naor (Jerusalem, 1985), pp. 56-57, 141-142; Rabbi M.M. Kasher, *Mefa'ne'ah Tsefunot* (New York, 1959), p. 14; A. Altmann, "Moses Narboni's 'Epistle on *Shi'ur Qoma'*" in *Jewish Medieval and Renaissance Studies*, ed. Altmann (Cambridge, Mass: Harvard University Press, 1967), pp. 225-288; Rabbi David Cohen, *Kol ha-Nevu'ah* (Jerusalem: Mossad Harav Kook, 1979), pp. 140-141; Rabbi Abraham Isaac Hakohen Kook, *Orot ha-Kodesh*, ed. Rabbi David Cohen, vol. 2 (Jerusalem: Mossad Harav Kook, 1985), end p. 603.

Allusions to limbs of the Creator measured in millions of parasangs or even megaparasangs are sure to offend the sensibilities of modern readers. Yet, dare we write off the work *Shi'ur Komah* as simply a foreign intrusion on native Jewish soil, the way the mature Rabbi Moses Maimonides and Rabbi Moses Taku did? (See Rabbi Moses Taku, *Ketav Tamim*, published in *Otsar Nehmad*, ed. Raphael Kirchheim, vol. III [Vienna, 1860], pp. 61-62.) For the former, *Shi'ur Komah* was the work of a Byzantine preacher; for the latter, it was a forgery by heretics. Current scholarship views *Shi'ur Komah* as very much a part of the *Heikhalot* literature and would set its date of composition as the second or third century C.E. Here too there is speculation that perhaps Gnostics who stood outside of rabbinic tradition were somehow able to graft their "measurement of the Creator" on to older, authentic *Merkavah* texts which restrict themselves to the Throne of Glory and venture no further. (It goes without saying that the *Heikhalot* of which we speak are not the *Heikhalot* of the *Zohar*; Rabbi Nahman vouched for the exactitude of the numbers of chambers reported in the latter. See *Hayyei MOHaRaN* [Jerusalem: Keren R. Israel Dov Odesser, n.d.], p. 442, par. 14.)

If Rabbi Nahman accepted *Shi'ur Komah* as mainstream Judaism, that would place him in the company of Sherira Gaon and his son Hai Gaon; perhaps a reluctant Sa'adyah Gaon; Rabbi Yehudah Halevi; Rabbi Abraham Ibn Ezra; the juvenile Maimonides (before his retraction); RABaD of Posquières, first in a distinguished line of kabbalists; Rabbi El'azar Roke'ah of Worms, spokesman of *Hasidei Ashkenaz*; the anonymous author of *Ma'arekhet ha-Elohut*; Rabbi Simeon ben Tsemah Duran, preeminent Algerian halakhist; and untold Jewish mystics over the centuries. See B.M. Levin, *Otsar a-Ge'onim* IV (Jerusalem, 1932), *Teshuvot*, pp. 10-12 (responsum of Sherira and Hai to the sages of Fez); *Otsar ha-Ge'onim* I (Haifa, 1928), *Teshuvot*, p. 17 (responsum of Sa'adyah); Rabbi Yehudah Halevi, *Kuzari*, ed. Even-Shmuel (Tel-Aviv: Dvir, 1972), IV, 3, end (pp. 165, 286); Rabbi Abraham Ibn Ezra, *Commentary of Ibn Ezra to Pentateuch*, ed. Asher Weiser (Jerusalem: Mossad Harav Kook, 1977), Exodus 33:21 (p. 216); idem, *Yesod Mora ve-Sod Torah*, ed. Cohen and Simon (Ramat Gan: Bar-Ilan University Press, 2002), pp. 84, 201; Maimonides, *Commentary to the Mishnah*, ed. Kafah, *Seder Nezikin* (Jerusalem: Mossad Harav Kook, 1963), p. 142, n. 42; *Otsar Nehmad*, ed. Raphael Kirchheim, IV (Vienna, 1864), p. 37 (Rabbi Asher ben David quoting his grandfather Rabbi Abraham ben David [RABaD] of Posquières); Rabbi El'azar Roke'ah, *Sodei Razayya* (Jerusalem, 2004), Part II, p. 39; anonymous, *Ma'arekhet ha-Elohut* (Mantua, 1558), 142b-144a; Rabbi Simeon ben Tsemah Duran, *Magen Avot* (Livorno, 1785), 21b, end; Rabbi Joseph Ergas, *Shomer Emunim* (Amsterdam, 1736), I, 65 (21a-c).

One of the major repositories of *Shi'ur Komah* fragments is *Sefer Raziel ha-Mal'akh* (Amsterdam, 1701). We know that Rabbi Nahman made some caustic remarks concerning that book: "*Sefer Raziel* is not from Adam; it was not handed by the angel to Adam, and has no power to save from fire. It has already happened that the book itself was burnt." Quoted in *Hayyei MOHaRaN* (Jerusalem: Keren R. Israel Dov Odesser, n.d.), p. 450, par. 34. But *Shi'ur Komah* fragments show up in other, less likely places as well. See *Midrash Mishlei*, ed. Buber (Vilna: Romm, 1893), 10 (34a).

Parenthetically, if there exists some doubt as to Rabbi Nahman's position concerning *Shi'ur Komah*, we have very clear positions regarding some other controversial theories of Kabbalah. Rabbi Nahman, as other Hasidic masters, embraced the "'*Olam ha-Malbush*" of Rabbi Israel Sarug. See *Sihot ha-RaN*, par. 225. Rabbi Nahman opposed the pre-Lurianic theory of "*Shemitot*" found in *Sefer ha-Temunah*; see *Hayyei MOHaRaN*, p. 420, par. 18. Cf. Rabbi Shneur Zalman of Liadi, *Torah 'Or* (Brooklyn: Kehot, 1972), *Shemot*, 51d, s.v. *Vayyomer Hashem elav mi sam peh la-adam*; Rabbi Dov Baer Shneuri, *Torat Hayyim* (Brooklyn: Kehot, 1980), *Shemot*, f. 59, s.v. *Vayyomer...lo' ish devarim anokhi*; Rabbi M.M. Schneerson, *Likkutei Sihot*, vol. 10 (Brooklyn: Kehot, 1981), p. 176; Rabbi David Cohen, *Kol ha-Nevu'ah*, pp. 192-193.

[8] *Ma'arekhet ha-Elohut* (Mantua, 1558), 142b-144a. This passage is quoted in the commentary of Rabbi Judah Hayyat (123b) with minor variations.

[9] *Likkutei MOHaRaN* I, 6:3. It is my hunch that Rabbi Nahman's remarks concerning the individual's growth and *teshuvah* inspired Rav Kook's vision of collective humanity evolving spiritually as more and more "shells" (*kelipot*) of

HASIDISM

corporeality fall away. See Rabbi Abraham Isaac Hakohen Kook, *Orot* (Jerusalem, 1950), p. 127; quoted in Naor, "Rav Kook and Emmanuel Levinas on the 'Non-Existence' of God," pp. 1, 3. See also Rav Kook's explanation of the mystery of *"pegimat ha-shemot"* as transmitted by Alexander Ziskind Rabinowitz (AZaR), in Elhanan Kalmanson, *Ha-Mahshavah ha-Yisraelit* (Jerusalem, 1920; photo-offset Jerusalem, 1967), p. 26.

10 Rabbi Abraham Isaac Hakohen Kook, *'Arpilei Tohar* (Jerusalem: Makhon RZYH Kook, 1983), p. 71; quoted in Zevi Yaron, *Mishnato shel Harav Kook* [*The Philosophy of Rabbi Kook*] (Jerusalem: W.Z.O., 1974), pp. 78-79. The passage is also to be found in *Orot ha-Kodesh*, ed. Cohen, vol. 1 (Jerusalem: Mossad Harav Kook, 1985), p. 110. (See now *Shemonah Kevatsim* 2:203.)

Cf. Rabbi Abraham Isaac Hakohen Kook, *Pinkas 13*, ed. Benzion Kahana-Shapira (Jerusalem: Makhon RZYH Kook, 2004), par. 137 (p. 96); reprinted in *Pinkesei ha-Rayah*, vol. 1, ed. Benzion Kahana-Shapira and Ze'ev Neuman (Jerusalem: Makhon RZYH Kook, 2008), *Pinkas 13* (*"Rishon le-Yaffo"*), par. 137 (pp. 294-295) = *Kevatsim mi-Ketav Yad Kodsho*, ed. Boaz Ofen (Jerusalem, 2006), *Pinkas Rishon le-Yaffo*, par. 137 (p. 152).

In the letters Rabbi Kook wrote to silence the Yemenite controversy concerning the *Zohar*, he explained at great length and with superb reasoning that the *meshalim* (tropes) of Kabbalah do not lead Jews astray. "Acceptance of the Kingdom of Heaven with simple unity, and the announcement *'Ein 'od milevado'* ('There is none other but Him') which is widespread in Israel, will save all those who walk in the way of the Torah and commandments from any stumbling block." From the endorsement of Rabbi Kook to the anonymous work, *Emunat Hashem* (Jerusalem, 1938); reprinted in *Haskamot ha-RAYaH*, ed. Yismah and Kahana (Jerusalem: Makhon RZYH Kook, 1988), pp. 46-47. See further *Ma'amrei ha-RAYaH*, vol. 2, ed. Rabbi Elisha Aviner (Langenauer) (Jerusalem, 1984), pp. 518-521 (on p. 521, for "R. Meir [Eisenstadt], author of *She'elot u-Teshuvot Panim Me'irot*," read "R. Meir Poppers"); and Rabbi David Cohen, *Kol ha-Nevu'ah* (Jerusalem: Mossad Harav Kook, 1979), pp. 219, 277-278.

AHAREI MOT (AFTER THE DEATH)

A DISCOURSE OF
RABBI AHARON HALEVI HURWITZ OF STAROSHELYE
FOR THE DAY OF ATONEMENT

Rabbi Aharon Halevi Hurwitz of Staroshelye (1766-1828), was the eminent disciple of Rabbi Shneur Zalman of Liadi, founder of HaBaD Hasidism. Rabbi Aharon studied under the master for thirty years. The *Alter Rebbe* ("Old Rabbi") referred to his dearly beloved disciple as *"Doreshei Yihudekha"* ("Seeker of Unity").[1] Rabbi Aharon authored works of Hasidism known for their depth: *Sha'arei ha-Yihud ve-ha-Emunah*; *Sha'arei 'Avodah*; and *'Avodat ha-Levi* (on the Pentateuch). Our reading is taken from the last-mentioned work, *'Avodat ha-Levi* (Lemberg, 1861-1862), *Aharei*, 35d-36c.

In the following *derush* (discourse) the Staroshelyer explains why Nadav and Avihu, the two sons of Aaron, who died in the process of offering incense in the Tabernacle, failed to achieve their goal, and why that goal can be achieved only by Aaron. The goal they sought is actually the reason that the world was created: in order that the divine unity be realized through all the details of Being (*Yesh*). This unity comes under the rubric of *Imma* (Mother). But in order to reach that unity, there must precede the realization of the divine unity at the level of Nothingness (*Ayin*). That unity is referred to as *Abba* (Father). By offering incense (whose eleven ingredients encompass the Other Side), the sons of Aaron hoped to achieve the unity of Being—for that after all, is the true purpose of Creation. Yet since that unity was not preceded by the unity of Nothingness, they failed in their mission. Only Aaron—who comes from a place of Nothingness, of *MaH* or *What* (as in *"Ve-Nahnu mah?"* / "We are what?")—can successfully achieve the sought divine unification.

At the end of the teaching, the Staroshelyer explains the kabbalistic significance of Yom Kippur (the Day of Atonement), when *Malkhut* ascends to *Binah*. He goes on to expound upon the Torah portion of *'Arayot* (forbidden incestuous relations) that is read that day at *Minhah* (the Afternoon Service).

Two leitmotifs of Rabbi Aharon's teaching are *hashva'ah* ("equality") and *peratei ha-yesh* ("the details of Being," or "the particulars of Being").

The first keyword, *hashva'ah*, refers to the ultimate level of reality where the binary of Being (*yesh*) and Nothingness (*'ayin*) collapses into a level unity.[2]

The second term, *peratei ha-yesh*, stresses that *Ein Sof* desires to be manifested precisely in the manifold particulars of Being, so that in a turnabout, Israel might reveal that this multifarious world of ours, this infinitely complex creation, is none other than *Ein Sof*! (One is tempted to conclude with the anonymous quote "God is in the detail.")

Rabbi Aharon Halevi of Staroshelye

TRANSLATION OF TEXT OF 'AVODAT HALEVI

> The LORD spoke to Moses after the death of the two sons of Aaron... (Leviticus 16:1)

We must first understand the significance of [the two divine names] *MaH* and *BaN*.³

MaH is an expression of essence (*mahut ve-'atsmut*).⁴ It is also an expression of nullification (*bittul*) and nothingness (*ayin*).⁵ It is the aspect of *Abba* (Father).⁶

BaN is the aspect of revelation of all the essence, and its extension. And it is the aspect of *Imma* (Mother).⁷

Let us illustrate this with a parable (*mashal*). When it comes to nullification (*bittul*) before a mortal king, there are two methods of nullification:

1) From the perspective of the king's essence; and
2) From the perspective of his revelation and extension, namely that several states and princes efface themselves before him.

Now in one respect, the nullification that proceeds from the essence of the king is superior, for [the subject] feels nothing except the very essence of the king. Yet in another respect, the nullification that proceeds from the extension of the king is superior, for the more one meditates on the greatness of the king as manifested through his extension, the more exalted the essence of the king becomes in [the subject's] eyes.

By the same token, it is understood in relation to service of the LORD, that in one respect, the aspect of *Abba* (Father)—which is the nullification itself,[8] beyond meditation[9] and intellect, i.e. from the perspective of His essence, blessed be He, inasmuch as He alone exists and none other, Heaven forbid—is superior to the nullification that proceeds from the aspect of *Imma* (Mother), which derives from meditation upon the *Yesh* (Being) and the worlds; upon the fact that all the worlds are insignificant [compared to Him].

The reason [that it is superior] is that in the act of meditation one senses the self and that there is someone who loves[10] [the LORD]—except that one nullifies it [i.e., one's ego] to the *Ein Sof* (Infinite), blessed be He. This is not the case when the nullification is from the perspective of *Abba* (Father); from the perspective of His essence. Then one experiences no ego at all.

Yet in another respect, the nullification from the perspective of *Imma* (Mother) is superior to that of *Abba* (Father), as explained in the parable above. This should suffice for the wise.

But there is more. The purpose of the Creation is precisely that there be revealed His perfection, blessed be He. And that revelation can only be to another. In other words, [the purpose is] that He be manifested and revealed in infinitely many details, and

[that] through the service of Israel the manifest reality be nullified to the *Ein Sof* (Infinite), blessed be He, from the perspective of His perfection that encompasses all—from the beginning of all levels to the end of all levels—equally (*be-shaveh mamash*).[11] Since in truth none other exists but Him, and it is inappropriate to refer to Him, blessed be He, as *"Ayin"* (No-Thing), for the contrary, He, blessed be He, is the source and root of Being (*Yesh*) in all its details. Thus, it is written "to bequeath to My lovers *Yesh*" [Proverbs 8:21]. However, Being (*Yesh*) is not separate [from Him] and corporeal, Heaven forbid, as it appears to our fleshly eyes. As it says, "Behold, there is a place with Me" [Exodus 33:21]; and "I am the first and I am the last" [Isaiah 44:6]. That means that even what is drawn down below so that it appears as "Being" (*Yesh*)—all is but the power of His essence, blessed be He.

As it is known, the revelation of *'Atik* (the Ancient of Days) is in [the *sefirah* of] *Binah*.[12] For the aspect of *Binah* exists to raise up all the details of the *Yesh* (Being) to the *Ein Sof* (Infinite), blessed be He. Its root is from the aspect of *'Atik*, which is His essence, blessed be He, that is removed (*ne'etak*) beyond any apprehension or cognition at all. So the *Yesh* (Being) too is not outside Him, as explained above. This should suffice for the wise.

※※※

But *Imma* (Mother)—"from her, judgments are aroused."[13] This means that since the meditation is from the perspective of the *Yesh* (Being) and the worlds—not from the perspective of the

'Etsem (Essence)—there can ramify from this *"dinim"* (judgments), which is to say, *yenikah la-hitsonim* (nourishment for the outsiders, i.e., the forces of evil). This would entail reckoning the *Yesh* (Being) as a separate entity (outside of *Ein Sof*). Even in the very act of nullification there can be self-consciousness that he is the one who is serving the LORD. Therefore, one must first activate the light of *Abba* (Father), i.e., the nullification from the perspective of His Essence, whereby the *Yesh* (Being) is totally insignificant, as mentioned above. Then, even in the light of *Imma* (Mother), i.e., in the meditation from the perspective of the *Yesh* (Being), the nullification will be clear and clean of any admixture [of ego]. One will totally nullify the *Yesh* (Being) to His Essence, blessed be He. This is the saying, "*Abba* (Father) and *Imma* (Mother) are two companions that are inseparable. They proceed as one and rest as one."[14] For the Supernal Father (*Abba 'Ila'ah*)—source of the *Ayin* (No-Thing)—and the Supernal Mother (*Imma 'Ila'ah*)—source of the *Yesh* (Being)—from the perspective of His Essence, blessed be He, are equally (*be-hashva'ah*) one.[15] The two [i.e., *Abba* and *Imma*] are in a state of true *bittul* (nullification), free of admixture [of ego]. This will be explained below in regard to Aaron.

This brings us to the matter of the Tree of Life and the Tree of Knowledge. It is seemingly incomprehensible why the Tree of

Knowledge was ever created, since the Holy One, blessed be He, never commanded that it be eaten.[16]

However, the Tree of Life represents the aspect of *Hokhmah*, [which is to say] *bittul* (nullification) from the perspective of the Essence (as explained above). [On the other hand,] the Tree of Knowledge represents nullification—intellectual and emotional—precisely from the perspective of the *Yesh* (Being), for this was the purpose of Creation (as explained above). As the saying of the *Zohar*: "One must know good and one must know evil, and return oneself to good."[17] What that means is, that the nullification must come through the evil, which is exactly the revealed *Yesh* (Being).

The sin of Adam consisted in his sense of self in the act of nullification, and reckoning *Yesh* (Being) as a reality. For this reason, it is stated before the Sin: "The two of them were naked."[18] *Naked* refers to *bittul* (nullification), devoid of any cloak or concealment. [In that state,] they did not reckon the *Yesh* (Being) as a separate reality. And after the Sin, it is written: "They knew that they were naked."[19] *They knew* means that they sensed themselves in the act of *bittul* (nullification), as mentioned above.

It is written in the sacred books that the sons of Aaron sought to rectify the sin of Adam.[20] For this reason, it is written, "when they approached before (*lifnei*) the LORD."[21] And it states in the *Zohar*[22] that wherever it is written "*lifnei*" ("before"), it refers to [the *sefirah*] of *Malkhut* (Royalty) as it exists at its source, which precedes [the name] *Havayah*.[23] It is known that *Malkhut* symbolizes His extension, blessed be He, in a revealed manner, in order to vivify the *Yesh* (Being). [The sons of Aaron] wished to raise up the *Yesh* (Being) to its root; to His essence, blessed be He. And that is the level of *Binah*, as mentioned above.

This is also the meaning of the [earlier] verse. When they offered the incense, it says: "They offered before the LORD a strange fire."[24] *Strange* refers to the *Yesh* (Being). The symbolism of the incense is known. The eleven ingredients [of the incense] represent the eleven sparks that enliven the Other Side.[25] [The sons of Aaron's] intention was to achieve *bittul* (nullification) precisely through the *Yesh* (Being), as was explained above at length.

But [the sons of Aaron] erred in this respect. The responsibility of raising up the *Yesh* (Being) and nullification through the *Yesh* (Being), was not assigned to them. The reason for that was that there did not shine in their souls the *bittul* (nullification) that proceeds from the light of the Supernal Father (*Abba 'Ila'ah*), namely essential *bittul*, from the perspective of His essence, blessed be He. Rather, [there shone in their souls] solely the light of *Imma* (Mother), and "from her, judgments are aroused," i.e., there is *yenikah la-hitsonim* (nourishment for the outsiders), whereby the *Yesh* (Being) is reckoned as a separate reality, as was explained above at length.

Therefore it is said of them, "They died."[26] Which is to say, there occurred the departure of the light from the vessel, because their intention surpassed the capacity of their vessels. As it is known in regard to the Primordial Kings, who[se vessels] were shattered because the lights were many and the vessels few.²⁷ This should suffice for the wise.

Only through Aaron [could this rectification come about]. In his soul, there shone the *bittul* (nullification) that proceeds from the light of the Supernal Father (*Abba 'Ila'ah*), as it is written: "What (*Mah*) are we?"²⁸ Which is to say, since [Aaron] was nullified from the perspective of His essence, blessed be He, before Whom the *Yesh* (Being) poses no concealment, for He is the Creator of all; of all the details of Being (as stated above)—therefore it was within the power of his soul to raise up and to nullify precisely through the *Yesh* (Being), without there entering into his *bittul* (self-nullification) any admixture of sense of self, as mentioned above.

It is in this context that the *Zohar* refers to Aaron as the "*Shushbina de-Matronita*" ("Bridal Escort of the Queen").²⁹ Just as the Bridal Escort conveys the Queen to the palace of the King, so Aaron's variety of *bittul* (nullification) was from the side of the *Yesh* (Being), to raise it up to the source of all: His essence, blessed be He.

This is what is written "after the death of the two sons of Aaron...he may not enter at any time...,"³⁰ only on Yom Kippur (the Day of Atonement), for then it is a propitious time, [a time of] complete refinement of the material, as the Rabbis observed: "On Yom Kippur there is no eating or drinking...."³¹ Then it states: "Before the LORD you shall be purified."³² I.e., the aspect of *Malkhut* at its source, referred to as "before *Havayah*" (as explained above),³³ is purified and uplifted to the source and root of all. This [comes about] inasmuch as on Yom Kippur [the Day of Atonement] there shines the Supernal Mother (*Imma 'Ila'ah*),[34] which is to say, the *bittul* (self-nullification) from the perspective of the *Yesh* (Being) [undergoing nullification] to His essence, blessed be He. This should suffice for the wise.

And therefore we also read the portion of the *'Arayot* (incestuous relations) on Yom Kippur (the Day of Atonement),[35] for *'ervah* is an expression for revelation, also an expression for shame. The meaning [of this coincidence] is that if one considers the *Yesh* (Being) a reality—even in one's service of the LORD, if one senses one's self in one's act of *bittul* (self-nullification)—it is a great shame, and the opposite of His unity, blessed be He. For His true unity [is] that no other exists but He, blessed be He. This is [the meaning of the verse]: "The nakedness of your sister...whether born at home, or born abroad, [you shall not reveal their nakedness....]"[36] *Born at home or born abroad (moledet bayit o moledet huts)*, i.e., both internally and externally (*hitsoniyut*), if one senses one's self, it is a great shame. This should suffice for the wise.

Even though the divine intention [in creating the world], as it were, was that *bittul* (self-nullification) would derive precisely from the *Yesh* (Being)—the *bittul* (self-nullification) must be clear and clean of any admixture of ego, Heaven forbid. One must nullify oneself to the LORD alone. And this aspect shines on Yom Kippur (the Day of Atonement). This should suffice for the wise.

Now even though the sons of Aaron did not rectify this aspect and it was not raised up through them as they thought, nonetheless, through them was effected the preparation for this raising up. And the rectification comes about precisely through Aaron in the course of the service of Yom Kippur (the Day of Atonement), as mentioned above. For this reason it states: "With this (*be-zot*) shall Aaron enter."[37] *Be-Zot* refers to the revelation of the *Yesod* (Foundation) of *Abba* (Father) in the aspect of *Nukva* (Female),[38] i.e., there shall shine the *bittul* (nullification) that proceeds from *Abba* (Father)—from the perspective of His essence, blessed be He—in the aspect of *Nukva* (Female), that is the revelation of the *Yesh* (Being) below. This should suffice for the wise.

---

[1] See the *haskamah* or approbation of Rabbi Tsevi Hirsch of Chashnik to Rabbi Aaron's *'Avodat ha-Levi*: "And in regard to him it was said: 'Seekers of Your unity (*Doreshei yihudekha*), watch over them as the apple of the eye.'"

According to Heilman, the HaBaD hagiographer, it was actually Rabbi Aaron's companion, Rabbi Dov Baer (known as the *"Mitteler Rebbe,"* the son of Rabbi Shneur Zalman), who, when uttering this line in the prayer *Ana be-Kho'ah*, would have in mind his friend Rabbi Aaron. See Hayyim Meir Heilman, *Beit Rabbi*, Part One (Berdichev, 1902), 67b, note 1.

[2] See Rachel Elior, *The Theory of Divinity of Hasidut HaBaD* (Hebrew) (Jerusalem: Magnes, 1982), pp. 37-43. Elior traces the origin of the term *hashva'ah* back to the early kabbalist Rabbi Azriel of Gerona, although she is puzzled how the teachings of Rabbi Azriel came to the attention of Rabbi Aaron Halevi of Staroshelye.

The most salutary solution, of course, would be that Rabbi Aaron was in possession of a manuscript of Rabbi Azriel's *Derekh ha-Emunah ve-Derekh ha-Kefirah*. There, Rabbi Aaron would have found spelled out in no uncertain terms the *hashva'ah* or equation of *yesh* (Being) and *'ayin* (Nothingness). The portion that treats of this topic has been published from Ms. Halberstam 444 (63b) by Rabbi Moshe Schatz in his introduction to Rabbi Azriel of Gerona, *Be'ur 'Eser Sefirot 'al Derekh She'elah u-Teshuvah* [also known as *Sha'ar ha-Sho'el*] (Jerusalem, 1997), pp. 15-16. (Earlier, it was published by Gershom Scholem in *Studies in Memory of Asher Gulak and Samuel Klein*, Jerusalem 1942. Today, the manuscript is available online through the catalog of the National Library of Israel. The JTSA designation is 1887; the film is designated 10985.)

The second best solution would be that Rabbi Aaron had in his possession a manuscript of Rabbi Azriel's *She'elot u-Teshuvot*. There, in Rabbi Azriel's response to the second question, he would have found the term *"hashva'ah gemurah*" ("absolute equality"). See Schatz, *Be'ur 'Eser Sefirot*, p. 30. Though the compendium *Likkutim me-Rav Hai Gaon* (Warsaw, 1798) includes Rabbi Azriel's *She'elot u-Teshuvot*, unfortunately the text begins with the fifth question (32b).

Short of that, the tracks of Rabbi Azriel's theory of *hashva'ah* (without reference to Being and Nothingness) are to be found in several printed works easily available to Rabbi Aaron Halevi:

- Rabbi Azriel of Gerona's commentary to *Sefer Yetsirah* 1:7, s.v. *Adon Yahid*. Misattributed to Rabbi Azriel's disciple Nahmanides, the commentary was first printed in Mantua in 1562, and was reprinted thereafter numerous times. See C.B. Chavel, *Kitvei Rabbeinu Moshe ben Nahman* (Jerusalem: Mossad Harav Kook, 1968), *Peirush le-Sefer Yetsirah*, p. 455.

This segment of the commentary, "that He is equal to all, and all is united in His (unity and) His equality (*hashva'ah*)," was excerpted by Rabbi Meir ibn Gabbai in his *'Avodat ha-Kodesh* (Venice, 1567). See *'Avodat ha-Kodesh* (Warsaw, 1891; photo offset Jerusalem 1973), I (*Helek ha-Yihud*), chap. 13 (bottom 15d).

- The pseudepigraphic *Sefer ha-'Iyyun* of Rabbi Hammai was first printed in the collection *Likkutim me-Rav Hai Gaon* in Warsaw in 1798. The term *"ahdut shaveh"* occurs there on 37a.

See further Gershom Scholem, *Origins of the Kabbalah* (Princeton University, 1990), pp. 439-442; Mark Verman, *The Books of Contemplation: Medieval Jewish Mystical Sources* (Albany: State University of New York, 1992), p. 34 (lines 3-4) and p. 39, note 10.

[3] Both names are *"millu'im"* (plene forms) of the Tetragrammaton, YHVH. *MaH* is the *"millui de-alphin."* By spelling out the four letters Yod Hé Vav Hé using alephs, the numerical value achieved is 45 or *MaH*. *BaN* is referred to as the *"millui de-hehin."* By spelling out the four letters Yod Heh Vav Heh using the letter *hé*, the numerical value becomes 52 or *BaN*.

[4] The Hebrew word *"Mah"* means "What?" *Mahut* (literally "whatness") is the medieval Hebrew term for quiddity or essence.

[5] In Exodus 16:7, speaking of himself and his brother Aaron, Moses said to the Children of Israel: "and we are what (*mah*)?" This was construed by the Rabbis as an extreme expression of humility. See *b. Hullin* 89a. Also below note 10.

[6] In terms of the *sefirot*, *Abba* would be associated with *"Hokhmah"* (Wisdom), the primal, seminal, undifferentiated thought. The verse in Job 28:12 states: *"Ve-ha-hokhmah me-'ayin timmatsei...."* According to the simple meaning, this is an interrogative statement: "And wisdom, from where shall it be found?" However, the kabbalists turned it into a declarative statement of fact: "And wisdom is found from *'ayin* [nothingness]."

[7] In terms of the *sefirot*, *Imma* would be linked to *"Binah"* (Understanding), whereby the germ of an idea (*Hokhmah*) is spun out and unpacked.

[8] The Hebrew phrase *'etsem ha-bittul* may be translated as "the nullification itself" or "the essence of nullification." The latter seems more likely. Elsewhere, Rabbi Aharon typifies the difference between *Abba* or *Hokhmah* and *Imma* or *Binah* in the following manner:

> *Abba* is the aspect of *Hokhmah*, which is the essence of nullification (*'etsem ha-bittul*) from the aspect of the Essence, without understand-

ing; and *Binah* is the understanding of the nullification (*havanat ha-bittul*).
(Rabbi Aharon Halevi Hurwitz, *Sha'arei ha-Yihud ve-ha-Emunah* [Shklov, 1820], Gate 1 [*Sha'ar Kelalut ha-Yihud*], chap. 5, *Hagahah* [16b])
Cf. *'Avodat ha-Levi, Derushim la-'Aseret Yemei Teshuvah*, s.v. *Shir ha-Ma'alot mi-ma'amakim* (I) (61c): "*Yod Hé* signify *Hokhmah* and *Binah*....*Yod* is...the essence of nullification (*'etsem ha-bittul*)...and *Hé* is...the understanding of the nullification (*havanat ha-bittul*)...."

[9] Hebrew, *hitbonenut*. I have consistently translated *hitbonenut* as "meditation," although a better translation might be "contemplation."

[10] Hebrew, *yesh mi she-ohev*. Rabbi Shneur Zalman's teaching concerning the "*yesh mi she-ohev*" ("there is someone who loves") syndrome, is found in *Torah 'Or (Hosafot), Vayakhel* 114d; *and Likkutei Torah, [Ki] Tavo* 42c.
In HaBaD teaching, this peculiar form of egoism is symbolized by the Biblical character Re'umah, concubine of Nahor (Genesis 22:24). This woman's name is broken down into two words: *Re'u mah!* ("See what!") One boasts that one has achieved a level of self-effacement: "See the *mah*, the *bittul*, the self-annihilation that I have achieved!" Rabbi Shneur Zalman equates Re'umah with *Kelipat Nogah de-Atsilut*. See *Ma'amrei Admor Hazaken—Et-halekh Liozhna* (Brooklyn, 2012), pp. 8-9, s.v. *U-filagsho u-shemah Re'umah*; *Likkutei Torah, Tazri'a* 23d; *Behar* 43a.

[11] This is a central teaching of Rabbi Aharon: *Hashva'ah* (Equality). From the perspective of ultimate reality, Being (*Yesh*) and Nothingness (*Ayin*) are equal.

[12] Cf. Rabbi Aharon Halevi Hurwitz, *Sha'arei ha-Yihud ve-ha-Emunah*, Gate 1 (*Sha'ar Kelalut ha-Yihud*), chap. 5, *Hagahah* (16a). See further Rabbi Shneur Zalman, *Torah 'Or, Lekh Lekha*, 11b; idem, *Likkutei Torah, Derushim le-Rosh Hashanah*, 57a.

[13] In HaBaD literature, the common expression is: "*Binah, minah dinin mit'arin.*" ("*Binah*—from her, judgments are aroused.") See *Zohar* III, 10b. The *partsuf* of *Imma* is synonymous with the *sefirah* of *Binah*. See above note 7.

[14] See *Idra Zuta* in *Zohar* III, 290b; Rabbi Hayyim Vital, *Peri 'Ets Hayyim, Sha'ar ha-Tefillin*, chap. 16.

[15] See above note 2.

[16] This question was asked by one of the great teachers of medieval Ashkenazic Jewry, Rabbi Judah ben Kalonymus of Mayence (the father of Rabbi El'azar of Worms, author of *Roke'ah*). See Levi Yitzhak Charitan, "*Sha'ar Simukhim le-Rabbeinu El'azar mi-Germaiza (Ha-Rokeah)*," in *Hitsei Giborim*, vol. 10 (Nissan, 5777/2017), pp. 370-373, 413-416.

[17] *Zohar* II, 34a.

[18] Genesis 2:25.

[19] Genesis 3:7.

[20] See Rabbi Hayim Vital, *Sha'ar ha-Gilgulim, hakdamah* 33. According to Lurianic teaching, the two sons of Aaron, Nadav and Avihu, were the soul of Adam. This is the import of the verse (Numbers 9:6): "There were men who were defiled by the soul of a man (*le-nefesh adam*)." This refers literally to the soul of Adam!

[21] Leviticus 16:1.

[22] The reference was not found.

[23] On Yom Kippur (the Day of Atonement), *Malkhut* ascends to its source in *Binah*, which precedes the name *Havayah*, symbolized by the *sefirah* of *Tif'eret* (or *Ze'ir Anpin*). See *'Avodat ha-Levi, Derushim la-'Aseret Yemei Teshuvah*, s.v. *Shir ha-Ma'alot mi-ma'amakim* (II) (62c); and *Derushim le-Yom Kippur*, s.v. *Ilmale lo zakhu Yisrael* (1d). See further below note 34.

[24] Leviticus 10:1.

[25] See Rabbi Hayyim Vital, *Sefer ha-Likkutim, Terumah* (Exodus 26:7), s.v. *Ve-'Asita yeri'ot 'izim...'ashtei 'esreh yeri'ot*; idem, *Peri 'Ets Hayyim, Sha'ar 'Olam ha-'Asiyah*, chap. 4, s.v. *Pitum ha-Ketoret*. And see Rabbi Shneur Zalman of Liadi, *Torah 'Or, Bereshit*, 5c; *Toledot*, 20b-c; *Vayyishlah*, 25c-d; *Esther*, 92a; idem, *Likkutei Torah, Shir ha-Shirim*, 7c-d, 10a.

This concept is dealt with at length in my article, "The Curtains of the Tabernacle: R. Shelomo Zalman of Kopyst," in *Orot: A Multidisciplinary Journal of Judaism*, vol. 1 (5751/1991), pp. 33-41.

[26] Leviticus 16:1.

[27] The Mystery of the Death of the Kings is expounded in the section of the *Zohar* known as the *Idra*. HaBaD explains that this came about due to a preponderance of light together with a paucity of vessels (*ribbui 'or u-mi'ut kelim*). The correction (*tikkun*) is the opposite scenario: A reduction of light and an abundance of vessels (*mi'ut 'or ve-ribbui kelim*).

[28] Exodus 16:7. Those words were uttered by Moses in regard to himself and his brother Aaron. Thus, it is established that Aaron reached the level of *bittul* (self-nullification) referred to as *MaH*.

[29] *Zohar* III, 53b.

[30] Leviticus 16:1-2.

[31] *Shabbat* 119a.

[32] Leviticus 16:30.

[33] See above note 22.

[34] On Yom Kippur, *Malkhut* ascends to *Binah*. See *Peri 'Ets Hayyim*, Gate 27 (*Sha'ar Yom ha-Kippurim*), chap 1. "The main theme of this day is the building of *Malkhut* (*binyan ha-Malkhut*) and her correction from her Supernal Mother (*Imma 'Ila'ah*)" (Ibid., chap. 5).

[35] At *Minhah*, the Afternoon Service. See *Megillah* 31a and *Tosafot* ad loc. s.v. *Be-Minhah korin ba-'Arayot*.

[36] Leviticus 18:9.

[37] Leviticus 16:3.

[38] See *'Avodat ha-Levi, Derushim la-'Aseret Yemei Teshuvah*, s.v. *Shir ha-Ma'alot mi-ma'amakim* (II) (62c); and *Derushim le-Yom Kippur*, s.v. *Ilmalé lo zakhu Yisrael* (1c-2a).

The Rebbe of Radzyn and Rav Kook on Doubt

Both Rabbi Gershon Henoch Leiner (1839-1891), Hasidic master of Radzyn, Poland and Rabbi Abraham Isaac Hakohen Kook (1865-1935), first Ashkenazic Chief Rabbi of the Holy Land, have much to say on the subject of doubt as an existential category.[1] Let us examine various texts in their respective *oeuvres*, in order to glean some insight into the *Weltanschauungen* of these two spiritual giants.

The Rebbe of Radzyn is most famous for his attempt to reinstitute the *mitsvah* of *tekhelet*, the blue thread in the *tsitsit* or ritual fringes, a practice unheard of for well over a millennium. Rabbi Leiner traveled to Naples, Italy, in search of the lost *hilazon*, the aquatic creature which had once served the Israelites of old as the source for the precious blue dye. In the Naples aquarium the Rebbe observed the cuttlefish (*Sepia officinalis*) which he believed satisfied the Talmudic, but especially the Maimonidean criteria for *hilazon*. (Maimonides specified that the the blood of the *hilazon* is "black as ink." According to Rabbi Leiner, Maimonides was referring to the sepia ink that the cuttlefish emits when threatened. In German, the cuttlefish is known as *"Tintenfische"* or "Ink Fish.")

In the final analysis, there was no way that the Rebbe could prove beyond a shadow of a doubt that this creature was indeed the *hilazon* of antiquity. Undeterred, the Rebbe resorted to the Rabbinic principal of *"sefeika de-oraita le-humra."* When in doubt regarding a Torah matter (as opposed to a Rabbinic matter), we are stringent. Whereas *tekhelet*, the blue thread, is a Biblical command, *Halakhah* would demand that we don it out of doubt. So argued the Rebbe.

The Rebbe of Radzyn did not rest with this halakhic argument. In his final work, *'Eyn ha-Tekhelet* (published posthumously by his son in Warsaw in 1891), designed as a response to the numerous critiques of his contemporaries, the Rebbe waxed philosophic, revealing the tip of his outlook on life and the centrality of doubt.

Responding to an anonymous authority known to delve into the mysteries of the Kabbalah, who refused to accept that Heaven should require one to exert oneself to perform a commandment whose outcome is dubious, Rabbi Gershon Henoch cited a passage in the *Zohar* concerning the sounds of the *shofar*:

> These Babylonians do not know the mystery of the *yevava* [i.e., *shevarim*] and the *yelala* [i.e., *teru'ah*], and do not know that both are needed: *Yelala* which represents harsh judgment; [and] the three broken sounds [i.e., *shevarim*] which represent soft judgment. The groaning sounds are soft. They do not know, and do both; and we know and do both.[2]

Clearly the *Zohar* is commenting on the doubt ascribed to Rabbi Abahu in the Babylonian Talmud whether the *"teru'ah"* of the Torah refers to a groaning sound (*ganuhei ganah*) or to an ululation (*yalulei yalal*). In the end, to cover all bases, Rabbi Abahu instituted in Caesarea that we blow both sounds.³

Rabbi Gershon Henoch derived from the passage in *Zohar* that at times what appears on the surface level of the *Halakhah* as a doubtful situation, is truly warranted on high for its intrinsic value. Rabbi Gershon Henoch sums up by saying:

> In truth, all the doubts have a place at the root, for the LORD, blessed be He, desires that Israel serve Him and bear his awe, and even through so many concealments. And doubts are included in the will of the LORD, blessed be He, who desired that they serve Him from the midst of the doubt (*ratsah she-ya'avdu 'oto mi-tokh ha-safek*). For if it were not His desire that Israel serve Him from the midst of the doubt, He would have revealed to them explicitly what is His will. And since Israel serve the LORD, blessed be He, even through the doubt—they arouse greater [divine] compassion.⁴

Doubts too have a part to play in the divine service. This is but the tip of the iceberg. In his Hasidic commentary to the Pentateuch, the Rebbe of Radzyn exposes the depth of his new theology of doubt. At the very beginning of the volume, we are introduced to the novel term *"Ilan ha-Safek"* (the Tree of Doubt), the Rebbe's transcription of the "Tree of Knowledge Good and Evil."⁵ There resonates here the key phrase from the halakhic work, "He desired that they serve Him from the midst of the doubt" (*"ratsah she-*

ya'avduhu mi-tokh ha-safek"),⁶ but in this retelling of the Genesis myth, we are treated to an entire metaphysic.

Rabbi Gerson Henoch draws on the extensive Lurianic cosmology, whereby the limitless light of *Ein Sof* is diminished as it descends through the *sefirot*, *partsufim* and worlds,

> until there is created the *Ilan ha-Safek* (the Tree of Doubt), which is the entire existence of the apprehension of man, for the term "tree" in the Holy *Zohar* signifies anything that has within it an entire structure of head, middle and end; any system of influencing and receiving in the form of a whole man is referred to as "tree." And since the LORD, blessed be He, desired the existence of the lowly world, in the *Ilan ha-Safek* (the Tree of Doubt) too—which is the Tree of Knowledge Good and Evil—there is an entire structure.
>
> The matter of this *Ilan ha-Safek* (Tree of Doubt) is as follows:
>
> The certainty (*vada'ut*) of the existence of the Creator and His true essence is clear only to Him. To the creations, the certainty of His existence is not that certain. His true essence, only He knows. Only His existence (*metsi'uto*) He revealed, imparting the knowledge that there is a Creator, but He did not impart the knowledge of His essence (*mahuto*) and quiddity.
>
> However, even in regard to His existence (that there exists a Creator), there are immeasurably many levels of

knowledge, as it states in the *Kedushah* of *"Keter"* that the angels on high also ask: "Where is the place of His glory?" Until in this World of Doubt, the entire knowledge of His existence is in doubt. For so He desired the service of the creations, that they serve Him out of the midst of the doubt. And in this Tree, and the World of this Tree, it constitutes a doubt.

However even in this doubt, there is an entire structure and all the instruments of influencing and receiving. Since the LORD, blessed be He, wished the creation of the doubt—in the knowledge of the doubt of His existence there is also a structure, and in direct proportion to one's ascent in this knowledge, one acquires perfection. For even after several services and intellectual attainments on the part of Man—all this is but knowledge of doubt in comparison with the higher worlds. Only that the LORD, blessed be He, in His abundant compassion, desirous as He is of the service of Man, illumines him in this doubt from His light, in relation to the vessel that Man will have prepared by His service.[7]

The Rebbe does not leave Man hanging in this nebulous state forever. Light beckons in the form of the Tree of Life:

And just as the LORD, blessed be He, created the *Ilan ha-Safek* (Tree of Doubt) in the lowly world, so there is a way that leads from this Tree to reach the light. For this very Tree itself—after the clarifications (*birurim*) and the services of Man—is the Tree of Life.⁸

At the end of the day, man's existential state remains one of doubt. Rabbi Gershon Hanokh's father, Rabbi Ya'akov Leiner of Izbica and Radzyn, drew upon a Talmudic anecdote to illustrate this point:

> Rabbi Pinhas ben Ya'ir was going to ransom captives. He came to the River Ginai. He said to it: "Ginai, split your waters that so that I might cross you."
>
> [The River] said to him: "You are going to do the bidding of your Creator, and I am going to do the bidding of my Creator. In your case, it is doubtful (*safek*) whether you will succeed.⁹ In my case, it is certain (*vadai*) that I shall succeed.¹⁰

From an isolated example of doubt concerning success in a mission of mercy, the story becomes emblematic of the human condition in general. As opposed to the natural elements (in this case, the river) which are not tasked with contending with uncertainty, man is forever forced to come to terms with the insecurity and perplexity of freedom.

In the Book of Daniel, Daniel writes in an autobiographic vein:

And I saw in the vision; now it was so, that when I saw, I was in Shushan the capital, which is in the province of Elam; and I saw in the vision that I was by the stream Ulai.[11]

Rav Kook (as earlier the *Tikkunei Zohar*), plays on the word "Ulai." Besides the geographic designation, in Hebrew the word *"ulai"* means "perhaps" or "maybe."[12] Rav Kook reads the passage as a confession of perplexity on Daniel's part.[13] In this reading, there emerges through a series of aquatic images, a vision of the descent from the original Edenic state of certitude to one of doubt. (The River that departs from Eden cascades down eventually to the Stream of Ulai.) By a process of emanation (similar to the one described by Rabbi Gershon Henoch on the basis of Lurianic teaching), clarity is progressively blurred with each downgrade. With each lessening of the light, the impact of divine existence is blunted once more. But as on Jacob's ladder, the traffic is two-way. Man may either ascend or descend on these levels of certainty:

> There are ascending levels of certainty. No level of certainty resembles the other in either quantity or quality. Conceptions and beliefs are separated from one another by the degree of certainty that enlivens them.
>
> Absolute certainty resides at the pinnacle of the world, in the secret strength of the World to Come: "I shall be that I shall be,"[14] "Whose name is certainty, so His praise."[15] Many streams diverge from it. They are all intertwined, until they come to the stream Ulai (Maybe),

"*Kulei hai ve-'ulai*" ("With all of this, perhaps").[16] Yet the Stream of Ulai (Maybe) is certainty relative to the creations that proceed from it; in relation to all that emanates and extends from its light. And they too, in all of their branches, are relatively certain. And all is fed from the source of certainty that flows from the absolute certainty, certainty above certainty.

In every world, in every man, with [spiritual] ascent, comes increasing certitude. The Stream of Ulai (Maybe) combines with "the River that goes out of Eden,"[17] from the foundation of certainty. And all together draw the sap of life from the source of all the certainties and from the source of all the doubts; from the source of all the certainty—from which all the doubts draw: to enliven them, to raise them up, to refresh them, to beautify them in the Life of the World.

And there is the dwelling place of joy, "strength and joy in His place."[18] "There is no joy like the resolution of doubts."[19] The doubts are revealed at their exalted root in their supernal form; in their positive, healthy, fresh form; in a form that enlivens all their sides. And through those very selfsame doubts,[20] will appear the extraordinary light; the source of worldwide joy; the absolute certainty in its ideal form....[21]

In the following chapter in *Orot ha-Kodesh*, we discover that despite all the intervening *sefirot* of doubt, the first *sefirah* of

Hokhmah (Wisdom) and the final *sefirah* of *Malkhut* (Royalty) connect in certainty. There is a jump from "the supernal wisdom" to the execution of the deed; a leap from "the rarefied thought" to concrete action. In the language of the *Zohar*: "Father established Daughter."[22] All the uncertainty that reigns in the intervening spheres of intellect and emotion, is resolved in the decisiveness and unambiguity of action:

> The levels of certainty do not resemble one another. Each individual according to the level of his own spirit, knows the certain values in each subject.
>
> The secret of faith extends [downward] from the beginning of absolute certainty; it illumines all the branches until it achieves its effect in the certainty that is hidden in the stream Ulai, *"Kulei hai ve-'ulai"* ("With all of this, perhaps").
>
> The more man (and the world) ascends, [the more] he discovers that all those doubts owe their weakness only to their outer aspect, but in their interior—certainty grows stronger. And the bottommost foundation of the deeds is built specifically upon the inner mystery of the values, from the foundation of the supernal wisdom, "Father established daughter."[23] [Thus,] we discover that they [i.e., the deeds] are included in the absolute certainty, "an eternal covenant."
>
> And by the interpenetration of these two wonderful powers—the beginning and the end; the rarefied thought

and the action that leaves a mark upon the world and life—certainty penetrates and pierces all those intermediary pathways and aspects, and all shine in the light of [the LORD] "Whose name is certainty, so His praise."[24]

The relativity of certainty and doubt was given splendid expression in a reflection that was incorporated in Rav Kook's commentary to the prayer book:

> The concepts of certitude and doubt correspond to revealed illumination and hidden revelation. Whatever is beheld as certainty in the revealed state becomes increasingly obscure when we come to the hidden world. The certainties ascend to a hidden state whereby they are beheld from a distance, as if in the form of doubts; and these doubts continue to ascend until they subsequently shine in the form of a certainty clearer and more decisive. And this path, by which we pass from the foundation of certainty which is revealed and lowly, to the foundation of certainty which is exalted, is the way of "the House of Doubt" (*beit ha-safek*),[25] which is covered by clouds of purity ('*arpilei tohar*).[26]

Rav Kook describes a process, a spiritual journey whereby one attains higher and higher levels of certainty. As one ascends, each level of certainty is followed by a subsequent level of skepticism and doubt. What appeared as certainty soon crumbles into doubt.

Beyond that questioning and uncertainty, there looms a higher, more recondite certainty. Though not spelled out, one senses that for Rav Kook this ascent is without end. There is not a single "House of Doubt," but many such houses of doubt.

The House of Doubt is covered by "clouds of purity." This enigmatic phrase, which comes out of the liturgy for *Mussaf* of Rosh Hashanah, served as the title of a work Rav Kook published in 1914 on the eve of World War One. This marriage of two antithetical images—clouds and purity, darkness and light, obscurity and enlightenment—beggars the imagination. Is Rav Kook suggesting that the fog itself is sown with an eery light?

The fact that this existential state is referred to as "the *house* of doubt," tells us that this is a permanent abode. For all of its anxiety and insecurity, this is the house in which mortal man resides more or less permanently. Compare this to Rav Kook's description of the spirituality of the *sukkah*, the booth or *"dirat 'ara'i"* (temporary lodgings), as composed of a series of successive, yet discontinuous and fleeting illuminations.[27]

Doubt, fog is the "house," the *"dirat keva',"* the permanent lodging; certainty, illumination, is the "booth," the *"dirat 'ara'i,"* the temporary lodging.

In the second part of *Reish Millin*, an independent *midrash* on the letters of the Hebrew alphabet,[28] Rav Kook makes some cryptic remarks about the interdependency of certainty (*vadai*) and doubt (*safek*). His remarks are occasioned by the two Hebrew words *'o* (or) and *'im* (if).

It seems that Rav Kook alludes to the *sefirot* represented by the Hebrew letters. *Aleph*, the first letter of the Hebrew alphabet, symbolizes the *sefirah* of *Hokhmah*[29] or Wisdom (also the *partsuf* of *Abba*, or Father) which he associates with the certainty of the beginning. Numerically, *aleph* signifies "one." The conjunctive letter *vav*, corresponding to the *sefirah* of *Tif'eret* or Beauty (also the *partsuf* of *Ze'ir Anpin*), with its numerical value of six (the *shesh ketsavot* or "six directions" of Kabbalistic terminology),[30] signals multiplicity. Thus in the transition from oneness to plurality there is a move from certainty to uncertainty. Choice opens up doubt. When we put the two letters *aleph* and *vav* together, we get the word *o* (or). Rav Kook concludes on a mysterious note: "We find that the doubt is itself the foundation of certainty."[31]

In the much lengthier meditation on the word *'im* (if) Rav Kook addresses several themes, including gender: masculinity and femininity.[32] We are introduced to the world of the mother, as opposed to the world of the father, for *'im* re-vocalized spells the word *'em*, or mother. And since the second letter of the word, *mem*, is derived from *mayim* (water), we are likewise immersed in an aquatic environment.

The transition from the first letter, *aleph*, to the second letter, *mem*, involves a descent from the certainty (*vadai*) of intellect to the uncertainty (*safek*) of emotion and passion.

Running through Rav Kook's meditation is the myth of the reduction of the moon. Once sun and moon were equal in stature.

Alas, at the time of creation, a cataclysmic event took place whereby the moon was diminished in size. Rav Kook, as all kabbalists, longingly awaits the day when the moon will be restored to its former grandeur. Then, sun and moon will once again shine as the "two great luminaries" (*"shnei ha-me'orot ha-gedolim"*).[33] Here, as elsewhere in his writings, Rav Kook understands sun and moon as symbols of reason and feeling.[34]

As we begin our descent from the universe of the *aleph*, associated with *Hokhmah* (Wisdom), we take leave of the certainty of reason and logic, and are confronted with a dimension of doubt. We are leaving behind the Face of Father (*Partsuf Abba*) and encountering the Face of Mother (*Partsuf Imma*). This is a world where emotion reigns supreme.

Here, the element of water presides. Water, with its ability to dissolves differences and individual identities. And out of this undifferentiated, diluvian consciousness, this tidal wave of maternality, comes confusion and—uncertainty.

Yet, within the depth of feeling lies hidden a certainty, for *Abba* and *Imma*, Father and Mother, are truly inseparable. In the *Zohar*'s portrayal, they are "two companions who never separate" (*"trein re'in de-lo mitparshin le-'almin"*).[35] So ultimately, both intellect and emotion will shine with the light of certainty.

Once again,[36] Rav Kook concludes with a quote from *"Ve-Khol ma'aminim"* ("And All Believe"), a liturgical poem recited on the Days of Awe, Rosh Hashanah and Yom Kippur:

Whose name is certainty (*vadai*);[37] so His praise.

In context, "Whose name" would refer to the transcendental state of divinity alluded to by the *aleph*. "His praise" (*tehillato*), on the other hand, refers to the reflected light of divinity that is our immediate reality.[38] Wonder of wonders, *both* arrive at certainty.

---

[1] Rabbi David Cohen ("the Nazirite"), the editor of Rav Kook's magnum opus, *Orot ha-Kodesh*, entitled an entire section of the work, *"Ha-Vada'ut ha-Mekorit"* ("The Original Certainty" or "The Sourceful Certainty"). See *Orot ha-Kodesh*, vol. 1 (Jerusalem: Mossad Harav Kook, 1985), pp. 201-219.

[2] *Zohar* III, 231b.

[3] See the discussion in *b. Rosh Hashanah* 34a. It should be pointed out that the enactment itself took place in Erets Israel in the city of Caesarea. By "Babylonians" the *Zohar* refers to the Babylonian Talmud's reconstruction of the logic that informed Rabbi Abahu's decision. The *Zohar* holds that the underlying reasoning of Rabbi Abahu is other than that arrived at by the Babylonian *sugya*.

[4] Rabbi Gershon Henoch Leiner, *Ma'amar 'Eyn ha-Tekhelet* (Warsaw, 1891; photo offset New York, 1954), chap. 41 (90b).

[5] To the very best of my knowledge, the term *"Ilan ha-Safek"* ("the Tree of Doubt") was coined by Rabbi Gershon Henoch. The appearance of the Aramaic version *"Ilana di-Sefeika"* in the recently published writings of Rabbi Isaac Hutner has the fingerprints of the Radzyner Rebbe all over it. See *Ma'amrei Pahad Yitzhak: Sha'ar Yerah ha-Eitanim* (Sukkot) (New York, NY, 2002), 9:6 (p. 25).

Elsewhere, I have written about the intellectual indebtedness of Rabbi Hutner to Rabbi Yeruham Leiner, the Radzyner Rebbe of Brooklyn. (Rabbi Yeruham Leiner was the nephew of Rabbi Gershon Henoch, son of Rabbi Gershon Henoch's brother, Rabbi Abraham Joshua Heschel Leiner of Chelm.) A disciple of Rabbi Hutner, Rabbi Yitzhak Alster (may he live and be well) testified to me that he would drive Rabbi Hutner to Rabbi Leiner's home in the Boro Park section of Brooklyn. (What the two rabbis discussed together was unknown to Rabbi Hutner's *chauffeur*, who remained sitting outside in the car.) And on the other side of the equation, I was told by Rabbi Yeruham Leiner's son and successor, the late Rabbi Mordechai Yosef Leiner of Boro Park, that whenever he publishes a work of Radzyner Hasidism, the first copy off the press must go to Rabbi Hutner. "It's a standing order from Rabbi Hutner."

A preliminary search, though by no means exhaustive, produced the follow occurrences of the term *"Ilana di-Sefeika"*: Rabbi Gershon Henoch Leiner, *Petihah* to his father, Rabbi Ya'akov Leiner's work, *Beit Ya'akov, Bereishit* (Warsaw, 1890), 14d; Rabbi Gershon Henoch Leiner, *Sod Yesharim, Rosh Hashanah*

(Warsaw, 1902), par. 28 (19b) (quoting Grandfather); and Rabbi Mordechai Yosef El'azar Leiner, *Tif'eret Yosef*, *Ta'anit* 7a (quoting Grandfather).

In *Beit Ya'akov, Bereishit*, par. 59 (18c) we find the almost identical term, *"'Alma di-Sefeika"* ("World of Doubt").

What is beyond doubt is that the expression *"Ilana di-Sefeika"* originated with the Leiner dynasty, which is to say the Rebbes of Izbica and Radzyn. How far back in that line it goes, is difficult to determine. Ostensibly, it originated with the founder of the dynasty, Rabbi Mordechai Yosef of Izbica, since he is quoted in this connection by his grandson Rabbi Gershon Henoch of Radzyn in *Sod Yesharim, Rosh Hashanah*. However, this may not be an exact quote but a paraphrase of the grandfather's saying. One must not exclude the possibility that the specific term *"Ilana di-Sefeika"* was coined by Rabbi Gershon Henoch and placed in the mouth of his grandfather. By the same token, though Rabbi Mordechai Yosef El'azar of Radzyn quotes *his* grandfather (Rabbi Ya'akov Leiner of Izbica and Radzyn), employing the term *"Ilana di-Sefeika"* to define this world of ours, it is possible that too is not an exact quote but a paraphrase. Finally, even the work *Beit Ya'akov, Bereishit*, which certainly contains the teachings of Rabbi Ya'akov Leiner of Izbica and Radzyn, was edited by his son Rabbi Gershon Henoch of Radzyn (see *Hakdamah*, 11b-c).

In his commentary to the Pentateuch, *Ma'or va-Shamesh*, Rabbi Kalonymos Kalman Epstein of Cracow (1751-1823) wrote that halakhic doubt (*sefeika de-dina*) arose as a result of Adam partaking of the forbidden fruit of the Tree of Knowledge. However, the Radzyner's coinage *"Ilana di-Sefeika"* (Aramaic, or in Hebrew *"Ilan ha-Safek"*), "the Tree of Doubt," does not occur there. See *Ma'or va-Shamesh* to Deuteronomy 17:8-9. The quote from *Ma'or va-Shamesh* has been translated into English by Ariel Evan Mayse. See Ariel Evan Mayse, "Tree of Life, Tree of Knowledge: Halakha and Theology in *Ma'or va-Shamesh*," *Tradition* 51:1 (2019), p. 13.

Also, it seems to me that the Radzyner worked *"safek"* up to an existential category whereas in *Ma'or va-Shamesh* it is restricted to the legal realm of *Halakhah*.

[6] Rabbi Gershon Henoch Leiner, *Sod Yesharim 'al ha-Torah* (Brooklyn, NY, 1971), *Bereshit*, 5b (unpaginated). The volume was published posthumously by the author's great nephew, Rabbi Mordechai Yosef Leiner of Brooklyn. Cf. Rabbi Gershon Henoch Leiner, *Petihah* to *Beit Ya'akov, Bereishit* (Warsaw, 1890), 14d: "...that man should serve the LORD, blessed be He, from the midst of this doubt" ("...*she-ya'avod ha-adam et Hashem, yitbarakh, mi-tokh ha-safek ha-zeh*").

[7] *Sod Yesharim 'al ha-Torah*, loc. cit.

[8] Ibid. 5b-6a.

[9] Rashi explains that the captors may not be willing to free their captives in exchange for the ransom money.

[10] b. *Hullin* 7a; Rabbi Ya'akov Leiner, *Seder Haggadah shel Pesah 'im Sefer ha-Zemanim* (Jerusalem, 2010), '*Inyan 'Omer*, s.v. *Torei zahav na'aseh lakh* [Song of Songs 1:11], 247b.

[11] Daniel 8:2.

[12] See *Tikkunei Zohar, tikkun* 69 (Vilna 1869 ed., 116b): "This is the *Shekhinah* which is called 'Ulai,' concerning which it is said, '*Kulei hai ve-'ulai*' ('With all of this, perhaps'), and concerning which it is said, 'by the stream Ulai.'"

In *Shemonah Kevatsim* 2:29, Rav Kook refers to this level as *"Tsedek ha-Tahton"* ("the Lower Righteouness") which is code for the *sefirah* of *Malkhut*, as opposed to *"Tsedek 'Elyon,"* "the Higher Righteousness," synonymous with the *sefirah* of *Binah*. (See Rabbi Moses Cordovero, *Pardes Rimonim* 23:18, s.v. *Tsedek*.) In that piece, simple faith (*emunah peshutah*) is equated with doubt. From that doubt-ridden faith, one graduates to the higher faith (*emunah ha-'elyonah*); from the hard riverbed of doubt and perplexity, man arrives at the Eden of certainty.

[13] The interpretation of the verse in Daniel is reminiscent of Rav Kook's famous interpretation of the first verse in Ezekiel: "And I am in exile." There too, Rav Kook engages in a *jeu de mots*. "The inner, essential 'I' of the individual and of the collective" is in exile, "alienated from its essence." See *Orot ha-Kodesh*, vol. 3, pp. 140-141 = *Shemonah Kevatsim* 3:24. In *Orot ha-Kodesh*, the piece was entitled by the editor, Rabbi David Cohen ("the Nazirite"), "The Quest for the Essential I."

In *Lamentations Rabbah*, the pronoun *"Ani"* ("I") in Ezekiel 1:1 was interpreted as referring to God Himself, as it were. See end *Petihata* to *Lamentations Rabbah* (34); quoted in *Tosafot, Sukkah* 45a, s.v. *Ani ve-hu*.

[14] Exodus 3:14.

[15] Line from the liturgical poem, *"Ve-Khol Ma'aminim"* ("And All Who Believe") recited in Ashkenazic congregations in the repetition of the *Mussaf* service of Rosh Hashanah and Yom Kippur. The poem has been attributed to the early Erets-Israeli poet Yannai (late 5th—early 6th centuries).

In his endnotes, the editor of *Orot ha-Kodesh*, Rabbi David Cohen, quotes from Rabbi Meir Popper's *Me'orei 'Or* (a kabbalistic lexicon) that *"Vadai"* has the numerical value of the divine name *"Ehyeh"* (21). See Rabbi Meir Poppers, *Me'orei 'Or*, s.v. *Vadai*; and *Orot ha-Kodesh*, vol. 2 (Jerusalem: Mossad Harav Kook, 1985), p. 591.

[16] A Talmudic expression. See *b. Hagigah* 4b.

[17] In terms of the *sefirot*, Eden translates to *Hokhmah* (Wisdom) and the River to *Binah* (Understanding).

[18] 1 Chronicles 16:27.

[19] A colloquial proverb.

[20] For the sake of emphasis Rav Kook reinforces this statement fourfold: *"ve-'al yadam, u-mehem, u-vahem, ve-'imam."*

[21] *Orot ha-Kodesh*, vol. 1, pp. 205-206 = *Shemonah Kevatsim* 5:116. In *Orot ha-Kodesh*, the editor, Rabbi David Cohen, entitled the piece, "The Levels of Certainty." In the editor Rabbi David Cohen's arrangement, this chapter is the second in a section entitled, *"Ha-Vada'ut ha-Mekorit,"* or "The Original Certitude."

In the remaining lines (indicated in our quote by ellipsis), Rav Kook lists the seven lower *sefirot* in descending order: *Gevurah, Hesed, Tif'eret, Netsah, Hod, Yesod, Malkhut* (for some reason, *Gevurah* precedes *Hesed* in the list). These are followed by the four worlds, again in descending order: *Atsilut, Beri'ah, Yetsirah* and *'Asiyah*. (*Gevurat* appears once again, this time preceding the world of *Atsilut*.)

In the kabbalistic rendering of the Seven Primordial Kings in Genesis 36:31-39, *Gevurah* does precede *Hesed*. See *Be'ur ha-GRA* to *Sifra di-Tseni'uta* (Vilna and Horadna, 1820), chap. 1 (4a). However, that hardly seems germane to the topic at hand. Much more pertinent is Rav Kook's discussion of his neologism *"Arieliyut"* in *Reish Millin;* see *Iggerot ha-RAYaH,* vol. 3 (Jerusalem: Mossad Harav Kook, 1965), Letter 896 to Rabbi Menashe Hakohen Adler (p. 207).

22 *Zohar* III, 256b *(Ra'ya Mehemna): "Be-Abba yasad Barta."* This is, in a sense, an Aramaic paraphrase of the quote there from Proverbs 3:19: "[The LORD] by wisdom established the earth" *("be-hokhmah yasad arets").*

"Abba" ("Father") is code for the *sefirah* of *Hokhmah* or Wisdom, while *"Barta"* ("Daughter") symbolizes the *sefirah* of *Malkhut*, or Royalty.

This passage from *Ra'ya Mehemna* was quoted by Rav Kook to a fellow Lithuanian kabbalist, Rabbi Pinhas ha-Kohen Lintop; see *Iggerot ha-RAYaH,* vol. 1 (Jerusalem: Mossad Harav Kook, 1962), Letter 112 (p. 142).

23 See the note above.

24 *Orot ha-Kodesh,* vol. 1, p. 207 = *Shemonah Kevatsim* 5:231.

For the significance of the name *"Vadai,"* see above note 15.

25 The expression *"Beit ha-Safek"* comes from the Halakhic literature. See Mishnah, *Kereitot* 6:3; *b. Kereitot* 25a-b. Rabbi Jonathan Eybeschuetz adopted *Beit ha-Safek* as the title of the appendix to *Kereiti u-Peleiti* (Altona, 1763), his commentary to *Shulhan 'Arukh, Yoreh De'ah* (until chap. 111). In that appendix, the author collected various halakhic principles governing cases of doubt.

Inter alia, Rav Kook was very taken with the depth displayed in Rabbi Jonathan Eybeschuetz's work *Urim ve-Tummim,* his commentary on *Shulhan 'Arukh, Hoshen Mishpat.* Rav Kook once told someone that his (Rav Kook's) works of thought should be studied with the same concentration that one studies a *Tummim!*

26 *'Olat Re'iyah,* ed. Rabbi Tsevi Yehudah Hakohen Kook (Jerusalem, 1939) vol. 1, p. 32. This particular section of the *'Olat Re'iyah* commentary appeared earlier in Rav Kook's halakhic manual on the commandment of *tefillin* (phylacteries), *Hevesh Pe'er.* See the second edition of *Hevesh Pe'er,* ed. Rabbis Yitzhak Arieli and Uri Segal Hamburger (Jerusalem, 1925), *"'Olat Re'iyah,"* 51b.

See also the first chapter in our section of *Orot ha-Kodesh,* entitled by the editor Rabbi David Cohen, *"She'elat ha-Vada'ut ha-Mekorit"* ("The Question of Original Certitude"). It occurs in volume 1 of *Orot ha-Kodesh,* pages 203-204 = *Shemonah Kevatsim* 5:183.

The process Rav Kook describes whereby a level of certainty is replaced by doubt, only to be replaced in turn by a higher level of certainty, ad infinitum, is reminiscent of the Mitteler Rebbe's *"he'elem ahar he'elem"* ("concealment after concealment"). See Rabbi Dov Baer Shneuri of Lubavitch, *Sha'arei Orah* (Johannisburg, n.d.; photo offset Brooklyn, NY, 1979), *Sha'ar ha-Hanukkah,* pars. 54-55 (22b-23a).

27 *'Arpilei Tohar* (Jerusalem, 1983), p. 74 = *Shemonah Kevatsim* 2:212. Cf. Maimonides' introduction to the *Guide of the Perplexed* (Pines transl., p. 7): "We are like someone in a very dark night over whom lightning flashes time and time again. Among us, there is one for whom the lightning flashes time and time again, so that he is always, *as it were,* in unceasing light. Thus, night appears to him as day" [italics—BN].

28 *Reish Millin* was first published in London in 1917. That first edition is restricted to individual letters of the alphabet. However, in 1987, a second

edition appeared with additional material, including *"Shorashim"* ("Roots") or words (designated "Part Two"). The method of interpretation in Part One was extended to interpreting whole words based on their constituent letters.

29 See Job 33:33: *"va-a'alefkha hokhmah"* ("and I shall teach you wisdom"). Cf. Rabbi Moses Cordovero, *Pardes Rimonim*, Gate 27 (*Sha'ar ha-'Otiyot*), chap. 4.

30 *Pardes Rimonim* 27:9.

31 *Reish Millin*, ed. Ben-Zion Shapira (Jerusalem: Makhon RZYH Kook, 1987), p. 119.

32 The characterization of the male is "activity," whereas the female is characterized by "passivity." Rav Kook may also be alluding to intellect (the Active Intellect or *"sekhel ha-po'el"*) versus emotion and passion (*"hitpa'alut"*).

33 Genesis 1:16; *b. Hullin* 60b. Cf. Rav Kook's remarks in Part One of *Reish Millin* (including the *"Havrakah"*) apropos of the two horizontal vowel points of the *tsereh*.

34 See *Shemonah Kevatsim* 1:279.

35 *Zohar* III, 4a. The reference there is to the two *sefirot* of *Hokhmah* and *Binah*. In Lurianic Kabbalah these become the *partsufim* of *Abba* and *Imma*.

36 See above note 24.

37 For the kabbalistic significance of the name *"Vadai,"* see above note 15.

38 Although etymologically unsound, Rav Kook, like many authors before him, supposed that the word *tehillah* (praise) is derived from the root *h-l*, which is an expression for the shining of light (Isaiah 13:10; Job 29:3). See *Siddur 'Olat Re'iyah*, vol. 1, p. 197, s.v. *ha-mehullal befi 'amo*; vol. 2, p. 62, s.v. *avorkhah et Hashem be-khol 'et, tamid tehillato be-fi*; and *Metsi'ot Katan*, (Jerusalem: Maggid, 2018), para. 124 (p. 205), note 393. Cf. Rabbi Menahem Mendel Schneersohn of Lubavitch, *Derekh Mitsvotekha* (*Ta'amei ha-Mitsvot*) (Poltava, 1911; photo offset Kefar Habad, 1973), *"Hallel"* (f.148).

BATI LE-GANI
("I CAME TO MY GARDEN")
TWO DISCOURSES OF
RABBIS SCHNEERSOHN AND HUTNER
COMPARED

In the year 5710/1950, in honor of the tenth of Shevat, the *yahrzeit* of his paternal grandmother Rebbetzin Rivkah, Rabbi Yosef Yitzhak Schneersohn, the Lubavitcher Rebbe, composed and distributed a *ma'amar* (discourse) to be studied on that day. As Divine Providence would have it, the tenth of Shevat (which fell on a Sabbath that year) became the Rebbe's own *yahrzeit*, for in the early hours of Shabbat morning he passed to his eternal reward.

Understandably, this discourse entitled *Bati le-Gani* ("I Came to My Garden"), after the verse in Song of Songs 5:1, was viewed thereafter as Rabbi Yosef Yitzhak's last will and testament. When a year later, on the tenth of Shevat, 5711/1951, the first *yahrzeit* of Rabbi Yosef Yitzhak, his son-in-law Rabbi Menachem Mendel Schneerson, formally succeeded him as Rebbe of Lubavitch, his "inaugural address," so to speak, was this *Ma'amar Bati le-Gani*. The discourse became the "mission statement" of the movement, and in years to come, this *ma'amar* would be revisited and reexamined annually on *Yud Shevat*.

The text which serves as the basis for the Rebbe's discourse is the Midrash in *Song of Songs Rabbah* which describes how as each epoch sinned, the *Shekhinah* or divine presence became further removed from our mundane reality:

> Adam sinned and the *Shekhinah* departed to the first heaven.
> Cain sinned; it departed to the second heaven.
> Enoch sinned; it departed to the third heaven.
> The generation of the Flood sinned; it departed to the fourth heaven.
> The generation of the Tower sinned; it departed to the fifth heaven.
> The inhabitants of Sodom sinned; it departed to the sixth heaven.
> The Egyptians sinned in the days of Abraham; it departed to the seventh heaven.

It then took another seven generations, starting with Abraham and culminating with Moses, to bring the *Shekhinah* back down to earth, the final dwelling place or "garden" of the *Shekhinah* being the *Mishkan*, the Tabernacle in the Wilderness:

> Opposite them stood seven *tsaddikim* (righteous) and brought her [back] to earth.
> Abraham lowered her from the seventh to the sixth.
> Isaac lowered her from the sixth to the fifth.
> Jacob lowered her from the fifth to the fourth.
> Levi lowered her from the fourth to the third.

Kehath lowered her from the third to the second.
Amram lowered her from the second to the first.
Moses lowered her to the earth.
And when did the *Shekhinah* rest on her [i.e., the earth]?
On the day that the Tabernacle was erected!

Front and center in the Midrash is a statement essential to the philosophy of HaBaD Hasidism: "The main [dwelling] of the *Shekhinah* is down below." ("*Ikkar Shekhinah ba-tahtonim.*") In the Midrash, it occurs as a rhetorical statement: "Was not the main [dwelling] of the *Shekhinah* down below?" This mirrors the statement at the core of *Tanya*, the primer of HaBaD Hasidism: "The Holy One, blessed be He, desired to have a dwelling place down below."[1] Unlike some other strands within Hasidism, HaBaD is not starry-eyed. It is determined to transform this lowly plane of existence into a Godly abode.

The discourse *Bati le-Gani* is by now very famous. The heirs to Rabbi Yosef Yitzhak, spiritual if not biological, understood its relevance to this generation. They viewed themselves as the seventh generation counting from the *Alter Rebbe*, Rabbi Shneur Zalman, author of *Tanya* and founder of HaBaD Hasidism. And their leader, the seventh Rebbe of HaBaD, Rabbi Menachem Schneerson, was Moses Redivivus.

Unbeknown to many, there is another *ma'amar* which though untitled, might as well be titled *"Bati le-Gani,"* by a contemporary of Rabbi Menachem Schneerson. His name is Rabbi Isaac Hutner. It appears in the volume *Pahad Yitzhak: Hanukkah*.[2]

It too is based on the verse in Song of Songs, "I came to My garden, my sister-bride," and on the Midrash to that verse. In fact, where Rabbi Schneersohn's quotation from the Midrash ends, Rabbi Hutner's quotation begins.

The thought occurred to this writer—wild though it appear—that by juxtaposing these two *ma'amarim* to one another, it might be possible to restart the conversation between two old friends, Rabbi Menachem Schneerson and Rabbi Isaac Hutner. We know for a fact that there was a time that the two of them studied together *be-havruta*. This was in the years before the son-in-law succeeded his father-in-law as Rebbe of Lubavitch. The two men would delve together into Hasidic texts.

How far back did their friendship go? Hard to say. Some have them acquainted with one another in their student days in Berlin before the War.

How long did their friendship persist? In the aftermath of the Six Day War in 1967, when the by then Lubavitcher Rebbe launched his *tefillin* campaign (*"Mivtsa' Tefillin"*), the two men exchanged letters in that regard.[3] In September of 1970, when Rabbi Hutner (together with many other Jewish plane passengers) was hijacked to Jordan by Palestinian terrorists, Rabbi Schneerson remarked at a *farbrengen*, a public gathering, that one of the captives is an expert in the writings of the legendary Maharal of Prague, who was known to perform wonders. Over the years, many letters went back and forth. Rabbi Hutner requested of the Rebbe clarification of various passages in his ancestor's magnum opus *Likkutei Torah* (often of a kabbalistic nature), and the Rebbe responded. (The responses are available in Rabbi Schneerson's multivolume *Iggerot Kodesh*.)

There were recently made public the letters Rabbis Schneerson and Hutner traded in 1977. On Purim of that year, the Rebbe sent as a gift, a volume of Hasidic teachings collected from the writings of his ancestor (and namesake) Rabbi Menachem Mendel Schneersohn (*"Tsemah Tsedek"*). Acknowledging receipt of the gift, Rabbi Hutner wrote that the word *"hit'anyenut"* or "interest" (which the Rebbe used in his cover letter) does not do justice to Rabbi Hutner's connection to HaBaD Hasidism. "A good portion of my soul world is planted on springs of HaBaD. Were one to empty me of this nourishment, this would cause a change in my entire existence."[4]

I shall not engage in historical revisionism. Along with abiding friendship, there was also deep revulsion on Rabbi Hutner's part brought on by a Lubavitch Messianism that became increasingly pronounced with the passage of time.

I will, in the course of this presentation, invoke literary license to magnify the *ma'amar* in *Pahad Yitzhak* from the local level of Hanukkah when it was first taught, to the global level, whereby—no less than the Lubavitch *Ma'amar Bati le-Gani*—it may be taken as a mission statement for an entire generation that has witnessed and lived through the birth of the modern State of Israel. Hopefully, by the end of our presentation, we will succeed in identifying the radical theology in these two discourses and discussing their relevance to our day.

※※※

Rabbi Hutner's discourse begins with a *diyyuk*, an analysis of a curious phrase in Maimonides' *Hilkhot Hanukkah*. (In fact, much of the *ma'amar* pivots on Maimonides' *Mishneh Torah*.) Maimonides wrote:

> The commandment of the candle of Hanukkah is a very beloved commandment.[5]

Rabbi Hutner questions why this commandment should be more beloved than all other commandments. Waxing romantic, he notes that there is something unique, something extraordinary about the love relation at its beginning. *Hanukkah*, which means "dedication," launches a new love between the Holy One, blessed be He, and *Knesset Israel*. As such, it fits into a pattern of many such *hanukkot* in Jewish history: the dedication of the Tabernacle in the Wilderness; the dedications of First and Second Temples (the First by King Solomon, the Second by Ezra the Scribe), and finally, the future dedication of the long-awaited Third Temple by King Messiah. All these dedications share a common denominator: an element of the extrajudicial. And that's where *Bati le-Gani* comes in.

The Midrash runs through a list of halakhic irregularities at the time of the dedication of the Tabernacle. Of that list, Rabbi Hutner singles out for mention the fact that the Princes offered *ketoret* (incense) as an individual offering, when in normative *Halakhah* it is strictly a communal offering.[6] We are presented with Rashi's rendition of the Midrash which is both pointed and poetic:

> **I came to my garden**—in the days of the dedication of the House…
>
> It refers to the incense which the Princes offered as an individual incense upon the outer altar, and it was accepted—though it is something that is not the procedure for the generations [to come].
>
> Therefore it says, "I ate my wood with my honey." There is a honey that grows in stalks…They suck out the sugar and throw away the wood.
>
> "And I, out of great love, ate my wood with my honey. I ate the cane with the sugar; that which is unfit—the voluntary incense that the Princes offered—together with that which is fit. And I accepted them on that day."[7]

The exceptional love that God has for Israel at the time of the dedication of a new sanctuary calls for exceptional, extrajudicial offerings. Rabbi Hutner goes so far as to suggest that this overarching principle of *"Bati le-Gani,"* as developed in the Midrash, was the guiding light of Maimonides' remarkable *tour de force* of Jewish history in *Hilkhot Ma'aseh ha-Korbanot*:

> All the measures of the libations mentioned in the Book of Ezekiel, and the numbers of those sacrifices, and the sacrificial orders written there—are all *milu'im* (dedications), and do not obtain for generations, rather the prophet commanded and elaborated exactly how they will sacrifice at the dedication of the altar in the days of King Messiah when the Third Temple will be built.
>
> And just as the Princes offered, at the dedication of the altar, things whose likes do not continue for generations, and they sacrificed on the Sabbath, so the Prince [i.e., King Messiah] will offer his dedicatory sacrifice on the Sabbath in the future, as stated explicitly there [i.e., in the Book of Ezekiel].
>
> And so the sacrifices offered in the days of Ezra by those returning from [Babylonian] captivity—were dedications, and do not obtain for generations.[8] But the things that obtain for generations are the words of the Torah that we explained, as transcribed from the mouth of Moses our Teacher. They are not to be added to or detracted [from].[9]

Rabbi Hutner fills out Maimonides' overview of history by including the eating on the fast of Yom Kippur at the time Solomon dedicated the Temple in Jerusalem.[10]

The same extraordinary love (*hibah* or *havivut*) came into play at the time of the Hasmonean dedication (or perhaps re-dedication) of the altar in the Second Temple era. That divine affection too was expressed in something which by normal standards would be "quasi-prohibited" (*"me-'ein issur"*), namely the lighting of a *menorah* or candelabrum (albeit an eight-branched as opposed to seven-branched candelabrum)[11] outside the Temple precincts in commemoration of the miraculous occurrence in the Temple.

What comes out of the discourse is that the dedication of a new Temple consistently brings about an incursion of prophecy whose mandate is extralegal (*hora'at sha'ah*);[12] an exposure to the divine mystery that defies human logic and rational investigation.

Drawing an analogy between the construction of the Tabernacle and the creation of the world, Rabbi Hutner reasons that just as the onset of creation comes under the rubric of "the glory of God to conceal a matter" (*"Kevod Elohim haster davar"*), and the continuation of creation comes under the rubric of "the glory of kings to search out a matter" (*"kevod melakhim hakor davar"*)[13]—by the same token, the dedication of the House of the LORD must partake of the hidden, the inscrutable, the mysterious, as opposed to the continuation of the House, which must be legislated by normative, rational, logical *Halakhah*.

This is a "rough-and-ready" summary of a lengthy disquisition with many ingenious twists and turns along the way. I think I am on safe ground when I say that it is one of the most scintillating discourses in *Pahad Yitzhak*.

The reader of *Pahad Yitzhak* is left wondering. Is this *ma'amar* restricted to *Hilkhot Hanukkah*? Is it but a highly imaginative *diyyuk ba-Rambam*; nothing more than a resourceful commentary on Maimonides' language? Or are there broader implications? Is Rabbi Hutner perhaps alluding to the mysterious events, the God-awful breakdown of *Halakhah* that—painfully—accompanied the birth of the State of Israel (viewed by some as the "beginning of redemption")?[14] This paradox continues to exercise Orthodox Jewish theologians to this day. Does this *ma'amar* of the mature thinker in some way—however circuitous—reflect the teaching of the controversial Chief Rabbi of Erets Israel, Rabbi Abraham Isaac Hakohen Kook, to which Isaac Hutner was exposed in his youth?[15]

When challenged concerning the legitimacy of the Zionist enterprise, Rav Kook quoted the famous halakhic principle: "We build [the Temple] with unconsecrated materials and afterwards sanctify." (*"Bonim ba-hol ve-ahar kakh makdishim."*)[16] In a personal letter to his beloved disciple Moshe Seidel, Rav Kook penned a line that has since become a slogan: "The old will be renewed, and the new—made holy." *("Ha-Yashan yithadesh, ve-he-hadash—yitkadesh.")*[17]

Perhaps Rav Kook's optic on the renewal of the Land was refracted through Rabbi Hutner's consciousness and contributed to this fascinating *ma'amar*.

Rav Kook envisioned a redemption which would unfold in two distinct phases: an earlier secular state that would be followed by a sacred state.[18] In the first phase, the emphasis is upon renewal. Later, the emphasis shifts to sacralization or sanctification. To evoke Rashi's graphic imagery, in the initial phase, the God of Israel ingests a lot of wood along with the honey.[19]

Rabbi Yosef Yitzhak drew attention to the fact that the Tabernacle was constructed of acacia wood (*'atsei shittim*). Etymologically, he linked *shittim* to *shetut*, folly or madness. He was rehashing the teaching of his illustrious father, Rabbi Shalom Dov Baer, who earlier, in his *Kuntres u-Ma'ayan mi-Beit Hashem*,[20] developed the theme of *"shetut di-kedushah"* or "holy madness."

Rabbi Yosef Yitzhak retold the Talmudic anecdote concerning Rav Shmuel bar Rav Yitzhak who at weddings would juggle three myrtle sprigs before the bride in order to gladden her heart. At the time, he was criticized by Rabbi Zeira who felt that such behavior was undignified for a Torah scholar. After Rav Shmuel bar Rav Yitzhak's death, at his funeral procession a "pillar of fire" separated between the bier and the mourners—a heavenly honor reserved for only one or two in a generation. Thereupon, Rabbi Zeira was forced to recant his previous judgment: "His folly (*shetuteh*) earned him this honor."[21]

Rabbi Yosef Yitzhak touched briefly on the term of derision by which the prophet was sometimes referred to in *TaNaKh*: *"meshuga'"* ("madman").[22]

The Rebbe was calling upon the faithful to deviate from the dictates of polite, "sane" society, if need be. The spiritual power that had fearlessly stood up to the might of the Soviet empire would not be deterred by the *politesse* of Western civilization. For the divine presence to reside inside each and every one of us, our inner Temple must be constructed of *'atsei shittim*. We have to step outside of ourselves, outside of our "comfort zone." If need be, we must take leave of our senses, lapsing like the prophets of yore into "temporary insanity."

There is a dovetailing of the two *ma'amarim* based on *Bati le-Gani*, that of the Rebbe and that of the Rosh Yeshivah. Both men understood that the generation of renewal will be confronted with unprecedented challenges that will require a suspension of the senses, of normal judgment.

Besides Rav Kook, there was another teacher with whom Rabbi Hutner studied and whose theology—or that inherited from his ancestor, the famed Izhbitser Rebbe—exerted a profound influence upon him, and that was Rabbi Yeruham Leiner, Rebbe of Radzyn (1888-1964).[23] One suspects that it was in the *Beit Midrash* of Izhbitsa-Radzyn that Rabbi Hutner learned the "mystery of the incense."

Rabbi Ya'akov Leiner of Izhbitsa-Radzyn contrasted the clear, pellucid olive oil of the *menorah* to the cloud of incense.[24] By now, it should not come to us as a surprise that precisely through the murky, impenetrable smoke of the incense shines the love of the Holy One, blessed be He:

> Oil alludes to clear, pure fear of the LORD. Oil is the light...by which man may understand what the LORD has spoken, whether one should do an act or refrain from it.

Oil represents intellect and wisdom that erects fences before man.

Incense alludes to the LORD's love for and cleaving to Israel. *Ketoret* (incense) is *kitura*, a bond.[25] Let man be certain that he is not disconnected from the LORD, even at the time of forgetting, of involuntary stumbling. Even then, he is stuck to the LORD....

The mystery of incense (*raza di-ketoret*) surpasses in greatness the mystery of the oil (*raza de-shemen*), which symbolizes intellect. Therefore it is said of the *menorah*, "outside the curtain of the ark,"[26] and of the altar of incense, "before the curtain...before the ark"[27] (though the incense altar is also outside the curtain).... It is as if it stands all the way inside (*lifnai ve-lifnim*)...

If one does not believe that even at a time of distraction, when one is not in a settled state of mind (*yishuv ha-da'at*), there is a depth beyond his intellect, and that the LORD desires to teach him thereby new matters of Torah and ways of the LORD—then, in this regard, it is said, "He who loves wine and oil, shall not become rich."[28]... Should man desire to avoid all doubt and conduct himself purely in the way of light—he will never become [spiritually] rich.

Who is to say that only when one is in a lucid, settled state of mind, one is connected to the LORD, and at a time of distraction, one is disconnected from the LORD?

Are there not times that man cannot be in a settled state of mind? And this applies even to *gedolim* (great men).²⁹

---

¹ Rabbi Shneur Zalman of Liadi, *Tanya*, chap. 36 (45b). The quote comes from *Midrash Tanhuma, Nasso* 16. That Midrash parallels the Midrash in *Song of Songs Rabbah*.
² Rabbi Isaac Hutner, *Pahad Yitzhak: Kuntres ve-Zot Hanukkah* (New York, NY, 1989), *ma'amar* 12 (pp. 106-117). As a rule, the *ma'amarim* in *Pahad Yitzhak* are untitled. They are also undated. There is every indication that this particular *ma'amar* was delivered before 1961.
³ The halakhic correspondence between them concerning the Rebbe's *Mivtsa' Tefillin* was published some years ago in a handsome volume entitled *Mi-Beit ha-Genazim*, ed. S.D. Levin (Brooklyn, 2009). Rabbi Hutner called into question the halakhic validity of wrapping phylacteries on a Jew who is totally oblivious to their significance. The Rebbe defended his initiative on halakhic grounds.
⁴ Rabbi Isaac Hutner, writing from Brooklyn, "Monday, *Va-Yakhel—Pekudei*, 5737." Published (complete with facsimiles) in *Heikhal ha-Besht*, Year 11, no. 35 (Tishri 5774/2014), pp. 75-77.
⁵ *MT, Hil. Hanukkah* 4:12.
⁶ *b. Menahot* 50a.
⁷ Cf. *Numbers Rabbah* 13:2; *Midrash Tanhuma, Naso* 20. Rabbi Shelomo Fisher *shelit"a* offered the novel suggestion that though the incense of the Princes was not a communal offering (*korban tsibbur*) in the strict sense, it was the closest thing: *bi-kenufya* (à la *b. Yoma* 51a). See Rabbi S.Y.Y. Fisher, *Beit Yishai: Derashot* (Jerusalem, 2003), chap. 2 (p. 29); chap. 54 (pp. 408-409).

Perhaps the Midrash concerning the desirability of individual incense at the time of the dedication of the Tabernacle can shed light on a curious comment of the *Torat Kohanim* (*Vayikra, Dibbura de-Hovah* 3:11) as spelled out by Rabad of Posquières in his commentary thereto:

> If [the incense altar] was dedicated with the incense of a private individual, then it is as if it was not dedicated, for he transgresses [the prohibition of] "Do not bring upon it a strange incense" [Exodus 30:9].

Rabbi Yosef Dov Halevi Soloveitchik of Jerusalem found the Rabad's remarks inscrutable because the incense of an individual is not reckoned incense at all! Quoted in Rabbi Ze'ev Dov Tchetchik, *Torat Ze'ev: Zevahim* (Zikhron Moshe, 1985), chap. 21 (p. 89).

For lack of a better explanation, I would say that the *Torat Kohanim* sought to forewarn that the *ketoret yahid* (individual incense), however desirable it might have been as a *hora'at sha'ah*, cannot serve for posterity as a *hinnukh ha-mizbe'ah*, a normative dedication of the altar.

In another vein, *Tosafot* point out that the burning of the *hat'at yahid* (individual's sin-offering) during the *shiv'at yemei ha-millu'im* (seven days of installation) was a *hora'at sha'ah* (ad hoc legislation). See *Tosafot, 'Avodah Zarah* 34a, s.v. *Ba-Meh shimesh Moshe.*

[8] Concerning irregularities (*"hora'ot sha'ah"*) in the Book of Ezra, see Rabbi Leib Rutta, *Reshimot Lev,* vol. 1 (Brooklyn, NY, 2000), *Pesah* 5730 (p. 3).

[9] *MT, Hil. Ma'aseh ha-Korbanot* 2:14, 15. Rabbi Hutner believed that he thereby solved the problem posed by Rabbi Meir Simhah Kohen (*'Or Same'ah* ad loc.): How is it possible for a prophet to legislate across eons of time, when in principle, the legislative power of the prophet is restricted to *ad hoc* measures (*hora'at sha'ah*)? (See earlier Rabbi Tsevi Hirsch Chajes, *Torat Nevi'im* [Zolkiew, 1836], 10b-11a.)

Within the parameters of Maimonides' system, which maintains strict separation of *Halakhah* and *Nevu'ah* (Prophecy), there remain several unresolved issues. Some light was shed on the broad topic by Rabbi Tsevi Hirsch Chajes (subject of Rabbi Hutner's daughter, Bruria Hutner David's doctoral dissertation, *The Dual Role of Rabbi Zvi Hirsch Chajes: Traditionalist and Maskil*, Columbia University 1971).

Yet there remains much to be clarified within Maimonides' system. For example, several students of Rabbi Isaac Ze'ev Halevi Soloveitchik ("Brisker Rov") recorded in his name that the commandment to annihilate Amalek cannot be executed without an "on site" command from a prophet. (See the recent *Reshimot Talmidim me-Rabbi Yitzhak Ze'ev Halevi Soloveitchik 'al Seder ha-Torah* [Rehovot: Da'at Sofrim, 2016], *Beshallah,* pp. 242-243.) This clearly flies in the face of what Maimonides wrote in his Introduction to the *Commentary to the Mishnah* that the prophet Samuel's command to Saul to wage war against Amalek comes under the rubric of "commands that are not in matters of religion, such as instructing to war against a certain city or a certain nation now" (Kafah ed. p. 4, s.v. *ve-ha-helek ha-sheni*). This statement is insupportable if—as maintained by Rabbi Isaac Ze'ev—the prophet plays an integral part in the religious observance. Maimonides is most emphatic that the role of Samuel on that occasion was restricted to the temporal aspect; to the practical execution and implementation of the commandment. Samuel played no part whatsoever in the halakhic legislation of the commandment.

In the opposite direction, Rabbi Aryeh Pomerantchik, a devoted disciple of the Brisker Rov, entertained the notion that the prophet and Urim and Thummim necessary for adding on to the city [of Jerusalem] or the Temple precincts, did not act in a consultatory capacity but were present purely as a formality. See *Yehegeh ha-Aryeh* (Jerusalem, 1999), *b. Shavu'ot* 14b (pp. 89-90). See further *Hiddushei ha-Gram ve-ha-Grid* [Soloveitchik]: *'Inyenei Kodashim* (Jerusalem, 1993), *Hil. Beit ha-Behirah* 4:1 (pp. 16-17); Rabbi Yosef Dov Halevi Soloveitchik [of Boston], *Iggerot ha-Grid Halevi* (Jerusalem, 2001), beg. *Hil. Melakhim* (pp. 266-267, 269-270).

Inter alia, see the glosses of Rabbi Tsevi Hirsch Chajes (*b. Shavu'ot* 15a) and Rabbi Samuel Strashun (*b. Shavu'ot* 16a); and the discussion in Rabbi

Yehiel Mikhel Charlop, *Torat ha-Hof Yamim: Sefer ha-Zikaron* (New York, 1985), pp. 281-285.

[10] *b. Mo'ed Katan* 9a. Gersonides wrote that the eating on Yom Kippur on that occasion was a *hora'at sha'ah* on the part of the prophets present there. See Ralbag, 1 Kings 8:65; and Rabbi A.M. Alter, *Mikhtevei Torah me-Admor mi-Gur*, ed. Z.Y. Abramowitz and I.M. Alter (Tel Aviv, 1987), Letter 3 (p. 11).

[11] See Maimonides, *MT, Hil. Beit ha-Behirah* 7:10; and Rabbi Abraham Isaac Hakohen Kook, *Mitsvat Re'iyah, Orah Hayyim* 670:1.

[12] Rabbi Hutner exerted much effort to bring Hanukkah into line, knowing only too well that the events of Hanukkah occurred after the cessation of prophecy. In Rabbi Hutner's reading of Jewish History, the extralegal practices associated with the dedication of a new House, are commanded either by prophets, or after the cessation of prophecy, by sages.

In Rav Kook's reading of the rebirth of Erets Yisrael, in lieu of prophecy, there is a *pirtsah* or breach of the law:

> Only when prophecy rests on Israel is it possible to fix such a matter by a *hora'at sha'ah*; then it is done in a manner that is permissible and an express commandment. Because of the blocking of the light of prophecy, this fixing is accomplished by a long-term breach that pains the heart with its exterior, and gladdens the heart with its interior.
> (Rav Kook, *'Arpilei Tohar*, Jerusalem 1914 = *Shemonah Kevatsim* 2:30)

(Cf. Rabbi Aharon Halevi Hurwitz of Staroshelye, *Sha'arei 'Avodah* 4:10: "This thing is either through a *hora'at sha'ah* or a command of the LORD, or done unwittingly, such as a *ba'al teshuvah* who committed a sin because of a spirit of folly.")

This would be a fundamental difference between Rav Kook's and Rabbi Hutner's readings of history.

[13] Proverbs 25:2; *Genesis Rabbah* 9:1; Rabbi Judah Löw (Maharal), *Gevurot Hashem*, First Introduction.

[14] The term *"athalta di-ge'ulah"* ("beginning of redemption"), contrary to what some assume, is not of modern coinage but appears in *b. Megillah* 17b. See the letter of Rav Kook to Moshe Seidel in *Iggerot ha-Rayah*, vol. 3 (Jerusalem: Mossad Harav Kook, 1965), p. 155 (Letter 871). The letter, datelined "19 Shevat, 5678, London," was written in the aftermath of the Balfour Declaration.

For positive attitudes of both Sephardic and Ashkenazic luminaries toward Zionism and the establishment of the State of Israel, see the two volumes of Rabbi Yitzhak Dadon's collection, *Athalta Hi* (Jerusalem, 2006, 2008).

As is public knowledge, Rabbi Hutner's own attitude toward Zionism and the secular State of Israel became increasingly hostile with the years. See Rabbi Hutner's famous anti-Zionist article, "'Holocaust'—A study of the term and the epoch it is meant to describe," *Jewish Observer* XII (8), 3-9 (October 1977). Recently, the article was analyzed by Rabbi Gamliel Shmalo, *"Radikaliyut filosofit be-'olam ha-yeshivot: Harav Yitzhak Hutner 'al ha-Sho'ah"* ("Philosophical Radicalism in the World of the *Yeshivot*: Rabbi Isaac Hutner on the Holocaust"), *Hakirah*, vol. 19, pp. 35-56.

Steven Schwarzschild, an interpreter of Hutnerian thought, wrote:
> I have notes of a long conversation with R. Hutner in Jerusalem in February 1975, which makes his extremely critical stance toward Zionism and the State of Israel very clear.
> (Steven Schwarzschild, "Isaac Hutner" in *Interpreters of Judaism in the Late Twentieth Century*, ed. Steven T. Katz [Washington, D.C.: B'nai B'rith Books, 1993], p. 164, n. 12)

For Schwarzschild's understanding of Rabbi Hutner's nuanced approach to the State, see ibid. pp. 161-163.

15 There was a familial relation between Rav Kook and the young Isaac Hutner. They were *"mehutanim"* (related by marriage). Rav Kook's daughter-in-law, married to his only son Tsevi Yehudah, was Hava Leah née Hutner. Rabbi Isaac Hutner and Havah Leah Hutner were cousins. Despite the fact that they both shared the same last name of "Hutner," that was not how they were related. Their common ancestor's last name was not Hutner but Segal. Hava Leah's maternal grandfather, Rabbi Yehudah Segal, a Warsaw *dayyan*, and Rabbi Isaac Hutner's paternal grandmother, Rahel Hutner (née Segal) were brother and sister, making Havah Leah Kook and Rabbi Isaac Hutner second cousins.

16 *Me'ilah* 14a; Maimonides, *MT, Hil. Me'ilah* 8:4. See further *y. Sanhedrin* 1:3 (differing opinions of Rabbi Yohanan and Reish Lakish). By way of this halakhic principle, Rabbi Tsevi Yehudah Kook interpreted the fact that Noah first dispatched the raven, an impure bird, and after sent out the dove, a pure bird. "This is a divine instruction, to make use also of the impure raven." See Rabbi Hayyim A. Schwartz, *Mi-Tokh ha-Torah ha-Go'elet*, vol. 2 (Jerusalem, 1989), *Parashat Noah 5732*, p. 14.

17 *Iggerot ha-Rayah*, vol. 1 (Jerusalem: Mossad Harav Kook, 1962), p. 214 (Letter 164).

18 In his famous eulogy for Theodor Herzl, *"Ha-Misped bi-Yerushalayim"* ("The Lamentation in Jerusalem"), Rav Kook interpreted the legend of the two Messiahs—Messiah son of Joseph followed by Messiah son of David—as symbolic of the material and spiritual phases of the Redemption. See Bezalel Naor, *When God Becomes History: Historical Essays of Rabbi Abraham Isaac Hakohen Kook* (New York, NY: Kodesh, 2016), pp. 38-56.

See also Rav Kook's *Shemonah Kevatsim* 2:88. (The piece first appeared in print in the undistributed *'Arpilei Tohar* in 1914.)

19 Recently a letter of Rav Kook's eminent disciple (*talmid muvhak*) Rabbi Jacob Moses Harlap to Rabbi Hayyim Ya'akov Levene was published, in which he reveals "the mystery of the abandonment by many of Torah and *mitsvot.*" Referring to the passage in the Talmud (*b. Niddah* 30b), whereby the fetus is taught the entire Torah, only to forget it at birth when an angel administers a slap on the baby's mouth, Rabbi Harlap concludes: "They are the result of the slap." He trails off on an optimistic note: "We must hope that soon all of our treasures will return to us and all Israel will grow." See *Yeshurun*, vol. 30 (Nissan, 5774/2014), p. 501 (facsimile).

Rabbi Hutner was familiar with Rabbi Harlap. (There are some who go so far as crediting Rabbi Harlap with inspiring Rabbi Hutner to pursue the study of Maharal's works. Rabbi Harlap taught Maharal in Merkaz Harav, Rav Kook's *yeshivah* in Jerusalem.) There are definite similarities between the oeuvre of

Rabbi Harlap, *Mei Marom*, and Rabbi Hutner's oeuvre *Pahad Yitzhak*. Both works approximate the style and syntax of Maharal of Prague. Rabbis Harlap and Hutner were influenced by Maharal not only syntactically, but what's more significant, substantively. Their *Weltanschauung* was shaped by Maharal.

[20] Rabbi Shalom Dov Baer Schneersohn delivered the discourse in Lubavitch in 1903, in which year it was distributed in the handwriting of Rabbi Shmuel Sofer in a limited stencil edition of 300 copies. It was first printed forty years later in Brooklyn (1943). See *Kuntres u-Ma'ayan mi-Beit Hashem* (Brooklyn: Kehot, 1958), pp. 4, 56-57.

The title *U-Ma'ayan mi-Beit Hashem* comes from the verse in Joel 4:18: "And a spring shall come forth out of the house of the LORD, and shall water the valley of Shittim."

[21] b. *Ketubot* 17a. (Cf. *Genesis Rabbah* 59:4.)

[22] 2 Kings 9:11. (See also Hosea 9:7.)

[23] Reports of Rabbi Hutner's intellectual interface with Rabbi Yeruham Leiner, Radzyner Rebbe of Brooklyn, have come to the writer (BN) from both sides. First, the latter's son and successor, Rabbi Mordechai Yosef Leiner, once confided that every time he publishes a *sefer* of his ancestors, the first copy must go to Rabbi Hutner, who has a "standing order." Second, Rabbi Yitzhak Alster, a disciple of Rabbi Hutner, revealed that he was the *"ba'al 'agoloh"* (chauffeur) who drove Rabbi Hutner to Rabbi Leiner's home for their meetings. Rabbi Alster was not privy to the actual discussions as he remained outside in the car.

Rabbi Leib Rutta, *Reshimot Lev* (Brooklyn, NY) recorded that on Pesah of 5732, Rabbi Hutner recounted a tradition concerning Rabbi Zadok Hakohen of Lublin and his master Rabbi Mordechai Joseph of Izhbitsa (author *Mei ha-Shilo'ah*) that Rabbi Hutner had heard from the Radzyner Rebbe, who received it from his father (Rabbi Abraham Joshua Heschel Leiner). (The wording differs somewhat in the two editions of *Reshimot Lev*. In the softcover 1997 edition, p. 60, the text reads: "An anecdote that he heard from the Rav of Radzyn." In the hardcover 2000 edition, vol. 1, p. 63, the text reads simply: "From the Rav of Radzyn." A phone conversation with Rabbi Rutta clarified that the language of the first edition is a faithful rendition. The slightly different version of the second edition should be chalked up to stylistic rather than substantive change.) For other traditions concerning Rabbi Zadok Hakohen of Lublin transmitted by Rabbi Abraham Joshua Heschel Leiner, see Rabbi Yeruham Leiner, *Tif'eret Yeruham* (Brooklyn, NY, 1967), pp. 156-164.

[24] One resists the temptation to juxtapose the Western term "cloud of unknowing."

[25] *Zohar* III, 37b. (Cf. *Genesis Rabbah* 61:4 concerning Keturah.)

[26] Leviticus 24:3.

[27] Exodus 30:6.

[28] Proverbs 21:17.

[29] Rabbi Ya'akov Leiner, *Beit Ya'akov*, vol. 2 (Lublin, 1903), *Tetsaveh*, par. 6 (182c-d). See further Bezalel Naor, "Ascent and Descent in the Yom Kippur Rite: From the Hasidic Thought of Izbica-Radzyn," in idem, *From A Kabbalist's Diary* (Spring Valley, NY: Orot, 2005), pp. 92-96.

VII

THE THOUGHT OF RAV KOOK

Reflections on *Yom ha-'Atsma'ut*
Based on the Works of Rav Kook
5 Iyyar, 5773

The fifth of Iyyar commemorates the establishment of the State of Israel in 1948. When it came to the State of Israel, the Orthodox community adopted three different stances. At one extreme was Rabbi Abraham Isaac Hakohen Kook who viewed the rebirth of Israel in its ancestral land as an *event* of major, even Messianic proportions.[1] At the opposite extreme was Rabbi Joel Teitelbaum, the Rebbe of Satu Mare, who saw in the Zionist entity an *anti-event*, once again of mythic proportions, evoking images of the anti-Messiah, Shabbetai Tsevi.[2] The middle ground was the position adopted by Rabbi Abraham Isaiah Karelitz (*"Hazon Ish"*) and Rabbi Isaac Ze'ev Halevi Soloveitchik ("Brisker Rav"), which was basically to treat the establishment of the State as a *non-event*.[3]

Let us leave aside for the moment the rhetoric of redemption and think in less romantic, more pragmatic terms of *transvaluation*. What is undeniable by all camps is that the State represents a transvaluation, an introduction of new values to Jewish life. What are these values, what is their import, and how are they to be contextualized within the ongoing history of the Jewish People?

It is to Rav Kook's credit that in several important essays he undertook the herculean task of identifying these elements that surfaced with twentieth-century Zionism and grappled with their larger significance. To the table he brought prodigious erudition in both the exoteric and esoteric traditions of Judaism, coupled with a talent for engaging in historiosophy.[4] Three major essays were devoted to this task:

- *The Lamentation in Jerusalem* (1904)
- *The Way of Renascence* (1906)
- *To the Process of Ideas in Israel* (1912)[5]

Different elements and emphases come to the fore in each essay.

In *The Lamentation in Jerusalem*, Rav Kook examines the rabbinic and kabbalistic notion that there are two Messiahs, Messiah Son of Joseph and Messiah Son of David. In Rav Kook's analysis, Messiah Son of Joseph symbolizes the physical as well as universal aspect of the Jewish People, while Messiah Son of David represents the spiritual as well as particularist or Torahitic aspect of the nation. Rav Kook boldly situated political Zionism, brainchild of Herzl, within the tradition of Messiah Son of Joseph.[6] Recalling the prophecy of Ezekiel 37, Rav Kook appealed for a unity of the "Tree of Joseph" and the "Tree of Judah," expressing at the same time the fervent hope that the secular leaders of the Jewish People would recognize the authority of the great Torah sages.

In *The Way of Renascence*, Rav Kook views Jewish history as a pendulum swinging back and forth between the two poles of "charisma" (Rav Kook actually employs this term), raw, unmediated experience, and book-learning with all of the discipline and rigor that it demands. Rav Kook recognizes in the Zionist romance of return to the Land yet another outburst in a series of spiritual eruptions, some ignoble, such as early Nazarene Christianity, Sabbatianism, and Frankism, while others noble, such as Beshtian Hasidism. These are instances of the spirit bursting the envelope of Torah learning. Whereas Rav Kook views Rabbi Akiva with his emphasis on Torah study as the corrective to the wild, unbridled charisma of Jesus; and the Gaon of Vilna with his call for devotion to Torah learning as the foil to the Hasidism of the Ba'al Shem Tov—in the case of the People's meeting up once again with its land, Rav Kook feels a different kind of solution is called for. The People are in need, not of rabbis who will dispense a dry, legalistic teaching, but exactly charismatic leaders who will be capable of channeling revelatory experience through the inwardness of Torah!

In any case, Rav Kook has identified in the new Israel the element of charisma, of untutored, direct apperception of God.[7] Coming from his background in the Volozhin Yeshivah,[8] which continued the tradition of the Vilna Gaon, whereby Torah learning is the bedrock of Jewish existence, there is a remarkable openness here to alternative models. (One might counter that Rav Kook's view was never as monastic as that of the true Volozhiner, for in his youth Abraham Isaac was exposed by his maternal grandfather Rabbi Raphael to HaBaD Hasidism.)

In *To The Process of Ideas in Israel*, Rav Kook embarks upon exploration of the three "Houses," or Temples (or Commonwealths) of Israel—*Bayit Rishon* (the First Temple Period), *Bayit Sheini* (the

Second Temple Period), and *Bayit Shelishi* (the Third Temple Period)—the last period (our own) to be, according to Rav Kook, a synthesis of the more salient features of the first and second.

This is a lengthy essay which deserves much study. In a nutshell, the "idea" (Rav Kook employs this exact term, Greek in origin, in the Hebrew essay) of the First Temple was nation; the idea of the Second Temple was religion. Conveniently, by the insertion of a hyphen, this yields in the Third Temple the national-religious idea. Rav Kook is acknowledging that whereas in Exile, Judaism was restricted to a strictly religious phenomenon, in the modern era of the Return to Zion, Judaism once again (as in the First Temple Period) assumes the role of a nation. And whereas Second Temple religion focuses on personal salvation and afterlife, the earlier edition of Judaism—brought back to life by Zionism—trains its sights on the eternity of the People.

Yet this is an extremely superficial reading of the essay. If one reads with proper concentration, one discovers that Rav Kook is saying that in the Third Temple period—our very own era—we shall discover the higher idea which subsumes and unites these two ideas of nation and religion, and that is: *"ha-idea ha-Elohit"* (the divine idea, or the idea of God).[9]

CONCLUSION

During his tenure as Rabbi of Jaffa (1904-1914), considered by many his most fruitful years in terms of Jewish Thought, Rav Kook penned three essays designed to place the modern Return to Zion in historic perspective. Taken together as a unit, they identify in the Zionist enterprise the following elements:

- Physicality and universalism, as opposed to disembodied spirituality and particularism rooted in Torah perspective
- Charismatic or experiential spirituality, as opposed to didactic book-learning
- National, collective consciousness, as opposed to personal, religious consciousness

---

[1] Though Rabbi Abraham Isaac Hakohen Kook died in 1935, thirteen years before the proclamation of the State, he could clearly see the "handwriting on the wall," and in his writings (perhaps prophetically) enunciated the name *"Medinat Yisrael."* See *Orot ha-Kodesh*, vol. 3, p. 191 = *Shemonah Kevatsim* 1:186. His legacy and viewpoint were continued by his biological and/or spiritual heirs, Rabbi Tsevi Yehudah Hakohen Kook and Rabbi Ya'akov Moshe Harlap, who lived to see the establishment of the State.

[2] Shabbetai Tsevi (1626-1676), Turkish pseudo-Messiah.

[3] Rabbi Dr. Zvi A. Yehuda, a student of the *"Hazon Ish,"* shared with this writer (BN) that the *"Hazon Ish"* would poke fun at the term *"athalta di-ge'ulah"* ("beginning of redemption") popular in Religious Zionist circles. He would say that with each day gone by, we inch ever closer to the redemption, but who is to determine whether we are in the beginning, the middle or the end?

Rabbi Dr. Joseph B. Soloveitchik, nephew of the Brisker Rav, in his eulogy for his uncle, *"Mah Dodekh mi-Dod,"* observed stoically that from his uncle's perspective, the *Medinah* (State) had no halakhic relevance because it did not occur in Maimonides' code *Mishneh Torah*. Thus the eulogist explained the fact that unlike the *"Hazon Ish"* who received Prime Minister David Ben-Gurion in his home in B'nei Berak, the Brisker Rav refused to countenance Ben-Gurion.

[4] A brilliant student of Rav Kook, Rabbi Shim'on Starelitz referred to his mentor's work as a *"historiosophia di-mehemnuta"* ("historiosophy of faith").

[5] All three essays were translated by this writer and included in his collection *When God Becomes History: Historical Essays of Rabbi Abraham Isaac Hakohen Kook* (New York, NY: Kodesh, 2016).

[6] Perhaps in the recesses of Rav Kook's mind was the saying of the *Midrash Tanhuma, Vayyigash* (10): "Whatever happened to Joseph, happened to Zion." The commentators elucidate that "Zion" has the same numerical value as "Joseph" (156). By an extension, Zionism becomes Josephism.

[7] Compare the opening salvo of *Reish Millin* (London, 1917), Rav Kook's mystical meditation on the letters of the Hebrew alphabet:

"יודעת היא הנשמה שכל הבא בלימוד—איננו מקורי".

"The soul knows that whatever comes through learning—is not of the source."

In his lectures on the *Book of Kuzari*, Rav Kook railed against "learning in translation" (*"limmud targumi"*) as opposed to "learning from the source" (*"limmud mekori"*). These lectures were preserved in the notes of Rabbi Mordechai Gimpel Barg and published in *Ma'amrei ha-RAYaH*, vol. 2, ed. Rabbi Elisha Aviner (Langenauer) (Jerusalem, 1984), pp. 485-495. See ibid., p. 490, beginning chap. 5, and p. 488, end chap. 3.

See too Rav Kook's paraphrase of the Midrash: "In the past, I gave you Torah; in the future, I shall give you life" (*Shemonah Kevatsim* 6:198). The original wording of the *Midrash Exodus Rabbah* (48:4) reads: "Said the Holy One, blessed be He: 'In this world My spirit gives you wisdom, but in the future, My spirit will enliven you, as it says, *I will put My spirit in you, and you shall live* [Ezekiel 37:14].'"

[8] Himself a product of the Volozhin Yeshivah, Rav Kook prided himself that his paternal ancestor Rabbi Dov Baer Jaffe of Turetz and Utian had been one of Rabbi Hayyim Volozhiner's original ten students.

On the title page of *Elef ha-Magen* (Warsaw, 1912), co-authored by Rabbi Mordechai Gimpel Jaffe and his brother-in-law Rabbi Nathan Nota Luria, we read that Rabbi Mordechai Gimpel was "the son of the famous *maggid* (preacher) Rabbi Dovid Baer, of blessed memory, who served as rabbi in Utian, Karelitz and Turetz; who was called 'Rabbi Baer Maggid of Utian,' a *talmid-haver* (disciple-companion) of the Gaon Rabbi Hayyim of Volozhin, of blessed memory, and a companion of the Gaon Rabbi David Tevel of Stoiptz, of blessed memory, *mara de-'atra* (rabbi) of Minsk."

[9] While at a glance one might think that MK Ruth Calderon in her recent inaugural speech before the Knesset, or Israeli Parliament, on February 2, 2013, essentially captured Rav Kook's picture of the Third Temple, with a little probing we see that this is not so.

Calderon recounted that she grew up in a household imbued with Zionism, for which the study of *Tanakh* (Bible) was of paramount importance. After pronouncing a personal and collective *mea culpa* on behalf of secular Israelis for jettisoning the study of Talmud, Calderon held up a tome of Talmud, which, in her words, "transformed her life." She then proceeded to teach a homily from the Talmud, Tractate *Ketubot* 62b, concerning Rav Rehumai, whose extreme devotion to his study of Torah was at the expense of his conjugal duties to his poor wife, for which Rav Rehumai was punished by accidentally falling to his death when the roof of the study house collapsed. Calderon's point was that it is inhumane and unconscionable for Torah students not to fulfill their responsibility toward their partners in society, in this case the military service incumbent upon Israeli citizens.

With all due respects to MK Calderon, I believe that her presentation is flawed for two reasons. First, it fails to grasp that just as the study of Bible is not value-neutral but carries with it responsibility (in her words, *"mi-Tanakh le-Palmah,"* "from Bible to military service"), so the study of Talmud cannot be reduced to an academic exercise, to an appreciation of the humor and linguistic subtleties of the Talmud as she has demonstrated, but rather carries with it the *"'ol mitsvot"* ("yoke of commandments") and *"shi'buda de-'oraita"* ("obligation of the Torah").

But beyond that criticism, even if we should arrive at a hyphenation of the two Judaisms, Biblical Judaism and Rabbinic Judaism, à la *dati-le'umi* (national-religious), or more recently HaRDaL (acronym of *haredi-le'umi*, or national-Orthodox), we would come up short, for we would not have realized the unifying principle, the supernal root of these two ideas, nation and religion, and that is the God idea, or as Judah Halevi termed it in Arabic, *al-'amr al-ilahi* (translated by Ibn Tibbon into Hebrew as *"ha-'inyan ha-elohi"*).

Searching for the Lost Dimensions of Judaism
Thoughts on Rav Kook's 80th Yahrzeit
3 Ellul, 5775

Abraham Isaac Hakohen Kook (1865-1935) served as the first Ashkenazic Chief Rabbi of Erets Israel. He was a preeminent Talmudist and Halakhist, as well as mystic and poet. Revered as the seer of the rebirth of Israel in its land, Rav Kook had a rare gift for reaching out to even the most alienated sectors of the nation.

I ask myself: How would Rav Kook wish to be remembered today?

Certainly he would not want us to dredge up old animosities surrounding his person. It was he who taught that the *tikkun* or remedy for the abominable sin of *sin'at hinam* (senseless hatred) is *ahavat hinam* (senseless love).

Rather, I imagine that the Rav would want us to learn and practice the most salient features of his teaching. Rav Kook was a man who in the course of a lifetime grew spiritually by quantum leaps, and he would demand of us our own spiritual growth and development.

By nature, he was a *homo mysticus* drawn inexorably to the mysteries of the Torah. His core learning was obtained in the bastion of Lithuanian scholarship, the famed Volozhin Yeshiva. To his dying day, he would remain faithful to the legacy of the Vilna Gaon as embodied in that great Torah institution. But as time went on, this *Litvak* broadened his being. A sea change occurred in Rav

Kook's consciousness at the time of his 'aliyah to Erets Israel in 1904, when he assumed the rabbinate of Jaffa (precursor to Tel-Aviv) and the outlying communities. This spiritual 'aliyah (ascent) is reflected in the abrupt shift in style. In Lithuania, Rav Kook wrote prose. In Erets Israel, Rav Kook's writing assumed the flowing stream of consciousness that has become his hallmark. Rav Kook is first and foremost a poet, and admission to his inner sanctum hinges on ability to tune in to the wavelength of his poetry. The shift in style is symbolic of a much deeper phenomenon: the search for the lost dimensions of Judaism.

(It is no mere coincidence that during that same Jaffa period, the works of Rabbi Nahman of Breslov became a staple of Rav Kook's spiritual diet. Rabbi Nahman of Breslov was experimenting with new forms of expression, whether it be converting the *torot*, or teachings, in *Likkutei MOHaRaN* into *tefillot*, or prayers; or his foray into the enchanted world of storytelling, which he expressed it in Yiddish as *"dertzehlen ma'asiyos."*)

Rav Kook was thirsty for the *nishmata de-'oraita* (the soul of the Torah). His spiritual quest took him beyond the "dry" *Halakhah* to the "moist" environment of the *Aggadah*. Beyond that, he expressed a longing for the resumption of *nevu'ah*, outright prophecy. All those who had substantive exposure to the Rav; all those who warmed to this great luminary, experienced this *"hitpashtut kedushah,"* this expansion of holiness. To Rabbi Ya'akov Moshe Harlap, suffocating within the confines of the Old Yishuv of Yerushalayim, the *"Yaffo'er Rov"* ("Jaffa Rabbi") appeared as a breath of fresh air. Under Rav Kook's guidance, Lithuanian Yeshiva students such as Rabbi Yehudah Gershuni ("Yudel Grodner" of the Kamenets Yeshiva) and Rabbi Isaac Hutner ("Itche Varshaver" of the Slabodka Yeshiva) were turned on to works of Jewish Thought generally beyond the purview of the average yeshiva man. And an unusual seeker such as Rabbi David Cohen (the "Nazirite"), who had studied in both *yeshivot* and universities, and was yet thirsting for the Living God, received validation from the Rav for his "vision quest," a trek in the inhospitable Judean wilderness with a select group of students of Merkaz Harav. If you allowed him to touch your soul, Rav Kook would broaden your horizon so that you too might experience a quantum leap.

Rav Kook's spiritual journey encompassed all these dimensions and more: ecstatic song and dance (à la Hasidism), body work, a love for the green vegetation of the Earth, animal welfare, etc. Rav Kook stretched the limits of "book learning," but furthermore, impressed upon his listeners the importance of recapturing dimensions of Judaism that go beyond the book, to the body and the soul, and ultimately "to the wellspring of prophecy" (*"el ma'ayan ha-nevu'ah"*).

Lest anyone surmise that Rav Kook was out to create an elite cadre of *hasidim* who would be clones of the master, let it be stated in no uncertain terms that this clearly was not his goal. On more than one occasion, the Rav said outright that he had no interest in producing "Kookists." When the Rebbe of Gur, Rabbi Abraham Mordechai Alter (*"Imrei Emet"*), duly impressed by Rav Kook's many talents, remarked that Rav Kook could have 100,000 *hasidim* (perhaps the number of Gerrer Hasidim in pre-Holocaust

Poland), Rav Kook was quick to reply: "I think only about *Kelal Yisrael*, the Jewish People as a whole!"

If we had to sum up Rav Kook's teaching in a single word (which became the *bon mot* of his son Rabbi Tsevi Yehudah), it would be: *"Kelaliyut"* (Universality). It was that unitive vision that enabled Rav Kook to open the conversation between the disciples of the Vilna Gaon and the disciples of the Ba'al Shem Tov; between pietists and secularists; between Russian Jews and Yemenite Jews; and between Jews and Arabs.

Does Rav Kook have all the answers? No! But he can certainly point us in the right direction.

Rabbi Isaac Hutner wrote in a by now famous letter that it took him forty years to properly grasp Rav Kook's *de'ah* or opinion.[1] And now, on the eightieth *yahrzeit* of Rav Kook, we collectively respond: Ditto.

---

[1] See *b. 'Avodah Zarah* 5b.
  Rabbi Hutner's letter to Rabbi Tsevi Yehudah Hakohen Kook was published in *Iggerot la-RAYaH*, ed. Ben-Zion Shapira (2nd edition, Jerusalem, 1990), Appendix, Letter 47 (p. 585).

The Scribal Art of Rabbi Meir:
A Study in Metanomianism
(Rav Kook's Pre-Purim Talk 5677/1917)

INTRODUCTION

In a personal letter to his son Tsevi Yehudah, dated "11 Adar, 5677," Rav Abraham Isaac Hakohen Kook shared a talk he delivered the previous Sabbath (*Parashat Zakhor*) before a London audience, concerning the commandment to erase or obliterate Amalek.[1] The hero of this discourse is the second-century sage Rabbi Meir. By cobbling together various references to Rabbi Meir in *Talmud Bavli*, *Talmud Yerushalmi* and *Midrash Rabbah*, Rav Kook is able to deftly paint a vivid portrait of the *tanna* (sage of the *Mishnah*) Rabbi Meir.[2] It is possible that some of what Rav Kook arrived at concerning writing and erasing, will jibe with postmodern deconstructionist literary theory.[3]

Before we launch into study of the actual discourse, we should point out that which, though unstated, may be obvious to some readers, namely that Rav Kook identifies with the protagonist. This is of extreme interest because just four years later, the Hasidic Rebbe of Gur (Gora Kalwaria, Poland), Abraham Mordechai Alter, in a letter to his family, published in the Jewish press of the day, would compare Rav Kook to—Rabbi Meir. It is highly unlikely that the Rebbe read our epistle of Rav Kook to his son. How did the

Rebbe so uncannily size up the situation? Was it something that Rav Kook let drop in conversation? Did the *tsaddik* (righteous man) read the "root" of Rav Kook's soul? (In Kabbalah, the term would be *"shoresh ha-neshamah."*) Whatever the answer, the Gerrer Rebbe took it with him to his eternal reward.

I quote the Rebbe of Gur's impression of Rav Kook, whom he had just met for the first time in Jerusalem in Nissan of 1921:

> The Rav, the Gaon, R. Avraham Kook, may he live, is a man of many-sided talents in Torah, and noble traits. However, his love of Zion surpasses all limit and he "declares the impure pure and adduces proof to it,"[4] reminiscent of the one [=Rabbi Meir] who the rabbis said in the first chapter of *'Eruvin* (13b) "had no equal in his generation," and therefore, "the final *halakhah* did not follow his opinion."[5]

TRANSLATION OF TEXT OF *IGGEROT HA-RAYAH*

> I spoke this holy Sabbath before an attentive audience concerning the erasing of Amalek, as a means of purifying all the values of existence; all the systems laden with the burden of the impurities, the pollution of wickedness, that extends from the "first of nations" [i.e., Amalek][6] even into the contents of the holy—which are corrupted by the evil influence of the wicked of the world.

The Scribal Art of Rabbi Meir

This is the reason[7] for the prohibition of putting *kankantum*[8] into the ink.[9] The law requires "'And he shall write....and he shall erase'—a writing that is able to be erased."[10] [This is] on account of the particles of wickedness that infect the values of holiness. If the hand of wickedness would pollute the entire foundation [of holiness] with its actions, then we would burn it [i.e., the Torah scroll] and the names of God contained therein, so as not to preserve the memory[11] of the sectarians and their deeds.[12] [But] the totality of the holy is merely *touched* by wickedness, as Jacob was touched by the man who wrestled him,[13] and for the purpose of this erasure there suffices a *potential* erasing (*mehiyah kohanit*), "a writing that is able to be erased."[14]

In the Torah scroll written by Rabbi Meir, "whose contemporaries were not able to fathom his thinking,"[15] instead of *"kotenot 'or"* (with an *'ayin*), "tunics of skin," it was written *"kotenot 'or"* (with an *aleph*), "tunics of light."[16] And in the Jerusalem Talmud, he referred to himself by saying: "Here is your Messiah."[17] In other words, the illumination of his soul was from the [future] state that the world will ascend to after the light of Messiah will shine "and the wickedness will be consumed as smoke."[18]

In the case of Rabbi Meir, there was no need to prevent the placing of *kankantum* [in the ink]. (We could even go so far as to say that without *kankantum*, something would have been missing.) The very possibility and capability of erasing stands in opposition to the pure light, the supernal light,[19] "that illumines and lights up the eyes of the sages in *Halakhah*."[20] So, true to his character, Rabbi Meir used to put *kankantum* into the ink.

But Rabbi Akiva[21] said to him that the [present] state of the world still requires—even in the values of holiness—the potential of erasure, so that there might ramify from it the absolute erasure: the erasure of the memory of Amalek in all its branchings, and the existence of the darkness of Amalek. [This darkness consists of] the spread of all the evil characteristics (*ha-middot ha-ra'ot*) in the national soul of every people,[22] which brings about all the tragedies, individual and collective.[23] In the words of the *Pesikta*: "As long as there is Amalek in the world, a wing (*kanaf*) covers the face [of God]. Only with its erasing, will it be said, 'No longer shall your Teacher be hidden (*yikanef*).'"[24]

At that time, the light of the Oral Torah shall unite with [the light of] the Written Torah; the lights shall interpenetrate.

"Write this a remembrance in the book"—Written Torah. "And place in the ears of Joshua"—Oral Torah.[25]

We are not allowed to write any of the Written Torah [from memory] without having an exemplar of the Scripture before us[26]—so as not to confuse [the realms of] scripture and orality. This concept [of not confusing the written with the oral] is explained in the *Yerushalmi*, [Tractate] *Megillah*.[27]

But none of this applies to the great of stature, "who see their eternity in their lifetime."[28] "Whoever possesses knowledge, it is as if the Holy Temple were rebuilt in his days."[29] And the light of Messiah shines upon him. And [thus] Rabbi Meir, concerning whom it is said, "And your eyelids [look] straight before you,"[30] wrote [by heart] without consulting Scripture[31]—just as he placed *kankantum* into the ink.

And in the days of Purim, when the erasing of Amalek intensified, the foundation of the Oral Torah was united with the Written Torah. The Torah that had been accepted under duress on Mount Sinai, was once again accepted *willingly* in the days of Ahashverosh.[32] In the well-known words of the [Midrash] *Tanhuma*, the coercion on Mount Sinai was directed at the Oral Torah.[33]

(Iggerot ha-RAYaH, Vol. III [Jerusalem, 1965], Letter 808 [pp. 86-87])

COMMENTARY

Rabbi Meir was a *lavlar* or scribe by profession.[34] Rav Kook, by marrying two *sugyot* of the Talmud (*'Eruvin* 13a and *Megillah* 18b) drew a composite sketch of Rabbi Meir, whereby he deviated from the norms prescribed by the sages in two respects: He added *kankantum* to his ink rendering it indelible; and wrote scripture from memory. The simple explanation for these deviations was his exceptional, flawless recall of the text of the Scripture. But Rav Kook chalks up Rabbi Meir's unusual behavior to the fact that his soul was from a future, Messianic time. (Thus, on one occasion Rabbi Meir referred to himself as the Messiah.) For that reason, in the verse in Genesis which narrates how after the Primordial Sin, the LORD fashioned for Adam and Eve tunics of animal skins, Rabbi Meir substituted in his Torah scroll "light" (*'or*) for "skin" (*'or*).[35] In Rabbi Meir's reality, the outer *"levushim"* or garments have shed their opacity; they have become translucent.[36]

Our world is tainted by the wickedness of Amalek. So insidious is this influence of Amalek that it penetrates even into the inner precincts of holiness. Even our Torah has been infected by the corrupting influence of Amalek. *Horribile dictum.*

(Some years ago, there appeared a popular film, *The Matrix* [1999], which envisioned a dystopia whose reality had been thoroughly subverted by aliens.)

In this vein, Rav Kook interprets the prohibition of adding *kankantum* to the ink. In our present reality, the Torah is subject to corruption; therefore, the Torah must carry within itself the capability of being erased.

But Rabbi Meir's Torah is a scroll from the future, the Messianic future which basks in the light of the Face of God, no longer obscured by the wing of Amalek. That scroll is not subject to corruption and is in no need of erasure. Rabbi Meir adds *kankantum* to the ink, rendering it permanent.

Collateral damage resulting from the "wing of Amalek" is the wedge that it drives between Written and Oral Torah. Here it would be almost impossible to glean Rav Kook's meaning, were it not for a passage in the writings of his beloved disciple, Rabbi Ya'akov Moshe Harlap, which serves as a "Rosetta Stone" to decipher the master's allusion.

Employing Kabbalistic terminology, Rabbi Harlap informs us that the Written Torah is code for the *"kelim"* ("vessels"), while the Oral Torah is code for the *"'orot"* ("lights").[37] In other words, the Written Torah represents the outer manifestation, the material side of existence; the Oral Torah is evocative of the inner content, the spiritual aspect of existence.

Amalek drives a wedge between those two. And in an era in which the Face of God is eclipsed by the Wing of Amalek, we are told to maintain the separation of the two realms of Written Law and Oral Law. In the words of the Babylonian Talmud: "Words that are in writing, you are not permitted to recite orally; words that are oral, you are not permitted to commit to writing.[38] Once again, Rabbi Meir, who lives already in the Messianic Era, recognizes no such opacity. In his reality, the Written Torah and the Oral Torah collapse into one. In Rabbi Meir's world there is total transparency. The "tunics of skin" have been transcribed into "tunics of light."

On Mount Sinai, there yet existed separation of Torah into two distinct realms: the Written and the Oral. On Purim, with the erasing of Amalek, this gap between the Written Law and the Oral Law is bridged; the two dimensions dissolve into one.

CONCLUSION

Contained in this pre-Purim talk of Rav Kook is radical theology, the assertion that the Torah of our age—as opposed to the Torah of the eschatological future[39]—has been tainted by the evil of Amalek, and therefore requires by halakhic mandate (no less!) the potential of erasure. Rav Kook makes very clear that he is not referring to a Torah scroll written by a sectarian with improper intention (which the *halakhah* would have us consign to flames), but rather a "kosher" Torah scroll written with the most holy of intentions. The thought that the quintessence of holiness, the Torah, is subject to corruption, is a prospect so frightening as to cause us to shudder. But that very outlook may also be a source of hope, reminding us that "hardwired" into the script of the Torah is the capability of catharsis.

---

[1] See Exodus 17:14; Deuteronomy 25:19; Maimonides, *Sefer ha-Mitsvot*, positive commandment 188; idem, *MT, Hil. Melakhim* 5:5; and the anonymous *Sefer ha-Hinnukh*, commandment 604.
  Rabbi Hadari included this talk on *Parashat Zakhor* in *Shemu'ot RAYaH*. See *Shemu'ot RAYaH: Bereshit/Shemot*, ed. Kalman Eliezer Frankel and Hayyim Yeshayahu Hadari (Jerusalem: WZO, 2015), *Parashat Zakhor*, pp. 334-338.

[2] Cf. Rav Kook's spiritual sketch of Rabbi Meir, written a decade earlier, in a letter to fellow Lithuanian kabbalist, Rabbi Pinhas Hakohen Lintop. Datelined "Jaffa, 11 Adar Rishon 5668 [i.e., 1908]," the letter was published in *Iggerot ha-RAYaH*, vol. 1 (Jerusalem: Mossad Harav Kook, 1962), Letter 111 (pp. 140-141).

[3] See Marc-Alain Ouaknin, *The Burnt Book: Reading the Talmud*, transl. Llewelyn Brown (Princeton, 1995).

[4] For Rabbi Zadok Hakohen's thoughts regarding this passage in *'Eruvin* 13, see *Dover Tsedek* (Piotrków, 1911), 4a-c. In brief, Rabbi Meir had the power to reveal the underlying unity of all existence, and from that perspective of the divine unity, the duality of pure versus impure is transcended.

[5] The letter was published in serial form in three successive issues of *Der Jud*,

the Warsaw newspaper of the Agudat Yisrael movement (27 May, 3 June and 10 June, 1921). (The English translation is from my introduction to Rav Kook's *Orot*.) To this day, in at least some Agudist circles, the Rebbe of Gur's assessment of, and pronouncement upon Rav Kook is considered well-nigh authoritative.

[6] Numbers 24:20.

Cf. Rabbi Michael Eliezer Hakohen Forshlager, *Torat Michael* (Jerusalem, 1967), "*Derush be-'inyan mehiyat zikhro shel 'Amalek*," 250a: "'The first of nations is Amalek,' for he is the first of, and includes all the evil." (Rabbi Forshlager was a disciple of Rabbi Abraham Bornstein of Sochatchov, author of Responsa *Avnei Nezer*. Cf. below note 22.)

[7] The Hebrew word is "*ta'am*." Rav Kook contributed much in the area of "*Ta'amei ha-Mitsvot*" (rationales of the commandments), beginning with his essay "*Afikim ba-Negev*," published in the Berlin journal *Ha-Peless* in 1903-1904 (reprinted in Rabbi Moshe Zuriel, *Otserot ha-RAYaH*, vol. 2 [Tel-Aviv, 1988], pp. 733-779), and continuing with his essay "*Talelei Orot*," published in the Bern journal *Tahkemoni* in 1910 (reprinted in *Ma'amrei ha-RAYaH*, vol. 1 [Jerusalem, 1980], pp. 18-28). See also the collection entitled *Orot ha-Mitsvot* in Rabbi Moshe Zuriel, *Otserot ha-RAYaH*, vol. 4 (Ashdod, 1992), pp. 31-47. And see now Don Seeman, "Evolutionary Ethics: The *Taamei Hamitzvot* of Rav Kook," *Hakirah* 26 (Spring 2019), pp. 13-55.

For a survey of the earlier literature, see Isaak Heinemann, *Ta'amei ha-Mitsvot be-Sifrut Yisrael* (Jerusalem, 1966).

In this particular instance, I do not believe that Rav Kook intended to supplant the practical reason for the law forbidding adding *kankantum* to the ink, which is simply to allow erasure in the case of scribal error. Rather, it appears that Rav Kook wrote in a homiletic vein.

[8] Medieval opinions were divided as to the identity of *kankantum*. Rabbi Nathan of Rome, '*Arukh*, s.v. *kalkantum*, and Rashbam opined that the substance is vitriol. See the various opinions in *Tosafot*, '*Eruvin* 13a; idem, *Megillah* 18b; Rashi, *Shabbat* 104b; idem, *Sotah* 17b; Maimonides, *Commentary to the Mishnah*, *Shabbat* 12:4 (Kafah ed., p. 41); *Megillah* 2:1 (Kafah ed., p. 231); *Gittin* 2:3 (Kafah ed., p. 141); *Teshuvot ha-Rambam*, ed. Freimann (Jerusalem, 1934), no. 126.

For our purposes, we need not concern ourselves with the *realia*. However one identifies *kankantum*, the upshot is that it renders the ink indelible.

[9] *b. 'Eruvin* 13a; *Sotah* 20a.

[10] Numbers 5:23; *m. Sotah* 2:4; *b. 'Eruvin* 13a; *Sotah* 17b, 20a; Maimonides, *MT, Hil. Sotah* 3:8; 4:9.

Originally stated in regard to the *Megillat Sotah* (the Scroll of the Suspected Adulteress), Rabbi Yishmael extended this requirement to the entire Torah scroll. *Tosafot* speculate by what Biblical exegesis Rabbi Yishmael accomplished this extrapolation. The alternative is that Rabbi Yishmael merely stated a matter of rabbinic law. See *Tosafot*, '*Eruvin* 13a, s.v. *huts mi-parashat sotah*.

Maimonides ruled that as a *mitsvah min ha-muvhar*, *kankantum* (or in his reading, *kalkantum*) should not be added to the ink of the Torah scroll; however, those who would invalidate a Torah scroll written with indelible ink, err in their judgment. In both his *Commentary to the Mishnah* and in a responsum

to Rabbeinu Ephraim of Tyre, Maimonides fleshed out his decision by explaining that the *halakhah* follows the *lishna batra* (later statement) of the Talmud:
> Rabbi Judah says, "Rabbi Meir used to say: 'For all [Scripture] we may place *kankantum* into the ink, except for the portion of the suspected adulteress (*parashat sotah*).'"

See Maimonides, *Commentary to the Mishnah, Sotah* 2:4 (Kafah ed., pp. 171-172); *MT, Hil. Tefillin* 1:4; *Teshuvot ha-Rambam*, ed. Freimann (Jerusalem, 1934), no. 126.

Par contre, the admixture of *kankantum* to the ink of the *Megillat Sotah* (Scroll of the Suspected Adulteress) does invalidate the scroll. See Maimonides, *Hil. Sotah* 4:9.

[11] Rav Kook wrote literally: "so as not to leave room" (*"kedei she-lo lehani'ah makom"*). However, the wording of Maimonides, *Hil. Yesodei ha-Torah* 6:8 (which is the source for Rav Kook's statement) is: "so as not to leave a name" (*"kedei she-lo lehani'ah shem"*).

[12] *b. Shabbat* 116a; *Gittin* 45b; Maimonides, *MT, Hil. Yesodei ha-Torah* 6:8; *Hil. Tefillin* 1:13.

Rabbi Aharon Soloveichik wrote that in our contemporary society, burning a Torah scroll written by a heretic would be counterproductive. In so many words, Maimonides wrote that the reason for doing so would be to prevent Jews from being drawn to heresy. But today we have the opposite scenario. Burning the Torah scroll would make heresy that much more attractive!

> All this applies only in a situation where by burning the Torah scroll written by the heretic, Jews will be prevented from being drawn to heresy. But if there should arise a situation (such as ours today) that by burning the Torah written by the heretic, Jews with limited commitment to the commandments will be drawn to heresy, as a result of the influence of the Reform and Conservative rabbis, who will say that the *"gedolim"* (great men) are intolerant and wish to coerce everyone into performing the commandments against their will—not only is it not a *mitsvah* (commandment) to burn the Torah scroll written by the heretic, but this would be a great desecration of the Name (*hillul hashem*).
> (Rabbi Aharon Soloveichik, *Perah Mateh Aharon*, novellae to Maimonides, *Sefer Madda'* [Jerusalem, 1997], *Hil. Yesodei ha-Torah* 6:8 [pp. 49-50])

Rabbi Soloveichik cites as his source the by-now famous ruling of the sage of B'nei Berak, Rabbi Abraham Isaiah Karelitz (*Hazon Ish*) regarding the inapplicability of the law of *"moridin ve-lo ma'alin"* in modern society:

> ....But in the time of the concealment, when belief has been cut off from the feeble of the people, the act of *horadah* [elimination of heretics] does not constitute a fence against the breach, but rather an addition to the breach, for in their eyes it will appear as a wanton act of violence, God forbid. Since our whole striving is to remedy, the law does not apply at a time when this is no remedy. [Rather,] we must return them with cords of love and stand them in the light (*leha'amidem be-keren 'orah*), to the extent of our ability.
> (*Hazon Ish, Yoreh De'ah* 2:16; cited in *Perah Mateh Aharon*, p. 5)

See further Benjamin Brown, *The Hazon Ish: Halakhist, Believer and Leader of the Haredi Revolution* (Hebrew) (Jerusalem, 2011), pp. 708-719. (The phrase *"leha'amidem be-keren 'orah"* derives from *b. Berakhot* 17a.)

In the Table of Contents, this chapter of *Perah Mateh Aharon* is summarized: If the burning of Torah scrolls of heretics will alienate Jews because of the impression of extremism, it is forbidden to burn them.

[13] Genesis 32:25.

[14] Although Rav Kook discusses the Torah scroll rather than the *"Megillat Sotah"* (Scroll of the Suspected Adulteress), it may interest the reader to learn that even in the latter regard (which is the source of our law), the verse "And he shall write....and he shall erase" (Numbers 5:23) is interpreted strictly *in potentia* ("that the ink is *capable* of being erased"), but the actual total erasure is derived from another verse: "'And after he shall give drink' [Numbers 5:26]—provided that no imprint [of the writing] be discernible" (*b. Sotah* 19b). See the clarification in *Tosafot Sens* (ibid.)—which differs with our *Tosafot, Sotah* 19a, s.v. *ve-ahar yashkeh*; Rabbi Hayyim Joseph David Azulai, *Hayyim Sha'al*, vol. 2 (Livorno, 1795), no. 5(3) (to Maimonides, *MT, Hil. Sotah* 4:14); Rabbi Pinhas Epstein, *Minhah Hareivah* (Jerusalem, 1923), *Sotah* 19a (93a).

Concerning the two *Tosafot* to Tractate *Sotah* ("our" *Tosafot* versus *Tosafot Sens*), see *Hayyim Sha'al*, vol. 2, no. 41. (Azulai's father possessed a manuscript of *Tosafot Sens* and remarked to his son that *Piskei Tosafot, Sotah* are based on *Tosafot Sens*.)

[15] *b. 'Eruvin* 13b.

[16] Genesis 3:21; *Genesis Rabbah* 20:12. Cf. *Genesis Rabbah* 9:5: "In the Torah of Rabbi Meir they found written [for] *'Ve-hinneh tov me'od'* ('And behold it was very good')—*'Ve-hinneh tov mot'* ('And behold it is good to die').

Saul Lieberman discussed at length "the book of Rabbi Meir." See his study, "The Texts of Scripture in the Early Rabbinic Period," in Saul Lieberman, *Hellenism in Jewish Palestine* (New York, 1994), pp. 24-26.

[17] *y. Kil'ayim* 9:3. The context was that Rabbi Meir, who had traveled to Asya, was about to die. He sent a message to his disciples in *Erets Yisrael* to bury him in the Land. The sense of his statement was: "Here is your rabbi." (See *P'nei Moshe* ad locum.) Rav Kook seizes upon Rabbi Meir's peculiar use of the word "Messiah."

[18] From the prayer of Rosh Hashanah and Yom Kippur.

[19] Aramaic, *"nehora 'ila'ah."*

[20] *b. Shabbat* 147b; *'Eruvin* 13b.

[21] It seems that Rav Kook's prodigious memory deceived him. It was not Rabbi Akiva but Rabbi Yishmael who had the exchange with Rabbi Meir. See *b. 'Eruvin* 13a and *Sotah* 20a.

In the very different *Yerushalmi* account, "Said Rabbi Meir, 'All the days that I studied under Rabbi Yishmael, I did not place *kankantum* into the ink.'" See *y. Sotah* 2:4; quoted in *Tosafot, Sotah* 17b, s.v. *she-ne'emar*. Maimonides explained in a responsum to Rabbeinu Ephraim of Tyre that the *Yerushalmi* refers to the practice of the student Rabbi Meir; later, the mature Rabbi Meir did add *kankantum* to the ink. See *Teshuvot ha-Rambam*, ed. Freimann (Jerusalem, 1934), no. 126.

[22] Cf. Rabbi Abraham Bornstein of Sochatchov: "This is Amalek, 'the first of

nations,' head of the seven evil characteristics" (*Ne'ot ha-Deshe*, vol. I [Tel-Aviv, 1983], *Parashat Zakhor*, p. 179, par. 6). The editor, Rabbi Aharon Israel Bornstein, clarifies that the seven Canaanite nations symbolize the seven evil characteristics and Amalek is the head of these nations. Ibid., n. 45.

[23] Rav Kook penned these lines at the height of World War One. He witnessed how the phenomenon of nationalism decimated Europe. Cf. *Orot*, "*Ha-Milhamah*" ("*The War*").

[24] Isaiah 30:20; *Pesikta Rabbati* 12:9. Rav Kook paraphrased. The exact wording of the *Pesikta* reads: "As long as the seed of Amalek exists, the Face is covered, as it were; once his seed is removed from the world, the Face that was covered, is revealed. 'No longer shall your Teacher be hidden (*yikanef*), but your eyes shall see your Teacher' [Isaiah 30:20]." See *Pesikta Rabbati*, ed. Meir Ish-Shalom (Vienna, 1880), chap. 12, "*Zakhor*" (51a).

[25] Exodus 17:14.

Cf. Rabbi Isaac Ze'ev Halevi Soloveitchik, *Hiddushei Maran RIZ Halevi 'al ha-Torah, Beshallah*, s.v. *Ketov zot zikaron ba-sefer ve-sim be-'oznei Yehoshua* (I). The author juxtaposes the comment of the *Sifré, Pinhas*: "'*Ve-Tsav et Yehoshua*' ('And charge Joshua') [Deuteronomy 3:28]—*Tsavehu 'al divrei Talmud* (Charge him concerning the Oral Law)." See *'Emek ha-Netsiv* ad loc. Rabbi Soloveitchik (the "Brisker Rav") supposed that the *Sifré* is the source of Maimonides' statement in the Introduction to *Mishneh Torah*: "To Joshua, his disciple, Moses, our teacher, delivered the Oral Law and charged him concerning it."

The verse in Exodus 17:14 follows upon Joshua's armed conflict with Amalek. Rav Kook suggests that the separation and bifurcation into two distinct entities of Written Law versus Oral Law, came about under the spell of Amalek's influence.

[26] b. *Megillah* 18b; *Menahot* 32b; Maimonides, *MT, Hil. Tefillin* 1:12.

[27] y. *Megillah* 4:1:

> Rabbi Haggai said: "Rabbi Samuel bar Rav Yitzhak entered the synagogue. He saw a scribe reading the *Targum* [the Aramaic translation of Scripture] from a book. He said to him: 'It is forbidden for you [to read the *Targum*—an oral transmission—from a book]. Words that were said orally, [must be transmitted] orally; words that were said in writing, [must be transmitted] from writing.'"

Cf. b. *Gittin* 60; *Temurah* 14b. Rav Kook might as well have made his point from the *Talmud Bavli*. Perhaps the *Yerushalmi Megillah* was uppermost in his mind, because his talk preceded Purim (and the incident concerning Rabbi Meir writing a Scroll of Esther by heart in Asya, occurs later in that passage of *Yerushalmi*).

But there is another possibility. Alfasi transcribed the *Yerushalmi* in his *Halakhot, Megillah*, chap. 4 (14a). (See Rabbi Solomon ben Simon Duran, *She'elot u-Teshuvot ha-RaShBaSh* [Livorno, 1742], no. 277.) Perhaps Rav Kook, like his mentor Rabbi Naphtali Tsevi Yehudah Berlin (NeTsIV) of Volozhin, was especially conversant with Alfasi. (According to anecdote, one Friday night in the Volozhin Yeshiva, the lights went out, yet Netsiv was able to continue studying, having committed Alfasi to memory.)

Confirmation of this theory comes from Rabbi Shim'on Glitzenstein, who acted as Rav Kook's secretary during the latter's stay in London. Glitzenstein attests that an Alfasi in small format never left the Rav's hands during his medically prescribed walks. The custom of daily study of Alfasi goes back to the Vilna Gaon. See Rabbi Moshe Tsevi Neriyah, *Sihot ha-RAYaH* (Jerusalem, 5755/2015), pp. 184-185.

And then the question arises why Rabbi Isaac Alfasi (RIF) quoted the *Yerushalmi* and not the *Bavli*. This question of Alfasi was asked by Rabbi Chaim Zimmerman, *Binyan Halakhah* (New York, 1942), *Hakdamat ha-Rambam* (p. 2).

Here too (as above note 7) it is unwarranted to assume that Rav Kook rode roughshod over the simple reason for the sages' prohibition of writing Scripture from memory, namely to prevent scribal error. (See Rabbeinu Menahem ha-Me'iri, *Beit ha-Behirah, Megillah*, ed. Rabbi Moshe Hershler [Jerusalem: Makhon ha-Talmud ha-Yisraeli, 1968], *Megillah* 18b.) Rather, Rav Kook wrote in a homiletic vein.

[28] *b. Berakhot* 17a.
[29] *b. Berakhot* 33a.
[30] Proverbs 4:25; *b. Megillah* 18b.
[31] *b. Megillah* 18b.

Rav Kook stopped short of the *sugya*'s conclusion, which is that "an exigency is different" ("*she'at ha-dehak shanei*"). Provisionally, the Talmud assumed that Rabbi Meir, because of his phenomenal recall of Torah, was *sui generis* (as correctly quoted by Rav Kook). However, when challenged by the example of Rav Hananel, whose total command of Torah was certainly comparable to that of Rabbi Meir, the Talmud was forced to retract, attributing Rabbi Meir's writing of Scripture (in the case in question, the Scroll of Esther) from memory to the extraordinary circumstances in which he found himself. In 'Asya, there simply was no preexisting *Megillah* to refer to.

In the final analysis, we may say that that there were two factors that contributed to Rabbi Meir's writing Scripture by heart: 1) "*she'at ha-dehak*" (exigency); and 2) the fact that Rabbi Meir was "*shalem she-bi-shelemim*" ("perfect among perfect"), in the words of Me'iri. See *Rabbeinu Menahem ha-Me'iri, Beit ha-Behirah, Megillah* 18b (p. 51, right column).

Rabbi Ya'ir Hayyim Bachrach equated the waiving of the prohibition of writing scripture by heart in the case of *she'at ha-dehak* (*b. Megillah* 18b), to the waiving of the prohibition of writing down the *Aggadeta* in an "'*et la'asot la-Adonai—heferu toratekha*," "A time to do for the [sake of] the LORD—they annulled your Torah" (Psalms 119:126; *Temurah* 14b). The same permission that makes allowances for turning the oral into the written, allows turning the written into the oral in extenuating circumstances. They are but two sides of the same coin. See *Havot Ya'ir*, no. 175.

The parallel *sugya* in *Yerushalmi, Megillah* 4:1 offers an alternative solution to the problem of how Rabbi Meir in 'Asya could write the Scroll of Esther by heart. Besides "*Ein lemedin mi-she'at ha-dehak*" ("We do not learn from an exigency"), as in *Bavli*, there is proffered the following ingenious solution: "And some say that [Rabbi Meir] wrote two [*megillot*]; the first, he wrote by heart, and the second from the first, and archived (*ganaz*) the first."

Rabbeinu Nissim (in pagination of Alfasi, *Megillah*, 5b, s.v. *heikhi damei mitnamnem*) ruled that other than a *she'at ha-dehak*, it is forbidden to read from Scripture that had been written by heart. Rabbeinu Manoah, on the other hand, wrote that the law of not writing by heart is strictly at the outset (*lekhatehillah*), but the Scripture is not invalidated thereby. The two opinions are brought in Rabbi Joseph Karo, *Beit Yosef* on *Tur, Yoreh De'ah* 274.

[32] *b. Shabbat* 88a.

[33] *Midrash Tanhuma*, Noah, 3.

According to the Talmud *(Shabbat* 88a), at Mount Sinai, God held the mountain over the heads of the people "as a vat" and threatened that if they did not accept the Torah, that would be their burial place. *Tosafot* (ibid.) raise the question that the Children of Israel had already willingly accepted the Torah by saying, "We shall do and we shall hearken" (Exodus 24:7). The *Midrash Tanhuma* resolves this difficulty by differentiating between Written and Oral Law. The Israelites' voluntary acceptance extended only to the Written Law; the heavy-handed tactic was required to force their submission to the Oral Law as well. On Purim, this situation was remedied, when the Jews lovingly committed to the Oral Law.

[34] *b.'Eruvin* 13a; *Sotah* 20a. See also *Ecclesiastes Rabbah* 2:17: "Rabbi Meir was an excellent scribe" (*"Rabbi Meir havah katvan tav muvhar"*). Quoted in Lieberman, op. cit., p. 25.

[35] Genesis 3:21; *Genesis Rabbah* 20:12.

Perhaps this Midrash was the inspiration for the phrase "rags of light" in Leonard Cohen's song "If It Be Your Will."

[36] See Rabbi Zadok Hakohen Rabinowitz of Lublin, *Dover Tsedek* (Piotrków, 1911), 4b.

[37] Rabbi Jacob Moses Harlap, *Mei Marom*, Vol. 10 (Leviticus) (Jerusalem, 1997), *ma'amar* 41, *"Ihud Torah she-bi-khetav 'im Torah she-be-'al peh"* (p. 131, para. 2). Earlier in that discourse, Rabbi Harlap writes: "The Written Torah is the essence of the worlds, the essence of all existence; and the Oral Torah, the light of existence....In the hands of Israel is the power to unify the essence of existence with the light within, and combine them into one unit, with the result that existence itself will be synonymous with the light, the Oral Torah...." (p. 128).

[38] *b. Gittin* 60; *Temurah* 14b; Maimonides, *MT, Hil. Tefillah* 12:8; idem, *Guide of the Perplexed*, transl. Schwarz (Jerusalem, 2002), I, 71 (pp. 185-186).

Rav Kook demonstrated an abiding interest in the problematic of committing the Oral Law to writing, revisiting this theme on more than one occasion in his halakhic *oeuvre*. On the issue of whether the prohibition of writing down the Oral Law is biblical or rabbinic in origin, he wavered. See Rav Kook's earliest halakhic work, *'Ittur Soferim*, vol. 1 (Vilna, 1888; photo offset Jerusalem, 1974), 7a (*"Lishkat ha-Sha'ar"*) and 20a (*"Lishkat ha-Sofer"*). See the earlier literature: Rabbi Eliezer of Metz, *Yere'im*, chap. 128; Rabbi Ya'ir Hayyim Bachrach, *Havot Ya'ir* (Frankfurt am Main, 1699), no. 175; Rabbi Hayyim Joseph David Azulai, *Birkei Yosef*, vol. I (Livorno, 1774), *Orah Hayyim*, chap. 49, para. 2; idem, *Mahazik Berakhah* (Livorno, 1785), *Orah Hayyim*, chap. 49, para. 1.

And then there is Rav Kook's scintillating explanation of the passage in Maimonides' Introduction to *Mishneh Torah*:

> From the time of Moses to that of *Rabbeinu ha-Kadosh* [i.e., Rabbi Judah the Prince], no work had been composed from which the Oral

Law was publicly taught. But in each generation, the head of the court or the prophet of that generation wrote down for his private use a memorandum of the traditions which he had heard from his teachers, while teaching orally in public.

Rav Kook's commentary thereto was transcribed by Rabbi Ya'akov Filber in his work *Le-'Oro* (Jerusalem, 1995), pp. 164-167; reprinted (in a truncated version) in Rabbi Moshe Zuriel, *Otserot ha-RAYaH*, old series, vol. 2 (Tel-Aviv, 1988), pp. 849-850, and (in a lengthier version) in idem, *Otserot ha-RAYaH*, new series, vol. 3 (Rishon le-Zion, 2002), pp. 11-13. In both *'Ittur Soferim* (loc. cit.) and the commentary to Maimonides, Rav Kook probed whether the prohibition consists in the initial act of writing the Oral Law or in the subsequent act of teaching it in public from a written text, or both.

For a scholarly treatment of the subject, see Saul Lieberman, "The Publication of the *Mishnah*," in idem, *Hellenism in Jewish Palestine* (New York, 1994), pp. 83-89.

Inter alia, in Jerusalem, in the 1930s, Rav Kook and the young, budding scholar Saul Lieberman studied together *be-havruta* on a regular basis *Tur* with the commentary of *Beit Yosef*. The precondition for this arrangement was that neither would prepare the text beforehand. (Heard from Dov Zlotnick, disciple of Lieberman and executor of his will—BN.)

[39] Cf. the work ascribed to Rabbi Moses Hayyim Luzzatto, *KaLaH Pithei Hokhmah*, ed. Spinner (Jerusalem, 1987), *petah* 30 (pp. 93-94), referencing Isaiah 51:4 and *Leviticus Rabbah* 13:3.

The Hasidism of Rav Kook

We usually associate the term "Neo-Hasidism" with thinkers such as Martin Buber, Hillel Zeitlin, and Abraham Joshua Heschel. It may come to many of us as a surprise that Rabbi Abraham Isaac Hakohen Kook also proposed a new Hasidism, but it should not.[1] During Rav Kook's lifetime, there were those who perceived him as the founder of a new Hasidic movement. Both admirers and detractors understood that this charismatic teacher embodied a renewed spirituality.

Rabbi Ya'akov Moshe Harlap, eminent disciple of Rav Kook, wrote a letter intended for the Gerrer Rebbe, in which he portrayed his mentor as a modern-day Hasidic master reaching out to alienated Jews in an attempt to bring them back to the fold.[2] A cynical writer of the Agudah camp, critiquing Rav Kook's seminal work *Orot* (1920), segued to the secular *"tsaddik"* Martin Buber and expressed fear lest there develop around Rav Kook yet another mystery religion.[3]

What are the facts? How did Rav Kook himself envision the new Hasidism? Was it to be a reincarnation of the East European variety attributed to Rabbi Israel Ba'al Shem Tov?

Untrained observers have the answer ready. One need merely point to the *spodik*, the tall fur hat perched on his head, to determine that Rav Kook viewed himself as a Hasidic rebbe. However there is an historical context to the headwear. Rav Kook's predecessors in the Ashkenazic Jerusalem rabbinate—his father-in-law, Rabbi Elijah David Rabinowitz-Te'omim (ADeReT), and Rabbi Samuel Salant, staunch Lithuanian *Mitnagdim*—wore the identical fur hat. Excuse the cultural confusion and move on to Rav Kook's own words.

In his much calumniated *Orot*, Rav Kook threw down the gauntlet, calling for a "great Hasidism," "very superior Hasidim" and "great Hasidim, unique in greatness of knowledge."[4] He even pushed the term to its extreme limits, signing off: "Give strength to the higher knowledge; to the exalted, radical, godly Hasidism (*Hasidut ha-elohit ha-radikalit ha-romemah*)!"[5] And with that, the reader is left wondering where exactly Rav Kook's *poignard* is pointing.

This year, yet another heretofore unknown journal of Rav Kook was released in Jerusalem.[6] An entry in the journal fleshes out Rav Kook's vision of a new Hasidism.

We should pay careful attention to this recently released passage. It should disabuse us of many well-intentioned but ill-conceived attempts to reduce Rav Kook to the status of one more Hasidic rebbe with a fur hat on his head. The entry, which is easily an essay in its own right, contains several subtle nuances which might be missed in our contemporary popular culture. Evidently, Rav Kook anticipated our ability to manufacture facile acronyms such as *HaBaKUK* (HaBaD, Breslov, Kook). In a "preemptive strike," he unleashes his own byword, *KeMaH*, the initials of *Kabbalah, Madda', Hasidut* (Kabbalah, Science, Hasidism).

The Hasidism of Rav Kook

Early on in the piece, Rav Kook holds up as a lodestar the book *Sha'ar ha-Shamayim* by Abraham Cohen de Herrera (a.k.a. Alonso Nunez de Herrera).

Herrera (d. 1635) studied in Ragusa (today Dubrovnik, Croatia) under Rabbi Israel Sarug, a peripatetic teacher who transmitted a form of Lurianic Kabbalah to several distinguished students in Italy, the greatest being Rabbi Menahem Azariah of Fano.[7]

Herrera's Spanish work of Kabbalah, *Puerta del Cielo* (*Gate of Heaven*), remained until recently an unpublished manuscript. Luckily, Rabbi Isaac Aboab da Fonseca (1605-1693), eventual *Hakham* of the Spanish-Portuguese community of Amsterdam, translated the work (which is to say, portions thereof) into Hebrew at Herrera's behest. The book was printed in Amsterdam in 1655 under the title *Sha'ar ha-Shamayim*.

What strikes the reader of *Sha'ar ha-Shamayim* is the ease with which Herrera juxtaposes arcane Lurianic Kabbalah and Neo-Platonic philosophy, prompting Alexander Altmann to title his 1982 study of *Puerta del Cielo*, "Lurianic Kabbalah in a Platonic Key." Herrera shuttles between Israel Sarug and Marsilio Ficino without batting an eyelash.

The reader may find curious the fact that Rav Kook, rather than viewing this Spanish work of Kabbalah, chock-full of Western philosophy, as an aberration or serious departure from tradition, regards it as mainstream. Furthermore, Rav Kook holds it up as a role model for the direction in which he wishes to lead us. As he writes regarding *Sha'ar ha-Shamayim*, "So did the great throughout the ages."

Rav Kook's perception of *Sha'ar ha-Shamayim* may have been influenced by the publisher's introduction to the Warsaw 1865 edition. Israel Jaffe of Kalisz wrote: "All that was investigated by the great godly geniuses—Rabbi Moshe Hayyim Luzzatto; the Vilna Gaon; his disciple Rabbi Hayyim of Volozhin; Rabbi Shneur Zalman of Liadi; his son Rabbi Dov; and his disciple Rabbi Aaron, all of blessed memory—all their systems are gathered together in this book." Jaffe certainly engaged in hyperbole, but his point was well taken. Herrera's book did in fact set the tone for an entire approach to Lurianic Kabbalah that came to be known as *"hasbarah,"* or conceptualization. In Padua, Vilna, Volozhin, Liadi, Lubavitch, and Staroshelye, Kabbalah was demythologized and translated to the language of reason and discourse.

But that is not exactly what Rav Kook is saying. Rav Kook asserts that *Sha'ar ha-Shamayim* represents a rapprochement between Kabbalah and the science of the day. In this respect, Rav Kook may be barking up the wrong tree. In the seventeenth century, in Holland as well as in Italy, there was a demarcation (however blurred) between philosophy and science. Rather than choosing Herrera as his role model, Rav Kook might have done better opting for Herrera's contemporary, Joseph Solomon Delmedigo (or as he is known in Hebrew, *"YaShaR mi-Candia"*) as an exemplary amalgam of Kabbalah and science. (By the way, Delmedigo's Kabbalah too is of Sarugian lineage.)

Be that as it may, Rav Kook advocates the marriage of Kabbalah and science. Where does Hasidism enter into the discussion?

Midway through the essay, Rav Kook rather abruptly quotes the rabbinic maxim, "The greater the man, the greater his inclination (*yetser*)."[8] *Yetser* is usually understood as *yetser ha-ra'*, the evil inclination. In truth, *yetser* derives from the root *yatsar*, "create." Rav Kook seems to be saying that the new creativity unleashed by the fresh synthesis of Kabbalah and *madda'* (science) demands a new ethic.[9]

Rather than the mediocre *Mussar* of the masses, Rav Kook writes, a new Hasidism is called for. Here, both the terms *Mussar* and Hasidism beg definition. What *Mussar*? What Hasidism?

By "*Mussar*," Rav Kook undoubtedly refers to the *Mussar* movement founded in Lithuania by Rabbi Israel Salanter. Rav Kook was a product of the Volozhin Yeshiva, whose heads (Rabbi Naftali Tsevi Yehudah Berlin and Rabbi Hayyim Soloveitchik) rejected the *Mussar* movement. Rav Kook finds *Mussar* enervating. The new Hasidism he proposes is empowering. "It takes them out from fear and darkness to confidence and light; from servitude and weakness to sovereignty and strength of spirit."[10]

To put his new Hasidism into clearer perspective, Rav Kook juxtaposes it to the previous Hasidism. "Such a Hasidism will certainly not be lacking all the (spiritual) wealth of the latter-day Hasidism." "The latter-day Hasidism" (*ha-hasidut ha-me'uharah*) is code for the Hasidism that originated with the Ba'al Shem Tov (BEShT). In *Orot*, Rav Kook refers to Beshtian Hasidism as "the latest Hasidism" (*ha-hasidut ha-aharonah*).[11] This is done to distinguish between East European Hasidism and earlier pietist movements, such as *Hasidei Ashkenaz*, the medieval Pietists of the Rhineland.

So what would Rav Kook's Hasidism look like? Perhaps the Hasidism advocated in Rabbi Moshe Hayyim Luzzatto's classic, *Mesillat Yesharim (Path of the Just)* could serve as an analog. In its original form, *Mesillat Yesharim* consisted of a dialog between a *hakham*, a wise man, and a *hasid*, a pious man.[12] Luzzatto, a Renaissance man in the tradition of Italian Jewry, combined Kabbalah and the science of his day. In Padua, a university town renowned for its medical school, Luzzatto's immediate circle included physicians Moshe David Valle and Yekutiel Gordon. In *Mesillat Yesharim*, Luzzatto included an entire section on *Hasidut* (chaps. 18-21). So enamored was Rav Kook of Luzzatto's work, that he penned a digest, *Kitsur Mesillat Yesharim*.[13]

Many years ago, a famous Rosh Yeshivah by the name of Rabbi Abba Berman (quoting his father who led a *metivta* in Lodz, Poland before World War Two), told this writer (BN) in private conversation: "The only Hasidism is that of the *Mesillat Yesharim*."

Speaking of his new Hasidism, Rav Kook writes:
> It must be expansive. It must reach to the depth of its source in the nation and the individual, and it must reach to the heights of God's loving-kindness (*hesed*).

This is Rav Kook's way of reminding us subtly (or not so subtly)—as did Luzzatto in *Mesillat Yesharim*—that the word *"hasidut"* (piety) derives from *"hesed"* (loving-kindness).[14]

In his *modus vivendi*, Rav Kook certainly internalized the words of the "*Hasid* Rabbi Moshe Hayyim Luzzatto"[15]:

> It is worthy for every *hasid* to intend with his actions for the good of his entire generation, to acquit them and protect them...for the Holy One, blessed be He, loves only the one who loves Israel; and the more a person loves Israel, the more the Holy One, blessed be He, loves that person.[16]

TRANSLATION OF THE TEXT OF *PINKESEI HA-RAYAH*

Kabbalah must bond with all the sciences; to live with them and through them. So did the great [sages] throughout the ages; and more than they achieved—it is obligatory upon us to achieve. The spiritual world that bestows its spirit upon the thinking man, was enhanced by constant appearances of the light of intellect. This enhancement dulls the oppositions between one science and another, and once the barriers have come down—the different sciences actually come to one another's aid.

Science in all of its breadth, in all of its various aspects—spiritual and practical, societal and global—must find its place alongside the supernal wisdom [i.e., Kabbalah].

A shining example of this would be the book *Sha'ar ha-Shamayim* by Rabbi Abraham Cohen Errera (!), who was the second in a line extending from the ARI [i.e., Rabbi Isaac Luria] through Rabbi Israel Sarug, disciple of the ARI.[17] [Herrera] was inspired to write his book in Spanish, in full view of the cultured world of the day. With a breadth of intellect and feelings of respect and affection, the author toured all the philosophical studies that represented the finest literature of his time. Rabbi Isaac Aboab [da Fonseca] who admired him [i.e., Herrera]—translating the work into Hebrew for the benefit of Hebrews—followed in his spirit, which is the spirit of true culture worthy of Torah scholars who are truly "men of holiness."

It is understood that according to the changes of the *Zeitgeist*, so must the synthesis (between the supernal, divine wisdom and all the human thoughts that proceed from the sciences) shift, but the principle remains the same. The preparedness of the thinker—pure of knowledge and holy of thought—to absorb into his midst the best thoughts of the finest writers, the thinkers, the sages of every people and language, of every subject of science; and to shine upon them, from them and through them, the divine light—this is the unchanging way of the world, upon which we are obligated to travel.

Only "if you have heard the old, will you hear the new."[18] The old must be studied and researched, and it will bring the new, good and fundamental.

[This synthesis of] science and the supernal illumination that expands the soul, produces a strong character in our entire organic unity, spiritual and material.

Through the supernal splendor and the fullness of life that beats in its midst, the natural inclinations of the soul and the body, and all its senses and faculties, are invigorated, strengthened and expanded. "The greater the man, the greater his inclination (*yetser*)."[19]

In order to purify great powers; to refine powerful, luminous, lofty ambitions, much preparation is required. So the synthesis of Kabbalah and science immediately beckons us to—Hasidism (Pietism).

We need now a rich, broad, luminous Hasidism to illumine us!

Such a Hasidism will certainly not be lacking all the [spiritual] wealth of the latter-day Hasidism [i.e., of Rabbi Israel Ba'al Shem Tov], but it must be expansive. It must reach to the depth of its source in the nation and the individual, and it must reach to the heights of God's lovingkindness (*hesed*).

[We need] a Hasidism that negates no good; no science, peace, Torah or talent, but rather crystallizes and purifies all. When understood as such, people with heart will not oppose it.

This Hasidism is needed by men of powerful spirit, just as the average *Mussar* (Ethics) is necessary for the masses. This Hasidism contains all the ways of *Mussar*, but it surpasses them; it takes them out from fear and darkness to confidence and light; from servitude and weakness to sovereignty and strength of spirit. This Hasidism must be combined with Kabbalah and science, so that greatness of spirit not grow inimical to routine ethics (which the average acquire through revulsion brought on by fear).

When we will have this order in hand—first in theory, and later in action—we will have the basis for all the light of Torah; for the theory of *Halakhah* and for all the parameters of action, education and true *hiddush* (creation). A *hiddush* that is at once sharp and esthetic, straight and clever.

And the more enhanced the knowledge and understanding of Torah—real Torah, permeated with the everlasting Holy Covenant—the more the ideal soul will expand, as it fills with the splendor of Kabbalah, the sciences and Hasidism.

In this regard I invoke the adage: "If there be no *KeMaH* (Flour), there be no Torah; if there be no Torah, there be no *KeMaH* (Flour)."[20] [*KeMaH* being an acronym for *Kabbalah, Madda', Hasidut*, or Kabbalah, Science, Hasidism.]

This is the straight way of the LORD that the new life and the feelings of freedom ringing throughout the sacred soil at this time require us to embark upon.

And a highway shall be there, and a way, and it shall be called the way of holiness....the redeemed shall walk there. (Isaiah 35:8-9)[21]

---

[1] Incidentally, both Buber and Zeitlin met with Rav Kook in Jerusalem and were favorably impressed.

[2] See my introduction to *Orot* (Maggid, 2015), p. 33.
   The letter was addressed directly to the Rav of Bendin, Rabbi Hanokh Tsevi Hakohen Levin, brother-in-law of the Gerrer Rebbe, Rabbi Abraham Mordechai Alter (author of *Imrei Emet*).

[3] Ibid., p. 53.

[4] *Orot ha-Tehiyah*, beginning chap. 4.

[5] Ibid. end chap. 4.

[6] *Pinkesei ha-RAYaH* 4, ed. Tsevi Mikhel Levin and Benzion Kahana-Shapira (Jerusalem, 5777/2017).

[7] Gershom Scholem lavished much scholarly attention on both Herrera and his teacher Sarug. In the first case, Scholem published a small biography, *Abraham Cohen Herrera: Leben, Werk und Wirkung* (1978). As for Sarug, in an early essay, caustically entitled, "Israel Sarug: Student of the Ari?" (1940), Scholem attempted to expose this sketchy figure as a fraud. Scholem presumed that Sarug was an impostor who passed himself off to unsuspecting Europeans as an erstwhile disciple of Rabbi Isaac Luria in either Egypt or Erets Israel. Lately, researchers such as Ronit Meroz and Yosef Avivi have made some headway in rehabilitating Sarug's image as a genuine conduit of Lurianic teaching.

[8] *b. Sukkah* 52a.

[9] Rav Kook revisits this theme later in that volume:

> One who feels in his soul that he needs much divine illumination, many ethical studies, and much contemplation, let him not delude himself by saying that he can throw off this burden and be like everyone else and like the masses of *"b'nei Torah"* (Torah students); that he can engage totally or for the most part in practical affairs, and that will suffice for him. *"The greater the man, the greater his inclination."* In direct proportion to the potential that one has for spiritual ascent, are the deficiencies, the strange desires and the pull to gross corporeality—that have no comparison among the average. The only way that one can be spared them (and even profit from them, inasmuch as their mighty power can be harnessed to pull one to a supernal loftiness) is if one fortifies one's character, raising thereby one's essence to its proper place: to "stroll in the Garden of Eden" of lofty matters, and the splendor (*Zohar*) of the joy of the LORD shall be his strength. But if one should wish to be like the masses of *"b'nei Torah,"* one will actually end up much lower than them, descending to the depth of bad traits. He shall find himself extremely corrupted—

until he reassumes the spiritual quality that is unique to him.

(*Pinkesei ha-RAYaH* 4 [Jerusalem, 5777/2017], *Pinkas ha-Dapim* 2:14 [p. 232])

[10] Rav Kook's critique of Rabbi Israel Salanter's Mussar movement deserves a separate study. I hope one day to treat that subject at length. For now, one would do well to consult Rabbi Moshe Zuriel's collection, *Otserot ha-RAYaH* (Rishon le-Zion, 2002), vol. 2, pp. 311-312, 314, 329-330.

(See now Rabbi Abraham Isaac Hakohen Kook's commentary to *The Legends of Rabbah bar Bar Hannah*, ed. Bezalel Naor [New York, NY: Orot/Kodesh, 2019], Appendix 6, "Rav Kook's Critique of the Mussar Movement," pp. 214-221. Add now to the references cited in that appendix, Rav Kook's Introduction to *'Eyn Ayah*, ed. Rabbi Ya'akov Filber, vol. 1 [Jerusalem: Makhon RZYH, 1987], p. 23.)

[11] *Orot ha-Tehiyah*, chapter 35.

[12] See Rabbi Moshe Hayyim Luzzatto, *Mesillat Yesharim* (Dialogue Version from Ms. Günzburg 1206, Russian State Library, Moscow; and Thematic Version from first edition, Amsterdam, 1740), ed. Avraham Shoshana (Jerusalem: Ofeq, 1994).

[13] First published as an appendix to Rabbi Tsevi Yehudah Kook's *Li-Sheloshah be-Elul*, vol. 2 (5707/1947), pp. 23-31, *Kitsur Mesillat Yesharim* has since been reprinted in *Ma'amrei ha-RAYaH*, vol. 2 (Jerusalem, 5744/1984), pp. 273-276; and Rabbi Moshe Zuriel, *Otserot ha-RAYaH*, new series, vol. 2, pp. 297-300.

[14] Rabbi Moshe Hayyim Luzzatto, *Mesillat Yesharim*, ed. Avraham Shoshana (Jerusalem, 1994), chap. 19 (p. 282).

[15] Thus did Rav Kook refer to the author of *Mesillat Yesharim*. See Rav Kook's eulogy for Rabbi Israel Salanter in *Ma'amrei ha-RAYaH*, vol. 1 (Jerusalem, 1980), p. 121; and Rabbi Moshe Zuriel, *Otserot ha-RAYaH*, vol. 2, p. 311.

[16] Rabbi Moshe Hayyim Luzzatto, *Mesillat Yesharim*, end chap. 19 (p. 296).

[17] In a letter to Rabbi Shemariah Menashe Hakohen Adler, who penned a commentary to Rav Kook's mystical tract *Reish Millin*, Rav Kook quoted from the "book *Beit Elohim* by the kabbalist, the philosopher, Rabbi Abraham Errera (!), disciple of Rabbi Israel Sarug, disciple of the ARI [i.e., Rabbi Isaac Luria], of blessed memory." See *Iggerot ha-RAYaH*, vol. 3 (Jerusalem: Mossad Harav Kook, 1965), Letter 896 (p. 208).

Like *Sha'ar ha-Shamayim*, *Beit Elohim* was written by Herrera in Spanish. The author titled his work, *Casa de la Divinidad* (House of Divinity). It was titled *Beit Elohim* by Rabbi Isaac Aboab da Fonseca in his Hebrew translation, published in Amsterdam in 1655 (after Herrera's death). Concerning the significance of the original Spanish title, see Nissim Yosha, *Myth and Metaphor: Abraham Cohen Herrera's Philosophic Interpretation of Lurianic Kabbalah* (Hebrew) (Jerusalem: Magnes, 1994), pp. 51-54.

Obviously, Rav Kook accepted at face value Rabbi Israel Sarug's claim that he was a bona fide disciple of Rabbi Isaac Luria. See too Rabbi Isaac Hutner's *haskamah* (encomium) to Rabbi Menahem Azariah of Fano's work, *Alfasi Zuta*; reprinted in Rabbi Isaac Hutner, *Pahad Yitzhak: Iggerot u-Ketavim*, ed. Rabbi Yonatan David (Brooklyn, NY, 2016), no. 80 (pp. 147-148). Rabbi Hutner accepted the theory of Rabbi Zadok Hakohen (Rabinowitz) of Lublin that Rabbi Israel Sarug studied under Rabbi Isaac Luria before Rabbi Hayyim Vital was apprenticed to the master. (See Rabbi Zadok Hakohen of Lublin, *Sefer ha-Zikhronot*, appended to idem, *Divrei Soferim* [Lublin, 1913; photo-offset B'nei Berak, 1967], 31a.) In order to determine that Sarugian Kabbalah was embraced in the "study-house of the Gaon Rabbi Elijah [of Vilna]," Rabbi Hutner referred to the work of the *Leshem* (i.e., Rabbi Solomon Eliashov), who demonstrated that *Nefesh ha-Hayyim* by Rabbi Hayyim of Volozhin, the Gaon's premier disciple, incorporates elements of Sarugian Kabbalah (*"'Olam ha-Malbush,"* etc.). See Rabbi Solomon Eliashov, *Sefer Hakdamot u-She'arim* (Piotrków, 1909), Introduction to *Sha'ar ha-Poneh Kadim* (f.59).

Perhaps it should be pointed out that Rabbi Zadok Hakohen advised maintaining distance from works that mix Kabbalah with gentile philosophy. After censuring Delmedigo's *Novelot Hokhmah*, Rabbi Zadok continues: "And so, in my opinion, it is advisable to stay far away from the book *Beit Elohim* and the book *Sha'ar ha-Shamayim*, composed by Rabbi Abraham Cohen Errera (!), who invented theories on his own and from what he derived from the early philosophers of the nations, and wished to unite them with the wisdom of Kabbalah, attained through prophecy and the divine spirit" *(Sefer ha-Zikhronot*, 36b).

For the positive reception of Sarugian Kabbalah by the masters of HaBaD Hasidism, see the exchange between Rabbi Dan Tumarkin of Rogatchov (a Lubavitcher Hasid) and the Kopyster Rebbe, Rabbi Shelomo Zalman Schneerson (author of *Magen Avot*), in Rabbi Mordechai Menashe Laufer, *Ha-Melekh bi-Mesibo*, vol. 2 (Kefar Habad, 1993), pp. 273 (*Magen Avot* quoting Rabbi Naftali Bacharach's *'Emek ha-Melekh*), 287 (i.e., 286, Rabbi Shelomo Zalman of Kopyst discussing the controversy surrounding Sarugian Kabbalah and its endorsement in Mezritch), 290 (Rabbi Shelomo Zalman of Kopyst quoting Sarug's teaching of a second *Tsimtsum*, and the *Alter Rebbe*'s excited quotation from *'Emek ha-Melekh*), 291 (Rabbi Shelomo Zalman of Kopyst referring to Sarugian Kabbalah), 292 (Rabbi Menahem Mendel Schneerson of Lubavitch-Brooklyn noting that the references to *'Emek ha-Melekh* emanate from the *Tsemah Tsedek*), 293 (*Tsemah Tsedek* quoting from *'Emek ha-Melekh* and from Rabbi Meir Poppers in *Zohar ha-Raki'a*).

The last reference is of special interest. Contained in the Korets 1785 edition of Rabbi Jacob Tsemah's *Zohar ha-Raki'a* is a section of commentaries to *Zohar* by his student Rabbi Meir Hakohen Poppers (starting on 19b). The passage that *Tsemah Tsedek* cites is found there at 20a. After briefly alluding to the *'Olam ha-Malbush* of Rabbi Israel Sarug, Rabbi Meir Poppers distances himself by saying:

> But I do not study these discourses [i.e., of Sarug] for so commanded Rabbi Hayyim Vital in the introduction to *'Ets Hayyim* that we not study the works of any other man. And it is a *mitsvah* to fulfill his words. Therefore, you will not find in any of my compositions a discourse outside of the holy words of Rabbi Hayyim Vital, of blessed memory. I just came to show you that I did not say anything of my own theorizing, for it is true and correct.

[18] *b. Berakhot* 40a.
[19] *b. Sukkah* 52a.

[20] *m. Avot* 3:17.
[21] *Pinkesei ha-RAYaH*, vol. 4, ed. Z.M. Levin and B.Z. Kahana-Shapira (Jerusalem, 5777/2017), *Pinkas ha-Dapim* 1:34 (pp. 88-92).

The Universalism of Rav Kook

Stereotypes are difficult to overcome. Until recently, the stereotype of Rav Avraham Yitzhak Hakohen Kook (1865-1935) was of a nationalist (perhaps even ultranationalist) who lent his rabbinic aegis to the Zionist enterprise in the first third of the twentieth century.

In his seminal work *Orot [Lights]* (Jerusalem, 1920), the very first section of the book is entitled *"Erets Yisrael."* The punchline of the first chapter reads:

> The expectation of salvation (*tsefiyat ha-yeshu'ah*) is the force that preserves exilic Judaism; the Judaism of the Land of Israel is salvation itself (*ha-yeshu'ah 'atsmah*).

Thus, Rav Kook placed Israel's return to its ancestral homeland front and center, and provided it with theological underpinnings sorely lacking in the secular Zionist movement.

In this respect, Rav Kook's bold initiative, courageous and outspoken, at times alienated him from his more conservative-minded rabbinic peers. The Gerrer Rebbe, Avraham Mordechai Alter (1866-1948), wrote in a much publicized letter:

> The Rav, the Gaon R. Avraham Kook, may he live, is a man of many-sided talents in Torah, and noble traits. Also, it is

public knowledge that he loathes money. However, his love for Zion surpasses all limit and he "declares the impure pure and adduces proof to it."... From this, came the strange things in his books.

With the passage of time and the publication of many hitherto suppressed manuscripts, we become increasingly aware of another facet to the extremely complex personality of Rav Kook: the cosmopolitan or universalist.[1] Rav Kook's passionate love for his land and his nation of Israel in no way vitiated the larger scope of his Messianic or utopian vision. Such an illuminating manuscript is that designated *Pinkas 5*, published this year of 2018 by Boaz Ofen in volume 3 of his ongoing series *Kevatsim mi-Ketav Yad Kodsho* (*Journals from Manuscript*). The *Pinkas* has been dated by the editor to the years 1907-1913, during which time Rav Kook served as Rabbi of Jaffa.

In the following *pensée* (perhaps "essay" is the better word), Rav Kook argues that just as the "seventy nations" of the world form an organic unity, the proverbial "family of man," so too the various faith communities or religions complement one another in a parallel organic unity.

Though Rav Kook probably never heard of the mythic bird Simorgh—which figures prominently in the twelfth-century work *The Conference of the Birds* by the Persian poet Farid ud-Din Attar—Rav Kook's imagery is roughly reminiscent. In that allegorical tale, the birds of the world set out to find a leader. It has been suggested to them that they appoint as their king the legendary

Simorgh. To reach the remote mountain abode of the Simorgh, the birds must embark on a perilous journey. Most of the birds succumb to the elements along the way. At journey's end, there remain but thirty birds. They discover that they themselves, together, form the sought Simorgh. In Farsi, *"Simorgh"* means "thirty birds" (*si-morgh*).

Lest the reader mistakenly surmise that Rav Kook suggests that the faith of Israel will in some way be subordinated to a higher unity, Rav Kook writes at the intermezzo:

> And with this, automatically the horn of Israel must be uplifted.
> *"Bow down to Him, all gods"* [Psalms 97:7].

Rav Kook sees no contradiction between the aspiration of Israel to settle their land and the blessing of peace for all mankind. On the contrary, he believes that precisely from its ancestral homeland the Nation of Israel will broadcast this prophetic message of global reconciliation to all the inhabitants of the planet. As he writes: "So the turn of Israel to shine has come—together with the demand of its independence, the desire of its renascence upon the holy soil, the source of the opinions and beliefs most worthy of spreading in space, and of taking up time and epochs in the life of all mankind."

The Thought of Rav Kook

TRANSLATION OF THE TEXT OF
KEVATSIM MI-KETAV YAD KODSHO

The aspiration to bring peace to the world, has forever been the aspiration of Israel. This is the interior of the soul of *Knesset Israel* (*Ecclesia Israel*), which was given full expression by the chosen of her children, the Prophets who foresaw at the End of Days humanity's happiness and world peace.

However, light advances slowly. The strides made are not discernible because divine patience is great, and that which appears in the eyes of flesh insignificant—is truly exalted from the vantage of the supernal eye. "In the place of its greatness, there you find its humility."[2] Even in the worst life; the hardest, lowest, most sinful life—there is abundant light and sufficient place for the divine love to appear. That life need not be erased from existence, but rather uplifted to a higher niveau. There is no vacuum,[3] no empty space; every level needs to be filled.

Truly, world peace, in the material sense, comes into our vision. The nationalism that ruled supreme during the days of "barbarism," when each nation perceived a foreign nation as uncivilized,[4] [and held] that all man's obligations to man are cancelled in regard to the "barbarians"—this evil notion is being erased. On the other hand, with the passing of generations, the intellect, the light of fairness, and the necessity of life—which together comprise the windows through which the divine light wends its way—all together impress the stamp of universal peace upon the national character. Gradually, there arrives the recognition that humanity's division into nations does not pit them against one another, such that nations cannot dwell together on the planet Earth. Rather, their relation is organic—just as individuals relate to the nation, and the limbs to the body. This notion, when completely manifest, shall renew the face of the world, purifying hearts of their wickedness and uplifting souls.

However, the relation of nations—their pacification—must correspond to the relation of religions. A complete nationalism is not possible without correlate feelings of holiness. Those sentiments—whether few or many—change opinions; those sentiments are sensitive to the variables of geography and genetics.[5]

Peace between nations cannot come about by minimizing the value of nationalism. On the contrary, people of good will recognize that just as the feeling for family is respectable and pleasant, holy and pure, and were it to be lost from the world, humanity would lose with it a great treasure of happiness and holiness—so the loss of the "national family" [i.e., nationalism] and all the sentiments and delicate ideas bound to it, would leave in its place a destruction that would bring to the collective soul a frustration much more painful than all the pains that it suffered on account of the demarcation of nationalism.

Humanity must receive the good and reject the evil. The force of repulsion and the force of attraction together build the material world; and the cosmopolitan[6] and national forces together build the palace of humanity and its world of good fortune.[7]

As it is in regard to nationalism, so it is in regard to religions. It is not the removal of religion that will bring bliss, but the religious perceptions eventually relating to one another in a bond of friendship. (With the removal of religion there would pass from the world a great treasure of strength and life; inestimable treasures of good.) Every thought of enmity, of opposition, of destruction, will dissipate and disappear. There will remain in the religions only the higher, inner, universal purpose, full of holy light and true peace, a treasure of light and eternal life. The religions will recognize each other as brothers; [will recognize] how each serves its purpose within its boundary, and does what it must do in its circle. The relation of one religion to another will be organic.[8] This realization automatically brings about (and is brought about by) the higher realization of the unity of the light of *Ein Sof* [the Infinite], that manifests upon and through all. And with this, automatically the horn of Israel must be uplifted.

"*Bow down to Him, all gods*" [Psalms 97:7].

This teaching of peace, which broadens the heart and refines the soul; which brings life and light to all the nations of the earth and to the "chambers of the heart" of each individual; which shines light on every home and family, every society and association—requires much study from the source of light. Humanity has hardly opened the first page of this teaching of peace; has yet to invoke the name of the Holy One, blessed be He, *"Shalom"* ("Peace").[9]

There was no opportunity for this as long as the blossom of national peace had not appeared. Now it has appeared, brought about by the humanistic[10] notions that grew stronger in the world for the past century and more. Yet they could not maintain their stand because they did not reach the pinnacle; they could not find firm footing in the peace of religions, that which would bring life and light, the blessing of heaven to individuals and to collectives, increasing true faith, love of God and the creations, the strength of life and joy of souls.

So the turn of Israel to shine has come—together with the demand of its independence, the desire of its renascence upon the holy soil, the source of the opinions and beliefs most worthy of spreading in space, and of taking up time and epochs in the life of all mankind. Once this encompassing light,[11] full of holiness and strength, appears upon them, the entire world of man, from one end to the other end, must be moved thereby, for light and for good, for the blessing of life and peace.

"Like the dew of Hermon descending upon the mountains of Zion, for there the LORD commanded the blessing, life eternal."[12]

(Kevatsim mi-Ketav Yad Kodsho, ed. Boaz Ofen, vol. 3 [Jerusalem, 2018], *Pinkas* 5, par. 43 [pp. 96-98])

---

[1] In Rav Kook's seminal work, *Orot* (1920), there was a chapter which I entitled in my edition, "The Three Wrestlers—Orthodoxy, Nationalism, and Liberalism—and the Referee." See Rabbi Abraham Isaac Hakohen Kook, ed. Bezalel Naor (Maggid, 2015), *Orot ha-Tehiyah* (Lights of Renascence), chap. 18 (pp. 320-327). A key sentence reads: "The Holy, the Nation, and Humanity—these are three major demands of which all life, our own and every man's, is composed" (ibid, p. 321).

[2] A play upon the saying of Rabbi Yohanan in *b. Megillah* 31a: "Wherever you find the strength of the Holy One, blessed be He, you find His humility."

[3] Based on the saying attributed to Aristotle: "Nature abhors a vacuum."

[4] Rav Kook explains the meaning of the original Greek word *"barbaros"* (βάρβαρος).

[5] Cf. this passage in *'Arpilei Tohar*:

> Messiah will interpret the Torah of Moses, by revealing in the world the vision how all the peoples and divisions of mankind derive their spiritual nourishment from the one fundamental source, while the content conforms to the spirit of each nation according to its history and all its distinctive features, be they temperamental or climatological; [according to] all the economic vagaries and the variables of psychology—so that the wealth of specificity lacks for nothing. Nevertheless, all will bond together and derive nourishment from one source, with a supernal friendship and a strong inner assurance. "'The LORD will give a saying; the heralds are a great host' [Psalms 68:12]—Every word that emitted from the divine mouth divided into seventy languages" [*b. Shabbat* 88b].
> And the absolute reconciliation of the spiritual unity of the entire human world—in a fashion that affirms the good of individual and collective freedom—is the beginning of that which is more exalted: the grand conception that flows from the revelation of the rich unity of the entirety of existence....

(*'Arpilei Tohar* [Jerusalem, 1983], pp. 62-63)

'Arpilei Tohar was first printed in Jerusalem in 1914, before the outbreak of World War One. For various reasons that we need not go into, that edition remained unbound and uncirculated. Random copies found their way into private collections. In 1983, *'Arpilei Tohar* was reprinted in a slightly censored fashion. The complete contents of *'Arpilei Tohar* are now available in the unexpurgated collection, *Shemonah Kevatsim*, where it is designated *"Kovets 2."*

This particular passage occurs in *Shemonah Kevatsim* (Jerusalem, 2004), 2:177.

Parenthetically, it seems to this writer that Rav Kook's vision of the Messiah differs significantly from that of Rabbi Nahman of Breslov, as becomes apparent from the latter's recently revealed *Megillat Setarim*. In Rav Kook's scheme, the Messiah reveals *retroactively* how the various peoples' spiritual paths are appropriate, given their national psychology; in Rabbi Nahman's scheme, the Messiah will act *proactively* to produce for the various peoples prayers befitting their respective mentalities:

> Afterwards he will travel to all the kings...and he will make for them customs similar to Israel's religion. Also there will be prayers that the nations will pray. (*Ahar kakh yisa' le-khol ha-melakhim...ve-ya'aseh lahem nimus samukh le-dat Yisrael. Gam yiheyu tefillot she-yitpallelu ha-'ummot.*)
> (Zvi Mark, *The Scroll of Secrets: The Hidden Messianic Vision of R. Nachman of Breslav* [Brighton, Mass.: Academic Studies Press, 2010], pp. 52-53)

Later, during World War One, in his place of exile, St. Gallen (Switzerland), Rav Kook would revisit this theme of spiritual diversity:

> [The] foundation was established in Israel, a holy nation, and from its ramifications, many peoples can receive nourishment, each nation according to its content, its ethics, and its natural, historic and racial disposition; according to its education and geographic and economic situation, and all the social and personal factors that combine with this.
> (*Shemonah Kevatsim* 7:45; *Orot, Yisrael u-Tehiyato* (Israel and Its Renascence), chap. 15 [Maggid edition, pp. 194-195])

[6] The loanword *"kosmopoliti"* occurs in Rav Kook's manuscript.

[7] Rav Kook likens nationalism and cosmopolitanism to the repulsive and attractive forces of a magnet.

[8] Rav Kook employs the loanword *"organi."*

[9] Rav Kook quotes Gideon in Judges 6:24: "[Gideon] called it [i.e., the altar] '*YHVH Shalom.*'"

The Talmud (*b. Shabbat* 10b) adduces this verse to establish that *"Shalom"* is a name of God of sufficient sanctity that it is forbidden to mention it in the bathroom. Maimonides' omission of this *halakhah* is curious; see Rabbi Joseph Karo, *Kesef Mishneh* to *MT, Hil. Keri'at Shema'* 3:5, and Maimonides' commentary to the *Mishnah, Berakhot* 9:7 (Kafah ed., p. 52, n. 27).

See further *Leviticus Rabbah* 9:9; *Numbers Rabbah* 11:7; Rabbi Nathan of Rome, *'Arukh*, s.v. *'et*; and Rashi, *Makkot* 23b, s.v. *u-she'elat shalom be-shem*.

Tosafot (*Sotah* 10a, s.v. *ela me-'atah lo yimaheh*) were of the opinion that the name *"Shalom"* must not be erased. For this reason, some have the custom of not writing the full name, substituting a slash for the final letter *mem*; see the gloss of Rabbi Moses Isserles to *Shulhan 'Arukh, Yoreh De'ah* 276:13.

[10] *Humaniyot* occurs in the Hebrew original.

[11] The Hebrew *"'or makif"* ("encompassing light") is a term borrowed from Lurianic Kabbalah.

[12] Psalms 133:3.

Rav Kook's Space Odyssey

"I am certain that one day men will fly from one planet to another, for this is something good and beautiful, and everything which is good and beautiful—will be!"

(Rav Kook)[1]

This year marks the fiftieth anniversary of the appearance of the classic film *2001: Space Odyssey* (1968), a collaborative work by science fiction writer Arthur C. Clarke and filmmaker Stanley Kubrick. The film traces the evolution of mankind "from ape to angel," starting with prehistoric hominids and ending with the Star Child, while much attention is lavished on the intervening species we call *Homo sapiens*. The development of man is carefully monitored from outer space by vastly superior unseen aliens who from eon to eon accelerate the process of evolution through the intervention of a mysterious monolith. Indeed, the iconic black monolith is the motif that remains with most viewers of this cinematic wonder.

To this day, interpreters are divided as to whether *Space Odyssey* is optimistic or pessimistic in outlook. According to the latest filmography by Michael Benson, *Space Odyssey: Stanley Kubrick, Arthur C. Clarke, and the Making of a Masterpiece* (New York: Simon and Schuster, 2018), the two collaborators brought to the project diametrically opposed perspectives. Kubrick, hot on the heels of his 1964 satire, *Dr. Strangelove* (a noir comedy concerning the nuclear arms race), had a rather dark vision of humanity. Clarke on the other hand, was the eternal optimist. In Benson's words: "It was an idea both could get behind, Clarke with his innate optimism about human possibilities, and Kubrick with his deeply ingrained skepticism" (p. 3). The unlikely alliance between a Jewish boy from the Bronx and an English gentleman (later knighted by Queen Elizabeth II as Sir Arthur C. Clarke), "was the most consequential collaboration in either of their lives" (p. 13). The savage brutality of prehistoric man on the African savanna may be credited to Kubrick; the beatific, almost messianic, image of the Star Child at the film's conclusion was Clarke's contribution. "The single most optimistic vision in [Kubrick's] entire body of work—2001's Star Child—was Clarke's idea" (ibid.).

By all accounts, Abraham Isaac Hakohen Kook (1865-1935) was a child of the cosmos. This is apparent to any student of his works. His famous *pensée*, *Shir Meruba'* or *Fourfold Song* (the title was provided by his disciple, the Nazirite), bespeaks the evolution of human consciousness in ever-widening circles from individualism to nationalism to humanism to a loving embrace of the universe as a whole. The *pensée* ends on this note:

Space Odyssey

The Song of the Soul,
the Song of the Nation,
the Song of Man,
and the Song of the World –
all combine....[2]

(*Space Odyssey* has its own four movements marked by the appearance of the monolith at four crucial junctures in the film.)

What is certainly less known is that as a young man, Rav Kook actually composed a poem (in free verse), "*Sihat Mal'akhei ha-Sharet*" ("The Conversation of the Angels"), which well before Kubrick, traces the trajectory of man from earthbound existence to future space travel. In 1968, when *Space Odyssey* took the "silver screen" by storm, travel beyond the earth's atmosphere was already a reality. NASA's Apollo program was well under way and, just a year later, on July 20, 1969, Neil Armstrong and Buzz Aldrin would be the first men to walk on the surface of the moon. But when Rav Kook composed his poem, space travel was truly visionary.

The recurring image of Rav Kook's overview of human history—written from the perspective of the angels above—is the dyad of "speck of dust" (*garger avak*) and "shining disk" (*'adashah notsetset*), i.e., earth and sun. It will take many "revolutions" (*sibbuvim*) of the speck of dust around the shining disk; many "changings of creatures" (*halifot yitsurim*), which is to say generations of man, in order to break free of the hold the dyad clamps on human consciousness. Progressing from the primitive state, "the creature" is subjected to a rude awakening when the Copernican Revolution reveals that its "home" (*ma'on*) is in motion around the sun. However, the supposed "lesson in humility" fails to unify mankind. Instead, as Rav Kook points out, in the several centuries that have passed since Copernicus published *De Revolutionibus orbium coelestium* (*On the Revolutions of the Celestial Spheres*) in 1543, territorial disputes, fratricide and warfare have been the order of the day.

Coming from Rav Kook, this stark realism is refreshing. Too often, his presentations have been stereotyped as Pollyannish. While yet he lived, he was on occasion ridiculed by his rabbinic contemporaries for being overly optimistic. The Ashkenazic Rabbi of Tiberias, Moshe Kliers, quipped: "Dots appear to him as lights." (The reference was to the title of Rav Kook's seminal work, *Orot*, or *Lights*, his messianic vision of the renascence of Israel.) Surprisingly, Rav Kook's narrative of the human race seems spot-on.

Though the road to intellectual maturity may be bumpy, eventually man will make it to the stars. Rav Kook is confident that the humbling discovery of how infinitesimally small we truly are will register with an unbelieving humanity. In the final stanza, the angels acknowledge, perhaps begrudgingly, that the "mighty among midgets," by dint of its intellect and imagination, and above all, its sheer willpower, shall one day overtake them.

Postscript: When I read Rav Kook's coinage, "mighty among midgets" (*abbir nanasim*), I was reminded of Rabbi Isaac Hutner's response to someone who argued that those who bitterly opposed his mentor Rav Kook in Jerusalem were *gedolim* (greats): *"Velkher gedolim? Zei zennen alle geven Lilliputen!"* "Which greats? They were all Lilliputians!" (The *Rosh Yeshivah* was well acquainted with Jonathan Swift's satire, *Gulliver's Travels*.)

Sihat Mal'akhei ha-Sharet
The Conversation of the Angels
Abraham Isaac Hakohen Kook

Translated and adapted by Bezalel Naor

A speck of dust
orbits a shining disk.
Some fragile creatures call it "Earth."
The disk they revere as "Sun."

As tiny as the speck is,
it is great
compared to its neighbor
circling it about.

Of the creatures there is one
possessing language and logic.
It named itself "Man,"
mighty among midgets.

It stands erect.
So does it walk,
moving parts of its body.
It calls them "legs."

The Thought of Rav Kook

From the rays of the disk
enveloping the speck
there is light,
perceptible by a small circle,
aqueous and fleshly.
The creature calls it the "eye."

This tiny creature
is full of powerful imagination,
as it rises up on its speck of dust
facing the shining disk.

The speck is great in its eyes
and to the disk it accords the glory of a god.
The creature is filled with
feelings of pride.

It measures the speck's orbit around the disk
to mark "Time"
sufficient to gauge
its habitation upon its speck.

The rays of the disk
also stream heat
that the creature and its neighbors on the speck
might live.

Space Odyssey

The duration of its life
amounts to so many orbits
of the speck
around the shining disk.

Life is in flux.
A creature dies.
And others replace it.
Wondrously, they are all of a single image.

This wonderful creature,
mighty among midgets,
has a conception, a thought
and a very mighty will.

Among the flock of this creature
the will differs much.
And so the conception.
What a wonder!

And in the fluctuation of these wondrous creatures
a conception settles in.
It continues to grow
and to expand its horizon.

The Thought of Rav Kook

After many orbits of
the speck around the disk,
the secret is known:
Man's manor is in motion!

The discovery is great.
A mystery has been divulged:
The entire speck
revolves around the shining disk.

The creature is so proud
of its wonderful discovery.
As if it created
worlds for eternity.

When these creatures meet
upon parts of the speck,
sometimes there breaks out an altercation,
a mighty disagreement.

They all come up with
the novel idea of fratricide.
They meet to plan
terminating life.

Space Odyssey

They quarrel over a piece of the speck.
Who should rule?
"Sovereignty" they call it.

After many orbits
and many changings of the creatures,
the conception grows,
the thought takes wing.

It appears from their movements
that they've begun to appreciate their petty value
and their pride in the speck-and-the-disk
has been reduced.
It's but a few more orbits until their intelligence
is sharpened.

When these puny creatures
will inherit the earth of "Truth,"
their spirit will soar
despite their humble abode.

They will recognize their true measure,
these tiny creatures.
Then they will truly grow in spirit.
When they will search for habitation
upon the terrain of "Truth."

"Truth is the living spring
to which we angels
accord honor."

With intelligence they will ascend
beyond the orbit of the speck,
beyond the compass of the disk.
In infinite expanses they will dwell.

Love will nestle in their midst,
strength of spirit from the Life of Worlds.
When they fully comprehend
how miniscule they are.

"These diminutive creatures
surpass us in knowledge and *élan*;
in mighty will,
full of unbounded expanses."

Eternal life shall start flowing in them.
Mighty horizons shall open for them.
From world to world they'll garner strength
and the spirit of the Living God will pulsate in them.[3]

[1] Quoted by his disciple in Boisk (Bauskas, Latvia), Dr. Moshe Seidel; see Hayyim Lifschitz, *Shivhei ha-RAYaH* (Jerusalem, 1995), p. 70.
[2] *Orot ha-Kodesh*, ed. Rabbi David Cohen, vol. 2 (Jerusalem: Mossad Harav Kook, 1971), p. 445.
[3] *Otserot ha-RAYaH*, ed. Rabbi Moshe Zuriel, vol. 2 (Rishon le-Zion, 2002), pp. 575-577.

Rav Kook
On Teaching Torah to Girls

The following letter of Rav Kook, addressed to his son, Tsevi Yehuda, and daughter, Freida Hannah, then residing with Rav Kook's in-laws in Jerusalem, discusses the Rav's educational philosophy. It touches upon the subject of teaching Torah to girls in particular, and on the goals of education in general.

Rav Kook maintains that in an ideal state—past and future—mankind would have no need of external learning; the individual would find all the necessary spiritual nourishment within the soul. Only with the "downfall" (*"nefilah"*) of mankind and distancing from its soulful resources does an artificial form of education become a necessity.

The Rav makes some very bold statements, referring to books as "medicaments," and schools as "prisons" and "hospital rooms."

From this perspective, the women of Israel, who traditionally were not subjected to the artifices of book-learning, were more fortunate. They continued to be taught by their own innate spiritual gifts, while their brothers were put through the contortions of formal education.

Though Rav Kook's epistle strikes the modern reader as anti-feminist, Rabbi Ari Shvat rightfully defends Rav Kook as neither a misogynist nor an apologist for rabbinic law, which discouraged a father from teaching Torah to his daughter.

The ideas conveyed in this letter must be viewed against the backdrop of other such statements spread throughout the vast literary *oeuvre* of Rav Kook. A decade later, in his petite mystical work, *Reish Millin*, Rav Kook fires this opening salvo:

> The soul knows that whatever comes through learning is not from the source. Sourceful is the inner idea that is not expressed, that will be the world's inheritance on the great day that no more shall a man teach his brother and a man his neighbor to know the LORD, for all shall know Him from the least of them to the greatest of them.[1]

Another passage in *Shemonah Kevatsim* (*Eight Journals*) resounds with this same sentiment:

> The truly great men find within them an inner opposition to being taught (*hitlamdut*), for all is alive in their midst and flows from their spirit. They must constantly delve deeper into their inner spirit. In their case, the aspect of learning is but an aid and ancillary; the main thing that brings about their perfection is their very own Torah (*Torah didehu*). "And in *his* Torah he shall meditate day and night."[2] Sometimes a man does not realize his worth and turns his back on his very own Torah (*Torah dileh*), and desires specifically to be taught (*melummad*), either because of habit or a learned theory, such as, "Inquire and

receive reward."³ Then the angst of the descent begins to darken the world of these weak greats (*gedolim halashim*).⁴

Though one cannot say with any certainty that Rav Kook was aware of the writings of Jean-Jacques Rousseau, some of the ideas expressed in our letter are definitely reminiscent of Rousseau's theory of the "noble savage."⁵ But then again, a strong case could be made that Rav Kook developed his ideas from the prophetic tradition of Judaism.

This call for direct apperception of divinity without recourse to sacred literature will become even more pronounced in the intimate diaries of Rav Kook's disciple, Rabbi David Cohen ("the Nazirite"):

> The prophets and the disciples of the prophets went into isolation in the mountains and valleys, taking in the view of fields and pure skies. A fresh breeze blows, reviving the soul, to pay attention, to hear the holy word of the LORD. For shelter from rain and the cold of night, they would gather in caves.
>
> They did not have with them many books. They did not require libraries of works such as Talmud, codes and commentaries. This burden of books that stuff the soul with paper, and that divert attention from the uplifted and exalted, the purity of the heavens of the LORD—not by this will be revealed and revived the spirit of prophecy, rather by oral Torah, by studies in the mountains and the

valleys, upon fields of holiness, in full view of the heavens of the LORD.[6]

Before the Nazirite, similar sentiments were expressed by the medieval mystic Abraham Abulafia, an elusive figure whom Rabbi David Cohen would come to greatly appreciate.[7] (He was treated to Abulafian manuscripts by Gershom Scholem, librarian of Hebrew University in Jerusalem.)[8] Abulafia, famous as the founder of the school of "Prophetic Kabbalah," evidently prized more knowledge transmitted from Above (*"bat kol"*) than that obtained from books of Kabbalah (*sifrei ha-kabbalah*).[9]

In what is perhaps the most surprising statement of the entire letter, Rav Kook confides that on rare occasions he is able to get in touch with "the Torah of your mother" within him. Rav Kook is alluding to the verse in Proverbs: "Hear, my son, the reproof (*mussar*) of your father and forsake not the teaching (*torah*) of your mother."[10] If we follow through, Rav Kook believes that a human walks around with both of these introjected voices; the voice of the father and the voice of the mother. In the male, while it is the voice of the father, which represents book-learning, that predominates, nevertheless, the maternal voice, of a more soulful nature, remains intact, though its influence is more subtle and thus more difficult to tap into.

The confession sounds somewhat Jungian. Carl Gustav Jung theorized that every human possesses an animus and an anima, a male and female aspect. In the male, the animus is dominant and the anima recessive; in the female, the anima presides and the animus becomes the shadow side of the personality.

Finally, one detects that there runs through the letter an aversion to orthodox medicine ("textbook medicine") and perhaps an attraction to alternative medicine. (Once again, it seems that this outlook on the *ars medica* was amplified in Rav Kook's disciple, the "Nazirite," who famously said: *"Rofé hinam* [free physician] is the numerical value of *Shekhinah* [divine presence].")[11]

The letter was published for the first time in its entirety by Rabbi Ari Shvat, a researcher at Beit Harav in Jerusalem.[12]

Jaffa, 2 Shevat 5667 [i.e., 1907]

With the help of God

My son and daughter, the apples of my eye, may you live well,

My parsimony of letters—brought about by various botherances ill-suited to my disposition and inner desire, that forcefully invade my domain and seek action of a man who neither knows them nor desires to know them—has affected you too, my beloved children, causing you aggravation because of the paucity of my writing. Beloved children, you must forgive. I imagine that you recognize how much my heart desires to fulfill your wishes in general, and specifically your ideal wish to enjoy my words, to reflect upon them, and perhaps even to learn from them. But the surrounding situation oftentimes drives me from my "house of pleasure." My soul hopes for the salvation of the LORD to restore to me the joy of my salvation and to avail me a mood fitting my soul's yearning.

Beloved of my soul, I do not want to write to you separately, for the spiritual things which are the main foundation, should always apply in some aspect to both of you. Knowledge is universal; it knows no differences of gender, except for the specific ramifications; it is in those ramifications that there arise divisions based upon the individual's value, and upon the character of each gender. And I generally elude the specifics and seek to latch on to the universals of the ideas, which are dimly present in the soul of each of us, except that most people are too lazy to roll away the curtain in their midst in order to know how great is the treasure that lives in their soul. I, and those who are like-minded, try our utmost—in every time and place—to drive away this lassitude that prevents thousands upon thousands of humans from illuminating the splendor of their lives, the wealth and goodness that is in their very midst. [This lassitude] causes them to go in ways of darkness—pettiness, hatred, envy and competitiveness—which suffocate even more the light of clear, pure life. Therefore, the difference [of gender] is not taken into account by me; thank God that both of you are—each in his/her own way—intelligent and sensitive, whether more or less, but thank God, at least [you] are accustomed to see and to hear the inner desire of straight living, of purity, justice and universal love. One in whose soul these good plants are absorbed, is ready to hear things much higher and more exalted than the convention of the marketplace. The inner understanding is not measured by the pages or the books but by the dimension of goodwill that lives inwardly within the soul. Certainly, there will be found things that are specific to one gender or the other of you, but the benefit derives from the knowledge that encompasses both worlds, that of the brother and that of the sister; and this unifies the form of the letters.

The main difference, my dear daughter, between the souls of man and woman, is only in regard to the necessity of studies. On their own, books are not the natural nourishment of the human spirit. They are, at best, medicines for a humanity already sickened long ago. "I am the LORD your healer."[13] The healthy inner feeling that emerges in its pure nature through uncorrupted education, should teach man what there is within him sufficiently. Not for one moment in life do the brain and the heart cease to work; if they are straight, their entire natural, perpetual work is learning and Torah. However, we have descended much, the deeds have become crooked, the life impoverished; the disease of materialism has attacked all of humanity, so that they cannot conduct their physiological affairs without doctors and medicines learned from textbooks and uncertain theories. The spirituality in us has generally arrived at this unfortunate state. We are forced to imprison our beloved children from the "morning dew of their youth"[14] for several hours each day in schoolrooms; to tie them to books and letters—just as we are forced to place the sick in hospital rooms and harsh confinement chambers (of textbook medicine).

The Holy One, blessed be He, acted charitably with His world by bestowing upon woman more understanding than man.[15] [This added understanding is expressed] through her domestic sense being deeper, though by the same token it does not extend outward as much. There is no advantage to a "woman of valor"[16] observing worldly affairs of princes and kings, and their cruel wars, which add several chapters to books[17] and increase the work of tender children, chaining them ever more to prison, and in no small measure injecting in their spirit the pollution of murder and misanthropy that darkens the splendor of life. A "woman of valor" is exempted from all this catastrophe. She was created to oversee the affairs of her house; to extend her palm to the poor and needy; to clothe her household. These deeds are beautiful; they are pleasant, and a "fragrance of Lebanon"[18] and natural holy idealism encompasses them all about. If life were healthy and whole, there would be no need for any learning to supplement the beautiful, delicate domestic character.

But life has become so deficient, the human heart has so lost its feeling that it does not know how to find peace in the tranquil tent that is entirely love and generosity. In proportion to the fall (*nefilah*), we need to strengthen the hands of our daughters too by broadening the education. Yet Heaven forefend that a delicate daughter destined to be a true "woman of valor"—especially a daughter of Israel whose inner tent is destined to be a holy sanctuary—exchange her living world for books; nourishment for medicaments.

The wide circle of human society—in which a man is called to work based on his physiological and psychological makeup—is already so dark, that were it not for luminaries from on high, and generally, from outside of life, not a single ray of light would penetrate its midst. [Mankind] is so sick that its diet consists of drugs and its raiment is the bandages to bind broken bones. [Mankind] must teach and learn. And the more devoted it is to its healing, the more it shall advance, until with time, its health will be restored and it shall live an Edenic life as of yore, "a world that is entirely Sabbath and eternal rest."[19]

But the inner world—which is also great and wide if one be but capable of beholding its myriad details that gladden and pleasure every straight soul—especially in Israel, is yet close to its purity and natural happiness. And the European confusion that imprisons daughters as well in the prime of their youth in a prison called "school," produces generations weak in spirit and in body. From both aspects [i.e., spirit and body] there is extinguished in their midst the last spark of straight and holy naturalness. Thus, when the honored daughter—whose honor is inward, inward within her tent, inward in the chambers of her heart,[20] where there is an entire living world, yet perfect, "a semblance of the World to Come"[21]— forgets her worth; or a foolish cruelty, a false pride of her parents, causes her to forget her worth, and insists upon teaching her on a permanent basis, by tying her to the school, to the "hospital," to the book, then "it is as if [the father] teaches her folly."[22]

I desired to write and write, my dear ones, but what shall I do? Here they come, my cruel overseers, my nuisances, and interrupt me, dragging me from my peaceful inner tent—where fortunately, I sometimes find the maternal side in me, "the Torah of your mother"[23]—and bring me to the harsh atmosphere of the outer, corrupt life, compounded with troubles and woes, stress and strain, plaints and complaints.[24] I must go; they push me with force.

I pray to the LORD that He show me His broad salvation.

My dear daughter and son, please inform me of all the good and blessing that come your way. Gladden my soul with your dear words. Write and write as much as you are able. Every letter, every word of yours, showers upon me the "dew of lights"[25] and gladdens my soul.

Blessed is the LORD for the life and peace which is ours. Were it not [for the fact] that I must be brief because I must stop, I would certainly [write] at more length regarding sacred and secular matters. But for the time being, this is not possible. May the Master of Peace bless you with all manner of goodness, and may we merit to see from you much satisfaction, blessing and peace. As is your dear wish and the wish of your father who looks forward to your happiness and good all the days.

Avraham Yitzhak Ha[Kohen] K[ook]

---

[1] Rav Kook paraphrases the verse in Jeremiah 31:33: "And they shall teach no more every man his neighbor, and every man his brother, saying, 'Know the LORD,' for all shall know Me, from the least of them to the greatest of them, says the LORD."
  Rabbi Abraham Isaac Hakohen Kook, *Reish Millin* (London, 1917), *"Aleph"* (p. 2). The occasion for this striking remark is the fact that the first letter of the Hebrew alphabet, *Aleph*, means "teach" in Aramaic, which traditionally is the language of translation (*Targum*) from the original language of Hebrew. (In Hebrew, the word for "teach" is *lamed*.)
[2] Psalms 1:2; b. *Kiddushin* 32b; b. *'Avodah Zarah* 19a.
[3] b. *Sanhedrin* 71a; *Zevahim* 45a.
[4] Rabbi Abraham Isaac Hakohen Kook, *Shemonah Kevatsim* 2:172.
[5] See now Emanuel Haronian, *The Attitude to Human Self in the Teaching of Rav Kook and Rav Harlap* (Hebrew), M.A. Thesis, Ben-Gurion University, February 2020, p. 23, note 179. Available at: academia.edu
[6] Rabbi David Cohen, *Mishnat ha-Nazir*, ed. Harel Cohen and Yedidyah Cohen (Jerusalem: Nezer David, 2005), pp. 52-53.
[7] See the section on *"Kabbalah Nevu'it"* (Prophetic Kabbalah) in Rabbi David Cohen, *Kol ha-Nevu'ah* (Jerusalem: Mossad Harav Kook, 1979), pp. 158-160.
[8] *Mishnat ha-Nazir*, p. 75.
[9] Abraham Abulafia, *Sefer ha-Heshek*, ed. Matityahu Safrin (Jerusalem, 1999), p. 7; quoted in Moshe Idel, "Maimonides' *Guide of the Perplexed* and the Kabbalah," *Jewish History* 18 (2004), p. 213.
[10] Proverbs 1:8.
  Cf. Rabbi J.B. Soloveitchik, "A Tribute to the Rebbetzin of Talne," *Tradition* 17:2 (Spring 1978), pp. 73-83.
[11] They share the numerical value of 385. See Hilah Wolberstein, *Harav ha-Nazir: Ish ki yafli'* (Jerusalem: Makhon Nezer David, 2017), p. 286. The source of the *gematria* is Rabbi Aaron Berechiah of Modena's *Ma'avar Yabok* (Mantua, 1626), *ma'amar* 1 (*Siftei Tsedek*), chap. 21 (19b): "But the true physician is the *Shekhinah* (divine presence) for numerically it is *rofé hinam.*"
  Apparently, the Nazirite expressed his thoughts on psychosomatic or alternative medicine in an essay entitled *"Megillat ha-Rof'im ve-ha-Refu'ot"* ("Treatise on Doctors and Medicines"). See Wolberstein, p. 285. Dr. Joshua Ritchie told this writer (BN) that when he paid a visit to the Nazirite, the latter began to expound to him his original theory of medicine.
[12] Ari Yitzhak Shvat, *"Iggeret Harav Kook be-Nose' Talmud Torah le-Nashim,"*

in *Me'orot li-Yehudah* (Rabbi Yehudah Feliks Festschrift), ed. M. Rehimi (Elkanah, 2012), pp. 343-362.

[13] Exodus 15:26.
[14] Cf. Psalms 110:3. In other words, from early childhood.
[15] *b. Niddah* 45b.
[16] Proverbs 31:10.
[17] Rav Kook's caustic remarks in this regard may have been influenced by Maimonides' earlier disparagement of the Arabic chronicles of kings. Maimonides thought reading such literature a complete waste of time. See Maimonides, *Commentary to the Mishnah, Sanhedrin* 10:1 (Kafah ed., pp. 140-141), and *Avot* 1:16 (Kafah ed., p. 273, "the third division").
[18] I.e., the fragrance of the legendary cedars of Lebanon. Cf. Hosea 14:7; Rabbi Abraham Isaac Hakohen Kook, *Orot, Orot ha-Tehiyah* (Lights of Renascence), chap. 38 (Naor ed., p. 363).
[19] *m. Tamid* 7:4 in version of Maimonides.
[20] Rav Kook paraphrases Psalms 45:14. See the rabbinic interpretation of the verse in *b. Gittin* 12a; *Yevamot* 77a; *Shavu'ot* 30a.
[21] The phrase *"me-'eyn 'olam ha-ba"* occurs in various hymns for the Sabbath. See *b. Berakhot* 57b: "The Sabbath is one sixtieth of the World to Come."
[22] m. *Sotah* 3:4; *b. Sotah* 21b; Maimonides, *MT, Hil. Talmud Torah* 1:13.
[23] Proverbs 1:8.
[24] Hebrew, *tevi'ot ve-kublanot*. Possibly an allusion to Rav Kook's position as *Av Beit Din*, or Chief Justice, of the Jaffa rabbinical court.
[25] Cf. Isaiah 26:19.

Rav Kook and Rav Harlap:
Truth and the Pursuit of Truth

In a poetic flourish—even more poetic than most of his personal *pensées*—Rav Kook let out this *cri de coeur*:

> I thirst for truth (emet), *not for the attainment of truth* (hasagat ha-emet).[1]

The syntactical combination *"hasagat ha-emet"* is difficult to define. Prominent use of it is made by Maimonides in the first chapter of *Misneh Torah* in regard to comprehending the truth of God's existence.

First, there is Maimonides' categorical pronouncement: "And the truth of (*'amitat*) the thing, man's mind cannot comprehend (*le-hasig*) and investigate."[2]

Having posited that this is an impossible goal to achieve, Maimonides then probes what exactly Moses sought when he asked of God, "Show me please Your glory."[3] In Maimonides' paraphrase of Exodus 33:20 ("You cannot see My face, for man cannot see Me and live"), God's definitive response was: "It is not within the power of the intellect of a living man, composed of body and soul, to comprehend the truth of (*le-hasig amitat*) this thing with clarity."[4]

Finally, Maimonides attempts to explicate the enigmatic concession granted Moses by God, "You shall see My back, but My face shall not be seen."[5] "[The Holy One], blessed be He, let

[Moses] know that which no man before or after knew, until he comprehended of the truth of (*hisig me-'amitat*) His existence such that the Holy One, blessed be He, was distinguished in his mind from the rest of the existent things, just as a man who has been viewed from behind (his entire body and clothing) is distinguished in one's mind from other men."[6]

⁂

Though lexically the reference to *Mishneh Torah* might work, it does not seem that Rav Kook is reacting to Moses Maimonides. It is much more likely that Rav Kook is responding to something written by Moses Mendelssohn's lifelong friend, Gotthold Ephraim Lessing. (It is accepted that Mendelssohn is the protagonist portrayed in Lessing's play *Nathan the Wise*.) In 1778, Lessing boldly asserted:

> The true value of a man is not determined by his possession, supposed or real, of Truth, but rather by his sincere exertion to get to the Truth. It is not possession of the Truth, but rather the pursuit of Truth by which he extends his powers and in which his ever-growing perfectibility is to be found. Possession makes one passive, indolent, and proud.
>
> If God were to hold all Truth concealed in his right hand, and in his left only the steady and diligent drive for Truth, albeit with the proviso that I would always and for-

ever err in the process, and offer me the choice, I would with all humility take the left hand, and say: "Father, I will take this one—the pure Truth is for You alone."[7]

To employ Lessing's imagery, it seems that Rav Kook would choose what is in the right hand of God ("Truth"), rather than what is contained in the left ("the diligent drive for Truth").

Whether Rav Kook was aware of the quote from Lessing is open to speculation. Some years ago, Eliezer Goldman published a groundbreaking article in which he investigated Rav Kook's familiarity with European philosophy.[8]

As I have written elsewhere,[9] Rav Kook was eminently familiar with the *Pantheismusstreit* (Pantheism Controversy) that broke out between Friedrich Heinrich Jacobi and Mendelssohn concerning Spinozism. What sparked the controversy was the alleged death-bed confession of Lessing, confirming his pantheistic belief. As Lessing was Mendelssohn's dearest friend, Jacobi hoped by publicizing Lessing's confession to discomfit and unseat the regnant "German Plato." Jacobi placed Mendelssohn in a bind. If Mendelssohn were to reject pantheism outright, he would thereby dishonor his departed friend's memory. If, on the other hand, he upheld Lessing's legacy, he would have to embrace Spinoza's doctrine which was widely construed as atheism. Mendelssohn tried to find a middle ground by casting Spinoza's doctrine in a different, favorable light. The grief caused Mendelssohn by Jacobi's assault on his integrity was considerable; some credit Jacobi with precipitating Mendelssohn's sudden death (at age fifty-six).

In one of Rav Kook's journals, he alluded to Moses Mendelssohn's attempt to "purify" Spinoza.[10] Did Rav Kook also look into the works of Lessing? I have no way of knowing.[11]

There is another avenue to explore in our attempt to contextualize Rav Kook's abrupt remark.

In his birthplace of Grieva, a suburb of Dvinsk, Latvia, Rav Kook was exposed at an early age to HaBaD Hasidism. His maternal grandfather, Rabbi Raphael Felman, was a Lubavitcher Hasid. (His particular allegiance was to the Rebbes of Kopyst, Rabbi Yehudah Leib Schneerson, and after his passing, his son Rabi Shelomo Zalman Schneerson, author of *Magen Avot*. These were the son and grandson of the famed "*Tsemah Tsedek*," Rabbi Menahem Mendel Schneersohn of Lubavitch.)[12]

The *Tsemah Tsedek* recorded in his writings that his grandfather Rabbi Shneur Zalman of Liadi, the founder of the HaBaD school, could be overheard uttering these words in his meditation before commencing the morning prayer:

Ich vill zhe gor nisht.
Ich vill nit dein Gan Eden.
Ich vill nit dein Olam Habo.
Ich vill mehr nit az Dich alein.

I want nothing.
I don't want Your Garden of Eden.
I don't want Your World to Come.
I want nothing but You alone.[13]

A slightly different, lengthier version was recorded by a Hasid close to the *Tsemah Tsedek*, Rabbi Peretz Chein:

I do not want the hasagah *of the ophanim.*
I do not want the hasagah *of the seraphim.*
I do not want Your Garden of Eden.
I do not want Your World to Come.
"Who is there for me in heaven, and beside You I desire none on earth."[14]

In his *cri de coeur*, Rav Kook might have been reverberating the anguished cry of the *Alter Rebbe* ("Old Rabbi"). Just as the founder of HaBaD had no interest in the *hasagot* of the ophanim and the seraphim, so Rav Kook had no interest in the *hasagah* of truth. Like the *Alter Rebbe* who desired God alone, Rav Kook thirsted for "truth" *tout court*.

Though the word *"hasagah"* does not occur in the shorter version of Rabbi Shneur Zalman's meditation, it may be implicit in the reference to the Garden of Eden. According to the teaching of Rabbi Shneur Zalman, there is not one Garden of Eden awaiting the soul after its departure from the body, but infinitely many. And each time that the soul is about to graduate from a lower Garden (*Gan 'Eden ha-Tahton*) to a higher Garden (*Gan 'Eden ha-'Elyon*),[15] it must first immerse itself in the *Nehar di-Nur*,[16] the River of Fire, which results in memory loss. In order to assimilate the new *hasagot*, the new consciousness, one must first forget the old and familiar, as Rabbi Zeira who fasted one hundred fasts to forget the learning of Babylonia so that he might absorb the higher learning of *Erets Yisrael*.[17] Thus, for Rabbi Shneur Zalman, the Garden of Eden is not a final destination but a station along a way with no end in sight.[18]

And one daresay, it was the unending process of perception upon perception, *hasagah* upon *hasagah* of truth that Rav Kook— perhaps not unlike the *Alter Rebbe*—wished to dispense with. This impassioned soul longed to bypass the process and finally, definitively arrive at—the truth.

As the *Alter Rebbe*, Rav Kook desperately desired to break the heavens wide open, to put an end once and for all to "process theology." "You alone." "The truth."

Rabbi Moshe Tsevi Neriyah, who studied under Rav Kook in his *yeshivah* in Jerusalem, recorded that during the afternoon banquet of *Simhat Torah*, a time of great exultation, Rav Kook suddenly got up from the table and began pacing the length of the hall while singing with emotion the *Alter Rebbe*'s paraphrase of the verse in Psalms 73:25:

"*Mi li va-shamayim ve-'imkha lo haftsti va-'arets.*"
Ich vill nit hoben dem Olam Hazeh,
Ich darf nit hoben dem Olam Habo,
Nor Dir alein,
Nor Dir alein.[19]

"Who is there for me in heaven, and beside You I desire none on earth."
I do not want this world,
I do not need the World to Come,
Only You,
Only You!

※

There is yet another angle to examine. Rav Kook expressed a predilection for the Talmud of *Erets Yisrael* (referred to by academicians as the "Palestinian Talmud") over the Babylonian Talmud. As he wrote to the historian Rabbi Yitzhak Isaac Halevi Rabinowitz (author of *Dorot ha-Rishonim*):

> So in *Erets Yisrael*, which is the place of prophecy, the flow of prophecy leaves a mark upon the discipline (*seder ha-limmud*), and the sense [of the text] is explained through an inner gaze and does not require such lengthy investigation....The wisdom of prophecy...was much more active in *Erets Yisrael* than in Babylonia, which is unworthy of prophecy....Now those influenced by the roots of the wisdom of prophecy—for them brevity is an advantage. The halakhic analysis and inference is accomplished by them with a wide view. For them, a subtle hint is sufficient to decide the law. This was the foundation of the discipline

(*seder ha-limmud*) of the [Talmud] *Yerushalmi*. For those fortunate to benefit from the light above, short inferences sufficed to clarify the *halakhah* (*birur ha-halakhah*). But for the Babylonians, upon whom the roots of prophecy did not exert so much influence, brevity was insufficient and there was required a lengthy discussion.[20]

The consensus among modern historians today is that the *sugyah* (Talmudic discussion) of the *Yerushalmi* is abbreviated in comparison to its Babylonian counterpart, not because of an influx of prophetic inspiration in *Erets Yisrael*, but for the more prosaic reason that the conversation in Babylonia continued for a century longer, during which time the next generations of *amoraim* had opportunity to join the discussion. In addition to that, the Babylonian Talmud underwent an editorial process by anonymous *"stammaim"* (as they are currently referred to) who provided the mortar to the bricks of the Talmud.

Yet Rav Kook persisted in his belief that the discipline of Talmudic study could yet be revolutionized in *Erets Yisrael*, "the place of prophecy." It is certainly no coincidence that in his first *yeshivah* in *Erets Yisrael* (that which existed in Jaffa when he served as rabbi there between the years 1904-1914), Rav Kook made a point of teaching Rabbi Yehudah Halevi's *Kuzari*.[21] The *Kuzari* states boldly: "Whoever prophesied did so either in the [Holy] Land, or concerning it."[22]

To the end of streamlining the process of halakhic decision-making, Rav Kook undertook the painstaking task of transcribing to the margins of the Talmud the pertinent quotes from Maimonides' code of law and Rabbi Joseph Karo's *Shulhan 'Arukh*. In his Central Universal Yeshivah in Jerusalem (today known as "Merkaz Harav"), Rav Kook rebuffed all attempts to import from Europe the type of conceptualization (*"Hasbarah"*) that was all the rage in the Lithuanian *yeshivot* of the day. (For this reason, Rav Kook was loath to endorse Rabbi Shimon Shkop's appointment as *Rosh Yeshivah*.) Instead, Rav Kook wished his students to adhere to the method of *"peshat"* (simple meaning) that was personified by the Vilna Gaon.[23] (Rav Kook himself penned a super-commentary [*Be'er Eliyahu*] to *Be'ur ha-Gra*, the Gaon's skeletal notes to *Shulhan 'Arukh, Hoshen Mishpat*.)

Today, we regard with some wonderment Rav Kook's idealization of the Talmud *Yerushalmi* over and against the *Talmud Bavli*. There is a tendency in some quarters to cut Rav Kook loose from his HaBaD roots. Scholars who are truly objective and disinterested would do well to compare Rav Kook's thoughts on the *Yerushalmi-Bavli* divide to an especially pithy passage in the writings of the *"Mitteler Rebbe"* ("Middle Rabbi"), Rabbi Dov Baer Shneuri, a master of HaBaD known for his depth.

In his work *Sha'arei 'Orah*, Rabbi Dov Baer discusses at length the protracted dialectic, the alternating stages of light and darkness, clarity and obfuscation, revelation and concealment that the sages of Babylonia would endure before they finally arrived at some halakhic conclusion. As they observed, considering their predicament: "'He sat me down in darkness.' This refers to the Talmud of Babylonia."[24] The sages of *Erets Yisrael*, on the other hand, were able to arrive at the finish line and reach halakhic decisions without the *pilpul* (dialectic). While the *Mitteler Rebbe* does not attribute this ability to the remnants or roots of prophecy as does Rav Kook, he does draw on kabbalistic tradition to account for the different disciplines of *Erets Yisrael* and Babylonia:

> This is the difference between the inhabitants of Babylonia and the inhabitants of *Erets Yisrael*: Outside the Land, the air of the nations is impure from *kelipat nogah*,[25] etc. The true light from the source of wisdom cannot come to them as it is without recourse to *pilpul*....But in *Erets Yisrael* where *kelipat nogah* does not rule in such a coarse manner (only through a thin veil, as is known), inasmuch as they are more separated from *kelipat nogah*,[26] the true light is able to be revealed in the vessels of their minds...without such lengthy *pilpul*.[27]

The *Mitteler Rebbe* describes the chiaroscuro process of the *Bavli* as one of *hasagah* mounted upon *hasagah* (or conversely as "*he'elem ahar he'elem*," "one concealment after another"), as opposed to the *Yerushalmi*'s brilliant flash of "*emet*" (truth).

Just as Rabbi Nahman of Breslov had once told his premier disciple Rabbi Nathan of Nemirov, so Rav Kook revealed to his premier disciple Rabbi Ya'akov Moshe Harlap that they had known each other in a previous lifetime.

On another occasion Rav Kook remarked that when he and Rabbi Harlap are alone together in a room, there is only one person there, not two. Such was the intimacy and closeness of master and acolyte.

Yet at the end of the day, no two people think alike. As the Rabbis expressed it: "Just as their faces are not alike, so their opinions are not alike."[28] In stark contrast to Rav Kook's one-liner, we find in the writings of Rav Harlap this reflection:

> However, one must ponder the *hasagot* (realizations) at their foundation: Is the realization the main thing, or is seeking the realization (*bakashat ha-hasagah*) the main thing. And if one should say that seeking the realization is the main thing, one must still see if the seeking must be restricted to that which it is possible to realize, or also—and essentially—that which it is impossible to realize.[29]

Rav Harlap presents his case that what enlivens man—if you would have it, the élan vital—is not the attainment of the realization but the unceasing striving for the unattainable.[30]

As Yeshayahu Leibowitz pointed out when reading aloud from the text of Rav Harlap, the author never heard of Lessing, yet independently arrived at Lessing's conclusion.[31] These words of Rav Harlap were very dear to Leibowitz because in them he heard (or wished to hear) a resonance of his own idiosyncratic Messianic vision, one of infinite striving. In Leibowitz's reading, Messiah tarries because he must; because, by definition, his arrival must be forever delayed. In the more popular and pointed version, Leibowitz notoriously defined a false Messiah as a Messiah who comes.

When Leibowitz attempted to ascribe his controversial version of Messianism to Maimonides, he was called out by Professor Ze'ev Harvey. Harvey demonstrated that Maimonides firmly believed in "perfectibility" and in a Messiah who in fact arrives.[32]

As is well known, despite Professor Yeshayahu Leibowitz's immense respect for Rav Kook's spiritual and intellectual stature, he could never agree to his philosophy. Needless to say, Rav Kook's "thirst for truth, not the striving for truth" could never become the "*Hazon Yeshayahu*," "the vision of Yeshayahu."[33]

---

[1] *Shemonah Kevatsim* 3:280. That particular *pensée* was first made available to the public in a collection of Rav Kook's poetry published by A.M. Habermann in *Sinai* 17 (1945). The poems were made available to Habermann by the poet's son, Rabbi Tsevi Yehudah Kook. (The ostensible dates of their composition were also provided by Rabbi Tsevi Yehudah.) In Habermann's edition, paragraphs 279 and 280 of *Shemonah Kevatsim* were conjoined (separated only by a dash) and entitled *"Merhavim, Merhavim"* ("Expanses, Expanses"), the first two words of paragraph 279.

[2] Maimonides, *MT, Hil. Yesodei ha-Torah* 1:9.

[3] Exodus 33:18.

[4] *Hil. Yesodei ha-Torah* 1:10.

[5] Exodus 33:23. Maimonides' nemesis, Rabad of Posquières, quipped: "'My face' and 'My back' is a great mystery and it is not fitting to reveal it to every man. And perhaps this author [i.e., Maimonides] did not know it." See *Hasagot ha-Rabad le-Mishneh Torah*, ed. Bezalel Naor (Jerusalem, 1985), *Hil. Yesodei ha-Torah* 1:10 (p. 15).

[6] *Hil. Yesodei ha-Torah* 1:10.

[7] *Anti-Goeze* (1778), as quoted in *God Is Not Great* (2007), by Christopher Hitchens, chap. 19.

[8] Eliezer Goldman, "Zikato shel ha-Rav Kook la-Mahshavah ha-Eropit" in *Yovel Orot*, ed. Binyamin Ish-Shalom and Shalom Rosenberg (Jerusalem: WZO,

1988), pp. 115-122.
9 Bezalel Naor, *The Limit of Intellectual Freedom* (Spring Valley, NY: Orot, 2011), pp. 22-23.
10 Rabbi Abraham Isaac Hakohen Kook, *Kevatsim mi-Ketav Yad Kodsho*, ed. Boaz Ofen, vol. 1 (Jerusalem, 2006), *Pinkas "Rishon le-Yaffo,"* par. 117 (p. 146).
11 In a letter to Rabbi Ya'akov Moshe Harlap, a young Tsevi Yehudah Kook (aged nineteen) quotes a saying of Lessing. Tsevi Yehudah explains to Rabbi Harlap that Lessing (and Kant, also quoted in that letter) lived in the generation of the Vilna Gaon. The quote from Kant was heard from Tsevi Yehudah's uncle, Shaul Hanna Kook. See *Tsemah Tsevi: Iggerot Harav Tsevi Yehudah Hakohen Kook*, vol. 1 (1907-1919), ed. Landau, Neuman, and Rahmani (Jerusalem, 1991), Letter 9 (p. 25).
12 Rabbi Menahem Mendel Schneersohn of Lubavitch (1789-1866) was referred to as *"Tsemah Tsedek,"* the title of his collection of halakhic responsa.
13 Rabbi Menahem Mendel Schneersohn, *Derekh Mitsvotekha*: *Ta'amei ha-Mitsvot* (Poltava, 1911; photo offset Kefar Habad, 1973), *Shoresh Mitsvat ha-Tefillah*, chap. 40 (138a). See further ibid. *Kedoshim* 5562 (154a).

Rav Kook borrowed *Derekh Mitsvotekha* (yet in manuscript) from his neighbor, Rabbi Shneur Zalman Slonim, Rabbi of the HaBaD community of Jaffa. See *Iggerot la-RAYaH* (Jerusalem, 1986), Letter 169 (p. 146): "Sometimes he borrowed from me [i.e., S.Z. Slonim] a manuscript, the *Sefer ha-Mitsvot* [Book of Commandments] by the *Tsemah Tsedek.*"
14 *Ha-Mashpi'a* (biography of Rabbi Shelomo Zalman Havlin) (Jerusalem, 1982), pp. 126-127. The line of transmission went from the *Tsemah Tsedek* to Rabbi Peretz Chein to his son Rabbi David Tsevi Chein, Rabbi of Chernigov. The final line is a quote from Psalms 73:25.
15 In one recension of the *Alter Rebbe*'s meditation, he spurns the lower Garden of Eden (*Gan 'Eden ha-Tahton*) and the higher Garden of Eden (*Gan 'Eden ha-'Elyon*). See Moshe Hariton in *Heikhal ha-Besht*, no. 4, year 3 (Tishri 5766), p. 167.
16 In his vision of the "four great beasts," Daniel saw a river of fire, *"Nehar di-Nur"* (Daniel 7:10).
17 *b. Bava Metsi'a* 85a; Rabbi Shneur Zalman of Liadi, *Torah 'Or, Yitro*, s.v. *mar'eihem u-ma'aseihem*, 69c.
18 See Rabbi Shneur Zalman of Liadi, *Torah 'Or, Mikets*, 32d:

> Therefore even though in general there are but two levels, the higher Garden of Eden in [the World of] *Beri'ah* and the lower Garden of Eden in [the World of] *Yetsirah*, to be specific, there are unlimited *hasagot* (attainments)....There are innumerable *hasagot*....And each time that the soul must ascend from one Garden of Eden to another there must precede the level of *Nehar di-Nur* (the River of Fire) in order that all the previous attainments be nullified, for the previous *hasagah* is incomparable to the *hasagah* above....With each added *hasagah*, the *hasagah* below becomes inconsequential.

The *Alter Rebbe* revisits this theme several times. See Rabbi Shneur Zalman, *Torah 'Or, Mikets*, 31a-b; *Megillat Esther*, 96a; idem, *Likkutei Torah, Beshallah*, 1d; *Derushim li-Shemini 'Atseret*, 83d, 84d.

[19] Rabbi Moshe Tsevi Neriyah, *Sihot ha-RAYaH* (Tel-Aviv, 1979), p. 258. Rabbi Neriyah juxtaposed a passage in Rabbi Shneur Zalman's *Tanya*, chap. 43 (62a).
  When subsequently challenged by HaBaD Hasidim who knew of no such *niggun*, Rabbi Neriyah countered that Rav Kook must have heard the tune in his youth from the Kopyster Hasidim in his hometown of Grieva. There is another possibility, namely that Rav Kook composed the melody himself, perhaps on the spur of the moment.

[20] *Iggerot ha-RAYaH*, vol. 1 (Jerusalem: Mossad Harav Kook, 1962), Letter 103 (pp. 123-124).

[21] See my edition of *Orot* (Maggid, 2015), p. 454, n. 174. See also Rabbi M.G. Barg's incomplete notes of Rav Kook's lectures on the *Book of Kuzari* delivered in Jerusalem in 1921; in *Ma'amrei ha-RAYaH*, vol. 2, ed. Rabbi Elisha Aviner (Langenauer) (Jerusalem, 1984), pp. 485-495.

[22] Judah Halevi, *Book of Kuzari*, transl. Hartwig Hirschfeld (New York: Pardes Publishing House, 1946) II, 14 (p. 78).

[23] See the response of Rabbi Ya'akov Moshe Harlap to Rabbi Hizkiyahu Yosef Mishkovksi of Krinik regarding the appointment (or dis-appointment) of Rabbi Shim'on Shkop, famous for his method of *Higayon* or Talmudic logic; in *Zeved Tov* [*Festschrift* for Rabbi Zevulun Charlop] ed. Ari S. Zahtz (New York: Yeshiva University Press, 2008), Letter 7 (p. 103). The letter is datelined "2nd Day of Rosh Hodesh Adar, 5686 [i.e., 1926], Jerusalem."

[24] Lamentations 3:6; *b. Sanhedrin* 24a. Quoted in Rabbi Dov Baer Shneuri, *Sha'arei 'Orah* (Johannisburg, n.d.; photo offset Brooklyn: Kehot, 1979), *Sha'ar ha-Hanukkah*, chaps. 54-58 (pp. 22b-24a).

[25] Literally, "shell of brightness," or "translucent shell." A Lurianic kabbalistic term for the borderline level intervening between *kedushah* (holiness) and the full-fledged *"shalosh kelipot teme'ot,"* or "three impure shells."

[26] See *Zohar* II, 140b-141a. Cf. Rabbi Abraham Azulai, *Hesed le-Avraham* (Lvov, 1863; photo offset Jerusalem, 1968), 3:9 (20a-b).

[27] *Sha'arei 'Orah*, chap. 58 (24a).

[28] *y. Berakhot* 9:1; *b. Berakhot* 58a.

[29] Rabbi Ya'akov Moshe Harlap, *Mei Marom*, vol. 1 (Commentary to Maimonides' *Shemonah Perakim*) (Jerusalem: Beit Zevul, 1982), 7:6 (p. 136).

[30] Ibid. pp. 136-139.
  Cf. Rabbi Harlap's letter to a young Rabbi Yehudah Klein (who later changed his surname to "Amital"). There, the point is made that that which is incomprehensible (*bilti-mussag*) is greater than that which is comprehensible (*mussag*) and more pleasurable. The letter is datelined "6 Adar I, 5706 [i.e., 1946]." First published in *'Alon Shevut*, Year 5, no. 20 (Adar 5734), pp. 18-21, it was later included in a 64-page brochure on Rabbi Harlap issued by the Israeli Ministry of Education, edited by Rabbi Aryeh Strikovsky, no. 271 (Tishri 5767), pp. 45-46. The brochure is available online: http://meyda.education.gov.il/files/tarbut/pirsumeagaf/kitveet/271pdf.pdf?fbclid=IwAR2uIdw9XhInuL_bW8LyHDq77j9JQGkNxBgG4WorTDjbXHulQKlgLL5l1KU
  In his letter, Rabbi Harlap refers to an early work of his, *Hed ha-Hayyim ha-Yisraeliyim* (Jerusalem, 1912).
  In this respect, Rav Kook and Rav Harlap would be in total agreement.

Rav Kook embraced Maimonides' "negative attributes" (*to'arei shelilah*). See *Reish Millin* (Jerusalem: Makhon RZYH Kook, 2003), Part Two (*Ha-Shorashim*), s.v. *Aleph Lamed* (p. 122):

> It is the spiritual negation, by which the logical mind negates from the highest concept (*musag*), that informs it [i.e., the mind] of its [i.e., the concept's] truth (*amitato*) and reveals its power and light.
> Negation in divine attributes is the source of truth, by which the soul stands on a basis filled with light, freedom, and eternal joy.

[31] See the video of the dialogue between Professors Yeshayahu Leibowitz and Zev (Warren) Harvey of 30/5/1993 at 28:45-32:30. Available at Youtube: https://www.youtube.com/watch?v=wkcnXAsFUgA

[32] See Warren Zev Harvey, "Leibowitz's Anti-Greek Concept of the Messiah," *Iyyun*, vol. 42 (October 1993): 517-520 (Hebrew); and the video cited in the previous note.

[33] Isaiah 1:1.

Zion and Jerusalem:
The Secular and the Sacred

Much has been written about Rav Kook's short-lived movement, *Degel Yerushalayim* (Banner of Jerusalem), which he envisioned as the complement or counterpart to the Zionist movement.[1] The bulk of the third volume and a good portion of the fourth volume of *Iggerot ha-RAYaH*, the collected letters of Rav Kook, are devoted to explicating and promoting the fledgling movement.[2] To Rav Kook's thinking, the two movements would work side by side in perfect symmetry. The secular Zionist movement founded by Herzl would address the physical building of the Land of Israel, while the movement with Rav Kook at its helm would focus on the spiritual rebirth to take place in the ancestral land.

This symmetry would be reflected in the respective names "Zion" and "Jerusalem." Zion symbolizes the political entity of statehood; Jerusalem is synonymous with the spiritual aspirations associated with the sacred place.[2*]

Historians tell us that the impetus for the movement came from none other than Nahum Sokolow, who, together with Chaim Weizmann, led the Zionist movement in London in World War One. When Rav Kook, then residing in London, pressed Sokolow to include the traditional Judaic vision in the Zionist platform, Sokolow responded in writing with the witticism, "A vessel used for the secular, may not be used for the sacred" ("*Keli she-mishtamshim bo hol, ein mishtamshim bo kodesh*"), while encouraging Rav Kook to found his own independent movement devoted solely to the sacred.[3]

What was apparent to Rav Kook's rabbinic peers was that a spiritual vacuum had been left by political Zionism. What required some explaining on Rav Kook's part was why yet another religious movement was called for. There existed already the Mizrachi (Religious Zionist) movement, founded by Rabbi Jacob Reines of Lida, and *Agudat Yisrael* (or simply the *Agudah*), founded by Jacob Rosenheim of Frankfurt. Rav Kook pointed out the shortcomings of these two movements. Mizrachi never emerged as a separate entity but always worked within the framework of Zionism, which is essentially secular in character. *Agudat Yisrael*, on the other hand, while clearly independent of and even antagonistic to Zionism, failed to make Erets Yisrael its priority.[4]

Conceptually, Rav Kook presented what appeared a coherent picture. Semantically, there was a problem with his construct, this being of a kabbalistic nature.

An acquaintance of Rav Kook from his sojourn in London during World War One, raised the following concern. According to Kabbalah, Zion represents the internal and Jerusalem the external. How, then, could Rav Kook reverse the significance of these terms, attributing the inner dimension to Jerusalem and the outer dimension to Zion?

The man who voiced this vexatious problem was Rabbi Shemariah Menashe Hakohen Adler. A native of Poland, he emigrated to Fuerth, Germany, where he engaged in commerce. At the outbreak of World War One, he arrived in London as a refugee.[5] As Rabbi Adler was an erudite Talmudist and halakhist (besides being knowledgeable in Kabbalah), he would go on to author several volumes of responsa, entitled *Mar'eh Kohen*. Unfortunately, his prodigious intellect was blighted by unattractive character traits. Shemariah Menashe Adler was known to be of a cantankerous nature. He publicly insulted Dayan Hillman,[6] and later, his successor in the London Beth Din, Dayan Abramsky.[7] Though Rabbi Shemariah Menashe Adler could be quite disdainful of celebrated rabbis, to Rav Kook's credit, it must be said that the ill-natured controversialist was quite fond of him,[8] even going so far as penning a commentary to Rav Kook's slight kabbalistic work *Reish Millin* (London, 1917). Rav Kook responded to Rabbi Adler on that occasion, complementing him on his work, while spelling out the true kabbalistic significance of the neologism *"Arieliyut"* in the introduction to the tract, *Reish Millin*, and correcting a theological error in Rabbi Adler's wording concerning the *Ein Sof*.[9]

Here, once again, we have Rav Kook engaging with Rabbi Adler in a kabbalistic discussion, this time concerning the terms "Zion"

and "Jerusalem."[10] Although Rav Kook addresses Rabbi Adler with the customary honorifics reserved for an outstanding rabbinic scholar ("the *gaon*, sharp and encyclopedic, et cetera"), from the tone of the letter, it sounds as if Rav Kook is somewhat miffed by the challenge to his proficiency in Kabbalah: "Regarding his comment that 'Zion' is an attribute more inward than 'Jerusalem,' *this is a simple matter, and every beginner in Kabbalah knows* that 'Zion' is the attribute of *'Tsaddik Yesod 'Olam'* [i.e., *Yesod*][11] and 'Jerusalem' is [situated] in *Malkhut*...."[12] (Italics mine—BN.) In fact, the question that Rabbi Adler poses is so basic that it is only with the greatest ingenuity that Rav Kook succeeds in answering it.

What follows is nothing less than a bouleversement. Rav Kook begins by offering an instructive example:

> Just as the days of the workweek correspond to the "six edges" (*vav ketsavot*)[13] and the Sabbath is the attribute of *Malkhut* which is the last [of the ten *sefirot*], nevertheless, for this very reason, the sanctity of the Sabbath is more revealed in the world, because the height of the upper attributes [i.e., the "six edges"] does not let them reveal their sanctity in the world. Only the attribute of *Malkhut* is fitting for such, and for this reason, the sanctity of the Sabbath is so severe.

Rav Kook would have us accept that the kabbalistic scheme is actually counterintuitive. That which in the kabbalistic reckoning is "higher," manifests in our mundane world as profane (*hol*); that which is sefirotically "lower," comes across in our plane of reality as sacred (*kodesh*). Having established the topsy-turvy relation of the six days of work to the seventh day of rest, Rav Kook proceeds to elucidate the relation of Zion to Jerusalem:

> Similarly, since the attribute of "Zion" is inner, in this world it is not recognized as being sacred. Therefore, here [i.e., in this world] it is the place of the kingdom (*mamlakhah*), and not the place of the Temple (*mikdash*), as is famous to those who stand in the Holy City.[14] And certainly the innermost holiness sanctifies the earthly kingdom as well, but the attribute of "Jerusalem"—because it is external at its root, in comparison to "Zion"—manifests below [i.e., in this world] with the power of holiness, and therefore we say, "[Bring us] to Zion, Your city, and to Jerusalem, Your Holy Temple."[15]

To digest Rav Kook's reconstruction, at its root on high, the secular aspect of Erets Yisrael ("Zion") with all the trappings of statehood, is actually "higher" and more "inward." On the other hand, the sacred aspect ("Jerusalem"), that which is manifestly holy in our world, is "lower" in the sefirotic realm, and more "outward."

The implications of Rav Kook's kabbalistic analysis are bold indeed. From the view above, that which manifests in the world as secular (*hol*) is "higher" than that which is revealed on our plane as sacred (*kodesh*)![16]

The next segment in Rav Kook's epistle appears to be a *non sequitur*. Rav Kook writes:

> ... and though there is the "word of the LORD" that is prophecy,[17] from *Netsah* and *Hod*,[18] below the Written Torah, which is the attribute of *Tif'eret*,[19] nevertheless, there is also the "word of the LORD" that is the root of creation and the source of Torah from heaven (*Torah min ha-shamayim*),[20] and "By the word of the LORD the heavens (*shamayim*) were made,"[21] which includes as well the supernal heavens (*ha-shamayim ha-'elyonim*).[22] "And the matters are ancient."[23]

Rav Kook explains that the Biblical phrase, "the word of the LORD," is a homonym.[24] It can have two different meanings. On occasion it refers to the Prophets (whose status is lower than that of the Torah), but it can also refer to the primordial Word which is the root of the Creation and the source of the Torah.

Though lexically interesting, this discussion seems off-topic. Why has Rav Kook suddenly segued to defining the term "the word of the LORD"?

I would venture a guess that Rabbi Shemariah Menashe Adler challenged Rav Kook's assignation of Zion to the secular and Jerusalem to the sacred, by quoting the famous verse, "For from Zion shall go forth Torah, and the word of the LORD from Jerusalem."[25] I imagine that Rabbi Adler marshaled the verse as proof that "Zion" represents a higher spiritual level than "Jerusalem." From Zion goes out "Torah," the Written Torah (*Torah she-bi-Ketav*), whereas from Jerusalem goes out the lower level of divine inspiration, "the word of the LORD" ("*devar Hashem*"), i.e., the *Nevi'im* or Prophets.[26] Rabbi Adler might have gone so far as to translate this into kabbalistic terms: "Torah" is synonymous with *Tif'eret*; the *Nevi'im* are directly below in *Netsah* and *Hod*. Thus, Rabbi Adler found incongruous Rav Kook's equation of Zion with the material aspect of the Land, and Jerusalem with the spiritual aspect.

To counter this supposed proof, and maintain the spiritual superiority of Jerusalem over Zion, Rav Kook had to show that the "the word of the LORD" need not refer to the *Nevi'im* or Prophets, who rank below the Torah; it might as well refer to the original "word of the LORD," which registers above the Torah.

***

The plot thickens. In 2018, there was released *Metsi'ot Katan* (*Findings of a Minor*), one of Rav Kook's earliest works, containing his thoughts from the years 1889-1895, when he served as Rabbi of Zeimel, Lithuania.[27] There, to our surprise, Rav Kook maintains that Zion is the site of the Temple, while Jerusalem is the site of the secular court. This is borne out in the verse, "For from Zion shall go forth Torah, and the word of the LORD from Jerusalem." Writes a youthful Rav Kook:

> When Israel were in their land....there were the priests, the teachers of Torah,[28] who would judge the people based on Torah law, and the officials appointed by the government would judge the law of the land. In Zion—the place of the priests—was the seat of Torah rule, and in Jerusalem was the political rule. They too [i.e., the statesmen] would judge for the sake of heaven by stabilizing the state.[29] And when Israel were settled [in their land] and performed the will of the Omnipresent, the law of the government was also aligned with the will of the LORD,[30] though it was not exactly perfectly Torah. And so it is written, "For from Zion shall go forth Torah, and the word of the LORD from Jerusalem." So, Zion was the source of instruction that transcends human intellect, greatly surpassing it...."[31]

Rav Kook repeats his interpretation of the verse once again:

> "For from Zion shall go forth Torah, and the word of the LORD from Jerusalem." The meaning is that Zion is called the site of the Temple, as it is said in the prayer of the Temple service: "May our eyes see when You return to Zion with compassion." And in Jerusalem, the site of the secular (*hol*), there sat the Sanhedrin, for half of the Chamber of Hewn Stone (*Lishkat ha-Gazit*) was situated

in the area of the profane, and the seating [of the Sanhedrin] was in the area of the profane.³² And also [situated in Jerusalem were] all the kings of Israel with the power to enforce [observance of] the holy religion even by those who were disobedient.³³

The reader will appreciate that by the time Rav Kook penned his epistle to Rabbi Shemariah Menashe Adler, he had reversed his thinking concerning the roles played by Zion and Jerusalem. In the interim, there had been born the Zionist movement, which laid claim to the secular realm, forcing Jerusalem—id est *Degel Yerushalayim*—to assume the role of the sacred. And it was necessary to explain to fellow kabbalists such as Rabbi Shemariah Menashe Adler how such a bouleversement played itself out "in all the worlds."

A few months after writing the response to Rabbi Shemariah Menashe Adler, on April 1st, 1925 (7 Nissan, 5685), Rav Kook would speak at the historic opening of Hebrew University on Mount Scopus in Jerusalem. He would conclude with the verse from the Prophets, "For from Zion shall go forth Torah, and the word of the LORD from Jerusalem."³⁴ Rav Kook's enemies seized the opportunity, beating his well-meant words into one more weapon in their arsenal. To invoke this prophecy in regard to the secular studies about to be taught at the University was nothing less than blasphemy! Rav Kook tried to explain that it was not in regard to the University that he waxed prophetic, rather in regard to the incipient Yeshivah with its Torah studies.[35] Indeed, an inspection of Rav Kook's letters from this period, reveals that this was the very time that he advocated for the Central Universal Yeshivah (*Ha-Yeshivah ha-'Olamit ha-Merkazit*), known today as *"Merkaz Harav."* From the time that he arrived back in the Land from his long sojourn in America, he wrote tirelessly to individuals and to the general public, begging to bring this dream to fruition.

Based on his recently released writings, we may now say that Rav Kook—unlike both the secular and religious camps—heard in the words of Isaiah's prophecy that there would issue from the Holy City—from two different locations within her, namely Zion and Jerusalem—the secular *and* the sacred, the temporal *and* the eternal.

Poignantly, the Aramaic *Targum* of Psalm 133:1 ("How good and how pleasant it is for brothers to dwell together in unity!") paraphrases: "How good and how pleasant it is for *Zion* and *Jerusalem* to dwell as two brothers yet as one!"

---

[1] See recently Rabbi Abraham Wasserman, *Koré ha-Degel* (2020).
   Incidentally, Jacob Agus entitled his biography of Rav Kook, *Banner of Jerusalem* (New York: Bloch, 1946). Later, he retitled the book, *High Priest of Rebirth* (New York: Bloch, 1972).

[2] See *Iggerot ha-RAYaH*, vol. 3 (1916-1919), ed. Rabbi Tsevi Yehudah Hakohen Kook (Jerusalem: Mossad Harav Kook, 1965); vol. 4 (1920-1925), ed. Rabbi Ya'akov Filber (Jerusalem: Makhon RZYH Kook, 1984).
   In Rabbi Tsevi Yehudah Kook's preface to the third volume, he writes that it pertains to the period of the Balfour Declaration and to the establishment of *"Degel Yerushalayim*, for the sanctification of Zionism" (*"kiddushah shel ha-*

Tsiyoniyut").

2* Rav Kook expressed this dichotomy succinctly in his address to the Agudat ha-Rabbanim in New York on 10 Iyyar, 1924, as recorded in *Ha-Tor*, year 4, no. 38, p. 12. See Yehoshua B. Be'ery, *Ohev Yisrael bi-Kedushah* (Tel-Aviv, 1989), vol. 1, p. 371; vol. 5, p. 248.

3 Nahum Sokolow's letter to Rav Kook, dated "5 Tevet, 5678" (i.e., December 20, 1917), was penned in the immediate aftermath of the Balfour Declaration of November 2, 1917. The whereabouts of the letter—once in the possession of Rav Kook's son, Rabbi Tsevi Yehudah Hakohen Kook—is today unknown. Rabbi Moshe Tsevi Neriyah excerpted the letter in his *Likkutei ha-Rayah*, vol. 1, p. 117. See further idem, *Mo'adei ha-Rayah*, pp. 396-397; *Entsiklopedia shel ha-Tziyonut ha-Datit*, p. 200. (Communication from Rabbi Zuriel Hallamish, researcher at Beit Harav, Jerusalem.)

Sokolow, who, in his youth, received the traditional Talmudic education, inverted the Talmudic saying (*b. Bava Metsi'a* 84b), "A vessel that was used for the sacred, should be used for the secular?" ("*Keli she-nishtamesh bo kodesh, yishtamesh bo hol?*"). Cf. *b. 'Avodah Zarah* 52b: "Since it was used for the sacred (*gavo'ah*) it is inappropriate to use it for the secular (*hedyot*)." However, essentially, Sokolow's statement is found in the *Tosefta, Megillah*, chap. 3 (Zuckermandel ed., p. 224); and *Menahot*, end chap. 9 (Zuckermandel ed., p. 526), though the wording differs: "Vessels that were made originally for the secular (*hedyot*), we may not make them for the sacred (*gavo'ah*)." The *Tosefta* is quoted verbatim in Maimonides, *MT, Hil. Beit ha-Behirah* 1:20.

4 *Iggerot ha-RAYaH*, vol. 4, Letter 1000 (p. 32). The letter, datelined "25 Kislev, 5680 [i.e., 1920]," is addressed to Rabbi Mendel Yitzhak Behrman and the members of *Degel Yerushalayim* in Manchester, England.

5 See the introduction to Rabbi Shemariah Menashe Hakohen Adler, *Mar'eh Kohen, Mahadura Telita'ah*, vol. 1 (*Piotrków*, 1931), 3b.

6 Rabbi Shemariah Menashe Adler unsuccessfully attempted to convince Rabbi Joseph Hayyim Sonnenfeld of Jerusalem that Dayan Shmuel Yitzhak Hillman should be disqualified as *Av Beit Din* based on the ignorance displayed in his Talmudic commentary *'Or ha-Yashar*! See *Mar'eh Kohen, Mahadura Telita'ah*, vol. 2 (Warsaw, 1933), nos. 130-131.

For a discussion of Rabbi Sonnenfeld's diplomacy in general, and vis-à-vis Rabbi Adler in particular, see Eitam Henkin's study of Rabbi Joseph Shapotshnick, "Ki hekhin beit haroshet lehatir 'agunot," *Asif* 2 (2015), pp. 379-382.

Rabbi Adler feigned surprise when Rabbi Dr. Isaac Halevi Herzog of Dublin, Dayan Hillman's son-in-law, returned the book (*Mar'eh Kohen, Mahadura Telita'ah*) to its sender! See Rabbi Shemariah Menashe Hakohen Adler, *'Emek ha-Bakha* (Keidan, 1935), 10:1 (p. 138). *'Emek ha-Bakha* is an attempt to prohibit the recent Soncino translation of the Talmud to English under the editorship of Rabbi Isidore (Yehezkel) Epstein of Jews' College. In lieu of a *haskamah* (approbation), Adler prefaced his work with a letter from the famed Rogatchover Gaon, Rabbi Joseph Rosen of Dvinsk, forbidding teaching Talmud to non-Jews. The letter is reprinted in *She'elot u-Teshuvot Tsafnat Pa'ne'ah ha-Hadashot*, vol. 2 (Modi'in 'Ilit, 5772/2012), nos. 109-110 (pp. 304-313). Unfortunately, both the Rogatchover and the editor of the new edition of his collected responsa accepted at face value Rabbi Adler's libelous accusation that the Soncino translation of the Talmud was directed primarily at non-Jews; see ibid., the bold print in note 48 on page 313.

Adler's work, *Maror de-Rabbanan* (*Bitter Herb of the Rabbis*), appended to *Mar'eh Kohen Tinyana* (London, 1928), is a diatribe against the Chief Rabbi and the London Beth Din.

7 For starters, in the introduction to *Mar'eh Kohen, Mahadura Hamisha'ah* (London, 1945), p. 20, the author trashes Dayyan Abramsky's work on the *Tosefta, Hazon Yehezkel*. (See earlier, *'Emek ha-Bakha*, 10:12 [p. 158], where Adler is just "warming up" for the full-blown attack on *Hazon Yehezkel*.) In a later volume of *Mar'eh Kohen*, concerning the *Herem de-Rabbeinu Gershom* (London, 1953), the author once again spews venom on Rabbi Abramsky, who by that time no longer resided in England but in Erets Yisrael, and may merely have acted in a consultant capacity on a visit to London. In the introduction to that volume (p. 3), Rabbi Adler records a dream in which the *Sefat Emet* appeared to him. (Prof. Marc B. Shapiro informs me that Rabbi Adler was a *hasid* of the Gur dynasty.) The volume deals with the problem of men whose wives disappeared in the Holocaust. Rabbi Adler, based on a responsum of the *Hiddushei ha-RIM* (founder of the Gur Hasidic dynasty) to Rabbi Hayyim Halberstam of Sanz (author of the responsa *Divrei Hayyim*), required a *heter me'ah rabbanim* (permission of one hundred rabbis) to allow the husbands to remarry. He accused Dayan Abramsky of obviating the requirement.

8 In letters to Rav Kook published in the first volume of *Mar'eh Kohen* (London, 1919), nos. 30, 32 (pp. 91, 96), Rabbi Adler addresses him as *"Ha-Rav ha-Ga'on ha-Tsaddik."* So too in the header to Rav Kook's approbation in *Zikhron Elhanan* (London, 1920), and ibid. pp. 5-6.

However, after Rav Kook's refusal to get involved in Rabbi Adler's campaign to unseat Dayan Hillman, one senses deep disappointment on the part of Rabbi Adler, if not outright bitterness. (Rav Kook's title, *"Tsaddik,"* conveniently disappears.) Rabbi Adler had hoped that in 1924, when Rav Kook stopped off in London on his way back from America, he would adjudicate the matter, but that did not happen. Rabbi Adler quotes Rav Kook as having told him in Yiddish on that occasion: *"Ikh kon mikh nisht shtellen mit dem Beis Din de-London veil Ikh broikh fun zei shtitze in fershidene inyonim."* ("I cannot get involved with the London Beth Din as I need from them support in various matters.") Rabbi Adler reminds Rav Kook of his past kindnesses, how during World War One, he had once hosted the Rav and Rebbetsin in his home in Oxford, at which time he served them personally. He also brought up the fact that it was he who publicly defended Rav Kook and the other rabbis in the press when the madman Joseph Shapotshnick defamed them. See *Mar'eh Kohen, Mahadura Telita'ah*, vol. 2 (Warsaw, 1933), nos. 132-133:1, 4 (f.231, 232d). The exchange of letters between Rabbis Kook and Adler took place at the end of 1928. For Rav Kook's experience with Shapotshnick, see Henkin, op. cit.

9 See *Iggerot ha-RAYaH*, vol. 3, Letter 896 (pp. 207-208); *Haskamot ha-RAYaH* (1897-1928), ed. Rabbis Ari Yitzhak Shvat, Zuriel Hallamish, and Yohanan Fried (Jerusalem: Beit Harav, 2017), no. 81 (pp. 174-176). See further Bezalel Naor, *"Reish Millin—Mekorot ve-He'arot," Sinai* 97 (Nissan-Ellul 5745/1985), pp. 69-76; also issued as *Zikhron RAYaH* (Memorial Volume on Rav Kook's Fiftieth *Yahrzeit*), ed. Yitzhak Rafael (Jerusalem: Mossad Harav Kook, 1986).

Rav Kook's letter to Rabbi Adler is datelined *"Erev Rosh Hodesh Mena-*

hem-Av, 5678 [i.e., 1918], Harrogate." During the summer months, Rav Kook, suffering from poor health, would rest in the famed spa town.

Years later, Rabbi Adler later confronted Rav Kook with the fact that Rav Kook had once written to him in a letter that his work *Reish Millin* came about in a revelatory manner (*"be-derekh hofa'ah ve-hitnotsetsut"*). See *Mar'eh Kohen, Mahadura Telita'ah*, vol. 2 (Warsaw, 1933), no. 133:1 (231c).

Rabbi Tsevi Yehudah Kook told the present writer (BN) that his father had received a *"tsav"* ("command") from above to write *Reish Millin* and also the more prosaic work, *Halakhah Berurah*.

Rabbi Adler's commentary to *Reish Millin* ran to some three hundred pages. Sometime after 1925, he offered it to Rabbi Yitshak Arieli of Jerusalem for publication. When Rabbi Arieli consulted with Rav Kook, his response was: "It is a commentary based on the kabbalistic side but does not touch on the philosophical side." See *'Eynei Yitzhak* (biography of Rabbi Yitzhak Arieli), ed. Aharon Ilan (Jerusalem, 2018), p. 177.

Despite that supposed disparagement, evidently the Rav's son, Rabbi Tsevi Yehudah Kook, thought highly enough of the commentary that on the 6th of Tishri, 5696 [i.e., 1935], barely a month after his father's passing (on the 3rd of Ellul), he reached out in writing to Rabbi Adler, requesting a copy of the commentary in its entirety, with an eye to its publication. See the introduction to the recently issued *Iggerot ha-RAYaH*, vol. 5 (1922), ed. Ze'ev Neuman (Jerusalem: Makhon RZYH Kook, 2019), pp. 10-11. See also *Iggerot ha-RAYaH*, vol. 3, Letter 874 (p. 162).

In *Iggerot ha-RAYaH*, vol. 3, Letter 916 (p. 228) consists of a *haskamah* (approbation) to an unnamed work by Rabbi Adler, datelined "London, 1st day of *Rosh Hodesh* Marheshvan, 5679" [1918]. Rav Kook's *haskamah* was published in Rabbi Adler's *Kuntres Zikhron Elhanan* (London, 5680). (However, the colophon of the book reads: Marheshvan, 5681 [i.e., 1920].) Zikhron Elhanan consists of notes to *Shulhan 'Arukh, Even ha-Ezer*, composed during the rabbi's three-week incarceration. The *haskamah* has been reprinted in *Haskamot ha-RAYaH* (1897-1928), no. 82 (p. 177) under the header, *"Peirush 'al Sefer Reish Millin"* (Commentary to *Reish Millin*). Actually, according to Rabbi Adler, Rav Kook's *haskamah* was an endorsement of his work, *Keter Torah*, on the *Otiyot de-Rabbi Akiva* (*Zikhron Elhanan*, p. 6). (Parenthetically, in the version printed in *Zikhron Elhanan*, the words *"bi-netivot lo yad'u,"* missing from the verse in Isaiah 42:16, have been supplied.)

Later, on the 18th of Tevet, 5681 [i.e., December 29, 1920], at the height of the controversy surrounding Rav Kook's seminal work, *Orot*, Rav Kook penned an additional *haskamah*, published in Rabbi Adler's sequel volume of *Mar'eh Kohen* (London, 1928). See *Haskamot ha-RAYaH* (1897-1928), no. 95 (p. 198).

Several years ago, I asked the renowned bibliophile Abraham Halevi Schischa of London if he knew what became of Rabbi Menashe Adler's manuscript of the commentary to *Reish Millin*. Sometime later, Schischa reported back to me that by sheer serendipity he "bumped into" a descendant of Rabbi Adler who said that the rabbi's sons did not care much for their father and after his passing, destroyed his manuscripts!

Recently, I published on the Orot website a facsimile of a letter from Rav Kook to Rabbi Yehudah Newman. Datelined "London, 21 Tevet, 5679" [i.e.,

December 24, 1918], the letter mentions *en passant* a Talmudic interpretation of Rav Kook's friend, R[abbi] S[hemariah] M[enashe]. The postscript contains a reference to *"histadruteinu ha-kedoshah"* ("our holy organization"), clearly *Histadrut Yerushalayim*, or the Jerusalem Organization, as it was known.

See http://orot.com/newly-acquired-manuscript-rav-kook/

[10] *Iggerot ha-RAYaH*, vol. 4, ed. Rabbi Ya'akov Filber (Jerusalem: Makhon RZYH Kook, 1984), Letter 1277 (p. 217). The letter is datelined "23 Tevet, [568]5" (i.e., January 19, 1925). Rav Kook mentions that he has not yet had time to rest up from his journey. Evidently, the reference is to Rav Kook's fundraising mission to America, where he spent the better part of the year 1924. See Rabbi Joshua Hoffman, "Rav Kook's Mission to America," *Orot: A Multidisciplinary Journal of Judaism*, vol. 1 (5751/1991), pp. 78-99. On the way back from America to Erets Yisrael, the indefatigable Rav Kook stopped over in London (where he made an appeal for his colleague Rabbi Nahman Shlomo Greenspan's Yeshivah 'Ets Hayyim) and Paris (where he persuaded Baron Edmond de Rothschild to halt desecration of the Sabbath on the newly installed train from Ras al-'Ayn to Petah Tikvah). See *Iggerot ha-Rayah*, vol. 4, Letter 1268 (pp. 211-212) and Letter 1266 (pp. 210-211).

[11] See Rabbi Meir Poppers, *Me'orei 'Or*, *Tsade*-15, s.v. *"Zion,"* that Zion has the numerical value of "Yosef." Joseph is identified with the *sefirah* of *Yesod*.

[12] See Rabbi Joseph Gikatilla, *Sha'arei Orah*, ed. Joseph Ben-Shlomo (Jerusalem: Bialik Institute, 1970), vol. 1, *Sha'ar Hamishi* (p. 205), note 53; idem, *Gates of Light*, transl. Avi Weinstein (San Francisco, CA: HarperCollins, 1994), Fifth Gate, p. 176 (regarding Psalm 135:21); *Zohar* III, 31a; 171a; 296 (*Idra Zuta*); Rabbi Moses Cordovero, *Pardes Rimonim*, Gate 23 (*Sha'ar 'Erkei ha-Kinuyim*), s.v. *Yerushalayim* and s.v. *Zion*; Rabbi Hayyim Vital, *'Ets Hayyim*, Gate 35 (*Sha'ar ha-Yare'ah*), chap. 3; Gate 34 (*Sha'ar Tikkun ha-Nukva*), chap. 2, *kelal* 18; idem, *Peri 'Ets Hayyim*, *Sha'ar ha-Lulav*, chap. 4; Rabbi Elijah Gaon of Vilna, *Likkutei ha-GRA 'al Seder Alpha Beta*, ed. Rabbi Nehemiah Feffer (New York, NY: Makhon HaGRA, 1999), *Tsade*-2, s.v. *Tsiyon vi-Yerushalayim*; Rabbi Menahem Mendel Schneerson (*"Tsemah Tsedek"*), *Reshimot 'al Shir ha-Shirim, Rut, Kohelet* (Brooklyn, NY; Kehot, 1960), *"Tse'enah u-Re'enah"* I (p. 79); Rabbi Levi Isaac Schneerson, *Likkutei Levi Yitzhak: Iggerot Kodesh* (Brooklyn: Kehot, 2004), Letter datelined "Dnepropetróvsk, 9 Kislev, 5695 [i.e., 1934]," pp. 340-341.

[13] The six *sefirot* of *Hesed*, *Gevurah*, *Tif'eret*, *Netsah*, *Hod* and *Yesod* are referred to as the "six edges (or extremities)" (of a cube). The term is taken from *Sefer Yetsirah* 1:13.

[14] Zion was associated with the City of David and the ancient seat of government, as opposed to the Temple Mount, which was the place of worship. See 1Kings 8:1, and *Seder 'Olam Rabbah*, ed. Moshe Ya'ir Weinstock (B'nei Berak, 1990), chap. 14, in commentary *"Seder Zemanim,"* pp. 230-231. (According to the very latest archeological findings, during the reign of King Hezekiah—who was a contemporary of the Prophet Isaiah—the administrative headquarters were outside of the City of David.)

However, see below the quotations from the earlier work, *Mets'iot Katan*, where Rav Kook wrote the exact opposite, that Zion is the site of the Temple and Jerusalem the site of the secular government.

[15] *Mussaf* (Additional Prayer) for festivals.

[16] In broad terms, one might say that this kind of inversion, whereby the "root" of the secular is higher than the "root" of the sacred, is reminiscent of HaBaD Hasidic teaching.

See, for example, Rabbi Shneur Zalman, *Tanya*, Part Four [*Iggeret ha-Kodesh*], chap. 20, where the root of the *mitsvot*, or commandments, is higher than the root of the Torah. In that regard, the *Tanya* employs the image of "a seal in reverse" (*hotam ha-mit-hapekh*), and quotes from *Sefer Yetsirah* (1:7): "Their beginning is embedded in their end."

An expression that has gained great currency is: "The root of the vessels is higher than the root of the lights." See Rabbi Aaron Halevi Hurwitz of Staroshelye, *Sha'arei ha-Yihud ve-ha-Emunah* (Shklov, 1820), Fourth Gate (*Sha'ar Orot ve-Kelim*), chap. 14 (15b); and chap. 29 (where it is explained that the root of the vessels is from the *"reshimu"* and the root of the lights is from the *"kav"*). In the latter regard, see also Rabbi Shneur Zalman of Liadi, *Likkutei Torah, Hosafot* (Addenda) to the Book of Leviticus, s.v. *Lehavin mah she-katuv be-'Otserot Hayyim*, 54a; Rabbi Menahem Mendel Schneersohn of Lubavitch (*"Tsemah Tsedek"*), *'Or ha-Torah, Tetse*, vol. 2, *Derush Kan Tsipor* (pp. 924-925) (transcribed in M.M. Laufer, *Ha-Melekh bi-Mesibo*, vol. 2, pp. 284-285); and Rabbi Isaac Dov Baer Schneerson of Liadi, *Siddur MaHaRID* (Berdichev, 1913; facsimile edition Kefar Habad, 1991), Part 2, *Mussaf le-Shabbat*, 69b, s.v. *u-be-Siddur ha-ARI z"l*.

In his famous essay, "The Souls of the World of Chaos," reprinted in the 1950 edition of *Orot*, Rav Kook writes: "The souls of Chaos (*neshamot de-Tohu*) are higher than the souls of Establishment (*neshamot de-Tikkun*)" (*Orot*, "*Zer'onim*," chap. 3 [p. 122]). In an endnote (on the final page of the volume, p. 192), the editor, Rabbi Tsevi Yehudah Kook, sourced this statement in RSZ, *Torat Hayyim, Vayyishlah*. *Torat Hayyim*, misattributed to Rabbi Shneur Zalman, is actually by his son, Rabbi Dov Baer, known in Lubavitch circles as the *"Mitteler Rebbe,"* or "Middle Rabbi." In that work of HaBaD Hasidism, we learn that the soul of Esau (*Tohu*) is higher than that of Jacob (*Tikkun*).

And see below, note 22, the inversion of the Written Torah and the Oral Torah.

Yet, to the best of my knowledge, the application to the particular realms of *kodesh* versus *hol*, is without precedent in the annals of Kabbalah and is uniquely Kookian. One might say that it is the response of a Kabbalist to the secular age in general, and specifically to the phenomenon of secular Zionism.

For the influence of HaBaD Hasidism upon the development of Rav Kook's thought, see my essay, "The Curtains of the Tabernacle: R. Shelomo Zalman of Kopyst," in *Orot: A Multidisciplinary Journal of Judaism*, vol. 1 (1991), pp. 33-41.

[17] See e.g. 1Samuel 3:1. Also, *b. Shabbat* 138b.

[18] According to Kabbalah, the source of the Prophets' inspiration is from the *sefirot* of *Netsah* and *Hod*. See Rabbi Joseph Gikatilla, *Sha'arei Orah*, Gates 3-4 (Ben-Shlomo ed., vol. 1, p. 158; Weinstein ed., p. 130); *Tikkunei Zohar* with commentary of Vilna Gaon (Vilna, 1867), Introduction, 13a, and *Tikkunim mi-Zohar Hadash*, 46b; Rabbi Moses Cordovero, *Pardes Rimonim* 6:6, 13:6, and 23:14 (s.v. *nevi'ei ha-emet*).

[19] See Rabbi Joseph Gikatilla, *Sha'arei Orah*, Fifth Gate (Ben-Shlomo ed., vol.

1, p. 248; Weinstein ed., p. 220).

Cf. Rav Kook's commentary to *The Legends of Rabbah bar Bar Hannah*, ed. Bezalel Naor (Monsey, NY: Orot/Kodesh, 2019), English, p. 91; Hebrew, p. 20.

One should add that halakhically, as well, the status of the Prophets (*Nevi'im*) is below that of Torah. For this reason, one must not place the Prophets on top of the Torah. See *t. Megillah* 4:20 (Zuckermandel ed., p. 227); *y. Megillah* 3:1; *b. Megillah* 27a; Maimonides, *MT, Hil. Sefer Torah* 10:5.

[20] *m. Sanhedrin* 10:1. See Rabbi Abraham Isaac Hakohen Kook, *Shemonah Kevatsim* 1:633.

In the present context, *"Torah min ha-shamayim"* means that the Written Torah emanates from the *sefirah* of *Tif'eret*, which is symbolized by *"shamayim,"* or heaven.

[21] Psalms 33:6. See Introduction to *Zohar* I, 5a.

[22] In the kabbalistic lexicon, the heavens (*shamayim*) are synonymous with the *sefirah* of *Tif'eret*, which, as Rav Kook explained earlier, is where the Written Torah (*Torah she-bi-ketav*) is situated. On the other hand, earth (*erets*) is synonymous with the *sefirah* of *Malkhut*, the location of the Oral Torah (*Torah she-be-'al-Peh*).

Rabbi Joseph Ibn Waqar quotes Rabbi Azriel of Gerona that in the verse in 1 Chronicles 29:11, *"shamayim"* signifies *Tif'eret* and *"arets"* signifies *Malkhut*. (This verse is basic to Kabbalah, as it provides the names of five *sefirot*: *Gedulah* [i.e., *Hesed*], *Gevurah, Tif'eret, Netsah, Hod*.) See Rabbi Joseph B. Abraham Ibn Waqar, *Shorashei ha-Kabbalah* (*Principles of the Qabbalah*), ed. Paul B. Fenton (Los Angeles: Cherub Press, 2004), p. 152, s.v. *limmudei Hashem*. Cf. *Zohar* I, 31; II, 116a.

It is explained that the Hebrew word *"shamayim"* is a combination of *esh* (fire) and *mayim* (water). See *b. Hagigah* 12a; *Genesis Rabbah* 4:7; Rashi, Genesis 1:1, 8. Since water is the symbol of *Hesed* and fire is the symbol of *Gevurah*, their synthesis, *shamayim*, symbolizes the synthesis of those two attributes: *Tif'eret*. See Rabbi Joseph Gikatilla, *Sha'arei Orah*, Gates 3-4 (Ben-Shlomo ed., p. 156; Weinstein ed., p. 127).

In *Shemonah Kevatsim* 1:98, Rav Kook writes: "The Written Torah is the attribute of 'Heaven' (*'shamayim'*)." The kabbalistic association of the Written Torah with Heaven (*"Tif'eret"*) and the Oral Torah with Earth, is borne out in the first chapter of *Orot ha-Torah* ("The Written Torah and the Oral Torah"), culled by the editor, Rabbi Tsevi Yehudah Hakohen Kook, from various passages in *Shemonah Kevatsim*.

The first paragraph in the chapter was taken from *Shemonah Kevatsim* 2:56, 57. By the way, in the very first line of *Orot ha-Torah*, the word *"ha-tsinor"* ("the pipeline") now reads *"ha-tsiyyur"* ("the conception"). This alteration was unnoticed by the editor of *Shemonah Kevatsim* in the *"He'arot Nusah"* or *variae lectionis* at the end of the volume.

The second paragraph in the chapter (taken from *Shemonah Kevatsim* 2:223) makes the point that the root of the Oral Law is higher than the root of the Written Law (yet another example of the topsy-turvy in Rav Kook's Kabbalah). In this connection, Rav Kook quotes the saying of the *Talmud Yerushalmi* (*Berakhot* 1:4; *Sanhedrin* 11:4; *'Avodah Zarah* 2:7): "The words of the scribes are more beloved than the words of the Torah." This *pensée* may have been inspired by a teaching of the *"Alter Rebbe,"* Rabbi Shneur Zaman of Liadi, founder of HaBaD Hasidism. See Rabbi Shneur Zalman, *Likkutei Torah, Shir ha-Shirim,* s.v. *Shehorah Ani ve-Navah* II, par. 3 (7a). Rav Kook once remarked to Rabbi Shim'on Glitzenstein—the HaBaD Hasid who served as his secretary during the years in London—regarding this particular *ma'amar* in *Likkutei Torah*: *"Do iz ofener ru'ah ha-kodesh."* (Yiddish, "Here is open divine inspiration.") Quoted in Rabbi Moshe Tsevi Neriyah, *Sihot ha-RAYaH* (Tel-Aviv, 1979), p. 256. According to Rabbi Glitzenstein's description, Rav Kook was so enraptured by the Hasidic discourse that he was pacing the length of his study in an emotional state!

In this paragraph, as well, the variants have gone unnoticed by the editor of *Shemonah Kevatsim*. *"Mats'ah et darkah"* ("she found her way") has become *"mats'ah et birkatah"* ("she found her blessing"); *"segulah 'ofit"* ("characteristic treasure") is rendered *"segulah Elohit"* ("Godly treasure").

23 1 Chronicles 4:22. This is an expression for the arcane.

24 See *b. Shabbat* 138b, where three different interpretations of *"devar Hashem"* ("the word of the LORD") are given.

25 Isaiah 2:3; Micah 4:2; *y. Nedarim* 6:8; *b. Berakhot* 63b.

26 Cf. Malbim's interpretation of the verse in Isaiah 2:3, whereby "Torah" refers to the judgment of the Sanhedrin in the Chamber of Hewn Stone (*Lishkat ha-Gazit*), as opposed to the "word of the LORD," which refers to the inspiration of the prophets, who did not sit in the Chamber of Hewn Stone, but circulated throughout the entire city of Jerusalem.

27 Rabbi Abraham Isaac Hakohen Kook, *Metsi'ot Katan*, ed. Harel Cohen (Israel: Maggid, 2018).

As Rav Kook was born in 1865, he was between the ages of 24 and 30 when he penned *Metsi'ot Katan*.

28 Hebrew, *tofesei ha-Torah*. See Jeremiah 2:8.

29 See Rabbeinu Nissim Gerondi, *Derashot ha-RaN*, ed. Leon A. Feldman (Jerusalem: Shalem, 1973), *derush* 11 (189ff.). According to Rabbeinu Nissim, the Torah provided for two parallel systems of jurisprudence: strict Torah law (*mishpat ha-Torah*) and the law of the monarchy or state (*mishpat ha-melukhah*).

Earlier, Rabbi David Kimhi envisioned the covalent institutions of King Messiah, the temporal authority, and the Aaronide High Priest, who would provide instruction in Torah law. See the commentary of RaDaK to Psalm 133. In this scheme, "Zion" is the seat of the monarchy.

30 Rav Kook understands the "word of the LORD" to refer in this context to the judgment rendered not strictly according to Torah law but nonetheless aligned to the will of the LORD.

31 *Metsi'ot Katan*, par. 99 (pp. 167-168). Rabbeinu Nissim made the point that the laws of the Torah transcend logic; see *Derashot ha-RaN*, loc. cit. (pp. 190-191).

32 *m. Middot* 5:4; *b. Yoma* 25a; *Sanhedrin* 88b. Rav Kook's scheme diverges from that of Rabbeinu Nissim (p. 191), who understood that the Sanhedrin sat in the Chamber of Hewn Stone in order to be in the place of divine inspiration (as opposed to the kings who sat in judgment at a far remove from the Temple Mount).

33 *Metsi'ot Katan*, par. 155 (pp. 249-250). See *Derashot ha-RaN*, cited in the

previous note.

[34] See *Ma'amrei ha-RAYaH*, vol. 2, ed. Elisha Aviner (Langenauer) (Jerusalem, 1984), pp. 306-308; English translation in *When God Becomes History: Historical Essays of Rabbi Abraham Isaac Hakohen Kook*, ed. Bezalel Naor (New York, NY: Kodesh Press, 2016), pp. 141-145.

[35] Ibid. pp. 147, 150.

In 1924, Rav Kook issued a 12-page prospectus, *Ha-Yeshivah ha-Merkazit ha-'Olamit bi-Yerushalayim*. Evidently, the booklet was issued simultaneously in New York and Jerusalem (at the press of Y.A. Weiss). The final line of the brochure is the verse, "For from Zion shall go forth Torah, and the word of the LORD from Jerusalem." See *Ma'amrei ha-RAYaH*, vol. 1 (Jerusalem, 1980), pp. 62-65. In the Jerusalem edition, the verse also appears alone as the motto on page (2).

Rav Kook's Shattered Vessels and Their Repair

Undoubtedly, Rav Kook's most important discussion of the *Zohar*'s Myth of the Primordial Kings (*Sod Malkin Kadma'in*), is the passage in *Shemonah Kevatsim* (1:164). In *Orot ha-Kodesh*, it was aptly titled, *"Shevirat ha-Kelim ve-Tikkunam"* ("The Shattering of the Vessels and Their Repair") by the editor, Rav Kook's disciple, Rabbi David Cohen, "the Nazirite."[1]

Recognizing the significance of this passage, the great researcher of Kabbalah, Yosef Avivi, devoted an entire chapter of his work, *Kabbalat ha-RAYaH*, to parsing it.[2] Avivi retitled the *pensée*, *"Kilkul ve-Tikkun,"* or "Corruption and Correction."[3] He then divided the material in two thematically, subtitling the first half, *"Mishtabrim ha-Kelim, Metim ha-Melakhim"* ("The Vessels Shatter, the Kings Die"), and the second half, *"Hesed 'Olamim ve-'Or Hadash"* ("Eternal Love and a New Light"). I have followed suit and divided the piece in two. The first half is Rav Kook's narrative of the shattering of the vessels; the second half is the story of their repair.

The account of the Kings of Edom occurs at the end of *Vayyishlah* (Genesis 36:31-39): "And these are the kings who reigned in the land of Edom before any king reigned over the Children of Israel...." There follow seven kings who reign and die (*"Vayyimlokh ... vayyamat"*), until finally, we come to the eighth king, Hadar, who reigns and does not die. This signifies that his reign is permanent. The previous seven kings, whose reign is fleeting and unstable, symbolize the previous world order which came crashing down, the *'Olam ha-Tohu*, the World of Chaos. Hadar will come to signify the new world order, noted for its stability and integrity, *'Olam ha-Tikkun*, the World of Establishment. The portion of the *Zohar* which treats this myth is called the *Idra*.[4] This is what we would call a creation myth. Roughly, it runs along the lines of the Midrash that God was "building worlds and destroying them."[5]

For Rav Kook, the mystery of the Death of the Kings is a trope for the death of the gods. As Rav Kook writes: "The vessels shatter, the kings die, the gods die...." (*"Mishtabrim ha-kelim, metim ha-melakhim, metim ha-elim...."*)

What does Rav Kook mean by the death of the gods? Is it merely that the names that mortals have assigned to the deity no longer serve their purpose, no longer signify what they were once intended to? The mystic loses patience with these signifiers that have worn thin. None of the names can satisfy the seeker's relentless quest for that which is ultimately beyond names. Thus, we have a breakdown of language.[6]

Or is it something deeper, something much more profound than the letters coming apart? Not only the various names of God come undone, but the gods themselves are dead to us. And here, various possibilities open up.

Is Rav Kook saying that the Kings of Edom were thought to be divine? Rav Kook may have had a historiosophical sense that the age of the gods had passed. Was Rav Kook familiar with the philosophy of history espoused in Vico's *Scienza Nuova* (1725)? Rav Kook's disciple, Rabbi David Cohen ("the Nazirite") speculated that Rabbi Moshe Hayyim Luzzatto had imbibed some of the theory of his countryman, Giambattista Vico (1668-1744).[7]

Or, might Rav Kook—like the modern Hebrew writers with whom he contended (Berdichevsky, Brenner, Tchernichovsky, even Zeitlin)—have been feeling the sting of Nietzsche's "death of God." Is *"metim ha-elim"* Rav Kook's Hebrew rendition of Zarathustra's barbed statement, *"Gott is tot"* ("God is dead")?[8]

In Rav Kook's writings (that have surfaced to date), there is but a single mention of Nietzsche's name. Juxtaposing Nietzsche to Shabbetai Tsevi, Rav Kook states the obvious, that "Nietzsche took leave of his senses."[9] However, in an all-important essay entitled, *"Yissurim Memarkim"* ("Purifying Tribulations"),[10] Rav Kook maintains that the modern phenomenon of atheism is a necessary stage in the spiritual evolution of mankind, whereby all the dross (Rav Kook employs the kabbalistic image of the *"kelipah,"* or outer shell) that has managed to creep into the conception of the *Ein Sof*, the Infinite, is purged. Playing on the Hebrew word for atheism, *"kefirah,"* and the word for frost, *"kefor,"* Rav Kook waxes poetic:

One who recognizes the inside of *kefirah*, sucks its honey, and returns it to the root of its holiness; and beholds the majesty of "the terrible ice" (*"ha-kerah ha-nora"*)[11]—"the frost of heaven" (*kefor shamayim*).[12]

In his poetic rendition of the Myth of the Primordial Kings, Rav Kook has given us to understand that the movement from *Tohu* to *Tikkun* is not linear but cyclical.[13] Time and time again the vessels (the divine names) are shattered, emptied of meaning, only to be repaired and reconstructed once again, which is to say, invested with new significance and infused with new divine soul. As Rav Kook expressed it, "as [man's] soul lifts higher and higher" (*"be-hinasé nishmato le-ma'alah le-ma'alah"*).

※○※

Though one cannot be certain, there appears to be Kantian influence in this musing of Rav Kook. We are struck by his ardent desire to break free of the phenomenon ("the light of God through the world, through existence, that penetrates into the eyes") and somehow latch on to the noumenon, the *Ding an sich* (*"emet she-hu le-'atsmo,"* or "truth in itself").[14]

In Lurianic Kabbalah, the *shevirah*, or shattering, occurred in the light of the eyes of *Adam Kadmon*.[15] For Rav Kook, the eyes are a symbol of the phenomena (as opposed to the noumena). For Rav Kook's disciple, "the Nazirite," the eye symbolizes Western thinking, which is visual, as opposed to the ear, which symbolizes

Hebrew prophetic acoustic logic (*ha-higayon ha-'Ivri ha-shim'i ha-nevu'i*).[16]

Before we embark on a study of this seminal *pensée*, I must state at the onset that I differ with Avivi in terms of general orientation. Where Avivi situates Rav Kook's script solidly within the tradition of Lurianic Kabbalah, I understand Rav Kook's *Sitz im Leben* to be much more eclectic than that of the "lion whelps" (*gurei ha-ARI*). While Rabbi Isaac Luria certainly provided the template, in the relatively free atmosphere created by Rav Kook's creative writing (which forever oscillates between the wavelengths of poetry and prose) there is room aplenty for improvisation and variations on the theme. To state it differently, though Lurianic Kabbalah is the mainstream which comes gushing through the sluice of Rav Kook's mystical experience, that stream is fed by many unnamed tributaries yet identifiable by telltale signs. A suggestive phrase, sometimes a single word, is sufficient to uncover a hidden sphere of influence. Rav Kook read widely and many souls are nested within this *neshamah kolelet*: Rabbi Moses Cordovero, Rabbi Isaac Luria, Abraham Herrera, the Vilna Gaon and his disciples, the Ba'al Shem Tov and his disciples. All these distinguished visitors to the Kook residence left their calling cards.[17]

I should like to discuss two important points left unaddressed by Avivi.

In the first half, from the stress that Rav Kook places upon the words *"mit-hader, mehader,"* it is apparent that he alludes to the eighth king of Edom, Hadar. But then, the very next sentence, *"Molekh ve-met"* ("Reigns and dies") is mystifying, for in Genesis 36:39, the eighth and last king of Edom, Hadar, does not die. This is crucial to the symbolism of the *Idra*.[18]

For lack of a better solution, I suggest that Rav Kook alludes to a profound teaching of his mentor in Kabbalah, Rabbi Shelomo Eliashov. Rabbi Eliashov (author of the series, *Leshem Shevo ve-Ahlamah*) lavished much attention on the discrepancies between the accounts in Genesis 36:31-39 and 1 Chronicles 1:43-51, chief of which may be the fact that in Chronicles, Hadad (not Hadar) dies.[19]

In the second half, Rav Kook writes the phrase *"hesed 'olamim."* Obviously, Avivi understood what a crucial part it plays, for he incorporated it in his subtitle. Yet he chalked it up to a *"kinnui mehuddash,"* or neologism, of Rav Kook.[20] In fact, in the text of the *Idra* (Zohar III, 142a), *"hesed"* (albeit *"hesed 'ila'ah,"* not *"hesed 'olamim"*) is of paramount importance in effecting *Tikkun*. Elsewhere, Avivi has discussed the significance of *hesed 'ila'ah* in this context.[21]

This *pensée*, fraught with kabbalistic symbolism and terminology, was included in A.M Habermann's collection of Rav Kook's poetry that appeared in the journal *Sinai*.[22] The poems (and their supposed dates of composition) were transmitted to Habermann by the Rav's son, Rabbi Tsevi Yehudah Kook. Our poem was dated "5672?" (i.e., "1912?").

Subsequently, Habermann's collection comprised the section of *Poems* in Ben Zion Bokser's anthology, *Abraham Isaac Kook*.[23] The translation which follows is my own. In a couple of instances, I noted Bokser's translation of a twist of language where I found it apposite.

BN

Text

I am full of love for God. I know that what I seek, what I love, is not called by any name. That which is more than all, more than the good, more than the essence, more than existence. And I love. And I say, I love God.

The light of *Ein Sof*[24] resides in the expression of the name, in the expression of "God," and in all the names and epithets that the heart of man conceives and utters, as his soul lifts higher and higher.

I cannot satisfy my soul with that love that comes from the knots of logic,[25] from searching the light of God through the world, through existence, that penetrates into the eyes.[26]

There are born in our souls, godly lights, many gods (*elohim rabbim*) in the vision of our spirit; one true God, "and before one"[27] in the depth of its truth.[28] God is revealed, controls us, conquers all our spirit, the spirit of all being. Wherever there is an idea, a feeling, a thought, a will; wherever there is exalted spiritual life—there a godly light reigns (*molekh*), rules (*moshel*),[29] conquers, sparkles, is beautiful (*mit-hader*), beautifies (*mehader*)[30] and glorifies,[31] enlivens, uplifts—all through the clarity of the light of existence. [The godly light] reigns and dies. The kingdom is limited, as long as it comes from the midst of the world, from the midst of existence.

Sometimes the light is overpowering. The will desires a light that is more refined, more inward, more truth in itself (*emet she-hu*

Shattered Vessels and Their Repair

le-'atsmo),[32] more mightful in the content of its inwardness. The light appears upon the vessel, the thought (*ha-mahshavah*)[33] upon existence—the situation cannot endure, the content does not fit. The vessels shatter, the kings die, the gods die. Their soul departs, taking flight to the heavens.[34] The bodies descend to the World of Separation (*'Alma de-Piruda*).[35] Existence stands naked, lonely, torn, scattered.

※○※

In [existence's] interior, there is hidden an eternal desire for a supernal light. In the broken vessels, an eternal love (*hesed 'olamim*) has deposited its light, its sparks. In every movement, in every life form, in every "is" (*yesh*), there is a spark, a spark of a spark (*nitsots shel nitsots*), finer than fine.

The inner light, the supernal light of God, builds and founds (*meyased*),[36] gathers in the dispersed, repairs worlds without end, arranges and pieces together. There is revealed an eternal kingdom (*malkhut*),[37] from the light of *Ein Sof* that is in the inwardness of the soul, from God to the world.[38] A new light is born,[39] the light of the splendor of the beauty (*hadar*)[40] of the Face of God (*p'nei El*).[41]

---

[1] See *Orot ha-Kodesh*, vol. 4, ed. Rabbis David Cohen and Yohanan Fried (Jerusalem: Mossad Harav Kook, 1990), pp. 400-401, "*Shevirat ha-Kelim ve-Tikkunam.*"
    Those exact words occur in the classic, *KaLaH Pithei Hokhmah* (attributed to Rabbi Moshe Hayyim Luzzatto), *petah* 37.
[2] See Yosef Avivi, *The Kabbalah of Rabbi A. I. Kook* (Hebrew) (Jerusalem: Yad

Ben-Zvi, 2018), vol. 3, chap. 39 (pp. 851-870).
3 This too is in conformity to *petah* 37 of the *KaLaH*. (See above note 1.)
4 The Greater *Idra*, or *Idra Rabbah*, is printed in *Naso*; the Lesser *Idra* or *Idra Zuta* is printed in *Ha'azinu*.

One notes with interest that Maimonides (*Guide* III, 50) considered the account of "the kings who reigned in the land of Edom" (Genesis 36:31) as belonging to the "mysteries of the Torah" *("sitrei Torah")* (Pines translation, p. 613). However, as is evident, Maimonides' understanding of this mystery is totally different from that of the *Zohar*.

5 *Genesis Rabbah* 3:7.
6 Of late, there is much speculation in literary circles that the Lurianic myth of the shattering of the vessels may have influenced the thinking of the celebrated critic Walter Benjamin (who would have been introduced to the imagery by his friend Gershom Scholem). The passage in question reads (in the translation of Harry Zohn):

> Fragments of a vessel that are to be glued together must match one another in the smallest details, although they need not be like one another. In the same way a translation, instead of imitating the sense of the original, must lovingly and in detail incorporate the original's way of meaning, thus making both the original and the translation recognizable as fragments of a greater language, just as fragments are part of a vessel.
>
> (Walter Benjamin, "The Task of the Translator," in *Walter Benjamin: Selected Writings*, vol. 1 [1913-1926], ed. Marcus Bullock and Michael W. Jennings [Cambridge, Mass.: Harvard University Press, 1996], p. 260)

See further Naomi Seidman, *Faithful Renderings: Jewish-Christian Difference and the Politics of Translation* (Chicago: University of Chicago Press, 2006), pp. 187-198.

7 See Rabbi David Cohen, *Kol ha-Nevu'ah* (Jerusalem: Mossad Harav Kook, 1979), p. 307, n. 452. (For some reason, the names of both Leibniz and Vico have been elided in that footnote.)
8 Friedrich Nietzsche, *Also Sprach Zarathustra (Thus Spoke Zarathustra)*, in *Nietzsche*, ed. Walter Kaufmann (New York, 1968), II, p. 202; IV, pp. 373, 375, 398, 399. See Bezalel Naor, "Rav Kook and Emmanuel Levinas on the 'Non-Existence' of God," in idem, *From a Kabbalist's Diary* (Spring Valley, NY: Orot, 2005), pp. 75-90.
9 Rabbi Abraham Isaac Hakohen Kook, *Kevatsim mi-Ketav Yad Kodsho*, vol. 1, ed. Boaz Ofen (Jerusalem, 5766/2006), *Pinkas "Aharon be-Boisk,"* par. 40 (p. 56).

Rabbi Tsevi Yehudah Hakohen Kook, on the other hand, mentioned Nietzsche by name on several occasions. See *Tsemah Tsevi* (Jerusalem, 1991), Letter 71 (p. 181); quoted in my introduction to *Orot* (Maggid, 2015), in the section entitled, "The Man Who Wore *Tefillin* All Day—And Nietzsche?" See ibid., pp. 63-64 and p. 450, n. 128.

Recently, there came to my attention that a line in a letter of Rabbi Tsevi Yehudah was censored. See *Tsemah Tsevi*, Letter 41 (p. 109). The letter, addressed to his father, Rav Kook (then in London), was written from Basel,

Switzerland in 1916. In the crucial passage, Rabbi Tsevi Yehudah quotes Rabbi Nahman of Breslov's famous statement regarding Erets Yisrael: *"Ich mein takeh dos Erets Yisroel mit die shtieber, mit die heizer."* ("I mean this Land of Israel with these homes, with these houses.") The omitted sentence reads: "In this respect, one may find basis for the comparison of [Rabbi Nahman] with Nietzsche, that was expressed in the new literature." See the facsimile on page 98 of Moshe Nahmani's *Shnei ha-Me'orot* (2019).

Probably, by "the new literature," Rabbi Tsevi Yehudah intended the writings of Hillel Zeitlin, who was wont to juxtapose Rabbi Nahman and Nietzsche. (Rabbi Tsevi Yehudah was very fond of Hillel Zeitlin, as was conveyed to this writer [BN] in oral conversation. See Rabbi Tsevi Yehudah's eulogy of Zeitlin, *"Zekher le-Mikdash ke-Hillel,"* which touches on Zeitlin's faithful presentation of Rabbi Nahman of Breslov. *"Zekher le-Mikdash ke-Hillel"* was reprinted in the collection of Rabbi Tsevi Yehudah's essays, *Li-Netivot Yisrael*, vol. 2 [Jerusalem, 1979], pp. 24-27.) Zeitlin saw similarities between Nietzsche's *Ubermensch* and Rabbi Nahman's *"Tsaddik,"* inasmuch as both enjoy a freedom denied lesser men. See Jonatan Meir's annotated edition of Zeitlin's 1910 essay, *"Rabbi Nahman mi-Breslov: Hayyav ve-Torato,"* chap. 16, p. 59, n. 117. In *Rabbi Nahman of Bratslav: World Weariness and Longing for the Messiah: Two Essays by Hillel Zeitlin*, Introduction and Critical Notes by Jonatan Meir (Hebrew) (Jerusalem, 2006). Meir noted that Aaron Zeitlin deleted the term *"adam ha-'elyon"* when he reissued his father's essay, because of its Nietzschean association.

[10] The essay was included in the collection *"Zer'onim,"* which first appeared in the literary journal *Ha-Tarbut ha-Yisraelit* in 1913. Subsequently, the chapters of *"Zer'onim"* were included in the 1950 edition of *Orot*. One may now consult the original texts that comprised *"Yissurim Memarkim"* in *Shemonah Kevatsim (Eight Journals)*.

Ben Zion Bokser translated the title of the essay as "The Pangs of Cleansing." See Bokser, *Abraham Isaac Kook* (Mahwah, NJ: Paulist Press, 1978), pp. 261-269.

[11] Ezekiel 1:22.

[12] Job 38:29.

Rabbi Abraham Isaac Hakohen Kook, *Orot* (Jerusalem: Mossad Harav Kook, 1963), p. 127; *Shemonah Kevatsim* 1:179.

This is comparable to Rabbi Nahman of Breslov's interpretation of Numbers 23:21, as transmitted by his disciple Rabbi Nathan Sternhartz:

> "and the shouting for the King is in him" *("u-teru'at melekh bo")*— *Teru'ah* is an expression of breaking, as it says, *"tero'em be-shevet barzel"* ("You shall break them with a rod of iron") (Psalms 2:9). This is to say that when we break *kefirot* (denials), then the King is in it. In other words, we discover the King, blessed be He, even within the denials themselves, for even in the denials themselves is garbed His vitality, blessed be He.
> (*Sihot ha-RaN*, par. 102)

Rav Kook gratefully acknowledged receipt of the work *Sihot ha-Ran* (from his son Tsevi Yehudah), which he read. See Moshe Nahmani, *Shnei ha Me'orot* (2019), pp. 93-94. On page 25, Nahmani wrote that the letter of acknowledgment was written in 1906 (when Tsevi Yehudah was fifteen).

[13] One might glean this sense from reading Rabbi Yitzhak Eizik Haver's *Pithei She'arim*, Part One, *Netiv 'Olam ha-Tikkun*, chap. 5 (66a): "Close to the end of the sixth millennium, evil will grow very strong... and then there will reincarnate sparks of the *'Olam ha-Tohu*, the brazen-faced of the generation who are from the side of the Mixed Multitude *('Erev Rav)*; and heresy and informing will wax; and 'impudence *(hutspah)* will increase' [m. Sotah 9:15]." This reference was provided in the notes to Rav Kook's essay, "Neshamot shel *'Olam ha-Tohu*" ("Souls of the World of Chaos"); see *Orot* (Jerusalem: Mossad Harav Kook, 1963), p. 181.

[14] Rav Kook discusses the Kantian revolution in philosophy in a letter to Samuel Alexandrov of Bobruisk, published in *Iggerot ha-RAYaH*, vol. 1 (Jerusalem: Mossad Harav Kook, 1962), Letter 44 (pp. 47-48); available in the English translation of Tzvi Feldman, *Rav A.Y. Kook: Selected Letters* (Ma'aleh Adumim, 1986), p. 92.

[15] Rabbi Hayyim Vital, *'Ets Hayyim* 8:1.

[16] See Rabbi David Cohen, *Kol ha-Nevu'ah*, pp. 225-226 ("*Shevirat ha-Kelim ve-Tikkunam*").

Cf. Rabbi Tsevi Elimelech of Dynów, *Igra de-Pirka*, chap. 297 (who equates "seeing" with *hakirah* or philosophical investigation, as opposed to simple faith, symbolized by "hearing"); quoted in Rabbi David Yitzhak Eizik Rabinowitz of Skolya-Vienna-Brooklyn, *Mekor ha-Berakhah* (Brooklyn, 1967), Introduction, 4a, and *Hashmatah* from Introduction, 11a.

[17] Rav Kook's eclectic approach was attested to by the Lithuanian kabbalist Rabbi Shelomo Eliashov, author of *Leshem Shevo ve-Ahlamah*:

> Once in conversation, the name of Rav Kook came up. Rabbi Shelomo [Eliashov] said to me: "Just as there are different lines *(shitot)* in Halakhah, so there are lines in Kabbalah, as well. RABaD [of *Posquières*] has a specific way and so does Nahmanides. The line of Rabbi Isaac Luria is different from that of Rabbi Moses Cordovero. And so throughout the generations: Rabbi Menahem Azariah of Fano, Rabbi Moshe Hayyim Luzzatto, the Vilna Gaon. However, Rav Kook encompassed and knew all the lines together, and in regard to him, one can say: 'No mystery escapes him.'"
>
> (Rabbi Aryeh Levine, quoted in Rabbi Moshe Tsevi Neriyah, *Sihot ha-RAYaH* [Tel-Aviv, 1979], p. 164)

The Jerusalemite saint (*"Tsaddik Yerushalmi"*) Rabbi Aryeh Levine was very close to Rabbi Shelomo Eliashov. Eventually, Rabbi Levine's daughter was wed to Rabbi Eliashov's grandson, Rabbi Yosef Shalom Elyashiv. (Rav Kook was the *shadkhan*, or matchmaker, and *mesader kiddushin*, which is to say that he officiated at their wedding ceremony.)

[18] See *Idra Rabba* in *Zohar* III, 142a, and *Idra Zuta* in *Zohar* III, 292a.

[19] See Rabbi Shelomo Eliashov, *Sefer ha-De'ah* [=*Hu Derushei 'Olam ha-Tohu*] (Piotrków, 1912), Part 1, *ma'amar kelali*, par. 1 (1a); and Part 2, *derush* 1, 2:3-3:4 (4a-5b). See also Rabbi Reuven Margaliyot, *Nitsutsei Zohar* to *Zohar* III, 142a (*Idra Rabba*), note 6; Rabbi Menahem Menkhin Heilprin, *Hagahot u-Be'urim* to Rabbi Hayyim Vital, *'Ets Hayyim* (Warsaw, 1891), 10:3 (*Mahadura Tinyana*), note 9; and the ingenious solution of Malbim, 1 Chronicles

1:43. And see Rabbi Gedaliah Levi, *"Kibbuts Derushei ha-Melakhim de-Mitu,"* in Rabbi Jacob Tsemah, *Kol be-Ramah,* ed. Eliyahu Attiah (Jerusalem: Makhon B'nei Yissachar, 2001), p. 232ff.

[20] *The Kabbalah of Rabbi A. I. Kook,* p. 864.

[21] See Yosef Avivi, *Kabbalat ha-GRA* (Jerusalem, 1993), p. 85.

The Vilna Gaon juxtaposes the Idra's *"hesed 'ila'ah"* to the verse in Psalms 89:3: *"'Olam hesed yibaneh."* See *Sifra di-Tseni'uta* with *Be'ur ha-GRA,* ed. Samuel Luria (Vilna, 1882), chap. 1 (4a-b). Rav Kook's neologism, *"hesed 'olamim,"* is referential to the verse in Psalms.

[22] A.M. Habermann, *"Shirat Harav," Sinai,* 17 (5705/1945).

[23] See Abraham Isaac Kook, ed. B.Z. Bokser (Mahwah, NJ: Paulist Press, 1978), pp. 367-386. Our poem appears there on pages 373-374.

[24] Literally, "Without End," "Infinite." The kabbalistic term for the deity.

[25] Hebrew, *"kishrei ha-higayon."* Ben Zion Bokser translated loosely, "the web of logic."

There is the remote possibility that this phrase is an echo of the *Zohar*'s play on the verse in Song of Songs 7:6: *"melekh assur ba-rehatim"* ("the King is bound by the tresses")—*"bi-rehitei moha"* ("by the channels of the mind"). The *Zohar* (and later *Tikkunei Zohar*) refer to the phylacteries (*tefillin*) by which God is, as it were, bound. (The allusion is to the channels [*rehatim*], or troughs of water, of Jacob in Genesis 30:38.) Cf. *Leviticus Rabbah* 31:4 and *Song of Songs Rabbah* to Song 7:6 (*"rehitin shel Ya'akov Avinu"*).

See *Hakdamat Sefer ha-Zohar, Zohar* I, 14a (*"kashir 'ihu ve-'ahid be-'inun batei"*); *Zohar* III, 136a (*Idra Rabba*); 269b; 293a-b (*Idra Zuta*); *Tikkunim* appended to *Tikkunei Zohar 'im Be'ur ha-GRA* (Vilna, 1867), *tikkuna shetita'ah* (169a); Rabbi Shneur Zalman of Liadi, *Tanya, Iggeret ha-Teshuvah,* chap. 7 (96b).

Remarkably, this image of God bound by phylacteries was appropriated by the Hebrew poet Shaul Tchernichovsky in his poem "Before the Statue of Apollo" (1899). Tchernichovsky bemoans the fact that "the people has grown old—its God grown old with it." He calls for the "light of *Yah* and life" (*"'or-Yah ve-hayyim"*). The last two lines deliver the punch. Tchernichovsky longs for

> God, God of the conquerors of Canaan by storm—
> And they bound Him in straps of phylacteries
> (*va-ya'asruhu bi-retsu'ot shel tefillin*).

Written at the *fin siècle* back in Odessa (and Heidelberg), this sentiment (shall we call it Nietzschean?) would resonate in secular circles for generations to come. Eventually, there arose in Israel a movement known as "Canaanites" (*"Kena'anim"*). Like the poet Tchernichovsky, these "neo-Canaanites" sought to return to a pre-Israelite rootedness in the land and nature. Their neo-pagan deity would be freed of the fetters of Judaic religion (symbolized by the "straps of *tefillin*").

It is more than likely that Rav Kook's famous poem *"Lahashei Havayah"* ("Whispers of Existence"), first published in the journal *"Ha-Tarbut ha-Yisra-elit"* in 1913, was in some sense a direct response to Tchernichovsky's poem. Rav Kook too hears the call of life (*"hayyim"*) emitting from the Land, but the Land issues a stern warning against those who come to her with impure intentions. She spurns suitors who are aroused by her beauty to paganism ("a foreign fire, *"esh zarah"*): "Get away from me! Get! To you I am forbidden." She accepts only that suitor who is filled with the light of holiness; in his ear she will whisper her secret, the mysteries of existence: "My chosen, to you I am permitted." See Avi Batt, *"Lahashei ha-Havayah,"* available at: https://bmj.org.il/wp-content/uploads/2019/12/2.51.BAT_.pdf

It is told that Rav Kook's son, Rabbi Tsevi Yehudah Kook once encountered Shaul Tchernichovsky aboard a ship voyaging from Europe to Erets Yisrael. Tchernichovsky attempted to engage Rabbi Tsevi Yehudah in conversation. Tchernichovsky pressed, saying, "Doesn't your father attempt to bridge the gap between *kodesh* and *hol*, between the sacred and the secular?" Young Rabbi Kook shot back: "Yes, indeed, but not the gap between *kodesh* and *tum'ah*, between the sacred and the impure!"

26 According to Lurianic Kabbalah, the *shevirah* (shattering) occurred in the light of the eyes of *Adam Kadmon*. See *'Ets Hayyim* 8:1; Rabbi David Cohen, *Kol ha-Nevu'ah*, pp. 225-226.

27 Hebrew, *"ve-lifnei ehad."* A quote from *Sefer Yetsirah* 1:2: "And before one (*ve-lifnei ehad*), what do you count?"

28 In Lurianic Kabbalah, the shattering of the vessels produces a diffuse state of *"reshut ha-rabbim"* (the public domain); after the *Tikkun*, this is transformed into a *"reshut ha-yahid"* (private domain; literally "domain of the one"). See Rabbi Yitzhak Eizik Haver, *Pithei She'arim*, Part One (Warsaw, 1888; photo offset Tel-Aviv, 1964), *Netiv Shevirat ha-Kelim*, chap. 13 (54a); Avivi, p. 855. Further in *Netiv Shevirat ha-Kelim*, chap. 15 (56a), the author returns to the theme of the *reshut ha-rabbim*, juxtaposing it to the saying of the Rabbis (*Hullin* 60b) "that they desired many gods" (*"she-'ivvu le-'elohot harbeh"*).

29 The Vilna Gaon differentiated between the Hebrew synonyms *melekh* and *moshel*, as follows. *Melekh* is one who rules with the consent of the people; *moshel* is one who rules by force, against the will of the people. See *Be'ur ha-Gra* to *Sefer Mishlei*, edited by his disciple Rabbi Menahem Mendel of Shklov, Proverbs 27:27. See too the commentary of the Gaon's son, Rabbi Abraham, to Psalms 89:10, 95:1; in *Sefer Tehillim 'im peirush...Be'er Avraham*, ed. Samuel Luria (Warsaw, 1887), 81b, 86.

The Gaon was preceded in this differentiation by Rabbi Abraham Ibn Ezra to Genesis 37:8 (also quoted and rejected by Nahmanides ad loc.). See also Rabbi Isaac Dov Baer Schneerson of Liadi, *Siddur 'im Peirush MaHaRID* (Berdichev, 1913; photo offset Kefar Habad, 1991), vol. 2, *Sha'ar ha-Hanukkah*, s.v. *Ha-Malokh timlokh 'aleinu*, 178a.

It is possible that Rav Kook was influenced by Maimonides' reading of the Kings of Edom, whereby they were, in fact, foreign tyrants who imposed their rule upon the nation of Edom. See *Guide of the Perplexed* III, 50 (Pines translation, p. 615).

30 *Mit-hader* and *mehader* both conjure up the eighth king of Edom, Hadar (Genesis 36:39).

Rabbi Tsevi Elimelekh Spira of Dynów explained the term *"mehadrin"* in regard to the kindling of the Hanukkah lights (*b. Shabbat* 21b) as an allusion to Hadar, the eighth of the primordial Kings, who represents *Tikkun* and the ascent of the sparks from the shattering. See *B'nei Yissachar, Ma'amrei Hodshei Kislev-Tevet*, *ma'amar* 3, par. 27. So too Rabbi Shelomo Hakohen of Radomsk, *Tif'eret Shelomo 'al Mo'adim* (Jerusalem, 1992), *Le-Zot Hanukkah*, s.v. *Zot hanukkat ha-mizbe'ah*, 165b; Rabbi Yitzhak Dov Baer Schneerson of Liadi, *Siddur 'im Peirush MaHaRID*, vol. 2, *Sha'ar ha-Hanukkah*, s.v. *Ha-Mehadrin*, 177b; Rabbi Shemariah Noah Schneerson of Bobruisk, *Shemen la-Ma'or* (Kefar Habad, 1964), *Hanukkah*, 58a.

[31] Elsewhere, Rav Kook expressed his glowing admiration for the Spanish work of Abraham Herrera, *Puerta del Cielo*, known to Rav Kook in Rabbi Isaac Aboab da Fonseca's Hebrew translation as *Sha'ar ha-Shamayim*. See *Pinkesei ha-RAYaH*, vol. 4, ed. Z.M. Levin and B.Z. Kahana-Shapira (Jerusalem, 5777/2017), *Pinkas ha-Dapim* 1:34 (pp. 88-92). My English translation of that piece appears in the present collection of essays under the title, "The Hasidism of Rav Kook."

In *Iggerot ha-RAYaH*, vol. 2 (Jerusalem: Mossad Harav Kook, 1961), Letter 447 (p. 91), Rav Kook includes Herrera's *Sha'ar ha-Shamayim* in a roster of kabbalistic works that speak of Erets Yisrael and the redemption. The footnote refers the reader to *Sha'ar ha-Shamayim* 6:9.

In *Iggerot ha-RAYaH*, vol. 3 (Jerusalem: Mossad Harav Kook, 1965), Letter 896 (p. 208), Rav Kook quotes a teaching from Herrera's other work, *Beit Elohim*, in order to drive home a point to Rabbi Shemariah Menashe Hakohen Adler. The subject is the utter indescribability of *Ein Sof*. (See *Beit Elohim* [Jerusalem, 2007], gate 1, chap. 3 [p. 6].)

Totally unrelated to King Hadar, Herrera characterized the *sefirot* as *hadar* in the sense of beauty. As explained by Yosha, Herrera was influenced in this regard by Marsilio Ficino's commentary on Plato's *Symposium*. See *Sha'ar ha-Shamayim* (Jerusalem, 2006), *ma'amar* 7, chap. 6 (pp. 163-165); Nissim Yosha, *Myth and Metaphor: Abraham Cohen Herrera's Philosophic Interpretation of Lurianic Kabbalah* (Hebrew) (Jerusalem: Magnes Press, 1994), pp. 256-257.

[32] Bokser translated, "the truth as it is in itself." Rav Kook's usage of the term is reminiscent of Kant's *Ding an sich*.

On the other hand, the thought occurs to this writer that the phrase *"emet she-hu le'atsmo"* may betray Breslov influence. During the years in Jaffa, Rav Kook took a keen interest in Breslov Hasidism. In Rabbi Nahman of Breslov's *Likkutei MOHaRaN* I, 9 (*"Tehomot yekhasyumu"*) we read:

> Know, that all is according to the greatness of the truth, for the main light is the Holy One, blessed be He, and the Holy One, blessed be he, is the essence of truth (*'etsem ha-emet*), and the main longing of God is only for truth.

The term *"'etsem ha-emet"* echoes in the disciple, Rabbi Nathan's *Likkutei Tefillot* (chap. 9). (Regarding *Likkutei Tefillot*, see the Letters of Rabbi Tsevi Yehudah Hakohen Kook, *Tsemah Tsevi* [Jerusalem, 1991], p. 26.) The themes in this Torah recur in *Likkutei MOHaRaN* I, 112 (*"Tsohar ta'aseh la-teivah"*). There we find the term *"emet ha-amiti"* ("the true truth"). There too, Rabbi Nahman issues the bold challenge: "One should pray all one's days that one merit once in one's lifetime to speak one word of truth before the LORD!"

In Rabbi Nathan's *Likkutei Halakhot, Hil. Hanukkah, halakhah* 6 (which parallels *Likkutei MOHaRaN* I,9), the thought is given this expression: "And truth is the light of the LORD Himself" (*"Ve-Emet hu 'or Hashem, yitbarakah, be-'atsmo"*) (par.1). Finally, the ascending number of Hanukkah candles is interpreted symbolically: "Every day the light increases, for every day the truth illuminates more" (par. 9).

[33] Rav Kook may be referencing the Cordoveran interpretation of the *Idra*. As opposed to Rabbi Isaac Luria's Kabbalah which tends to the mythic, his predecessor, Rabbi Moses Cordovero, developed an intellectual approach to Kabbalah. Specifically, the death of the primordial kings is viewed as a description of the intradivine intellectual process, whereby a thought was aborted. As Rabbi Moses Cordovero points out: "Do not say that they died, rather they were suppressed" (Aramaic, *"its-tan'u,"* literally, "hidden away"). Furthermore, Cordovero understands *"melakhim"* in this context as *"'etsot,"* advice or counsel, as in the Aramaic verse in Daniel 4:24: *"milki yishpar 'alakh."* These divine thoughts (Cordovero coins the term, *"kohot mahshaviyot,"* "thought potentialities") are fleeting, as they are subject to revision. See Rabbi Moses Cordovero, *Elimah* (Lvov, 1881), 4:1:20 (109b-d). Cf. idem, *Shi'ur Komah* (Warsaw, 1883), s.v. *boneh 'olamot u-maharivan* (65c-66a). Earlier, in his magnum opus, *Pardes Rimonim*, Cordovero translates the Aramaic *its-tan'u* into Hebrew, *ne'elmu*; see *Pardes Rimonim* (Munkatch, 1906?; photo offset Jerusalem, 1962), 5:4 (25d).

Rav Kook, as his mentor in Kabbalah, Rabbi Shelomo Eliashov (author of *Leshem Shevo ve-Ahlamah*) made ample use of Cordoveran Kabbalah, as well as Lurianic Kabbalah (as opposed to those kabbalists who held that the latter had obsoleted the former). See Bezalel Naor, *Kana'uteh de-Pinhas* (Spring Valley, NY: Orot, 2013), pp. 25, 106-107.

(An aside: one speculates that the Cordoveran term *"kohot mahshaviyot"* and the like later influenced the development of Nathan of Gaza's theology of *'or she-yesh bo mahshavah* versus *'or she-'ein bo mahshavah*.)

[34] Cf. the Vilna Gaon's Hebrew description of the death of the kings: "...Their soul returned above to their place (*ve-nishmatam hazrah lema'alah bi-mekomam*), and their vessels below, which is the mystery of 'death'" (*Sifra di-Tseni'uta* with *Be'ur ha-GRA*, ed. Samuel Luria [Vilna, 1882], chap. 1 [11a]). See also Rabbi Yitzhak Eizik Haver, op. cit., *Netiv Shevirat ha-Kelim*, chap. 29 (62b).

[35] A kabbalistic term.

[36] An allusion to the *sefirah* of *Yesod*. In the Vilna Gaon's commentary to *Sifra di-Tseni'uta*, Hadar is equated with *'Ateret ha-Yesod*. See *Sifra di-Tseni'uta* with *Be'ur ha-GRA*, chap. 1 (10a).

[37] An allusion to the *sefirah* of *Malkhut*. In *Idra Zuta* (printed in *Zohar* III, 292a), Hadar is equated with *"peri 'ets hadar."* In the *Zohar*, *"peri 'ets hadar"* (Leviticus 23:40), identified by the Sages as the *etrog*, or citron, symbolizes *Malkhut*. For the Vilna Gaon's understanding of this passage in the *Idra*, see the note above. (The Gaon differentiates between the *Malkhut di-Ze'ir Anpin* and *Malkhut de-'Eser Sefirot*, which is to say that Hadar is the *Malkhut* of *Ze'ir Anpin* [i.e., *'Ateret ha-Yesod*], but not the *Malkhut* of the Ten *Sefirot*.)

In the Gaon's understanding, there is no *Malkhut* per se in the World of *Tohu*. The revelation of *Malkhut* (*gillui Malkhut*) is the new dimension of the World of *Tikkun*. For the symbolism of this statement, see Rabbi Yitzhak Eizik Haver, *Pithei She'arim, Netiv Shevirat ha-Kelim*, chap. 18 (58a).

[38] A letter written by Tsevi Yehudah Kook (aged nineteen) to Rabbi Ya'akov Moshe Harlap, might shed some light on the direction his father Rav Kook is taking in our *pensée*:

In regard to what I wrote about the concept of good and the concept of love from the perspective of the height of universality (*kelaliyut*), it seems to me that this is the true intention of the saying of the Sages, of blessed memory: "Great is the power of the prophets, that they compare the form to its Creator." (But I still do not know whether this fits properly the context of the words, for I have forgotten their location.)

In the eyes of many, these words are inscrutable. What is the comparison of the form to the Creator? On the contrary, the prophets compare the Creator to the form, not the opposite. Also, the "greatness" is not so understandable.

But in truth, this is the main greatness of prophets, that they do not scholastically infer from the creation to the Creator—which is merely the way of human investigation—rather, since their soul ascends to the heights of the heavens of the LORD, from the higher awareness of the might of the LORD; [from] the awareness of the universality (*kelaliyut*) of existence and the love; in short, from their proximity to the LORD, to the Creator, from this, precisely from this, they are able to understand and recognize, to view and know the form, the creation....

Precisely from their ascent to the "higher worlds" and from their recognition and love of the Creator, the source of the form, they come to love and recognize the form. This is above the aspect of "From my flesh, I shall see God" [Job 19:26]. The opposite: From the vision of God, I shall know my flesh. Only from recognition and love of the divinity, the universality (*kelaliyut*) and the eternal, will the individual, finite existents come to [the prophets'] awareness and love.... Without the light of God that appears within its midst, life remain a riddle without solution, something lacking all attraction.

So, once again: They compare the form to the Creator; the creation corresponds for them to the system of God, the Creator; the specifics correspond for them to the generalities; "Jerusalem below" corresponds to "Jerusalem above" [*b. Ta'anit* 5a]....—This is the special value of the prophets; this is their great power.

(Rabbi Tsevi Yehudah Hakohen Kook, *Tsemah Tsevi* [Jerusalem, 1991], Letter 9 [datelined "Jaffa, 16 Av 5670," i.e., 1910], pp. 24-25)

Like his father, Rabbi Tsevi Yehudah believed that rather than proceeding from the world to God ("from searching the light of God through the world, through existence, that penetrates into the eyes"), as do the philosophers, those truly close to God (i.e., the prophets) are able to proceed "from God to the world."

The Midrash quoted by young Tsevi Yehudah ("Great is the power of the prophets, that they compare the form to its Creator") is from *Genesis Rabbah* 27:1. For a recent discussion of the import of the Midrash attributed to Rabbi Yudan, see Yair Lorberbaum, "Anthropomorphisms in Early Rabbinic Literature: Maimonides and Modern Scholarship," in *Traditions of Maimonideanism*, ed. Carlos Fraenkel (Leiden: Brill, 2009), pp. 334-340.

[39] The new light is the new name *MaH* (*millui de-Alphin*); see *'Ets Hayyim* 10:2 (*Mahadura Tinyana*); Avivi, p. 869.

[40] An allusion to Hadar, the eighth king of Edom (Genesis 36:39), who, in the kabbalistic interpretation of the *Idra*, represents *Tikkun* (Repair).

[41] Cf. Genesis 32:31: "And Jacob called the name of the place *Peniel*, 'for I have seen God face to face, and my life was preserved.'"

Rabbi Yitzhak Eizik Haver discusses the light of Peniel, based on the teachings of the Gaon (in his commentary to the *Heikhalot* in *Zohar, Pekudei*). *'Or Peniel* has the numerical value of *malbush* and of *hashmal* (378). See *Pithei She'arim, Netiv Shevirat ha-Kelim*, chap. 16 (f.56); Elijah Gaon of Vilna, *Yahel 'Or*, ed. Naphtali Herz Halevi of Bialystok (Vilna, 1882), *Be'ur ha-Heikhalot, Heikhal* 2 (*Zohar* II, 247a), s.v. *hakha kaymin kol inun levushin*: "*Hashmal, Orpeniel*, and *malbush* all have one [numerical] amount" (bottom 20a). And See Rabbi Reuven Margaliyot, *Mal'akhei 'Elyon* (Jerusalem: Mossad Harav Kook, 1988), s.v. *Orpeniel*, pp. 10-11.

VIII

RAV KOOK: HISTORICAL STUDIES

The Mysterious "Meir":
Rav Kook's Missing Student[1]

Recent years have seen a breakthrough regarding the elusive identity of "Monsieur Chouchani," the mysterious vagabond who, in the capacity of mentor, exerted such an incredibly profound effect upon the Nobel-laureate novelist Elie Wiesel as well as the philosopher Emmanuel Levinas in the post-war, post-Holocaust years in France. I am referring to the identification of Chouchani as none other than Hillel Pearlman, an early student of Rav Kook in his short-lived Jaffa *Yeshivah*.[2]

Pivotal to the identification (which we shall not enter into here) is a letter that Rav Kook penned from exile in St. Gallen, Switzerland, to two students of the *Yeshivah*. We offer the letter in our English translation:

> With the help of God
>
> 6 Tishri 5676 [i.e., 1915]
>
> A good conclusion[3] to my beloved soul-friends, each man according to his blessing,[4] the dear "groom," the Rabbi, sharp and encyclopedic, crowned with rare qualities and character traits, our teacher, Rabbi **Hillel**, may his light shine; and the dear "groom," exceptional in Torah and awe of heaven, modest and crowned with rare character traits, Mr. **Meir**, may his light shine.

Peace! Peace! Blessing with abundant love.

My dear friends, for too, too long I delayed the response to your dear letter. In your goodness you will give me the benefit of the doubt. Only as a result of the preoccupation brought on by the pain of exile and the heart's longing produced by the general situation (God have mercy), were things put off.

Many thanks to you, our dear Mr. **Meir**, for your detailed letter, whereby you deigned in your goodness to write to us in detail the state of our family members in the Holy Land, especially the state of the girls, may they live.[5] May the LORD repay your kindness and gladden your soul with every manner of happiness and success, and may we together rejoice in the joy of the Land of Delight upon the holy soil, when the LORD will grant salvation to His world, His land and His inheritance, speedily, speedily, soon.

And you, my beloved Mr. **Hillel**, all power to you for your dear words, upright words, pronounced with proper feeling and the longing of a pure heart. We are standing opposite a great and powerful vision previously unknown in human history. There is no doubt that changes of great value are hidden in the depths of this world vision. There is also no doubt that the hand of Israel through the spirit, the voice of Jacob,[6] must be revealed here. Far be it from us to treat as false all the deeds and events, the longing for general life, that we experienced the past years. As much as they are mixed with impurities; as much as they failed to assume their proper form, their living description, their true life—we see in them in the final analysis, correspondence to the holy vision, unmistakable signs that things are happening according to a higher plan. The hand of the LORD holds them, to pave a way for His people, weary from its multitudinous troubles, and also for His world, crouching under the weight of confused life.

It is certainly difficulty at this time to trace which is the way of the process, but in this respect we may be certain: The terrible wandering of such great and essential portions of our nation residing in Eastern Europe, where the spiritual life of Israel is concentrated, and the necessity of rebuilding physically and spiritually new communities, educational institutions and Torah academies—will bring numerous new results, certainly for good. From those new winds that have been blowing in our world for the past half-century and more, something is to be derived, if we can purify them, erecting them upon foundations of purity and holiness. The opinions and longing for spiritual and physical building of Israel; the mighty desire of building the Land and the Nation, despite external and internal obstacles; the visions tucked away in the hearts of numerous thinkers to uplift the horn of Israel and its spirit, to bind together the strength of life with the sanctity of the soul, the talent of understanding with the depth of faith, immediate implementation with longing for salvation—all these are things that will bear fruit, and the Master of Wars, blessed be He, will grow from all of them His salvation.[7]

One thing we know for certain, that we are invited to great projects: philosophic projects; literary and publicistic projects; practical and social projects; projects at the interior of eternal life and projects of temporal and secular life; projects that remain within the border of Israel; and projects that overflow and touch the streams of life of the world at large and their many relations with the world of Israel, which was, is, and will be a blessing to all the families of earth,[8] as the word of the LORD to our ancestor [Abraham] in antiquity.

My beloved, I request that you write to us whatever is [happening] to you, your situation in detail, whether in spiritual or material matters; whatever you imagine might interest us, whether of private or public affairs. For all I will be exceedingly grateful to you, with God's help.

I am your fast friend, looking for your happiness and success, and your return together with all our scattered people to the holy soil in happiness and success. May the LORD bless you with all good and extend to you peace and blessing and a good conclusion, as is your wish and the wish of one who seeks your peace and good all the days, longing for the salvation of the LORD,

Abraham Isaac Ha[Kohen] K[ook][9]

MISSING STUDENT

In order to understand the contents of the letter, the better to grasp the identities of its two recipients, we must first acquaint ourselves with the circumstances in which it was written.

For one decade, from 1904 to 1914, Abraham Isaac Hakohen Kook served as Rabbi of the port city of Jaffa (precursor to Tel-Aviv). During those years in Jaffa he taught a select group of students in a *yeshivah* of his own making. (This *yeshivah* is not to be confused with the famous Yeshivah Merkaz Harav founded by Rav Kook in Jerusalem in the early 1920s.) In summer of 1914, Rav Kook set sail for Europe to attend the *Knessiyah Gedolah* or World Congress of the recently organized Agudath Israel movement. Due to the outbreak of World War One (on Tish'ah be-Av of that year), the conference was cancelled. Unable to return to Jaffa, Rav Kook remained stranded in Europe for the duration of the War, first in St. Gallen, Switzerland, where his needs were provided for by a sympathetic Mr. Abraham Kimhi, and later in London, where Rav Kook served as Rabbi of the Mahzikei Hadat synagogue in London's East End.[10]

Much concerning the Jaffa *yeshivah* remains shrouded in mystery. No archive remains of this short-lived institution.[11] Thus we are pretty much left in the dark as to the curriculum,[12] enrollment, and even location. Fortunately, significant headway has been made in this direction in the recent article by Moshe Nahmani of the Yeshivat Hesder of Ramat Gan, *"She'areha Ne'ulim—Yeshivat Harav Kuk be-Yaffo"* ("Closed Gates—The *Yeshivah* of Rabbi Kook in Jaffa").[13] Through painstaking research, the author was able to put together a list of students. Researchers had no difficulty identifying the "Hillel" of the letter as Hillel Pearlman. It was merely a case of "connecting the dots."[14] But Nahmani was baffled by the "Meir" who is one of two co-addressees in our letter.[15]

I believe that I have solved the mystery of the missing Meir. In 1977, I was a visitor to the home of Rabbi Mayer Goldberg of Oakland, California. Rabbi Goldberg was a successful businessman (at that time in real estate) and a Jewish philanthropist, especially supportive of *yeshivot* or rabbinical academies. Rabbi Goldberg revealed to me that he had studied under Rav Kook in Jaffa.[16] He then went on to share with me a teaching of Rav Kook that I have since repeated on many an occasion. He said that before being exposed to Rav Kook's teaching, the term *"yir'at shamayim"* ("fear of heaven") had only a restrictive, narrowing connotation. Rav Kook explained the term in a totally different light. By the term *"yir'at shamayim,"* Rav Kook conveyed to his young listeners the vastness, the enormity, the infinitude of the universe.

Reading Moshe Nahmani's article concerning Rav Kook's *yeshivah* in Jaffa, and his bafflement as to the full identity of the student named simply "Meir," I recalled my meeting with Rabbi Mayer Goldberg. I resolved that during my forthcoming visit to the East Bay area (as it has come to be known) I would meet with the late Rabbi's children to learn from them more details of their father's involvement with Rav Kook. What emerged from our discussion (conducted on February 14, 2013) is the following reconstruction of events.

Missing Student

Mayer Vevrick was born circa 1890 "near Kiev."[17] At some time before World War One, Mayer boarded a ship from Odessa to Jaffa. In the words of his daughter Rachel Landes:

> Once he arrived in Jaffa, he sought out the yeshiva of Rabbi Kook. Rabbi Avraham Kook was a world renowned scholar and it was there my father headed to study further. He became a "hasid," a follower of the Rabbi, and thoroughly enjoyed his studies there. He lived in Rabbi Kook's home.[18] He studied Talmud...with Rashi and the commentaries, for many hours a day with the other young men. These were the happiest days of his life, with uninterrupted Torah study, and the joy of learning with Rabbi Kook. Mayer adopted [Rabbi] Kook's philosophy and was guided by it for the rest of his life.[19]

In World War One, Mayer left Jaffa for Egypt. There he was held by the British in an internment camp. Eventually, with some ingenuity, he was able to book passage on a boat to the United States.[20] Initially he resided on the East Coast. In Boston, he received a *ketav semikhah* (writ of ordination) from Rabbi Joseph M. Jacobson. The *semikhah* was written by Rabbi Jacobson on the spot in recognition of Mayer's knowledge of Torah.[21] Later, Rabbi Mayer relocated to the West Coast, first to Washington State and finally to California.[22]

What becomes apparent from the letter of Rav Kook is that "Meir" remained in Jaffa after Rav Kook's departure for Europe (followed almost immediately by the outbreak of World War One), and thus was in a position to give the Rav an update on the welfare of his daughters left behind in Jaffa. What also becomes apparent is that in the fall of 1915, "Meir" and his companion Hillel were no longer in the Land of Israel but somewhere else, for in his concluding remarks Rav Kook expresses the wish that they return to the Holy Land. This is consistent with Rabbi Goldberg's biography, whereby he (along with countless other Jews of Erets Israel) was forced to flee the Holy Land at that time.[23] This also coincides with the reconstructed biography of Hillel (Pearlman). Both students of Rav Kook, Hillel (Pearlman) and Meir (Goldberg) ended up in the United States in World War One. Whereas we are being told that Hillel (Pearlman) later left the United States for Europe and North Africa, reinventing himself as the mysterious "Monsieur Chouchani," Mayer Goldberg remained in the United States.

Rabbi Mayer Goldberg passed away on September 25, 1992, a centenarian.[24] Shortly before his passing, Rabbi Goldberg had published in Jerusalem a collection of kabbalistic insights (culled from his marginalia in the books of his library), entitled *Margaliyot shel Torah (Pearls of Torah)*. Much of the material in the book is attributed to the kabbalistic work *Yalkut Re'uveni*.[25] My attention was riveted to an unattributed piece, which would appear to originate with Rabbi Mayer Goldberg himself:

In Exodus 2:12 we read that Moses slew the Egyptian (who was beating a Hebrew) and buried him in the sand. The Hebrew words are: *"Vayyakh et ha-mitsri vayyitmenehu ba-hol."*

Rabbi Goldberg observes that the word *"ha-mitsri"* ("the Egyptian") has the same numerical value (*gematria*) as the word *"Moshe"* ("Moses"): 345. In other words, Moses slew himself! The Rabbi then goes on to explain that what is truly conveyed by the verse, is that Moses slew the opinions of Egypt. Moses, growing up in the house of Pharaoh, had imbibed secular knowledge stripped of Godliness. So in other words, on a deeper level, what Moses was actually slaying was himself, or a part of himself that was thoroughly Egyptian in outlook. He then buried that secular learning devoid of Godliness "in the sand." Here the Rabbi plays on the word *"hol,"* which may have another meaning besides "sand": the secular. This is to say, Moses buried that tainted learning in the secular realm.[26]

---

[1] The writer wishes to express his gratitude to Eve Gordon-Ramek and Robert H. Warwick, children of the late Rabbi Mayer Goldberg, for their invaluable contribution to the preparation of this article.

[2] Prof. Shalom Rosenberg, Professor of Jewish Philosophy at Hebrew University in Jerusalem, who was present at the time of Chouchani's death in Uruguay, was so convinced of the identification that he named his son "Hillel" after his revered master. See Moshe Nahmani, *"Mi Kan Hillel,"* Mussaf Shabbat, Makor Rishon, 3 Ellul, 5771 [2.9.2011]; Yair Sheleg, "Goodbye, Mr. Chouchani," *Haaretz*, Sept. 26, 2003; Solomon Malka, *Monsieur Chouchani: L'énigme d'un maitre du XXème siècle* (Paris, 1994). Recently, a website has been devoted exclusively to Chouchani. At www.chouchani.com we are told that Michael Grynszpan is in the process of producing a documentary film on the life of M. Chouchani.

I have two anecdotes to contribute to the growing literature on Chouchani, the first heard from Prof. Andre Neher (1914-1988), the second from Rabbi Uziel Milevsky (former Chief Rabbi of Mexico).

- My dear friend André (Asher Dov) Neher, *z"l*, had been a distinguished professor of Jewish studies at the University of Strasburg. I knew him in his last years after his retirement to Jerusalem. Neher told me that in his youth, his father had hired Chouchani to teach him Talmud. At their initial meeting it was decided that they would study Tractate *Beitsah*. Chouchani said to the young Neher: "In the next hour I can either teach you the first folio of the Tractate, or sum up for you the entire Tractate!"

- Similarly, in the final phase of Chouchani's career (in Montevideo, Uruguay), Rabbi Aaron Milevsky (1904-1986), Chief Rabbi of Uruguay, hired Chouchani to tutor his young son Uzi in Talmud. Chouchani rewarded Uzi's diligence by allowing him to quiz him on any entry in the dictionary. Uzi asked Chouchani for the Latin name of some obscure butterfly, which Chouchani was able to supply without hesitation! (Heard from Rabbi Nachum Lansky of Baltimore, *shelit"a*, quoting Rabbi Uziel Milevsky, *z"l*.)

At the onset of this article I wish to clarify one point. Should the identification of Hillel Pearlman with "Monsieur Chouchani" one day prove incorrect, that would in no way affect the positive identification of Rav Kook's addressee "Meir" as Rabbi Mayer Goldberg of Oakland, California. The identification of the mysterious "Meir" as Rabbi Meir Goldberg is in no way contingent upon the identification of Hillel Pearlman as "Chouchani," but rather stands on its own merits.

[3] Traditional blessing for the New Year uttered between Rosh Hashanah and Yom Kippur.

[4] Cf. Genesis 49:28.

[5] While Rav Kook and his Rebbetzin (as well as their only son Tsevi Yehudah) were together in Europe, their daughters were left behind in Jaffa, and Rav Kook was most anxious as to their welfare. The family would not be reunited until after World War One, when Rav Kook returned from European exile to the Holy Land.

[6] Genesis 27:22.

[7] Allusion to the conclusion of the *Yotser* prayer recited in the morning service: "*ba'al milhamot, zore'a tsedakot, matsmi'ah yeshu'ot*" ("Master of wars, planter of righteousness, grower of salvations"). A year into World War One, Rav Kook already envisioned that the outcome of the War would be a shifting of the center of Jewish life from Eastern Europe elsewhere, as well as the further advancement of the building of the Holy Land.

[8] Genesis 12:3.

[9] *Iggerot ha-RAYaH*, vol. 3 (Jerusalem: Mossad Harav Kook, 1965), Letter 740 (pp. 2-3).

[10] Mr. Jacob Rosenheim, organizer of the *Knessiyah Gedolah*, subsequently penned a letter of apology to Rav Kook, for by extending the invitation to him to attend the conference, Rosenheim had indirectly brought about Rav Kook's misfortune.

[11] Moshe Nahmani posits that it existed for 6-7 years from 1909/10-1915.

[12] We do know that one subject on the curriculum, namely *Kuzari* by Rabbi Judah Halevi, aroused the ire of the Jerusalem zealot Rabbi Yeshayah Orenstein. See my edition of *Orot* (Maggid, 2015), p. 454, n. 174.

[13] Available on the website www.shoresh.org.il, dated 4/17/2012 or 25 Nissan, 5772.

According to Moshe Nahmani, the true reason that so little is known of this earlier *yeshivah* of Rav Kook is that Rav Kook himself suppressed publicity concerning its inner life, for fear that should word of the curriculum leak out, the *yeshivah* would come under attack from the ever vigilant rabbis of Jerusalem. (In fact, Rav Kook's teaching of *Kuzari* to the students was sharply criticized by the zealous Rabbi Yeshayah Orenstein of Jerusalem.) Nahmani believes that Rav Kook was dispensing the arcane wisdom of Kabbalah to the students—sufficient grounds for keeping publicity away from the *yeshivah*. (But the Kabbalah may not have been the standard Kabbalah as taught in Jerusalem. We know that one of the instructors in the *yeshivah* was Shem Tov Geffen [1856-1927], an autodidactic genius who fused the study of Kabbalah together with mathematics and physics.) Of course, this is mere speculation on Nahmani's part. What is factual, is that Rav Kook taught in Jaffa the *Kuzari* of Rabbi Judah Halevi and Maimonides' *Eight Chapters* (Maimonides' introduction to his commentary to Tractate *Avot* or Ethics of the Fathers)—which in themselves represented a departure from the standard curriculum of the contemporary *yeshivot*.

In a letter to Shem Tov Geffen, then fundraising for the Jaffa *yeshivah* in Russia, Rav Kook reported that he had added to the curriculum lectures in *Kuzari* three times a week. Rav Kook refers to this study as "the beloved and fundamental subject of the inner wisdom of our holy religion." See *Iggerot ha-RAYaH*, vol. 2, ed. RZYH Kook (Jerusalem: Mossad Harav Kook, 1961), Letter 339 (p. 4). The letter is datelined "Jaffa, 22 Marheshvan 5671 [i.e., 1910]." The letter was reprinted in Yedidyah Wengrover, *R' Shem Tov Geffen* (Metula: Nezer David, 2017), Letter 29 (p. 137). And see ibid. Letter 25 (p. 131, n. 436). More than two years later (in 1913), the *shi'urim* in *Kuzari* a few times a week, were still going on. Rav Kook explained to his brother (Rabbi Dov Kook?) that he used the book as a springboard for discussion of *"hilkhot de'ot,"* or theological issues. See *Iggerot ha-RAYaH*, vol. 2, Letter 501 (p. 139).

[14] In one day, 26 Iyyar, 5675, Rav Kook sent two letters from St. Gallen to America (*Iggerot ha-RAYaH*, vol. 2 [Jerusalem: Mossad Harav Kook, 1961], Letters 733-734 [pp. 329-330]). The first letter is addressed to Rabbi Meir Berlin asking that he lend assistance to Rav Kook's student, newly arrived immigrant Hillel Pearlman. The second letter is addressed to Hillel Pearlman himself, expressing pain that he too was exiled from the Holy Land, and offering encouragement, as well as the practical suggestion that he establish contact with Rabbi Meir Berlin, and with Rav Kook's staunch friend Dr. Moshe Seidel, who might be in a position to help. In a postscript, Rav Kook, noting that Hillel Perlman had spent some time in the house after Rav Kook's own absence, asks for details concerning the welfare of the two Kook daughters left behind in Jaffa, Batyah Miriam and Esther Yael. Logic dictates that our Hillel is Hillel Pearlman of the earlier letters. What eventually became of Hillel Perlman and whether he in fact "morphed" into "Monsieur Chouchani" remains something of a mystery. See Moshe Nahmani, *"Mi Kan Hillel?"*

[15] *"She'areha Ne'ulim—Yeshivat Harav Kuk be-Yaffo,"* Part II, note 51. So too in Nahmani's earlier article *"Mi Kan Hillel?"*

[16] Meir Goldberg told this writer (BN) that before arriving in Jaffa from his native Russia, he had studied under the *"Gadol* of Minsk." (That would have been Rabbi Eliezer Rabinowitz [1859-1924], who inherited the rabbinate of his deceased father-in-law, Rabbi Yeruham Yehudah Leib Perlman [1835-1896]. Both men were referred to by the sobriquet *"Ha-Gadol Mi-Minsk."*)

According to the memoir of Rabbi Goldberg's daughter, Rachel Landes, "My Father, Mayer Goldberg" (October 15, 2009), her father grew up in Krementchug, Ukraine. She also writes that at one point in his career, her father studied in a *yeshivah gedolah* under Rabbi Zimmerman. Though Landes does not specify that the *yeshivah* was located in Krementchug (to the contrary she writes that the *yeshivah* was in Kiev), one ventures a guess that this *yeshivah* of Rabbi Zimmerman was actually that of Rabbi Abraham Isaac Halevi Zimmerman, Rabbi of Krementchug.

Rabbi Abraham Isaac Halevi Zimmerman of Krementchug was the paternal grandfather of Rabbi Dr. Aharon Chaim Halevi Zimmerman (1915-1995), *Rosh Yeshivah* of Beit ha-Midrash le-Torah (Hebrew Theological College) in Skokie, Illinois. (Rabbi Dr. Zimmerman's father, Rabbi Ya'akov Moshe Halevi Zimmerman was the son of Rabbi Abraham Isaac Halevi Zimmerman of Krementchug.) Rabbi Chaim Zimmerman published a collection of his grandfather's novellae on Maimonides' *Mishneh Torah*, two volumes of *Hiddushei ha-RAYaH* (Jerusalem, 1988).

(According to Rabbi Chaim Zimmerman, a young Menahem Mendel Schneerson, the son of the Rabbi of Yekaterinoslav [later Dnepropetrovsk], who would one day become the Lubavitcher Rebbe, briefly visited the *yeshivah* of Rabbi Zimmerman in Krementchug, though he was never officially enrolled there. I have been unable to corroborate this story from other sources.)

Rabbi Abraham Isaac Halevi Zimmerman of Krementchug was the father-in-law of Rabbi Baruch Baer Leibowitz (*talmid muvhak*, or premier disciple, of Rabbi Hayyim Halevi Soloveitchik, known as "Rabbi Hayyim of Brisk"). Rabbi Baruch Baer Leibowitz served as *Rosh Yeshivah* of Knesset Beit Yitzhak, originally located in Slabodka, a suburb of Kovno, Lithuania, and between the two World Wars in Kamenets. During World War One, Knesset Beit Yitzhak was located in Krementchug, where the Rosh Yeshivah, Rabbi Baruch Baer Leibowitz, acted also as Rabbi of the community. See Shulamit Ezrahi's biography of her father, Rabbi Meir Hadash, *Ha-Mashgi'ah Rabbi Meir* (Jerusalem: Feldheim, 2001), p. 93.

[17] According to Rachel Landes' memoir, her father was born in Krementchug. In his Application for a Certificate of Arrival and Preliminary Form for Petition for Naturalization (1940), Mayer writes that he was born in "[illegible] near Kiev." Mayer adopted the surname "Goldberg" in the United States.

[18] The fact that Meir (or Mayer) resided in the Kook home would explain how he was able to supply Rav Kook with information concerning the Rav's daughters. Nahmani noted that Rav Kook had earlier asked Hillel Perlman for details concerning the girls, the assumption being that Hillel Perlman had resided in the Rav's home (though that is not explicitly stated in Rav Kook's letter to Hillel Pearlman). See Moshe Nahmani, *"Mi Kan Hillel?"*

[19] Rachel Landes, "My Father, Mayer Goldberg" (2009), p. 2.

[20] According to Mayer Warwick Goldberg's Application for a Certificate of Arrival and Preliminary Form for Petition for Naturalization (1940), he booked passage on a Greek steamship from Alexandria, Egypt to New York under the assumed name "Othniel Kaplan" in spring of 1915 or 1916. Writing twenty-five years after the fact, Mayer could no longer recall the precise date, whether the arrival in New York had taken place in spring of 1915 or spring of 1916. We are now in a position to aid his memory. We know from Rav Kook's letters to Rabbi Meir Berlin and to Hillel Pearlman, both datelined "St. Gallen, 26 Iyyar 5675," that as of spring 1915, Hillel Perlman was in America.

In order for Rav Kook's letter of 6 Tishri, 5676, to be addressed jointly to Hillel and Meir, Meir too would have had to reside in America by fall of 1915. That could only be so if Meir (or Mayer) arrived in New York in spring of 1915—not 1916!

21 The fact that Rav Kook does not address Meir by the title "Harav" in the salutation (as he does Hillel) indicates that Meir was not yet an ordained rabbi in the fall of 1915.

22 According to information supplied in his 1940 Application for Naturalization, Mayer resided in New York City and Brooklyn from 1916 to 1917; in New Haven and Colchester, Connecticut from 1917 to 1919; in Seattle and Tacoma, Washington from 1919 to 1922; in San Francisco from 1922 to 1930; and in Oakland from 1930 to 1940.

23 To quote from Rachel Landes' memoir (p. 2): "…World War I broke out. The Turks, who were in control of Palestine, sided with Germany, and Russia was on the side of the Allies. My father, being from Russia, found himself classified as an enemy alien. The Turks began to round up all foreign nationals. It became clear that my father could not stay there."

24 At the 24th Annual Banquet of the Hebrew Academy of San Francisco, held on Sunday, December 6, 1992, a moving tribute was paid to the recently departed Rabbi Mayer Goldberg.

25 *Yalkut Re'uveni* (Wilmersdorf, 1681), by Reuben Hoshke HaKohen (Sofer) of Prague (died 1673), is a kabbalistic collection on the Pentateuch.

26 Rabbi Mayer Goldberg, *Margaliyot shel Torah* (Jerusalem, 5750), p. 112. The Hebrew original reads:

וי"ך – כמנין ל"ו כריתות [משנה, כריתות א, א], משה כרת את המצרי, כרת את החיצונים, ויטמינם בחולין. המצרי שהרג משה – הדעות של מצרים שמשה למד, חיצוניות בלי אלוהות – הרג וטמן בחולין, כי מש"ה בגימטריא המצר"י.

When Rav Kook Was the Zealot *(Kannai)* and His Opponent the Advocate *(Melits Yosher)*[1]

In 1891, there appeared in Warsaw an anonymous work[2] entitled *Hevesh Pe'er*,[3] whose sole objective was to clarify for the masses the proper place on the head to don the *tefillah shel rosh* or head-phylactery. According to *halakhah*, the *tefillah* must be placed no lower than the hairline and no higher than the soft spot on a baby's head (i.e., the anterior fontanelle).[4] In ancient times, there were sectarian Jews who deliberately placed the *tefillah* on the forehead, as attested to by the *Mishnah*: "If one placed it [i.e., the *tefillah*] on his forehead, or on his hand, this is the way of sectarianism *(minut)*."[5] These Jews interpreted literally the verse, "You shall bind them for a sign upon your hand, and they shall be for frontlets between your eyes."[6] Adherents to Rabbinic Judaism are punctilious about placing the hand-phylactery on the biceps of the forearm opposite the heart,[7] and the head-phylactery above the hairline. East European Jews who placed their phylacteries on the forehead did so not out of conviction, as the Sadducees of old, but out of sheer ignorance of the law. The slim book (all of 24 leaves or 48 pages) was thus an elaborate educational vehicle to educate the masses how to properly observe the law.[8]

According to the approbation to *Hevesh Pe'er* by Rabbi Elijah David Rabinowitz-Te'omim (ADeReT) of Ponevezh, the book was published [but not authored] by his former son-in-law (presently his brother's son-in-law), Rabbi Abraham Isaac Hakohen Kook of Zeimel.⁹

Wares in hand, the young rabbi of Zeimel (aged twenty-six) assumed the role of an itinerant bookseller, travelling from town to town in Lithuania. Wherever he went, he preached concerning the importance of fulfilling the commandment of *tefillin*. Historically, there was precedent for a rabbi promoting that specific *mitsvah*. In the thirteenth century, Rabbi Moses of Coucy (author of *Sefer Mitsvot Gadol* or *SeMaG*), circulating in the communities of France and Spain, was able to turn the tide and convince Jews, hitherto lax in their observance of the commandment, to don *tefillin*.¹⁰ As for an author posing as an itinerant bookseller, Rav Kook's older contemporary, Rabbi Israel Meir Kagan of Radin, had done exactly that, thus earning himself the sobriquet *Hafets Hayyim*, after the book by that name that he peddled. (*Hafets Hayyim* tackles the problem, halakhic and otherwise, of malicious gossip.)

It is recorded that Rav Kook's sermons had such a positive influence upon his audience that the Rebbe of Slonim, Rabbi Shmuel Weinberg, offered to support him if he would devote himself full-time to acting as a *maggid* or peripatetic preacher.¹¹

One would never have imagined that this halakhic work would meet with any rabbinic opposition.¹² The point it makes that wearing the head-phylactery below the hairline on the forehead invalidates the performance of the commandment, seems rather clear-cut in the sources. (In fact, but a few years earlier, in 1884, Rabbi Israel Meir Kagan in his work *Mishnah Berurah* had advised wearing the phylactery higher on the head, at a remove from the hairline, just to be on the safe side.)[13]

However, five years later, Rabbi Ze'ev Wolf Turbowitz of Kraz (Lithuanian, Kražiai; Yiddish, Krozh)[14] devoted the very first of his collected responsa, *Tif'eret Ziv*, to pummeling the anonymous work *Hevesh Pe'er*.[15] Rabbi Turbowitz prefaces his remarks by saying: "The intention of this author [i.e., the author of *Hevesh Pe'er*] is for [the sake of] Heaven, but nonetheless he has spoken shabbily of the people of the LORD. May the LORD forgive him. For Israel, 'if not prophets, are the children of prophets.'"[16] Rabbi Turbowitz goes on to argue that the commandment is invalidated only if the majority of the phylactery is placed below the hairline. If, on the other hand, the majority is situated above the hairline and only a minority below, then the halakhic principle of *"rubbo ke-khullo"* ("the majority as the whole") applies, and the commandment is fulfilled.[17] One of the rabbi's supposed proofs is the ruling of the *Turei Zahav* that one must recite the blessing once again only in a case where the entire phylactery or the majority thereof has slipped down, but if only a minority of the phylactery has been displaced, with the majority still within the prescribed area, one does not recite another blessing upon readjusting the phylactery.[18]

Rav Kook (now outed as the author of *Hevesh Pe'er*) responded to the onslaught of *Tif'eret Ziv*. His lengthy rejoinder, entitled *"Kelil Tif'eret,"* appeared in the periodical *Torah mi-Zion* (Jerusalem, 1900).

In *"Kelil Tif'eret,"* Rav Kook makes a strong case that the principle of *rubbo ke-khullo* cannot justify a minority of the head-phylactery descending below the hairline onto the forehead. *Rubbo ke-khullo* has no bearing on *shi'urim* or measurements. In support of his position, Rav Kook quotes two sources: Rabbi B.H. Auerbach's *Nahal Eshkol*,[19] and the recent responsa of Rabbi Eliezer Don-Yahya of Lutzin, *Even Shetiyah*.[20] (Rav Kook seems to have overlooked the earlier authority Rabbi Moses Schreiber, who writes explicitly: "We do not say in regard to *shi'urim* [the principle of] '*rubo ke-khullo*.'")[21]

Rav Kook dismantles Rabbi Turbowitz's supposed proof from the fact that another blessing is unwarranted as long as the majority of the phylactery is still in its proper place. Rav Kook reasons that we must distinguish between the essential commandment ("*'etsem ha-mitsvah*") and the action of the commandment ("*ma'aseh ha-mitsvah*"). The fact that one does not recite an additional blessing does not necessarily mean that the commandment ("*'etsem ha-mitsvah*") is still being fulfilled. What it does imply, is that the action of the commandment ("*ma'aseh ha-mitsvah*") is ongoing. The blessing addresses renewed action ("*ma'aseh ha-mitsvah*"). In a case where only a minority of the phylactery has been displaced, the action required to readjust it does not warrant a blessing. "And the *Turei Zahav*[22] holds that since in the entire Torah, '*rubbo ke-khullo*,'[23] once most of the action has been nullified, the action as a whole is nullified, but if most of the action remains, even though the commandment has been nullified, still the action exists…"[24]

As is typical for Rav Kook, he signs himself, "Abraham Isaac Hakohen Kook, servant to the servants of the LORD…Bausk."[25]

Evidently, Rabbi Turbowitz was not one to take something lying down. He came back at Rav Kook with a stinging reply, integrated into *Ziv Mishneh*, his commentary to Maimonides' *Mishneh Torah*.[26] There, in *Hilkhot Tefillin* (4:1), he maintains that since "*rubbo ke-khullo* is a universal principle in the entire Torah,"[27] this applies to *tefillin* as well. He reiterates once more his proof from the *Turei Zahav*, who ruled that the blessing is recited once again only in a scenario where the *tefillin* are totally displaced. He mentions the opinion of "one wise man" ("*hakham ehad*") who wrote that even the slightest deviation disqualifies the *mitsvah*, and disagrees. According to Rabbi Turbowitz, *lekhathillah* (*ab initio*), the entire phylactery should be above the hairline with none of it extending down to the forehead, but *be-di-'avad* (*ex post facto*), if a minority of the phylactery is below the hairline, one has nonetheless fulfilled the commandment. And therefore, the anonymous sage was wrong to criticize the masses, who are remiss in this respect, and their spiritual leaders, who look the other way and do not protest. "He spoke shabbily of the people of the LORD and will in the future be called to judgment!" After summing up rather concisely the position he took earlier in *Tif'eret Ziv*, Rabbi Turbowitz now lambastes Rav Kook for what he wrote in *Torah mi-Zion* (Jerusalem, 1900), no. 4, chap. 4, accusing Rav Kook of deliberately misquoting him.

In 1925, two disciples of Rav Kook, Rabbi Yitzhak Arieli[28] and Rabbi Uri Segal Hamburger,[29] reissued *Hevesh Pe'er* in Jerusalem with Rav Kook's permission.[30] Appended to the work was Rav Kook's rebuttal "*Kelil Tif'eret*." (In addition, this edition was graced by the comments of Rav Kook's deceased father-in-law, ADeReT, and of Rav Kook's admirers in Jerusalem: Rabbis Tsevi Pesah Frank, Ya'akov Moshe Harlap, and Yehiel Mikhel Tukachinsky. Finally, there are the substantial "Comments upon Comments" [*"He'arot le-He'arot"*] of the editor, Rabbi Yitzhak Arieli.)[31]

In 1939, Rabbi Yosef Avigdor Kesler of Rockaway (Arverne to be precise)[32] published a second collection of his deceased father-in-law, Rabbi Ze'ev Turbowitz's numerous responsa. Whereas the first collection of *Tif'eret Ziv* covered only *Orah Hayyim*, this collection covered all four sections of *Shulhan 'Arukh*.[33] In addition, it contained a supplement (*Kuntres Aharon*) entitled *"Mele'im Ziv."* In the supplement, Rabbi Kesler published a letter from ADeReT to Rabbi Turbowitz that turned up in the latter's papers.

ADeReT's letter is datelined "Monday, *Vayyetse*, 5657 [i.e., 1896]." In the letter, ADeReT gratefully acknowledges receipt of the recently published book *Tif'eret Ziv*. Regretting that he is unable to send monetary payment for the book because he is presently inundated with works of various authors, ADeReT nonetheless wishes to at least offer some comment on the contents of the book.[34]

Referring to the very first responsum in *Tif'eret Ziv*, ADeReT rejoices that Rabbi Turbowitz sought to advocate on behalf of the Jewish People regarding the commandment of *tefillin*. He is especially overjoyed that Rabbi Turbowitz was not cowed, but dared to differ. ADeReT holds up as role models Rabbi Zerahyah Halevi (*Ba'al ha-Ma'or*) who critiqued Rabbi Isaac Alfasi (RIF), only to be attacked himself by RABaD of *Posquières*; RABaD of *Posquières* who critiqued Maimonides; et al. Since this is the "way of Torah" (*darkah shel Torah*), why should he harbor any resentment toward Rabbi Turbowitz for disagreeing with him?[35] (ADeReT, though not the author of *Hevesh Pe'er*, had wholeheartedly endorsed and sponsored its publication.)

The sterling character of ADeReT is best summed up in the following lines:

> God forbid, I am not deluded to think that truth resides with me. I wholeheartedly acknowledge the truth. I have not a thousandth part of resentment towards one who differs with me. And the opposite, I love him with all my soul when he points out to me the truth.[36]

Since Rabbi Turbowitz acted as a true *talmid hakham* (Torah scholar) who uninhibitedly speaks truth, ADeReT wonders why he failed to mention the name of the work he critiqued, *Hevesh Pe'er*. This would have provoked neither the author nor ADeReT.[37]

In this vein of truth-seeking, ADeReT proceeds to explain why the argument presented in *Tif'eret Ziv* failed to dissuade him from the position adopted both by him and by the author of *Hevesh Pe'er*. Since the *shi'ur* or measurement of the area on the head where the phylactery is to be placed is *Halakhah le-Moshe mi-Sinai* (a law to Moses from Sinai), the principle of *"rubbo ke-khullo"* is of no consequence in this regard.[38]

Realizing the historic importance of the contents of the letter, Rabbi Kesler provided a photograph of the crucial passage in the letter, which reads as follows:

> About two years ago, the thought occurred to me to reprint the booklet *Hevesh Pe'er*. I wrote to its author, my son-in-law, my soul-friend (today the Rabbi of Bausk, may he live) and asked him if he has anything new to add to it. He wrote me an article, brief in quantity but great in quality, that it is possible to say *"rubbo ke-khullo."* In the summer of 5655 [i.e., 1895] when I was in Warsaw, I already spoke with a printer and also notified the [government] censor, and I was thinking to print. But after this, I reversed myself, and the two of us [i.e., ADeReT and Rav Kook] agreed that it is not worthwhile to print leniencies (*kulot*).[39]

ADeReT explains that if we show any leniency, it will prove a slippery slope. He reveals to Rabbi Turbowitz his unusual experience with Hasidim in particular: "From this, there came about in places where the Hasidim reside [the custom] to wear large *tefillin*.[40] Not one in a thousand bears most of the *tefillah* within the hairline. In most cases, but a small fraction (*mi'uta de-mi'uta*) [is within the hairline]. I have seen with my own eyes the entirety upon the forehead. They laughed at my rebuke, saying: 'Thus is the *mitsvah*.' 'So we saw our fathers doing.'"[41]

The letter concludes with this salutation:

His friend who is honored by his love, appreciates his genius and his Torah, and blesses him with all good,

Elijah David Rabinowitz Te'omim

...Mir[42]

---

[1] These are the exact words of Rabbi Joseph Avigdor Kesler in the introduction to his father-in-law Rabbi Ze'ev Wolf Turbowitz's work of responsa, *Tif'eret Ziv* (Brooklyn: Moinester Publishing Company, 1939), p. 7, par. 5.

By the time of his passing in 1935, Rav Kook would be immortalized as a twentieth-century Rabbi Levi Isaac of Berdichev, the great advocate of the Jewish People, forever defending their practices in the heavenly tribunal. Today, Rav Kook is famous for his leniency concerning the *Shemittah* or Sabbatical year, the *heter mekhirah*, which allows sale of the land to a non-Jew for the duration, whereby agricultural work, or at least some forms thereof, may take place. The model for this contract is the prevalent *mekhirat hamets* or sale of leaven to a non-Jew before Passover, so that it need not be removed from the home of the Jew.

However, in general, if one studies the *teshuvot* (responsa) of Rav Kook, he does not come across as extraordinarily lenient in his *pesakim* or halakhic decisions. *Par contre*, someone whose work is chock-full of startling leniencies is Rabbi Aryeh Tsevi Frumer of Kozhiglov, *Hashem yikom damo* (1884-1943), *Rosh Yeshivah* of Yeshivat Hakhmei Lublin and a disciple of Rabbi Abraham Bornstein (the author of responsa *Avnei Nezer*). Rabbi Fromer designed his work of responsa, *Erets Tsevi* (Lublin, 1938), to be *melammed zekhut*, to find some halakhic justification (however farfetched) for certain otherwise anomalous practices within the Jewish community. This is apparent from the very first responsum, where the author attempts to justify the prevalent practice of wearing a *tallit katan* that fails to meet the prescribed *shi'ur* or measurement.

[2] The title page credits as author: "KDY (*Kohen Da'ato Yafah*)." The expression "*kohen she-da'ato yafah*" comes out of the *Mishnah, 'Avodah Zarah* 2:5. Thus, the title alludes to the author being a *kohen* or member of the priestly caste.

The thought occurs to this writer (BN) that "*Yafah*" might be an allusion to Rav Kook's descent from Rabbi Mordechai Yaffe (author of the *Levush[im]*). Rav Kook was immensely proud of his pedigree which reached back to the *Levush*. The pedigree to the *Levush* was something that Rav Kook had in common with his father-in-law ADeReT (who was the *éminence grise* of the publication). See Rabbi Moshe Tsevi Neriyah, *Sihot ha-RAYaH* (Tel-Aviv, 1979), note on p. 134; and idem, *Tal ha-RAYaH* (Tel-Aviv, 1993), p. 75.

In the letter written by Rav Kook's paternal great-uncle, Rabbi Mordechai Gimpel Yaffe of Rozhinoy, to the Trisker Maggid, Rabbi Abraham Twersky, Rabbi Yaffe mentions their remote common ancestor, the *Levush*. See *The Legends of Rabbah bar Bar Hannah with Commentary of Rabbi Abraham Isaac*

Kook, ed. Bezalel Naor (Orot/Kodesh, 2019), pp. 202-203.
3 The title is taken from the verse in Ezekiel 24:17: *"Pe'erkha havosh 'alekha"* ("Bind your head-tire upon you"). The Rabbis interpreted the head-tire as a reference to the head-*tefillah*; see b. *Mo'ed Katan* 15a.
4 y. *'Eruvin* 10:1; b. *Menahot* 37a; Maimonides, *MT, Hil. Tefillin* 4:1; Rabbi Joseph Karo, *Shulhan 'Arukh, Orah Hayyim* 27:9.
5 m. *Megillah* 4:8.
6 Deuteronomy 6:8.
7 *Shulhan 'Arukh, Orah Hayyim* 27:1.
8 In *Hevesh Pe'er*, chap. 2, the author points out that there already appeared in print a small booklet with diagrams, *"Tikkun 'Olam 'im tsiyurim,"* but writes that the error persists depite that.
9 Rav Kook's first wife, Alta Batsheva, daughter of ADeReT, died at a young age, leaving him to raise their infant daughter, Freida Hannah. ADeReT suggested to Rav Kook that he marry Reiza Rivkah, ADeReT's niece, daughter of his deceased twin brother, Tsevi Yehudah, Rabbi of Ragola. ADeReT had raised Reiza Rivkah in his home after her father's death.
10 Rabbi Jacob of Coucy, *Sefer Mitsvot Gadol*, positive commandment 3; *Hevesh Pe'er*, chap. 2. At the end of positive commandment 3, Rabbi Jacob gives the exact year of his campaign in Spain: 4996 *anno mundi* or 1236 C.E.

Urbach writes that this role of the itinerant preacher, or *darshan*, is without precedent among the French Tosafists. He conjectures that in this respect, Rabbi Moses of Coucy came under the influence of *Hasidei Ashkenaz*. See E.E. Urbach, *Ba'alei ha-Tosafot* (Jerusalem: Bialik Institute, 1995), pp. 466-470. Concerning specifically French Jewry's laxity when it came to observing the commandment of *tefillin*, see ibid. p. 469, n. 13 (citing *Tosafot, Shabbat* 49a, s.v. *ke-Elisha Ba'al Kenafayim*, and *Rosh Hashanah* 17a, s.v. *karkafta de-lo manah tefillin*). The *SeMaG* refutes Rabbenu Tam's understanding of *"karkafta de-lo manah tefillin."*
11 Rabbi Ya'akov Moshe Harlap, quoted in Rabbi Moshe Tsevi Neriyah, *Sihot ha-RAYaH* (Tel-Aviv, 1979), p. 191, and idem, *Tal ha-RAYaH* (Tel-Aviv, 1993), p. 116. According to Rabbi Harlap, the Slonimer Rebbe reached out to ADeReT, hoping that he could prevail upon his former son-in-law (and present nephew by marriage) to accept this magnanimous offer.
12 Rav Kook's erstwhile mentor in the Volozhin Yeshivah, Rabbi Naphtali Tsevi Yehudah Berlin (NeTsIV), was so enamored of *Hevesh Pe'er* that he kept it in his *tallit* bag. See the Introduction of Rabbis Yitzhak Arieli and Uri Segal Hamburger to the Jerusalem 1925 edition of *Hevesh Pe'er*, p. 2.
13 See Rabbi Israel Meir Kagan, *Mishnah Berurah* (Warsaw, 1884) to OH 27:9. In the *Be'ur Halakhah*, Rabbi Kagan sought support for this prescription in the manuscript glosses of "the Gaon Rabbi El'azar Harlap" to *Ma'aseh Rav* (a collection of the practices of the Vilna Gaon). If I am not mistaken, these notes would have been penned by the Gaon (and *Mekubbal*) Rabbi Ephraim Eliezer Tsevi Harlap of Mezritch.
14 Rabbi Ze'ev Wolf Turbowitz was born *Rosh Hodesh Iyar*, 1840 in Baboina near Kletsk and was known in his youth as the *"'Illui* of Baboina." His first wife was from Izilian. After his marriage, he devoted himself exclusively to study of Torah, whereby he was then known as the *"Porush* of Izilian." At a tender age he began to study Kabbalah. (Among his writings was found a work on

Zohar.) In 1863, he was appointed as a *rosh metivta* in Minsk. In 1866, he received his first rabbinical position in Swislowitz. In 1875, he assumed the rabbinate of Kletsk. Afterward, he served a stint in Wolpa. And finally in 1889, he was elected rabbi of Kraz, where he served until his death on the 14th of Kislev, 5682 [i.e., 1921]. These biographical details were gleaned from his son-in-law Rabbi Yosef Kesler's introduction to the Brooklyn 1939 edition of *Tif'eret Ziv*, p. 4.

Rabbi Eitam Henkin, *Hashem yikom damo*, wrote of the interface between Rabbi Turbowitz and Rabbi Eliyahu Goldberg, mentor of Rabbi Yehiel Mikhel Epstein (author of *'Arukh ha-Shulhan*). Besides corresponding with Rabbi Goldberg in halakhic matters, Rabbi Turbowitz delivered a moving *hesped* (eulogy) for Rabbi Goldberg in 1875 in the town of Kletsk, Rabbi Goldberg's birthplace. See Rabbi Eitam Henkin, *Ta'arokh Lefanai Shulhan* (Israel: Maggid, 2018), pp. 359-360, 363.

[15] See Rabbi Ze'ev Wolf Turbowitz, *Tif'eret Ziv* (Warsaw, 1896), no. 1. *Ziv* is an acronym for *Ze'ev Yekhuneh Volf*.

The responsum is datelined "Wednesday, 16 Tammuz, 5651 [1891]," which means that it was penned the same year that *Hevesh Pe'er* was published. Rabbi Turbowitz does not mention the book by name, referring to it as "a new book that has appeared" (*"sefer ehad hadash she-yatsa la-'or"*).

By the same token, in responsum 12 of *Tif'eret Ziv*, where Rabbi Turbowitz engages with another early work of Rav Kook (in fact, his first), *'Ittur Soferim*, he refers to that work obliquely as *"sefer ehad katan"* ("a small book"). Rabbi Abraham Joshua of Pokroi had raised the question whether one who becomes *bar mitsvah* at night must recite once again the blessing for studying Torah (*birkat ha-Torah*), though he already recited it that morning. The editor, Rav Kook, devoted a few pages to resolving this problem. See *'Ittur Soferim*, Part Two (Vilna, 1888), 9a-10b. Rabbi Turbowitz made short shrift of the question. At the same time, he tackled the Vilna *dayan*, Rabbi Shelomo Hakohen, who had also raised the question in his work, *Binyan Shelomo*. In the Brooklyn 1939 edition of *Tif'eret Ziv*, the first two responsa are to Rabbi Shelomo Hakohen, who had defended his position to Rabbi Turbowitz.

According to Rabbi Turbowitz's son-in-law, Rabbi Yosef Avigdor Kesler, the famous "*Gadol* of Minsk" (i.e., Rabbi Yeruham Yehudah Perlman) read Rabbi Turbowitz's responsum concerning the placement of the head-phylactery before it went to print and approved its contents. See the supplement to the Brooklyn 1939 edition of *Tif'eret Ziv*, *Kuntres Aharon*, "*Mele'im Ziv*," 2d-3a, footnote.

[16] *Tif'eret Ziv*, 6a. The quote is from *b. Pesahim* 66b: "Leave Israel alone! If they are not prophets, they are the children of prophets." Rabbi Turbowitz's remark is quoted in Yehudah Mirsky, *Rav Kook: Mystic in a Time of Revolution* (New Haven: Yale University Press, 2014), p. 23.

[17] *Tif'eret Ziv* 1:3 (6c).

[18] *Tif'eret Ziv* 1:16-21 (8c-9b). See Rabbi David Halevi (*TaZ*), *Magen David* to OH 8:15; cited in *Mishnah Berurah* to OH 25:12.

[19] Rabbi B.H. Auerbach, *Sefer ha-Eshkol* with commentary *Nahal Eshkol*, Part Two (Halberstadt, 1868), *Hil. Tefillin*, pp. 92-94.

[20] Rabbi Eliezer Don-Yahya, *Even Shetiyah* (Vilna, 1893), nos. 12-13.

As a teenager, Rav Kook came under the influence of Rabbi Eliezer Don-Yahya (1838-1926) in Lutzin (Latvian, Ludza). See Rabbi Moshe Tsevi Neriyah, *Sihot ha-RAYaH* (Tel-Aviv, 1979), pp. 58-65; idem, *Tal ha-RAYaH* (Tel-Aviv, 1993), pp. 20-21; idem, *Bi-Sdeh ha-RAYaH* (Tel-Aviv, 1991), pp. 526-528, 537-540; and *Haskamot ha-RAYaH*, ed. Y.M. Yismah and B.Z. Kahane (Jerusalem, 1988), nos. 79, 94 (pp. 97, 112). In *"Kelil Tif'eret,"* Rav Kook refers to Rabbi Eliezer Don-Yahya as "my friend" (*"yedidi"*). This is explained by the fact that the Rabbi of Lutzin related to the young men who studied there not as an authority figure but "as an older brother." So wrote his son Rabbi Benzion Don-Yahya; see *Sihot ha-RAYaH*, pp. 62-63.

This writer (BN) had the privilege of enjoying the friendship of Rabbi Eliezer Don-Yahya's grandson, Shabtai Don-Yahya, a disciple of Rav Kook in Merkaz Harav. As editor of *Ha-Tzofeh*, he would sign his articles with the *nom de plume*, "Shin Daniel." (The Hebrew surname "Daniel" was bestowed upon him by Rabbi David Cohen, the "Nazirite.")

For other members of this distinguished rabbinical family, see below, "The Religious-Zionist Manifesto of Rabbi Yehudah Leib Don Yahya."

[21] *She'elot u-Teshuvot HaTaM Sofer, Orah Hayyim*, no. 140. See also the discussion of *"Rubo ke-khullo"* by Rabbi Hayyim Soloveitchik (and the proof brought by Rabbi Zelig Reuven Bengis), in *Hiddushei ha-GRaH he-Hadash*, vol. 3 (stencil, Jerusalem, 1967), p. 90.

[22] See above note 18.

[23] It may strike the reader as ironic that Rav Kook introduced at this point in the discussion the concept of *rubbo ke-khullo* when he had earlier rejected its application. But from Rav Kook's standpoint (and that of his father-in-law ADeReT, see below note 38), that principle simply could not be applied to the *area* of the phylactery with its precise dimensions. *"Shi'urim halakhah le-Moshe mi-Sinai,"* "Measurements are a law to Moses from Sinai" (*y. Pe'ah* 1:1, *Hagigah* 1:2; *b. 'Eruvin* 4a, *Yoma* 80a, *Sukkah* 5b).

[24] Rabbi Abraham Isaac Hakohen Kook, *"Kelil Tif'eret"* in *Hevesh Pe'er*, ed. Rabbis Yitzhak Arieli and Uri Segal Hamburger (Jerusalem: Mossad Harav Kook, 1985), p. 46. Of course, the element of *hesah ha-da'at*, i.e., whether one has "removed one's awareness," plays a crucial part in determining whether one must recite the blessing on the *tefillin* once again. See ibid.

Rav Kook's *hilluk* (differentiation) between *"'etsem ha-mitsvah"* and *"ma'aseh ha-mitsvah"* (especially the terminology) is somewhat remarkable, issuing as it did from the pen of Rav Kook, who studiously avoided the school of *Hasbarah* with its abstract constructs and neologisms, then in vogue in the Lithuanian *yeshivah* world. The most famous proponent of *Hasbarah* was Rabbi Hayyim Soloveitchik (who would one day inherit his father Rabbi Yosef Dov Soloveitchik's rabbinate in Brisk, whereupon he would be known as "Reb Hayyim Brisker"). The latter's methodology of Talmudic analysis came to be known as the *"Brisker derekh [ha-limud],"* "the Brisker way [of learning]."

Rav Kook's biographers have duly noted that his first mentor back in Dvinsk (since Rav Kook's *bar mitsvah*), Rabbi Reuven Ha-Levi Levin (known as "Reb Ruvaleh Denaburger") had, so to speak, "immunized" Rav Kook against the trend of *"sevarot"* or newfangled "concepts." Rabbi Reuven Levin was highly suspicious of *sevarot* that had not been enuciated already by the *rishonim*, the medieval authorities. (See Rabbi Kesler's introduction to *Tif'eret*

Ziv, Brooklyn 1939, p. 8, par. 9, quoting Rabbi Reuven Levin, and ibid. sec. *Hoshen Mishpat*, responsum 46:6 [116c]: "It is not my way to say *sevarot* of my own cognizance.")

And thus, when later Avraham Yitzhak Kook arrived at Volozhin, "the mother of *yeshivot*," he gravitated to the elder *Rosh Yeshivah*, Rabbi Naphtali Tsevi Yehudah Berlin (NeTsIV), known as a *pashtan*, a champion of the simple understanding of the text, rather than to his grandson-in-law, Rabbi Hayyim Soloveitchik, who was surrounded by budding scholars attracted to the exciting new method of Talmudic analysis that he was developing.

Although Rav Kook was never so outspoken as Rabbi Ya'akov David Wilovsky (or "Reb Yankel Dovid Slutsker"), known by the acronym RIDBaZ, who satirized the new method as "chemistry," Rav Kook was clearly on the other side of the great divide between Lithuanian Talmudists. This aversion of Rav Kook to the method of *"hasbarah"* was given eloquent testimony in recently unearthed correspondence concerning the unsuccessful attempt of Rabbi Shim'on Shkop (a *rosh yeshivah* in Telz and later head of his own *yeshivah* in Grodno) to be accepted as *Rosh Yeshivah* of Merkaz Harav in Jerusalem. Speaking in Rav Kook's name, his devoted disciple Rabbi Ya'akov Moshe Harlap conveyed to Rabbi Hizkiyahu Yosef Mishkovski of Krinik (who had interceded on Rabbi Shim'on Shkop's behalf) the following laconic response:

> Regarding the proposal concerning the Gaon Rabbi Shim'on Shkop, may he live, to accept him as *Rosh Yeshivah* of Merkaz Harav, there is certainly nothing to discuss, for since the founding of the *Yeshivah*, this position is reserved for *Maran* [our master, i.e., Rav Kook], may he live, who plans to fill it himself. For *Maran*, may he live, wishes— and this is a strong desire—that the main method of learning of the *Yeshivah* be according to the order and method of the GRA [i.e., the Gaon Rabbi Elijah of Vilna], of blessed memory. Though he [i.e., Rav Kook] knows and feels also the great necessity of developing the methods of *"hasbarot"* (conceptualizations) and *"havanot hegyoniyot"* (logical understandings), he wants the main spirit of the *Yeshivah* to be based on his method, etc. Today I showed *Maran*, may he live, his honor's letter, and what I wrote here is his response.

Rabbi Harlap's letter is datelined "Monday, 2nd day of *Rosh Hodesh Adar*, 5686 [i.e., 1926], Jerusalem." It was published in a *Festschrift* for his grandson, Rabbi Zevulun Charlop, *Zeved Tov*, ed. Ari S. Zahtz (New York: Yeshiva University Press, 2008), p. 103.

Inter alia, "Z. Wein" mentioned in the letter from Rabbi Shkop to Rabbi Tobolsky, expressing Rabbi Shkop's desire to settle in the Holy Land (ibid. p. 101), is none other than [Rabbi] Ze'ev Wein, *a"h*, father of Rabbi Berel Wein, *shelit"a*. Rabbi Ze'ev Wein (1906-2004), a disciple of Rabbi Shkop, went on to study in Rav Kook's Merkaz Harav in Jerusalem. He served for many years as a distinguished rabbi in Chicago.

Rabbi Shim'on Shkop was famous for his method of *"higayon"* (logic), displayed in his magnum opus, *Sha'arei Yosher*. (Rabbi Hershel Shachter, *shelit"a*, revealed to this writer [BN] that his father-in-law, Rabbi Yeshayah Shapiro, a *rosh yeshivah* at Torah Vodaath in Brooklyn, was instrumental in writing that work.)

This is not the place to discuss in any depth the differences between

Rabbi Shim'on Shkop's method and that of Rabbi Hayyim Brisker and his heirs. Two anecdotes should suffice. The Briskers quipped that Rabbi Shim'on "had looked at the world and created the Torah" (*"Istakel be-'alma u-vara 'oraita"*), a reversal of the *Zohar*'s adage, "[God] looked at the Torah and created the world" (*"istakel be-'oraita u-vara 'alma"*). On one occasion, Rabbi Yitzhak Ze'ev Soloveitchik ("Reb Velvel," known as the "Brisker Rov," for he inherited from his father Rabbi Hayyim the rabbinate of Brisk) met Rabbi Shim'on Shkop and told him: "I removed from your student Rabbi Leib Malin the last sinew (*gid*) left from your teaching." (The imagery is that of de-veining or *nikkur*. Reb Velvel probably used the Yiddish verb, *"treiberen."*) Both anecdotes were heard from Rabbi Shelomo Fisher, *shelit"a*, of Jerusalem.

[25] In 1895, Rav Kook left the town of Zeimel for the large city of Bausk, Latvia.

[26] Rabbi Ze'ev Wolf Turbowitz, *Ziv Mishneh* (Warsaw, 1904). The author has the rather unique distinction of viewing Maimonides as a kabbalist and finding kabalistic "sources" for his rulings. (Similarly, the introduction to the Warsaw 1896 edition of *Tif'eret Ziv* demonstrates the author's proficiency in Lurianic kabbalah.) Though not unique in this respect, Rabbi Turbowitz is perhaps the most outspoken proponent of this peculiar methodology of studying Maimonides' *Mishneh Torah*. Another Maimonidean commentator who occasionally resorts to this method of sourcing is Rabbi Joseph Rosen (the Rogatchover Gaon). See his *Tsaphnat Pa'ne'ah, Hil. 'Avodah Zarah* 12:6. Nowadays, Rabbi Hayyim Kanievsky's *Kiryat Melekh*, a work that provides sources for *Mishneh Torah*, is replete with references to *Zohar*.

[27] b. *Horayot* 3b; and Rashi, *Zevahim* 26a, s.v. *hikhnis rosho ve-rubbo*. Both are referenced by Rabbi Turbowitz.

[28] Rabbi Yitzhak Arieli was one of the founders of Yeshivat Merkaz Harav and acted in the official capacity of *"Mashgiah"* of the *Yeshivah*. He is most famous for his work on the Talmud, *'Eynayim le-Mishpat*. Recently, Aharon Ilan, a great-grandson of Rabbi Yitzhak Arieli, brought out his biography, *'Eynei Yitzhak* (Jerusalem, 2018).

[29] Rabbi Uri Segal Hamburger was a descendant of Rabbi Moshe Yehudah Segal Hamburger of Novemeste (a disciple of the *HaTaM Sofer*) who came to *Erets Yisrael* in 1857. Rabbi Uri Segal Hamburger resided in the Old City of Jerusalem until its conquest by the Jordanians in 1948. He penned a memoir of that tragic event, *"Be-Tseiti mi-Yerushalayim."* One may find a short biography and a photograph of Rabbi Hamburger in *'Eynei Yitzhak*, pp. 136-137.

[30] Rav Kook's biographer and disciple, Rabbi Moshe Tsevi Neriyah, records that Rav Kook wrote in his *haskamah* (letter of approbation) to the publishers the following disclaimer: "In our holy land, which thank God, is full of Torah and fear of heaven, the admonition (*azharah*) is not so necessary. Nevertheless, I have not prevented re-issuing the book, for the benefit of our brothers in the Diaspora, in areas where the matter is yet in need of correction" (*Sihot ha-RAYaH* [Tel-Aviv, 1979], pp. 189-190). This disclaimer does not appear in the printed version of the *haskamah*. Where did Rabbi Neriyah obtain it? The mystery was cleared up in the new edition of *Sihot ha-RAYaH* (2015) published after Rabbi Neriyah's passing. Rabbi Arieli's son, Prof. Nahum Arieli, wrote to Rabbi Neriyah that he has in his possession much material that went into the making of the Jerusalem edition of *Hevesh Pe'er* edited by his father, including a *"petek"* (note) with those exact words. Rabbi Neriyah's daughter,

Tsilah Bar-Eli, granted Aharon Ilan permission to include a facsimile of Nahum Arieli's letter to her father (on stationery of Bar-Ilan University) in the biography of Rabbi Arieli, *'Eynei Yitzhak*, p. 139.

[31] Rabbi Arieli's promised *"Kuntres Aharon"* was never published. Remnants of the manuscript are in the possession of his heirs. Rabbi Neriyah speculated that financial considerations prevented its publication in *Hevesh Pe'er*. See *'Eynei Yitzhak*, p. 138, n. 102.

[32] On the inside of the book, Rabbi J. Kesler's address is given as: "146 Beach 74th Street, A[r]verne, Long Island."

[33] It is important to note that the two collections do not overlap. The responsa on *Orah Hayyim* that appeared in the Warsaw 1896 edition of *Tif'eret Ziv*, were not included in the Brooklyn 1939 edition. In their stead, appear more recent responsa on *Orah Hayyim*. In terms of sheer quantity, the second collection by far outstrips the first. The first Warsaw edition has 122 pages; the second Brooklyn edition, 488 pages.

[34] *"Mele'im Ziv,"* 2a-b.

[35] *"Mele'im Ziv,"* 2b-2c.

[36] *"Mele'im Ziv,"* 2d.

[37] *"Mele'im Ziv,"* 3a.

[38] *"Mele'im Ziv,"* 3a-b.

[39] The facsimile occurs in Rabbi Kesler's introduction to the book on p. 7. It is transcribed in *"Mele'im Ziv,"* 3b.

If not for the evidence of the facsimile, it would indeed be difficult to accept that Rav Kook once entertained even the remote possibility of invoking the principle of *rubbo ke-khullo* in this regard.

[40] To this day, Lubavitcher Hasidim wear very large *tefillin*.

[41] *"Mele'im Ziv,"* 3b-c.

[42] *"Mele'im Ziv,"* 3d.

In 1893, ADeReT left the community of Ponevezh to assume the rabbinate of Mir.

IX

MESSIAH

The Two Faces of Messianism[1]

In Messiah Son of Joseph is revealed the characteristic of Israel's nationalism per se. However, the ultimate goal is not the isolation of nationalism, but the longing to unite all the inhabitants of the world into a single family, that all may call upon the name of the LORD. And despite the fact that this too requires a special center, nonetheless the intention is not the center, but its effect upon the great collective. Now when the world must transition from the concept of nationalism to universalism, there must be a sort of destruction of the things that were rooted in narrow nationalism, which carries with it the drawbacks of excessive self-love. Therefore in the future, Messiah Son of Joseph will be killed, and a true and enduring kingdom will be [that of] Messiah Son of David.

(Rabbi Abraham Isaac Hakohen Kook)[2]

In this brief pensée, our great teacher Rav Kook (1865-1935) has provided the key to at once penetrate the arcane mysteries of the Rabbinic tradition (with its oblique references to two Messiahs, "Messiah Son of Joseph" and "Messiah Son of David") and unlock the secrets of the human heart. Every individual human and every nation on this planet of ours must somehow come to terms with the sometimes seemingly insurmountable conflict between the ideals of nationalism and universalism, peoplehood and humanity. We are at once citizens of our respective nations and of Planet Earth. The conflict is not a particularly Jewish one; it affects everyone on the globe. (Although historically, the conflict may have been intensified in the nation of Israel—even before the advent of Zionism.)

By decoding "Messiah Son of Joseph" as nationalism (though unstated, the reference is likely to Jewish nationalism or even Zionism) and "Messiah Son of David" as universalism, Rav Kook envisioned a humanity transitioning from a tribal or ethnocentric consciousness to a global or planetary consciousness. The present writer on the other hand, is disinclined to view mankind's historical process as a unilateral progression from the confines of nationalism to the expanses of universalism, and proposes an alternate model, whereby there is at work here a dialectic between the two poles of nation and planet.

The genesis of our essay is itself instructive in this regard. It came as a reverie to a young man traipsing about Switzerland, *en route* from West to East; from Berkeley, California, to Jerusalem, Israel. The geography is pregnant with symbolism. In Berkeley, the writer was exposed to a broad, global perspective. Yet he was travelling to Jerusalem to seek out a teacher of the Kabbalah, an esoteric discipline restricted to Jews, and then to only the most pious among them. The thought uppermost in the seeker's mind was: Would it be possible to find a teacher who could show the way to integrate the most expansive spiritual realizations with the treasures of the ancient tradition?

On his second day in Jerusalem, the writer (then in his early twenties) found himself sitting face to face with an octogenarian rabbi by the name of Tsevi Yehudah Hakohen Kook (1891-1982), only son of the famed Chief Rabbi. Thinking to impress the elderly gentleman with a good opening line, the writer blurted out: "How much *Ahavat Yisrael* (love of the Jewish People) your father had!"

Rabbi Tsevi Yehudah's response was a spontaneous outburst of hearty laughter. When he regained his composure, the ancient sage revealed what in that statement precipitated the sudden mirth:

"Ahavat Yisrael? Love of Israel? My father loved the entire world!"[3]

Rabbi Tsevi Yehudah then proceeded to retrace the great chain of being. *"Afilu tsome'ah!"* ("Even the vegetable kingdom!")

And then reaching down to rap on the stone floor for emphasis, he added, *"Afilu domem!"* ("Even the mineral kingdom!")

In the writings of Rav Kook, the present essayist, as many other seekers (Jews and non-Jews), discovers a master, who, torn as his soul may be (by his own admission),[4] brings to the esoteric discipline of Kabbalah the clever wisdom of the adult and the simple faith of the child, and attempts to synchronize the "little picture" with the "big picture," as he zooms in and out of a Cosmos[5] longing to be redeemed from Chaos; all the while envisioning a World of *Tikkun* bringing integration (*hitkalelut*) to a World of *Tohu* inhabited by primordial kings and self-mythologizing gods.[6]

Finally, a word about the style. The author traces the ongoing oscillation of Judaism between the tribal and the universal, utilizing raw materials of Bible, Midrash, Talmud, medieval philosophy, Kabbalah and Hasidism. The essay is written in a lyrical style not readily comprehensible to those seeking political analysis. In this respect, the author's role model was Rabbi Abraham Isaac Hakohen Kook.

Messiah

GENEALOGY

PARTICULARISM	UNIVERSALISM
RACHEL	LEAH
JOSEPH (AND BENJAMIN)	JUDAH
SAUL	DAVID
JEROBOAM	SOLOMON
MESSIAH SON OF JOSEPH	MESSIAH SON OF DAVID

MESSIAH SON OF JOSEPH AND MESSIAH SON OF DAVID

The history of the human race may be compared to a giant field through which the mighty winds of unification and atomization blow back and forth. Nations come together, confederate, aspire to commonality and cooperation, and once again there is raised the demand of nationalism or tribalism, and the member nations return "each man to his camp and to his flag."[7] So it has been throughout time. These two opposite *Zeitgeisten* are forever circulating in the unconscious and sometimes conscious thinking of those who shape the dominant ideas of any given historical period.

Messiah Son of Joseph is the atomizer, the separatist; Messiah Son of David is the unifier. Messiah Son of Joseph carries within his head a vision drawn along coordinates of national boundaries and bloodlines; Messiah Son of David envisions a reality that is supra-nationalist and planetary.

In the Book of Genesis we learn that Joseph, Viceroy of Egypt, would divine events by gazing into his goblet.[8] The Hebrew word for goblet is *gavi'a* (גביע). Broken down into its component letters, *gimmel, bet-yod, 'ayin* (ג-בי-ע), the word signifies the three patriarchs, twelve tribes and seventy souls that culminated in the formation of the Israelite nation.[9] This is what we might expect of the clairvoyance of Joseph (prototype of Messiah Son of Joseph). Within the statecraft of Joseph runs the desire to preserve national identities and narratives.

Joseph views a national entity (in this case, his own people of Israel) through the lens of biology. Israel descends from three patriarchs (Abraham, Isaac and Jacob), develops into twelve tribes (Reuben, Simeon, Levi, Judah, etc.), and at a later, critical stage of its evolution (the descent into Egypt), evolves into "seventy souls."[10] It is not mere happenstance that Joseph seats Egyptians and Hebrews separately at his dinner table,[11] or that later, he arranges that his brethren come to reside in the separate province of Goshen, apart from mainstream Egyptian life.[12] Joseph was identified as a "Hebrew man."[13] According to the Midrash, it was in this merit that Joseph was later buried in the Land of the Hebrews. (On the other hand, Moses who was identified as an "Egyptian man,"[14] did not merit interment in the land. As the Midrash expressed it so succinctly, "He who admitted to his land, was buried in his land; he who did not admit to his land, was not buried in his land."[15] But we are getting ahead of ourselves.)

Vastly different is the statecraft of David and his successor Solomon. Joseph *speaks* seventy languages; Solomon *marries* seventy languages. David, but even more so Solomon, are thinking in terms of global expansion, but ultimately—world union.

The comprehensive vision of unity has traditionally been the domain of the individual, of the gifted few. The atomistic, divided view of reality on the other hand, seems to fall quite naturally into the public domain. David's expansionist worldview prompts him to conquer Syria. The *Sifré* (a third-century halakhic commentary to the Book of Deuteronomy) censures David's conquest: "You did not lay claim to the immediate vicinity of your palace [in Jerusalem], yet you go and conquer Aram-Naharayim and Aram-Tsobah?"[16] The contentious conquest of Syria, a relic of Davidic ambition, would forever be subjected in the annals of the Talmud to the dubious distinction of a *"kibbush yahid,"* "a one-man conquest," unsanctioned by proper parliamentary procedure.[17] The collective Jewish People had its eyes trained on Jerusalem; it was that rare individual David (forerunner of Messiah Son of David) whose vision expanded to enfold an entire world. The "one-man conquest" forever remains a mystery.[18]

"HEAR O ISRAEL, THE LORD OUR GOD, THE LORD IS ONE" (DEUTERONOMY 6:4)

The most basic utterance of Jewish faith, the *Shema'*, the first thing that we are taught as children, and the last thing that we recite before dying, reads: "Hear O Israel, the LORD our God, the Lord is one." As a declaration of divine unity, the sentence is strangely disjointed. Rashi, a native of medieval Troyes (France), most beloved of Bible commentators, attempted to smooth over the disruption in thought: "The LORD Who is today our God [i.e., the God of Israel], will one day be one LORD over all the nations."

"The LORD our God" is the call of Messiah Son of Joseph. "The LORD is one" is the call of Messiah Son of David.

If we should be even more exacting, the word "one" itself is given to two opposite interpretations: "One," in the sense of uniqueness, to the exclusion of all others; as opposed to "one" in the sense of unity, comprehending and including all.[19]

From an historic perspective, the Messianisms of Joseph and David interact and reciprocate, and the relations between them as well as their concatenations tend to be extremely complex. Nonetheless, we shall attempt to point out a few directions that these interactions have taken over the centuries.

"MOSES TOOK THE BONES OF JOSEPH WITH HIM" (EXODUS 13:19)

If ever there was a man deserving of the title "cosmic visionary," it was Moses. Could it be otherwise? Is it conceivable that the prophet unequalled in having spoken to the LORD "face to face," was not privy to some sense of the eternal destiny of the globe? The God of Moses, *Ehyeh asher Ehyeh* ("I am that I am," or "I shall be that I shall be," as it is variously translated into English) is not a local, regional deity, but the LORD of Necessary Existence (as Maimonides explained so well),[20] an existence at once simple and abstract. And yet, paradox of paradoxes, this prophet of cosmic proportions, a "Davidic" Messiah if ever there was one, is sent to perform a mission purely "Josephic" in character, namely that of national liberation. He is dispatched to Egypt to take the oppressed Hebrew nation out of the House of Bondage. "Moses took the bones of Joseph with him." In Hebrew, the word for "bones," "*atsmot*," slightly re-vocalized becomes "*atsmut*" or "essence." Moses took the essence of Joseph with him. "There was in Jeshurun a king. When the heads of the people assembled. The tribes of Israel together."[21] According to some commentators, the "King" of Jeshurun refers to Moses.[22] Moses acted in the capacity of a monarch over Israel.[23]

But at the end of Moses' career, there is revealed retroactively who Moses truly is. Moses is relieved of his duties as national liberator. The actual entry into the Promised Land will not be accomplished by Moses. Rather, the national deliverance is entrusted to Moses' successor Joshua, appropriately enough an Ephraimite, descended from Joseph. It is Joshua, not Moses, who will complete the mission, the *"mitsvah,"* of depositing the bones of Joseph in their final resting place in Shechem.

Rather than meriting burial in Israel, Moses' mysterious crypt is situated rather nebulously "opposite Beit Peʻor,"[24] a site tied to the idolatrous cult of Peʻor. At day's end, we find Moses working to uplift cosmic sparks dispersed in the depths of depravity, rather than being entombed in sacred soil.

One may almost palpably feel Moses' final frustration, his anxiety, his discomfiture. More than most of us, he is torn between the godly and the all too human. "*'The man of God.'* Said Rabbi Abin: From the waist down, man; from the waist up, God."[25] The prophet who looks through a "clear speculum,"[26] is godly; the national liberator, is human. Moses must descend from the Mountain of God illuminated in eternal light, to the camp of the Hebrews, in order to set in motion events that will birth a nation of Israel. However, as the curtain closes on his career, Moses is informed from on high that he will not be granted the privilege of completing this national mission; he will not enter into the land. A prophet of Moses' caliber must be ready to abandon his "humanity" and revert back to his "divinity," expressed symbolically in death by the kiss of God[27]—in the very middle of the act.[28]

MESSIAH SON OF JOSEPH IS KILLED

Throughout its history, the Jewish People is forced to battle enemies. Joshua battles Amalek; Saul, Agag and his people; Mordechai and Esther, Haman; and at the End of Days, Messiah Son of Joseph contends with Armilus the Wicked.[29] (Some say that Armilus is a thinly veiled reference to Romulus, the legendary founder of Rome.)[30] "The House of Jacob shall be a fire, and the House of Joseph a flame; and the House of Esau straw; and they shall burn them and consume them."[31]

It is the job of Josephic Messianism to protect the Israelite character from inimical forces and currents. This mission is entrusted to the Children of Rachel.[32] In Kabbalah, Rachel symbolizes "the Revealed World" (*'Alma de-Itgalya*)—the world of division and differentiation—and the *sefirah* (attribute) of *Malkhut* (Kingship). At the opposite pole, Messiah Son of David descends from Rachel's sister Leah, who, in turn, symbolizes "the Hidden World" (*'Alma de-Itkasya*), a world of unity associated with the *sefirah* (attribute) of *Binah* (Understanding).

Before the arrival of Messiah Son of David, there precedes him Messiah Son of Joseph, which is to say in so many words, before there will commence in earnest a cosmic unification, there will precede an arousal of particularist nationalism. The Talmud describes the death of Messiah Son of Joseph.[33] Yet the greatest kabbalist of all time, Rabbi Isaac Luria, prescribed a prayer (to be recited during the silent devotion, the *Shemoneh 'Esreh* or *'Amidah*) asking that Messiah Son of Joseph be spared death on the battlefield at the hand of Armilus the Wicked.[34] As Maimonides judiciously wrote concerning the Days of Messiah, ours is not to know "the order of these events, nor their specifics,"[35] but this much we do know. The discussion in the Talmud and in the Lurianic writings revolves around this question: What will be the nature of the transition from the particularist to the universalist; from the nationalist to the global? Must the epoch of Messiah Son of Joseph die a violent death in order to pave the way for the epoch of Messiah Son of David? Or is it possible (as was the fervent prayer of Rabbi Isaac Luria) that there might develop a peaceful coexistence of Joseph and Judah, Saul (the Benjaminite, descendant of Rachel) and David (the Judahite, descendant of Leah); that in the imagery of the Talmud, there might result a seamless, uninterrupted transition from "redemption" to "prayer" (*semikhat ge'ulah li-tefillah*)?[36] To put it into our contemporary jargon, must there be violent revolution, or can the "birth pangs of Messiah" take the form of peaceful evolution?

JUDAH AND JOSEPH

> **Judah approached him [Joseph] and said, "Please, my master (*bi adoni*)." (Genesis 44:18)**
>
> (Or translated differently, "Mine the mastery [*bi adoni*]!")

Two Faces of Messianism

What is the nature of the struggle, the conflict that erupted between Judah and Joseph? Joseph is an acculturated Hebrew who works for the cause of the nationalist dream; Judah conversely is a *"heimishe Yid"* (Yiddish, a homey Jew), whose progeny will take up global concerns. The hermeneutic method of Joseph is from the universal to the particular; the method of Judah, from the particular to the universal. The line of Judah is a series of endogamous, even incestuous relations: Lot and his daughters, Judah and his daughter-in-law Tamar. It would be hard to find a more inbred family. Yet, from these unions emerges King David, who aspires to redeem the world at large in all its breadth and externality. The turning point from endogamy to exogamy was the intermarriage of Boaz and Ruth the Moabitess. (Rabbinic tradition made Ruth's adventure the very paradigm of halakhic conversion to Judaism.)[37] In Kabbalah, their union bespeaks the marrying of "redemption" (Boaz the Redeemer) to "prayer" (Ruth, grandmother of David, "who satiated [*rivah*] the Holy One, blessed be He, with songs and praises").[38] Boaz represents ancestral land claims, while Ruth, a landless alien, symbolizes the universal.

The tribes of Judah and Joseph would evolve into two kingdoms: the Kingdom of Joseph (consisting of ten tribes) in the North and the Kingdom of Judah (consisting of two tribes, Judah and Benjamin) in the South. Which of the two kingdoms was more universalist in scope; which more particularist or nationalist? Reading the Bible, it becomes apparent that the Northern Kingdom was more prone to adopting surrounding idolatries. Yet this steady seduction to the worship of Baʻal and Asherah does not seem to have bestowed a more cosmopolitan outlook. The Kingdom of Judah on the other hand, centered on Solomon's Temple in Jerusalem, might actually have been less parochial in outlook.

Take the Tree of Joseph and the Tree of Judah, and they shall be as one in your hand.[39]

MORDECHAI: A BENJAMINITE JUDEAN

Before we analyze his personality, we must develop somewhat the historical and political backdrop from which Mordechai emerges.

The Scroll of Esther is dominated by King Ahashverosh. This near-mythic king heads a list of several "cosmocrats" (to employ the Greek loanword *"kosmokrator"* imported by the Rabbis of the Midrash).[40] The "dark side" of cosmocracy usually spells trouble for the Jews. What about the "bright side" of this phenomenon? How does Judaism fare under a "benevolent despot" such as Alexander the Great, or Napoleon, for that matter?

To this day, devout Jewish men bear the name "Alexander" (bestowed upon them at the time of their circumcision). That itself is indication of a fondness for this historic figure. The Talmud tells a charming tale of an encounter in Erets Israel between Alexander the Macedonian and the leader of the Jews, the High Priest Simeon the Just. Alexander was astonished to behold the visage of the saintly man. It was that very face that would appear to Alexander in dream on the eve of a major victory. Thus positively predisposed,

Alexander granted Simeon his request that the Temple in Jerusalem be spared destruction.[41]

Moving on to Napoleon and the Jews, there are many different versions of this complex relationship. Tomes have been written concerning this intriguing chapter in history. Was Napoleon bent on the extirpation of Judaism and the forceful absorption of the Jews into European civilization? Was he sympathetic to the Jews' return to their land?

As romantically told by Martin Buber in the historic novel *For the Sake of Heaven* (entitled in Hebrew, *Gog u-Magog*), the great Hasidic masters of Russia and Poland were divided in their opinions of Bonaparte. While some Rebbes viewed him as a gentile Messiah, a modern-day Cyrus,[42] others looked upon him as Satan incarnate. Rabbi Shneur Zalman of Liadi was shown on the first day of Rosh Hashanah (before *Mussaf*) that Napoleon's victory would bring economic prosperity to the Jews while spelling spiritual destruction. Contrariwise, Tsar Alexander's victory would bring economic ruin to the Jews, yet their faith would survive intact. Rabbi Shneur Zalman opted for the latter and was forced to flee to the interior of Russia, always one step ahead of the *Grande Armée*. Finally, the Old Rabbi succumbed in the remote village of Piena.[43]

The Messiah and the cosmocrat share much in common. How did Alexander and Napoleon hope to juggle the opposed currents of union and diversity, empire and nationalism? In the Scroll of Esther, Ahashverosh, "who rules from India to Ethiopia over a hundred and twenty-seven states,"[44] encourages each man to "speak the language of his people."⁴⁵ If language is an indication, then Alexander and Napoleon lie at the opposite end of the spectrum from the Persian emperor Ahashverosh, the one imposing Hellenization, the other Gallicization upon the subjects of their respective realms. Assimilation to the dominant culture was the price of admission to these latter two cosmocracies. Napoleon's bold new synthesis, while tearing down the walls of the ghetto, sought to homogenize ethnic Jews into Frenchmen of the Mosaic faith.

Back to Mordechai. When confronted with the dark side of the Persian Empire, with "Haman," Mordechai functions as a Josephic Messiah (though technically not descended from Joseph, but from Benjamin, Rachel's younger son),⁴⁵* throwing all the forces at his disposal—both physical and spiritual—into the fray against Haman the Agagite. As for the bright side of the Empire, Mordechai, as Joseph before him, serves as viceroy to the King. According to rabbinic tradition, Mordechai of the *Megillah* is one and the same as Mordechai Bilshan (Mordechai the Linguist) of Ezra 2:2 and Nehemiah 7:7, whereby it was deduced that he was a gifted linguist.⁴⁶

Mordechai is in the final analysis a hybrid: a Benjaminite Judean. As a Benjaminite, he falls into the tradition of Messiah Son of Joseph; as *"Mordechai ha-Yehudi"* ("Mordechai the Judean") he longs for a world of unity. Drawing on the interchangeability of the letters *hé* and *ḥet*, the Midrash is able to interpret *Yehudi* (יהודי), or Judean, as *Yiḥudi* (יחודי), or Unifier.⁴⁷

Two Faces of Messianism

"THE SCEPTER SHALL NOT DEPART FROM JUDAH, NOR THE RULER'S STAFF FROM BETWEEN HIS FEET, UNTIL SHILOH COMES" (GENESIS 49:10)

Many have wondered at this mysterious ancient prophecy. Great French commentators offered the solution that the verse alludes to the ongoing competition between Joseph and Judah, later embodied in the establishment of the Northern Kingdom by Jeroboam I upon the death of King Solomon. The establishment of the kingdom of Jeroboam (an Ephraimite, thus a descendant of Joseph) put an end to the hegemony of Judahite rule. Furthermore, that kingdom of Jeroboam was prophesied by Ahijah the Shilonite. Thus, it was precisely at the time of the arrival of the Shilonite (from Shiloh) that the royal scepter departed from Judah, which is to say, that the undivided rule of the Davidic dynasty ceased.[48]

The excesses of King Solomon, an early experiment with the model of cosmocracy, demanded that the pendulum swing in the opposite direction. Israel would once again toil in the vineyard of nationalism, except this time the "nationalism within nationalism" of a divided kingdom. The tribal consciousness of King Jeroboam I was subject to extreme pride. There are those who view the two golden calves of Jeroboam, the one erected in Dan, the other in Bethel, as symbolic of Menasseh and Ephraim, Joseph's two sons.[49] (Earlier, the Golden Calf in the Desert was linked in rabbinic tradition to Joseph himself.)[50]

There would seem to be a dialectic at work here. As far as the genius of Messiah Son of David advances in the direction of unification and synthesis, so must the talent of Messiah Son of Joseph achieve in the opposite direction of breakdown and fragmentation.

A quaint *aggadah* or legend of the Talmud bears out this point:

> The Holy One, blessed be He, grabbed Jeroboam by his garment and said to him: "Repent, and I and you and [David] the son of Jesse will stroll together in the Garden of Eden."
> Jeroboam asked Him: "Who shall lead?"
> "The son of Jesse shall lead."
> "If so, I am not interested."[51]

True to character to the bitter end, even to the point of sounding ludicrous, Jeroboam will not be enticed by the promise of a utopian confederation with David at its helm. Jeroboam had been divinely appointed to be the instrument of dismantling David's kingdom. He is forever nitpicking at the details of the proposed structure. "Who shall lead?"

CROSSCURRENTS

The winds of unification and fragmentation blow to and fro. At times, all the valiant efforts and campaigns of Messiah Son of Joseph are but a preparation for an advanced, elevated consciousness that will flourish in the Days of Messiah Son of David. "Therefore it shall be said in the Book of the Wars of the Lord—love (*vahev*) in the end."[52] And the opposite scenario exists as well. There are times in history when the work of unification, the superb governmental architecture of David and Solomon paves the way for the fault-finding and fissuring of Jeroboam. "The scepter shall not depart from Judah, nor the ruler's staff from between his feet, until Shiloh comes, and to him an assembly of peoples."[53] And, "Who shall lead?"

CONCLUSION

[Jacob] had a dream, and behold, a ladder was set on the earth and its top was reaching to the heavens, and behold, the angels of God were ascending and descending on it (*bo*). (Genesis 28:12)

According to the Midrash, the angels of the Land of Israel were ascending and the angels of Beyond the Land were descending.[54] It is possible that the final word of the verse *"bo"* refers not to Jacob's ladder but to Jacob himself. The angels were ascending and descending within him (*bo*)![55] Within each of us there are these ascending and descending angels (the Greek word *angelos*, as the original Hebrew word *mal'akh*, conveys the sense of "messenger"), angels of the Land, and angels of Beyond the Land.

When Jacob later reenters the land, the process reverses itself: "And Jacob went on his way, and angels of God encountered him. Jacob said when he saw them, 'This is the camp of God.' So he called the name of that place *Mahanayim* [Two Camps]."[56] Once again, the Midrash explains that the angels of the Land of Israel came out to greet him and to accompany him to the Land. The two camps refer to the two groups of angels: the angels of Beyond the Land who escorted him up to this point, and the angels of the Land of Israel who came to receive him.[57]

Each spiritual process is unique. There are those, such as Herzl and Joseph, Viceroy of Egypt, whose focus (like that of Jacob reentering the Land) shifts from the cosmopolitan to the ancestral.

At a certain point in their career, the angels of Beyond the Land take leave of them and they are embraced by the angels of the Land of Israel.

And then there are those, such as Rav Kook and the Biblical Judah, whose spiritual evolution takes them beyond the confines of the ghetto to encompass the globe. In a portentous dream, like our Father Jacob, they witness a changing of the guard: angels of the Land of Israel ascending and angels of Beyond the Land descending. Within themselves they experience a shift of consciousness, a change of perception. Ultimately, their calling, their mission broadens.

And finally, there are the hybrids among us who, as *Mordechai ha-Yehudi*, attempt to fuse the two aspirations of nationalism and cosmocracy.

---

[1] Adapted by the author from *"Du-Partsufin shel ha-Meshihiyut,"* which first appeared in Bezalel Naor, *Avirin* (Jerusalem, 5740/1980), pp. 16-24.

[2] Rabbi Abraham Isaac HaKohen Kook, *Orot Yisrael* (Jerusalem, 1942), 6:6; reprinted in *Orot* (Jerusalem, 1950), p. 160.

    Cf. Rabbi Zadok Hakohen Rabinowitz of Lublin, *Mahshevot Haruts* (Piotrków, 1912); 35c-36b; idem, *Dover Tsedek* (Piotrków, 1911), 40d-41c.

[3] In one of his journals Rav Kook recorded this confession:

> I love all. I am incapable of not loving people, all the peoples. In all the depths of my heart I want the glory of all, the mending of all. My love for Israel is more ardent, more profound, but the inner desire extends with its mighty love to all, literally. I have no need to force this feeling of love; it flows straight from the holy depth of the wisdom of the godly soul."
> (*Shemonah Kevatsim* 2:76)

    This *pensée* first appeared in *'Arpilei Tohar* (Jerusalem, 1914).

[4] The writer Alexander Ziskind Rabinowitz (AZaR), a great admirer of Rav Kook during his days as Rabbi of Jaffa, recollected Rav Kook confiding:

> Whoever said about me that my soul is torn, expressed it well. Certainly it is torn. A human whose soul is not torn is inconceivable. Only the mineral is whole. But a human possesses opposite aspirations; a

constant war is waged in his midst. The entire work of man is to unify the oppositions in his soul through a universal idea, by whose greatness and loftiness all is encompassed and arrives at total harmony. Understandably, this is but an ideal to which we aspire; no mortal can ever achieve it. Yet by our striving, we can come ever closer. It is this that the kabbalists refer to as *"yihudim"* ("unifications").

(Quoted in Elhanan Kalmanson, *Ha-Mahshavah ha-Yisraelit* [Jerusalem, 1920; photo offset Jerusalem, 1967], p. 13)

[5] This ability is visualized in the short film *Cosmic Zoom* (1968) directed by Eva Szasz.

Rav Kook wrote that our amazement at the minuscule should in no way lag behind our amazement at the magnitude of the universe. He paralleled the Psalmist's exclamation, "How great are Your works, O LORD" (Psalms 92:6) with "How tiny are Your works, O LORD!" See *Orot ha-Torah* 3:8, and *'Eyn AYaH*, vol. 4, ed. Rabbi Ya'akov Filber (Jerusalem: Makhon RZYH, 2000), *Shabbat* 54b (chap. 5, par. 12), p. 23.

[6] See our essay "Rav Kook's Shattered Vessels and Their Repair."

[7] Numbers 1:52.

[8] Genesis 44:5.

[9] Rabbi Hayyim Joseph David Azulai, *Devash le-Fi* (Livorno, 1801), s.v. *gavi'a*, quoting the kabbalist Rabbi Nathan Shapira Yerushalmi.

[10] Deuteronomy 10:22.

[11] Genesis 43:32.

[12] Genesis 46:34.

[13] Genesis 39:14.

[14] Exodus 2:19.

[15] *Deuteronomy Rabbah* 2:8.

[16] *Sifré, 'Ekev*.

[17] b. *Gittin* 8b, 47a; Maimonides, *MT, Hil. Terumot* 1:3; Nahmanides, Deuteronomy 11:24.

[18] As foreseen by Rabbi Moses Hayyim Luzzatto, in the future, the entire earth will enjoy the status of Syria, *"kibbush yahid,"* whereby the lands outside of Israel will be purified. Yet the sanctity of *"kibbush rabbim"* will still be restricted to *Erets Yisrael* proper. See Rabbi M.H. Luzzatto, *Ma'amar ha-Ge'ulah*, ed. H. Touitou (n.p., 2002), p. 37.

[19] For this latter understanding of the word *ehad* (one), the reader is referred to the vast Sufic literature concerning the practice of *tawhid*, and to the equally voluminous Hasidic literature concerning the meditative discipline of *yihud*. In both *tawhid* and *yihud* the adept arrives at the realization that all is God. As that great teacher of HaBaD Hasidism, Rabbi Eizik of Homel, unabashedly ejaculated in the Yiddish vernacular: *"Altz iz Gott!"* "All is God!" See Rabbi Yitzhak Eizik Halevi Epstein of Homel, *"Iggeret Kodesh"* (Holy Epistle), printed at the conclusion of *Hannah Ariel—Amarot Tehorot (Ma'amar ha-Shabbat*, etc.) (Berdichev: Sheftel, 1912), 4b.

[20] Maimonides, *Guide of the Perplexed* I, 63.

[21] Deuteronomy 33:5.

[22] *Exodus Rabbah* 2:6, 48:4; *Leviticus Rabbah* 31:4; Ibn Ezra, Hizkuni, Nahmanides (quoting "some *aggadot"*) and Rabbeinu Behaye (Bahya ben Asher ibn Halawa) to Deuteronomy 33:5. See also Ibn Ezra and RaShBaM (Rabbi

Samuel ben Meir) to Genesis 36:31. And see Maimonides, *Commentary to the Mishnah, Shavu'ot* 2:2 (Kafah ed., p. 169).

23 *Seder 'Olam Rabbah,* chap. 7; *b. Zevahim* 102a.

24 Deuteronomy 34:6.

25 Deuteronomy 33:1; *Deuteronomy Rabbah* 11:4.

26 *b. Yevamot* 49b.

27 *b. Mo'ed Katan* 28a; *Bava Batra* 17a; Maimonides, *Guide of the Perplexed* III, 51.

28 In my perception of Moses as torn between universalism and nationalism, I seem to have been preceded by Rabbi Samuel Alexandrov of Bobruisk. See his *Mikhtevei Mehkar u-Bikoret,* vol. 3 (Jerusalem, 1932), pp. 18-21, 23. Alexandrov finds support for Moses' aloofness from Israel in the writings of MaHaRaL of Prague. See Rabbi Judah Löw, *Gevurot Hashem* (London: L. Honig & Sons, 1954), chap. 15 (75b): "In addition, when you know the level of Moses our Teacher, peace be unto him, inasmuch as he was set apart from *Kelal Yisrael* (the collective of Israel) by his level, and did not share the level of the rest of Israel, [Pharaoh's astrologers] could not know whether [Moses] was from Israel or from the nations, because according to his level, he had nothing in common with the rest of Israel. Understand this well."

29 Sa'adyah Gaon, *Emunot ve-De'ot* 8:5 (Kafah edition, p. 246).

30 See Yehudah Even-Shmuel, *Midreshei Ge'ulah* (Giv'atayim-Ramat Gan: Mossad Bialik, 1968), Introduction, p. 51, n. 67.

31 Obadiah 1:18; *b. Bava Batra* 123b.

32 "It is a tradition that Esau falls only by the hand of the children of Rachel" (*Genesis Rabbah* 73:7; 75:5). See also *Pesikta Rabbati,* ed. Meir Ish-Shalom (Vienna, 1880), chap. 13, *"Mini Ephraim Shoresham Amalek"* [Judges 5:14], 54a: "The seed of Amalek falls only by the hand of the children of Rachel." And see ibid. 54b.

33 *b. Sukkah* 52a.

34 See Rabbi Hayyim Vital, *Peri 'Ets Hayyim* (Dubrovna, 1804), *Sha'ar ha-'Amidah,* chap. 19, s.v. *ve-kissei David 'avdekha* (58c).The fervent wish that Messiah Son of Joseph not be killed was expressed earlier in *Zohar* III, 223a, 277b, and *Tikkunim me-Zohar Hadash* (Vilna, 1867), 27a.

35 Maimonides, *MT, Hil. Melakhim* 12:2.

36 *y. Berakhot* 1:1; *b. Berakhot* 4b, 9b, 42a; *Zohar* I, 132b, 205b (see commentary of *Sulam* there); Rabbi Hayyim Vital, *Peri 'Ets Hayyim* (Dubrovna, 1804), *Sha'ar Keri'at Shema',* chap. 29 (50b), *"ge'ulah—Yesod; tefillah—Malkhut";* Rabbi Levi Yitzhak Monson of Ozerna, *Bekha Yevarekh Yisrael* (Przemysl, 1905), Introduction and *Vayyeshev* (16c-d).

Rabbi Zadok Hakohen Rabinowitz of Lublin wrote: "Then David would have been Messiah, and Saul would have been worthy of being Messiah Son of Joseph, as Jonathan said [to David], 'And I shall be your second [in command]' [1 Samuel 23:17]'" (*Peri Tsaddik,* vol. 2 [Lublin, 1907], *Parashat Zakhor* [bot. 91b]).

37 *b. Yevamot* 47b.

38 *b. Berakhot* 7b, *Bava Batra* 14b.

39 See Ezekiel 37.

40 *Esther Rabbah* 1:12.

41 *b. Yoma* 69a.

Two Faces of Messianism

[42] See Isaiah 45:1.

According to Buber, Rabbi Menahem Mendel of Rymanów viewed Napoleon favorably.

A descendant of Rabbi Shneur Zalman of Liadi recounted to the latter's biographer, Hayyim Meir Heilmann, that it was the Maggid of Kozienice (Rabbi Israel Hopstein) that locked horns with the Alter Rebbe concerning Napoleon. See H.M. Heilman, *Beit Rabbi* (Berdichev, 1902), Part One, chap. 22 (45b, note 1).

[43] Ibid., chap. 22.

[44] Esther 1:1.

[45] Esther 1:22.

[45*] Esther 2:5. See commentary of Rabbi David Kimhi (RaDaK) to 2 Samuel 19:21 s.v. *le-khol Beit Yosef*.

[46] m. *Shekalim* 5:1; *Menahot* 65a. And see *Tosafot*, *Menahot* 64b, s.v. *amar lehu Mordechai*, and *Bava Kamma* 82b, s.v. *ve-'al otah sha'ah*.

[47] *Esther Rabbah* 6:2.

[48] See Hizkuni, Rabbi Samuel ben Meir (RaShBaM) and *Da'at Zekenim mi-Ba'alei ha-Tosafot* to Genesis 49:10. (The verse quoted by Hizkuni in his first interpretation, *"Va-yavo'u Shiloh va-yamlikhu 'aleihem et Yarav'am"* ["They came to Shiloh and appointed as king over them Jeroboam"] is not to be found in the Bible.)

[49] Abrabanel, 1 Kings 12:28.

[50] Rashi, Exodus 32:4 quoting *Midrash Tanhuma, Ki Tissa* 19. See Deuteronomy 33:17 and Psalms 106:20.

[51] b. *Sanhedrin* 102a.

[52] Numbers 21:14; b. *Kiddushin* 30b.

[53] Genesis 49:10.

[54] Rashi, Genesis 28:12, quoting *Genesis Rabbah* 68:12.

[55] In *Genesis Rabbah* (ibid.), Rabbi Hiyya and Rabbi Yannai disagreed whether the angels were ascending and descending on the ladder, or ascending and descending on Jacob.

Ibn Ezra (Genesis 28:12) quotes Rabbi Shelomo ha-Sepharadi as saying: "The ladder alludes to the supernal soul, and the angels of God—the thought of wisdom."

[56] Genesis 32:2-3

[57] Rashi ad locum, quoting *Midrash Tanhuma, Vayyishlah* 3.

"My Beloved is Like a Gazelle"
(Domeh Dodi li-Tsevi): The Esthetic Messiah
An *Essai* in Rabbinic Surrealism,
or Another Jewish Bestiary[1]

In the Song of Songs, King Solomon writes:

> My beloved is like a gazelle or a young hart; behold, he stands behind our wall, he looks in through the windows, he peers through the lattice.[2]

According to the Midrash, the verse describes the elusive character of the Redeemer: "Just as a deer appears and disappears and reappears, so the first Redeemer is revealed and occulted and revealed."[3] The commentators limn for us the timetable of the first Redeemer, Moses, who after an initial contact with the Children of Israel subjugated in Egypt, absented himself, only to reappear on the scene at a later time.[4] (Some make the astute observation that in the Bible code known as *ATBaSh*, the Hebrew word *tsevi* [deer] is permutated to *Moshe*.) And so too, we are told, the *future* process of redemption will be a symphony in three movements: revelation/occultation/revelation.[5]

Yet there is another sense in which the Beloved is compared to a deer. Besides its elusive behavior, the deer symbolizes the entire esthetic dimension. Part and parcel of the redemption of the soul of mankind is the redemption of the esthetic (perhaps erotic is the better word) dimension of being.

I will not commit the *faux pas* of writing that the Hebrew word for "deer," *tsevi*, has an additional meaning of "beauty." Though they look alike, these are actually two different words derived from separate proto-Semitic roots.

Be that as it may, the works of Solomon, Song of Songs and Proverbs (but especially the former) are replete with the image of the Beloved portrayed as a deer.

> Your two breasts are like two fawns that are twins of a gazelle, which feed among the lilies.[6]
>
> I adjure you, O daughters of Jerusalem, by the gazelles, and by the hinds of the field, that you awaken not, nor stir up love, until it please.[7]
>
> A lovely hind and a graceful doe, let her breasts satisfy you at all times; with her love be you ravished always."[8]

This fascination with the gazelle is common to both Hebrew and Arabic literature. Classical Arabic poetry abounds with the imagery of the graceful gazelle, a symbol of female pulchritude. (It has been theorized that *"ghazal,"* the word for love poetry in Arabic, is related to the word for gazelle.)

In medieval Arabic and Persian civilization the fawning (pun intended) on the graceful hind did not remain restricted to the realm of poetry (as in Hebraic civilization), but extended into the visual arts as well. In the Jewish world, the deer as visual image would be kept waiting in the woods for several centuries.

Belated as its arrival may have been, come the seventeenth century the icon of the deer exploded upon the Jewish world with full force. In 1666 ("the year of the beast" from the perspective of English Protestant millenarians),[9] a Turkish Jew by the name of "Tsevi" (first name "Shabbetai") captured the Messianic imagination of the Jewish People the world over. The symbolism of the deer was lost neither on Shabbetai Tsevi (he signed himself *"Tavya de-vei 'ila'ah,"* Aramaic for "celestial deer")[10] and his admirers, nor on his eventual critics (after the necessary sobering) who punned on his name *"tsevi shavur"* ("a broken deer," a Mishnaic reference).[11] Sabbatian iconography (the little that has survived in frontispieces of books) makes ample use of deer representation.[12]

The great visionary of Israel's rebirth, Rabbi Abraham Isaac Hakohen Kook (1865-1935), first Ashkenazic Chief Rabbi of Erets Israel, saw a similarity between Shabbetai Tsevi and Nietzsche.

> What Nietzsche is to humanity, Shabbetai Tsevi (may the name of the wicked rot) is to Judaism; and just as Nietzsche took leave of his senses, so Shabbetai Tsevi took leave of his religion. One shell (*kelipah*) related to the Footsteps of Messiah.[13]

Rav Kook's intriguing *pensée* has left many of us in suspense. Could he by some stretch be alluding to Nietzsche's triumphing of the Dionysian element over the Apollonian element?[14]

Messiah

Speaking of Rav Kook, in his seminal work, *Orot* (1920), Rav Kook would devote two crucial chapters to the "power of imagination" (*"ko'ah ha-medammeh"*) and the role it is destined to play in the redemptive process.

Initially, Rav Kook's survey of the contemporary scene assumes a rather pessimistic tone:

> All of contemporary culture is built on the foundation of the imaginative faculty. This is the pagan legacy of the civilized nations caught up in the imaginative faculty, from which developed physical beauty, both in action and in representation. The imaginative faculty progresses, and with it, the applied and empirical sciences, and in proportion to the ascendance of the imaginative faculty and its hold upon life, the light of intellect recedes, because the entire world supposes that all happiness depends on the development of the imaginative faculty. So things continue gradually, until the remains of reason in the spirit of secular wisdom are also converted to the imaginative faculty. The speakers and raconteurs, the dramaturges and all engaged in *les beaux arts*, assume prominence in society, while philosophy hobbles and totters because pure reason disappears. As much as reason recedes, so "impudence increases, and the wisdom of sages rots, the sin-fearing are reviled and truth is absent, and the face of the generation is as the

face of a dog."[15] That inner gentleness, which comes from the spirit of wisdom, disappears. The longing for spirituality and transcendence; for divine communion; for the higher world; for the clarity of ethics in the apex of its purity; for the concepts of intellect in and of their eternal selves, become a rare spectacle. This global phenomenon is reflected proportionately in Israel *vis-à-vis* divine inspiration and love of Torah with an inner spirit and essential freshness of faithful Judaism. There rules in the world a material spirit. *Woe unto you, O land, when your king is a lad and your princes eat in the morning!*[16]

And then in an abrupt turnabout, we are treated to a glint of the brilliant ironic wit which is the signature of Kookian vision:

> But all of this is a far-reaching plan, the LORD's plan to perfect the imaginative faculty, for imagination is the healthy basis for the supernal spirit that will descend on it… the supreme divine spirit destined to come through King Messiah. Therefore, now the imaginative faculty is being firmly established. When it is completely finished, the seat will be ready and perfect for the supernal spirit of the LORD, fit to receive the light of the divine spirit, which is the spirit of the LORD, *a spirit of wisdom and understanding, a spirit of counsel and strength, a spirit of knowledge and awe of the LORD.*[17]

Not content with sociological study and survey of modern intellectual history, Rav Kook, a kabbalist of note, goes on to provide Lurianic underpinnings to his observations, whereby the harlotry first addressed by Joshua (or rather his spies) with only partial success, is later confronted by King Solomon, with complete (or near complete) success. In the Kookian interpretation of this Lurianic myth, Rahab the Harlot and the two harlots who appeared before King Solomon symbolize the unbridled power of imagination:[18]

> When the time had as yet not arrived for all the purity to appear at the final heights, there were sent by Joshua two spies to reconnoiter the land, and they came to the home of a harlot by the name of Rahab.[19] All is tied together with holiness and the highest good, but the attribute of judgment is aroused and true fear of punishment is required in proportion to the empowerment of the imagination and its deepening. But in the essence of the national will, the imaginative dimension—which entails the embodiment of knowledge on the one hand, and all description of beauty on the other—was still not completed at that time. This was brought to completion in the days of Solomon: *Then two harlots came* before the judgment of the King of Israel, who sits on the throne of the LORD.[20]

Rav Kook continues to trace the historic process of *"birur ko'ah ha-medammeh,"* the clarification of the power of imagination (to employ the terminology of Rabbi Nahman of Breslov),[21] through the idolatrous leanings of King Solomon in the First Temple period (attributed by the Bible to the influence of his foreign wives), which in turn prompted the hamstringing of imagination by the Men of the Great Assembly at the beginning of the Second Temple period, and finally culminating in the re-emergence and re-empowerment of imagination at the time of the national renascence in the Land of Israel:

> However, through the interference of the foreign women,[22] together with the inability to digest foreign things, there resulted the wickedness that caused the founding of the great city of Rome,[23] and the siftings of elements had to be stretched out for eons, until the imagination was disempowered in Israel. The drive for idolatry was captured in a "lead pot" and "slaughtered."[24] By the same token, *there is no more any prophet*,[25] and the flame of love for nation and land is not felt in the same profound way as in the good days. This is related to the pain of the entire world. Until at the End of Days, the traces of the power of imagination are revealed and the love of the Land is aroused. The thing appears with its dregs, but it is destined to be purified. *The smallest will become a thousand, and the youngest, a powerful nation, I am the LORD; in its time I will hasten it.*[26]

In Rav Kook's vision, a reactivation of the imagination is necessary for the return of prophecy to Israel. *"U-ve-yad ha-nevi'im adammeh."* "By means of the prophets I have spoken in images."[27]

Rav Kook is indebted to Maimonides for placing the *ko'ah ha-medammeh*, the imaginative faculty, front and center, rendering it an essential component, perhaps even *the* essential component of prophecy.[28] While a dormant imagination may not pose an obstacle to the intellectual pursuit of Torah study, Israel's renewed quest for prophecy in its land makes the revival of the moribund *"medammeh"* an absolute necessity.

Rav Kook may not have been alone in the belief that the non-cerebral (or right-hemispheric) dimension, so long missing from Judaism, would play a vital part in the national renascence. There is an intriguing remark of the Rebbe of Sokhatchov that leads one to suspect that he too may have been thinking in such terms, that Israel in its struggle for final redemption must encompass a dimension hitherto almost alien to its being. His oral remarks (which fortunately, were preserved for posterity) take the form of commentary to the *Haftarah*, the reading from the Prophets for the Intermediate Sabbath of the Festival of *Sukkot* (Booths). According to Talmudic tradition, on that Sabbath morning we read *Be-Yom bo' Gog*,[29] Ezekiel's apocalyptic vision of the confrontation between the army of Gog and Magog on the one hand, and Jerusalem on the other.[30] Rav Hai Gaon, quoted in the *Tur*, explained that this occasion was deemed appropriate for that reading, because the War of Gog and Magog will take place on Sukkot.[31]

Rabbi Samuel Bornstein (1855-1926), the Rebbe of Sokhatchov (a school of Polish Hasidism known for its penetrating thought) could not leave matters at that. He probed for some intrinsic connection between the prophesied cosmic struggle and the observance of the commandment of *sukkot*, those booths or huts that serve as temporary residences throughout the festival.

But first, there arises the more basic question: Who are Gog and Magog? Some say that they symbolize the seventy nations of the world, all lined up against Israel. (The Hebrew words "*Gog u-Magog*" have the numerical value of 70.)[32] The Sokhatchover, drawing on a Midrash, traces Gog back to his ancestor Yephet, son of Noah. Likewise, Israel is traced back to Shem, son of Noah.[33] In the postdiluvian world, Yephet received the dimension of *"hitsoniyut"* ("outwardness"), and Shem, the dimension of *"penimiyut"* ("inwardness").[34] In the apocalyptic struggle of titans, Israel's eleventh-hour salvation will hinge on its ability to take hold of the outward dimension, symbolized by the commandment of the *sukkah* or booth, which may be fulfilled by the mere act of sleeping in the *sukkah*. In sleep, one is stripped of the cerebral and reduced to the external, bodily aspect of one's being.[35] (Though the Sokhatchover does not couch it in such terms, sleep is also a window of opportunity for unbridled imagination; for the soul to enter the imaginal world.)[36]

Rabbi Gershon Hanokh Leiner (1839-1890), the Rebbe of Radzyn, in *his* analysis of the confrontation between Gog and Israel, focuses specifically on the Greek connection. In this regard, the Radzyner quotes the Talmud: "Our rabbis permitted [to write a Torah scroll in] Greek."³⁷ As is well known, the civilization of *Yavan*, or Greece, excelled in the arts and appreciation of the esthetic dimension of being. The Talmud will justify the practice of writing a Torah scroll in Greek by invoking the verse, "*Yapht Elohim le-Yephet ve-yishkon be-'aholei Shem*" ("May God enlarge the boundaries of Yephet, and may he dwell in the tents of Shem"), which they paraphrased as, "*Yaphyuto shel Yephet yehé be-'aholei Shem*" ("The beauty of Yephet shall be in the tents of Shem").³⁸ To the Radzyner's thinking, implicit in Ezekiel's prophecy, "And it shall come to pass on that day that I will give unto Gog a place there for a grave in Israel,"³⁹ is the prediction that the good, positive element of Gog—or Greece—once extracted from the dross, will be incorporated within Israel's collective consciousness. Gog being buried in Israel, which is to say, the soil of Israel receiving into its midst the body of Gog, symbolizes the introjection of Greek civilization—or rather the salient, redeeming feature thereof—into the nation of Israel.⁴⁰ "And the precious, the good, found in this victory, will remain in Israel for eternity."⁴¹

There is no denying that *HaZaL*, the Sages of blessed memory, were open to allowing the *'or hozer*, the reflected light of Hellenic (or Japhetic) civilization to shine upon Hebraic (or Semitic) civilization, but we find in the writings of the Rabbis another strain of thought whereby beauty shines upon Zion not as an *'or hozer*, a reflection of a foreign civilization, but as an *'or yashar*, a direct illumination from the source of Israel, whose rays extend to the entire world.

> The Sages say: "From Zion was created the world, for it is said, 'A psalm of Asaph. The God of gods, the LORD, spoke, and called earth, from the rising of the sun until its setting. Out of Zion, the perfection of beauty (*mi-Tsiyon mikhlal yophi*)'—from it is perfected the beauty of the world (*mimenu mukhlal yophyo shel 'olam*)."[42]
>
> Ten measures (*kabin*) of beauty (*yophi*) descended to the world; nine, Jerusalem took, and one, the rest of the world."[43]

In the mystical *Heikhalot* literature, we discover that the name of the "Prince of Torah" (*Sar ha-Torah*) is *Yophiel*, or in other texts *Yepheiphiyah*.[44] At first glance, this might strike us as a strange name for an angel: "The Beauty of *Yah*." However, as scholars have pointed out, the setting for the visionary experiences recorded in the *Heikhalot* is the Holy Temple in Jerusalem.[45] A student of the Talmud will recall that on the seventh day of Sukkot (or *Hoshana Rabba*) in the Temple, at the conclusion of the seven *hakafot* or circumambulations, they would bid farewell: *"Yophi lakh, mizbe'ah! Yophi lakh, mizbe'ah!"* ("Beauty to you, Altar! Beauty to you, Altar!"). According to the opinion of Rabbi Eliezer [ben Jacob], they would say: *"Yophi le-Yah ve-lakh, mizbe'ah! Yophi le-Yah ve-lakh, mizbe'ah!"* ("Beauty to *Yah*, and to you, Altar! Beauty to *Yah*, and to you, Altar!").[46] One speculates that the name of the angel

Yepheiphiyah derived from this salutation: *"Yophi le-Yah!"* Verily, the Temple in Jerusalem is the source of all beauty in the world.

> Said Rav Hisda: "What is written, 'The LORD loves the gates of Zion more than all the dwellings of Jacob'?⁴⁷ The LORD loves gates distinguished by *Halakhah* more than synagogues and study-houses."
>
> This is what Rabbi Hiyya bar Ammi said in the name of 'Ulla: "From the day the Temple was destroyed, the Holy One, blessed be He, has naught in His world except the four ells of *Halakhah*."⁴⁸

With the return of the lovely *Shekhinah* to Zion, all of the beauty and romance which are hers will reappear in the Gates of Zion. If, as the Sages say, the *Sha'arei Tsiyon* (Gates of Zion) are *"she'arim metsuyanim ba-halakhah"* ("gates distinguished by *Halakhah*"), then they are also *"she'arim metsuyanim"* ("decorative gates") without further modification.⁴⁹ With the destruction of the Temple, the Holy One's world was reduced to "four ells of *Halakhah*,"⁵⁰ but with the national rebirth, the Holy One's world broadens to encompass other dimensions as well. *"Ohev Hashem Sha'arei Tsiyon."* "The LORD loves the Gates of Zion."

And my Beloved, the Messiah, with his nose pressed up against the glass window like that of a fawn, is taking it all in.

[1] In 2012, I published *The Kabbalah of Relation: "We Would Have Learned the 'Way of the Earth' From the Cock"* (A Jewish Bestiary), which dealt with the symbol of the cock in Talmud, Kabbalah and the surrealist art of Marc Chagall.
[2] Song of Songs 2:9. Cf. ibid. 2:17.
[3] *Numbers Rabbah* 11:2; *Song of Songs Rabbah, Parashah* 2.
[4] See Rabbi Ze'ev Wolf Einhorn, *Peirush MaHaRZU* to *Exodus Rabbah* 5:19.
[5] *Numbers Rabbah* and *Song of Songs Rabbah*, loc. cit.
[6] Song of Songs 4:5.

The recent shocking statement by author Melissa Mohr is an apt description of the contortions like verses are put through in various quarters: "Some of these euphemisms are obvious, as in the Song of Songs...It is almost painful to watch scholars insist that this passage has nothing at all to do with sex. No, it is truly and only about God's love for Israel ... or the soul's spiritual union with God" (Melissa Mohr, *Holy Sh*t: A Brief History of Swearing* [New York: Oxford University Press, 2013], pp. 83-84).

[7] Song of Songs 2:7, 3:5. I am still undecided whether the comment by some that *"tseva'ot"* is a pun on the divine name *Tseva'ot* and *"ayelot ha-sadeh"* a pun on the divine cognomen *El Shaddai*, constitutes genuine Bible commentary or merely *leitsanut* (comedy).

[8] Proverbs 5:19.

[9] The reference is to the Book of Revelations by John of Patmos, wherein the number 666 is the mark of the beast, interpreted by Protestant millenarians to refer to the Antichrist. Recently, it has been speculated that the beast is actually a veiled reference to the Roman Emperor Nero.

[10] b. *Hullin* 59b.

[11] m. *Bava Metsi'a* 1:4.

[12] See Bezalel Naor, *Post-Sabbatian Sabbatianism* (Spring Valley, NY: Orot, 1999), pp. 79-82, concerning the frontispiece to Rabbi Tsevi Chotsh, *Hemdat Tsevi* (Amsterdam, 1706).

[13] Rabbi Abraham Isaac Hakohen Kook, *Kevatsim mi-Ketav Yad Kodsho*, vol. 1, ed. Boaz Ofen (Jerusalem, 5766/2006), *Pinkas "Aharon be-Boisk,"* par. 40 (p. 56).

[14] See Friedrich Nietzsche, *The Birth of Tragedy* (1872).

[15] m. *Sotah* 9:15.

[16] Ecclesiastes 10:16.

[17] Isaiah 11:2.

Rabbi Abraham Isaac Hakohen Kook, *Orot* (1920), *Yisrael u-Tehiyato* (Israel and Its Renascence), chap. 17.

[18] See Shlomo Katz, "Rahav and Yehoshua: Imagination and Intellect," *Orot: A Multidisciplinary Journal*, vol. 1 (5751/1991), pp. 49-64, and Editor's Apercu, pp. 65-67.

[19] Joshua chap. 2.

[20] 1 Kings chap. 3. See Rabbi Hayyim Vital, *Sefer ha-Likkutim*, Joshua chap. 2; 1 Kings chap. 3; idem, *Likkutei Torah*, Joshua chap. 2; 1 Kings chap. 3.

[21] *Likkutei MOHaRaN* II, 8:7. See further below note 28.

Known as *"Tik'u Tokhahah,"* this was the last public discourse delivered by Rabbi Nahman before his passing. Rabbi David Sears speculates that it served as the template for Rabbi Nahman's one and only poem, *Shir Na'im*. See Rabbi Nachman of Breslov, *Shir Na'im/Song of Delight*, ed. Rabbi David

Sears (Spring Valley, NY: Orot, 2005).

On the other hand, in *Likkutei MOHaRaN* I, 26 *("Ahavei lan mana")*, Rabbi Nahman takes an extremely dim view of the imaginative faculty, equating it with the *yetser ha-ra'*, or evil inclination. In that discourse, the key term is not *"birur ko'ah ha-medammeh"* ("clarification of the imaginative faculty") but *"shevirat ko'ah hamedammeh"* ("breaking of the imaginative faculty"), indicating its unredeemable character.

[22] 1 Kings 11:1-8.

[23] *b. Shabbat* 56b, *Sanhedrin* 21b. However, a different version of the founding of Rome is recorded in Rashi, *Megillah* 6b.

[24] *b. Yoma* 69b, *Sanhedrin* 64a, *'Avodah Zarah* 17.

[25] Psalm 74:9. According to the *Sefer Hasidim*, Vilna Gaon and Rabbi Zadok Hakohen of Lublin, the cessation of prophecy was linked to the eradication of idolatry. See Bezalel Naor, *Lights of Prophecy/Orot ha-Nevu'ah* (1990).

[26] Isaiah 60:22. *Orot, Yisrael u-Tehiyato*, chap. 18.

In *Shemonah Kevatsim* 5:190 the conclusion reads: "The smallest will become a thousand," "the thousand for you, Solomon" [Song of Songs 8:12]. This is actually the more logical conclusion. Logic would dictate that Solomon reappear in the conclusion to the *pensée*.

[27] Hosea 12:11.

[28] See Moses Maimonides, *Guide of the Perplexed* II, 36. Another latter-day visionary who pursued this line (while downplaying the indebtedness to Maimonides) was Rabbi Nahman of Breslov. Rabbi Nahman, as Rav Kook (who was very attached to and inspired by the writings of Breslov), is intent on the rectification and clarification of imagination as a means to reviving prophecy. See, e.g., *Likkutei Moharan* II, 8 (*Tik'u Tokhaha*), pars. 7-8. See now Zvi Mark, *Mistikah ve-Shiga'on bi-Yetsirat R. Nahman mi-Breslov* (*Mysticism and Madness in the Work of R. Nahman of Bratslav*) (Tel Aviv, 2003), chap. 5 (*"Dimyon, Nevu'ah ve-Emunah"*), especially pp. 86-95.

[29] Ezekiel 38:18.

[30] *b. Megillah* 31a.

[31] Rabbi Jacob ben Asher, *Arba'ah Turim, Tur Orah Hayyim*, chap. 490.

[32] *Midrash Tanhuma*, end *Korah*.

[33] *Genesis Rabbah* 36:6. See Genesis 10:2: "The children of Yephet: Gomer and Magog and Media and Yavan and Tubal and Meshekh and Tiras." Cf. Ezekiel 39:1: "...Gog, chief prince of Meshekh and Tubal."

[34] Rabbi Samuel Bornstein recorded this insight in the name of his father Rabbi Abraham Bornstein, author of the Responsa *Avnei Nezer*.

It would be apposite to point out that Noah's blessing to Yephet bespeaks the assignation of outwardness to Yephet and inwardness to Shem. "May God enlarge Yephet and may he dwell in the tents of Shem." In the Hebrew original it reads: *"Yapht Elohim le-Yephet ve-yishkon be-'aholei Shem"* (Genesis 9:27).

Yapht may, by a stretch, be related to the Hebrew word for "beauty," *yophi*. As the Rabbis paraphrased the verse: "The beauty (*yaphyuto*) of Yephet shall be in the tents of Shem" (*b. Megillah* 9b). The halakhic discussion there concerns the permissibility of writing Torah scrolls in the very esthetic Greek script. But this Rabbinic interpretation of the term is the stuff of *derash* or homily.

From a perspective of *peshuto shel mikra*, the simple sense of the verse, *yapht* as a verb (*p-t-h*) is an expression of width or spatial extension. (See Onkelos, Rashi and Ibn Ezra to Genesis 9:27; the last-mentioned in opposition to Sa'adya Gaon.) At the other extreme stand the "tents of Shem," archetypical domiciles symbolic of inwardness.

One notes that whereas in the Sokhatchover analysis Yephet and Shem in their new incarnations of Gog-and-Magog and Israel are pitted against one another, in the passage from the Talmud cited above there is expressed an ideal marriage of the two *Weltanschauungen*. Out of the confrontation of the two ideational continents of Yephet and Shem may yet come a synthesis, or better yet, a creative tension.

[35] Rabbi Samuel Bornstein, *Shem mi-Shemuel, Rosh Hashanah—Sukkot* (Jerusalem, 5734/1974), *Yom Shabbat Hol ha-Mo'ed Sukkot*, Year 5677 (191b-192a).

[36] The Arabic term *'alam al-mithal* (literally "the world of likeness"), rooted in Islamic philosophy (especially in the writings of Ibn Sina or Avicenna), was translated by Henri Corbin into Latin as *mundus imaginalis* or imaginal world. See Henri Corbin, "Mundus Imaginalis or, the imaginary and the imaginal," *Cahiers internationaux de symbolisme*, vol. 6 (1964), pp. 3-26.

[37] *b. Megillah* 9a.

[38] Genesis 9:27; *b. Megillah* 9b.

[39] Ezekiel 39:11.

[40] Rabbi Gershon Hanokh Leiner, *Sod Yesharim, Sukkot* (Warsaw, 1903), *Shalosh Se'udot shel Hol ha-Mo'ed Sukkot*, par. 39, s.v. *Ve-hayah ba-yom ha-hu be-yom bo' Gog 'al admat Yisrael* (63c-64a).

Historically speaking, Sokhatchov and Radzyn were on opposite sides of the barricades that went up after the Kotsk-Izhbitsa (Polish, Kock-Izbica) schism in 1839. Rabbi Abraham Bornstein of Sokhatchov (Polish, Sochaczew) was the son-in-law of the Kotsker Rebbe, Menahem Mendel Morgenstern. Rabbi Gershon Hanokh Leiner of Radzyn was the grandson of Rabbi Mordechai Joseph Leiner of Izbica, author of *Mei ha-Shilo'ah*. Both the Kotsker and the Izhbitser had studied under Rabbi Simha Bunem of Pshiskha (Polish, Przysucha). It was in Pshiskha that this uniquely intellectual form of Polish Hasidism was born.

[41] *Sod Yesharim, Sukkot*, end par. 39 (64a).

[42] Psalms 50:1-2; *b. Yoma* 54b. In Lurianic Kabbalah, the beauty of Zion is associated with Joseph, of whom it was said, "And Joseph was handsome in form and handsome in appearance (*yephé to'ar vi-yphé mar'eh*)" (Genesis 39:6). See Rabbi Hayyim Vital, *'Ets Hayyim* 32:5 (=*Sha'ar He'arat ha-Mohin*, chap. 5). There is Midrashic precedent for equating Zion with Joseph: "Whatever befell Joseph, befell Zion" (*Midrash Tanhuma, Vayyigash* 10). Astute commentators point out that both Joseph and Zion share the numerical value of 156.

An exploration of the esthetic dimension of the Biblical Joseph in Midrash and Kabbalah would make for a fascinating study. The famed Gaon of Rogatchov (1858-1936) dropped some tantalizing hints in this connection. See Rabbi Joseph Rosen, *Tsaphnat Pa'ne'ah, Bereshit* (Jerusalem, 1967), *Vayyeshev*, Genesis 39:2, 6 and *Haphtarat Vayyeshev* (pp. 143-147). In those spartan notes, the Rogatchover atypically references Lurianic Kabbalah, and sketches the features of an androgynous Joseph!

43 *b. Kiddushin* 49b.

44 See Reuben Margaliyot, *Mal'akhei 'Elyon* (Jerusalem, 1945), s.v. *Yophiel* (pp. 65-67) and s.v. *Yepheiphiyah* (p. 68); Gershom G. Scholem, *Jewish Gnosticism, Merkabah Mysticism and Talmudic Tradition* (New York, 1965), pp. 12-13. In Targum Pseudo-Jonathan to Deuteronomy 34:6, both Yophiel and Yepheiphiyah occur as *"rabbanei hokhmeta"* ("teachers of wisdom"). The enigmatic Galician kabbalist who perished in Siberian exile during the Second World War, Isaac Messer (1891-1942), lavished great attention on the Prince of Torah, Yophiel/Yepheiphiyah. See Isaac Messer, *U-Mi-Midbar Matanah*, ed. Moshe Hallamish (Jerusalem, 1985), pp. 40, 43-44. Concerning this mysterious student of Hillel Zeitlin, see Bezalel Naor, *Kabbalah and the Holocaust* (Spring Valley, NY, 2001), pp. 103-117.

The Lithuanian kabbalist, Rabbi Eizik Haver offered an explanation for the association of *yophi* or beauty with *"razin de-'oraita"* (mysteries of Torah). See Rabbi Yitzhak Eizik Haver (Wildman), *Afikei Yam*, vol. I (Jerusalem, 1994), *Kiddushin* 49b, s.v. *'Asarah kabin yophi* (p. 300). Note that his explanation differs from those of the Vilna Gaon (whom he quotes). See Elijah Gaon, *Yahel 'Or*, ed. Naphtali Herz Halevi [Weidenbaum] (Vilna, 1882), *Zohar* II, 247b (*Heikhalot*) (20d).

45 See Michael D. Swartz, *Scholastic Magic: Ritual and Revelation in Early Jewish Mysticism* (Princeton, 1996), pp. 64-65; Elliot R. Wolfson, *Through A Speculum That Shines: Vision and Imagination in Medieval Jewish Mysticism* (Princeton, 1994), pp. 19-20; Moshe Idel, *Kabbalah: New Perspectives* (New Haven, 1988), p. 168.

Also Ithamar Gruenwald, *"Mekoman shel masorot kohaniyot bi-yetsiratah shel ha-mistikah shel ha-merkavah ve-shel shi'ur komah"* in *Early Jewish Mysticism*, ed. Joseph Dan (Jerusalem, 1987) [=*Jerusalem Studies in Jewish Thought*, vol. 6, nos. 1-2], pp. 65-120; Rachel Elior, *"Sifrut ha-heikhalot ve-ha-merkavah: zikatah la-mikdash, la-mikdash ha-shamaymi u-le-mikdash me'at,"* *Retsef u-Temurah* (2004), pp. 107-142; idem, "The priestly nature of the mystical heritage in *Heykalot* literature," *Expérience et écriture mystiques dans les religions du livre*, ed. Fenton and Goetschel (2000), pp. 41-54; idem, "The Merkavah tradition and the emergence of Jewish mysticism: from Temple to Merkavah, from Hekhal to Hekhalot, from priestly opposition to gazing upon the Merkavah," *Sino-Judaica* (1999), pp. 101-158; idem, *"Bein ha-heikhal ha-artsi la-heikhalot ha-shamaymiyim: ha-tefilah ve-shirat ha-kodesh be-sifrut ha-heikhalot ve-zikatan la-masorot ha-keshurot ba-mikdash,"* *Tarbiz* 64:3 (1995), pp. 341-380.

Inter alia, see Bezalel Naor, *The Limit of Intellectual Freedom: The Letters of Rav Kook* (Spring Valley, 2011), p. 109, concerning the focus of *Talmud Yerushalmi* on the Temple in Jerusalem.

46 *t. Sukkah* 3:2; *b. Sukkah* 45b. Though this passage occurs in some versions of the *Mishnah*, *Sukkah* 4:5 (not Maimonides', to be sure), it is actually not a *mishnah* but a *beraita*. See *Hagahot B[ayit] H[adash]*; N.N. Rabbinowicz, *Dikdukei Soferim*; S. Lieberman, *Tosephta ki-Pheshutah*; Y. Kafah, *Peirush ha-Mishnah la-Rambam*. Though it should be obvious enough, my inclusion of the word *"Yophi"* in the opinion of Rabbi Eliezer [ben Jacob] is spelled out in Rabbeinu Menahem ha-Meiri, *Beit ha-Behirah, Sukkah*, ed. Liss (Jerusalem, 1966), p. 161 (col. a).

Rabbi Jacob Ettlinger was perplexed why Maimonides omitted this farewell salutation from his *Mishneh Torah, Hil. Lulav* 7:23. His proffered solution that Maimonides restricts his remarks to legal obligations, omitting mere custom, is less than satisfactory. (In that very *halakhah*, Maimonides mentions a *minhag Yisrael!*) See Rabbi J. Ettlinger, *'Arukh la-Ner, Sukkah* 45a.

My own suspicion is that Maimonides was squeamish about a formula that so readily lent itself to syncretistic interpretation. See the objection raised by the Talmud: *"Ve-ha ka meshattef shem shamayim ve-davar aher?"* "Is he not combining the name of Heaven and something else [i.e., combining *Yah* and the altar in a single salute]?" (*Sukkah* 45b). And though the Talmud reconciles the practice, Maimonides may have found the answer given to be forced, and being hypersensitive to any practices at all smacking of syncretism, saw fit to omit the custom from his code (for as *'Arukh la-Ner* pointed out, it was but a custom, not an obligation). In *Sefer ha-Mitsvot*, positive commandment 7, Maimonides quotes the *beraita* marshalled by the Talmud (ibid.): "Whoever combines the name of Heaven with something else, is uprooted from the world." (See further Maimonides, *Moreh Nevukhim*, ed. Michael Schwarz [2002], vol. I, pp. 142-143, n. 3.)

I surmise that deciding the *halakhah* in favor of the *tanna kamma* over Rabbi Eliezer ben Jacob was not an option for Maimonides, in view of the accepted principle of Talmudic jurisprudence that the *halakhah* is in accordance with Rabbi Eliezer ben Jacob, for "the Mishnah of Rabbi Eliezer ben Jacob is trim and clean *(kav ve-naki)*" (*b. Yevamot* 49b, *Gittin* 67a).

Postscript: I once heard from Rabbi J.B. Soloveitchik of Boston that his grandfather Rabbi Hayyim Soloveitchik of Brisk refused to utter the prayer *"Berikh Shemeh"* (a passage from *Zohar* II, 369a) before the open ark because he found syncretistic the passage *"sagidna kammeh u-mi-kamma di-ykar 'oraiteh"* ("I prostrate myself before Him and before the honor of His Torah"). Evidently, from the perspective of Halakhah, not only the altar, but the Torah too, is subject to syncretism.

(Recently Avishai Bar-Asher revealed that *"Berikh Shemeh"* is not integral to the text of the *Zohar* but is rather a printer's insertion. See A. Bar-Asher, *"Berikh Shemeh," Tarbiz*, vol. 86 [5779], pp. 147-198.)

For the same reason, Rabbi Hayyim Soloveitchik opposed singing on Simhat Torah the *piyyut "Ein Adir."* Rabbi Hayyim felt that its lumping together God, Moses, Torah and Yisrael smacks of syncretism. See Rabbi Mikhel Zalman Shurkin, *Harerei Kedem*, vol. 1 (Jerusalem, 2000), chap. 154 (p. 267).

[47] Psalms 87:2.
[48] *b. Berakhot* 8a.
[49] See Rashi, *Shabbat* 145b, s.v. *metsuyyanin—mekushatin*.

As Rabbi Nahman of Breslov expressed it in Yiddish: *"Ikh mein takeh dos Eretz Yisroel mit die shtieber, mit die heizer."* ("I mean literally this Land of Israel, with these homes, with these houses.")

[50] However, Rabbi Joseph Engel noted that both the anonymous author of the *Halakhot Gedolot* and Maimonides (Introduction to the *Commentary to the Mishnah*) do not have in their text of the Talmud the words *"Mi-yom she-harav beit ha-mikdash"* ("From the day the Temple was destroyed"). See Rabbi Joseph Engel, *Gilyonei ha-Shas, Berakhot* 8a.

The Philosopher King and the Poet Messiah: Hellenic and Hebrew Republics Compared

In Honor of *Yom Yerushalayim* 5777
Fiftieth Anniversary of the Reunification
of Jerusalem 1967-2017

The Holy One, blessed be He, sought to make Hezekiah the Messiah, and Sennacherib—Gog and Magog.

The Attribute of Judgment remonstrated with the Holy One, blessed be He: "Master of the World, If You did not make David, King of Israel—who recited several songs and praises before You—the Messiah, then Hezekiah—for whom you performed all these miracles and he did not utter a single song before You—You shall make the Messiah?"

(Babylonian Talmud, *Sanhedrin* 94a)

In this legend of the Talmud we are told that King Hezekiah had all the makings of the Messiah but one—his failure to utter a song of thanksgiving. It would have been appropriate at the time of the miraculous deliverance of Jerusalem from the siege of Sennacherib, the King of Assyria, to compose a paean of praise to the Almighty in recognition of this momentous event. Failure to set the victory to song was deemed an offense so grievous that it disqualified the otherwise righteous king from a Messianic role. This is the simple interpretation of the passage in the Talmud. But might it tell us something deeper, more essential about the character of the long-awaited Messiah?

In Plato's *Republic*, the ruler of the ideal state will be a philosopher. In that tract, Plato takes advantage of the opportunity to express his utter disdain for poets:

> There is an old quarrel between philosophy and poetry. (*Republic*, 607b5-6)

The greatest Jewish philosopher of the medieval era, Moses Maimonides (1138-1204), was also dismissive of poets. In a response to Rabbi Jonathan Hakohen of Lunel, Maimonides wrote that "the way of 'the poets and the poetesses' (*ha-sharim ve-ha-sharot*) is not right in my eyes."[1] Maimonides' sensibilities were offended by the ambiguities ('the riddles and the parables") of poetry. His correspondent, Rabbi Jonathan, had written him a lengthy epistle gushing with the panegyric then in vogue in Provence. Maimonides was put on the spot. Mentioning the fact that his former colleagues back in *Sefarad* were wont to write in rhyme, and invoking the adage "When in Rome, do as the Romans do,"[2] Maimonides responded in kind, and one must say, his own verse does not lag behind.[3]

In his *Commentary to the Mishnah*, Maimonides grouped "books of poetry" (without differentiation) together with "those books found among the Arabs....that are devoid of wisdom or practical avail, just a waste of time." (The roster of trashy literature includes "chronicles, customs of the kings and genealogies of the Arab tribes.")[4]

Later in that same work, remarking upon the sage's advice, "All my days I grew up among the wise men and I found for the body no good but silence," Maimonides launches into a lengthy classification of the types of poetry:

> Know that the poems that are composed in any language are classified solely by their topics....I need to explain this—though it is simple—because I observed that if the great and pious of our nation are invited to a banquet or wedding or the like, and someone desires to sing in Arabic—even if that song be in praise of strength or willpower (which is desirable) or in praise of wine—then they put up a vocal protest and do not allow it to be heard. [On the other hand,] if the singer sings one of the Hebrew poems, none protests. They see nothing wrong with that, though the contents be forbidden or reprehensible. This is absolute folly, for what makes speech forbidden or permitted, desirable or repugnant, is not the language in which it is expressed, but the content. If the content of the song is exalted, then it is obligatory to say it in any language; and if it is inferior, then it should be avoided in any language.[5]

Maimonides goes on to explain his view that if there are two erotic poems, one in Hebrew, and the other in Arabic or Farsi, the Hebrew version is the more reprehensible in the Torah's opinion, precisely because of the sanctity of the tongue:

> It is not fitting to use it [i.e., Hebrew] for other than exalted matters. It is even more reprehensible if a verse of Torah or Song of Songs is used for that purpose [i.e., erotic poetry]. Then it is not merely reprehensible but forbidden, for the Torah forbade turning the prophetic language into lowly songs.[6]

Finally, in his philosophic work, *Guide of the Perplexed*, Maimonides took a jab at the poets who allow themselves unwarranted liberties by ascribing human attributes to the divinity.[7]

※

Given Maimonides' dim view of the poet, it is hardly surprising that what defines the Messiah in Maimonides' *Hilkhot Melakhim* (Laws of Kings) is first and foremost his study of Torah:

> If there should arise a king of the House of David *who studies the Torah* and performs the commandments as David his ancestor....[8]

Note that David's distinction as the "sweet-singer of Israel" has been dropped from the definition of Messiah. (In 2 Samuel 23:1 David is referred to as "Messiah of the God of Jacob and sweet-singer of Israel.")

In *Hilkhot Teshuvah* ("Laws of Return"), Maimonides fleshes out the personal attributes of King Messiah, endowing him with wisdom greater than that of Solomon, and prophecy approaching that of Moses:

> ....That king that shall arise from the seed of David, shall be a master of wisdom greater than Solomon, and a great prophet approaching Moses our Teacher, and therefore he shall teach the entire people and instruct them in the way of the Lord, and all the nations shall come to hearken to him, as it says: "And it shall be at the end of days, the mountain of the House of the LORD shall be established at the head of the mountains" [Isaiah 2:2].[9]

There is robust discussion in the secondary literature whether Maimonides subscribed to Plato's notion of the philosopher king. In the *Guide*, Maimonides cites but a single work of Plato: *Timaeus*.[10] If Maimonides was at all familiar with the drift of the *Republic*, it was only through the channeling of al-Farabi.[11] And while al-Farabi—whom Maimonides held in the highest esteem after Aristotle[12]—embraced the Platonic notion of placing the philosopher as ruler of the state, in Maimonides' own system, as laid out in the

Guide, it seems that the prophet has replaced the philosopher as ruler.[13] (Unable to find presence of the philosopher ideal in the *Guide*, both Shlomo Pines and Steven Harvey resorted to the *ad hominem* argument, finding Maimonides to have led the lifestyle of a philosopher-statesman.)[14]

It should not come as a shock that undoubtedly one of the most imaginative of charismatic teachers, the master storyteller Rabbi Nahman of Breslov, greatly enhanced Maimonides' depiction of the Messiah. In some respects their Messianic scenarios tally, but in other respects they diverge widely.

For two centuries, the contents of Rabbi Nahman's prophecy concerning the Messiah were kept secret within the confines of the Breslov community. In the recently released *Scroll of Secrets* (*Megillat Setarim*), wherein Rabbi Nahman paints a vivid picture of the future redeemer, we read that the Messiah "will be accepted as the halakhic authority throughout Israel" (starting at age twelve!).[15] Thus, the Messiah is well within Maimonides' framework of "studying Torah." Or, as Rabbi Nahman puts it: "He begins to scrutinize the Torah until he attains deep insights."[16]

Not all of the Messiah's day will be devoted to fielding *"she'elot u-teshuvot"* (questions of Jewish Law). "The daily schedule" will include "an hour in which...he will practice contemplative religious introspection (*hitbodedut*)."[17] Even that is not revolutionary from the Maimonidean perspective. Maimonides had prescribed solitude and contemplation as part of the daily regimen.[18]

However, beyond the scholarly and introspective side to Messiah's personality, Rabbi Nahman has restored his musical ability:

> And he will make new musical instruments and songs, for his genius in song will be very great. He will innovate in this art such that the souls of those who hear his songs will faint.[19]

The Sages may have been as contemptuous of Homer as Plato was (though for perhaps different reasons),[20] but that did not prevent them from envisioning the ruler of the future Hebrew republic as a poet in addition to Teacher of the Law.

As we have seen, Maimonides' role model for the Messiah was King David. The *Midrash Tehillim* has David praying "that men not read his words [i.e., the Psalms] as they read the books of Homer, but read them and study them so that they receive reward for them as they would for studying *Nega'im* and *Ohalot* (titles of two tractates of the Mishnah)."[21]

Let us return to King Hezekiah. Hezekiah is portrayed by the Sages as an unequalled disseminator of Torah:

He stuck a sword at the entrance to the study house and declared: "Whoever does not engage in study of Torah shall be stabbed by this sword!"

[Subsequently,] they inspected from Dan to Beer Sheba and found no ignoramus; from Gevat to Antipras and found no lad or lass, man or woman, who was unfamiliar with the laws of purity and impurity.[22]

Yet this truly amazing accomplishment, the phenomenal propagation of Torah study, was deemed insufficient when deciding Hezekiah's final status as Messiah. Though missing from Maimonides' *Laws of Kings* (*Hilkhot Melakhim*), a definite desideratum of King Messiah is that he be an accomplished *poet*.

---

[1] The Hebrew phrase, *"ha-sharim ve-ha-sharot,"* is a quote from 2 Chronicles 35:25.

[2] *Genesis Rabbah* 48:14; *Exodus Rabbah* 47:5. In the Midrash, Rabbi Meir quotes the maxim in Aramaic.

[3] See *Teshuvot ha-Rambam*, ed. Alfred Freimann (Jerusalem: Mekize Nirdamim, 1934), p. lix; quoted in Samuel K. Mirsky, *Commentary by R. Jonathan of Lunel on Mishnah and Alfasi Tractates Megillah and Mo'ed Katan* [Hebrew] (Jerusalem: Sura, n.d. [1956]), p. 12.

[4] Moses Maimonides, *Commentary to the Mishnah, Sanhedrin* 10:1 (Kafah edition, pp. 140-141). In his note, Rabbi Yosef Kafah writes that it is known that Maimonides was not an aficionado of "the poets and poetesses" (understatement) and refers the reader to *Pe'er ha-Dor*, no. 41. Published in Amsterdam in 1765, *Pe'er ha-Dor* is an early arrangement of Maimonides' responsa. Perhaps ironically, Rabbi Kafah would later impugn the ostensible exchange between the sages of Lunel and Maimonides. Thereupon, Rabbi Yitzhak Shilat took up the cudgels on behalf of the responsa to the sages of Lunel, defending their authenticity. See *Sefer Zikaron le-Harav Yitzhak Nissim*, ed. Meir Benayahu, vol. 2 (Jerusalem, 1985), pp. 235-252, 253-256.

For further reading on Maimonides' attitude toward poetry, see: H.

Schirmann, "Maimonides and Hebrew Poetry" (Hebrew), *Moznayim* 3 (1935):433-436; Yosef Tobi, *Between Hebrew and Arabic Poetry: Studies in Spanish Medieval Hebrew Poetry* (Leiden: Brill, 2010), pp. 422-466 ("Maimonides' Attitude Towards Secular Poetry, Secular Arab and Hebrew Literature, Liturgical Poetry, and Towards Their Cultural Environment").

[5] Moses Maimonides, *Commentary to the Mishnah, Avot* 1:16 (Kafah edition, pp. 273-274).

[6] Ibid. p. 274. See *b. Sanhedrin* 101a.

[7] Moses Maimonides, *Guide of the Perplexed* I, 59 (Pines translation, p. 141).

[8] *Mishneh Torah, Hil. Melakhim* 11:4.

[9] *Mishneh Torah, Hil. Teshuvah* 9:2.

It is possible that at this early stage of his writings, Maimonides had in mind to combine the Platonic ideal of the philosopher-king (assuming Solomon was a philosopher) and the ideal of the prophet-ruler that would later be espoused in the *Guide*. On Solomon in contradistinction to Moses, see *Guide* III, 54 (Pines translation, p. 633).

[10] Moses Maimonides, *Guide of the Perplexed* II, 13 (Pines translation, p. 283).

Inter alia, young Josef Solowiejczyk originally planned to write his doctoral dissertation at the Friedrich-Wilhelms-Universität of Berlin on the topic of "Maimonides and Plato," to demonstrate that Maimonides had been misconstrued as an Aristotelian, but unfortunately could find no *Doktorvater* to sponsor the project. See Aharon Lichtenstein, "R. Joseph Soloveitchik," in *Great Jewish Thinkers of the Twentieth Century*, ed. Simon Noveck (Clinton, Mass: B'nai B'rith, 1963), p. 285.

[11] See Leo Strauss, *Philosophie und Gesetz* (Berlin, 1935); idem, «Quelques remarques sur la science politique de Maimonide et de Farabi,» *Revue des Etudes Juives*, C (1936), pp. 1-37; Moses Maimonides, *Guide of the Perplexed*, transl. Shlomo Pines (Chicago: University of Chicago Press, 1964), Translator's Introduction, pp. lxxvi, lxxviii-xcii; Steven Harvey, "Maimonides in the Sultan's Palace" in *Perspectives on Maimonides: Philosophical and Historical Studies*, ed. Joel L. Kraemer (Oxford: Oxford University Press, 1991), p. 51, n. 16.

[12] Shlomo Pines, op. cit., p. lxxviii (referring to Maimonides' letter to Ibn Tibbon on p. lx).

[13] See Pines, op. cit., pp. lxxxviii-lxxxix.

[14] Pines, op. cit., p. lxxxix; Harvey, "Maimonides in the Sultan's Palace," pp. 47-75.

[15] Zvi Mark, *The Scroll of Secrets: The Hidden Messianic Vision of R. Nachman of Breslav* (Brighton, Mass.: Academic Studies Press, 2010), p. 55. Rabbi Nahman's vision of the Messiah as a *"moreh hora'ah"* (halakhic authority) may have been inspired by the portrayal of King David in rabbinic lore. See *b. Berakhot* 4a.

[16] Mark, pp. 55-56.

In an appendix to Rabbi David Sears' study of Rabbi Nahman's single poem, I explored how Rabbi Nahman interfaces with Maimonides. See Bezalel Naor, *"Shir Na'im* as a Reply to Maimonides," in Rabbi Nachman of Breslov, *Shir Na'im/Song of Delight*, transl. David Sears (Spring Valley, NY: Orot, 2005), pp. 123-126. (Available in the present collection on pp. 237-246.)

[17] Mark, p. 53.

[18] See *Guide of the Perplexed* III, 51; Harvey, "Maimonides in the Sultan's Palace," p. 68ff.
[19] Mark, p. 59.
   Though Rabbi Nahman may have expressed reservations concerning the medium of poetry, he did bequeath to us a single magnificent poem, *Shir Na'im*. Rabbi David Sears viewed the poem as a summation of Rabbi Nahman's teachings over the course of a lifetime. See Rabbi Nachman of Breslov, *Shir Na'im/Song of Delight*, transl. David Sears, especially pp. 115-117 ("Rabbi Nachman and Poetry").
[20] See *m. Yadayim* 4:6; commentary of Hai Gaon *ad locum*; and discussion in Saul Lieberman, *Hellenism in Jewish Palestine* (New York, 1994), pp. 105-114. Unlike the Gaon who read in the Mishnah *"Homeros,"* Maimonides read *"Miram,"* for which he supposed a Hebrew derivation. (See Maimonides, *Commentary to the Mishnah*, Kafah ed., pp. 442-443.) This is less baffling than Maimonides' acceptance of an Aramaic provenance for "Epicurus" in the Mishnah, *Sanhedrin* 10:1 (Kafah ed., p. 140). Cf. Rashi, *Sanhedrin* 99b, s.v. *megalleh panim ba-Torah*.
[21] *Midrash Tehillim*, chap. 1 (Buber ed., 5a); quoted in Lieberman, op. cit., pp. 110-111.
[22] *b. Sanhedrin* 94b.

Messiah's Donkey of a Thousand Colors

To the State of Israel
on its Seventieth Birthday
1948-2018

In *Perek Helek*, the final chapter of Tractate *Sanhedrin* (98a), famous for its discussions of eschatological issues, we find a focus on the speed of Messiah's arrival (or lack thereof).

Rabbi Joshua ben Levi juggles two sets of seemingly opposite prophecies. In the first opposition, we have Isaiah prophesying: "In its time, I will hasten it."[1] Which is it? Will the redemption be on time or speeded up? Rabbi Joshua ben Levi reconciles the two by saying that this depends on the merits of Israel. If they merit, it will be accelerated; if they do not merit, it will be on schedule.

Next, the Rabbi is bothered by the discrepancy between Zechariah's vision and Daniel's vision. Daniel depicted the Messiah "coming with the clouds of heaven like a son of man."[2] The implication is, as Rashi put it succinctly: *"Bi-mehirut."* ("With speed.") Zechariah, on the other hand, pictured a plodding Messiah, "poor and riding on a donkey."[3] Rashi supplies the key word: *"Be-'atslut."* ("With lassitude.") Once again, Rabbi Joshua ben Levi judiciously mediates between the conflicting reports: "If they merit, 'with the clouds of heaven'; if they do not merit, 'a poor man, riding on a donkey.'"

Messiah

This segment of the Talmudic discussion is fairly well known. It is the third and final paragraph of this seminar on Messianism, which though less quoted in the literature, may prove most fascinating.

> Shabur Malka (King Shapur I) said to Samuel: "You say that Messiah comes on a donkey. I will send him a lightning-fast horse (*susa barqa*) that I have."
>
> Samuel replied to him: "Do you have one of a thousand colors?"

Rashi fleshes out Samuel's retort: "Do you have a horse of a hundred colors such as Messiah's donkey?"

(The discussion between the Persian king and the Babylonian sage took place in Farsi. Where Rashi has a hundred colors, we will adopt Rabbi Nathan ben Yehiel of Rome's more precise translation from the Farsi, *"khar hazar gawna"* ["a donkey of a thousand colors"]. Thus Samuel replied: "Do you have a donkey of a thousand colors?")[4]

Rashi sums up by saying that Samuel pushed back with any old response. In other words, Shapur was cynical about the Jews' belief in Messiah and, accordingly, received from Samuel an equally flippant reply. Evidently, Rashi did not attach much significance to the variegated donkey.

While Rashi left it at that, one of our greatest theologians, Maharal of Prague, took up the challenge: "And I say that [Samuel] returned to him *a very deep wisdom* by saying that it has a hundred colors."⁵ Emboldened by Maharal's example, let us re-examine the dialogue or religious disputation between Shapur and Samuel.

Shapur offers his lightning-fast steed (*susya barqa*). This is tantalizingly reminiscent of *Al-Buraq*, the flying horse of the Islamic hadiths.⁶ In Greek mythology, there was Pegasus. Scholars assume that Islamic tradition drew on older myths. Perhaps Shapur's *susya barqa* prefigures Muhammad's *Al-Buraq* (from the Arabic *barq* for "lightning"). Assuming the identification is correct, this Persian Pegasus travelled from Iran to the Arabian Peninsula where it became the vehicle for Muhammad's night journey and ascent to heaven. Later with the Islamic conquest, *Al-Buraq* returned to Iran, where it figures prominently in Persian iconography.

The Sasanid monarch was chiding the Jewish People for their Messiah dragging his feet, so to speak. Samuel revealed a dimension of the Messiah of which the king was totally unaware: The donkey of Messiah possesses a thousand colors.

What does the donkey of Messiah symbolize? Rav Kook, in his eulogy for Herzl the man (and Zionism the movement) explained that the *hamor* of Messiah is the *homer*, the raw material, the naturalistic setting which serves as the vehicle of the redemption.⁷ (Earlier, Maharal made the connection between *hamor* and *homer*.)⁸

There were sages who whimsically exclaimed: "*Yeitei ve-lo ahmineh!*" "May Messiah come and may I not see him!"⁹ The advent of Israel's redemption will be fraught with such trials and tribulations—"*hevlei Mashiah*" ("birth pangs of Messiah")—that more than one sage dreaded to see Messiah in the flesh.

Rav Yosef—the hero of Rav Kook's eulogy—shot back a stunning reply: "May Messiah come, and may I merit to sit in the shadow of the dung of his donkey!"[10] Rav Yosef was willing to descend three levels just to participate in the redemption. If the donkey is not lowly enough, then the droppings of the donkey; and if the droppings are not dark enough, then the shadow cast by those droppings.

For Rav Kook, secular Zionism, with its emphasis on the material aspect of nationhood, was the symbolic "Donkey of Messiah." And if Rav Kook's unpacking of the Messianic mythos is on the mark, then a "donkey of a thousand colors" is a State of Israel which is variegated.

Recently there was revealed to the outside world Rabbi Nahman of Breslov's *Scroll of Secrets* (*Megillat Setarim*). This is the great Hasidic master's prophecy concerning the Messiah. The document, heavily encrypted, was handed from generation to generation within the confines of the tight-knit Breslov community. Recently, Zvi Mark gained access to the *Scroll* and published it in book form.[11] Initially, the *Scroll* elicited disappointment. Readers expected that Rabbi Nahman, like Nostradamus before him, would assign dates or perhaps precise coordinates. Actually, Rabbi Nahman provided us with something more valuable: a glimpse into the "thousand colors" of the Messiah. Patterned after the paradigm of King Solomon and to an extent Rabbi Nahman's own personality— as Professor Mark observes—the Messiah envisioned by Rabbi Nahman exhibits genius in many different fields. He excels in realms as diverse as *Halakhah* and horticulture, medicine and music.

When we extrapolate to the collective "Donkey of Messiah," the modern State of Israel, we discover that it too is at the forefront of multiple fields of endeavor: agriculture, medicine, the military, music, and cyber-technology, to name a few.

Israel's redemption is no flying horse, no *susya barqa*. It is in Kookian terminology, a *tahalikh ha-go'el*, a redemptive process, slow and arduous. But it has something unknown to the King of Persia. Our redemption is a polychromatic phenomenon. "A donkey of a thousand colors."

---

[1] Isaiah 60:22.
[2] Daniel 7:13.
[3] Zechariah 9:9.
[4] See Rabbi Nathan ben Yehiel of Rome, *'Arukh*, s.v. *khar*; and Alexander Kohut, *Aruch Completum*, Part Four, (Vienna 1891), p. 178, s.v. *kar*.
[5] Rabbi Judah ben Bezalel Löw, *Hiddushei Aggadot* ad loc.
[6] The remarkable linguistic similarity was duly noted by the lexicographer Alexander Kohut. See his *Aruch Completum*, Part Two (Vienna 1878), p. 201, s.v. *barqa* 4.
[7] See "The Lamentation in Jerusalem," in Bezalel Naor, *When God Becomes History: Historical Essays of Rabbi Abraham Isaac Hakohen Kook* (New York, NY; Kodesh Press, 2016), p. 49.
[8] See Rabbi Judah ben Bezalel Löw, *Netsah Yisrael*, chap. 36; and idem, *Hiddushei Aggadot, Sanhedrin* 98.
[9] *b. Sanhedrin* 98b.
[10] Ibid.
[11] Zvi Mark, *The Scroll of Secrets: The Hidden Messianic Vision of R. Nachman of Breslav* (Brighton, Mass.: Academic Studies Press, 2010).

X

BOOK REVIEWS

The Maggid of Kozhnits

Rabbi Israel ben Shabtai Hopstein. *'Avodat Yisrael*
(B'nei Berak: Pe'er mi-Kedoshim, 5773/2013)

Rabbi Israel ben Shabtai Hopstein, the Maggid of Kozienice (or more commonly, the "Kozhnitser Maggid") (d. 1814) was a major figure in the third generation of East-European Hasidism founded by Rabbi Israel Ba'al Shem Tov, and specifically, a towering luminary within Polish Hasidism.

Like his contemporary, Rabbi Shneur Zalman of Liozhno (and later Liadi), Rabbi Israel studied under Rabbi Dov Baer, the Maggid of Mezritch (who led the Hasidic movement after the death of the founder, Ba'al Shem Tov). Interestingly enough, Rabbi Kalonymos Kalman Shapira of Piaseczna, who achieved immortality as the "Rebbe of the Warsaw Ghetto," viewed those two as leading expositors of Kabbalah, juxtaposing "the Kabbalah of the Rav [Shneur Zalman] and the Kabbalah of the Maggid of Kozienice."[1]

However, whereas Rabbi Shneur Zalman's most famous work, *Tanya*, has earned the sobriquet (at least among HaBaD Hasidim) "the Written Torah of Hasidism" (*"Torah she-bi-Ketav shel Hasidut"*), unfortunately, Rabbi Israel's magnum opus, *'Avodat Yisrael* (*Service of Israel*), a commentary on the Pentateuch, has suffered neglect. Until today, the book has been an example of poor typography. First published in 1842, *'Avodat Yisrael* has been reissued periodically with pitifully broken letters of "Rashi" script (today unfamiliar to Hebrew readers without rabbinic training). About now, the cognoscenti will chime in, *"Afilu Sefer Torah she-be-heikhal tsarikh mazal"* ("Even a Torah scroll in the ark requires luck") and *"Habent sua fata libelli"* ("Books have their fates").

Thankfully, this horrendous situation has now been remedied. Enter Pe'er mi-Kedoshim, a publishing concern headed by Rabbi Israel Menachem Alter of Gur. Pe'er mi-Kedoshim has committed itself to re-issuing the classic texts of Hasidic thought in deluxe, state-of-the-art editions. The Kozhnitser Maggid's *'Avodat Yisrael* is the premier volume in a series envisioned to include: *Degel Mahaneh Ephraim* by Ba'al Shem Tov's grandson, Rabbi Moshe Hayyim Ephraim of Sudilkov (next on the agenda); *No'am Elimelekh* by Rabbi Elimelekh of Lizhensk; *Zot Zikaron* by Rabbi Jacob Isaac Horowitz (the "Seer of Lublin"), et cetera.

The book displays all the benefits that the modern age of Hebrew printing has brought to the sacred realm. The cursive "Rashi" script has been replaced by the square characters familiar to every Hebrew reader, which have then been provided with vowel points and modern punctuation. Sidebars caption the highlights of the Maggid's comments. Footnotes reference sources in rabbinic and kabbalistic literature, as well as cross-referencing to parallel passages in the Maggid's own works. As is customary, the book is preceded by the *"Toledot"* (Biography) of the Author and followed by *"Maftehot"* (Indices). (At present these indices are purely topical. It is hoped that in the future there will be included an index of the works cited by the Maggid, which will allow students of his thought a glimpse of his library, and the horizon of his intellectual world.)

Quoting the Psalmist, "Who can understand errors?" (Psalms 19:12), the editors have encouraged readers to offer constructive criticism, including pointing out errata in the present printing. Let us take them up on their kind offer.

In *Parashat Bereshit*, end s.v. *vayyasem Hashem le-Kayin 'ot* (6a), the Maggid observes "that there are times when miracles are performed by the Other Side, as we find in the *Gemara*, and in the *Midrash, Parashat Toledot*, that through Arginiton miracles were performed for Rabbi Judah the Prince and his companions, and the Omnipresent has many emissaries." Where the Maggid alludes to an unspecified "*Gemara,*" the editors have supplied within the text itself, within parentheses, "*Me'ilah* 17b." If one consults the text of that passage in the *Talmud Bavli*, one discovers that it concerns miracles wrought by Ben Temalyon (name of a demon) for Rabbi Shim'on ben Yohai during his mission to Rome. When offered the demon's help, rather than rebuffing him, Rabbi Shim'on resigned himself to accepting his intervention by saying: *"Yavo' ha-ness mi-kol makom."* ("Let the miracle come from any place.") This statement of Rabbi Shim'on is similar in tenor to the Maggid's conclusion: *"Harbeh sheluhim la-Makom."* ("The Omnipresent has many emissaries.") Clearly, the editors have read the text of *'Avodat Yisrael* in a disjointed fashion, interpreting that the "*Gemara*" and the "*Midrash, Parashat Toledot*" refer to two different stories.

My own reading of the situation is that the "*Gemara*" and the "*Midrash, Parashat Toledot*" refer to the identical story whereby

Rabbi Judah the Prince and his companions were spared the imperial wrath of Diocletian through the intervention of the demon Arginiton (or in the version of the *Yerushalmi*, "Antigris").[2] The "*Gemara*" of course is not the *Gemara Bavlit*, but the *Gemara Yerushalmit*, and the reference is to the *Talmud Yerushalmi* at the end of the eighth chapter of *Terumot*.[3]

In *Parashat Shemot*, beginning s.v. *ve-sham'u le-kolekha* (91a), the Maggid writes that Moses was confronted with a conundrum. On the one hand, he was pressing for some kind of divine assurance that his mission to Egypt be crowned with success and that the Hebrews indeed hearken to his voice. On the other hand, he was concerned that by its very nature a divine guarantee would rob the Hebrews of their free will, forcing them into belief. The assumption is that the Hebrews were redeemed from Egypt in the merit of their faith or *emunah*. (See *Exodus Rabbah*, *Beshallah* [*parashah* 23] playing on the words *"tashuri me-rosh Amanah"* [Song of Songs 4:8].) It is a tribute to the originality of the Kozhnitser Maggid that while most Biblical commentators busied themselves with the philosophic problem of God's hardening the heart of Pharaoh, thereby depriving him of the free will to respond affirmatively to the divine demands, the Maggid explored in the opposite direction the problem of preserving the Hebrews' free will to disbelieve. The Maggid's solution to the problem involves some rather esoteric doctrines of Kabbalah, namely *"hanhagat gadlut"* ("governance of greatness") versus *"hanhagat katnut"* ("governance of smallness"), best left for the adept in Jewish mysticism. I would just point out for the record that the editors missed a cue here. When the Maggid writes *"'Ve-hen' she-hu ahat,"* he is clearly referencing the *Talmud*

Bavli, Shabbat 31b: *"She-ken bi-leshon yevani korin le-ahat 'hen.'"* (*"Hen* in Greek is one.")

In the section for the festival of *Shavu'ot,* s.v. *u-Moshe 'alah el ha-Elohim* (200a), the Maggid writes: "Since all Israel prepared themselves for the sanctity of the Lord, and a leader is commensurate to his generation, therefore Moses was able to ascend above." Now the crucial words, the key to understanding this thought, *"parnas lefi doro"* ("a leader is commensurate to his generation"), have been emended by the editors to: *"kol ehad le-fi koho"* ("each according to his ability"). Granted that in the old edition there was some fuzziness concerning these words (*"parush lefi doro"*), they could still be made out simply by correcting *"parush lefi doro"* to *"parnas lefi doro,"* a well-known Hebrew adage. In the present version, one is at a loss to glean the Maggid's meaning. (I see now that the wording *"kol ehad lefi koho"* does occur in the Warsaw 1878 edition of *'Avodat Yisrael*. Unfortunately, the edition I possess is without place or date. Unable to locate a copy of the *editio princeps* of 1842, I have no way of knowing which version occurs there.)

In *Parashat Mas'ei,* end s.v. *elleh mas'ei v'nei Yisrael* (240a), in regard to *Tish'ah be-Av,* the Maggid discusses the difference between the *"batei gava'ei"* ("inner chambers") and the *"batei bara'ei"* ("outer chambers"), alluded to by the Rabbis in *b. Hagigah* 5b. The Maggid's remarks in this passage are consonant with what he wrote elsewhere in *Ner Israel,* his commentary to the *Likkutim me-Rav Hai Gaon* (2a): "In the outer chambers there is sadness and mourning, but for one who is able to ascend to the inner chambers, to the will of the Creator, blessed be He, certainly there is happiness." (By the way, the kabbalists' reading of the passage in

Hagigah, while opposite Rashi's, coincides with the version of Rabbeinu Hananel. See Rabbi Shelomo Eliashov, *Hakdamot u-She'arim* [Piotrków, 1909], *sha'ar* 6, chap. 6, "*avnei milu'im*" [24b-27b].)

In *Parashat Devarim*, end s.v. *eleh ha-devarim* (246a) there is a quote from Rabbi Isaac Luria's commentary to the *Idra Zuta*. The Maggid supplies the exact page number: folio 120. The problem is that the passage does not occur there. The editors have left the reference in the text untouched. At least in a footnote we should be told that the quote may be found in Rabbi Jacob Zemah, *Kol ba-Ramah* (Korets, 1785), 122a.[4] See also Rabbi Hayyim Vital, *Sefer ha-Derushim* (Jerusalem, 5756/1996), 214 (left column); and Rabbi Shalom Buzaglo, *Hadrat Melekh* (London, 5530/1770; photo offset B'nei Berak, 5734/1974), 139a.

In the section for *Tu be-Av*, s.v. *meyuhasot she-bahen* (256b-257a), the Maggid writes that there are times that *ki-ve-yakhol* (as it were), God so delights in Israel that He becomes as a young man (*bahur*). The Maggid writes that he has dealt with this in his commentary to the line in *Avot* (beginning chap. 6), "*Barukh she-bahar bahem u-ve-mishnatam.*" As the editors point out, the comment is not to be found in the Maggid's remarks on *Avot*. Instead, they refer us to a parallel passage in *Re'eh*, s.v. *ve-hinneh ha-Midrash* (270a). By the same token, they might have referred us to *Ner Israel* (commentary to *Likkutim me-Rav Hai Gaon*), 4b: "*Ve-nikra bahur ka-arazim....*"

In the section for Rosh Hashanah, there is a lengthy kabbalistic homily, the thrust of which is that on that day we ask the Holy One, blessed be He, to reinvest himself in the particular role of "*Elohei Yisrael*" ("God of Israel").

"The God of these [Jews] is asleep." Which is to say, [the nations] were not foolish enough to assert that the *Sibbat kol ha-Sibbot* (Cause of All Causes) is in a state of slumber, only "the God of these [Jews]," in other words, this particular *hanhagah* (governance) referred to as *"Elohei Yisrael"* (the God of Israel) is in a state of sleep...and unconsciousness, and He is but *"Elaha de-Elahaya"* (the God of Gods). Based on this, you will understand the *kavvanah* (mystical meditation) of Rabbi Isaac Luria for Rosh Hashanah, and we awaken Him by the *shofar* (ram's horn).[5]

The editors duly noted the reference to Rabbi Hayyim Vital, *Peri 'Ets Hayyim, Sha'ar ha-Shofar*, chap. 1. But what they should have noted is the following reference which would have been even more instructive:

> Now in the days of Mordechai was the mystery of the time of *dormita* of *Ze'ir Anpin*, and the mystery that Haman said, "There is (*yeshno*) one people spread and separated among the peoples" [Esther 3:8]. The Rabbis, of blessed memory, commented on the word *"yeshno,"* that Haman alleged "their God is asleep."
> (Rabbi Hayyim Vital, *Peri 'Ets Hayyim, Sha'ar ha-Purim*, beginning chap. 5)

The Holy Maggid loaded the *kavvanot* of Purim on to the *kavvanot* of Rosh Hashanah!

The Kozhnitser Maggid was a preeminent halakhist (specializing in *hetter 'agunot*, permitting wives of missing husbands to remarry), kabbalist, thinker (penning commentaries to the works of Maharal of Prague), and statesman. With all that, the following anecdote sent a shiver down my spine:

The Kozhnitser Maggid was on friendly terms with several prominent members of the Polish nobility. In the eighteenth century, Poland, dismembered and subjected to a tripartite division—whereby Prussia annexed the western portion of Poland; Austro-Hungary annexed Galicia in the south; and Russia annexed the east—simply ceased to exist. A certain Polish nobleman importuned the Maggid to intercede with Heaven on behalf of the Polish nation. The gentleman would not leave the Maggid's home until promised Polish independence. Finally, the Maggid foretold that at a time in the future Poland would once again be a sovereign nation—for a span of "three *shemitin*" (three sabbatical cycles or 21 years). When the Jews of Warsaw were being subjected to aerial bombardment by the Luftwaffe in September of 1939, they recalled the Maggid's prediction. In the aftermath of World War I, in 1918 to be precise, Poland once again declared its independence. Three *shemitin* had passed from 1918 until 1939. Warsaw capitulated to the Nazis on the eve of *Sukkot*, the *yahrzeit* of the Kozhnitser Maggid! This anecdote was told by a survivor of the Warsaw Ghetto, Joseph Friedenson, editor of *Dos Yiddishe Vort*, the Yiddish magazine of Agudath Israel of America (*"Toledot,"* p. 37).

THE MAGGID OF KOZHNITS

[1] Kalonymos Kalmish Shapira, *Hovat ha-Talmidim* (Jerusalem, 1990), p. 217. Besides being a descendant of the Kozhnitser Maggid, Rabbi Kalonymos Kalmish was the son-in-law of the Rebbe of Kozhnits of the day, Rabbi Yerahmiel Moshe Hopstein.

[2] See *Genesis Rabbah* 63:8. Rabbi Nathan of Rome, *'Arukh*, s.v. *Arganatin*, writes that this demon is a denizen of the bathhouse. Alexander Kohut's etymology, whereby the name is a compound of two Greek words, "argos nautis" (αργός ναύτης), or "swift sailor," is hardly convincing. (The same goes for the earlier suggestion of Benjamin Musafia.)

[3] In the biographical introduction to the book we are told that Rabbi Hayyim of Volozhin attested that the Kozhnitser Maggid was "familiar with *Talmud Yerushalmi*" (*"baki be-Shas Yerushalmi"*) (p. 30).

According to Rabbi El'azar Mordechai Kenig, a Kozhnitser Hasid, Rabbi Hayyim of Volozhin visited the Kozhnitser Maggid on several occasions. On one of those occasions, they exchanged views on the relative merits of the Hasidic leadership. See Rabbi Gedaliah Aaron Kenig, *Hayyei Nefesh* (Tel-Aviv, 1968), p. 89.

[4] I am indebted to Prof. Menachem Kallus for the correct address.

[5] *'Avodat Yisrael*, 290b.

Historians will have a field day trying to figure out how this element of Cardozan theology found its way into the writings of the Kozhnitser Maggid. The writings of Abraham Miguel Cardozo are forever offsetting the deistic notion of the other peoples ("philosophers and Ishmaelites") against the particularistic God of Israel (*Elohei Yisrael*), though the term Cardozo typically employs is the *"Sibbah Rishonah"* (First Cause), not the *"Sibbat kol ha-Sibbot"* (Cause of All Causes). See David J. Halperin, *Abraham Miguel Cardozo: Selected Writings* (Mahwah, NJ: Paulist Press, 2001), pp. 173-175. And when Cardozo does refer to the "Cause of all Causes," the Hebrew term he invariably employs is *"'Illat kol ha-'Illot,"* not *"Sibbat kol ha-Sibbot."*

An exception to this rule is found at the beginning of Cardozo's treatise, *Boker de-Avraham*. Discussing the belief system of "the second class, of the philosophers," he employs the term *"Sibbah le-khol ha-Sibbot"* for "Cause of all Causes." The treatise begins with the words, *"Bati le-faresh emunat avoteinu"* ("I have come to explain the faith of our fathers"). It is available in several manuscripts: See Library of the Hungarian Academy of Sciences, Budapest, Ms. Kaufmann A 232, p. 40; London Beth Din Ms. 124 = National Library of Israel Ms. Heb. 28°7405, f.1v.; Russian State Library, Moscow, Ms. Guenzburg 660, f.1v.; and Ms. Guenzburg 1109, f.2v.

(Scholem seems to equivocate whether the "Cause of all Causes" is identical in Cardozan theology with the "First Cause"; see Gershom Scholem, *Sabbatai Sevi: The Mystical Messiah* [Princeton, NJ: Princeton University Press, 1975], pp. 912-913.)

This opposition of the *Sibbah Rishonah* to *Elohei Yisrael* pervades the works later attributed (correctly or incorrectly) to Rabbi Jonathan Eybeschuetz, *Va-Avo ha-yom el ha-'ayin* and *Shem 'Olam*.

It may well be that the Kozhnitser Maggid was influenced in this respect by reading Pinhas Elijah Hurwitz of Vilna's *Sefer ha-Berit* (Brünn 1797), a work which enjoyed great popularity. (It appears that the Kozhnitser Maggid's contemporary, Rabbi Nahman of Breslov, delved into *Sefer ha-Berit*; see Mendel Piekarz, *Studies in Braslav Hasidism* [Hebrew] [Jerusalem: Mossad Bialik, 1995], pp. 249-252.)

Hurwitz devoted an entire chapter to the opposition of the philosophic notion of the *Sibbah Rishonah* to the particularist revelation of *Elohei Yisrael*, while, ironically enough, vilifying the man who promulgated this opposition: Abraham Cardozo! See *Sefer ha-Berit*, Part 1, *ma'amar* 20, chap. 15 (109a-111a).

Inter alia, Hurwitz speaks glowingly of Immanuel Hai Ricchi's *Yosher Levav*: "If you wish, beloved reader, to know who your Creator is, consult the aforementioned work, *Yosher Levav*" (ibid. 110b). (The quote from *Yosher Levav* which offsets the *Sibbah Rishonah* against *Ze'ir Anpin*, beginning with the words *"Ha-Kelal ha-'oleh,"* is to be found in the *editio princeps* of *Yosher Levav* [Amsterdam 1742] on 34a.) Elsewhere, I have dealt with crypto-Sabbatian passages in Ricchi's *oeuvre*; see Bezalel Naor, *Post-Sabbatian Sabbatianism* (Spring Valley, NY: Orot, 1999), pp. 53-57. For an original analysis of Cardozo's theology, see ibid. pp. 14-20.

I must confess that at the time I wrote *Post-Sabbatian Sabbatianism*, I mistakenly assumed that the reference to "philosophers and Ishmaelites" in *Sefer ha-Berit*, 110a, occurred in the quote from Rabbi Meir ibn Gabbai's *Derekh Emunah*. Upon inspection of *Derekh Emunah* (Padua, 1563), 4a, I see that those words in brackets were not in the original but issued from the pen of Pinhas Elijah Hurwitz. Thus, my statement at the conclusion of note 16 on page 159 of *Post-Sabbatian Sabbatianism* is erroneous. Again, "philosophers and Ishmaelites" (or in Halperin's rendition, "philosophers and Muslims") is a signature juxtaposition of Cardozo; see, e.g., chap. 7 of Cardozo's *Derush Zeh Eli ve-Anvehu*, transcribed in Gershom Scholem, "Two new theological texts by Abraham Cardozo" (Hebrew), *Sefunot*, vols. 3-4 (1960), pp. 281-282; translated to English by Halperin, op. cit., pp. 201-203.

In truth, Cardozo's fingerprints are all over the aforementioned chapter in *Sefer ha-Berit*, starting with Pharaoh's familiarity with the First Cause but ignorance of the God of Israel. Cf. *Derush Zeh Eli ve-Anvehu*, chaps. 13-14; in Scholem, pp. 292, 294; in Halperin, pp. 226, 229-230. It may be possible with further research to ascertain specifically which of Cardozo's sixty (!) manuscript works influenced Hurwitz.

"The Jackals" and "The Lion": Animal Fables of Kafka and Rav Kook

In 1917, Franz Kafka (1883-1924), a surrealist writer living in Prague, published in Martin Buber's Zionist journal, *Der Jude*, a short story entitled "Jackals and Arabs." The plot of the story is rather simple; the meaning—like that of most of Kafka's works—continues to mystify readers to this day.

A European gentleman camped in the desert is approached by a pack of jackals who look to him as to the long-awaited savior. The oldest jackal explains that since time immemorial, generations upon generations of jackals have been waiting for his arrival. Momentarily, he presents the astonished guest "with a small pair of sewing scissors, covered with ancient rust," for the singular purpose of ridding the jackals of the Arabs, whom they detest, but whose yoke they are powerless to throw off. The interloper from the North politely demurs. In the next scene, an Arab chieftain arrives and proceeds to disabuse the European of the nonsense that the jackal blabbered to him. He explains that the Arabs keep jackals as pets, much as Europeans keep dogs. "They have the most lunatic hopes, these beasts; they're just fools, utter fools. That's why we like them; they are our dogs; finer dogs than any of yours." The Arab then cut up a camel carcass; the carrion was immediately snatched up by the jackals. "They had forgotten the Arabs, forgotten their hatred, the all-obliterating immediate presence of the stinking carrion bewitched them."

What is one to make of Kafka's parable? Given its context, it seems reasonable to assume that the Arabs are truly Arabs and the jackals—Jews. The Jews look to Europe to free them from Arab oppression in *Erets Yisrael*. The tool of their deliverance is sewing scissors, an unlikely choice of arms. Why scissors? Is Kafka poking fun at the Jews as being a nation of tailors?

(In a "contrapuntal" interpretation, Edward Said appropriated Kafka's parable for the cause of Palestinian liberation, whereby the "Arabs" become Jews, and the jackals—Palestinians. But then wouldn't Kafka have been guilty of mixing metaphors? Palestinians brandish a knife, not scissors. As they say in Yiddish: *"Nu, a kashya auf a mayseh!"* "A question on a tale!")

Some view Kafka's piece as uncannily prescient. Shortly thereafter in 1917, His Majesty's Government promised in the Balfour Declaration, "the establishment in Palestine of a national home for the Jewish people." Famous words. Unfortunately, the Balfour Declaration was a valueless paper. It would take another three decades for "Perfidious Albion" to lower the Union Jack and for General Sir Alan Cunningham, British High Commissioner for Palestine, to set sail from Haifa harbor for England. Kafka was right. Europe would not liberate the Jews of *Erets Yisrael*. How then, would the liberation be accomplished? That brings us to our next animal fable, by Abraham Isaac Hakohen Kook (1865-1935).

Not nearly as famous as Kafka's "Jackals and Arabs," Rav Kook's *"Ha-Aryeh ba-Sugar"* ("The Lion in the Cage") first appeared in print in Rabbi Moshe Zuriel's collection *Otserot ha-RAYaH* circa 1990. "The Lion in the Cage" is the story of an ancient lion, broken in spirit, living out his days within the confines of a cage. His cubs, who were born in captivity, know no better, and find their surroundings most comfortable, if not outright enjoyable. In fact, they are at a loss to understand what it is exactly that oppresses the spirit of the old lion. And then one day, the leonine patriarch reveals to them his secret:

> *There is a world full of light,*
> *Freedom and liberty prevail.*
> *There is a vast forest tall with trees*
> *And stately with mighty cedars.*
> *The fragrance is refreshing*
> *And free animals abound.*
> *When I was your age, my children,*
> *I ruled the forest with pride and might*
> *And all bowed before me.*
> *If not for my pursuers*
> *who broke my bones,*
> *and this cramped cage—*
> *I would still rule the forest,*
> *And you too would be free and proud.*

Learning the lie of their "gilded cage" existence, the lion cubs now look with deep dissatisfaction upon their environs. Eventually, this dissatisfaction will lead to a prison break:

The words of the Old One
strengthened the cubs' heart,
and with the might of lions
they began to break down the cramped cage.
With claws and jaws and the roar of lions
they frightened away their smug captors.
With a mighty spirit
imbued with the delight of the forest
they shattered the walls of the cramped cage.

And with that, lo and behold, the ancient lion was rejuvenated:

The Old One was suddenly alive,
his broken bones healed with joy.
Rebuking his enemies, he and his cubs returned
and established the kingdom of the forest.

Who is the ancient lion? Who are the lion cubs?

While lacking the haunting quality of a Kafkaesque story, neither is Rav Kook's tale totally transparent. Treading uncertain ground, we might say that the ancient lion represents the sages of Israel, who in exile preserved the memory of the homeland. The ancient sages were, alas, weak when it came to establishing facts on the ground. Yet they were able to communicate to the young an odium for exile, and to fan the spark of the longing for Zion. It was the youth of Israel, impudent, brazen Zionists, who, once their conscience, their Jewish identity had been pricked, threw off the yoke of the oppressor.

As for Kafka, today the *literati* debate whether this tormented genius was a Zionist or anti-Zionist. Perhaps it would be fair to say that Kafka lived in the elusive shadow of the legendary Golem of Prague, created by *Der Hohe Rabbi Loew* to act as a Jewish savior. When the Golem proved unruly, his creator was forced to pull the plug on him. A sleeping giant lying amid the *sheimos* ("sacred trash") up in the attic of the Altneuschul, the Golem is the stuff of which dreams are made.

Bridging the Kabbalistic Gap

Avinoam Fraenkel. *Nefesh HaTzimtzum* (2015)

Volume 1: Rabbi Chaim Volozhin's *Nefesh HaChaim* with Translation and Commentary
Volume 2: Understanding *Nefesh HaChaim* through the Key Concept of *Tzimtzum* and Related Writings

Recently there has been a spate of English translations of the classic of Mitnagdic philosophy, *Nefesh ha-Hayyim* by Rabbi Hayyim of Volozhin (1749-1821), eminent disciple of the Vilna Gaon. This is perhaps the most glorious—certainly the lengthiest—of the translations, one that attempts to rewrite the debate between Hasidim and *Mitnagdim*.

The present edition, the most extensive to date, is divided in two volumes. Volume One consists of a Hebrew-English edition of the entire book with the exception of the famous note by the author's son, Rabbi Isaac (Itzeleh) of Volozhin, known as *"Ma'amar Be-Tzelem."* That note and other related writings of Rabbi Hayyim have been translated in Volume Two. In a unique typesetting innovation, the translator divides the complex Hebrew sentences into phrases, easing the English reading.

In the lengthy introduction to Volume Two, entitled *"Tzimtzum—The Key to Nefesh HaChaim,"* Avinoam Fraenkel has carved out for himself a most ambitious goal: to tackle the perennial problem of latter-day Kabbalah, namely the Lurianic doctrine of *Tzimtzum* or divine self-contraction. Traditionally, there have been two schools of thought on the matter: those who hold *"Tzimtzum ki-peshuto,"* i.e., the doctrine is to be taken literally; and those convinced that *"Tzimtzum she-lo ki-peshuto,"* i.e., *Tzimtzum* is not to be taken literally. As Fraenkel points out, this terminology first gained currency in the debate between two Italian kabbalists, Rabbi Joseph Ergas (author of *Shomer Emunim*) and Rabbi Immanuel Hai Ricchi (author of *Yosher Levav*) back in 1736-7.[1]

Fraenkel's thesis is that even when things are *"pashut"* (simple), they truly are not so *"pashut"* (simple). Even when a kabbalist such as Rabbi Shelomo Eliashov (author of *Leshem Shevo ve-Ahlamah*) writes boldly that he understands the doctrine literally as did the author of *Yosher Levav*—that requires complexification.

You might ask: Of what concern is this rarefied debate to the masses of Jews living in the twenty-first century? Ah! It just so happens that many, if not most, historians have assumed that this debate, which translates into transcendentalist versus immanentist theology, was at the heart of the terrible controversy between the *Mitnagdim* and Hasidim that tore apart East European Jewry in the late eighteenth century. At that time, the Vilna Gaon issued a *herem*, an official rabbinic ban excommunicating the followers of the Ba'al Shem Tov.

If it can be proven that there is essentially no difference of theology between the *Tanya* (the "Bible" of Hasidism), written by Rabbi Shneur Zalman of Liadi, founder of the HaBaD school of

Hasidism, and the *Nefesh ha-Hayyim* (the *"Shulhan 'Arukh"* of Mitnagdic ideology), then we will have dissolved any continuing animus between Hasidim and *Mitnagdim*, and *"Shalom 'al Yisrael"* (Peace to Israel). This is the fondest wish of the author.

The truth is—as the author makes us aware—this is not the first attempt to smooth over theological differences between the *Tanya* and *Nefesh ha-Hayyim*. On the eve of World War Two, Rabbi Eliyahu Eliezer Dessler—a preeminent master of the Mussar school, *Mashgi'ah Ruhani* of Gateshead and later of the Ponevezh Yeshivah in B'nei Berak—then residing in London, wished to issue a proclamation to the effect that there is essentially no *mahloket*, no difference of opinion between Rabbi Shneur Zalman and Rabbi Hayyim regarding the correct interpretation of *Tzimtzum*. Rabbi Dessler's distinguished houseguest at the time was Rabbi Yitzhak Horowitz (known in Lubavitch as "Reb Itche Der Masmid," on account of his legendary *"hatmadah,"* or devotion to learning), who acted as fundraiser on behalf of the Lubavitcher Rebbe, Joseph Isaac Schneersohn. Rabbi Dessler asked Rabbi Horowitz to sign on the proclamation.

To make a long story short, eventually Rabbi Dessler's overtures were forwarded to the son-in-law of the Rebbe, Rabbi Menachem Mendel Schneerson (eventual successor to his father-in-law as Rebbe of Lubavitch), who penned a formal reply. For the life of him, Rabbi M.M. Schneerson could not fathom how someone with competence in Kabbalah (which Rabbi Dessler certainly did possess) could fail to see the obvious differences between the HaBaD and Volozhin understandings of *Tzimtzum*. (Rabbi Schneerson further outlined that there was a difference between the Vilna Gaon and his student Rabbi Hayyim of Volozhin regarding *Tzimtzum*, a point in the letter which continues to rile *Mitnagdim* to this day. In fact, Rabbi Yosef Zussman of Jerusalem, eminent disciple of Rabbi Ya'akov Moshe Harlap, wrote several unanswered letters to the Lubavitcher Rebbe, remonstrating how absurd it is to entertain the notion that Rabbi Hayyim, who adored his master the Gaon, disagreed with him on so basic an issue.)

Left without a "partner in peace" of the opposite camp, Rabbi Dessler's proclamation was buried. Where titans such as Rabbis Dessler and Schneerson could not see eye to eye, Avinoam Fraenkel certainly has his work cut out for him. Before we proceed further to the "nuts and bolts" of the *Tanya—Nefesh ha-Hayyim* debate, the reader may wish to listen to some music pleasing to the ear:

- When Rabbi Abraham Mordechai Alter, Rebbe of Gur (*"Imrei Emet"*) asked Rav Kook how he knew so much *Hasidut*, Rav Kook responded that he had studied *Nefesh ha-Hayyim*.
- Rabbi Michael Eliezer Forshlager of Baltimore, a foremost student of Rabbi Avraham Bornstein, Rebbe of Sokhatchov (author of Responsa *Avnei Nezer*) carried in his *tallit* bag a volume which consisted of *Tanya* and *Nefesh ha-Hayyim* bound together at Rabbi Forshlager's special request.
- Once around the family table in Brooklyn, Rabbi Menachem Mendel Schneerson (by then Lubavitcher Rebbe) spoke so enthusiastically of *Nefesh ha-Hayyim* that his brother-in-law, Rabbi Shemariah Gurary, said in jest:

"Then perhaps we Hasidim should take to studying *Nefesh ha-Hayyim*."

Back to the *mahloket*. What are the cold facts concerning the debate?

It is incontrovertible that Rabbi Hayyim has stood the *Zohar*'s terms *"memalé kol 'almin"* ("filling all worlds") and *"sovev kol 'almin"* ("surrounding all worlds") on their heads. What for the *Tanya* is *"memalé kol 'almin,"* is for *Nefesh ha-Hayyim*, *"sovev kol 'almin,"* and vice versa. Rabbi Shelomo Fisher of Jerusalem has written that this is merely semantics.[2] Others read into the shift of terminology a substantive controversy as to *Weltanschauung*. What for Hasidism is common experience, namely the immanence, the immediate presence of God, is for Mitnagdism a recondite mystery reserved for the elite.

In the words of Rabbi Eizik of Homel, a major disciple of Rabbi Shneur Zalman of Liadi and of his son, Rabbi Dov Baer of Lubavitch (*Mitteler Rebbe*):

> This belief is possessed by all the Hasidim, but the *Mitnagdim*, even those who are not etc. [the word etc. occurs in the original], do not have this faith, only in a very, very concealed manner, as Israel were in Egypt....They have no room for this faith that *Altz iz Gott* (All is God).[3]

Fraenkel observes that much of the "poisoning of the waters" was brought about by the publication of a spurious letter attributed to the *"Alter Rebbe,"* Rabbi Shneur Zalman, in the anonymous

Matzref ha-'Avodah (Koenigsberg, 1858). Later the letter was incorporated in Heilman's more responsible *Beit Rebbi* (Berdichev, 1902). In the forged epistle, Rabbi Shneur Zalman writes that it has come to his awareness that the Vilna Gaon understands *Tzimtzum* literally.

This letter contributed to Rabbi Menachem Mendel Schneerson's formulation concerning the Vilna Gaon's view of *Tzimtzum*. One might mistakenly assume that once the letter is exposed as a forgery, HaBaD should have no problem accepting that there truly was no disagreement between the two rival camps concerning *Tzimtzum*. But Fraenkel knows that this is not the end of his troubles.

There is the matter of the passage in the second part of *Tanya* (titled *Sha'ar ha-Yihud ve-ha-Emunah*) which reserves some pretty harsh language for the literalists:

> ...the error of some wise men in their own eyes, may the Lord forgive them, who erred and were mistaken in their study of the writings of the ARI [i.e., Rabbi Isaac Luria], of blessed memory, and understood the doctrine of *Tzimtzum* mentioned there literally, that the Holy One, blessed be He, withdrew Himself and His essence, God forbid, from this world, only that He supervises from above.[4]

Who are the unnamed villains of this passage? To endeavor to answer this question, we would do well to research the printing history of the *Tanya*. The passage in question was missing from all editions of the *Tanya* printed before the year 1900. In that year, the passage surfaced in the Romm edition printed in Vilna at the behest of Rabbi Shalom Dov Baer Schneersohn of Lubavitch. Until that time, it had been preserved in manuscript in the keeping of the heirs of the *Ba'al ha-Tanya*. That means that for over a century since the *Tanya* was first printed in Slavuta in 1796, this sensitive piece—a sort of *J'accuse*, if you will—was suppressed. Why was it ever suppressed to begin with, and why was it finally revealed in 1900?

An obvious solution would be that the passage obliquely lambasted the Vilna Gaon, and it was not until a century later that a direct descendant of the author felt that times had changed and that the sociological "climate" had warmed sufficiently to allow for an unexpurgated version of the *Tanya* to appear in print. This time, no *herem* would be issued in Vilna.

And for the record, Rabbi Menachem Mendel was not the first Schneerson to assume that the Gaon understood *Tzimtzum* literally. Earlier, the Rebbe of Kopyst, Rabbi Shelomo Zalman Schneerson (1830-1900), author of *Magen Avot*, wrote in a letter to Rabbi Don Tumarkin: "This is the entire subject of *Tzimtzum*, and this is the Hasidism of the Ba'al Shem Tov and the Maggid, may they rest in peace, that the *Tzimtzum* is not to be taken literally, as opposed to the opinion of the *Mishnat Hasidim* [i.e., Rabbi Immanuel Hai Ricchi] and the Gaon Rabbi Elijah, of blessed memory."[5]

Fraenkel is not willing to accept that the passage in *Tanya* is directed at the Vilna Gaon or earlier Rabbi Immanuel Hai Ricchi. He stands in good company. Upon receipt of Hayyim Yitzhak

Bunin's *Mishneh HaBaD* II (Warsaw, 1933), Rav Kook wrote back to the author requesting that he retract his statement that the pejorative "wise men in their own eyes" refers to the author of *Mishnat Hasidim* and the Gaon of Vilna.[6]

But then the question remains. Who are the "bad guys" of the *Tanya*? Fraenkel would have us believe that the reference is to the likes of the crypto-Sabbatian Nehemiah Hiyya Hayyon, against whom Ergas inveighed in his polemical works *Tokhahat Megulah* and *Ha-Tzad Nahash* (London, 1715).[7]

If that were the case, the language of the *Tanya* is too mild and reserved. Sabbatians (believers in the pseudo-Messiah Shabtai Tzevi) are usually treated to much more invective, such as "blasted be their bones." There is a parallel passage in the work of Rabbi Aaron Halevi Horowitz of Staroshelye, *Sha'arei ha-Yihud ve-ha-Emunah*. There the language is even more compassionate and conciliatory. It is hard to imagine that the *Ba'al ha-Tanya* and his prime pupil Rabbi Aaron Halevi Horowitz would show such empathy towards a Sabbatian heresiarch. With very few exceptions, members of the rabbinate were not *"melamed zekhut"* when it came to deviants of the Sabbatian persuasion. The passage reads:

> ...As it occurred to some latter-day kabbalists who attempt to be wise (*mithakmim*)...to understand *Tzimtzum* literally, as if He contracted Himself, and this is a crime, and their sin is too great to forbear, but their merit is that they have not spoken all these things with premeditation, God forbid, but from lack of understanding. May the LORD

forgive them, "for in respect of all the people it was done in error" [Numbers 15:26].[8]

Tzimtzum-literalism is not a characteristically Sabbatian posture, nor is it the exclusive domain of Sabbatians. Rabbi Jacob Emden, the arch-nemesis of the Sabbatians, took *Tzimtzum* literally, drawing an analogy to the vacuum created by a pump.[9] In fact, Emden excoriated Ricchi for belaboring the point, when "certainly, absolutely, it is not to be construed other than literally, and it is one of the *a priori* assumptions for the believer in our holy religion, if not for anti-religious *apikorsim* who do not concede the creation of the world."[10]

There is another problem with deflecting the *Tanya*'s critique away from the Gaon of Vilna toward Sabbatian kabbalists. If Sabbatians were being targeted, then why did the passage need to be suppressed at all? The Vilna Gaon and his disciples were certainly condemnatory of Sabbatianism in all its guises, so there would have been nothing in the passage to give offense to the *Mitnagdim*, the opponents of Hasidism.

Fraenkel's work is much more difficult than that of Rabbi Dessler, for Fraenkel has tasked himself with harmonizing the view of Rabbi Shelomo Eliashov (1841-1926), author of the *Leshem*, as well. Rabbi Shelomo Eliashov wrote—both in his *Helek ha-Be'urim* and in his recently published correspondence with fellow Mitnagdic kabbalist Rabbi Naftali Herz Halevi Weidenbaum—that he subscribes to the literalist interpretation of *Tzimtzum* as described in Ricchi's *Yosher Levav*.[11] The *Leshem* went so far as to cast aspersions on the *Likkutim* printed at the conclusion of *Be'ur ha-Gra* to *Sifra di-Tzeni'uta*, which present a non-literal reading of *Tzimtzum*.[12]

Professor Mordechai Pachter was struck by the most incongruous dovetailing of the perspectives of Lubavitch and the *Leshem* concerning the Vilna Gaon's interpretation of *Tzimtzum*. Both ascribe to the Gaon a literalist interpretation.[13]

"To cut to the chase," Fraenkel's strategy for reconciling what appear glaring differences of opinion, involves invoking the kabbalistic theory of relativity, namely the distinction between the divine perspective and the human perspective. The Aramaic expressions that convey this thought are *"le-gabei dideh"* versus *"le-gabei didan."*[14] (In *Nefesh ha-Hayyim*, the Hebrew terms *"mi-tsido"/"mi-tsideinu"* serve the same purpose.)[15] This distinction is certainly a valuable tool but it should not be overused. It strikes this reader as overly simplistic to assume that all writers (with the exception of Sabbatians) who grasp *Tzimtzum* literally are necessarily writing from the human perspective, while writers who understand *Tzimtzum* non-literally are necessarily writing from the divine perspective. And if the distinction should not be overused, *a fortiori* it should not be misused. To ascribe the human perspective (as opposed to divine perspective) to Rabbi Immanuel Hai Ricchi when he clearly writes the opposite, is to do violence to his words. A key passage in his *Yosher Levav* (quoted in fact by Fraenkel) reads:

Therefore relative to us (*le-gabei didan*), it is as if there was no *Tzimtzum* and we can say that the *Tzimtzum* is not literal. However, relative to the *Ein Sof* (*le-gabei ha-Ein Sof*) itself, it is literal.[16]

How it is then possible to flip around the author's mindset and reverse his stated position, is beyond me.

At day's end, the warring factions within *Knesset Yisrael* may have to make peace with their differences of opinion intact, even in the matter of *Tzimtzum*.

---

[1] Prof. Menachem Kallus confided to the writer (BN) that in his estimation the earliest discussion whether *Tzimtzum* was intended literally or not, is to be found in the notes to Rabbi Hayyim Vital's *'Ets Hayyim* penned by Rabbi Meir Poppers (ca. 1624-1662). Poppers writes that it sounds to him as if Luria's disciples Rabbi Hayyim Vital and Rabbi Yosef ibn Tabul understood from the Rav (i.e., Isaac Luria) that "the *Tzimtzum* is literal" (*"ha-tzimtzum ke-mishma'o"*). See Rabbi Meir Poppers, *'Or Zaru'a*, ed. Safrin and Sofer (Jerusalem: Hevrat Ahavat Shalom, 1986), *Sha'ar ha-'Iggulim ve-ha-Yosher*, chap. 2 (p. 29).

[2] See *"Derush ha-Tefillin"* in Rabbi Shelomo Fisher, *Beit Yishai—Derashot* (Jerusalem, 2004), p. 355.

[3] Rabbi Eizik of Homel, *"Iggeret Kodesh"* (Holy Epistle) printed at the conclusion of *Hannah Ariel—Amarot Tehorot* (*Ma'amar ha-Shabbat*, etc.) (Berdichev: Sheftel, 1912), 4b.

[4] *Tanya* II, 7 (83a).

[5] Published in M.M. Laufer, *Ha-Melekh bi-Mesibo*, vol. 2 (Kefar Habad: Kehot, 1993), p. 286.

Rabbi Shelomo Zalman's younger brother, Rabbi Shemariah Noah of Bobruisk, discusses the literalist interpretation of *Yosher Levav* (by Rabbi Immanuel Hai Ricchi, author of *Mishnat Hasidim*). See Rabbi Shemariah Noah Schneerson, *Shemen la-Ma'or*, vol. 1 (Kefar Habad, 1964), *Bo*, s.v. *ve-kakhah tokhlu 'oto*, par. 2 (f. 130).

[6] Rav Kook's manuscript, dated 3 Tamuz 5693 (i.e., 1933), was published in *Haskamot ha-RAYaH* (Jerusalem: Makhon RZYH Kook, 1988), no. 85 (pp. 104-105). In his letter to Bunin, Rav Kook insisted that at the earliest opportunity Bunin make amends for having slighted the honor of the authors of

Mishnat Hasidim and *Sha'arei Gan 'Eden* (and the Vilna Gaon).

Ironically, Rav Kook's maternal grandfather Raphael Felman was a *hasid* of the Rebbe of Kopyst.

Fraenkel dismisses out of hand the notion that the *Tanya* pilloried Ricchi because of the fact that references to Ricchi's *Mishnat Hasidim* figure prominently in the *Tanya*. See *Nefesh HaTzimtzum*, vol. 2, p. 79, n. 89. This argument is unconvincing. It is quite conceivable that the *Ba'al ha-Tanya* was fond of *Mishnat Hasidim*, a popular digest of Lurianic Kabbalah, while viewing Ricchi's other work *Yosher Levav* as being beyond the pale. And for the very reason that such a venerable kabbalist erred in his judgment concerning *Tzimtzum*, he was worthy of compassion. Cf. Rabbi Zadok Hakohen of Lublin:

> There were already found many great men, authors among the *mekubbalim* (kabbalists), who stumbled in this [i.e., *hagshamah*, or corporealization], including the author of *Yosher Levav*, who explained the matter of *Tzimtzum* and similarly many matters of Kabbalah in [terms of] total corporealization, as the understanding will recognize. I have spelled out his name, for some authors who came after him already publicized him in print, in order to clarify his errors in this respect. Behold he was a great and holy man, as is known, and erred only in his faith. Though this too is a great error and requires atonement (as explained above), nonetheless, it is not such a grievous sin, as explained in the words of the RABaD [i.e., Rabbi Abraham ben David of Posquières]...."
>
> (Rabbi Zadok Hakohen Rabinowitz, *Sefer ha-Zikhronot* in *Divrei Soferim* [Lublin, 1913], 32d)

The reference is to RABaD's animadversion to Maimonides' statement in *MT, Hil. Teshuvah* 3:7 that one who professes belief in a corporeal deity has the halakhic status of a *"min,"* or heretic. See *Hasagot ha-RABaD le-Mishneh Torah*, ed. Bezalel Naor (Jerusalem, 1985), pp. 56-58, 141-142.

*

In deference to *"Ha-Ga'on he-Hasid"* Rav Kook, in the second edition of *Mishneh HaBaD*, when explicating the *Tanya*'s oblique mention of "some wise men in their own eyes," Bunin omitted his previous reference to *Mishnat Hasidim* of Rabbi Immanuel Hai Ricchi and *Sha'arei Gan 'Eden* of Rabbi Jacob Koppel of Mezritch, while retaining the reference to the Vilna Gaon. Bunin explained that he felt justified in retaining the reference to the Vilna Gaon on the basis of the letter addressed by the *Ba'al ha-Tanya* to his Hasidim in Vilna, wherein we read that the Vilna Gaon understood *"Tzimtzum"* in the literal sense. Obviously, Bunin was unaware that the letter was a forgery. See Hayyim Yitzhak Bunin, *Mishneh HaBaD*, vol. 1, book 1, part 1 (Warsaw, 1936), pp. 68-69, note 5.

On the *Gnazim* website there is accessible Bunin's response to the letter of Rav Kook published in *Haskamot ha-RAYaH*. Bunin's letter is datelined "16 Marheshvan 5694 [i.e., 1933], Warsaw." Addressed to *"Ha-Rav ha-Ga'on he-Hasid"* Rav Kook, Bunin apologizes for not having responded sooner. Rav Kook's letter reached him only in Tishri and since then, "mighty burdens" prevented his responding.

Bunin respectfully differs with Rav Kook's opinion. In his work *Yosher*

Levav, Rabbi Immanuel Hai Ricchi (the author of *Mishnat Hasidim*) repeatedly reiterates that *Tzimtzum* must be taken literally. It is inconceivable that such a *ga'on* and *tsaddik* (as Ricchi) would dissemble. As for the author of *Sha'arei Gan 'Eden*, though his language is opaque, a straightforward assessment will turn up that he too was of the opinion that *Tzimtzum* is to be construed literally. Bunin then quotes verbatim several phrases from *Sha'arei Gan 'Eden* to prove his point.

Rav Kook made reference in his letter to Rabbi Meir Popper's gloss at the beginning of *'Ets Hayyim* concerning *Tzimtzum*: "Said Meir: The *Rav* [Luria] said this in relation to us (*be-'erkeinu*)." Bunin responded that the gloss represented an earlier understanding; this would not prevent those who came later (such as the Vilna Gaon) from understanding *Tzimtzum* differently. (Oddly enough, Rav Kook was under the mistaken impression that the gloss was written by Rabbi Meir Asch [Eisenstadt], author of *Panim Me'irot*. Bunin followed suit. This same blunder of Rav Kook occurs in a letter written two years earlier on 26 Tevet, 5691 [i.e., 1931] to Rabbi Yahya al-Kafah; see *Ma'amrei ha-RAYaH*, vol. 2, ed. Elisha Aviner [Langenauer] [Jerusalem, 1984], p. 521.)

Finally, against his better judgment, in deference to Rav Kook, Bunin promises in a future edition to publish a retraction.

See: http://gnazimorg.startlogic.com/1935-1865-קון-הכהן-יצחק-אברהם
[7] Fraenkel's "Shabbetian *Tzimtzum Kipshuto*" (as opposed to the "Acceptable *Tzimtzum Kipshuto*") strikes this writer as a "straw man" contrived for purposes of *pilpul*.
[8] Rabbi Aaron Halevi, *Sha'arei ha-Yihud ve-ha-Emunah* (Shklov, 1820), Part 1, Gate 1, chap. 21, note (f.51).
[9] Rabbi Jacob Emden, *Mitpahat Sefarim* (Altona, 1768), 35b-36a (i.e., 45b-46a).
[10] *Mitpahat Sefarim* 35b (i.e., 45b).

To the question of whether Ricchi himself was a crypto-Sabbatian, I devoted an entire chapter of my book *Post-Sabbatian Sabbatianism* (1999): "Immanuel Hai Ricchi—Literalist among Kabbalists." See now Tzvi Luboshitz, "An Early Version of the *Simsum* Debate in Immanuel Hay Ricchi's *Yosher Levav*," *Kabbalah*, 42 (2018), pp. 267-320.
[11] Rabbi Shelomo Eliashov, *Helek ha-Bi'urim* (Jerusalem, 1935), 3a-b. The letters of Rabbi Eliashov to Rabbi N.H. Halevi Weidenbaum were published in Rabbi Moshe Schatz, *Ma'ayan Moshe* (Jerusalem, 2011).
[12] *Helek ha-Bi'urim*, 5b. However, recently Yosef Avivi vouched for the authenticity of the manuscript; see Yosef Avivi, *Kabbalat ha-GRA* (Jerusalem, 5753 [i.e., 1993]), p. 27.
[13] Mordechi Pachter, "The Gaon's Kabbalah from the Perspective of Two Traditions" (Hebrew), in *The Vilna Gaon and his Disciples* (Ramat-Gan: Bar-Ilan University Press, 2003), pp. 119-136.
[14] See Rabbi Menahem Azariah da Fano, *Ma'amar ha-Nefesh*, Part 2, chap. 4 in *Ma'amrei ha-RaMA' mi-Fano* (Jerusalem: Yismah Lev, 1997), p. 339; Rabbi Immanuel Hai Ricchi, *Yosher Levav* (Amsterdam, 1737), chap. 15 (10a); Rabbi Moshe Hayyim Luzzatto (i.e., attributed to—), *KaLaH Pithei Hokhmah* (Koretz, 1785), *petah* 27 (31b); idem, *Peirush Arimat Yadai* in *Adir ba-Marom* II, ed. Spinner (Jerusalem, 1988), p. 74; Rabbi Aaron Halevi Horowitz, *Sha'arei ha-Yihud ve-ha-Emunah* (Shklov, 1820), Part 1, Gate 1, note to

chap. 21 (43b-44a); Rabbi Isaac of Volozhin, *"Ma'amar Be-Tzelem"* (note to *Nefesh ha-Hayyim*, Gate 1, chap. 1) in Avinoam Fraenkel, *Nefesh HaTzimtzum*, vol. 2, p. 397; Rabbi Abraham Isaac Hakohen Kook, *Shemonah Kevatsim* (Jerusalem, 2004), 2:120 (vol. 1, p. 284).

[15] *Nefesh ha-Hayyim* III, 6.

[16] Rabbi Immanuel Hai Ricchi, *Yosher Levav* (Amsterdam, 1737), chap. 15 (10a). Quoted in *Nefesh ha-Tzimtzum*, vol. 2, pp. 260-261. See also Fraenkel's discussion of Ricchi's position on pp. 63-71.

Maimonides:
Between Philosophy and Halakhah

Rabbi Joseph B. Soloveitchik's Lectures on the Guide of the Perplexed.
Edited with an Introduction by Lawrence J. Kaplan (2016)

In the late 1970s, Rabbi Joseph B. Soloveitchik entrusted Lawrence Kaplan with the formidable task of translating his classic Hebrew monograph *Ish ha-Halakhah* into English. It was published in 1983 under the title *Halakhic Man*. Now Professor Kaplan has stewarded this project: A student's notes of a course on the *Guide of the Perplexed* that Rabbi Soloveitchik offered in Yeshiva University's Bernard Revel Graduate School in the academic year 1950-1951.

Kaplan is much more than a translator or even editor of Rabbi Soloveitchik's works. Over the years, he has emerged as a leading interpreter of Soloveitchik's thought, as well as a gifted thinker in his own right. He is at once reverential towards and critical of his *Rav*'s thought. In the words of Dov Schwartz, in his Foreword to the book: "His admiration of R. Soloveitchik has not detracted from his critical sense. As a student, he transcends the scholar in him, and as a scholar, he transcends the student in him." I would go one step further in defining the role of Lawrence Kaplan. To employ the by now famous imagery of Rabbi Hutner, Kaplan is that "singular student who has the unique ability to grasp the thought of the *Rav* when he is silent; when he passes from speech to silence."[1]

Rabbi Soloveitchik opened the course with this salvo:

> There are two aspects to creativity in the realm of philosophy. The first is philosophical creativity, whereby one brings new thoughts to the totality of man's historical treasures. The second is creativity in the realm of philosophical style. Philosophical style refers to one's philosophical formulae and terminology, the choice of one's words, the literary categories one employs. If a philosopher is both philosophically creative and, as well, creates a new philosophical style, he will revolutionize philosophy.
>
> Sometimes, however, a philosophical genius is handicapped by the routine philosophical jargon that prevails in a particular climate. Literary categories are always needed as tools enabling one to express subjective ideas. Each epoch has its own jargon and categories....Not every creative genius will be able to fashion new tools. Some may be exceedingly creative in the area of philosophical analysis, but lack creativity in the field of literary inventiveness. They are unable to find a new medium or instrumentality to present their thought.

Maimonides Between Philosophy and Halakhah

> Maimonides was such a genius. He was a great genius in the realm of philosophical analysis and imagination. Indeed, in the *Mishneh Torah*, in the realm of *Halakhah*, he was able to mint new terms, to fashion new philosophic categories. There he was creative in all senses. But in the *Guide* there is sterility as to the form of presentation. He used the old, routine, Aristotelian philosophical jargon. Perhaps his use of Arabic hampered him; perhaps he was so overawed by Aristotle that he adopted his tools and took on his tradition.[2]

One can imagine students sitting on edge in shock and awe upon delivery of this candid appraisal of the book widely held to be the pinnacle of Jewish Philosophy! I will leave it to others more conversant with the Judeo-Arabic literary tradition to opine on the correctness of Rabbi Soloveitchik's assessment. It is not difficult to glean where Rabbi Soloveitchik was coming from and where he was going to with this bold, perhaps even brash statement. His grandfather Rabbi Hayyim Soloveitchik (known in the *yeshivah* world as "Reb Hayyim Brisker") was a genius in both senses. He excelled in originality of thought and expression. The *"Brisker Derekh,"* the revolutionary method of conceptualization that he bequeathed to coming generations of Talmudists, came equipped with an equally exciting lexicon: *heftsa/gavra, hiyyuv/kiyyum, shnei dinim, din mesuyyam*. And Rabbi Soloveitchik himself would prove a master at coining neologisms, of which the present volume has its fair share: "ethical-intellectual," "metaphysical-transcendental" (p. 82).

While the modern reader might find these hyphenated terms a bit old-fashioned or outlandish, in context they do serve their purpose.

Rabbi Joseph B. Soloveitchik was renowned for having inherited his grandfather's consuming passion for Maimonides' *Mishneh Torah*. It is public knowledge that in the realm of *Halakhah*, the Rabbi of Boston perpetuated Rabbi Hayyim's razor-sharp method of analyzing that *magnum opus*. What remains a little known fact is that Rabbi Hayyim Soloveitchik was an avid student of the *Guide* as well. In Volozhin, Rabbi Hayyim confided to a visitor, Rabbi Yosef Alexander—Rabbi of Darbian (today Darbenai, Lithuania) and author of a commentary to the prayer book, *Porat Yosef* (Warsaw, 1898)—that it had taken him two years to study the *Guide*.[3] Rabbi J.B. Soloveitchik shared with his students that not only was his grandfather Rabbi Hayyim expert in the *Guide* but that he wished to pen a commentary thereto—a wish that unfortunately remained unfulfilled due to the exigencies of time. On that occasion, Rabbi Soloveitchik related that he received directly from his grandfather guidance how to deal with contradictions between the *Guide* and *Mishneh Torah*.[4] It seems that at one point in time Rabbi Hayyim's study partner in the *Guide* was an enigmatic HaBaD Hasid by the name of Rabbi Hayyim Abraham Dov Baer Hakohen Levine (known in Hasidic circles as "the *Mal'akh*," "the Angel").[5]

Rabbi Hayyim Soloveitchik's enthusiasm for the *Guide* was shared by his contemporaries, Rabbi Meir Simhah Cohen and

Rabbi Joseph Rosen. These two, who served respectively as the Mitnagdic and Hasidic Rabbis of Dvinsk, produced monumental commentaries of their own on *Mishneh Torah*. While Rabbi Hayyim had no recourse to the *Guide* in his *Hiddushei Rabbenu Hayyim Halevi*, the *Tsaphnat Pa'ne'ah* of Rabbi Joseph Rosen (known as the "Rogatchover" after his birthplace in Belarus) and the *'Or Same'ah* of Rabbi Meir Simhah Cohen abound with references to the *Guide*.

There is a simple explanation why Rabbi Hayyim Soloveitchik's *Hiddushei Rabbenu Hayyim Ha-Levi* has no truck with the *Guide* while *'Or Same'ah* is replete with references to the *Guide*. The former deals only with the halakhic portions of *Mishneh Torah*, while the latter takes up with the philosophic sections of *Sefer ha-Madda'* as well.

In the case of *Tsafnat Pa'ne'ah*, the involvement with the *Guide* is much more complex. For starters, unlike Reb Hayyim Brisker who was prevented from writing a commentary to the *Guide*, Rabbi Joseph Rosen (or as he was referred to colloquially, "Reb Yoshe Denaburger," after Denaburg, the former name of Dvinsk, today Daugavpils, Latvia) penned notes to that philosophic work. While he rails time and time again against the heresies of Moses Narboni (Moses of Narbonne),[6] he has no problem with the *Giv'at ha-Moreh* of Solomon Maimon, whom he refers to simply as *"Ha-Mefaresh"* ("the Commentator"). It is conceivable that this HaBaD Hasid was simply unaware who authored the anonymous commentary to the *Guide*.[7]

But the relation of *Tsafnat Pa'ne'ah* to the *Guide* does not end there. Those same Aristotelian categories which Rabbi J.B. Soloveitchik found to be time-worn, routine, and hackneyed—*homer/tsurah, harkavah mizgit/harkavah shekhenit, 'etsem/mikreh, he'eder/metsi'ut*—were now introduced into Talmudic analysis! (Tail end of the story: The Rogatchover's method of analysis, plucked from the *Guide*, found one disciple in Rabbi J.B. Soloveitchik's long-standing friend, Rabbi Menahem Schneerson, the Lubavitcher Rebbe.)

Whereas numerous scholars perceive two distinct Maimonides—one, the halakhist of *Mishneh Torah*; the other, the phlosopher of the *Guide*—these three *Litvishe gedolim* (Lithuanian titans) saw no discontinuity, no disconnect, no split in personality.[8] Rabbi Meir Simhah concluded: "The words of *Rabbeinu* [i.e., Maimonides] in all of his books—the *Yad*, the *Guide*, and the *Commentary to the Mishnah*—one *Geist* runs through them."[9]

Rabbi Yehiel Ya'akov Weinberg had the audacity to tell Rabbi Moshe Soloveichik that though his father, Rabbi Hayyim Soloveitchik's interpretations of Maimonides' *Mishneh Torah* are certainly not what Maimonides intended, nonetheless Rabbi Hayyim's novellae are of interest in their own right. "Reb Hayyim was a new Maimonides in his own right."[10] We might be tempted to say something similar concerning Rabbi Joseph B. Soloveitchik's interpretation of Maimonides' *Guide*. While in places it leaves the reader far from convinced that this was Maimonides' original intention, it is fascinating in its own right. "Reb Yoshe Baer was a new Maimonides in his own right."[11]

Maimonides Between Philosophy and Halakhah

In his thorough Introduction, Professor Kaplan mentions *en passant* a *Yahrzeit Shi'ur* of Rabbi Soloveitchik, *"Be-'Inyan Mehikat Hashem,"* "devoted to an analysis of Maimonides' theory of divine attributes and the resulting obligation of imitating God" (p. 23). While Kaplan is certainly correct when he writes that it "takes the form of a commentary on the opening paragraphs of *Laws of the Foundations of the Torah*, Chapter 6," upon internal inspection we discover that the *shi'ur* is infused with the spirit and substance of the *Guide*. This is a summation from the *shi'ur*:

> A new light is shed, if so, upon all the twenty-four books of the *TaNaKh*. I always had difficulty with the role of the prophets of Israel. On the one hand, we hold that a prophet is not permitted to innovate, to add or detract by even an iota; on the other hand, the word of the LORD came to the prophets, they prophesied and their prophecy was written down for eternity. What is the purpose of their prophecy, since they cannot innovate any *halakhah*? True, they rebuked Israel, and exhortation was one of the purposes for which our prophets were sent. But I still find it difficult to say that in their prophecy they did not relate to Israel the word of the LORD in a halakhic sense. But now all is crystal clear. An entire teaching is contained in the Prophets—the teaching of the ways of the Holy One, blessed be He; the teaching of the attributes that obligates

man in *imitatio Dei*. Therefore Maimonides included the chapter dealing with erasing the Name—which essentially is the chapter of the proper names and attributes—in the *Laws of the Foundations of the Torah* before the explanation of the foundation of prophecy, because in the teaching of the names of the Holy One, blessed be He—"I will make all My goodness pass before you, and will proclaim the name of the LORD before you; and I will be gracious to whom I will be gracious, and will show mercy on whom I will show mercy."—is hidden the foundation of prophecy and its purpose. In brief, prophecy comes to teach man how to participate in the attributes of the Holy One, blessed be He, and merit to be called by the same.[12]

The Biblical quote is from Exodus 33:19. This verse is discussed by Maimonides in the *Guide*, Part I, Chapter 54. That chapter concludes:

> For the utmost virtue of man is to become like unto Him, may He be exalted, as far as he is able; which means that we should make our actions like unto His, as the Sages made clear when interpreting the verse, *You shall be holy*. They said: *He is gracious, so be you also gracious; He is merciful, so be you also merciful.*[13]

Rabbi Soloveitchik's discussion in *"Mehikat Hashem"* of the role that prophecy plays and of the two forms of *imitatio Dei* (behavioral versus characteriological) is seminal. It might be interesting to contrast that Maimonidean interpretation to Abraham Joshua Heschel's perception of the prophets, who express the word of an anthropopathic deity—a notion in direct contravention of the strictures set up by Maimonides in the *Guide*. For Rabbi Soloveitchik (as for Maimonides), God engages in activities designed to evoke and inculcate in man various character traits. In Rabbi Heschel's reading of the prophets, God goes so far as to share in the pathos, the emotion described so vividly by the *nevi'im*.[14]

In his Preface, Prof. Kaplan apprises us that the present volume takes us through the student's notes of the First Course, but there yet awaits "Course Two." This reviewer was privileged to hear Rabbi Soloveitchik hold forth on the *Guide of the Perplexed* one Saturday night in the Maimonides School that he founded in Boston. (On that memorable occasion, the Philosopher of Boston explored Maimonides' solution to the problem of evil in the *Guide*, Part III, Chapter 12.) Is there any chance that there exists a record of *that* series of lectures?

---

[1] Rabbi Isaac Hutner, *Pahad Yitzhak: Hanukkah* (New York, NY, 1989), 8:5 (pp. 64-65).
[2] *Rabbi Joseph B. Soloveitchik's Lectures on the* Guide of the Perplexed, pp. 75-76.
[3] Rabbi Uri Moinester, *Karnei Re'em* (New York, 1951), p. 104, note 1.
[4] Rabbi Hershel Reichman, *Reshimot Shi'urei Maran ha-GRID Ha-Levi: Sukkah*

(New York, 1990), p. 258.

[5] Rabbi Yisroel Besser, *Mishpacha*, no. 191 (2 Shevat, 5768/2008), p. 41. Rabbi Baruch Baer Leibowitz, eminent disciple of Rabbi Hayyim Soloveitchik, referred to Rabbi Levine as *"a mensch vos hot geshushket mit mein rebbe in Moreh."* Although the Yiddish is idiomatic and well-nigh untranslatable, the gist is "someone who whispered with my rabbi [i.e., Hayyim Soloveitchik] in the *Guide*."

See also the testimony of the *Mal'akh*'s son, Rabbi Raphael Zalman Levine, quoting Rabbi Baruch Baer Leibowitz: "[Rabbi Hayyim Soloveitchik] *flegt zikh shushkenen mit ihm* [i.e., *Mal'akh*] *gantze teg nokhanand."* The idiomatic Yiddish translates as, "[Rabbi Hayyim Soloveitchik] would whisper with him [i.e., the *Mal'akh*] for days on end." Rabbi Baruch Baer concluded by saying that no one knew what they discussed. See Rabbi C.S. Glickman, *Mi-Pihem u-mi-Pi Ketavam* (Brooklyn, NY, 2008), p. 145. The sense is that the two men (Rabbi Hayyim Soloveitchik and the *Mal'akh*) were sequestered, studying in private.

[6] The expressions that Rabbi Joseph Rosen reserves for Narboni are so vituperative that rather than print them in the commentary of *Tsafnat Pa'ne'ah*, the editor, Rabbi Kasher, saw fit to relegate them to an appendix to the work. See Rabbi Joseph Rosen, *Tsaphnat Pa'ne'ah*, Deuteronomy, Part Two/*Moreh Nevukhim*, ed. Rabbi Menahem Mendel Kasher (Jerusalem, 1965), p. 422.

[7] In the Sulzbach 1828 edition of *Moreh Nevukhim* in which Rabbi Joseph Rosen penned his notes, the commentary *Giv'at ha-Moreh* was printed without the author's name. Thus, Rabbi Rosen would have been unaware that the commentary was written by Solomon Maimon, a notorious renegade. See Rabbi Menahem M. Kasher's introduction to Rabbi Joseph Rosen, *Tsaphnat Pa'ne'ah*, *Moreh Nevukhim*.

[8] The three shared in common exposure to Rabbi Hayyim's father, Rabbi Joseph Baer Soloveitchik of Brisk (author of *Beit ha-Levi*). As a youth, Joseph Rosen of Rogatchov studied with the *Beit ha-Levi* when he served as Rabbi of Slutsk. As for Rabbi Meir Simhah Cohen, when he was a young man in Bialystok, his talent was duly noted by Rabbi Joseph Baer Soloveitchik, who recommended him for the (Mitnagdic) rabbinate of Dvinsk.

[9] Rabbi Meir Simhah Cohen, *Meshekh Hokhmah* (Riga, 1927), *Yitro*, s.v. *lo yiheyeh lekha* (44a).

[10] In letters to Dr. Gavriel Cohen written in the year 1965, Rabbi Weinberg recollected a conversation he had years earlier with Rabbi Moshe Soloveitchik concerning his father Rabbi Hayyim Soloveitchik's exegesis of Maimonides. See *Kitvei ha-Gaon Rabbi Yehiel Ya'akov Weinberg*, ed. Melekh Shapiro, vol. 2 (Scranton, 2003), p. 219, note 4. See also Marc B. Shapiro, *Studies in Maimonides and His Interpreters* (Scranton, PA: University of Scranton Press, 2008), Hebrew Section, pp. 30-31.

[11] In *yeshivah* circles, Rabbi Joseph Baer Soloveitchik of Boston was referred to colloquially as "Reb Yoshe Baer."

[12] Rabbi Joseph Dov Halevi Soloveitchik, *Shi'urim le-Zekher Abba Mari* (Jerusalem: Mossad Harav Kook, 2002), vol. 2, pp. 188-189.

[13] Maimonides, *Guide of the Perplexed*, transl. Shlomo Pines (Chicago: University of Chicago Press, 1964), p. 128.

[14] See Abraham Joshua Heschel, *The Prophets* (1962).

HALLEL FROM HEAVEN
AND HALLEL FROM HELL

THE POST-HOLOCAUST RESPONSES OF
PAUL CELAN, AHARON APPELFELD AND MESHULAM RATH

"Just as the praise of the Holy One ascends to Him from Heaven, so it ascends from Hell." (Midrash)

What do the poet Paul Celan, the novelist Aharon Appelfeld, and the religious legalist Meshulam Rath share in common? Two things.

First, they all emerged from Tchernowitz (today Chernivtsi, Ukraine), capital of Bukovina, a relic of the Habsburg era, located at the eastern extreme of the defunct Austro-Hungarian Empire. Tchernowitz, whose Jewish population was estimated at 50,000 in the interbellum (roughly half the total population). Tchernowitz, where Jews spoke German while their gentile neighbors spoke Ruthenian or Ukrainian, or maybe Romanian.

Second, these three men bequeathed a literary legacy of Holocaust response that deserves our careful attention.

※

Paul Celan (1920-1970), whose last name is an anagram of his original patronym Ancel (Antschel), would after the war reinvent himself in Paris as a German poet of distinction, hailed by many as the greatest of the postwar German poets. His existence was riddled with contradictions. A Jew living in France, writing in German, no less. He could not extricate himself from the tongue. The language of the murderers was also the language of his mother—a mother whose loss haunts his poetry. We may say that Celan was a survivor who did not survive. A quarter of a century later the Holocaust would catch up to him, plunging his body into the Seine, drowning out a voice that had been slowly drowning for half its life. As Katharine Washburn, one of Celan's many translators, wrote: "Celan described the trajectory of his own poetic career as *'still geworden,'* becoming silent."

Celan's poem *Todesfuge* (Death Fugue), written while the war yet raged, created a sensation when it was published in Germany in 1952 and established the poet's career. It captures the eerie incongruity of Jewish violinists being forced to perform concert music in the death camps. One of the most haunting images is the following:

> *Er ruft streicht dunkler die Geigen*
> *Dann steigt ihr als Rauch in die Luft*
> *Dann habt ihr ein Grab in den Wolken*
> *Da liegt man nicht eng.*

> He shouts strike the fiddles darker
> Then you'll rise as smoke in the air
> Then you'll have a grave in the clouds
> There you won't lie cramped.

As the years went by, Celan's poems became sparser. Begrudgingly few words and their meanings obtuse beyond comprehension. There was set in motion a total breakdown of language (running a course parallel to Celan's mental breakdown). Celan was being overtaken by silence, his voice being choked as a rehearsal for its final "stilling" in the Seine.

But before the total strangulation of sense, Celan's eye would light on the King within the Nothing.

> *Im Nichts—wer steht da? Der König.*
> *Da steht der König, der König.*
> *Da steht er und steht.*
> *Judenlocke, wirst nicht grau.*

> In Nothing—what dwells there? The King.
> There the King dwells, the King.
> There he dwells and dwells.
> Jew's curl, you'll turn not grey.[1]

Had Celan read Rabbi Nahman of Breslov?[2] Or had their minds' eyes shared a common vision of a King who reposes in the Void? And might Celan's cranium have yet retained the verses of Judah the Pious of Regensburg's *Hymn of Glory* sung in synagogue on the Sabbath:

> The tresses of His head are like His youthful days;
> His locks are black curls.

And maybe the two mystical visions of Nahman of Breslov and Judah the Pious collided in Celan's imagination, yielding a marriage of Heaven and Hell; the destruction of Jewry and its immortality.

※※※

Aharon Appelfeld (1932-) was a boy at the time of the Holocaust. Like Celan, he is eternally orphaned of his mother. Unlike Celan, he traded his maternal language of German for Hebrew. Since settling in Israel after the War in 1946, he has produced novel after novel in the "sacred tongue." In those novels, he returns time and again to Tchernowitz. The guises change from narrative to narrative; through the diaphanous veil we easily make out the features of the boy orphaned of his mother. (Both Celan and Appelfeld are openly Oedipal.) Appelfeld and his readers are forced to forever revisit the scene of the trauma; to reopen a wound that never heals.

Appelfeld was spared Celan's agony of taking German's infamously long words and dissecting them until they dissolve into nothingness. Instead, Appelfeld opted for a Hebrew language that is trim and laconic, a quality that persists in English translation. To quote the New York Times Book Review of *All Whom I Have Loved*, "he has an artfully spare writing style."

Though Appelfeld's silence is not as invasive as Celan's, it should not be underestimated:

> But in his heart Hugo knows that what had been would never be again. The time in the ghetto and in hiding is

already embossed on his flesh, and the power of the words he would use has faded. Now it isn't words that speak to him, but silence. This is a difficult language, but as soon as one adopts it, no other language will ever be as effective.[3]

A theme that runs through Appelfeld's novels is the sociological observation, usually made by devout Ukrainian peasants, that the Old Jews believed in God and prayed in the synagogue but the New Jews no longer believe and have no use of synagogues.

Finally, we come to Meshulam Rath (1875-1962), the elder Rabbi of Tchernowitz. He survived the inferno that engulfed Europe and settled in Israel in 1944, where he was frequently consulted by the Chief Rabbinate. (Since youth, Rath had been identified with the Religious Zionist movement.)

Even those who could not abide Meshulam Rath's Zionist sympathies dared not impugn his credentials as a world-class halakhic authority. Rabbi Meshulam Rath's most famous—and controversial—legal decision concerns reciting *Hallel* (Psalms of thanksgiving) on Israel's Independence Day. In 1952, at the behest of Rabbi Judah Leib Maimon, he penned a formal responsum wherein he expressed his bold opinion that it behooves Jews to recite *Hallel* with a blessing on *Yom Ha-'Atsma'ut*.

Rabbi Rath entitled his collection of responsa *Kol Mevaser* (*Voice of the Herald*):

I pray that just as I merited after the terrible Holocaust to see the beginning of the redemption, so may the LORD grant me the privilege to hear the voice heralding our complete redemption, speedily in our days.[4]

The poet who emerged from the Holocaust a young man, lapsed into silence, and eventually madness and suicide. The novelist who emerged from the vanished world an adolescent, also succumbed to silence. It was the old rabbi, the septuagenarian sage, who saw a world destroyed and rebuilt, that summoned the strings of King David's harp. And these strings would not establish for the Jews a space in the sky—as in Celan's *Death Fugue*—but a space on Earth.

Celan's cryptic remark proved true:

Judenlocke, wirst nicht grau.

Jew lock you'll turn not gray.

---

[1] *"Mandorla"* from *Die Niemandsrose* (1963); in *Paul Celan: Poems*, translated by M. Hamburger (New York: Persea Books, 1980), pp. 156-157.
[2] See *Likkutei MOHaRaN* I, 64 ("*Bo el Par'oh*").
[3] Aharon Appelfeld, *Blooms of Darkness*, translated by Jeffrey M. Green (New York: Schocken, 2010), p. 53.
[4] From the Introduction to *Kol Mevaser*, datelined B'nei Berak, 23 Menahem-Av 5715 (i.e., 1955).

When Elijah's Mantle Fell:
The Judaism of Leonard Cohen

Now that the dust has begun to settle on the freshly dug grave of Leonard Cohen (1934-2016), and we are hopefully past the hullabaloo, past the media circus which witnessed (in Leonard's own words) "all the lousy little poets coming round," we may begin to examine with some sobriety the literary legacy of this celebrated bard.

No, Leonard Cohen did not receive the coveted Nobel Prize for Literature. Instead, it was awarded to another Jewish poet, Bob Dylan (*né* Robert Zimmerman). But, about the same time that Dylan was announced a Nobel laureate, Cohen bequeathed to us what would become his farewell song, his *Kaddish*, "You Want It Darker." With that, the prodigal son returned home and was clutched to the bosom of his people. Complete with the Biblical Hebrew refrain *"Hineni"* ("I'm ready") and backed up by the cantorial rendition of the *hazan* of historic Congregation Shaar Hashomayim in Montreal, the synagogue Leonard grew up in as a boy, "this last song he left us is the most Jewish he ever wrote" (Rabbi Lord Jonathan Sacks). Indeed, as the Talmud put it, "There is one who acquires eternity in a single hour."[1]

Cohen's identity as a priest descended from Aaron, was not lost on him. Time and again, he invoked his priestly powers. At the conclusion of one memorable concert in Israel, Cohen actually extended his hands in priestly benediction, pronouncing—in the outlandish Ashkenazic pronunciation of his forebears—the three verses of the ancient formula.

Besides bestowing blessing, the High Priest in days of yore also acted as an oracle. In his prophetic imagination, the letters engraved in the precious and semi-precious stones on his breastplate would light up like a console, delivering a Delphic message to the nation. Cohen preserved this tradition as well in his literary *oeuvre*, referring to it self-deprecatingly as "entertainment for cryptologists."

Having properly vetted him as an authentic Jewish voice, one asks where exactly in the pantheon of Judaism does Leonard Cohen's God belong? Certainly Cohen's God is not the Lithuanian Mitnagdic God of his maternal grandfather, Rabbi Solomon Klonitzky-Kline, author of *Otsar Ta'amei Hazal*, a thesaurus of aggadic interpretations of the Pentateuch. Unlike classical rabbinic Judaism, with its transcendental vision of the deity, Cohen's faith is decidedly pantheistic. His God is embodied and incarnate. (Stated succinctly, Leonard's credo reduces to the belief that the divinity is splendid as a woman but pathetic as a god.) But neither is his the faith of the Hasidim. From the very beginning, the *Tanya* (referred to in HaBaD circles as "the Bible of Hasidism"), drives a wedge between the "animal soul" (*nefesh ha-behemit*) and the "divine soul" (*nefesh ha-elohit*). If there is a Judaism that can accommodate the enigmatic soul of Leonard Cohen, it is, Heaven shudder—Sabbateanism. In the wake of the appearance of the Messiah of Izmir, seventeenth-century Shabbetai Tsevi, there was constructed—and deconstructed—a kabbalistic universe in which lust, passion and sensuality interplay with the divine.

One of the vestments of the priest was the *avnet*, the belt or girdle. The Talmudic sages disagreed what fabric it consisted of, whether it was pure white linen (the garb of the angels on high) or mixed with multi-variegated wool, embracing all the sensual colors of life: crimson, blue and purple.[2] In fact, the great codifier Maimonides adopted the latter approach.[3] And the *avnet* was extremely long, which required it to be wrapped around the *cohen*'s frame several times. Thirty-two cubits in length, no less![4] Thirty-two (*Lamed Bet*) being the Hebrew word for "heart." It may have been richly colored, and it certainly was hearty, but a divide it was nonetheless, a barrier between the upper and lower parts of man.

In Leonard Cohen's art, we have a priestly wardrobe *sans* girdle. All the divine poetry of man's higher self and all the graphic detail of man's lower self, come together. No one is more aware of this ongoing battle, this war waged between the physical nature and the spiritual nature, than Leonard Cohen himself.

In *My Life in Art*, which contains an unpublished memoir of the time he spent in Israel during and in the aftermath of the Yom Kippur War, Cohen recorded the contents of a letter he received from "Asher," an all too sincere convert to Judaism, whose fundamental belief assaulted, challenged, disturbed, and provoked Leonard on so many levels of his being. One thing is certain. Cohen was unable to ignore the gauntlet thrown down by this unlikely acquaintance.

Just shy of his fortieth birthday, Cohen left behind his partner Suzanne Elrod and their infant son Adam on the idyllic Greek isle of Hydra, in order to be with his people in this dark hour of their history. In Athens airport, as he was about to board the plane bound for Tel-Aviv, Cohen met this strange man, Asher, who was himself leaving behind the comforts of California to show his solidarity with his new nation of Israel. Cohen would eventually head for the front to perform a concert for the Israeli soldiers. The troops begged him to sing "Suzanne" encore after encore. Cohen's appearance outside Ismailia, on the Egyptian side of the Suez Canal, has been preserved for posterity in the iconic photograph shot together with General Ariel Sharon. The mysterious gentleman's gravitation to the Holy Land, however, remains unrecorded. Asher vanishes —except in the annals of Cohen's memoir.

From Jerusalem, Asher addresses a letter to Leonard. The letter is oracular, but speaks in no uncertain terms. By some neat trick of ventriloquism, Asher becomes the voice of Cohen's conscience. In so many words, he imparts to Cohen this uncommon wisdom:

> *Now is the time to seize the opportunity and become the real Cohen you were always intended to be. Grab on to the cape of the Prophet Elijah thrown to you.*
>
> The Law requires that the High Priest be married. "'He shall atone for himself and for his house.' 'His house.' This is his wife."[5]

> *Having joined together physical and spiritual natures, the High Priest may then go on to serve in the rebuilt Temple of physical and spiritual Jerusalem.*

The letter resounds with a definite tone of celestial authority though at no point is it as brutal as the dictation of Joseph Caro's *maggid*.

Implicit in the letter is the rabbinic tradition whereby Elijah was a Cohen.[6] As much as Cohen may have reached for it, he was simply incapable of grasping the symbolic mantle of Elijah. It would continue to elude him. The singer decided to leave the Land of Israel.

Another Cohen, who earned the sobriquet "the High Priest of Rebirth," Rabbi Abraham Isaac HaCohen Kook (1865-1935), recorded *his* vision of Elijah heralding the Messianic Age:

> *Behold, I see with my eyes the light of Elijah's life rising. His power for his God is increasingly revealed. The holiness in nature breaks down fences. It proceeds to be united with the holiness that is above coarse nature; with the holiness that fights nature.*[7]

Rav Kook envisioned Elijah, "the Angel of the Covenant," the genius of holiness in the flesh, as holding the key to unlock the secrets of the flesh and of the divine seal inscribed in the Israelite body.[8] As Abraham Isaac HaCohen Kook was preparing to leave this world so fraught with contradictions, another Cohen was preparing to enter the fray of earthly existence and unravel—or perhaps complexify—its mysteries.

> *They said to him: "He is a hairy man, with a girdle of skin girded about his loins."*
> *And he said: "It is Elijah the Tishbite."*[9]
> *He lifted up the mantle of Elijah that had fallen from him.*[10]

The mantle of Elijah still waits to be lifted.
The loins have yet to be girded.

---

[1] *b. 'Avodah Zarah* 10b, 17a, 18a.
[2] *b. Yoma* 12b.
[3] Maimonides, *MT, Hil. Klei ha-Mikdash* 8:1.
[4] Ibid. 8:19.
[5] *m. Yoma* 1:1.
[6] *b. Bava Metsi'a* 114b.
[7] Rabbi Abraham Isaac HaKohen Kook, *Orot*, Lights of Renascence, chap. 30.
[8] *Orot*, Israel and Its Renascence, chap. 29.
[9] 2 Kings 1:8.
[10] 2 Kings 2:13.

The Religious-Zionist Manifesto of Rabbi Yehudah Leib Don Yahya

In 1901 there appeared in Vilna a 32-page booklet entitled, *Ha-Tsiyoniyut mi-nekudat hashkafat ha-dat* (*Zionism from the Viewpoint of Religion*). The author was Yehudah Don Yahya.[1] The final eight pages of the work contain a supplement (*Millu'im*) by one Ben-Zion Vilner, criticizing the anti-Zionism of the Rebbe of Lubavitch. (One ventures that "Ben-Zion Vilner" is a pseudonym.)

What is remarkable about this manifesto that argues that Zionism is totally compatible with traditional Judaism, is that the author, Rabbi Yehudah Leib Don Yahya, was an intimate student of Rabbi Hayyim Soloveitchik, a most outspoken opponent of the Zionist movement.[2]

To add to the intrigue, Don Yahya's grandfather, Rabbi Shabtai Don Yahya of Drissa, had been an ardent Hasid of Rabbi Menahem Mendel of Lubavitch (known by his work of Halakhic responsa as *"Tsemah Tsedek"*).[3] Yehudah himself would go on to serve as rabbi of the HaBaD Hasidic community of Shklov.[4] Although, as we shall see, within the HaBaD community, there were differing responses to Zionism along the fault line of the Kopyst—Lubavitch dispute.

Today, students who immerse themselves in the Torah novellae of Rabbi Hayyim Soloveitchik may come across the name of Rabbi Yehudah Leib Don Yahya, but they have no idea who this disciple was. Appended to *Hiddushei ha-GRaH he-Hadash 'al ha-Shas* (issued upon the ninetieth anniversary of Rabbi Hayyim's passing in 2008) are Don Yahya's memoirs of his beloved mentor in the Volozhin Yeshivah. In 2018 (coincidentally a century since Rabbi Hayyim's passing) there appeared in print a *Tagbuch* or diary, in which Rabbi Hayyim jotted down his insights on Talmud and Maimonides' code.[5] In his introduction to the volume, the editor, Rabbi Yitzhak Abba Lichtenstein, notes that Rabbi Hayyim would allow some scholars to copy down entries from the journal. Indeed, one such scholar was Rabbi Yehudah Leib Don Yahya. Two novellae that appear in the *Tagbuch* were previously published in Don Yahya's *Bikkurei Yehudah* (1939).[6]

One asks: What would prompt such a devoted disciple to break from his master's ideology concerning Zionism?

To understand how such a phenomenon as Yehudah Don Yahya was possible, one needs to trace his membership in Nes Ziyonah, the underground proto-Zionist movement that existed in the Volozhin Yeshivah from 1885 until its disbandment in 1890.

This was the era of Hovevei Zion (Lovers of Zion), a Russian Jewish movement to settle the Land of Israel that predated Herzlian political Zionism. Nes Ziyonah, which blossomed independently within the ranks of the student body of the famed Volozhin Yeshivah, interfaced with Hovevei Zion, presided over by Rabbi Samuel Mohilever of Bialystok. Members of Nes Ziyonah were sworn to secrecy. The membership included such illustrious scholars as Moshe Mordechai Epstein of Bakst,[7] Menahem Krakovsky,[8] and Isser Zalman Meltzer. Moshe Mordechai Epstein would eventually become Rosh Yeshivah of Slabodka. Menahem Krakowsky would one day assume the position of *"Shtodt Maggid"* of Vilna. Finally, Isser Zalman Meltzer would become Rosh Yeshivah of Slutzk and later 'Ets Hayyim of Jerusalem.[9] It was through the last-mentioned disciple, who was especially close to Rabbi Hayyim Soloveitchik, that Rabbi Hayyim was able to discover the identities of the students who belonged to Nes Ziyonah.[10]

Nes Ziyonah had sprung up without the knowledge of the elder dean of the Yeshivah, Rabbi Naftali Tsevi Yehudah Berlin (NeTsIV). In fact, according to Israel Kausner, who wrote a history of Nes Ziyonah, the members of the secret society prided themselves that they had been able to prevail upon Rabbi Berlin to join the greater Hovevei Zion movement and to assume a role of leadership alongside Rabbis Samuel Mohilever and Mordechai Eliasberg of Bausk.[11] In 1890, somehow Nes Ziyonah came to the attention of the Russian government authorities. One of its leaders (Yosef Rothstein) was arrested but subsequently released. When Rabbi Berlin learned that such a society had sprung up in the Yeshivah under his very nose, he was aghast. He feared that Nes Ziyonah might jeopardize the existence of the Yeshivah, which was under constant government scrutiny.[12] Leaving aside pragmatic considerations, in principle, Volozhin had always been a bastion of pure Torah learning; there was no room in it for Zionist activism.[13] Nes Ziyonah ceased to exist. (Hovevei Zion, with its office in Odessa, was legalized by the Tsarist government in 1890.)[14]

The idealistic young men who had formed Nes Ziyonah were not ones to easily give up. Nes Ziyonah morphed into Netsah Yisrael, whose express goal was to advocate on behalf of Zionism and religion. (Nes Ziyonah had restricted its activities to settling the Land of Israel.) Most prominent in this reincarnation of Netsah Yisrael was—Yehudah Leib Don Yahya.[15]

It is against this backdrop—the publicistic activity of Netsah Yisrael—that one must view Don Yahya's tract, *Zionism from the Viewpoint of Religion*.

Let us briefly sum up some of the more salient points of Don Yahya's booklet.

The author begins by clarifying that the return of the nation to its land can in no way be viewed as the *complete* redemption prophesied in Scripture. The prophets' vision, while including the ingathering of exiles, extends beyond that to global mankind's acknowledging God and embracing His Torah.[16]

On the other hand, Don Yahya is flummoxed by various rabbis who adopt an all-or-nothing attitude to the Zionist organization's striving to secure from the Ottomans a safe haven for Jews in the Holy Land. Just because the Zionist dream does not encompass the comprehensive vision of our prophets of old, is no reason to reject Zionism. Granted that the Zionist goals are much more modest in scope; that still does not justify opposing the movement. Don Yahya's own reading of the sources—Biblical and Rabbinic—is gradualist. He anticipates a phased redemption. The Jews' return to the Land is certainly the beginning, the first installment in a protracted process which will eventually—upon completion of "the full and encompassing redemption" (*"ha-ge'ulah ha-sheleimah ve-ha-kelalit"*)—culminate in the restoration of the Davidic dynasty in the person of King Messiah and the rebuilding of the Temple.[17]

The author adopts as his paradigm the Second Temple period. Taking issue with those who construe the return from Babylonian captivity as a "temporary remembrance" ("*pekidah li-zeman mugbal*"), Don Yahya maintains that the Second Commonwealth had the potential to develop into full-blown redemption. With that model in mind, he writes that return from exile and settling the Land can evolve beyond that to greater spiritual dimensions.[18]

After having made his case for the compatibility of the nascent Zionist movement and Judaism, Don Yahya tackles the painful question why some of the great Torah geniuses oppose Zionism.[19]

Don Yahya has a couple of explanations. First, knowledge of Torah is divided into *Halakhah* and *pilpul*, on the one hand, and matters of belief and opinion, on the other. Contemporary *ge'onim* (unlike their medieval predecessors Maimonides and Nahmanides) have devoted their lives to *Halakhah*, to the exclusion of *emunot ve-de'ot* (beliefs and opinions). "In regard to the portion of Torah which is beliefs and opinions, their view does not exceed the view of an average Jew."[20]

Rather conveniently, Don Yahya holds up as examples of recent Torah authorities who plumbed the depths of the beliefs contained in the *Aggadah*, and who concluded that the redemption shall begin with the Jews receiving permission to settle the Land of Israel—Rabbis Naftali Tsevi Yehudah Berlin and Mordechai Eliasberg—two rabbis who stood at the helm of Hovevei Zion.[21]

A second reason for the opposition of some *ge'onim* to Zionism is that they have been fed misinformation (or disinformation) by those of lesser stature who surround them. As the great men eschew reading newspapers, they must rely for information on extremists (*kana'im*) who skew their perception. They are told that the leaders of the Zionist movement are men who are not simply unobservant in their private lives, but furthermore, intent on uprooting Judaism.[22]

According to Don Yahya, the Zionist leaders profess no proficiency in matters of religion and are amenable to working with the great rabbis in matters pertaining to religion. He cites the example of a responsum from one of the great halakhic decisors of the generation to accommodate the Colonial Bank so that the prohibition of charging interest (*ribbit*) be not transgressed. Don Yahya personally witnessed both the question from Zionist officialdom and the responsum issued by the elderly *ga'on*.[23] (Undoubtedly, "the elderly *ga'on*" ["*ha-ga'on ha-yashish*"] was Don Yahya's own father-in-law, Rabbi Shelomo Hakohen, the *dayyan* or chief justice of Vilna.)[24]

Don Yahya points out the democratic character of the Zionist congresses. If more religious Jews would join the ranks of the Zionist movement, they would be able to turn the tide and steer the movement in a more religious direction.[25]

The author chides those religious elements opposed to Zionism not to gloat and say, "We told you so." In the event that Zionism deviates from Judaism, this will be a self-fulfilling prophecy of doom; the anti-Zionist agitators will then be held responsible for bringing about that outcome by instructing observant Jews to stay clear of the movement.[26]

II.

As stated above, the *Millu'im* or Excursus of the pamphlet is a harshly worded rejoinder to the Rebbe of Lubavitch, Rabbi Shalom Dov Baer Schneersohn (1860-1920), who had made public his vehement opposition to Zionism on religious grounds.[27]

Again, one asks: How is possible that a staunch HaBaD Hasid such as Rabbi Yehudah Leib Don Yahya appended such an excursus to his work? From a remove of more than a century this seems inconceivable.

We need once more to place this pamphlet within the context of the times. Today, HaBaD has assumed a monolithic character, but at the turn of the twentieth century there existed a great divide between two competing "courts" within HaBaD Hasidism: Kopyst and Lubavitch.[28] When Rabbi Menahem Mendel Schneersohn of Lubavitch (author of the responsa *Tsemah Tsedek*) passed in 1866, a dispute erupted over succession to the throne. The youngest son, Shmuel (MaHaRaSh), remained in Lubavitch and inherited control of that city. An older son, Yehudah Leib (MaHaRIL), moved to the city of Kopyst, taking some of the Hasidim with him.[29] When within a year of the *Tsemah Tsedek*'s passing, Yehudah Leib passed, his son Shelomo Zalman (author of the Hasidic work *Magen Avot*) became the Kopyster Rebbe. And when in 1900 the Kopyster Rebbe passed, he was succeeded by his younger brother Rabbi Shemaryah Noah Schneerson (author of the Hasidic work *Shemen la-Ma'or*). Though there was a brief attempt on the part of Rabbi Shemaryah Noah Schneerson to establish himself in the city of Kopyst, eventually he returned to his rabbinate in Bobruisk, which then became the center of this branch of HaBaD Hasidism.[30] With the passing of the Rebbe of Bobruisk in 1923, this branch ceased to exist, leaving only the Lubavitch faction. At that point, remnants of the Bobruisker Hasidim transferred their allegiance to the Lubavitcher Rebbe.

In the early years of the twentieth century there erupted a major financial dispute between Bobruisk and Lubavitch regarding control of the purse strings of Kollel HaBaD in Erets Yisrael. (One may find evidence of the dispute in letters of Rav Kook from this period, when as Rabbi of Jaffa, he offered guidance how to come to a compromise.)[31] The tension arose because each Rebbe wanted his representative in Erets Yisrael to be responsible for disbursement of the funds raised by the Hasidim in Russia for the support of their brethren in the Holy Land.

Thus, there are historians who would explain the tension between Bobruisk and Lubavitch as being purely financial.[32] Truth be known, there were ideological issues dividing the two cousins, Rabbi Shemariah Noah of Bobruisk and Rabbi Shalom Dov Baer of Lubavitch. In general, it may be said that the Bobruisker was more progressive, more forward-looking. The Lubavitcher was more old-school, more conservative in outlook. These different *Weltanschauungen* found expression on many fronts.

When the Russian government sought to demand of the rabbis proficiency in the Russian language, the Bobruisker (as Rabbi Meir Simhah Cohen of Dvinsk) found this a reasonable demand; the Lubavitcher (as Rabbi Hayyim Soloveitchik of Brisk and Rabbi

Israel Meir Kagan [a.k.a. *Hafets Hayyim*]) fought against this proposal tooth and nail.³³

When it came to deciding which city should serve as the center of HaBaD Hasidism in Erets Yisrael—Hebron or Jerusalem—Rabbi Shalom Dov Baer militated to retain the center in the provincial town of Hebron rather than allow the center to shift to Jerusalem.³⁴ In this way, the Lubavitcher Rebbe believed he could shield the Hasidim from the distractions of urban civilization. The Bobruisker did not think it realistic to keep the Hasidim "down on the farm." Willy-nilly, establishment of a *"bibliotek"* in Hebron would bring secular literature to the curious eyes of Hasidic youth.³⁵

And finally, we arrive at the issue with which we began: Zionism. While Lubavitch would have no truck with Zionism, out of the *"Kibbutz"* (study-hall for advanced rabbinic students) of Bobruisk there would emerge prominent rabbis of the Mizrahi or Religious Zionist movement.³⁶

The answer to the question how Rabbi Yehudah Leib Don Yahya, a fervent HaBaD Hasid, could oppose the Rebbe of Lubavitch is simple: Don Yahya was a Kopyster Hasid,³⁷ not a Lubavitcher Hasid.

---

¹ Yehudah Leib Don Yahya was born in Drissa (today Verkhnyadzvinsk, Belarus) in 1869 and passed in Tel-Aviv in 1941. Besides this Zionist manifesto, Rabbi Don Yahya published two volumes of *Halakhah* and essays and sermons: *Bikkurei Yehudah*, vol. 1 (Lutzin, 1930); vol. 2 (Tel-Aviv, 1939).

Volume One of *Bikkurei Yehudah* was published in Lutzin (Ludza) by the author's cousin, Rabbi Benzion Don Yahya, Rabbi of Lutzin. At that time,

Rabbi Yehudah Leib served as Rabbi of Chernigov, Soviet Russia. In his preface to the work, Benzion Don Yahya explains that the manuscript was sent to him for publication because there is no longer a Hebrew press in Russia. On pages 36-38, the editor traces the lineage of the Don Yahya family. We learn that his paternal grandfather was Rabbi Shabtai Don Yahya, Rabbi of Drissa for sixty years until his death at approximately age 90 in 1907. One of Rabbi Shabtai's sons, Rabbi Eliezer, became Rabbi of Lutzin (Ludza), a rabbinate inherited by his son, the editor (Rabbi Benzion). In 1840, there were born to Rabbi Shabtai twins: Menahem Mendel and Hayyim. Menahem Mendel served as Rabbi of Kopyst for some years, passing there in 1920. Hayyim served as Rabbi of Shklov, and after his father Shabtai's passing, as Rabbi of Drissa, until his own passing in 1913. Hayyim's son, Yehuda Leib, served as Rabbi in Shklov and Vietka, until he inherited from his father the Rabbinate of Drissa in 1913. (In *Bikkurei Yehudah*, vol. 2, f. 159, there is a letter dated 5673 [i.e., 1913] from Rabbi Meir Simhah of Dvinsk to Rabbi Don Yahya congratulating him on assuming the rabbinate of his father and grandfather in Drissa.) In 1925, Yehudah Leib was accepted as Rabbi of Chernigov.

In Shklov, Rabbi Yehudah Leib Don Yahya ministered to the *"Kehal Hasidim"* (exclusive of the Mitnagdim, who would have had their own *Rav*). (See below note 4.) However, it should be mentioned that the communities of Vietka and Chernigov as well figure prominently in the annals of HaBaD Hasidism.

The Rabbi of Vietka, Rabbi Dov Baer Lifshitz, author of an important commentary on Tractate *Mikva'ot*, *Golot 'Iliyot* (Warsaw, 1887), refers to Rabbi Shneur Zalman of Liadi as *"dodi zekeini"* ("my great uncle"). See ibid., Addendum to Introduction, and 7c. Rabbi Lifshitz's mentor and predecessor in the rabbinate of Vietka was Rabbi Nathan Gur-Aryeh, a premier disciple of Rabbi Shneur Zalman.

The man who immediately preceded Rabbi Don Yahya as Rabbi of Chernigov, Rabbi David Tsevi (Hirsch) Hen (referred to by the Hasidim as "RaDaTs") was acknowledged as one of the greatest of HaBaD Halakhists in his day. In 1925, through the intervention of Chief Rabbi Kook, he was able to emigrate from the Soviet Union to Erets Yisrael together with his daughter Rahel, son-in-law Rabbi Shalom Shelomo Schneerson (brother of Rabbi Levi Isaac Schneerson, Rabbi of Yekaterinaslav, today Dnieperpetrovsk, and uncle of Rabbi Menahem Mendel Schneerson, Lubavitcher Rebbe of Brooklyn), and granddaughter Zelda, who would later achieve fame as a Hebrew poet. See *Iggerot ha-RAYaH*, vol. 4 (Jerusalem, 1984), Letter 1330 (p. 251), in which Rav Kook attempts to install the recently arrived Rabbi S.S. Schneerson as Rav of Haderah. Rav Kook's involvement in bringing RaDaTs and family to Erets Israel is discussed in the recently published annals of the Hen Family, *Avnei Hen*, ed. Eliezer Laine and S.Z. Berger (Brooklyn, NY: Kehot, 2015).

Reviewing the second volume of *Bikkurei Yehudah*, Rabbi Zevin wrote an especially insightful appreciation of Rabbi Yehudah Leib Don Yahya. Rabbi Zevin, himself a HaBaD Hasid, noted how rare it was to find in the twentieth century a HaBaD Hasid who combined both persona of the *maskil* (intellectual) and the *'oved* (master of contemplative prayer). (In the latter connection, Rabbi Zevin observed that Rabbi Don Yahya wore daily three pairs of *tefillin*: Rashi, Rabbenu Tam, and *Shimusha Rabbah*.) Beyond HaBaD Hasidism, Don

Yahya mastered Rabbi Hayyim Soloveitchik's method of Talmudic analysis and the process of *pesikah* (halakhic decision) of Don Yahya's father-in-law, Rabbi Shleimeleh Hakohen, the Dayyan of Vilna. See Rabbi Shelomo Yosef Zevin, *Soferim u-Sefarim* (Tel-Aviv: Abraham Ziyoni, 1959), pp. 296-300.

It is noteworthy that the volume contains a responsum to Rabbi Mordechai Shmuel Kroll, the Rav of Kefar Hasidim in Erets Yisrael, and halakhic novellae of Rabbi Kroll. See *Bikkurei Yehudah*, vol. 2, ff. 121-129, 160-162. Rabbi Kroll was the eminent disciple of Rabbi Don Yahya.

[2] Rabbi Hayyim Soloveitchik's opposition to Zionism is well known. One particular statement should illustrate how extreme was Rabbi Hayyim's opposition to the new movement. The following incident took place in Minsk in 1915 (when many Jews were forced to flee their homes before the German invasion and seek refuge in the large city located farther east).

> Young Raphael Zalman Levine was walking down the street with his father, Rabbi Abraham Dov Baer Levine (known as the *"Mal'akh,"* the "Angel"). Pinned to the adolescent's lapel was an insignia of the *Keren Kayemet le-Yisrael* (Jewish National Fund), to which he had recently donated. The elder Levine was adamantly opposed to the Zionist enterprise and demanded that his son remove the pin, which he found offensive. Father and son were in the midst of an intense argument when, lo and behold, they saw approaching them from the opposite direction none other than the great Rabbi Hayyim Soloveitchik.
> Rabbi Levine said to Rabbi Soloveitchik: "My son wants to ask you a *she'elah* (question)."
> Rabbi Soloveitchik turned to Raphael Zalman: "You can ask your father." (Rabbi Levine and Rabbi Soloveitchik were friends.)
> Rabbi Levine persisted: "My son wants to ask you a *she'elah* in *emunah* (a matter of faith)."
> *"Emunah?"* Rabbi Soloveitchik's face now assumed a serious expression. Young Raphael Zalman was put on the spot and forced to ask Rabbi Hayyim what he thought of his donation to the Jewish National Fund. It just so happened that across the street was a church.
> Rabbi Hayyim responded to his young questioner: "If you have a few spare kopecks in your pocket, you can place them there rather than in the *pushke* of the *Keren Kayemes."*
> (Reported by Rabbi Yochanan Lefkowitz and by Prof. Richard Sugarman, who heard this anecdote on two separate occasions from the mouth of Rabbi Raphael Zalman Levine of Albany, NY)

The episode is also reported in Rabbi Raphael Zalman Levine's name in Rabbi C.S. Glickman, *Mi-Pihem u-mi-Pi Ketavam* (Brooklyn, NY, 2008), pp. 119-120.

Though the sharpness of Rabbi Hayyim Soloveitchik's statement is shocking, halakhic opposition to donating to the Zionist cause was shared by several East European rabbinic leaders. A decade later in 1925, four distinguished leaders of Polish Jewry, the Hasidic Rebbes of Gur, Ostrovtsa, Radzyn, and Novominsk, addressed a letter to Rav Kook adjuring him to curtail his support of *Keren Kayemet le-Yisrael* and *Keren ha-Yesod*. See *Iggerot la-RAYaH*, ed. B.Z. Shapira (Jerusalem, 1990), Letter 199 (pp. 303-304); facsimile on p. 590.

Rav Kook, unlike the Polish Rebbes, differentiated between the two funds, lending his support to *Keren Kayemet le-Yisrael*, which directed funds to the physical reclamation of the land, but not to *Keren ha-Yesod*, which funded secular (and perhaps anti-religious) culture. See Rabbi Tsevi Yehudah Hakohen Kook, *Li-Sheloshah be-Ellul*, vol. 1 (1938), par. 44 (p. 22); *Iggerot ha-RAYaH*, vol. 5: 5682, ed. Ze'ev Neuman (Jerusalem, 2019), pp. 407-413.

3 According to his namesake and great-grandson, journalist Shabtai Don Yahya (who wrote under the pen name of "Sh. Daniel"), the Rabbi of Drissa was known in Lubavitch as "Reb Shebsel Drisser." Sh. Don Yahya wrote that it was said that the Rabbi of Drissa might have become one of the great men of the generation in terms of Talmudic learning, but his Hasidic exuberance stunted his academic growth. See Shabtai Don Yahya, *Rabbi Eliezer Don Yahya* (Jerusalem, 1932), pp. 10-11.

(The title-page makes the point that the book bears the encomium of Chief Rabbi Kook. Shabtai Don Yahya was one of the first students of Merkaz Harav and a devoted disciple of Rav Kook. *Rabbi Eliezer Don Yahya* is a biography of the author's paternal grandfather, the Rabbi of Lutzin, son of Rabbi Shabtai Don Yahya. As a youth, Avraham Yitzhak Hakohen Kook studied under Rabbi Eliezer Don Yahya in Lutzin. Rabbi Eliezer Don Yahya was born 4 Tammuz 5598 [i.e., 1838] and passed on his birthday, 4 Tammuz 5686 [i.e., 1926]. A photograph of the funeral of Rabbi Eliezer Don Yahya in Lutzin in 1926 may be found in Rabbi Yitzhak Zilber's autobiography, *To Remain a Jew*. Zilber's original surname was "Ziyoni." Rabbi Eliezer Don Yahya inherited the rabbinate of Lutzin from his illustrious father-in-law Rabbi Aharon Zelig Ziyoni.)

Rabbi Yehudah Leib Don Yahya often quotes the *Tsemah Tsedek* in his halakhic responsa.

4 In the biography of Rabbi Yehudah Leib Don Yahya in Shmuel Noah Gottlieb's *Ohalei Shem* (Pinsk, 1912), p. 207, s.v. *Shklov*, it states that Don Yahya assumed the rabbinate of Shklov in 1906. However, as early as Friday, 17 Menahem Av [5]664," i.e., 1904, Rabbi Shelomo Hakohen addressed his son-in-law as *"Rav Av-Beit-Din* of the congregation of Hasidim of Shklov." See *Bikkurei Yehudah*, vol. 2 (Tel-Aviv, 1939), 145a.

In *Shklover Yidden* (1929) and *Feter Zhoma* (1930), the Yiddish and Hebrew poet and writer Zalman Shneur portrayed the Hasidim of his birthplace, Shklov.

Earlier, Rabbi Yehudah Leib's father, Rabbi Hayyim Don Yahya, had served as Rabbi of Shklov. A halakhic responsum of Rabbi Hayyim Don Yahya (datelined "5653 [i.e., 1893], Shklov") was published in the journal of the Skvere Kollel, *Zera' Ya'akov* 26 (Shevat 5766 [i.e., 2006]), pp. 17-21. On p. 20, Rabbi Hayyim mentions the learned opinion of his (twin) brother from Kopyst [i.e., Rabbi Menahem Mendel Don Yahya].

5 Rabbi Yitzhak Lichtenstein writes in the introduction to the volume that there were many such *Tagbikher* that were lost to posterity. This particular journal was inherited by Rabbi Hayyim's son, Rabbi Moshe Soloveichik. (Behind the scenes, the *Tagbuch* was made available to Rabbi Lichtenstein by his maternal uncle, Prof. Haym Soloveitchik of Riverdale, son of Rabbi J.B. Soloveitchik of Boston, son of Rabbi Moshe Soloveichik.)

6 See *Bikkurei Yehudah*, vol. 2 (Tel-Aviv, 1939), 142a-144b. The volume was edited by the author's son-in-law Rabbi Yitzhak Neiman. Rabbi Zevin explains

that though the volume was submitted for publication in 1939, it was not issued until 1941, a few weeks before the author's passing. See S.Y. Zevin, *Soferim u-Sefarim* (Tel-Aviv: Abraham Ziyoni, 1959), p. 297. The two novellae of Rabbi Hayyim Soloveitchik (to *Bava Kamma* 13a and *Ketubot* 21a) were reprinted in the memorial volume for Rabbi Neiman, *Zikhron Yitzhak* (Jerusalem, 1999), along with several novellae of his father-in-law, Rabbi Don Yahya.

[7] See Israel Klausner, *Toledot "Nes Ziyonah" be-Volozhin* (Jerusalem: Mossad Harav Kook, 1954), pp. 25, 65, 113. A young Moshe Mordechai Epstein appears in a group photo on p. 26.

[8] Ibid. p. 24.

[9] Rabbis Epstein and Meltzer would eventually become brothers-in-law by their marriage to two sisters, daughters of the Maecenas, Shraga Feivel Frank of Kovno.

[10] Heard from Rabbi Yosef Soloveichik of Jerusalem (son of Rabbi Ahron Soloveichik of Chicago), a great-grandson of Rabbi Hayyim Soloveitchik. Rabbi Yosef Soloveichik explained the exact halakhic reasoning whereby his ancestor was able to release young Isser Zalman Meltzer from his solemn oath.

Despite Rabbi Hayyim's disapproval of Nes Ziyonah, he rejoiced at the release of the ringleader Rothstein subsequent to the latter's arrest by the Russian police:

> Also the Gaon Rabbi Hayyim of Brisk, of blessed memory, greatly rejoiced over me. He received me with joy and brought me before the NeTsIV, of blessed memory, who was pleased by my return, though he did say to me that this is not the place [for activism]. "A *mitsvah* that can be performed by others, we do not cancel for it the study of Torah" [*MT, Hil. Talmud Torah* 3:4]....Evidently, the NeTsIV too was content but had to act as if he disapproved....
>
> (Yosef Rothstein, in Israel Klausner, *Toledot "Nes Ziyonah" be-Volozhin*, p. 123)

See earlier on p. 13, NeTsIV's opposition to students taking time out from their Torah study for activism—even on behalf of a cause as dear to NeTsIV's heart as *Yishuv Erets Yisrael*.

[11] Ibid. p. 14.

[12] Ibid. p. 19.

[13] See above note 10.

[14] Klausner, *Toledot "Nes Ziyonah" be-Volozhin*, p. 21.

[15] Ibid. pp. 22-24. The members of Netsah Yisrael were also sworn to secrecy. Netsah Yisrael lasted until the closing of the Volozhin Yeshivah by the Russian authorities in 1892.

[16] *Ha-Tsiyoniyut mi-nekudat hashkafat ha-dat*, pp. 5-6.

[17] Ibid. pp. 6-7.

[18] Ibid. pp. 7-10.

[19] Ibid. p. 15.

[20] Ibid.

[21] Ibid. p. 16.

[22] Ibid.

[23] Ibid. pp. 16-17. Don Yahya does not go into Halakhic details. The way to circumvent the problem of *ribbit* (interest) is by drafting a *"heter 'iska."*

Rabbi Tsevi Yehudah Hakohen Kook relates that when the Zionist Colonial Bank was founded, his father, Rabbi Avraham Yitzhak Hakohen Kook, entered into negotiations with the Zionist officials and rabbis, which resulted in a *"shtar heter 'iska."* See Rabbi Tsevi Yehudah Hakohen Kook, *Li-Sheloshah be-Ellul*, vol. 1 (1938), par. 17 (pp. 11-12).

[24] The elderly *Dayyan* of Vilna, Rabbi Shelomo Hakohen (author of *Heshek Shelomo*) was exceptionally respectful of Theodor Herzl when the latter visited Vilna, extending to him the priestly benediction at a reception in Herzl's honor. See Israel Cohen, *History of Jews in Vilna* (Philadelphia: Jewish Publication Society of America, 1943), p. 350; and Israel Klausner, *Vilna: "Jerusalem of Vilna," 1881-1939*, vol. 2 (Hebrew) (Israel: Ghetto Fighters' House, 1983), p. 339.

Another son-in-law of Rabbi Shelomo Hakohen, Rabbi Nahum Greenhaus of Trok (Lithuanian, Trakai), a suburb of Vilna, was, like Don Yahya, an outspoken advocate of Zionism. Because of their support of the movement, both Rabbi Shelomo Hakohen and Rabbi Nahum Greenhaus suffered persecution by anti-Zionist elements in Lithuanian Jewry. See Klausner, ibid. pp. 330-333.

Rabbi Nahum Greenhaus' namesake was Rabbi Nahum Partzovitz (known in his youth as "Nahum Troker"), who would one day become the illustrious Rosh Yeshivah of the Mirrer Yeshiva in Jerusalem. Rabbi Nahum Partzovitz's father, Rabbi Aryeh Tsevi Partzovitz, inherited the rabbinate of Trok from his father-in-law, Rabbi Nahum Greenhaus.

A third son-in-law of Rabbi Shelomo Hakohen of Vilna was Rabbi Meir Karelitz, the older brother of Rabbi Abraham Isaiah Karelitz (author of *Hazon Ish*). Rabbi Meir Karelitz was prominent in Agudah circles, both in Vilna and later in Erets Yisrael.

[25] *Ha-Tsiyoniyut mi-nekudat hashkafat ha-dat*, p. 17.

[26] Ibid.

This modern disagreement sounds vaguely reminiscent of the disagreement between Resh Lakish and Rabbi Yohanan in *Talmud Bavli, Yoma* 9b-10a. Resh Lakish said of Babylonian Jewry: "God hates you. If you had gone up to the Land of Israel *en masse* in the days of Ezra, the divine presence would have rested in the Second Temple and there would have been a resumption of full-blown prophecy. Now that you have gone up in pitifully small numbers (*dalei dalot*), but a remnant of prophecy remains, the *bat kol* (heavenly voice)." Rabbi Yohanan responded: "Even if all of Babylonian Jewry would have gone up to the Land in the days of Ezra, the divine presence would not have rested in the Second Temple, for it is written: 'God will broaden Japheth and dwell in the tents of Shem' [Genesis 9:27]. Though God will broaden Japheth, the divine presence rests only in the tents of Shem." Rashi explains that the divine presence was prevented from resting in the Second Temple because it was built by the Persians; the divine presence rested only in the First Temple which was built by Solomon of the seed of Shem.

(Interestingly enough, the great halakhist Rabbi Moses Schreiber extends Rabbi Yohanan's thinking by attributing the fragmentation of Torah and the proliferation of controversy between the House of Shammai and the House of Hillel — to Herod's construction of the Temple. See *Torat Moshe*, ed. Shim'on Sofer [Pressburg, 1906], *Vayyikra*, s.v. *Asham hu ashom asham la-*

Hashem [Lev. 5:19], 6c.)

Evidently, Rabbi Don Yahya (like Resh Lakish) was convinced that what was crucial to effecting a spiritual revolution in Erets Yisrael was a critical mass. His opponents (like Rabbi Yohanan) could not be swayed that it was merely a matter of numbers. To their thinking, non-Jewish influence at the very inception of the Zionist movement would preclude it from bringing about the hoped for spiritual renascence so woefully lacking in the Jewish collective.

[27] See '*Or la-Yesharim* (Warsaw, 1900), pp. 57-61. For other (later) recordings of Rabbi Shalom Baer Schneersohn's anti-Zionist stance, see Bezalel Naor, *When God Becomes History: Historical Essays of Rabbi Abraham Isaac Hakohen Kook* (New York, NY: Kodesh Press, 2016), p. 168, n. 10.

[28] Actually, there was another "court" contending for the legacy of HaBaD, that of Liadi. The Rebbe of Liadi, Rabbi Hayyim Shneur Zalman Schneerson, was a third son of the *Tsemah Tsedek*. After Rabbi Hayyim Shneur Zalman's passing, his son, Rabbi Yitzhak Dov Baer Schneerson (author of the commentary to the *Siddur*, *Peirush MaHaRID*), succeeded him as Rebbe of Liadi.

For the sake of simplification, I have restricted my remarks to the competition between Kopyst and Lubavitch.

[29] In his autobiography, Chaim Tchernowitz (*"Rav Tsa'ir"*) revealed some of the intrigue in the aftermath of the *Tsemah Tsedek*'s passing that led to the Kopyst-Lubavitch schism. See Ch. Tchernowitz, *Pirkei Hayyim* (New York, 1954), pp. 104-106.

[30] See Hayyim Meir Heilman, *Beit Rabbi* (Berdichev, 1902), vol. 3, chap. 9.

[31] See *Iggerot ha-RAYaH*, vol. 1 (1962), Letter 39, to Rav Kook's maternal uncle, Rabbi Yehudah Leib Felman of Riga, a Kopyster Hasid (pp. 34-36). The letter is datelined, "Jaffa, 3 Marheshvan, [5]667," i.e., 1906. At that time, the financial dispute was between the three competing "courts" of Bobruisk, Liadi, and Lubavitch. See ibid. p. 36.

In 1920, Rav Kook once again acted as an arbiter in the financial dispute between the *kollelim* of Bobruisk and Lubavitch. See *Iggerot ha-RAYaH*, vol. 4, ed. Rabbi Ya'akov Filber (Jerusalem: Makhon RZYH, 1984), Letter 1080 (p. 90). See also Letter 1165 (p. 154) of 22 Shevat, 5683 [i.e., 1923], addressed to HaBaD Hasidim in America, upholding the sterling reputation of Kollel Bobruisk, which had been maliciously besmirched. The administrator of Kollel Bobruisk was Rabbi Hayyim Eliezer Hakohen Bichovsky. See Rav Kook's letter to him in *Iggerot ha-RAYaH*, vol. 1, ed. Rabbi Tsevi Yehudah Kook (Jerusalem: Mossad Harav Kook, 1962), pp. 160-161 (Letter 132). (Eliezer has been misspelled "El'azar.")

[32] Roughly thirty years ago, I heard this monetary explanation from Rabbi Chaim Liberman, who had served as personal secretary and librarian of Rabbi Joseph Isaac Schneersohn of Lubavitch.

Interestingly enough, in the 1880s there emerged a theological dispute between the Rebbes of Kopyst and Lubavitch. The way it came about was in the following manner. After the passing of Rabbi Samuel (MaHaRaSh) of Lubavitch in 1882, his sons published an edition of their ancestor Rabbi Shneur Zalman of Liadi's *Torah 'Or* on the first three *parshiyot* or pericopes of the Torah (*Bereshit, Noah, Lekh Lekha*). Entitled *Likkutei Torah*, it was brought out in Vilna in 1884. The publishers took the liberty of incorporating into the text comments of the recently deceased Rabbi Samuel Schneersohn. The Kopyster Rebbe, Rabbi Shelomo Zalman Schneerson (author of *Magen Avot*), was outraged and penned a public letter of protest.

One comment of his uncle Rabbi Samuel (to *Parashat Noah*) in particular provoked the Kopyster Rebbe, this touching on the proper way to understand Rabbi Isaac Luria's metaphor of *Tsimtsum*. In three letters to Rabbi Dan Tumarkin of Rogatchov (a Lubavitcher Hasid), the Kopyster Rebbe clarified his position on *Tsimtsum* and how it differed from that of Rabbi Samuel Schneersohn. The correspondence is briefly alluded to in H.M. Heilman, *Beit Rabbi*, vol. 3, chap. 10, s.v. *Rabbi Dan Tumarkin*. The entire exchange is available in Rabbi Mordechai Menashe Laufer, *Ha-Melekh bi-Mesibo*, vol. 2 [Kefar Habad, 1993], pp. 283-293. (This truly fascinating correspondence was brought to my attention a generation ago by Baruch Thaler.)

Regarding the publication of *Likkutei Torah* (Vilna, 1884), see further Hayyim Meir Heilman, *Beit Rabbi*, vol. 1, 87a; vol. 3, 16a, 28a; Rabbi Yehoshua Mondshine, "'*Likkutei Torah*' le-Shalosh Parshiyot," *Kefar Habad*, nos. 931, 933. Available online at:
http://www.shturem.net/index.php?section=blog_new&article_id=29

[33] This issue was raised at the rabbinical conference held in St. Petersburg in 1910. The decisions reached by the delegates were relayed to Stolypin, Minister of the Interior. Some of the heated exchange between the Bobruisker and the Lubavitcher behind closed doors has been preserved in the memoirs of Isaac Schneersohn, one of the delegates to the conference; see I. Schneersohn, *Leben un Kamf fun Yiden in Tsarishen Rusland 1905-1917* (Paris, 1968). The chapters concerning the 1910 conference were translated from Yiddish into Hebrew by Rabbi Yehoshua Mondshine, "*Asifat ha-Rabbanim be-Rusya bi-Shenat 'Atar,*" *Kefar Habad*, no. 898. Available online at: http://www.shturem.net/index.php?section=blog_new&article_id=24

According to Isaac Schneersohn, it was none other than he (Crown Rabbi of Chernigov) who proposed abolishing the position of *Kazyonny Ravin* (in Hebrew, "*Rav mi-Ta'am,*" or Crown Rabbi), thus wresting authority from the secular-trained, modern "*Rabbiner*" and consolidating communal power in the hands of the Talmudically-trained traditional *Rav*—provided he be proficient in the Russian language.

[34] Historically, the HaBaD community in Hebron preceded that of Jerusalem. In 1823, Rabbi Dov Baer Shneuri of Lubavitch (*"Mitteler Rebbe"*), the second-generation leader of the HaBaD movement, founded a HaBaD community in Hebron. Later, in 1847, a group of HaBaD families from Hebron relocated to Jerusalem.

[35] See *Kuntres me-Admo"r shelit"a mi-Bobruisk: Teshuvot nitshiyot va-amitiyot 'al Kuntres Admo"r shelit"a de-Libavitz* (1907), pp. 18-19. I described the contents of the booklet in Kestenbaum Catalogue, Auction Sale 38 (Thursday, November 29th, 2007), Lot 85, p. 28. Available at:
https://www.kestenbaum.net/media/catalog/product/pdfs/Auction_38.pdf

[36] Two names come to mind: Rabbi Nissan Telushkin in the United States and Rabbi Shelomo Yosef Zevin in Erets Yisrael. Both studied in the *"Kibbutz"* of the Bobruisker Rebbe and received ordination from him. Eventually, with the extinction of Bobruisker Hasidism, both Telushkin and Zevin would transfer their allegiance to Lubavitch. However, their affiliation with the Religious

Zionist movement could at times place them in an unenviable position. Particularly Rabbi Zevin oftentimes found himself between a rock and a hard place. Rabbi Menachem Mendel Schneerson, the Lubavitcher Rebbe residing in Brooklyn, would on occasion expect of Rabbi Zevin to promote positions at variance with his Mizrahi colleagues in Erets Yisrael (such as Chief Rabbi Isaac Halevi Herzog). See Marc B. Shapiro, *Changing the Immutable: How Orthodox Judaism Rewrites Its History* (Oxford: Littman, 2015), pp. 235; 238, n. 87.

A brief autobiographical sketch of Rabbi Telushkin (a native of Bobruisk) is found at the conclusion of his halakhic work on *mikva'ot* (ritual baths), *Tahorat Mayim* (Brooklyn, NY: Kehot, 1990), pp. 355-356 *("Le-Zikaron")*.

37 In Rabbi Don Yahya's letter to Rabbi Shelomo Yosef Zevin concerning the counterintuitive thought process that informed Rabbi Hayyim Soloveitchik's halakhic decisions, Rabbi Don Yahya refers to himself as a "Hasid [of] Kopyst." The context is Rabbi Hayyim's desire to procure a *"Yanover esrog"* (citron from Genoa, Italy) to fulfill the commandment, in compliance with the tradition of HaBaD, and earlier the *HaTaM Sofer*, *Orah Hayyim*, no. 207. See *Hiddushei ha-GRaH he-Hadash 'al ha-Shas* (B'nei Berak: Mishor, 2008), p. 586.

However, in *Zikhron Yitzhak* (Memorial Volume for Rabbi Yitzhak Neiman) (Jerusalem, 1999), p. 141 (which is the source of *Hiddushei ha-GRaH*), Rabbi Don Yahya refers to himself as a "Hasid (HaBaD)." It would be interesting to see the original of the letter, which may yet be in the hands of the heirs of Rabbi Zevin. From the fact that the word "HaBaD" is placed in parentheses, one is inclined to assume that this is an addition on the part of an editor (Rabbi Zevin?). According to the Introduction *("Petah Davar")* to *Zikhron Yitzhak*, this is the first publication of the letter from Rabbi Don Yahya to Rabbi Zevin.

(Inter alia, elsewhere Rabbi Zevin quoted Rabbi Don Yahya concerning Rabbi Hayyim Soloveitchik's leniency in regard to fasting on Yom Kippur, which Rabbi Zevin followed up with a more comprehensive explanation by Rabbi Isaac Ze'ev Soloveitchik, the son of Rabbi Hayyim. See Rabbi Shelomo Yosef Zevin, *Ha-Mo'adim ba-Halakhah* [Tel-Aviv: A. Zioni, n.d.], *"Yom ha-Kippurim,"* p. 82.)

Klausner, *Toledot "Nes Ziyonah" be-Volozhin*, p. 17, records that in 1889, the members of Nes Ziyonah were able to elicit letters of support for the conception of *Yishuv Erets Yisrael* from the Hasidic Rebbes of Kopyst and Bohush (a branch of Ruzhin).

*

Postscript: By the time Rabbi Joseph Isaac Schneersohn of Lubavitch relocated to Riga, Latvia, old animosities between the remnants of Kopyster hasidim and the rival Lubavitch court were set aside. See Rabbi Eliyahu Hayyim Althaus' letter describing *Shemini 'Atseret* 1929 in Riga, when "even the critics, the *Kamats Kufin*" were overwhelmed. Facsimile in Rabbi Chaim Rapoport, *The Afterlife of Scholarship: A Critical Review of 'The Rebbe' by Samuel Heilman and Menachem Friedman* (2011), p. 208. "*Komats Kuf*" was Lubavitch code for "Kopyst."

See also Rabbi Shaul Shimon Deutsch, *Larger than Life* (New York, NY, 1997), p. 45 concerning Rabbi Ben-Zion Don-Yahya. In the document on p. 35 the Rabbi of Lutzin's name appears as "Ben-Zion Donhin."

Of Priests and Prophets:
The Way of Knowing
and the Way of Not-Knowing

Shnayor Z. Burton. *Mishnat Ya'akov: Derushim Nivharim be-Mo'adei ha-Shanah* (5779/2019)

Rabbi Shnayor Burton is a distinguished Talmudic scholar who resides in the Flatbush section of Brooklyn. This is his second work of Jewish Thought.

In 2017 he published *Orot Ya'akov: Derushim Nivharim be-Ma'asei Avot*. That volume focuses on the lives of the patriarchs of our nation, Abraham, Isaac and Jacob, whose sagas are recorded in the Book of Genesis.

The present sequel volume contains *derushim* (homilies) on the cycle of the year, the Sabbath and festivals.

In the introduction to the work, the author calls our attention to the first *derush*, "Torat Moshe ve-Derekh ha-Nevi'im" ("The Torah of Moses and the Way of the Prophets"). It is to this seminal thought that I shall devote my remarks.

The three outstanding Jewish theologians of twentieth-century America—Abraham Joshua Heschel, Isaac Hutner and Joseph Baer Soloveitchik (in alphabetical order of their last names)—in one context or another, all dwelled on the phenomenon of the prophets of Israel.

In the case of Rabbi Soloveitchik, it was the spartan yet incisive observation that the entire project of the prophets consists of a divulgence of the divine attributes, to the end of *imatatio dei*. Rabbi Soloveitchik's remarks are predicated on Maimonides, *Hil. De'ot* 1:6: "Thus too, the prophets described God by all the various attributes, 'long-suffering' and 'abounding in kindness,' 'righteous' and 'upright,' 'perfect,' 'mighty' and 'powerful,' and so forth, to teach us that these qualities are good and right, and that a human being should cultivate them, and imitate [God], as much as one can."[1]

Rabbi Hutner's perception of the prophets took the form of an intriguing exploration of their silence when confronted with the problem of theodicy. For the *Pahad Yitzhak* (as for Rashi earlier), the essence of the prophet is speech (*navi* from *niv*)[2] and the ability to describe the divine attributes. With the destruction of the Temple there occurred a cosmic breakdown and a muting of the prophetic voice.[3]

Finally, as a young man, Abraham Joshua Heschel wrote his doctoral dissertation on the subject. *The Prophets* is a massive work that attempts to arrive at the essence of Israelite prophecy. Painstakingly, we are introduced to a God who is—to employ Heschel's term—"anthropopathic." God commiserates with man and shares in man's suffering. This is a reversal of Maimonides' teaching.[4] The divine attributes are not virtual realities designed for human imitation. They are reality!

Priests and Prophets

Our author, whether consciously or not, continues the conversation. He sets up the opposition of the Torah of Moses and the Way of the Prophets. Some of the ideas are already familiar to us, but there is something fresh, something new here, specifically the value assigned to the *korbanot*, the sacrifices in the Temple. For Rabbi Shnayor Burton, the sacrificial cult is not just one aspect of the Torah, but its essence. And it is the sacrifices which are the escarpment between the two surfaces of the Torah and the Prophets.

The prophets—Isaiah, Jeremiah—rail time and time again against the sacrificial cult. Why? Simply, theirs is a critique not so much of the institution itself, but of the corruption and the moral turpitude that came to be associated with it.

In Rabbi Burton's presentation we wake up to the realization that the way of the priests and the way of the prophets are in a sense antithetical to one another. If the prophets bestowed upon us knowledge of God's ways, the sacrifice takes us beyond that to the unfamiliar and ultimately unknowable. The act of bringing a sacrifice is an act of surrender, an admission of ignorance. The way of the prophets is the way of knowing. The way of the sacrifices is the way of not-knowing.[5]

The prophets allow us to know God's goodness.[6] The Torah takes us beyond human ken, beyond earthbound notions of "God,"[7] beyond "good."[8] Torah is the Absolute, the Prophets are the attributes.

Perhaps this is the secret of Maimonides' downgrading of the sacrifices in his philosophic work, the *Guide*. Whereas in his halakhic work, *Mishneh Torah*, the sacrifices enjoy a robust life (something unseen in the several centuries intervening between the completion of the Talmud and Maimonides' own day), in the *Guide* the sacrifices suffer immensely, as they are held up to the scrutiny of comparative religion and reduced to the primitive state of Near Eastern civilization. Many over the centuries, including Maimonides' greatest admirers, have been perplexed how the same author could so abruptly shift gears.

I would suggest that in *Mishneh Torah* Maimonides writes from the perspective of Moses the legislator. In the *Guide*, which according to scholarly consensus is (or at least, contains) Maimonides' promised *Book of Prophecy*,[9] he writes from the perspective of the prophetic—not the Mosaic—tradition. And that tradition, which constitutes the way of knowing God, carries with it, *eo ipso*, an adversarial attitude to the very institution of sacrifice.

Unbeknown to our author, some of the themes that he addresses were encapsulated by Rav Kook in an enigmatic code.

The verse in Exodus 22:1 reads: "If the thief is discovered while tunneling in...." The Hebrew word for the underground (or tunnel) is *"mahteret."* Rav Kook envisioned this as two words: *mah torat*. *Mah* (*mem, het*) is the number forty-eight, symbolizing the forty-eight prophets.[10] *Torat* is Torah in the *nismakh* (construct)

PRIESTS AND PROPHETS

form. The thief is an allusion to Jesus, who was depicted in the old work *Toledot Yeshu* as a *"gonev shem shamayim,"* someone who absconds with the divine name.[11]

What appeared to Rav Kook in a kabbalistic reverie was that the "theft," the misappropriation perpetrated by Christianity, consisted in the prioritization of the Prophets over the Torah. In mainstream Judaism, the Torah is primary and the Prophets secondary. Christianity reversed the order, making the Torah secondary (*"nismakh"*) to the Prophets. Christianity latched onto the compassion of the prophets while obsoleting the laws of the Torah.[12]

(As a student of students of Rav Kook, I might add a postscript that in Catholicism, the singular divine "I" of *Anokhi*, the undefinable, indescribable Giver of the Torah, was fractured into a trinity of attributes.)

The saintly *"Hafets Hayyim,"* as he was known, Rabbi Israel Meir Kagan, pushed young Talmudists, especially *kohanim* such as himself, to become conversant with the fifth order of the Talmud, *Kodashim*, which deals with sacrifices. To this end, he himself authored the digest *Likkutei Halakhot*, accomplishing for the exotic order of *Kodashim* what Rabbi Isaac Alfasi in his *Halakhot* had accomplished for the other, actual orders of the Talmud.

The *Hafets Hayyim* explained that the rebuilding of the Temple is imminent and therefore, the teachers of Torah must be competent to rule in matters pertaining to the Temple service.

That the sacrifices have seized the imagination of a young, talented thinker with such force, may be indicative of our proximity to the Temple. The *Beit ha-Mikdash* will require not only *poskei halakhot* (decisors) to adjudicate thorny matters of ritual law, but also *hogei de'ot* (thinkers) to breathe life into an otherwise moribund service, and to make peace between the way of knowing and the way of not-knowing.[13]

---

[1] See Rabbi J.D. Halevi Soloveitchik, *Shi'urim le-Zekher Abba Mari*, vol. 2 (Jerusalem: Mossad Harav Kook, 2002), *"Mehikat Hashem"* (pp. 188-189).
Cf. Rabbi Nahman of Breslov, *Likkutei MOHaRaN* I, 212. (Elsewhere, we have discussed Rabbi Nahman's use of Maimonides' *Sefer ha-Madda'*. Although in this instance, Rabbi Nahman's remarks might also have been inspired by the *Shir ha-Kavod* [*"An'im Zemirot"*] attributed to the *Hasidei Ashkenaz*.)

[2] Rashi, Exodus 7:1.

[3] See Rabbi Isaac Hutner, *Pahad Yitzhak: Kuntres ve-Zot Hanukkah* (New York, NY, 1989), *ma'amar* 8 (pp. 63-75).
Textual problems arise in regard to this *ma'amar*. The key phrase *"ro'eh ve-shotek"* ("He sees and is silent") does not occur in the *Bavli* version of the crisis (*Yoma* 69b), rather in the *Yerushalmi* version (*Berakhot* 7:3, *Megillah* 3:7). And in the *Yerushalmi*, God's silence does not result in the muting of prophecy. On the contrary, "It is fitting to call this [God] *'gibbor'* ('mighty'), for He sees the destruction of His house and is silent!" By fusing *Bavli* and *Yerushalmi*, Rabbi Hutner has in effect created his own narrative.

[4] For Maimonides, the belief that God is anthropopathic is just as grievous as the belief that God is anthropomorphic. See *Guide of the Perplexed* I, beginning chap. 53.

[5] The thought occurs to this writer that perhaps this is implicit in the *halakhah*, "Any priest who does not admit to the service [of the sacrifices] has no portion in the priesthood" (*"Kol kohen she-eino modeh ba-'avodah, ein lo helek ba-kehunah"*) (*Hullin* 132b; *Menahot* 18b). The statement is problematic because such a *kohen* should be disqualified on grounds of heresy (*apikorsut*). See RaShI, RITBA, and other *rishonim* cited in Rabbi Yitzhak Goldstoff, *Mikdash ha-Kodesh*, vol. 2 (Jerusalem, 1999), 35:2 (118b-119b). Beyond the belief system of any Jew, there may be required of the priest a special belief in the sacrifices, involving *bittul*, or surrender, to that which is unknowable.

[6] One ventures that this is the significance of the term *"nevi'im tovim"* ("good prophets") in the blessing preceding the *haftarah*, the reading from the Prophets. The *raison d'être*, the entire project of the prophets, is to manifest the

goodness of God.

See also Rabbi Nehemiah's interpretation of the verse in Exodus 2:2: "'Tov' (good)—*hagun li-nevi'ut* (worthy of prophecy)" (*b. Sotah* 12a).

[7] See Exodus 6:3.

[8] See Maimonides, *Guide of the Perplexed* I, 2.

[9] See *Shemonah Perakim* (Maimonides' introduction to *Avot*), chap. 7 (Kafah ed., p. 260, col. a); the introduction to the *Commentary to the Mishnah*, Kafah ed., p. 5, col. a; and the introduction to *The Guide of the Perplexed*, transl. Shlomo Pines (Chicago: University of Chicago Press, 1964), pp. 9-10.

[10] *b. Megillah* 14a.

[11] In the legend recorded in *Toledot Yeshu*, Jesus made off with the secret divine name (*shem ha-meforash*) that was recorded in the Temple in Jerusalem, and subsequently employed the name for magical purposes.

This legend runs parallel to the Geonic tradition concerning Parvah Amgusha of the Talmud. In the tradition recorded by Rabbeinu Hananel, Parvah Magus tunneled under the Temple in order to observe the High Priest's behavior on the Day of Atonement, but was discovered in the process. See *b. Yoma* 35a, Rabbeinu Hananel ad loc. (quoted in Rabbi Nathan of Rome, *'Arukh*, s.v. *Parvah*, which in turn is quoted in *Tosafot, Yoma*, s.v. *Parvah Amgusha*); and Maimonides, *Commentary to the Mishnah, Middot* 4:8 (Kafah ed., p. 300). Though unstated, it is possible that Parvah sought to learn the *shem ha-meforash*, which would have been pronounced by the High Priest on the Day of Atonement.

The divine name was to remain a secret tradition zealously guarded by the priests in the Temple. See *b. Kiddushin* 71a. According to Rashi, *'Avodah Zarah* 17b, s.v. *'alav li-sereifah*, pronunciation of the name of forty-two letters enabled one to "do with it as one desires." See Ephraim Kanarfogel, "Rashi's Awareness of Jewish Mystical Literature and Traditions," in *Raschi und Seine Erbe*, ed. Krochmalnik, Liss and Reichman (Heidelberg: Hochschule für Jüdische Studien, 2007), pp. 29-30.

Concerning the name of forty-two letters, see Rashi, *Kiddushin* 71a, s.v. *shem ben shteim 'esreh; Sanhedrin* 60a, s.v. *shem ben arba' otiyot; Sanhedrin* 101b, s.v. *u-bi-leshon 'agah*, and *Margaliyot ha-Yam* ad loc.

[12] See Rabbi Abraham Isaac Hakohen Kook, *Kevatsim mi-Ketav Yad Kodsho*, vol. 1, ed. Boaz Ofen (Jerusalem, 2006), *Pinkas Rishon le-Yaffo*, para. 43 (pp. 98-99); Rabbi Hayyim Avihu Shvarts, *Mi-Tokh ha-Torah ha-Go'elet*, vol. 3 (Jerusalem, 1989), p. 225; Rabbi Tsevi Yehudah Hakohen Kook, *Li-Netivot Yisrael*, vol. 2 (Jerusalem, 1979), "*Ha-Pesha' be-Yisrael*" (pp. 60-61).

This same thought is conveyed in *Shemonah Kevatsim* 5:127, where the opposition is also between Halakhah and Aggadah.

[13] See Rabbi Nahman of Breslov, *Likkutei Moharan* I, 6:4, 7; II, 7:7.

The Two Luminaries:
Rabbi Nahman of Breslov and Rav Kook

Moshe Nahmani. *Shnei ha-Me'orot* (5779/2019)

Moshe Nahmani has distinguished himself as a foremost independent researcher of the annals of Rav Kook. Like Rav Kook, he has an affinity for Breslov Hasidism (something which alienates him from some disciples of Rav Kook, who would wish to distance and disentangle the Rav from Hasidism). The past several years, he has emerged as a most vocal and outspoken defender of animal welfare. (Again, this causes some friction between Nahmani and some representatives of Kookian tradition who regard the Rav's writings on vegetarianism as a *"hilkheta li-Meshiha,"* something that awaits the Messianic Era.)

We are all indebted to Moshe Nahmani for his latest work, a carefully documented presentation of the overlap and spiritual affinity between the elder Rav Avraham Yitzhak Hakohen Kook (and his son Rav Tsevi Yehudah Hakohen Kook) on the one hand, and Rabbi Nahman of Breslov, on the other. Besides invaluable anecdotes provided by disciples,[1] there are at least two great finds in terms of archival material. First and foremost are Rav Tsevi Yehudah's notes in the marginalia of his copy of *Likkutei MoHaRaN*, Rabbi Nahman's magnum opus. Second, is the lengthy letter Rabbi Avraham Sternhartz addressed to Rav Kook in the summer of

1934, seeking the Chief Rabbi's assistance in easing his immigration from Soviet Russia to Erets Yisrael.

※※※

Rabbi Avraham Sternhartz was the grandson of Rabbi Nathan Sternhartz of Nemirov and Breslov, who acted as Rabbi Nahman's *sofer* (scribe). But Rabbi Nathan was much more than just an amanuensis. Rabbi Nahman believed that the soul-connection between the two, Nahman and Nathan, extended back in time. Rabbi Nathan would become Rabbi Nahman's chief disciple and interpreter. After Rabbi Nahman's passing, Rabbi Nathan became the leader of the Breslover Hasidim.

After Rabbi Avraham Sternhartz's arrival in Erets Yisrael in 1936,[2] he transmitted the Breslov tradition to disciples, most notably Rabbi Gedaliah Kenig, who before his passing in 1980, initiated the establishment of the now thriving Breslov community in Tsefat.

What is most curious about Rabbi Sternhartz's letter of introduction to Rav Kook (on pages 69-72) is that he presents himself as a grandson, on his father's side, of the great Rabbi David Tsevi, *Av Beit Din* of several communities, and on his mother's side, of Rabbi [Nahman] of Tcherin, author of *Parpera'ot la-Hokhmah* [a commentary on *Likkutei MOHaRaN*]. It is definitely true that Rabbi Nathan's father-in-law was the esteemed halakhist Rabbi David Tsevi Auerbach of Sharigrad, Kremnitz, and Mohilev, but why not state the most obvious claim to fame, namely descent from Rabbi Nathan Sternhartz himself?

Rabbi Nahman and Rav Kook

I turn now to Rav Tsevi Yehudah's notes to *Likkutei MOHaRaN*.[3] Perhaps the most important contribution is Rav Tsevi Yehudah's finding that an important passage in *Likkutei MOHaRaN* I, 6:3 has its antecedent in the classic ethical work by Bahya ibn Pakuda, *Hovot ha-Levavot* (*Duties of the Heart*).

Rabbi Nahman writes:

> Even if one knows in oneself that one did complete *teshuvah* (repentance), nonetheless, one must repent of the first repentance, because in the beginning, when one did *teshuvah*, one did [so] according to one's understanding, and afterward, when one does *teshuvah*, one certainly recognizes and understands more *Hashem*, blessed be He. We find that according to one's present understanding, certainly the first understanding was a corporealization. We find that one must repent of one's first understanding for having corporealized the sublimity of the divinity.

Rav Tsevi Yehudah jotted down:

> See *Ho[vot] ha-L[evavot]*, *Sha'ar 'Avoda[t] H[ashem]*, chap. 3, fifth advantage of arousal of reason: "they renew repentance" ("*mehaddeshim teshuvah*").

Nahmani unpacks Rav Tsevi Yehudah's shorthand notation. In the aforementioned paragraph, Bahya recorded the practice of "some devotees[4] that spent their lifetimes doing repentance. Every day they used to find a new way of repentance,[5] as they increased their understanding of God's greatness and their neglect of their obligation to obey Him in the past."[6]

It is of course edifying to learn that Rabbi Nahman was preceded in his conception of ongoing repentance (perhaps "return" is the better translation of *"teshuvah"*) by the eleventh-century Spanish *dayyan*, Bahya ibn Pakuda. But it seems to me that there is an essential element in Rabbi Nahman's teaching lacking in the earlier *Hovot ha-Levavot*. That is the element of *"hagshamat Elohut"* (corporealization of divinity). This is the revolutionary thought of Rabbi Nahman of Braslav. And it is this same daring that we will encounter in the writings of Rav Kook (the elder).

In *Zer'onim*, one of the earliest collections of Rav Kook's *pensées*, published in the literary journal *Ha-Tarbut ha-Yisraelit* in Jaffa in 1913,[7] we find this striking statement:

> From epoch to epoch, the mixture of pure belief in the Unity [of the deity] with the darkness of corporealization (*hagshamah*) is increasingly clarified....[8]

What Rav Kook has done in few words is to apply the method of Rabbi Nahman, previously reserved for the individual, to mankind as a whole. For Rabbi Nahman, spiritual growth consists of shedding puerile conceptions of the divinity for more advanced, more rarefied notions. And for Rav Kook, this evolution of consciousness is written not just on the tablet of the individual heart but on the tablet of the heart of collective mankind.[9] And then, it is not just the individual Jew who is involved in an ongoing process of *teshuvah*, but *Knesset Yisrael*, and beyond that, the human race as a whole. In the writings of the two spiritual luminaries, Rabbi Nahman and Rav Kook, *teshuvah* achieves epic proportions.

In 1978, newlywed and newly arrived in Jerusalem (we made *'aliyah* upon completion of our *"Sheva' Berakhot"*), I was privileged to meet several times with Rav Tsevi Yehudah Kook in the privacy of his home at 30 Ovadyah Street in the Ge'ulah section of town. On one of these occasions, the octogenarian sage shared with me impromptu some of his reflections on Breslov.

Rav Tsevi Yehudah recounted in a humorous vein his experience with a certain unnamed rabbi from America who would daily stroll with him. This regimen of the daily walk went on for some time. Then one day during their outing together, Rabbi Tsevi Yehudah mentioned Rabbi Nahman of Breslov. The next day, the man did not arrive for the walk. So ended this *"havruta."* (Nahmani has the story on page 112 *sans* the "American" identity of the mystery man.)

The elder Rav Kook wrote a by now famous letter to his adolescent son Tsevi Yehudah,[10] advising some caution when studying the works of the "great man," Rabbi Nahman. Basically, the father communicated to his son that there is required "a healthy soul in a healthy body." Rav Kook also recommended that the study of Rabbi Nahman be balanced by studying opposed views.[11]

Perhaps it was for the sake of providing balance that Rav Tsevi Yehudah dropped on me that the wondrous *Sippurei Ma'asiyot*, the tales of Rabbi Nahman, were looked at askance both in Gur and HaBaD.

I later fact-checked this with Breslover Hasidim who informed me that indeed the *Hiddushei ha-RIM* (Rabbi Yitzhak Meir Rotenberg-Alter, the founder of Gerrer Hasidism) had made a study of the stories of Rabbi Nahman. The RIM was able to follow the storyline as far as it was based on the Kabbalah of the ARI (Rabbi Isaac Luria). But it seems that at a certain point Rabbi Nahman left the ARI behind and ventured out on his own, and there the RIM was lost.

As for HaBaD's rejection of Rabbi Nahman's stories, to this day I have no idea to what Rav Tsevi Yehudah, zt"l, was alluding.

Again for the sake of balance, when asked by a student as to the nature of Rabbi Nahman's *Stories*, Rav Tsevi Yehudah responded that contained within them are moral lessons (*divrei mussar*).[12]

Moshe Nahmani has put together a wonderful collection of anecdotes and documents (including, on page 16, a facsimile of Rav Kook's own copy of *Likkutei MOHaRaN*). Much maligned during their lifetimes and even after, these two great luminaries, Rabbi Nahman and Rav Kook, are now shining brightly. And we can rest assured that their lights will glow ever brighter with the passage of time.

¹ I wish to correct a slight imprecision of language in one of these quotes. Nahmani quotes Rav Kook's disciple, Rabbi Israel Porath. The latter's testimony is of paramount importance for the reason that Rabbi Israel Porath was one of three major Torah scholars who would journey from Jerusalem to study under Rav Kook in Jaffa, the other two being Rabbi Tsevi Pesah Frank and Rabbi Ya'akov Moshe Harlap. Eventually, Rabbi Porath went on to become Rabbi of Cleveland, Ohio, where he was esteemed by all members of the Jewish community, regardless of their affiliation. He also authored a multivolume work on the Talmud, *Mavo ha-Talmud (The Outline of the Talmud)*, whose peculiar methodology was inspired by Rav Kook.

In *Shnei ha-Me'orot* (p. 14) we read:

> According to what [Rav Kook] communicated to me in private....his heart was drawn to the ways of [spiritual] service of Hasidism, and he especially devoted himself to the mysticism of Rabbi Nahman of Breslov. He read and studied much his books *and conversations*, and delved deeply into his thoughts.

The quote is taken from *Hayyei ha-RAYaH*, a biography of Rav Kook by a later disciple, Rabbi Moshe Tsevi Neriyah.

However in Rabbi Porath's original appreciation, which appeared in *Sefer ha-Do'ar*, there is a slightly different wording:

> According to what [Rav Kook] communicated to me in private....his heart was drawn to the ways of [spiritual] service of Hasidism. He especially devoted himself to the mysticism of Rabbi Nahman of Breslov. He read and studied much his books, and delved deeply into his thoughts *and conversations*.
> (Rabbi Israel Porath, "Harav A.Y. Kook z"l," in *Sefer ha-Do'ar: Mivhar ma'amarim la-yovel ha-shishim 5682-5742*, ed. Miklishanski and Kabakoff [New York: *Histadrut ha-'Ivrit ba-Amerika*, 1982], p. 199, col. 1)

² For more details of Rabbi Avraham Sternhartz's narrow escape from Soviet Russia, see Bezalel Friedman's biography of Rabbi Levi Yitzhak Bender, *Ish Hasidekha* (Jerusalem, 1993), pp. 178-179. (It includes a photo of Rebbetzin Sternhartz's Soviet passport of December 1935.)

³ I should add that not only did Rav Tsevi Yehudah annotate his copy of *Likkutei MOHaRaN*, but in the marginalia of his copy of *Orot ha-Kodesh*, on two occasions found sources for his father's statements in *Likkutei MOHaRaN*. See Rav Tsevi Yehudah's notes to *Orot ha-Kodesh*, appended to vol. 4 of *Orot ha-Kodesh* (Jerusalem: Mossad Harav Kook, 1990), p. 595. These notes pertaining to *Likkutei MOHaRaN* appear (in somewhat abridged form) in *Shnei ha-Me'orot*, pp. 115-116.

⁴ Judah ibn Tibbon translated into Hebrew as *"perushim"* (ascetics). The reference is probably to Sufi ascetics.

⁵ In Ibn Tibbons' Hebrew translation (as that of Kafah): *"mehaddeshim teshuvah."*

⁶ Bahya ben Joseph ibn Pakuda, *The Book of Direction to the Duties of the Heart (Al-Hidaya ila Fara'id Al-Qulub)*, transl. Menahem Mansoor (London: Routledge & Kegan Paul, 1973), p. 184 (the fifth reason).

⁷ The editors were Alexander Ziskind Rabinowitz (*AZaR*) and Tsevi Yehudah Hakohen Kook.

[8] Reprinted in *Orot* (Jerusalem, 1950), p. 127.
In the continuation of that paragraph, Rav Kook writes:

> In the last days of the human spirit's return to the sphere of pure belief, the final, fine shell (*kelipah*) of corporealization falls away, which is the attribution of general being to the divinity. (Ibid., p. 127)

Cf. Rabbi Mordechai Gimpel Barg's notes of Rav Kook's lectures on the *Book of Kuzari*, where we encounter the startling neologism *"kelipat nogah di-kedushah"* ("translucent shell of sanctity"):

> During the time that the world exists, the coarse, thick shells (*kelipot*) have already fallen off faith. Our work now is to remove the fine shells, which at first glance are imperceptible: the translucent shell of sanctity (*kelipat nogah di-kedushah*).
> (*Ma'amrei ha-RAYaH*, vol. 2, ed. Elisha Aviner [Langenauer] [Jerusalem, 1984], p. 490, end chap. 4)

Rav Kook's contradistinction of *"kelipot gasot"* ("coarse shells") versus *"kelipot dakot"* ("fine shells") may very well have been influenced by chapter four of Rabbi Shneur Zalman's *Iggeret ha-Kodesh*. See *Tanya* IV, chap. 4 (105b-106a). According to the author of the *Tanya*, man has the ability to remove the coarse shells, but the fine shell, which only the LORD can remove, remains until the coming of the Messiah. (The context is the "circumcision of the heart" and the distinction between *"milah"* and *"peri'ah."*)

For further clarification of Rav Kook's project of de-corporealization, see (on page 242) our remarks concerning the Maimonidean term *"mehuyyav ha-metsi'ut"* and Rabbi Nahman of Breslov's adoption of that term.

[9] The following poetic piece does seem geared to the individual and to one's daily trials and tribulations in regard to *"hagshamah"* (corporealization):

> **Let us escape**
> Let us escape from the depth of corporealization.
> Corporealization shadows us
> day in and day out,
> hour by hour,
> moment by moment.
> Give us ethics free of unworldliness,
> belief free of corporealization!
> Give light!
> Give light!
> Air and life for the soul!
> Not suffocation of the breath.
>
> (Rabbi Abraham Isaac Hakohen Kook, *Hadarav*, ed. Ron Sarid [3rd edition, 2008], p. 44)

This striking *pensée*, composed in Jerusalem between the years 1921-1924, comes from a transcript of Rabbi Tsevi Yehudah Hakohen Kook; see ibid., p. 249.

[10] On page 25, Nahmani writes that the letter was sent in 1906. As Tsevi Yehudah was born in 1891, he would have been aged fifteen when he received the letter.

[11] Nahmani bemoans the fact that the manuscript of the letter has gone missing. See *Shnei ha-Me'orot*, p. 94.

On at least one occasion we find young Tsevi Yehudah seeking his father's explanation of a certain passage in *Likkutei MOHaRaN* (I, 4). See *Tsemah Tsevi* (Jerusalem, 1991), Letter 21 (datelined "Halberstadt, *Motsa'ei Shabbat ha-Gadol*, 5674 [i.e., 1914]"), p. 63; *Shnei ha-Me'orot*, pp. 95-96.

Another passage in *Tsemah Tsevi* understood by Nahmani as a query to the elder Rav Kook, was actually misinterpreted. In Letter 15, datelined "Jaffa, 22 Sivan 5673 [i.e., 1913]" (p. 45), Tsevi Yehudah requested Rabbi Ya'akov Moshe Harlap's assistance in obtaining a copy of Rabbi Nathan Sternhartz's *Likkutei Tefillot*. The three titles requested of Rabbi Harlap were: *Likkutei Tefillot*, *Shev Shma'teta*, and *Kuntres ha-Hitpa'alut*. *Shev Shma'teta* by Rabbi Aryh Leib Hakohen (author of *Ketsot ha-Hoshen* and *Avnei Milu'im*) is a work immensely popular in yeshivah circles. *Kuntres ha-Hitpa'alut* is a Hasidic work on meditation by Rabbi Dov Baer Shneuri of Lubavitch (*"Mitteler Rebbe"*). Rabbi Harlap's response is found in *Hed Harim*, p. 51. He felt confident that *Shev Shma'teta* and *Likkutei Tefillot* were readily obtainable in Jerusalem. He was in doubt as to *Kuntres ha-Hitpa'alut*.

[12] *Shnei ha-Me'orot*, p. 111.

Rabbi Nahman himself said upon concluding his thirteenth and final story, "The Seven Beggars" (which by all standards is his masterpiece), "This story... has in it much *mussar*."

Etatism and Halakhah:
Family Feud and Political Theory

Rabbi Yitzhak Goldstoff. *Mikdash ha-Kodesh.* 2 volumes: *Hilkhot Beit ha-Behirah; Hilkhot Klei ha-Mikdash.* Jerusalem 5754-5759 [1994-1999].

In what proved a controversial eulogy for his uncle, Rabbi Yitzhak Ze'ev Soloveitchik of Brisk and Jerusalem (1886-1959),[1] Rabbi Joseph Baer Soloveitchik of Boston attempted to provide explanation why the "Brisker Rov" refused to receive Israeli Prime Minister David Ben-Gurion in his home, when his counterpart in Bnei Berak, Rabbi Abraham Isaiah Karelitz (*"Hazon Ish"*) did receive the Prime Minister. According to the younger Soloveitchik, the reason was simple: *Medinat Yisrael* (the State of Israel) does not appear in Maimonides' Code of Law![2]

At the time that Rabbi Soloveitchik delivered the eulogy, a youthful Rabbi Dovid Cohen (a disciple of Rabbi Isaac Hutner, *Rosh Yeshivah* of Yeshivah Rabbi Chaim Berlin in Brooklyn) vocally protested to defend the honor of the *Hazon Ish,* and was bodily removed from the premises. (The next day in private phone conversation to his disciple, Rabbi Hutner told him to stand strong and "not be ashamed because of people who ridicule him [in the service of the LORD].")[3]

The nephew, Rabbi J.B. Soloveitchik, who figured as the ideologist of the *Mizrachi* (Religious Zionist) movement, on another occasion clearly defined his own position and that of the movement he represented: "The *Agudah* draw the line between *Erets Yisrael* (the Land of Israel) and *Medinat Yisrael* (the State of Israel). We draw the line between *Medinat Yisrael* (the State of Israel) and *Memshelet Yisrael* (the Government of Israel)." In other words, Rabbi J.B. Soloveitchik recognized the State of Israel; whatever qualms he had were not with the State *per se*, rather with the policies of the particular government at its helm.

What has all this to do with the book under review?

On the one hand, the work bears the formal *haskamah* (endorsement) of Rabbi Yehiel Mikhel Feinstein, the highly esteemed son-in-law of Rabbi Isaac Ze'ev Soloveitchik (the "Brisker Rov"). And indeed, the work excels in the so-called *"Brisker derekh"* ("Brisk methodology") of *diyyukim ba-Rambam*,[4] what a layman might describe as micro-managerial attention to the text of Maimonides (parenthetically, a method the *Hazon Ish* objected to). On the other hand, we find in this breathtakingly erudite work a new diagnostic tool not to be found in the traditional Brisker toolkit, namely the collective concept of *"malkhut"* (kingdom), as opposed to the individual *melekh*, or king.

Thus does the author explain the difference between the anointment of high priests and that of kings. Whereas each successive generation of high priest must be anointed anew, only the first king of the dynasty requires anointment; his heirs need not be anointed (except in the case of contention, or *mahloket*). The author explains that in the case of the priests, it is the individual priest who must be anointed. In the case of kings, at the other extreme, it is the institution of the kingdom that is anointed. This is an innovative understanding of Maimonides. The abstract concept of *malkhut* rather than the concrete person of the *melekh* is anointed.[5]

The author will implement this collectivizing tool in yet another regard: the difference between the institution of *kehunah*, or priesthood, and the individual priest. In *Hilkhot Klei ha-Mikdash*, Maimonides speaks about the establishment of the priesthood in general, abstract terms, not specifying who is to bestow honor upon the priesthood. In the following *halakhah*, Maimonides articulates the specific honors to be bestowed upon the priest. For Rabbi Goldstoff, the introductory *halakhah* demands respect for the institution of *kehunah* (collective *"ve-kidashto"*); the second *halakhah* addresses the respect to be shown the individual *kohen*. There is a practical outcome: Respect for the institution of *kehunah* must be accorded even by the priests themselves; respect for the individual *kohen* (individual *"ve-kidashto"*) comes from a Yisrael (Israelite; non-priest), not from a fellow priest.[6]

As stated above, this novel differential (which arguably may be inherent in Maimonides himself) is not the bequest of Brisk. Where, then, does it come from? Perhaps it is the influence of a thinker taboo in today's ultra-Orthodox world—Rav Kook, who famously differentiated between *kelal* (collective) and *perat* (individual). Or perhaps it is simply the *reshimu* (to employ a kabbalistic

BOOK REVIEWS

term), the residuum of the reality of the State and the etatism against which the Brisker Rov fought tooth and nail.[7]

---

[1] The *hesped* (eulogy) in Yiddish was delivered in Yeshiva University's Lamport Auditorium in the aftermath of the Brisker Rov's passing in Jerusalem on the Eve of Yom Kippur, 9 Tishri 5720 (i.e., 1959). A redacted Hebrew version of the eulogy, entitled *"Mah Dodekh mi-Dod,"* was published on the Brisker Rov's fourth *Yahrzeit*, 9 Tishri 5724 (i.e., 1963), in *Ha-Do'ar* (New York), pp. 752-759. Later, it was included in a collection of Rabbi Yosef Dov Soloveitchik's essays, *Divrei Hagut ve-Ha'arakhah* (Jerusalem, 1982), pp. 57-97.

[2] The version of *Ha-Do'ar* (p. 757) reads:
> They said of him [i.e., Rabbi Yitzhak Ze'ev Soloveitchik] that he was opposed to the State of Israel. This statement is not correct. Opposition to a State expresses adopting a position regarding a political body, which is itself a political act. My uncle was completely removed from all socio-political thought or response. What might be said of him, is that the State found no place within his halakhic thought system nor on his halakhic value scale. He was unable to "translate" the idea of a sovereign, secular State to halakhic properties and values.

I have utilized the English translation of Rabbi Jeffrey Saks with slight modifications. See Jeffrey Saks, "Rabbi Joseph B. Soloveitchik and the Israeli Chief Rabbinate: Biographical Notes (1959-60)," *B.D.D.* 17, September 2006, pp. 48-49.

Rabbi Sacks sums up: "It is not that Reb Velvel was an anti-Zionist, *per se*, but that, as a Halakhic Man and "Man of Pure Halakhic Truth," the secular State of Israel did not register on his radar screen" (ibid., p. 49).

*

In Maimonides' code, appointment of a king requires a *beit din* (court of law) of seventy sages and a prophet; see *Hil. Melakhim* 1:3.

In a by now famous responsum, Rav Kook argued that in the absence of monarchy, those powers revert to the nation of Israel as a whole. This responsum paved the way for viewing the eventual State of Israel, elected by the people, as invested with the powers of kingship. The operative principle is *"haskamat ha-'ummah"* ("consensus of the nation"). See Rabbi Abraham Isaac Hakohen Kook, *Mishpat Kohen*, 144:15:1 (336b-338a).

Remarkably, Rav Kook was preceded in this line of thinking by Rabbi Abraham Weinberg of Slonim; see *Hesed le-Avraham* to the Prophets (Jerusalem, 1986), 1 Samuel, chap. 8 (pp. 52-53).

Rabbi Shelomo Yosef Zevin brought support for Rav Kook's position from the wording of Nahmanides ("a commandment upon the king, or the judge, or whoever has authority over the people"). See Rabbi S.Y. Zevin, *Le-'Or Ha-Halakhah* (Jerusalem, n.d.), p. 16; *Sefer ha-Mitsvot 'im Hasagot ha-Ramban*, ed. C.B. Chavel (Jerusalem: Mossad Harav Kook, 1981), p. 409.

[3] A quote from Rabbi Moses Isserles' gloss to *Shulhan 'Arukh, Orah Hayyim* 1:1.

[4] This method with its hypercritical analysis of Maimonides' code was founded by Rabbi Hayyim Soloveitchik of Brisk (Brest-Litovsk) (1853-1918). In the United States, it was promulgated by his grandson, Rabbi Joseph Baer Soloveitchik of Boston (1903-1993). For a while, Rabbi Soloveitchik maintained in Boston an institute of higher learning, Heikhal Rabbeinu Hayyim Halevi (named after his grandfather). In 1941, Rabbi Soloveitchik invited the refugee Rabbi Mikhel Feinstein to teach there. (These two were second cousins. Rabbi Soloveitchik's mother, Pesha, and Rabbi Feinstein's father, Avraham Yitzhak, were first cousins. Later in Erets Yisrael in 1946, Rabbi Mikhel Feinstein would wed Lifsha, the daughter of the *Brisker Rov*, making him Rabbi Soloveitchik's first cousin by marriage.) That same year of 1941, Rabbi Soloveitchik succeeded his recently deceased father, Rabbi Moshe Soloveichik, as *Rosh Yeshivah* at Yeshivah Rabbi Yitzhak Elhanan in New York.

[5] The pertinent texts read as follows:

> ... Even a [high] priest, the son of a [high] priest, we anoint, as it says: "And the anointed priest that shall be in his stead from among his sons" [Leviticus 6:15].
> (*Hilkhot Klei ha-Mikdash* 1:7)
>
> ... And we do not anoint a king, son of a king, for the kingdom is the inheritance of the king forever, as it says: "He and his sons in the midst of Israel" [Deuteronomy 17:20].
> (*Hilkhot Klei ha-Mikdash* 1:11)

See *Mikdash ha-Kodesh*, vol. 2, chap. 8 (f.23).

[6] The pertinent texts read as follows:

> It is a positive commandment to set the priests apart and to sanctify them and prepare them for sacrifice, as it says: "And you shall sanctify him for he sacrifices the bread of your God" [Leviticus 21:8].
> (*Hilkhot Klei ha-Mikdash* 4:1)
>
> And every man of Israel must treat them with much respect and give them precedence for everything holy: to be the first to open the Torah [reading]; to bless first [after meals]; and to take the choice portion first.
> (*Hilkhot Klei ha-Mikdash* 4:2)

See *Mikdash ha-Kodesh*, vol. 2, chap. 55 (f.187 ff.)

[7] Although not his coinage, "etatism" was certainly the *bête noire* of Yeshayahu Leibowitz, who gave the term currency in Israeli discourse.

Rav Yosef Dov Soloveitchik ZT"L
ON THE *SEDER HA-'AVODAH* OF *YOM HA-KIPPURIM*
A SYNOPSIS OF
THE RAV'S YIDDISH *TESHUVAH DERASHAH* 5736 (1975)
BY BEZALEL NAOR

The thrust of Rav Soloveitchik's lecture is a fascinating exploration of our custom of reciting (and reliving) the ritual of the Day of Atonement in the Second Temple. The Rav described the *Seder ha-'Avodah* as "the climax of the sanctity of the day" (*"der hoikh-punkt fun kedushas ha-yom"*). It was the Rav's distinct impression that Jews were so "spellbound" (*"baki-shuft"*) by the recitation, that they found it difficult to take leave of it. This is borne out by the practice in Baghdad of old. The *Seder ha-'Avodah* was so beloved to the Jews of Baghdad that they recited *Seder ha-'Avodah* not only at *Mussaf* (the Additional Service), as is our custom, but at *Shaharit* (the Morning Service) and *Minhah* (the Afternoon Service) as well. Despite the efforts of several generations of Ge'onim to uproot this custom, they were unsuccessful in doing so.[1] This was also the impression conveyed to the young Soloveitchik growing up, by his grandfather, Rabbi Hayyim Soloveitchik, and father, Rabbi Moshe Soloveichik. The recitation of the *Seder ha-'Avodah* was so beloved to them, that it was only with the greatest difficulty that they were able to bid it farewell.

(At this point in his delivery, the Rav digressed, recalling nostalgically how the Modzhitser Hasidim in Warsaw prolonged the third

Sabbath meal well into the night. Evidently, it was very hard for them to take leave of the Sabbath Queen. One of the unforgettable scenes from this *derashah* is the Rav's vivid portrayal of one of the poverty-stricken Hasidim that he encountered in the Modzhitser *shtiebel* at *Shalosh Se'udot, Yankel der Treiger* [Yankel the Porter]. During the week, Yankel wore an outfit that was "more holes than material" [*"mehr lekher vie materiel"*]. Like his fellow porters in Warsaw, he was a human beast of burden. The Rav comically described how one would see a commode or other heavy furniture walking down the street with two little feet under it. But on Shabbat, at the Third Meal in the Modzhitser *shtiebel*, the same *Yankel der Treiger* was unrecognizable. He appeared a prince with a *shtreimel* on his head and a *kapote*.

The Rav's point was that once upon a time, Jews could not get enough of the Sabbath. They simply could not let go of her. Whereas today, we modern Jews say to her coolly, "Goodbye, I'll see you next week.")

Why was the *Seder ha-'Avodah* so extremely important? What is its significance? The Rav presented three *"ta'amim,"* or reasons for the custom. One is readily available in Rashi; the other two are original.

1. Rashi attributes the *sheli'ah tsibbur*'s (prayer leader's) recitation of the *Seder ha-'Avodah* to the principle of *"U-Neshalmah pharim sefateinu,"* "Our lips will pay bulls" (Hosea 14:3).[2] After the destruction of the Temple in Jerusalem, we compensate for our inability to offer physical sacrifices by reciting the Torah reading thereof.

The Rav found a difficulty with Rashi's explanation. If that were the reason for reciting the *Seder ha-'Avodah* in *Mussaf*, it should be incumbent upon each and every individual, just as *Mussaf* is incumbent upon the individual. In the controversy between Rabbi El'azar ben Azariah and the Sages in the Mishnah, the *halakhah* is in accordance with the opinion of the Sages. (Rabbi El'azar ben Azariah held that *Mussaf* is recited only *"be-haver 'ir"*; the Sages disagreed and held that the obligation of *Mussaf* devolves upon each individual.)³ Just as *Mussaf* is recited by each individual and not delegated to the *sheli'ah tsibbur* (prayer leader), so the recitation of the *Seder ha-'Avodah* should be the obligation of each individual. Why then is it recited by the *sheli'ah tsibbur*?

2. In the Temple, besides the offerings of the various sacrifices, there was also a Torah reading by the *kohen gadol* (high priest). This reading took place after the scapegoat had been dispatched to the wilderness to Azazel. The reading was considered of such paramount importance that the ruling is *"Keri'ah me'akevet."* The Torah reading is indispensable to the sacrifices.⁴

The Rav wondered aloud whether in the Second Temple the *kohen gadol*'s reading was accompanied by Targum, Aramaic translation. The practice of Targum was instituted at the very beginning of the Second Temple by Ezra the Scribe.⁵

The Rav reasoned that especially in the Second Temple when there were controversies between the Pharisees and the Sadducees as to the exact sequence of the high priest's actions on the Day of Atonement, it would have been imperative that his reading be supplemented by explanatory Targum, so that the common folk not suspect him of having deviated from the order of the Torah.[6]

The Rav proposed that the *sheli'ah tsibbur*'s recitation of the *Seder ha-'Avodah* is a commemoration of the *kohen gadol*'s Torah reading on *Yom ha-Kippurim*. But here a difficulty arises. The *kohen gadol*'s reading is from the Written Torah (*Torah she-bi-khetav*), whereas the *sheli'ah tsibbur*'s reading is from the Oral Torah (*Torah she-be-'al peh*).

At this point, the Rav relied on *derush sefarim* (homiletic literature), most notably *Beit Halevi* of his great-grandfather and namesake, Rabbi Yosef Dov Baer Halevi Soloveitchik,[7] to the effect that Yom Kippur is the manifestation of the Oral Torah; the celebration, the *"Yom Tov of Torah she-be-'al peh."*

This contention is constructed of many sources. First, there is the Mishnah, end *Ta'anit*: "There were never such festivals (*yamim tovim*) for Israel as the fifteenth of Av and Yom Kippur." The *Gemara* explains that the distinction of Yom Kippur is due to the fact that it is "the day the second tablets were given."[8] And yet, we celebrate *Shavu'ot* as the time of the giving of the Torah. What was the difference between the first and second tablets? The first tablets contained not only the Written Law but the Oral Law as well.[9] In fact, the letters that flew off the tablets, causing Moses to drop them and shatter them,[10] were not the letters of the Written Law but those of the Oral Law.[11] Subsequently, the second tablets contained only the Written Law.[12] So what was unique about the giving of the second tablets on Yom Kippur was that for the first time the *Torah she-be-'al peh* came into its own and emerged as a distinct entity.¹³ And it is the Torah *she-be-'al peh* that the *kohen gadol* manifests by his Torah reading on Yom Kippur. His concluding remarks, "More than I read before you is written here,"¹⁴ may allude to the Oral Law. And it is this same manifestation of *Torah she-be-'al peh* that the *sheli'ah tsibbur* accomplishes with his recitation of the *Seder ha-'Avodah*. (As opposed to *Amits Ko'ah*, the medieval *piyyut* by Rabbi Meshullam ben Kalonymos, recited in Ashkenazic congregations, the antique *Atah Konanta*, recited in Sephardic congregations, goes back to the Tannaitic era, and is attributed by some to a priest. Thus, it eminently qualifies as *Torah she-be-'al peh*.)¹⁵

The Rav anticipated that one might counter that *Sukkot*, not Yom Kippur, should rightly be termed the *Yom Tov* of *Torah she-be-'al peh*. The Rambam begins the laws of *Sukkah* with its physical dimensions, which are surely *Torah she-be-'al peh*. As we say, "*Shi'urin, hatsitsin u-mehitsin, halakhah le-Moshe mi-Sinai.*" ("Measurements… are oral tradition to Moses from Sinai.")¹⁶ And in regard to various observances of *Sukkot* there were controversies between the Pharisees and the Sadducees: *nisukh ha-mayim* (the water libation) and *'aravah* (the willow branch).¹⁷

The Rav's response was that, in truth, *Sukkot* is but the continuation, the extension of Yom Kippur. The Midrash comments on the verse in regard to the four species: "'And you shall take for you on the first day'—the first day of reckoning sins."¹⁸ The Jew emerges from Yom Kippur spiritually cleansed: "Before the LORD you shall be purified."¹⁹ And as Rabbi Akiva said: *"Ashreikhem Yisrael!* Happy are you, Israel! Before whom are you purified, and who purifies you? Your Father in heaven."[20] And it is this joy, this *simhah* that comes from having received from heaven the greatest gift, a gratuitous gift (*matnat hinam*), a sense of spiritual purity (*taharat ha-nefesh*), that pervades the ensuing Yom Tov of Sukkot.

3. Finally, quoting the Talmud Yerushalmi, the Rav offers a third *"ta'am"* for the speciality of the *Seder ha-'Avodah* on Yom Kippur. The Yerushalmi states: "Any generation in which the Temple is not rebuilt in its days, it is as if it is destroyed in its days."[21]

The Rav ventured that on Yom Kippur we must atone not only for our individual sins but for the historic, collective sin of not having rebuilt the Temple. *"Aval anahnu va-'avoteinu hatanu."* "We and our fathers have sinned."[22] This refers to the ongoing historic sin that nineteen hundred years later we are still bereft of the Temple in Jerusalem. Our recitation of the *Seder ha-'Avodah* followed by the *kinot*, the elegy of the Ten Martyrs (*'Asarah Harugei Malkhut*), is our way of expiating this historic sin.

If the Rav's portrayal of *Yankel der Treiger* is comedic, his depiction of the transition from the *Seder ha-'Avodah* is pathos-laden and starkly, brutally tragic. The abrupt transition from *"Mar'eh Kohen"*—the face of the high priest, when he emerged from the Holy of Holies, radiating the splendor of the divine presence (*ziv ha-Shekhinah*)—to the present reality, a world without Temple, without sacrifices, without Kohen, Levite and Israelite—was likened by the Rav to a rude awakening from a beautiful dream. For a brief, too brief moment, we were transported to the Temple in Jerusalem with all of its glorious splendor and pageantry. And then suddenly, with a clap, we find ourselves back in our spiritually impoverished waking life. *"Me-'igra ramah le-bira 'amikta!"* "From a mighty mountain to a profound pit!"

"Es iz geven, yeh. Ober es iz nit mehr."

"It was, yes. But it is no more."

"Dos iz geven azei, ober nisht itzter."

"This was so, but not now."

In order for us to appreciate the enormity of the loss, it would be necessary to recount the past glory. The Rav juxtaposed the verse in Lamentations 1:7: "Jerusalem remembered [in] the days of her affliction and of her anguish all her treasures that she had from the days of old."[23]

"All this occurred when the Temple was on its foundation and the Holy Sanctuary was on its site, and the *Kohen Gadol* stood and ministered—his generation (*doro*) watched and rejoiced."[24]

The Rav commented ruefully: "'His generation'—not ours."

"Ashrei 'ayin ra'atah kol eleh." "Fortunate is the eye that saw all these."[25]

"But our forefathers' iniquities destroyed the Temple, and our sins delayed the Final Redemption." (*"Aval 'avonot avoteinu heherivu naveh, ve-hat'oteinu he'erikhu kitso."*)[26]

"Any generation in which the Temple is not rebuilt in its days, it is as if it is destroyed in its days."

The Rav offered historical insight into Rabbi Akiva's proverb that concludes the Mishnah, Tractate *Yoma*. In the generation that followed the destruction of the Temple, the Jewish People could not imagine how it would be possible to celebrate Yom Kippur, a day which pivots on the service in the Temple. Rabbi Akiva appeared to us then as a great consoler, driving home the message that as important as the Temple ritual was, in the final analysis, it is the LORD who purifies Israel of all its sins, and the LORD we have not lost.

> *"Ashreikhem Yisrael!*
> Happy are you, Israel!
> Before whom are you purified, and who purifies you?
> Your Father in heaven."

---

[1] See the responsum of Hai Gaon in B.M. Lewin, *Otsar ha-Ge'onim, Yoma* (Jerusalem, 1934), no. 121 (p. 41); Natronai Gaon, quoted in *Seder Rav Amram Gaon*, ed. Daniel Goldschmidt (Jerusalem: Mossad Harav Kook, 2004), p. 169; and Rabbi Yosef Dov Halevi Soloveitchik, *Kuntres be-'Inyan 'Avodat Yom ha-Kippurim*, ed. Rabbi Aharon Lichtenstein (Jerusalem, 1986), *Yoma* 36b, s.v. *ha-hu de-nahit* (pp. 30-31).

[2] Rashi, *Yoma* 36b, s.v. *ha-hu de-nahit*.

[3] m. *Berakhot* 4:7.

[4] See b. *Yoma* 5b, "*Mikra parashah me'akev,*" and Rashi, *Yoma* 68b, s.v. *ba' likrot*. This is one of two opinions in Rabbeinu Menahem ha-Me'iri, *Beit ha-Behirah, Yoma*, beginning chap. 7.

[5] Maimonides, *Hil. Tefillah* 12:10.

[6] The Pharisees upheld the oral tradition of *"Hamesh tevilot va-'asarah kiddushin"* ("Five ritual immersions and ten washings of the hands and the feet"), whereby *ipso facto* the verse in the Torah portion is out of sequence. See *b. Yoma* 71a. The Sadducees, on the other hand, maintained the order spelled out in the Torah.

In the Rav's opinion, this Pharisaic practice would have appeared to the public much more egregious than the more famous controversy between the Pharisees and the Sadducees as to where the incense should be lit. According to the Sadducees, the high priest *"matkin mi-ba-huts,"* "lights outside" the *kodesh kodashim*, or Holy of Holies; the Pharisees, on the other hand, held that the high priest *"matkin mi-bifnim,"* "lights inside" the Holy of Holies. See *b.*

Yoma 19b, 53a.
7. See Rabbi Yosef Dov Baer Halevi Soloveitchik (of Brisk), *She'elot u-Teshuvot Beit Halevi*, Part Two, *derush* 18
8. *b. Ta'anit* 30b.
9. *y. Shekalim* 6:1, quoted in *Beit Halevi*.
10. *y. Ta'anit* 4:5.
11. This is the novel idea of *Beit Halevi*.
12. *Beit Halevi* relied on the *Yerushalmi, Shekalim*. However, according to *Exodus Rabbah* 46:1 it was the exact opposite: The first tablets contained only the Ten Commandments and the second tablets contained also *"halakhot, midrash,* and *aggadot."* See *Yefeh To'ar* ad loc. (This Midrash was brought to my attention by the indefatigable Torah scholar Rabbi Moshe Zuriel *shelit"a*.)
13. According to the *Beit Halevi*, since the Oral Law was not included in the second tablets, it was now to be written in the heart of Moses and the hearts of the Jewish People. Thereby, Israel ascended to a greater level. No longer would the Torah and Israel be two but one. (*"Ha-Torah ve-Yisrael kula had hu."*)
14. *m. Yoma* 7:1; *b. Yoma* 68b.
15. See Rabbi Yom Tov ben Abraham Asevilli, *Hiddushei ha-RITBA, Yoma* 56b, s.v. *Ha-hu de-nahit kameh de-Rava*, quoting *'Ittur*: "We hear from this that [the *sheli'ah tsibbur*] recites it in the language of the Mishnah *(leshon ha-Mishnah)*, such as *'Atah Konanta'* of Yosé ben Yosé."
16. *b. Sukkah* 5b.
17. *m. Sukkah* 4:9; *b. Sukkah* 43b-44a.
18. Leviticus 23:40; *Midrash Tanhuma, Emor*, 22.
19. Leviticus 16:30.
20. *m. Yoma* 8:9.
21. *y. Yoma* 1:1.
22. Preface to *Vidui* (Confession of sins).
23. The Rav directed us to Ibn Ezra's commentary ad locum.
24. Afterword to *Seder ha-'Avodah*.
25. Ibid.
26. Ibid.

A King's Palace

Aharon Hayyim Zimmerman. *Agra la-Yesharim*. Jerusalem, 1983.

Rabbi Aharon Hayyim Zimmerman (1915-1995) served as Rosh Yeshivah of Beit Midrash le-Torah (Hebrew Theological College) in Chicago. He was famed for his genius in both Talmud and mathematics. In his youth, he studied in his uncle Rabbi Baruch Dov Leibowitz's *yeshivah* in Kamenitz. (Rabbi Leibowitz was married to Rabbi Zimmerman's father's sister. Sister and brother were the children of Avraham Yitzhak Halevi Zimmerman, Rabbi of Kremenchug, Ukraine.)

Rabbi Zimmerman's first work, *Binyan Halakhah* (New York, 1942), on Maimonides' *Mishneh Torah*, bore the *haskamot* (endorsements) of Rabbi Baruch Dov Leibowitz and Rabbi Isaac Herzog, Chief Rabbi of Erets Israel, who was visiting the United States at the time. In his letter of recommendation, Rabbi Herzog implored Chicago Jewry to appreciate the young prodigy in their midst.

Later, Rabbi Zimmerman produced a massive work entitled *Agan ha-Sahar* (New York, 1955), which dealt with the halakhic problems associated with the international date line. In this ambitious undertaking, the author upheld the ruling of the sage of B'nei Berak, Rabbi Abraham Isaiah Karelitz (*"Hazon Ish"*), while lambasting his theoretical opponent, Rabbi Menahem Mendel Kasher (author of *Torah Sheleimah*).

The dilemma arose during the brief sojourn of the Mirrer Yeshivah in Kobe, Japan in 1941. From Japan, queries were sent to Erets Israel, both to Chief Rabbi Herzog and to the *Hazon Ish*. The majority of *posekim* (halakhic decisors) in Erets Yisrael, at a special session convened by Chief Rabbi Herzog, ruled that the Sabbath should be observed in Japan on Saturday by the local reckoning. The *Hazon Ish*, on the other hand, held that the new day begins in China (not at an imaginary line drawn in the Pacific Ocean), which means that the Sabbath should be observed on Sunday by Japanese standards. Eventually, the *Hazon Ish* penned a comprehensive study, *Kuntres Shmoneh 'Esreh Sha'ot* ("Eighteen Hours") explaining his reasoning (based on Rabbi Yehudah Halevi's *Kuzari*) that the day begins in the East in China six hours before Erets Israel, and ends in the West eighteen hours after Erets Israel.[1]

The present *sefer*, *Agra la-Yesharim*, advocates for reviving the *mitsvah* of *shemirat ha-mikdash*, guarding the Temple Mount. (Rabbi Zimmerman, a Levi, may have felt a personal connection to this particular commandment as it devolves upon the Levites.) In his code, Maimonides writes:

> Guarding the Temple is a positive commandment, and though there be no fear of enemies or brigands, for its

guarding is only for its honor; there is no comparison between a palace that has guards and a palace that has no guards.²

In truth, Rabbi Zimmerman was not the first to raise the issue of reviving this ancient practice of stationing guards outside the Temple. A century earlier, Rabbi Hillel Moshe Meshel Gelbstein (1833-1907), a Kotzker and later Lubavitcher Hasid, published a work *Mishkenot le-Abir Ya'akov* (Jerusalem, 1881), advocating for this lost commandment (what we would refer to as a *"mitsvah yetomah,"* or "orphan commandment"). Rabbi Gelbstein sent his work to the great authority Rabbi Abraham Bornstein of Sochaczew (1839-1910), son-in-law of the Kotzker Rebbe, Rabbi Menahem Mendel Morgenstern. The Sochaczewer's response to Rabbi Gelbstein (published in his collected responsa, *Avnei Nezer*) was negative. For various reasons, the Sochaczewer concluded that the commandment is not applicable at this time. The responsum in *Avnei Nezer* begins with a demurral:

> Regarding his honor's discussion whether it is obligatory at this time to station guards for the Temple. I shall answer him according to my limited intellect but not as a matter of practical halakhah (*halakhah le-ma'aseh*) for it is not my place to decide a matter that affects *Kelal Yisrael* (the Jewish People). Thank God, Israel is not a widower. [I.e., there are others more qualified to decide.] I write in a purely theoretical manner.³

Rabbi Zimmerman takes up the cudgels once again. A typical chapter (chap. 9) discusses whether a pedigreed Levite (*"Levi meyuhas"*) is required to guard the Temple.

At the present time, when guardianship over the Temple Mount is entrusted to the Jordanian *wakf*, it seems improbable that guard duty will be assigned to the Levites.

※

I should like to share with the reader the gist of the final chapter of *Agra la-Yesharim* (chap. 42). The paradoxical nature of the thought, which by the author's own assessment contains "very deep matters" (*"devarim 'amukim me'od"*),[4] goes to the heart of the philosophical problem of divine dictate versus free will.

Rabbi Zimmerman makes a strong case that ultimately the building of the Holy Temple must be "in the hands of heaven" (*"bi-yedei shamayim"*). Rashi and *Tosafot* adduced in this regard the verse in Exodus 15:17: "The Temple of the LORD Your hands established." However, Rashi and Tosafot referred to the future Third Temple which "will come from heaven."[5] Rabbi Zimmerman, based on the verse in 1 Chronicles 29:1, extends the definition to *all* Temples, including the First Temple built by Solomon, and the second built (or rather enlarged) by Herod. The verse in Chronicles reads: "... for the palace (*birah*) is not for man, but for the LORD God."

In regard to King Herod, we find the statement in the Talmud: "Without a king, the Temple cannot be built."[6] This might seem a prosaic statement of fact. However, the legendary *gaon*, Rabbi David Friedman of Karlin, interpreted the statement halakhically.[7] For Rabbi Zimmerman, this Talmudic statement is not only of halakhic significance, but theological significance as well. Since ultimately the construction of the Temple is accomplished by the Almighty, how is it possible that it be brought about by a human? The solution, according to our author, lies in the words of Proverbs 21:1: "The heart of a king is in the hand of the LORD." Only a king, who is stripped of the common man's free will, and is wholly subservient to the divine will, is uniquely suited to build the LORD's Temple, a task definitionally not "in the hands of man" (*"bi-yedei adam"*) but "in the hands of heaven" (*"bi-yedei shamayim"*).

In my humble opinion, the thought may betray Izhbitser-Radzyner influence. After leaving Chicago, and before his *'aliyah* to Erets Israel, Rabbi Zimmerman dwelled in the Boro Park section of Brooklyn and prayed in the *beit midrash* of the Rebbe of Radzyn. On the other hand, Rabbi Zimmerman writes that he presented the kernel of the idea (that a king is stripped of free will) to his *rebbe*, Rabbi Baruch Dov [Leibowitz], who concurred that this is the true interpretation (*"ha-peshat ha-amiti"*).[8] Rabbi Zimmerman also found support for this concept in the work of the famous Sephardic *gaon*, Rabbi Hayyim Palache, *Re'eh Hayyim*.[9]

---

[1] The *Kuntres Shemoneh 'Esreh Sha'ot* was published in *Hazon Ish, Orah Hayyim/Mo'ed*, ed. Rabbi Samuel Greineman (3rd edition, B'nei Berak, 1967), chap. 64 (ff. 93-96). The *Hazon Ish*'s study was written as a direct response to Rabbi Yehiel Mikhel Tukachinsky's work *Ha-Yomam be-Kadur ha-'Arets* (Jerusalem, 1943). Rabbi Tukachinsky, one of the sages of Jerusalem, was married to the granddaughter of Rabbi Samuel Salant, revered Ashkenazic Chief Rabbi of

Jerusalem for almost seventy years until his passing in 1909.

[2] Maimonides, *MT, Hil. Beit ha-Behirah* 8:1.
[3] Rabbi Abraham Bornstein, *Avnei Nezer, Yoreh De'ah* (Piotrków, 1913), no. 449.
[4] *Agra la-Yesharim*, 271a.
[5] See Rashi and *Tosafot, Rosh Hashanah* 30a; *Sukkah* 41a; and *Shavu'ot* 15b.

However, see the Vilna Gaon's interpretation of the verse "The Temple of the LORD Your hands established," in *Aderet Eliyahu* (Warsaw, 1887), Deuteronomy 1:10: "It appeared that they were making [the Temple] but they were not making [it] at all ... And so in the Temple... They were lifting the stone, but it was not they who were lifting, but the LORD gave strength and lifted their hand." The Gaon references the verse in 1 Kings 6:7 regarding the construction of Solomon's Temple. See *Numbers Rabbah* 14:3 and *Zohar* I, 74a.

[6] *b. Bava Batra* 4a.
[7] Rabbi David Friedman, Introduction to *Kuntres Derishat Zion vi-Yerushalayim*; published in idem, *She'elat David* (Piotrków, 1913), 14a. *Derishat Zion vi-Yerushalayim* is Rabbi Friedman's rebuttal of Rabbi Tsevi Hirsch Kalischer's *Derishat Zion* (Lyck, 1862).
[8] *Agra la-Yesharim*, 270b.
[9] Rabbi Hayyim Palache, *Re'eh Hayyim*, Part One (Saloniki, 1860), *Shemot*, 81a; quoted in *Agra la-Yesharim*, 270b-271a.

However, in the next paragraph, Rabbi Palache quotes from the works of Rabbi Hayyim Yosef David Azulai (HYDA) that the principle "The heart of a king is in the hand of the LORD" applies only to a righteous king; a wicked king remains a "master of free will" (*"ba'al behirah"*). This would throw a monkey wrench into Rabbi Zimmerman's remarks concerning King Herod, who most certainly was a wicked king.

Bibliography

Aaron Berechiah of Modena. *Ma'avar Yabok*. Mantua, 1626.

Abraham ben David of Posquières. *Hasagot ha-Rabad le-Mishneh Torah*. Ed. Bezalel Naor. Jerusalem: Zur-Ot, 1985.

Abraham ben Isaac of Narbonne. Sefer ha-Eshkol. Ed. Shalom and Hanokh Albeck. Jerusalem, 1935-1938.

Abraham Maimonides. *Birkat Avraham*. Responsa. Ed. Baer Goldberg. Lyck, 1859.

_____. *Ha-Maspik le-'Ovdei Hashem* (*Kitāb Kifāyah al-'Ābidīn*). Transl. Yosef Dori. Jerusalem, 1973.

_____. *Peirush Rabbeinu Avraham ben ha-Rambam 'al Bereshit u-Shemot*. Ed. Efraim Yehudah Wiesenberg. London: L. Honig & Sons, 1958.

_____. *Peirush ha-Torah, Bereishit*. Ed. Moshe Maimon. Monsey, NY, 2020.

Abraham son of Vilna Gaon. Commentary to Psalms. *Sefer Tehillim 'im peirush...Be'er Avraham*. Ed. Samuel Luria. Warsaw, 1887.

_____. *Tirgem Avraham*. Commentary on *Targum Onkelos*. Jerusalem 1896; photo-offset Tel-Aviv: Ya'akov A. Landa, n.d.

Abrams, Daniel. *The Book Bahir: An Edition Based on the Earliest Manuscripts*. Los Angeles: Cherub, 1994.

_____. *R. Asher ben David: His Complete Works and Studies in His Kabbalistic Thought*. Ed. Daniel Abrams. Los Angeles: Cherub, 1996.

Abulafia, Abraham. *Sefer ha-Heshek*. Ed. Matithyahu Safrin.

Jerusalem, 1999.

Adler, Shemariah Menashe. *'Emek ha-Bakha*. Keidan, 1935.

———. *Mar'eh Kohen*. London, 1919. *Mahadura Tinyana*. London, 1928. *Mahadura Telita'ah*, vol. 1. Piotrków, 1931. *Mahadura Telita'ah*, vol. 2. Warsaw, 1933. *Mahadura Hamisha'ah*. London, 1945. Concerning the Herem de-Rabbeinu Gershom. London, 1953.

———. *Maror de-Rabbanan*. Appended to *Mar'eh Kohen Tinyana*. London, 1928.

———. *Zikhron Elhanan*. London, 1920.

Agus, Jacob. *Banner of Jerusalem*. Biography of Rav Kook. New York: Bloch, 1946. Later retitled, *High Priest of Rebirth*. New York: Bloch, 1972.

Alexander, Yosef, of Darbian (Darbenai, Lithuania). Commentary to prayer book. *Porat Yosef*. Warsaw, 1898.

Alexandrov, Samuel. *Mikhtevei Mehkar u-Bikoret*. vol. 1. Vilna, 1907. vol. 2. Cracow, 1910. vol. 3. Jerusalem, 1932.

Algaze, Yom Tov. *Tosefet de-Rabbanan*. In *Kehillat Ya'akov*. Saloniki, 1786.

Alkalai, Judah Hai. *Minhat Yehudah*. (Pressburg) 1843.

Alter, Abraham Mordechai, of Gur. *Mikhtevei Torah me-Admor mi-Gur*. Ed. Z.Y. Abramowitz and I.M. Alter. Tel Aviv, 1987.

Alter, Judah Aryeh Leib. *Sefat Emet*. On Pentateuch. 5 vols. Piotrków-Cracow, 1905-1908.

Alter, Robert. *The Hebrew Bible*. Transl. with commentary. 3 vols. New York: W.W. Norton, 2019.

Alter-Rotenburg, Isaac Meir, of Gur. *Hiddushei ha-RIM 'al ha-Torah*. Ed. Judah Leib Levin. Jerusalem, 2010.

Altmann, Alexander. "Moses Narboni's 'Epistle on *Shi'ur Qoma*.'" In *Jewish Medieval and Renaissance Studies*. Ed. Altmann. Cambridge, Mass: Harvard University Press, 1967.

BIBLIOGRAPHY

Amram bar Sheshna. *Seder Rav Amram Gaon*. Ed. Daniel Goldschmidt. Jerusalem: Mossad Harav Kook, 2004.

Appelfeld, Aharon. *Blooms of Darkness*. Transl. Jeffrey M. Green. New York: Schocken, 2010.

Arieli, Yitzhak. *'Eynayim le-Mishpat*. Tractate *Makkot*. Jerusalem: Mossad Harav Kook, 1959.

_____. *'Eynayim le-Mishpat. Bava Batra*, Part Two. Jerusalem, 1975.

Aristotle. *Nicomachean Ethics*.

Asher ben David. In *Otsar Nehmad* IV. Ed. Raphael Kirchheim. Vienna, 1864, pp. 37-43.

_____. *R. Asher ben David: His Complete Works and Studies in His Kabbalistic Thought*. Ed. Daniel Abrams. Los Angeles: Cherub, 1996.

Asher ben Yehiel. *She'elot u-Teshuvot ha-ROSh*. Constantinople, 1517.

_____. *Tosefot ha-ROSh 'al Masekhet Sotah*. Ed. Ya'akov Lifshitz. Jerusalem: Makhon Harry Fischel, 1968.

Ashkenazi, Hayyim Eliezer. "Heker ve-'Iyun be-Sifrei Rishonim (4)." *Yeshurun*, vol. 40 (Nisan 5779).

Ashkenazi, Tsevi. *She'elot u-Teshuvot Hakham Tsevi*. Amsterdam, 1712.

Auerbach, Benjamin Hirsch. *Sefer ha-Eshkol* with commentary *Nahal Eshkol*. Halberstadt, 1868-9.

Auerbach, Menahem Natan Nota. *Orah Ne'eman*. On *Shulhan 'Arukh, Orah Hayyim*. Jerusalem, 1924-1931.

Avivi, Yosef. *The Kabbalah of Rabbi A. I. Kook* (Hebrew). 4 vols. Jerusalem: Yad Ben-Zvi, 2018.

_____. *Kabbalat ha-GRA*. Jerusalem, 1993.

_____. *Zohar Ramhal*. Jerusalem, 1997.

Azriel of Gerona. *Be'ur 'Eser Sefirot 'al Derekh She'elah u-Teshuvah*. (Also known as *Sha'ar ha-Sho'el*.) Ed. Moshe Schatz.

Jerusalem, 1997.

———. Commentary to *Sefer Yetsirah*. (Misattributed to Rabbi Azriel's disciple Nahmanides.) Mantua, 1562.

———. *Commentary on Talmudic Aggadoth*. Ed. Isaiah Tishby. Jerusalem: Magnes, 1982.

———. *Derekh ha-Emunah ve-Derekh ha-Kefirah*. Ms. Halberstam 444. In Azriel of Gerona, *Be'ur 'Eser Sefirot 'al Derekh She'elah u-Teshuvah*. Ed. Moshe Schatz.

———. *She'elot u-Teshuvot*. In *Likkutim me-Rav Hai Gaon*. Warsaw, 1798.

Azulai, Abraham. *Hesed le-Avraham*. Amsterdam, 1685; Lvov, 1863, photo offset Jerusalem, 1968.

Azulai, Hayyim Joseph David (HYDA). *Birkei Yosef*. Commentary to *Shulhan 'Arukh*. 2 vols. Livorno, 1774-1776.

———. *Devash le-Fi*. Livorno, 1801.

———. *Hayyim Sha'al*. Responsa. 2 vols. Livorno, 1792-1795.

———. *Mahazik Berakhah*. Commentary to *Shulhan 'Arukh*, *Orah Hayyim* and *Yoreh De'ah*. Livorno, 1785.

———. *Shem ha-Gedolim*. Bibliography. 2 vols. Livorno, 1774, 1786.

Babad, Joseph. *Minhat Hinnukh*. Commentary to *Sefer ha-Hinukh*. Lvov, 1869.

Bachrach, Naftali. *'Emek ha-Melekh*. Amsterdam, 1648.

Bachrach, Ya'ir Hayyim. *Havot Ya'ir*. Responsa. Frankfurt am Main, 1699.

Baden, Joel S. *The Book of Exodus: A Biography*. Princeton, NJ: Princeton University Press, 2019.

Bahir. Attributed to Rabbi Nehunyah ben ha-Kanah. Amsterdam 1651. Facsimile edition in *The Book Bahir*. Ed. Daniel Abrams. Los Angeles: Cherub Press, 1994.

———. "Hiddushei ha-Bahir." In Cremona 1558 edition of *Zohar*. Facsimile in Daniel Abram's edition of *Bahir*.

_____. *Sefer ha-Bahir.* Ed. Reuven Margaliyot. With Commentary *'Or Bahir.* Jerusalem: Mossad Harav Kook, 1951.

Bahya ben Asher ibn Halawa. Commentary to Pentateuch. Ed. C.B. Chavel. 3 vols. Jerusalem: Mossad Harav Kook, 1966-1968.

Bahya ben Joseph ibn Pakuda. *The Book of Direction to the Duties of the Heart (Al-Hidaya ila Fara'id Al-Qulub).* Transl. Menahem Mansoor. London: Routledge & Kegan Paul, 1973.

Bar-Asher, Avishai. "Berikh Shemeh." *Tarbiz*, vol. 86 (5779), pp. 147-198.

Barg, Mordechai Gimpel. Notes of Rav Kook's lectures on *Kuzari.* In *Ma'amrei ha-RAYaH*, vol. 2.

Baruch of Kosov. *'Ammud ha-'Avodah.* Czernowitz, 1863.

Batt, Avi. "Lahashei ha-Havayah." Available at: https://bmj.org.il/wp-content/uploads/2019/12/2.51.BAT_.pdf

Be'ery, Yehoshua B. *Ohev Yisrael bi-Kedushah.* 5 vols. Tel-Aviv, 1989.

Benjamin, Walter. "The Task of the Translator." In *Walter Benjamin: Selected Writings*, vol. 1 (1913-1926). Ed. Marcus Bullock and Michael W. Jennings. Cambridge, Mass.: Harvard University Press, 1996.

Benson, Michael. *Space Odyssey: Stanley Kubrick, Arthur C. Clarke, and the Making of a Masterpiece.* New York: Simon and Schuster, 2018.

Berger, Yisrael. *Simhat Yisrael.* Piotrków, 1910.

Berlin, Naftali Tsevi Yehudah. *'Emek ha-NeTSIV.* Commentary to Sifre. 3 vols. Jerusalem, 1959-1961.

Berlin, Saul. *Besamim Rosh.* Berlin, 1793.

Bernfeld, Shim'on. *Da'at Elohim.* Warsaw, 1897-1899.

Besser, Yisroel. In *Mishpacha*, no. 191 (2 Shevat, 5768/January 9, 2008).

Bodoff, Lippman. "Jewish Mysticism: Medieval Roots, Contemporary Dangers and Prospective Challenges." Available at: http://www.edah.org/backend/coldfusion/search/document.cfm?title=Jewish+Mysticism:+Medieval+Roots,+Contemporary+Dangers+and+Prospective+Challenges&hyperlink=Bodoff3_1.htm&type=JournalArticle&category=Orthodoxy+and+Modernity&authortitle&firstname=Lippman&lastname=Bodoff&pubsource=not+available&authorid=531&pdfattachment=Bodoff3_1.pdf

Bokser, Ben Zion. *Abraham Isaac Kook*. Mahwah, NJ: Paulist Press, 1978.

Bornstein, Abraham. *Avnei Nezer: Yoreh De'ah*. Piotrków, 1913.

Bornstein, Aharon Israel. *Ne'ot ha-Deshe*. 2 vols. Tel-Aviv, 1983.

Bornstein, Samuel, of Sochatchov. *Shem mi-Shmuel*. On Pentateuch and Festivals. 8 vols. Piotrków, 1927; photo offset Jerusalem, 1974.

Boyarin, Daniel. "Two Introductions to the Midrash on the Song of Songs" (Hebrew). *Tarbiz* 56:4 (1987), pp. 479-500.

Breuer, Mordechai. *'Ohalei Torah*. Jerusalem: Shazar Center, 2004.

Brill, Allan. "Auxiliary to *Hokhmah*: The Writings of the Vilna Gaon and Philosophical Terminology." In *The Vilna Gaon and His Disciples*. Ed. Hallamish, Rivlin, and Shuchat. Ramat Gan: Bar-Ilan University Press, 2003.

Brown, Benjamin. *The Hazon Ish: Halakhist, Believer and Leader of the Haredi Revolution*. Hebrew. Jerusalem, 2011.

Buber, Martin. *Bein 'Am le-Artso*. Jerusalem: Schocken, 1944. In English: *On Zion: The History of an Idea*. Syracuse, NY: Syracuse University Press, 1997.

_____. *Gog u-Magog*. Tel-Aviv, 1944. In English: *For the Sake of Heaven*. Philadelphia: Jewish Publication Sociey, 1945.

BIBLIOGRAPHY

———. *Ich und Du*. Berlin: Schocken, 1922. In English: *I and Thou*. Edinburgh, 1937.

Bunin, Hayyim Yitzhak. Letter to Rav Kook. Available at: http://gnazimorg.startlogic.com/1935-1865-קוק-הכהן-יצחק-אברהם

———. *Mishneh HaBaD*, vol. 1, book 1, part 1. Warsaw, 1936.

Buzaglo, Shalom. *Hadrat Melekh*. On *Zohar*. London 1770; photo offset B'nei Berak, 1974.

Cardozo, Abraham, *Boker de-Avraham*. In manuscripts: Library of the Hungarian Academy of Sciences, Budapest, Ms. Kaufmann A 232; London Beth Din Ms. 124; Russian State Library, Moscow, Ms. Guenzburg 660; and Ms. Guenzburg 1109.

———. *Derush Zeh Eli ve-Anvehu*. Transcribed in Gershom Scholem. "Two new theological texts by Abraham Cardozo." Hebrew. *Sefunot*, vols. 3-4 (1960).

Celan, Paul. *Paul Celan: Poems*. Transl. M. Hamburger. New York: Persea Books, 1980.

Chajes, Tsevi Hirsch. *Hiddushei MaHaRaTs Hayyot*. Novellae to Talmud. Published in Vilna edition of Talmud.

———. *Torat Nevi'im*. Zolkiew, 1836.

Charitan, Levi Yitzhak. "Sha'ar Simukhim le-Rabbeinu El'azar mi-Germaiza (Ha-Rokeah)." In *Hitsei Giborim*, vol. 10 (Nissan, 5777/2017).

Charlop, Yehiel Mikhel. *Torat ha-Hof Yamim: Sefer ha-Zikaron*. New York, 1985.

Chotsh, Tsevi. *Hemdat Tsevi*. Amsterdam, 1706.

Cohen, Bezalel (*Dayyan* of Vilna). *Reshit Bikkurim*. Vilna, 1869; photo offset Jerusalem, 1969.

Cohen, David. *Kol ha-Nevu'ah*. Jerusalem: Mossad Harav Kook, 1979.

———. *Mishnat ha-Nazir*. Ed. Harel Cohen and Yedidyah Cohen. Jerusalem: Nezer David, 2005.

Cohen, Israel. *History of Jews in Vilna*. Philadelphia: Jewish Publication Society of America, 1943.

Cohen, Meir Simhah. *Meshekh Hokhmah*. Riga, 1927.

_____. *'Or Same'ah*. Commentary on *Mishneh Torah*.

Cohen, Solomon (Dayyan of Vilna). *Binyan Shelomo*. Vilna, 1889.

Copernicus, Nicolaus. *De Revolutionibus orbium coelestium* (*On the Revolutions of the Celestial Spheres*). 1543.

Corbin, Henri. "*Mundus Imaginalis* or, the imaginary and the imaginal." *Cahiers internationaux de symbolism*, vol. 6 (1964).

Cordovero, Moses. *Elimah*. Lvov, 1881.

_____. *Pardes Rimonim*. Munkatch, 1906.

_____. *Shi'ur Komah*. Warsaw, 1883.

Dadon, Yitzhak. *Athalta Hi*. 2 vols. Jerusalem, 2006, 2008.

Dan, Joseph. "A Bow to Frumkinian Hasidism." *Modern Judaism*, May 1991, pp. 175-194.

_____. *History of Jewish Mysticism and Esotericism: The Middle Ages*. vol. 6. Jerusalem: Zalman Shazar Center for Jewish History, 2011.

Danzig, Abraham. *Hayyei Adam*. Vilna, 1810.

David ben Levi of Narbonne. *Sefer ha-Mikhtam*. In *Ginzei Rishonim / Berakhot*. Ed. Moshe Hershler. Jerusalem: Makhon ha-Talmud ha-Yisraeli, 1967.

David, Bruria Hutner. *The Dual Role of Rabbi Zvi Hirsch Chajes: Traditionalist and* Maskil. Ph.D. dissertation. Columbia University 1971.

Delmedigo, Yosef Shelomo (*YaShaR mi-Candia*). *Novelot Hokhmah*. Basel, 1631.

Deutsch, Shaul Shimon. *Larger than Life: The Life and Times of the Lubavitcher Rebbe Rabbi Menachem Mendel Schneerson*.

2 vols. New York, NY, 1995-1997.

Don-Yahya, Eliezer. *Even Shetiyah*. Vilna, 1893.

Don Yahya, Hayyim. Responsum datelined "5653 [i.e., 1893], Shklov." In journal of the Skvere Kollel, *Zera' Ya'akov* 26 (Shevat 5766 [i.e., 2006]), pp. 17-21.

Don Yahya, Shabtai. *Rabbi Eliezer Don Yahya*. Jerusalem, 1932.

Don Yahya, Yehudah Leib. *Bikkurei Yehudah*. vol. 1. Lutzin, 1930. vol. 2. Tel-Aviv, 1939.

Dov Baer of Mezritch. *'Or Torah*. Ed. Rabbi Isaiah Dinowitz. Korets, 1804.

Duran, Simeon ben Tsemah. *Magen Avot*. Livorno, 1785.

Duran, Solomon ben Simon. *She'elot u-Teshuvot ha-RaShBaSh*. Livorno, 1742.

Edels, Samuel Eliezer (MaHaRaShA). *Hiddushei Aggadot*. Commentary to legends of Talmud. 2 vols. Lublin-Cracow, 1627-1631.

Eisenstadt (Asch), Meir. *Panim Me'irot*. Responsa. Amsterdam, 1715.

El'azar of Worms (Roke'ah). "Sha'ar Simukhim le-Rabbeinu El'azar mi-Germaiza (Ha-Rokeah)." Ed. Levi Yitzhak Charitan. In *Hitsei Giborim*, vol. 10 (Nissan, 5777/2017).

———. *Sodei Razayya* I-II. Ed. Aaron Eisenbach. Jerusalem, 2004.

Eliashov, Solomon. *Hakdamot u-She'arim*. Piotrków, 1909.

———. *Helek ha-Be'urim*. Jerusalem, 1935.

———. Letters to Naftali Herz Halevi Weidenbaum. In Moshe Schatz, *Ma'ayan Moshe*. Jerusalem, 2011.

———. *Sefer ha-De'ah* (=*Hu Derushei 'Olam ha-Tohu*). Piotrków, 1912.

Eliezer ben Hyrcanus (attributed to—). *Pirke deRabbi Eliezer*. Translated and annotated Gerald Friedlander. New York: Sepher-Hermon, 1981.

Eliezer of Metz. *Yere'im.* Venice, 1566.

Elijah Gaon of Vilna. *Aderet Eliyahu.* Commentary to Pentateuch. Warsaw, 1887.

_____. *Be'ur ha-GRA* to Proverbs. Ed. Menahem Mendel of Shklov. Shklov, 1798. Edited from manuscripts. Moshe Philip. Petah-Tikvah, 1985.

_____. *Be'ur ha-GRA* to *Shulhan 'Arukh.*

_____. *Be'ur ha-GRA* to *Sifra di-Tseni'uta.* Ed. Jacob Moses of Slonim. Vilna and Horadna, 1820. Ed. Samuel Luria. Vilna, 1882. Ed. Bezalel Naor. Jerusalem, 1997.

_____. *Be'ur ha-GRA* to *Tikkunei Zohar.* Vilna, 1867.

_____. *Yahel 'Or.* Commentary to *Zohar.* Ed. Naphtali Herz Halevi [Weidenbaum] of Bialystok. Vilna, 1882.

Elior, Rachel. "*Bein ha-heikhal ha-artsi la-heikhalot ha-shamaymiyim: ha-tefilah ve-shirat ha-kodesh be-sifrut ha-heikhalot ve-zikatan la-masorot ha-keshurot ba-mikdash.*" *Tarbiz* 64:3 (1995), pp. 341-380.

_____. "The Merkavah tradition and the emergence of Jewish mysticism: from Temple to Merkavah, from Hekhal to Hekhalot, from priestly opposition to gazing upon the Merkavah." *Sino-Judaica* (1999), pp. 101-158.

_____. "The priestly nature of the mystical heritage in *Heykalot* literature." In *Expérience et écriture mystiques dans les religions du livre.* Ed. Paul B. Fenton and Roland Goetschel. Leiden: Brill, 2000. pp. 41-54.

_____. "*Sifrut ha-heikhalot ve-ha-merkavah: zikatah la-mikdash, la-mikdash ha-shamaymi u-le-mikdash me'at.*" In *Retsef u-Temurah: Yehudim ve-Yahadut be-Erets Yisrael ha-Bizantit-Notsrit* (Continuity and Renewal: Jews and Judaism in Byzantine-Christian Palestine). Ed. Yisrael L. Levin. Jerusalem: Yad Ben-Zvi, 2004. pp. 107-142.

_____. *The Theory of Divinity of Hasidut HaBaD.* Hebrew. Jerusalem: Magnes, 1982.

Emden, Jacob. *Mitpahat Sefarim.* Altona, 1768.

Emunat Hashem. Anonymous. Jerusalem, 1938.

Engel, Joseph. *Gilyonei ha-Shas.* 3 vols. Vienna, 1924-1937. 4th vol. Warsaw, 1938.

Entsiklopedia shel ha-Tziyonut ha-Datit. Ed. Yitzhak Raphael and Ge'ulah Bat-Yehudah. 6 vols. Jerusalem: Mossad Harav Kook, 1958-2000.

Epstein, Barukh. *Torah Temimah.* Commentary to Pentateuch. 5 vols. Vilna: Romm, 1902.

Epstein, Kalonymos Kalman. *Ma'or va-Shemesh.* Breslau, 1842.

Epstein, Pinhas. *Minhah Hareivah.* Commentary to Tractate *Sotah.* Jerusalem, 1923.

Epstein, Yitzhak Eizik, of Homel. *Hannah Ariel.* 3 vols. Berdichev: Sheftel, 1912.

_____. "*Iggeret Kodesh*" (Holy Epistle). Printed at conclusion of *Hannah Ariel*, Part 3: *Amarot Tehorot* (*Ma'amar ha-Shabbat,* etc.). Berdichev: Sheftel, 1912.

Ergas, Joseph. *Shomer Emunim.* Amsterdam, 1736.

Ettlinger, Jacob. *'Arukh la-Ner, Makkot.* Altona, 1855
_____. *'Arukh la-Ner, Sukkah.* Altona, 1858.

Even-Shmuel, Yehudah. *Midreshei Ge'ulah.* Giv'atayim-Ramat Gan: Mossad Bialik, 1968.

Eybeschuetz, Jonathan. *Kereiti u-Peleiti.* Commentary to *Shulhan 'Arukh, Yoreh De'ah.* Altona, 1763.

_____. (Attributed to—). *Shem 'Olam.* Pressburg, 1890-1.

_____. (Attributed to—). *Va-'Avo ha-yom el ha-'ayin.* Ed. Pawel Maciejko. Los Angeles, Cherub, 2014.

'Eyn Ya'akov. Legends of the Talmud. Ed. Jacob ibn Habib. 2 vols. Salonika, 1515-1522.

Ezra of Gerona. Commentary to Song of Songs. In *Kitvei Ramban*. Ed. C.B. Chavel, vol. 2.

Ezrahi, Shulamit. *Ha-Mashgi'ah Rabbi Meir*. Biography of Rabbi Meir Hadash. Jerusalem: Feldheim, 2001.

Falk, Marcia. "The *Wasf.*" In *The Song of Songs: Modern Critical Interpretations*. Ed. Harold Bloom. New York: Chelsea House Publishers, 1988.

Fano, Menahem Azariah da. *Ma'amar ha-Nefesh*. In *Ma'amrei ha-RaMA' mi-Fano*. Jerusalem: Yismah Lev, 1997.

Feldman, Tzvi. *Rav A.Y. Kook: Selected Letters*. Ma'aleh Adumim, 1986.

Ficino, Marsilio. *Commentarium in Convivium Platonis De Amore*. (Commentary on Plato's *Symposium on Love*.) Florence, 1484.

Filber, Ya'akov. *Le-'Oro*. Jerusalem, 1995.

Fisher, Shelomo Yehonathan Yehudah. *Beit Yishai*: *Derashot*. Jerusalem, 2003.

Forshlager, Michael Eliezer. *Torat Michael*. Ed. Dov Meir Krauser. Jerusalem, 1967.

Fox, Marvin. "Rav Kook: Neither Philosopher nor Kabbalist." In *Rabbi Abraham Isaac Kook and Jewish Spirituality*. Ed. David Shatz and Lawrence Kaplan. New York: NYU Press, 1995.

Fraenkel, Avinoam. *Nefesh HaTzimtzum*. 2 vols. Jerusalem: Urim, 2015.

Freimann, Avraham Hayyim. *Ha-ROSh ve-Tse'etsa'av*. Biography of Rabbi Asher ben Yehiel. Transl. Menahem Eldar. Jerusalem: Mossad Harav Kook, 1986.

Friedland-Ben Arza, Sarah. "*Shekhenut ve-korat gag—'al shnei 'ekronot darshanut tsuraniyim be-kitvei R' Zadok Hakohen mi-Lublin.*" In *Me'at la-Zaddik*. Ed. Gershon Kitsis. Jerusalem, 2000.

Friedman, Bezalel. *Ish Hasidekha*. Biography of Rabbi Levi Yitzhak Bender. Jerusalem, 1993.

Friedman, David, of Karlin. *She'elat David*. Piotrków, 1913.

Friedman, Shamma Yehudah. "Ha-Rambam ve-ha-Talmud." *Dinei Yisrael*, 26-27 (5769-5770).

Frumer, Aryeh Tsevi, of Kozhiglov. *Erets Tsevi*. Lublin, 1938.

Gabbai, Meir ibn. *'Avodat ha-Kodesh*. Venice, 1567; Warsaw, 1891, photo offset Jerusalem 1973.

———. *Derekh Emunah*. Padua, 1563.

Gelbstein, Hillel Moshe Meshel. *Mishkenot le-Abir Ya'akov*. Jerusalem, 1881.

Gellman, Jerome. "Buber's Blunder: Buber's Replies to Scholem and Schatz-Uffenheimer." *Modern Judaism*, February 2000, pp. 20-40.

Gershuni, Yehudah. "Be-'Inyan Keri'at Bikkurim." In *Kovets Ma'amarim*, included in *Shitah Mekubetset 'al Masekhet Pesahim*. Ed. Yehudah Gershuni. New York, 1966.

Gikatilla (Chiquitilla), Joseph. *Gates of Light*. Transl. Avi Weinstein. San Francisco, CA: HarperCollins, 1994.

———. *Ginat Egoz*. Ed. Mordechai Attiyah. Jerusalem: Yeshivat Ha-Hayyim ve-ha-Shalom, 1989.

———. *Sha'arei Orah*. Ed. Joseph Ben-Shlomo. 2 vols. Jerusalem: Bialik Institute, 1970.

Ginsburg, Aryeh Leib. "Hiddushei Sha'agat Aryeh 'al ha-Torah." *Arazim* 5 (Jerusalem, 2019), pp. 14-125.

———. *Turei Even*. Metz, 1781.

Glickman, C.S. *Mi-Pihem u-mi-Pi Ketavam*. Brooklyn, NY, 2008.

Goldberg, Mayer. *Margaliyot shel Torah*. Jerusalem, 1990.

Goldfeld, Lea Naomi. "Hilkhot Melakhim u-Milhamot u-Melekh ha-Mashiah." *Sinai* 96 (1985), pp. 67-79.

Goldman, Eliezer. *"Zikato shel ha-Rav Kook la-Mahshavah ha-Eropit."* In *Yovel Orot*. Ed. Binyamin Ish-Shalom and Shalom Rosenberg. Jerusalem: WZO, 1988.

Goldstoff, Yitzhak. *Mikdash ha-Kodesh*. 2 vols. *Hilkhot Beit ha-Behirah*; *Hilkhot Klei ha-Mikdash*. Jerusalem, 1994-1999.

Gottlieb, Efraim (Ed.). *The Hebrew Writings of the Author of* Tiqqunei Zohar *and* Ra'aya Mehemna. Hebrew. Jerusalem: The Israel Academy of Sciences and Humanities, 2003.

_____. *Mehkarim be-Sifrut ha-Kabbalah*. Ed. Joseph Hecker. Tel-Aviv, 1976.

Gottlieb, Shmuel Noah. *Ohalei Shem*. Pinsk, 1912.

Graetz, Heinrich. *Geschichte der Juden von den ältesten Zeiten bis auf die Gegenwart*. 11 vols. Leipzig: Leiner, 1853-1875.

_____. *History of the Jews from the Earliest Times to the Present Day*. Transl. Bella Löwy. London, 1891-1892.

Green, Arthur. "The Song of Songs in Early Jewish Mysticism." In *The Song of Songs: Modern Critical Interpretations*. Ed. Harold Bloom. New York: Chelsea House Publishers, 1988.

Grossman, Avraham. *Rashi: Religious Beliefs and Social Views*. Hebrew. Alon Shevut, 2016.

Gruenwald, Ithamar. "Mekoman shel masorot kohaniyot bi-yetsiratah shel ha-mistikah shel ha-merkavah ve-shel Shi'ur Komah." In *Early Jewish Mysticism*. Ed. Joseph Dan. Jerusalem, 1987. [=*Jerusalem Studies in Jewish Thought*, vol. 6, nos. 1-2, pp. 65-120.]

Habermann, Abraham M. "Shirat Harav." In *Sinai* 17 (5705/1945).

Halperin, David J. *Abraham Miguel Cardozo: Selected Writings*. Mahwah, NJ: Paulist Press, 2001.

Hariton, Moshe. "Ma'amar Rabbeinu ha-Zaken, 'Mi li ba-shamayim...'" Letter to Editor. *Heikhal ha-Besht*, no. 4, year 3 (Tishri 5766), pp. 167-168.

BIBLIOGRAPHY

Harlap, Jacob Moses. *Beit Zevul*. Part Six. Jerusalem: Beit Zevul and Harry Fischel Institute, 1966.

_____. *Hed Harim*. Letters to Abraham Isaac Kook. Ed. Tsevi Yehudah Kook. Jerusalem, 1953.

_____. *Hed ha-Hayyim ha-Yisraeliyim*. Jerusalem, 1912

_____. Letter to Hayyim Ya'akov Levene. In *Yeshurun* 30 (Nissan, 5774/2014), p. 501 (facsimile).

_____. Letter to Hizkiyahu Yosef Mishkovksi. In *Zeved Tov* (*Festschrift* for Rabbi Zevulun Charlop). Ed. Ari S. Zahtz. New York: Yeshiva University Press, 2008. Letter 7 (p. 103).

_____. Letter to Yehudah Klein (Amital). In *'Alon Shevut*, Year 5, no. 20 (Adar 5734), pp. 18-21. Included in 64-page brochure on Rabbi Harlap issued by the Israeli Ministry of Education. Ed. Aryeh Strikovsky, no. 271 (Tishri 5767), pp. 45-46. The brochure is available online: http://meyda.education.gov.il/files/tarbut/pirsumeagaf/kitveet/271pdf.pdf?fbclid=IwAR2uIdw9XhInuL_bW8LyHDq77j9J-QGkNxBgG4WorTDjbXHulQKlgLL5l1KU

_____. *Mei Marom*, vol. 1: Commentary to Maimonides' *Shemonah Perakim*. Jerusalem, 1945; photo offset Jerusalem: Beit Zevul, 1982.

_____. *Mei Marom*. vol. 5: Nimmukei ha-Mikra'ot. Jerusalem, 1981.

_____. *Mei Marom*. vol. 10: Leviticus. Jerusalem, 1997.

Haronian, Emanuel. *The Attitude to Human Self in the Teaching of Rav Kook and Rav Harlap*. Hebrew. MA Thesis. Ben-Gurion University, February 2020. Available at: www.academia.edu

Harvey, Steven. "Maimonides in the Sultan's Palace." In *Perspectives on Maimonides: Philosophical and Historical Studies*. Ed. Joel L. Kraemer. Oxford: Oxford University Press, 1991.

Harvey, Warren Zev. "Leibowitz's Anti-Greek Concept of the Messiah." Hebrew. *Iyyun*, vol. 42 (October 1993), pp. 517-520.

_____. Video of dialogue between Professors Yeshayahu Leibowitz and Zev (Warren) Harvey of 30/5/1993. Available at: https://www.youtube.com/watch?v=wkcnXAsFUgA

Haver (Wildman), Yitzhak Eizik. *Afikei Yam*. 2 vols. Jerusalem, 1994.

_____. *Pithei She'arim*. 2 parts. Warsaw, 1888; photo offset Tel-Aviv: Sinai, 1964.

Havlin, David. *Ve-Nitsdak Kodesh*. Jerusalem, 1981.

Havlin, Shelomo Zalman. *Ha-Mashpi'a*. Biography of Rabbi Shelomo Zalman Havlin. Jerusalem, 1982.

Hayes, Yitzhak. *Si'ah Yitzhak* to Tractate *Makkot*. Podgorze, 1900.

Hayyim ben Isaac, of Volozhin. *Nefesh ha-Hayyim*. Ed. Yissachar Dov Rubin. B'nei Berak, 1989.

Hazan, Abraham ben Nahman, of Tulchin. *Yemei ha-Tela'ot*. Jerusalem, 1933.

Heilman, Hayyim Meir. *Beit Rabbi*. 3 parts. Berdichev, 1902.

Heilprin, Menahem Menkhin. *Hagahot u-Be'urim* to Rabbi Hayyim Vital, *'Ets Hayyim*. Warsaw, 1891.

Heinemann, Isaak. *Ta'amei ha-Mitsvot be-Sifrut Yisrael*. Jerusalem, 1966.

Heller, Yom Tov Lipmann. *Tosefot Yom Tov*. Commentary to Mishnah. 6 vols. Prague, 1614-1617.

Henkin, Eitam. "Ki hekhin beit haroshet lehatir 'agunot." Study of Rabbi Joseph Shapotshnick. *Asif* 2 (2015).

_____. *Ta'arokh Lefanai Shulhan*. Biography of Rabbi Yehiel Mikhel Epstein, author of *'Arukh ha-Shulhan*. Israel: Maggid, 2018.

Herczeg, Yisrael. *Keren David, Makkot*. Jerusalem, 1982.

Herrera, Abraham Cohen de. *Casa de la Divinidad / Beit Elohim*. Translated from Spanish to Hebrew by Isaac Aboab da Fonseca. Amsterdam, 1655. Jerusalem, 2006.

———. *Puerta del Cielo / Sha'ar ha-Shamayim*. Translated from Spanish to Hebrew by Isaac Aboab da Fonseca. Amsterdam, 1655. Jerusalem, 2006.

Heschel, Abraham Joshua. "Did Maimonides Believe That He Attained Prophecy?" Hebrew. In *Louis Ginzberg Jubilee Volume*. Ed. Saul Lieberman et al. New York, 1945.

———. *The Prophets*. New York: Jewish Publication Society of America, 1962.

Hitchens, Christopher. *God Is Not Great*. (United Kingdom) Atlantic Books, 2007.

Hoffman, David Zvi. *Midrash Tanna'im* to the Book of Deuteronomy. Berlin, 1908.

Hoffman, Joshua. "Rav Kook's Mission to America." *Orot: A Multidisciplinary Journal of Judaism*, vol. 1 (5751/1991), pp. 78-99.

Hopstein, Israel ben Shabtai, of Kozhnits. *'Avodat Yisrael*. B'nei Berak: Pe'er mi-Kedoshim, 2013.

———. *Ner Israel*. Commentary to *Likkutim me-Rav Hai Gaon*. Piotrków, 1913.

Horowitz, Isaiah Halevi. *Shnei Luhot ha-Berit*. Amsterdam, 1648.

———. *Siddur ha-SheLaH*. Amsterdam, 1717. 2 vols. Jerusalem: Ahavat Shalom, 1998.

Hoshke, Reuben (Sofer) of Prague. *Yalkut Re'uveni*. Wilmersdorf, 1681.

Hoter ben Shelomo. *She'elot R. Hoter ben Shelomo*. Ed. Yosef Kafah. Jerusalem, 2001.

Hurwitz, Aharon Halevi, of Staroshelye. *'Avodat ha-Levi*. Commentary on Pentateuch. Lemberg, 1861-1862.

_____. *Sha'arei 'Avodah.* Shklov, 1821.

_____. *Sha'arei ha-Yihud ve-ha-Emunah.* Shklov, 1820.

Hurwitz, Pinhas Elijah, of Vilna. *Sefer ha-Berit.* Part 1. Brünn, 1797.

Hutner, Isaac. "'Holocaust'—A study of the term and the epoch it is meant to describe." *Jewish Observer,* October 1977.

_____. Letter to M.M. Schneerson. Datelined, "Monday, Va-Yakhel—Pekudei, 5737." In *Heikhal ha-Besht,* Year 11, no. 35 (Tishri 5774/2014), pp. 75-77.

_____. Letter to Tsevi Yehudah Hakohen Kook. Datelined, "28 Ellul 5722." In *Iggerot la-RAYaH.* Ed. Ben-Zion Shapira. 2nd edition, Jerusalem, 1990. Appendix, Letter 47 (p. 585).

_____. *Ma'amrei Pahad Yitzhak: Pesah.* Brooklyn, NY, 2017.

_____. *Ma'amrei Pahad Yitzhak: Sukkot.* New York, NY, 2002.

_____. *Pahad Yitzhak: Hanukkah.* New York, NY, 1989.

_____. *Pahad Yitzhak: Iggerot u-Ketavim.* Ed. Yonatan David. Brooklyn, NY, 2016.

_____. *Pahad Yitzhak: Rosh Hashanah.* New York, NY, 2003.

_____. *Reshimot Lev.* See *Rutta, Leibel.*

_____. *Sefer ha-Zikaron le-Maran Ba'al Pahad Yitzhak.* Ed. Yonatan David. Brooklyn, NY, 2014.

Ibn Ezra, Abraham. *Commentary to Pentateuch.* Ed. Asher Weiser. Jerusalem: Mossad Harav Kook, 1977.

_____. *Yesod Mora ve-Sod Torah.* Ed. Joseph Cohen and Uriel Simon. Ramat Gan: Bar-Ilan University Press, 2002.

Ibn Kaspi, Joseph. *'Ammudei Kesef u-Maskiyot Kesef.* Ed. Salomo Werbluner. Frankfurt am Main, 1848.

_____. *Mishneh Kesef* I. Ed. Isaac Last. Pressburg, 1905; photo offset Jerusalem, 1970.

_____. *Sefer ha-Mussar/Yoreh De'ah.* In Eliezer Ashkenazi of

Tunis, *Ta'am Zekenim*. Frankfurt am Main, 1854. In Isaac Last, *'Asarah Klei Kesef*. Pressburg, 1903.

———. *Shulhan Kesef*. Ed. Hannah Kasher. Jerusalem: Ben-Zvi Institute, 1996.

Ibn Sahula, Isaac. *Meshal ha-Kadmoni*. Venice, 1546.

Ibn Waqar, Joseph ben Abraham. *Shorashei ha-Kabbalah (Principles of the Qabbalah)*. Ed. Paul B. Fenton. Los Angeles: Cherub Press, 2004.

Idel, Moshe. *The Angelic World: Apotheosis and Theophany*. Hebrew. Tel-Aviv: Yedioth Ahronoth, 2008.

———. "The Kabbalah in Byzantium—Preliminary Remarks." In *Jews in Byzantium: Dialectics of Minority and Majority Cultures*. Ed. Robert Bonfil. Leiden: Brill, 2012.

———. *Kabbalah: New Perspectives*. New Haven: Yale University Press, 1988.

———. "Maimonides' *Guide of the Perplexed* and the Kabbalah." *Jewish History* 18 (2004).

———. *R. Menahem Recanati ha-Mekubal*. vol. 1. Jerusalem and Tel-Aviv: Schocken, 1998.

Ilan, Aharon. *'Eynei Yitzhak*. Biography of Rabbi Yitzhak Arieli. Jerusalem, 2018.

Ilan, Mordechai. *Torat ha-Kodesh*. 2 vols. B'nei Berak, 2006.

Isaac ben Abba Mari of Marseille. *'Ittur*. Venice, 1608.

Isaac ben Sheshet Perfet. *She'elot u-Teshuvot RIVaSh*. Constantinople, 1546-1547.

Isaac 'Or Zaru'a of Vienna. *'Or Zaru'a*. 2 vols. Zhitomir, 1862.

'Iyyun (Sefer ha-). Attributed to Rabbi Hammai. In *Likkutim me-Rav Hai Gaon*. Warsaw, 1798.

Jacob ben Asher. *Arba'ah Turim*. Piove di Sacco, 1475.

Jaffe, Mordechai Gimpel and Nathan Nota Luria. *Elef ha-Magen*. Commentary to Tractate *Horayot*. Warsaw, 1912.

James, William. *The Varieties of Religious Experience*. New York: Longmans, Green, & Co., 1902.

Jonathan ben David of Lunel. *Commentary by R. Jonathan of Lunel on Mishnah and Alfasi Tractates Megillah and Mo'ed Katan*. Hebrew. Ed. Samuel K. Mirsky. Jerusalem: Sura, n.d. (1956).

Judah ben Samuel of Regensburg. *Sefer Hasidim*. Ed. Jehuda Wistinetzki. Berlin: Mekitsei Nirdamim, 1893. With commentary *Mishnat Avraham* by Abraham Aaron Price. 2 vols. Toronto, 1955; New York, 1960.

⸺. *Sefer Hasidim*. Ed. Reuven Margaliyot. Jerusalem: Mossad Harav Kook, 1957.

Judah Halevi. *Book of Kuzari*. Transl. Hartwig Hirschfeld. New York: Pardes, 1946.

⸺. *Kuzari*. Transl. Yehudah Even-Shmuel. Tel-Aviv: Dvir, 1972.

Justman, Pinhas Menahem. *Siftei Tsaddik*. Piotrków-Bilgoraj, 1924-1935.

Kafah, Yahya ben Shelomo (Sliman). *'Amal u-Re'ut Ru'ah va-Haramot u-Teshuvatam*. Tel-Aviv, 1914; limited facsimile edition Jerusalem 1976.

Kafah, Yosef. "She'elot hakhmei Lunel u-teshuvot 'ha-Rambam' kelum mekoriyot hen?" In *Sefer Zikaron le-Harav Yitzhak Nissim*. Ed. Meir Benayahu. vol. 2. Jerusalem, 1985.

Kafka, Franz. "Jackals and Arabs." In *Der Jude*. Ed. Martin Buber. 1917.

Kagan, Israel Meir. *Mishnah Berurah*. Commentary to *Shulhan 'Arukh, Orah Hayyim*. 6 vols. Warsaw, 1884-1907.

Kahan, Moshe. "Joseph ibn Kaspi—From Arles to Majorca." *Iberia Judaica* VIII (2016), pp. 181-192.

Kalischer, Tsevi Hirsch. *Derishat Zion*. Lyck, 1862.

Kalmanson, Elhanan. *Ha-Mahshavah ha-Yisraelit*. Jerusalem,

1920; photo offset Jerusalem, 1967.

Kalmin, Richard. *Jewish Babylonia between Persia and Roman Palestine*. Oxford: Oxford University Press, 2006.

Kanarfogel, Ephraim. "Rashi's Awareness of Jewish Mystical Literature and Traditions." *Raschi und Seine Erbe*. Ed. Daniel Krochmalnik, Hanna Liss and Ronen Reichman. Heidelberg: Hochschule für Jüdische Studien, 2007. pp. 23-34.

Kanievsky, Hayyim. *Kiryat Melekh*. Commentary to *Mishneh Torah*. Bnei Berak, 1983.

Kaplan, Aryeh. *Meditation and Kabbalah*. York Beach, Maine: Samuel Weiser, 1985.

Kaplan, Lawrence J. *Maimonides—Between Philosophy and Halakhah: Rabbi Joseph B. Soloveitchik's Lectures on* The Guide of the Perplexed. Jerusalem: Urim, 2016.

Karelitz, Abraham Isaiah. *Hazon Ish, Orah Hayyim / Mo'ed*. Ed. Samuel Greineman. 3rd edition. B'nei Berak, 1967.

———. *Hazon Ish, Yoreh De'ah*. Ed. Samuel Greineman. B'nei Berak, 1962.

Karo, Joseph. *Beit Yosef*. Commentary on *Arba'ah Turim*. 4 vols. Venice-Sabbioneta, 1550-1559.

———. *Shulhan 'Arukh*. Venice: Bragadin, 1565.

Kasher, Menahem Mendel. *Mef'ane'ah Tsefunot*. New York, 1959.

———. *Torah Shelemah*. Talmudic-Midrashic encyclopedia on the Pentateuch. 42 vols. Jerusalem-New York, 1927-1992.

Kasher, Moshe Shelomo. *Ha-Ga'on ha-Rogatchovi ve-Talmudo*. Jerusalem, 1958.

Katz, Shlomo. "Rahav and Yehoshua: Imagination and Intellect." *Orot: A Multidisciplinary Journal*, vol. 1 (5751/1991).

(Keidaner, Ya'akov). *Matzref ha-'Avodah*. Koenigsberg, 1858.

Kenig, Gedaliah Aaron. *Hayyei Nefesh*. Tel-Aviv, 1968.

Kiener, Ronald C. "Jewish Mysticism in the Lands of the Ishmaelites: A Re-Orientation." In *The Convergence of Judaism and Islam: Religious, Scientific, and Cultural Dimensions*. Ed. Michael M. Laskier and Yaacov Lev. Gainesville: University Press of Florida, 2011.

Kitsis, Gershon. *"Mi-Peri Tsaddik."* Bibliography of Rabbi Zadok Hakohen. In *Me'at la-Zaddik*. Ed. Gershon Kitsis. Jerusalem, 2000.

Klausner, Israel. *Toledot "Nes Ziyonah" be-Volozhin*. Jerusalem: Mossad Harav Kook, 1954.

_____. *Vilna: "Jerusalem of Vilna," 1881-1939*. Hebrew. vol. 2. Israel: Ghetto Fighters' House, 1983.

Klonitzky-Kline, Solomon. *Otsar Ta'amei Hazal*. New York: Shulsinger, 1939.

Kohut, Alexander. *Aruch Completum*. 8 vols. Vienna, 1878-1892.

Kook, Abraham Isaac. *"Afikim ba-Negev."* In *Ha-Peless*. Berlin, 1903-1904. Photo offset in Moshe Zuriel. *Otserot ha-RAYaH*. Old series, vol. 2. Tel-Aviv, 1988, pp. 733-779.

_____. *'Arpilei Tohar*. Jerusalem, 1914. Jerusalem: Makhon RZYH Kook, 1983. Ed. Yitzhak Shilat (Greenspan).

_____. *"Ha-Aryeh ba-Sugar"* ("The Lion in the Cage"). Poem. In Moshe Zuriel. *Otserot ha-RAYaH*. Old series. vol. 3. n.p., n.d. [circa 1990], pp. 1281-1282.

_____. Commentary to *The Legends of Rabbah bar Bar Hannah*. Ed. Bezalel Naor. Monsey, NY: Orot/Kodesh, 2019.

_____. *'Ets Hadar ha-Shalem*. Ed. Judah Zoldan. Jerusalem, 1986.

_____. *'Eyn Ayah*. Commentary to *'Eyn Ya'akov* Legends of the Tamud. Ed. Ya'akov Filber. 4 vols. Jerusalem: Makhon RZYH, 1987-2000.

_____. *Hadarav*. Ed. Ron Sarid. Third edition. 2008

_____. *Haskamot ha-RAYaH*. Ed. Y.M. Yismah and B.Z Kahana. Jerusalem: Makhon RZYH, 1988.

____. *Haskamot ha-RAYaH* (1897-1928). Ed. Ari Yitzhak Shvat, Zuriel Hallamish, and Yohanan Fried. Jerusalem: Beit Harav, 2017.

____. *Hevesh Pe'er*. Ed. Yitzhak Arieli and Uri Segal Hamburger. Jerusalem, 1925.

____. *Iggerot ha-RAYaH*. Ed. Tsevi Yehudah Kook. vol. 1 (1888-1910). Second edition corrected. Jerusalem: Mossad Harav Kook, 1962.

____. *Iggerot ha-RAYaH*. Ed. Tsevi Yehudah Kook. vol. 2 (1911-1915). Second edition corrected. Jerusalem: Mossad Harav Kook 1961.

____. *Iggerot ha-RAYaH*. Ed. Tsevi Yehudah Kook. vol. 3 (1916-1919). Jerusalem: Mossad Harav Kook, 1965.

____. *Iggerot ha-RAYaH*. vol. 4 (1920-1925). Ed. Ya'akov Filber. Jerusalem: Makhon RZYH Kook, 1984.

____. *Iggerot ha-RAYaH*. vol. 5 (1922). Ed. Ze'ev Neuman. Jerusalem: Makhon RZYH Kook, 2019.

____. *Iggerot la-RAYaH*. Ed. Ben-Zion Shapira. Second edition expanded. Jerusalem: Makhon RZYH, 1990.

____. *'Ittur Soferim*. 2 vols. Vilna, 1888. In 1 vol. photo offset Jerusalem, 1974. With notes of Tsevi Yehudah Kook.

____. "Kelil Tif'eret." Rejoinder to Rabbi Turbowitz. In *Torah mi-Zion*. Jerusalem, 1900. Reprinted in *Hevesh Pe'er*. Ed. Yitzhak Arieli and Uri Segal Hamburger.

____. *Kevatsim mi-Ketav Yad Kodsho*. Ed. Boaz Ofen. 3 vols. Jerusalem, 2006, 2008, 2018.

____. *Kitsur Mesillat Yesharim*. Appended to Tsevi Yehudah Kook. *Li-Sheloshah be-Elul*. vol. 2. Jerusalem, 1947, pp. 23-31; reprinted in *Ma'amrei ha-RAYaH*. vol. 2. Jerusalem, 1984, pp. 273-276; and in Moshe Zuriel. *Otserot ha-RAYaH*. New series. vol. 2, pp. 297-300.

____. *The Koren Rav Kook Siddur*. Ed. Bezalel Naor. Jerusalem: Koren, 2017.

———. Letter to Yehudah Newman. Datelined "London, 21 Tevet, 5679" [i.e., December 24, 1918]. Available at: http://orot.com/newly-acquired-manuscript-rav-kook/

———. *Ma'amrei ha-RAYaH*. 2 vols. vol. 1. Ed. Elisha Langenauer and David Landau. Jerusalem, 1980. vol. 2. Ed. Elisha Aviner (Langenauer). Jerusalem, 1984.

———. *Metsi'ot Katan*. Ed. Harel Cohen. Israel: Maggid, 2018.

———. *Mishpat Kohen*. Jerusalem, 1937.

———. "*Ha-Misped bi-Yerushalayim*" ("The Lamentation in Jerusalem"). Eulogy for Theodor Herzl. In Bezalel Naor. *When God Becomes History: Historical Essays of Rabbi Abraham Isaac Hakohen Kook*, pp. 38-56.

———. *Mitsvat ha-RAYaH*. On *Shulhan 'Arukh, Orah Hayyim*. First published as appendix to Menahem Natan Nota Auerbach. *Orah Ne'eman*. Jerusalem, 1924-1931. Published separately in expanded edition. Ed. Tsevi Yehudah Kook. Jerusalem: Mossad Harav Kook, 1970.

———. *Orot*. Ed. Tsevi Yehudah Kook. Jerusalem, 1920. Enlarged Jerusalem, 1950.

———. *Orot*. Original 1920 edition. Transl. Bezalel Naor. Jerusalem: Maggid, 2015.

———. *Orot ha-Kodesh*. Ed. David Cohen. 3 vols. Jerusalem: 1938-1950. vol. 4. Ed. David Cohen and Yohanan Fried. Jerusalem: Mossad Harav Kook, 1990.

———. *Orot ha-Mitsvot*. In Moshe Zuriel. *Otserot ha-RAYaH*. Old Series, vol. 4. Tel-Aviv, 1992, pp. 28-47. Reprinted from *Be-Shemen Ra'anan* (Rabbi Natan Ra'anan-Kook Memorial Volume), vol. 1.

———. *Orot ha-Torah*. Ed. Tsevi Yehudah Kook. Jerusalem, 1940.

———. *Orot Yisrael*. Ed. Tsevi Yehudah Kook. Jerusalem, 1942.

BIBLIOGRAPHY

_____. *Otserot ha-Rayah.* Ed. Moshe Zuriel. Old series. 4 vols. Tel-Aviv, 1988-1992. New Series. 5 vols. Rishon le-Zion, 2002. vols. 6-7. Ed. Moshe Zuriel, Shai Hirsch, and Ari Shvat. Rishon le-Zion, 2016.

_____. *Pinkas Yod Gimel.* (Also *Pinkas Rishon le-Yaffo.*) Ed. Ben-Zion Shapira. Jerusalem: Makhon RZYH Kook, 2004. Reprinted in *Pinkesei ha-Rayah*, vol. 1, and in *Kevatsim mi-Ketav Yad Kodsho*, vol. 1.

_____. *Pinkesei ha-RAYaH.* 4 vols. Jerusalem: Makhon RZYH Kook, 2008-2017. vol. 1. Ed. Ben-Zion Shapira and Ze'ev Neuman. vol. 2. Ed. Ben-Zion Shapira and Levi Yitzhaki. vol. 3. Levi Yitzhaki. vol. 4. Tsevi Mikhel Levin and Ben-Zion Shapira.

_____. *Reish Millin.* London, 1917.

_____. *Reish Millin.* Part Two (*Ha-Shorashim*). Jerusalem: Makhon RZYH Kook, 2003.

_____. *Shabbat ha-Arets.* Jerusalem, 1910.

_____. *Shemonah Kevatsim.* 2 vols. Second Edition. Jerusalem, 2004.

_____. *Shemu'ot RAYaH: Bereshit/Shemot.* Ed. Kalman Eliezer Frankel and Hayyim Yeshayahu Hadari. 2nd edition. Jerusalem: WZO, 2015.

_____. *Siddur 'Olat Re'iyah.* Ed. Tsevi Yehudah Kook. 2 vols. Jerusalem, 1939, 1949.

_____. "Talelei Orot." In *Tahkemoni.* Bern, 1910. Reprinted in *Ma'amrei ha-RAYaH*, vol. 1. Jerusalem, 1980, pp. 18-28.

_____. *When God Becomes History: Historical Essays of Rabbi Abraham Isaac Hakohen Kook.* Ed. Bezalel Naor. New York, NY: Kodesh Press, 2016.

_____. *Ha-Yeshivah ha-Merkazit ha-'Olamit bi-Yerushalayim.* 12 pp. Jerusalem: Y.A. Weiss [1924].

_____. "Zer'onim." In *Ha-Tarbut ha-Yisraelit.* Ed. Alexander Ziskind Rabinowitz (*AZaR*) and Tsevi Yehudah Kook.

Jaffa, 1913. Reprinted in 1950 edition of *Orot*.

Kook, Tsevi Yehudah. *Li-Netivot Yisrael*. vol. 1. Tel-Aviv, 1967. vol. 2. Jerusalem, 1979.

⎯⎯⎯. *Li-Sheloshah be-Ellul*. Biography of Rabbi Abraham Isaac Kook. vol. 1. Jerusalem, 1938. vol. 2. Jerusalem, 1947.

⎯⎯⎯. *Mi-Tokh ha-Torah ha-Go'elet*. See *Schwartz, Hayyim Avihu*.

⎯⎯⎯. *Tsemah Tsevi: Iggerot Harav Tsevi Yehudah Hakohen Kook*. vol. 1 (1907-1919). Ed. Landau, Neuman, and Rahmani. Jerusalem, 1991.

Lachter, Hartley. "Spreading Secrets: Kabbalah and Esotericism in Isaac ibn Sahula's *Meshal ha-Kadmoni*." *Jewish Quarterly Review*, Vol. 100, No. 1 (Winter 2010), pp. 111-138.

Laine, Eliezer and S.Z. Berger. *Avnei Hen*. Annals of the Hen Family. Brooklyn, NY: Kehot, 2015.

Landau, Ezekiel. *Doresh le-Zion*. Ed. Samuel Landau. Prague, 1827.

Landes, Rachel. "My Father, Mayer Goldberg." October 15, 2009. Unpublished memoir.

Langermann, Y. Tzvi. "On Some Passages Attributed to Maimonides." Hebrew. In *Me'ah She'arim: Studies in Medieval Jewish Spiritual Life in Memory of Isadore Twersky*. Ed. Fleischer, Blidstein, Horowitz, and Septimus. Jerusalem: Hebrew University Magnes Press, 2001.

Laniado, Samuel. *Keli Yakar*. Commentary on Early Prophets. Venice, 1603.

Laufer, Mordechai Menashe. *Ha-Melekh bi-Mesibo*. 2 vols. Kefar Habad: Kehot, 1993.

Leiner, Gerson Hanokh. *'Eyn ha-Tekhelet*. Warsaw, 1891; photo offset New York, 1954.

⎯⎯⎯. Introduction to his father, Rabbi Ya'akov Leiner's *Beit*

Ya'akov, Bereishit. Warsaw, 1890. Also published separately as *Ha-Hakdamah ve-ha-Petihah*.
_____. *Sod Yesharim, Rosh Hashanah*. Warsaw, 1902.
_____. *Sod Yesharim, Sukkot*. Warsaw, 1903.
_____. *Sod Yesharim 'al ha-Torah*. Brooklyn, NY, 1971.

Leiner, Mordechai Yosef of Izbica. *Mei ha-Shilo'ah*. vol. 1. Vienna, 1860. vol. 2. Lublin, 1922.

Leiner, Mordechai Yosef El'azar. *Tif 'eret Yosef*. Jerusalem, 1961.

Leiner, Ya'akov. *Beit Ya'akov*. 3 vols. Genesis. Warsaw, 1890. Exodus. Lublin, 1903. Leviticus. Warsaw. 1937.
_____. *Seder Haggadah shel Pesah 'im Sefer ha-Zemanim*. Jerusalem, 2010.

Leiner, Yeruham. *Tif 'eret Yeruham*. Brooklyn, NY, 1967.

Lessing, Gotthold Ephraim. *Nathan der Weise* (*Nathan the Wise*). Berlin: C.F. Voss, 1779.

Levi, Gedaliah. "Kibbuts Derushei ha-Melakhim de-Mitu." In Jacob Tsemah, *Kol be-Ramah*. Ed. Eliyahu Attiah. Jerusalem: Makhon B'nei Yissachar, 2001.

Levin, Joshua Heschel. *'Aliyot Eliyahu*. Biography of Vilna Gaon. Jerusalem, 1989.

Levin, Sholom Dov Baer. *Mi-Beit ha-Genazim*. Brooklyn: Kehot, 2009.

Levinas, Emmanuel. *Difficile liberté: Essais sur le Judaïsme*. Paris, 1963.
_____. *Du sacré au saint : Cinq nouvelles lectures talmudiques*. Paris, 1977.
_____. *L'Au-delà du verset : Lectures et discours talmudiques*. Paris, 1982.
_____. *Quatre lectures talmudiques*. Paris, 1968.

Levinger, Jacob. *Maimonides' Techniques of Codification: A Study in the Method of* Mishneh Torah. Hebrew. Jerusalem: Magnes, 1965.

Lewin, Benjamin Menashe. *Otsar ha-Ge'onim*. 12 vols. Haifa-Jerusalem, 1928-1943.

Lichtenstein, Aharon. "R. Joseph Soloveitchik." In *Great Jewish Thinkers of the Twentieth Century*. Ed. Simon Noveck. Clinton, Mass: B'nai B'rith, 1963.

Lieberman, Saul. *Hellenism in Jewish Palestine*. New York, 1994.

_____. Letter to Louis Ginzberg. In Marc B. Shapiro, *Saul Lieberman and the Orthodox*.

_____. *Midreshei Teiman*. Jerusalem, 1940.

_____. *Mishnat Shir ha-Shirim*. Appendix to Gershom Scholem. *Jewish Gnosticism, Merkabah Mysticism and Talmudic Tradition*, pp. 118-126.

_____. *Sheki'in*. Jerusalem, 1939.

_____. *Tosefta ki-Fshutah*. Commentary to *Tosefta*. 10 vols. New York, 1955-1988.

Liebes, Yehuda. *Studies in the Zohar*. Albany: State University of New York Press, 1993.

Lifschitz, Hayyim. *Shivhei ha-RAYaH*. Jerusalem, 1995.

Lifshitz, Dov Baer. *Golot 'Iliyot*. On Tractate *Mikva'ot*. Warsaw, 1887.

Lifshitz, Jacob Koppel, of Mezritch. *Sha'ar Gan 'Eden*. Koretz, 1803.

Lintop, Pinhas. *Binyan ha-'Ummah*. Piotrków, 1907.

_____. *Kana'uteh de-Pinhas*. Ed. Bezalel Naor. Spring Valley, NY: Orot, 2013.

_____. *Yalkut Avnei Emunat Yisrael*. Warsaw, 1895.

Lobel, Diana. *A Sufi-Jewish Dialogue: Philosophy and Mysticism in Bahya Ibn Paquda's* Duties of the Heart. Philadelphia: University of Pennsylvania Press, 2007.

Löw, Judah ben Bezalel (MaHaRaL) of Prague. *Gevurot Hashem*. Cracow, 1582. London: L. Honig & Sons, 1954.

_____. *Hiddushei Aggadot*. 4 vols. London: L. Honig & Sons, 1960.

_____. *Netsah Yisrael*. Prague, 1599. London: L. Honig & Sons, 1957.

_____. *Tif'eret Yisrael*. Venice: Daniel Zanetti, 1599. London: L. Honig & Sons, 1955.

Luboshitz, Tzvi. "An Early Version of the *Simsum* Debate in Immanuel Hay Ricchi's *Yosher Levav*." *Kabbalah*, 42 (2018), pp. 267-320.

Luria, David. *Be'ur ha-RaDaL*. Commentary to *Pirkei de-Rabbi Eliezer*. Warsaw, 1852.

Luzzatto, Moses Hayyim. *Adir ba-Marom* II. Ed. Yosef Spinner. Jerusalem, 1988.

_____ (attributed to—). *KaLaH Pithei Hokhmah*. Koretz, 1785. Ed. Yosef Spinner. Jerusalem, 1987.

_____. *Ma'amar ha-Ge'ulah*. Ed. H. Touitou. n.p., 2002.

_____. *Mesillat Yesharim* (Dialogue Version from Ms. Günzburg 1206, Russian State Library, Moscow; and Thematic Version from first edition, Amsterdam, 1740). Ed. Avraham Shoshana. Jerusalem: Ofeq, 1994.

Ma'arekhet ha-Elohut. Mantua, 1558.

Maccoby, Hayyim Zundel. *Imrei Hayyim*. Ed. Max Mansky. Tel-Aviv, 1929.

Maimon, Solomon. *Giv'at ha-Moreh*. Commentary to *Moreh Nevukhim*. Sulzbach, 1828.

Malbim (Wisser), Meir Leibush. *Mikra'ei Kodesh*. Commentary on the Prophets and Hagiographa. Warsaw, 1874.

Malka, Solomon. *Monsieur Chouchani: L'énigme d'un maitre du XXème siècle*. Paris, 1994.

Margaliyot, Abraham Tsevi. *Keren 'Orah*. Commentary to Pentateuch. Jerusalem, 1986.

Margaliyot, Hayyim Mordechai. *Sha'arei Teshuvah*. Commentary to *Shulhan 'Arukh*. Dubno: Press of Hayyim Mordechai Margaliyot, 1820 (completed 1825).

Margaliyot, Reuven. *Mal'akhei 'Elyon*. Jerusalem: Mossad Harav Kook, 1988.

    _____. *Margaliyot ha-Yam*. On Tractate *Sanhedrin*. Jerusalem: Mossad Harav Kook, 1958.

    _____. *Nitsutsei 'Or*. Notes to *Zohar*. In *Zohar*. Ed. Reuven Margaliyot. Jerusalem: Mossad Harav Kook, 2002.

    _____. *Shem 'Olam*. Jerusalem: Mossad Harav Kook, 1989.

    _____. *Yesod ha-Mishnah va-'Arikhatah*. Lwów, 1933.

Mark, Zvi. *Mistikah ve-Shiga'on bi-Yetsirat R. Nahman mi-Breslov* (*Mysticism and Madness in the Work of R. Nahman of Bratslav*). Tel Aviv, 2003.

    _____. *The Scroll of Secrets: The Hidden Messianic Vision of R. Nachman of Breslav*. Brighton, Mass.: Academic Studies Press, 2010.

Marx, Karl. *The Portable Karl Marx*. Ed. Eugene Kamenka. New York: Penguin, 1983.

Mayse, Ariel Evan. "Tree of Life, Tree of Knowledge: Halakha and Theology in *Ma'or va-Shamesh*." *Tradition* 51:1 (2019).

Meir, Jonatan. "Hillel Zeitlin, William James and Hasidism." Lecture delivered March 7, 2016 at "Life as a Dialogue," International Conference in Honor of Ephraim Meir, Bar Ilan University. Available at youtube:

https://www.youtube.com/watch?v=h2TKkSbwcsA

Menahem ben Solomon ha-Me'iri. *Beit ha-Behirah, Berakhot*. Ed. Shmuel Dikman. Jerusalem: Makhon ha-Talmud ha-Yisraeli, 1965.

    _____. *Beit ha-Behirah, Megillah*. Ed. Moshe Hershler. Jerusalem: Makhon ha-Talmud ha-Yisraeli, 1968.

    _____. *Beit ha-Behirah, Sukkah*. Ed. Avraham Liss. Jerusalem: Makhon ha-Talmud ha-Yisraeli, 1966.

    _____. *Beit ha-Behirah, Yoma*. Ed. Yosef Klein. Jerusalem:

Makhon ha-Talmud ha-Yisraeli, 1970.

Messer, Isaac. *U-Mi-Midbar Matanah*. Ed. Moshe Hallamish. Jerusalem, 1985.

Meyuhas ben Elijah. Commentary to Exodus. Ed. A.W. Greenup. Budapest, 1929.

Midrash Debarim Rabbah (from Oxford ms.). Ed. Saul Lieberman. Jerusalem, 1940.

Midrash Mishlei. Ed. Solomon Buber. Vilna: Romm, 1893.

Midrash Tehillim. Ed. Solomon Buber. Vilna: Romm, 1891.

Mirsky, Yehudah. *Rav Kook: Mystic in a Time of Revolution*. New Haven: Yale University Press, 2014.

Mohr, Melissa. *Holy Sh*t: A Brief History of Swearing*. Oxford: Oxford University Press, 2013.

Moinester, Uri. *Karnei Re'em*. New York, 1951.

Mondshine, Yehoshua. "*Asifat ha-Rabbanim be-Rusya bi-Shenat 'Atar.*" *Kefar Habad*, no. 898. Available online at: http://www.shturem.net/index.php?section=blog_new&article_id=24

———. "*'Likkutei Torah' le-Shalosh Parshiyot.*" *Kefar Habad*, nos. 931, 933. Available online at: http://www.shturem.net/index.php?section=blog_new&article_id=29

Monson, Levi Yitzhak, of Ozerna. *Bekha Yevarekh Yisrael*. Przemysl, 1905.

Moses ben Hisdai Taku. *Ketav Tamim*. Ed. Raphael Kirchheim. In *Otsar Nehmad*, vol. 3. Vienna, 1860. Facsimile of manuscript of *Ketav Tamim*. Akademon, 1984.

Moses ben Maimon (Maimonides). *Commentary to the Mishnah*. Ed. Yosef Kafah. 3 vols. Jerusalem: Mossad Harav Kook, 1963-1968.

———. *The Guide of the Perplexed*. Transl. Shlomo Pines. Chicago: University of Chicago Press, 1963.

———. *Iggerot ha-Rambam*. Ed. Yitzhak Shilat (Greenspan).

2 vols. Ma'aleh Adumim, 1987-1988.

———. *Iggerot ha-Rambam*. Ed. Yosef Kafah. Jerusalem: Mossad Harav Kook, 1972.

———. *Mishneh Torah: The Book of Knowledge*. Transl. Moses Hyamson. Jerusalem: Feldheim, 1971.

———. *Moreh ha-Nevukhim*. Transl. Judah al-Harizi. Ed. S. Scheier and S. Munk. 2 vols. Tel-Aviv: Mossad Harav Kook, circa 1965.

———. *Moreh Nevukhim*. 2 vols. Transl. Michael Schwarz. Jerusalem: Tel-Aviv University Press, 2002.

———. *Moreh Nevukhim*. Transl. Samuel ibn Tibbon. With commentary *Giv'at ha-Moreh* (by Solomon Maimon). Sulzbach, 1828.

———. *Moreh ha-Nevukhim*. Transl. Yosef Kafah. 3 vols. Jerusalem: Mossad Harav Kook, 1972.

———. *Pe'er ha-Dor*. Amsterdam, 1765.

———. *Sefer ha-Mitsvot 'im Hasagot ha-Ramban*. Ed. C.B. Chavel. Jerusalem: Mossad Harav Kook, 1981.

———. *Teshuvot ha-Rambam*. Ed. Alfred Freimann. Jerusalem: Mekize Nirdamim, 1934.

———. *Teshuvot ha-Rambam*. Ed. Joshua Blau. 3 vols. Jerusalem: Mekitzei Nirdamim, 1958-1961.

Moses ben Nahman (Nahmanides). Commentary to Pentateuch. Ed. C.B. Chavel. 2 vols. Jerusalem: Mossad Harav Kook, 1959-1960.

———. *Kitvei Rabbeinu Moshe ben Nahman*. Ed. C.B. Chavel. 2 vols. Jerusalem: Mossad Harav Kook, 1963-1964.

———. *Sefer Iyov 'im Peirush ha-Ramban*. Commentary to Book of Job. Ed. Yehudah Leib Friedman. Israel: Feldheim, 2018.

———. "Torat Hashem Temimah." In *Kitvei Rabbeinu Moshe ben Nahman*. vol. 1.

Moses of Coucy. *Sefer Mitsvot Gadol (SeMaG)*. Rome, before 1480.

BIBLIOGRAPHY

Moshav Zekenim. Ed. Solomon David Sassoon. London, 1959.

Nahman ben Simhah, of Breslov. *Likkutei MOHaRaN.* Appended variants in Rabbi Nathan Sternhartz's manuscript. Ed. Nathan Tsevi Kenig. Jerusalem, 1985.

_____. *Shir Na'im/Song of Delight.* Ed. David Sears and Bezalel Naor. Spring Valley, NY: Orot, 2005.

Nahmani, Moshe. "Mi Kan Hillel?" *Mussaf Shabbat, Makor Rishon,* 3 Ellul, 5771 (2.9.2011).

_____. "She'areha Ne'ulim—Yeshivat Harav Kuk be-Yaffo." Available on the website www.shoresh.org.il. Dated 4/17/2012 or 25 Nissan, 5772.

_____. *Shnei ha-Me'orot.* 2019

Naor, Bezalel. "Ascent and Descent in the Yom Kippur Rite: From the Hasidic Thought of Izbica-Radzyn." In *From A Kabbalist's Diary.* Spring Valley, NY: Orot, 2005.

_____. *Avirin.* Jerusalem: Zur-Ot, 1980.

_____. "The Curtains of the Tabernacle: R. Shelomo Zalman of Kopyst." In *Orot: A Multidisciplinary Journal of Judaism,* vol. 1 (5751/1991), pp. 33-41. Ed. Bezalel Naor.

_____. *From A Kabbalist's Diary: Collected Essays.* Spring Valley, NY: Orot, 2005.

_____. *Kabbalah and the Holocaust.* Spring Valley, NY: Orot, 2001.

_____. *The Kabbalah of Relation: "We Would Have Learned the 'Way of the Earth' From the Cock"* (A Jewish Bestiary). Spring Valley, NY: Orot, 2012.

_____. *Lev Atsal.* Commentary to Maimonides' *Sefer ha-Madda'.* n.p., 5733/1973.

_____. *Lights of Prophecy/Orot ha-Nevu'ah.* New York: Union of Orthodox Jewish Congregations of America, 1990.

_____. *The Limit of Intellectual Freedom: The Letters of Rav Kook.* Spring Valley, NY: Orot, 2011.

_____. *Mahol la-Tsaddikim*. Jerusalem and Monsey: Makhon RaMHaL/Orot, 2015.

_____. *Post-Sabbatian Sabbatianism*. Spring Valley, NY: Orot, 1999.

_____. "Rav Kook and Emmanuel Levinas on the 'Non-Existence' of God." In *Orot: A Multidisciplinary Journal of Judaism*, vol. 1 (5751/1991), pp. 1-11. Reprinted in Bezalel Naor, *From a Kabbalist's Diary: Collected Essays*.

_____. "Reish Millin—Mekorot ve-He'arot." In *Sinai* 97 (Nissan-Ellul 5745/1985), pp. 69-76. Also issued as *Zikhron RAYaH* (Memorial Volume on Rav Kook's Fiftieth *Yahrzeit*). Ed. Yitzhak Raphael. Jerusalem: Mossad Harav Kook, 1986.

_____. "*Shir Na'im* as a Reply to Maimonides." In Nachman of Breslov, *Shir Na'im/Song of Delight*. Ed. David Sears and Bezalel Naor. Spring Valley, NY: Orot, 2005, pp. 123-126.

_____. *Shod Melakhim*. Jerusalem: Makhon RaMHaL/Orot, 2017.

_____. *When God Becomes History: Historical Essays of Rabbi Abraham Isaac Hakohen Kook*. New York, NY: Kodesh, 2016.

_____. "'Zedonot na'asot ke-zakhuyot' be-mishnato shel Harav Kuk." In *'Ofer ha-Ayyalim: Sefer Zikaron le-ha-Kadosh 'Ofer Eliyahu Cohen*. Ed. Dani Kokhav (Koch). Jerusalem, 1994.

Nasr, Seyyed Hossein (Ed.). *The Study Quran: A New Translation and Commentary*. New York: HarperOne, 2015.

Nathan ben Yehiel of Rome. *'Arukh*. n.p. (Rome?), n.d. (circa 1477).

Nathan of Gaza. *Sefer ha-Beri'ah*. Ed. Leor Holzer. Jerusalem: Holzer, 2019.

Neiman, Yitzhak. *Zikhron Yitzhak*. Memorial volume. Jerusalem, 1999.

Neriyah, Moshe Tsevi. *Bi-Sdeh ha-RAYaH*. Tel-Aviv, 1991.

———. *Hayyei ha-RAYaH*. Tel-Aviv, 1983.

———. *Likkutei ha-Rayah*. Tel-Aviv, 1990.

———. *Mo'adei ha-Rayah*. 1st edition. Bnei Berak, 1991. 2nd edition. Jerusalem, 2015.

———. *Sihot ha-RAYaH*. 1st edition. Tel-Aviv, 1979. 2nd edition. Jerusalem, 2015.

———. *Tal ha-RAYaH*. Tel-Aviv, 1993.

Nietzsche, Friedrich. *Also Sprach Zarathustra*. Leipzig, 1883-1885. In English: *Thus Spoke Zarathustra*. In *Nietzsche*. Ed. Walter Kaufmann. New York: Viking Press, 1968.

———. *Die Geburt der Tragödie aus dem Geiste der Musik*. Leipzig, 1872. In English: *The Birth of Tragedy*. Edinburgh, 1909.

Nirenberg, David. *Anti-Judaism: The Western Tradition*. New York: W.W. Norton, 2013.

Nissim ben Reuben Gerondi. *Derashot ha-RaN*. Ed. Leon A. Feldman. Jerusalem: Shalem, 1973.

Offenberg, Sarah. "On Heresy and Polemics in Two Proverbs in *Meshal Haqadmoni*." Hebrew. *Jewish Thought* 1 (2019).

Otto, Rudolf. *Das Heilige*. Breslau, 1917. In English: *The Idea of the Holy*. [London]: Oxford University Press, 1923.

Ouaknin, Marc-Alain. *The Burnt Book: Reading the Talmud*. Transl. Llewelyn Brown. Princeton, 1995.

Pachter, Mordechai. "The Gaon's Kabbalah from the Perspective of Two Traditions." Hebrew. In *The Vilna Gaon and his Disciples*. Ed. M. Hallamish, Y. Rivlin and R. Shuchat. Ramat-Gan: Bar-Ilan University Press, 2003. pp. 119-136.

Palache, Hayyim. *Re'eh Hayyim*. On Pentateuch. Part One. Saloniki, 1860. Part Two. Izmir, 1865.

Pardo, David. *Maskil le-David.* Super-commentary to Rashi. Venice, 1760.

Pesikta Rabbati. Ed. Meir Ish-Shalom. Vienna, 1880.

Piekarz, Mendel. *Studies in Braslav Hasidism.* Hebrew. Jerusalem: Mossad Bialik, 1995.

Plato. *Republic.*

———.*Timaeus*

Plotski, Meir Dan. *Keli Hemdah.* Piotrków, 1906.

Pomeranchik, Aryeh. *Yehegeh ha-Aryeh.* Jerusalem, 1999.

Poppers, Meir. *Me'orei 'Or.* In *Me'orot Natan.* 1st edition. Frankfurt am Main, 1709. 2nd edition. Warsaw, 1867; photo offset in *Sifrei ha-'Arakhim be-Kabbalah*, Jerusalem, 1995.

———. *'Or Zaru'a.* Ed. Safrin and Sofer. Jerusalem: Hevrat Ahavat Shalom, 1986.

Porath, Israel. "Harav A.Y. Kook z"l." In *Sefer ha-Do'ar: Mivhar ma'amarim la-yovel ha-shishim 5682-5742.* Ed. Miklishanski and Kabakoff. New York: Histadrut ha-[]Ivrit ba-Amerika, 1982.

———. *Mavo ha-Talmud (The Outline of the Talmud).* 7 vols. St. Louis, MO-New York, 1942-1960.

Price, Abraham Aaron. *Sefer Hasidim* with commentary *Mishnat Avraham.* 2 vols. Toronto, 1955; New York, 1960.

Ra'anan, Shalom Natan. *Be-Shemen Ra'anan.* Rabbi Natan Ra'anan-Kook Memorial Volume. Ed. Ben-Zion Shapira. 2 vols. Jerusalem: Makhon RZYH, 1990-1991.

Rabbinowicz, Raphael Nathan Nata. *Dikdukei Soferim. Variae lectiones* of Talmud. 16 vols. Munich, 1867-1886.

Rabinovitch, Nahum L. *Yad Peshutah.* Commentary to Maimonides' *Yad ha-Hazakah.* 21 vols. Jerusalem, 1984-2019.

Rabinowicz, Shelomo Hakohen, of Radomsk. *Tif'eret Shelomo.* 2 vols. Pentateuch; Festivals. Warsaw, 1867-1869. Reprinted

Jerusalem, 1992.

Rabinowitz, David Yitzhak Eizik, of Skolya-Vienna-Brooklyn. *Mekor ha-Berakhah*. On Tractate *Berakhot*. Brooklyn, 1967.

Rabinowitz, Zadok Hakohen, of Lublin. *Divrei Soferim*. Lublin, 1913; photo-offset B'nei Berak, 1967.

_____. *Dover Zedek*. Piotrków, 1911; photo-offset B'nei Berak, 1967.

_____. *Komets ha-Minhah*. Lublin, 1939; photo-offset B'nei Berak, 1967.

_____. *Mahshevot Haruts*. Piotrków, 1912; photo-offset Bnei Berak, 1967.

_____. *Peri Zaddik*. Commentary on Pentateuch. 5 vols. Lublin, 1901-1934; photo offset Jerusalem, 1972.

_____. *Poked 'Akarim*. Piotrków, 1922; photo-offset Bnei Berak, 1967.

_____. *Sefer ha-Zikhronot*. Appended to *Divrei Soferim*.

_____. *Sihat Mal'akhei ha-Sharet*. Lublin, 1927; photo offset B'nei Berak 1967.

_____. *Tsidkat ha-Tsaddik*. Lublin, 1902; Lublin, 1913, photo offset B'nei Berak 1967.

_____. *Yisrael Kedoshim*. Lublin, 1928; photo offset B'nei Berak 1967.

(Rabinowitz-Te'omim, Elijah David [ADeReT]). *Aharit ha-Shanim*. Warsaw, 1893.

Raccah, Mas'ud Hai. *Ma'aseh Rokah*. Commentary to *Mishneh Torah*. 3 vols. Venice-Livorno, 1742-1766. vol. 4. Tel-Aviv, 1964.

Rath, Meshulam. *She'elot u-Teshuvot Kol Mevaser*. Jerusalem: Mossad Harav Kook, 1955.

Rapoport, Chaim. *The Afterlife of Scholarship: A Critical Review of 'The Rebbe' by Samuel Heilman and Menachem Friedman*. 2011.

Raziel ha-Mal'akh. Amsterdam, 1701.

Ricchi, Immanuel Hai. *Yosher Levav*. Amsterdam, 1742.

Rivkin, Moshe Dov Baer. *Tif'eret Zion*. New York, 1975.

Roke'ah, El'azar. See *El'azar of Worms*.

Rosanes, Judah. *Mishneh le-Melekh*. Commentary to *Mishneh Torah*. Constantinople, 1731.

Rosen, Joseph, of Rogatchov and Dinaburg (Dvinsk). *Tsaphnat Pa'ne'ah*. Commentary to *Mishneh Torah*. Parts 1 and 2. Warsaw, 1902

———. *Tsafnat P'ane'ah*. Commentary to *Mishneh Torah*. Kuntres Hashlamah. Warsaw, 1909.

———. *Tsafnat P'ane'ah*. Commentary to *Mishneh Torah*. Mahadura Tinyana. Dvinsk, 1930.

———. *Tsafnat P'ane'ah*. Commentary to *Moreh Nevukhim*. Appended to Commentary to Pentateuch, vol. 6.

———. *Tsaphnat Pa'ne'ah*. Commentary to Pentateuch. Ed. Menahem Mendel Kasher. 6 vols. Jerusalem, 1960-1965.

———. *Tsaphnat P'ane'ah*. Tractate *Makkot*. Ed. Menahem Mendel Kasher. New York: Shulsinger Bros., 1959.

———. *She'elot u-Teshuvot Tsafnat Pa'ne'ah ha-Hadashot*. 3 vols. Modi'in 'Ilit, 2012.

Rosenberg, Shalom. *Darkhei Shalom* (Shalom Rosenberg Festschrift). Ed. Benjamin Ish-Shalom. Jerusalem, 2007.

Rosenfeld, Ben Zion. "*Yahaso shel ha-RAYaH Kook le-Hakhmei ha-Mizrah bi-Tekufat Yaffo 5664-5674 (1904-1914)*" ("Ha-Rav Avraham Isaac HaCohen Kook and his Attitude Regarding the Sephardi Sages During His Stay in Jaffa567–5664 1914–1904]4]"). *Libi ba-Mizrah* (*My Heart Is in the East*) 1 (2019), pp. 287-290.

Rosenwasser, Moshe Yehudah. "*Peirush ha-RaMBaN 'al ha-Torah le-'or ha-'imut 'im ha-Notsrut*." HaMa'ayan 47:2 (Tevet

5767), pp. 19-32.

Rotenberg, Moshe. *Bikkurei Aviv.* St. Louis, MO, 1942.

Rutta, Leibel. *Reshimot Lev.* Informal talks of Rabbi Isaac Hutner. 2 vols. softcover. Brooklyn, 1997. 2 vols. hardcover. Brooklyn, NY, 2000.

Sa'adyah ben Joseph al-Fayyumi. *Emunot ve-De'ot.* Ed. Yosef Kafah. Jerusalem: Sura/Yeshiva University, 1970.

Safran, Bezalel. "Maimonides on Free Will, Determinism and Esotericism." In *Porat Yosef: Studies Presented to Rabbi Dr. Joseph Safran.* Ed. Bezalel Safran and Eliyahu Safran. Hoboken, New Jersey: Ktav, 1992.

Saks, Jeffrey. "Rabbi Joseph B. Soloveitchik and the Israeli Chief Rabbinate: Biographical Notes (1959-60)." *B.D.D.* 17, September 2006, pp. 45-67.

Samson of Ostropolya. *Nitsutsei Shimshon.* Ed. Avraham Ya'akov Bombach. Jerusale, 2013.

Schäfer, Peter. *Synopse zur Hekhalot-Literatur.* Tübingen 1981.

Schirmann, Hayyim. "Maimonides and Hebrew Poetry." Hebrew. *Moznayim* 3 (1935):433-436.

Schneersohn, Isaac. *Leben un Kamf fun Yiden in Tsarishen Rusland 1905-1917.* Paris, 1968.

Schneersohn, Menahem Mendel, of Lubavitch (*"Tsemah Tsedek"*). *Derekh Mitsvotekha: Ta'amei ha-Mitsvot.* Poltava, 1911; photo offset Kefar Habad, 1973.

_____. *'Or ha-Torah. Derush Kan Tsipor.* In *Tetse,* vol. 2, pp. 924-925.

_____. *Reshimot 'al Shir ha-Shirim, Rut, Kohelet.* Brooklyn, NY: Kehot, 1960.

Schneersohn, Shalom Dov Baer. *Kuntres u-Ma'ayan mi-Beit Hashem.* Brooklyn: Kehot, 1958.

_____. In *'Or la-Yesharim* (anti-Zionist collection). Warsaw, 1900.

Schneerson, Isaac Dov Baer, of Liadi. *Siddur 'im Peirush Ma-HaRID.* 2 vols. Berdichev, 1913; photo offset Kefar Habad, 1991.

Schneerson, Levi Isaac. *Likkutei Levi Yitzhak: Iggerot Kodesh.* Brooklyn: Kehot, 2004.

Schneerson, Menahem Mendel, of Brooklyn. *Likkutei Sihot,* vol. 10. Brooklyn: Kehot, 1981.

———. *Likkutei Sihot* (Yiddish). vol. 24. Israel, 2006.

Schneerson, Shelomo Zalman, of Kopyst. Letters to Don Tumarkin of Rogatchov. In Mordechai Menashe Laufer, *Ha-Melekh bi-Mesibo,* vol. 2.

Schneerson, Shemariah Noah, of Bobruisk. *Kuntres me-Admo"r shelit"a mi-Bobruisk: Teshuvot nitshiyot va-amitiyot 'al Kuntres Admo"r shelit"a de-Libavitz.* 1907.

———. *Shemen la-Ma'or.* 2 vols. Kefar Habad, 1964.

Scholem, Gershom (Gerhard). *Abraham Cohen Herrera: Leben, Werk und Wirkung.* 1978.

———. *Das Buch Bahir.* Leipzig, 1923.

———. *Jewish Gnosticism, Merkabah Mysticism and Talmudic Tradition.* New York, 1965.

———. *Major Trends in Jewish Mysticism.* New York: Schocken, 1971.

———. *On the Kabbalah and Its Symbolism.* New York: Schocken Books, 1970.

———. *On the Mystical Shape of the Godhead.* New York: Schocken Books, 1991.

———. *Origins of the Kabbalah.* Princeton University Press, 1990.

———. *Sabbatai Sevi: The Mystical Messiah.* Princeton, NJ: Princeton University Press, 1975.

———. "Two new theological texts by Abraham Cardozo." Hebrew. *Sefunot,* vols. 3-4 (1960).

Schreiber, Moses. *She'elot u-Teshuvot Hatam Sofer, Orah Hayy-*

im. Pressburg, 1855.

_____. *Torat Moshe.* Commentary to Pentateuch. Ed. Shim'on Sofer. Pressburg, 1906. Photo-offset Brooklyn, NY, 1980.

Schwartz, Hayyim Avihu. *Mi-Tokh ha-Torah ha-Go'elet.* Teachings of Rabbi Tsevi Yehudah Kook. 4 vols. Jerusalem: Zur-Ot 1989.

Schwarzschild, Steven. "Isaac Hutner." In *Interpreters of Judaism in the Late Twentieth Century.* Ed. Steven T. Katz. Washington, D.C.: B'nai B'rith Books, 1993.

Schweid, Eliezer. "Prophetic Mysticism in Twentieth-Century Jewish Thought." *Modern Judaism,* May 1994.

Seder 'Olam Rabbah. Rabbi Yose ben Halafta. Ed. Moshe Ya'ir Weinstock. With commentary *"Seder Zemanim."* B'nei Berak, 1990.

Seeman, Don. "Evolutionary Ethics: The *Taamei Hamitzvot* of Rav Kook." *Hakirah* 26 (Spring 2019), pp. 13-55.

Sefer Yetzirah: The Book of Creation. Ed. Aryeh Kaplan. York Beach, Maine: Samuel Weiser, 1997.

Seidman, Naomi. *Faithful Renderings: Jewish-Christian Difference and the Politics of Translation.* Chicago: University of Chicago Press, 2006.

Shapira, Kalonymos Kalmish. *Hakhsharat ha-Avrekhim.* Jerusalem: Feldheim, 2001.

_____. *Hovat ha-Talmidim.* Jerusalem, 1990.

Shapiro, Marc B. *Changing the Immutable: How Orthodox Judaism Rewrites Its History.* Oxford: Littman, 2015.

_____. (Shapiro, Melekh.) *Iggerot Malkhei Rabbanan.* Scranton, 2019.

_____. *Saul Lieberman and the Orthodox.* Scranton, PA: University of Scranton Press, 2006.

_____. *Studies in Maimonides and His Interpreters.* Scranton,

PA: University of Scranton Press, 2008.

Sheleg, Yair. "Goodbye, Mr. Chouchani." *Haaretz*, Sept. 26, 2003.

Shilat, Yitzhak. "*Kelum teshuvot ha-Rambam le-hakhmei Lunel mezuyafot hen?*" In *Sefer Zikaron le-Harav Yitzhak Nissim*. Ed. Meir Benayahu. vol. 2. Jerusalem, 1985.

Shinawa (Sieniawa), Samuel. *Ramatayim Tsofim*. Commentary to *Tanna de-Vei Eliyahu*. Ed. Shmuel Tsevi Zinger. Jerusalem, 2016.

Shmalo, Gamliel. "*Radikaliyut filosofit be-'olam ha-yeshivot: Harav Yitzhak Hutner 'al ha-Sho'ah*" ("Philosophical Radicalism in the World of the *Yeshivot*: Rabbi Isaac Hutner on the Holocaust"). *Hakirah*, vol. 19.

Shneur Zalman ben Baruch, of Liadi. *Likkutei Torah*. Leviticus-Deuteronomy. Kehot: Kefar Habad, 1972.

———. *Likkutei Torah* (to first three portions of Genesis). Vilna, 1884.

———. *Ma'amrei Admor Hazaken—Et-halekh Liozhna*. Brooklyn, 2012.

———. *Siddur 'im DAH*. Ed. Dov Baer Shneuri of Lubavitch. New York, NY: Kehot, 1971.

———. *Tanya (Sefer shel Beinonim)*. Vilna, 1937.

———. *Torah 'Or*. Genesis-Exodus. Brooklyn: Kehot, 1972.

Shneur, Zalman (pen name of Shneur Zalkind). *Feter Zhoma*. Vilna: Kletzkin, 1930.

———. *Shklover Yidden*. Vilna: Kletzkin, 1929.

Shneuri, Dov Baer. *Be'urei ha-Zohar*. Brooklyn, NY: Kehot, 2015.

———. *Sha'arei Orah*. Johannisburg, n.d.; photo offset Brooklyn, NY: Kehot, 1979.

———. *Torat Hayyim, Bereshit*. Brooklyn: Kehot, 1993. *Shemot*. Facsimile of manuscript of R. Shmuel Sofer. 3rd printing. Brooklyn: Kehot, 1980.

Shurkin, Mikhel Zalman. *Harerei Kedem*. Teachings of Rabbi Yosef Dov Soloveitchik of Boston on Festivals. 2 vols. Jerusalem, 2000, 2004.

Shvat, Ari Yitzhak. "*Iggeret Harav Kook be-Nose' Talmud Torah le-Nashim.*" In *Me'orot li-Yehudah* (Rabbi Yehudah Feliks Festschrift). Ed. M. Rehimi. Elkanah, 2012.

Siddur Eitz Chaim: The Complete Artscroll Siddur (Nusach Sefard). Transl. Nosson Scherman. Brooklyn, NY: Mesorah Publications, 1985.

Sklarevski, Paulina Sarah. "*Hiddush ha-Kedushah: Ha-RAYaH Kook bi-re'i tefisat ha-tsiyonut shel Buber be-sefer 'Bein 'Am le-Artso.*'" Term Paper. Jerusalem: Hebrew University, July 31, 2013. Available at www.academia.edu.

Solomon ben Abraham ibn Adret (RaShBA). *Ma'amar 'al Yishmael*. Ed. Bezalel Naor. Spring Valley, NY: Orot, 2008.

_____. *She'elot u-Teshuvot Rabbeinu Shelomo ben Adret*. Rome, circa 1470.

Soloveichik, Ahron. *Perah Mateh Aharon*. Novellae to Maimonides. 2 vols: *Sefer Madda'; Sefer Ahavah*. Jerusalem, 1997, 1999.

Soloveichik, Moses and Soloveitchik, Yosef Dov. *Hiddushei ha-GRaM ve-ha-GRYD: 'Inyenei Kodashim*. Jerusalem, 1993.

Soloveitchik, Haym. "Interview with Professor Haym Soloveitchik by Rabbi Yair Hoffman." *Five Towns Jewish Times*, Wednesday, January 8th, 2014. Available at: http://www.theyeshivaworld.com/news/headlines-breaking-stories/209453/interview-with-professor-haym-soloveitchik-by-rabbi-yair-hoffman.html

Soloveitchik, Hayyim, of Brisk. *Hiddushei ha-GRaH he-Hadash*. Vol. 3. Stencil. Jerusalem, 1967.

_____. *Hiddushei ha-GRaH he-Hadash 'al ha-Shas*. B'nei

Berak: Mishor, 2008.

———. *Hiddushei Rabbeinu Hayyim Halevi*. Novellae to *Mishneh Torah*. 1936.

———. *Kitvei Rabbeinu Hayyim Halevi mi-Ketav Yad Kodsho* (*Tagbuch*). Ed. Yitzhak Abba Lichtenstein. Jerusalem, 2018.

Soloveitchik, Joseph Baer. *And From There You Shall Seek*. Translation of *"U-Vikkashtem mi-Sham*. Transl. Naomi Goldblum. Jersey City: Ktav, 2008.

———. *Halakhic Man*. Translation of *"Ish ha-Halakhah."* Transl. Lawrence J. Kaplan. Philadelphia: Jewish Publication Society of America, 1983.

———. *Maimonides between Philosophy and Halakhah: Rabbi Joseph B. Soloveitchik's Lectures on the* Guide of the Perplexed. Ed. Lawrence J. Kaplan. Brooklyn: Ktav; Jerusalem: Urim, 2016.

———. *"A Tribute to the Rebbetzin of Talne."* Tradition 17:2 (Spring 1978).

See also Soloveitchik, Yosef Dov, of Boston

Soloveitchik, Yitzhak Ze'ev, of Brisk and Jerusalem. *Hiddushei Maran RYZ ha-Levi 'al ha-RaMBaM*. Jerusalem, 1962.

———. *Hiddushei Maran RYZ Halevi 'al ha-Torah*. Jerusalem, 1962.

———. *Reshimot Talmidim me-Rabbi Yitzhak Ze'ev Halevi Soloveitchik 'al Seder ha-Torah*. Ed. Raphael Kook. Rehovot: Da'at Sofrim, 2016.

Soloveitchik, Yosef Dov, of Boston. *Harerei Kedem*. See Shurkin, Mikhel Zalman.

———. *Iggerot ha-GRYD Halevi*. Jerusalem, 2001.

———. *"Ish ha-Halakhah."* Talpiyot 1:3-4 (5704-5/1944).

———. *Kuntres be-'Inyan 'Avodat Yom ha-Kippurim*. Ed. Aharon Lichtenstein. Jerusalem, 1986.

———. *"Mah Dodekh mi-Dod?"* Eulogy of Rabbi Yitzhak

Ze'ev Soloveitchik. In *Ha-Do'ar* (1964), pp. 752-759; and in *Divrei Hagut ve-Ha'arakhah*. Jerusalem, 1982, pp. 57-97.

_____. *Reshimot Shi'urei Maran ha-GRYD Ha-Levi: Shavu'ot—Nedarim*. 2 vols. Ed. Tsevi Yosef Reichman. Union City, NJ, 1993, 1996.

_____. *Reshimot Shi'urei Maran ha-GRYD Ha-Levi: Sukkah*. Ed. Tsevi Yosef Reichman. New York, 1990.

_____. *Shi'urim le-Zekher Abba Mari*. 2 vols. Jerusalem: Mossad Harav Kook, 2002.

_____. "U-Vikkashtem mi-Sham." *Hadarom*, 1978.

See also *Soloveitchik, Joseph Baer*.

Soloveitchik, Yosef Dov Baer, of Brisk. *Beit Halevi*. On Genesis and Exodus. Warsaw, 1884.

_____. *She'elot u-Teshuvot Beit Halevi*. 3 vols. Vilna, 1863; Warsaw, 1874-1891.

Spiegel, Ya'akov Shmuel. *'Ammudim be-Toledot ha-Sefer ha-'Ivri: Hagahot u-Magihim*. Ramat Gan: Bar-Ilan University Press, 2005

Spielman, Mordechai. *Tif'eret Tsevi*. On *Zohar*. 6 vols. Brooklyn, 1981-2003.

Spira, Hayyim El'azar, of Munkatch. *Sha'ar Yissakhar 'al Mo'adim*. Brooklyn, NY, 1992.

Spira, Tsevi Elimelech, of Dynów. *Igra de-Pirka*. Lvov, 1858.

Sternhartz, Nathan, of Nemirov and Breslov. *Hayyei MO-HaRaN*. Jerusalem: Keren R. Israel Dov Odesser, n.d.

_____ (attributed to—). *Kin'at Hashem Tseva'ot*. Iasi or Lvov, 1852.

_____. *Likkutei Halakhot*. On *Shulhan 'Arukh*. [Iasi]-Zolkiew, 1843-1849.

_____. *Sihot ha-Ran*. B'nci Berak, 1976.

_____. *Yemei ha-Tela'ot*. See *Hazan, Abraham ben Nahman,*

of Tulchin.

Strashun, Samuel. *Hiddushei RaShaSh*. Novellae to Talmud. Published in Vilna edition of Talmud.

Strauss, Leo. "How To Begin To Study *The Guide of the Perplexed.*" In Moses Maimonides, *The Guide of the Perplexed.* Transl. Shlomo Pines. Chicago: University of Chicago Press, 1963.

_____. "Notes on Maimonides' *Book of Knowledge.*" In *Studies in Mysticism and Religion Presented to Gershom G. Scholem.* Ed. Urbach, Werblowsky, and Wirszubski. Jerusalem, 1967.

_____. *Persecution and the Art of Writing.* Glencoe, Illinois: The Free Press, 1952.

_____. *Philosophie und Gesetz.* Berlin, 1935.

_____. "Quelques remarques sur la science politique de Maimonide et de Farabi." *Revue des Etudes Juives,* C (1936), pp. 1-37.

Swartz, Michael D. *Scholastic Magic: Ritual and Revelation in Early Jewish Mysticism.* Princeton: Princeton University Press, 1996.

Swift, Jonathan. *Gulliver's Travels.* London, 1726.

Ta-Shma, Israel. *Ha-Nigleh she-ba-Nistar.* Tel-Aviv, 1995.

_____. *Rabbi Zerahyah Halevi (Ba'al ha-Ma'or) u-B'nei Hugo.* Jerusalem: Mossad Harav Kook, 1992.

Tchernichovsky, Shaul. "Before the Statue of Apollo." Poem. 1899.

Tchernowitz, Chaim. *Pirkei Hayyim.* New York, 1954.

Tchetchik, Ze'ev Dov. *Torat Ze'ev: Zevahim.* Zikhron Moshe, 1985.

Telushkin, Nissan. *Tahorat Mayim.* Brooklyn, NY: Kehot, 1990.

Tishby, Isaiah. *Mishnat ha-Zohar.* vol. 1. 2nd printing with corrections. Jerusalem: Mossad Bialik, 1949.

Tobi, Yosef. *Between Hebrew and Arabic Poetry: Studies in Spanish Medieval Hebrew Poetry*. Leiden: Brill, 2010.

Tsemah, Jacob. *Kol be-Ramah*. Korets, 1785. Jerusalem: Makhon B'nei Yissachar, 2001. Ed. Eliyahu Attiah.

———. *Nagid u-Metsaveh*. Lublin, 1881.

———. *Zohar ha-Raki'a*. Korets, 1785.

Tukachinsky, Yehiel Mikhel. *Ha-Yomam be-Kadur ha-Arets*. Jerusalem, 1943.

Turbowitz, Ze'ev Wolf. *Tif'eret Ziv*. Brooklyn: Moinester Publishing Company, 1939.

———. *Tif'eret Ziv*. Warsaw, 1896.

———. *Ziv Mishneh*. Warsaw, 1904.

Urbach, Ephraim Elimelech. *Ba'alei ha-Tosafot*. 2 vols. Jerusalem: Bialik Institute, 1995.

Verman, Mark. *The Books of Contemplation: Medieval Jewish Mystical Sources*. Albany: State University of New York, 1992.

Vico, Giambattista. *Scienza Nuova*. 1725.

Vidas, Elijah de. *Reshit Hokhmah*. Munkatch, n.d. [1895].

Vital, Hayyim. *'Ets Hayyim*. Ed. Menahem Menkhin Heilprin. 3 vols. Warsaw, 1891; stereotype Jerusalem, 1910, photo offset Jerusalem, 1975.

———. *Likkutei Torah*. Vilna, 1880; photo offset Jerusalem, 1972.

———. *Peri 'Ets Hayyim*. Dubrovna, 1804.

———. *Sefer ha-Derushim*. Ed. Ya'akov Moshe Hillel. Jerusalem: Ahavat Shalom, 1996.

———. *Sefer ha-Likkutim*. Ed. Ze'ev Wolf Ashkenazi. Jerusalem, 1913.

———. *Sha'ar ha-Gilgulim*. Jerusalem: Keren Hotsa'at Sifrei Rabbanei Bavel, 1990.

———. *Sha'ar ha-Hakdamot*. Ed. Menahem Menkhin Heilprin. Jerusalem, 1909.

_____. *Sha'ar ha-Kavvanot*. Ed. Menahem Menkhin Heilprin. Jerusalem, 1902.

_____. *Sha'ar ha-Mitsvot*. Ed. Ze'ev Wolf Ashkenazi. Jerusalem, 1905.

Volkovski, Elijah Mordechai. *Hezyonei Amatsyahu*. (Additional title: *Shnei ha-Me'orot ha-Gedolim*.) Keidan: Movshovitz and Kagan, 1934. Photo offset in Moshe Yehiel Zuriel. *Otserot ha-RAYaH*. vol. 2. Tel-Aviv, 1988.

Wasserman, Abraham. *Koré ha-Degel*. 2020.

Wasserman, Elhanan Bunim. "*Divrei Aggadah*," appended to *Kovets He'arot le-Masekhet Yevamot*. Piotrków, 1932.

Waxman, Meyer. "*Ha-Gaon mi-Vilna*." In *Sefer ha-Shanah li-Yehudei Amerika*, vols. X-XI (1949).

Weinberg, Abraham, of Slonim. *Hesed le-Avraham*. Commentary to Prophets. Jerusalem, 1986.

Weinberg, Yehiel Ya'akov. *Kitvei ha-Ga'on Rabbi Yehiel Ya'akov Weinberg*. Ed. Melekh Shapiro. 2 vols. Scranton, 2003.

Weintraub, Israel Elijah. *Nefesh Eliyahu: Hakdamot u-She'arim*. n.p., 2002.

_____. *Nefesh Eliyahu 'al Sifra di-Tseni'uta 'im Be'ur ha-GRA*. n.p., n.d.2012]].

Wengrover, Yedidyah. *R' Shem Tov Geffen*. Metula: Nezer David, 2017.

Wolberstein, Hilah. *Harav ha-Nazir: Ish ki yafli'*. Jerusalem: Makhon Nezer David, 2017.

Wolfson, Elliot R. *Through A Speculum That Shines: Vision and Imagination in Medieval Jewish Mysticism*. Princeton: Princeton University Press, 1994.

Yahuda, A.S. "A Contribution to Qur'an and Hadith Interpretation." *Ignace Goldziher Memorial Volume*, Part I. Ed. Samuel Löwinger and Joseph Somogyi. Budapest, 1948.

Yaron, Zevi. *Mishnato shel Harav Kook* (*The Philosophy of Rabbi Kook*). Jerusalem: W.Z.O., 1974.

Yom Tov ben Abraham Asevilli. *Hiddushei ha-RITBA*. Tractate *Yoma*. Constantinople, 1754; Berlin, 1860; Ed. Eliyahu Lichtenstein. Jerusalem: Mossad Harav Kook, 1976.

Yosef Hayyim of Baghdad (*"Ben Ish Hai"*). *Benayahu*. On Legends of Talmud. 3 vols. Jerusalem, 1998.

_____. *Ben Yehoyada'*. On Legends of Talmud. 4 vols. Jerusalem, 1998.

Yosha, Nissim. *Myth and Metaphor: Abraham Cohen Herrera's Philosophic Interpretation of Lurianic Kabbalah* Hebrew. Jerusalem: Magnes, 1994.

Zeilberger, Benjamin. *Nahalat Binyamin: Bikkurim*. Jerusalem, 2016.

Zeitlin, Hillel. *Be-Hevyon ha-Neshamah* (*In the Hiding Place of the Soul*). In *Netivot*, vol. 1. Warsaw: Ahisefer, 1913, pp. 205-235.

_____. *Hasidic Spirituality for a New Era: The Religious Writings of Hillel Zeitlin*. Ed. Arthur Green. Paulist Press: Mahwah, NJ, 2012.

_____. *Rabbi Nahman of Bratslav: World Weariness and Longing for the Messiah: Two Essays by Hillel Zeitlin*. Hebrew. Introduction and notes Jonatan Meir. Jerusalem, 2006.

Zevin, Shelomo Yosef. *Ha-Mo'adim ba-Halakhah*. Tel-Aviv: A[braham] Zioni, 1953.

_____. *Le-'Or ha-Halakhah*. 2nd edition. Jerusalem: Beit Hillel, n.d. [c.1980].

_____. *Soferim u-Sefarim*. Tel-Aviv: A[braham] Ziyoni, 1959.

Ziemba, Menahem. *Tots'ot Hayyim*. Warsaw, 1921; photo offset Brooklyn, 1976.

Zilber, Yitzhak. *To Remain a Jew*. Transl. Sherry Dimarsky. New

York: Feldheim, c. 2010.

Zimler, Richard. *The Last Kabbalist of Lisbon*. Woodstock, NY: The Overlook Press, 1998.

Zimmer, Yitzhak (Eric). "Tenuhot u-tenu'ot ha-guf bi-she'at Keri'at Shema'." In *Asufot* 8 (1994).

Zimmerman, Abraham Isaac Halevi, of Krementchug. Novellae on Maimonides' *Mishneh Torah*. 2 vols. *Hiddushei ha-RAYaH*. Jerusalem, 1988.

Zimmerman, Chaim. *Agan ha-Sahar*. New York, 1955.

———. *Agra la-Yesharim*. Jerusalem, 1983.

———. *Binyan Halakhah*. Novellae on *Mishneh Torah*. New York, 1942.

Zinberg, Israel. *A History of Jewish Literature*. 12 vols. Transl. Bernard Martin. Cleveland: Case Western Reserve University, 1972-1978.

Zitrin, Mendel. *Shivhei Tsaddikim*. Warsaw, 1884.

Ziyoni, Menahem. *Sefer Ziyoni*. Cremona.

Zohar. Pritzker edition. 12 vols. vols. 1-9 ed. Daniel Matt. vol. 10 ed. Nathan Wolski. vol. 11 ed. Joel Hecker. vol. 12 ed. Nathan Wolski and Joel Hecker. Stanford, California: Stanford University Press, 2004-2017.

Zohar. Ed. Reuven Margaliyot. 3 vols. Jerusalem: Mossad Harav Kook, 1940-1946.

Zohar Hadash. Ed. Reuven Margaliyot. Jerusalem: Mossad Harav Kook, 1953.

www.ingramcontent.com/pod-product-compliance
Lightning Source LLC
Chambersburg PA
CBHW031659230426
43668CB00006B/47